Europe by Rail

The Definitive Guide

by

Nicky Gardner and Susanne Kries

18th edition
October 2024

hidden europe publications

EUROPE BY RAIL: THE DEFINITIVE GUIDE

Eighteenth edition. Published in October 2024.

ISBN 978-3-945225-04-2

Copyright © 2024 Nicky Gardner and Susanne Kries. All rights reserved.

No part of this publication may be reproduced, stored in a retrieval system, or transmitted in any form or by any means without the prior consent of the publisher.

Nicky Gardner and Susanne Kries have asserted their right to be identified as the authors of this work in accordance with the Copyright, Designs and Patents Act 1988.

Published by
hidden europe publications
Gardner u. Kries GbR, Schäferstr. 2-A, D-14109 Berlin, Germany
www.hiddeneurope.eu

Design and layout by hidden europe editorial bureau of Berlin, Germany
Printed and bound by GraphyCems of Villatuerta (Navarra), Spain
Distribution by CBL Distribution Ltd of Birmingham, England
Colour maps on inside covers by David McCutcheon FBCart.S., www.dvdmaps.co.uk.

Our front cover image shows an SBB train on the Gotthard Railway near Faido in the Swiss canton of Ticino. This line is described in Route 41 in this book (photo © Leonid Andronov / dreamstime.com).

This book has a dedicated website with route maps at www.europebyrail.eu
There is an associated twitter account at www.twitter.com/europebyrail
Follow us on facebook at www.facebook.com/europebyrailguide and find us on Instagram at www.instagram.com/europebyrailguide

The authors can be contacted by e-mail at editors@europebyrail.eu

Disclaimer

The authors have done their level best to make sure that the information published in this book is accurate and up-to-date. But things can change. A hotel remembered with affection may have turned into a dive, and of course public transport timetables change. Entire rail routes may close. So always check details before setting out, and bear in mind that savvy local advice may be worth much more than what you read in a guidebook. If you feel that we have made a mistake somewhere, please do let us know. But do note that neither the authors nor the publisher can accept any responsibility for loss, damage, injury or inconvenience occasioned by material included, or anything not mentioned, in this book or on any websites maintained by the authors or publisher.

| **3**

A word of welcome	8
Over fifty years of Interrail	11
How to use this book	14
Overview: The 50 routes	16
Planning your itinerary	18
Crossing cities	21
Night trains	22
High-speed rail in Europe	25
Key shipping links	29
Europe in colour: Journeys of discovery	33

ROUTES 49

Discover Britain and Ireland 50

1. Following Brunel to Cornwall
London – Reading – Exeter – Plymouth – Penzance ... 52
SIDETRACKS A: CORNISH BRANCH LINES ... 58

2. Cathedrals, castles and glens
London – York – Durham – Edinburgh – Inverness – Kyle ... 59
SIDETRACKS B: THE HEBRIDES ... 68

3. The rural route to the West Highlands
Amsterdam – Newcastle – Carlisle – Edinburgh – Fort William – Mallaig ... 69

4. Across England and Wales to Ireland
Rotterdam – Harwich – Chester – Dublin – Killarney ... 78
SIDETRACKS C: IRISH QUESTIONS ... 87

5. West to Europe's Celtic fringe
London – Cotswolds – mid-Wales – Dublin – Galway ... 88

The Low Countries and Germany 96

6. Through Flanders to Amsterdam
Lille – Bruges – Antwerp – Den Haag – Amsterdam ... 97
SIDETRACKS D: BELGIUM'S COASTAL TRAMWAY ... 103

7. From Hauts-de-France to the Rhine
Lille – Brussels – Liège – Aachen – Cologne ... 104
SIDETRACKS E: CREATURE COMFORTS ... 109

8. From the Netherlands to Lake Geneva
Amsterdam – Maastricht – Luxembourg – Strasbourg – Lausanne ... 110

9. Exploring the Rhine Valley
Cologne – Koblenz – Heidelberg – Triberg – Zurich ... 117
SIDETRACKS F: RHINE VS MOSELLE ... 125

10. Across northern Germany
Cologne – Düsseldorf – Hannover – Helmstedt – Berlin ... 126

11. **Steaming through the Harz Mountains**
    Hannover – Goslar – Wernigerode – Quedlinburg – Magdeburg　　133
12. **From Berlin to the Alps**
    Berlin – Leipzig – Weimar – Würzburg – Munich – Salzburg　　138

A taste of France　　147

13. **From London to the Mediterranean**
    London – Paris – Nevers – Clermont-Ferrand – Nîmes – Marseille　　148
14. **Paris to Geneva – the slow way**
    Paris – Dijon – Beaune – Lyon – Annecy – Geneva　　156
    SIDETRACKS G: EXPLORING THE JURA　　163
15. **Exploring the French Riviera**
    Marseille – Bandol – Toulon – Cannes – Antibes – Nice　　164
16. **The Seine Valley and Normandy**
    Paris – Giverny – Rouen – Lisieux – Bayeux – Cherbourg　　171
    SIDETRACKS H: CARRIAGE DESIGN　　175
17. **The Loire Valley and Atlantic coast**
    Paris – Angers – Bordeaux – Biarritz – San Sebastián　　176
18. **To the Pyrenees**
    Paris – Dordogne – Toulouse – Latour de Carol – Barcelona　　182
19. **From Normandy to the Rhône Valley**
    Caen – Le Mans – Angers – Bourges – Lyon – Valence　　189
    SIDETRACKS I: FRANCE WITHOUT PARIS　　196

Iberian connections　　197

20. **From the Alps to Catalonia**
    Geneva – Aix-les-Bains – Avignon – Perpignan – Portbou – Barcelona　　198
    SIDETRACKS J: MEDITERRANEAN ISLANDS　　206
21. **Historic Spain**
    Barcelona – València – Despeñaperros – Córdoba – Seville – Cádiz　　207
    SIDETRACKS K: SOUTH FROM SPAIN　　214
22. **High-speed Spain**
    Barcelona – Madrid – Córdoba – Málaga　　215
23. **Not quite the pilgrim route to Santiago**
    San Sebastián – Burgos – Madrid – Zamora – Santiago de Compostela　　221
24. **The Atlantic coast of Iberia**
    Santiago de Compostela – Vigo – Porto – Lisbon – Seville　　227
    SIDETRACKS L: GRAND STATIONS　　235

Scandinavia and the Baltic　　236

25. **Great maritime cities**
    Amsterdam – Hamburg – Odense – Copenhagen – Stockholm　　237
26. **To the Skagerrak and beyond**
    Fredericia – Aarhus – Hirtshals – Oslo – Stockholm　　247
    SIDETRACKS M: SLOW BOAT TO ICELAND　　254

27. **Sampling Scandinavia**	
Copenhagen – Göteborg – Oslo – Bergen	255
28. **North to the Lofoten Islands**	
Oslo – Lillehammer – Trondheim – Bodø – Svolvær	263
29. **Night train to Narvik**	
Stockholm – Boden – Narvik – Svolvær	269
Sidetracks N: Norway's Far North	276
30. **A foray through Finland**	
Boden – Oulu – Tampere – Helsinki – Turku – Stockholm	277
Sidetracks O: The communal carriage	287
31. **Baltic adventure**	
Hamburg – Lübeck – Stralsund – Szczecin – Gdańsk – Warsaw	288
Sidetracks P: Baltic trains	297

Central and eastern Europe — 298

32. **Bohemian byways**	
Nuremberg – Plzeň – Karlovy Vary – Prague	299
33. **Four capitals in a day**	
Hamburg – Berlin – Prague – Bratislava – Budapest	305
Sidetracks Q: Named trains	313
34. **To the Black Sea**	
Vienna – Budapest – Sighişoara – Bucharest – Constanţa	314
35. **Exploring Slovakia**	
Vienna – Bratislava – Poprad – Košice – Budapest	323
Sidetracks R: Carpathian connections	331
36. **East from Berlin**	
Berlin – Poznań – Warsaw – Kraków – Przemyśl – Lviv	332
Sidetracks S: Through Ukraine	340
37. **From Saxony to the Tatra Mountains**	
Dresden – Görlitz – Wrocław – Kraków – Zakopane – Poprad	341
Sidetracks T: Crossing frontiers	349

Alpine adventures — 350

38. **Crossing the Alps**	
Munich – Mittenwald – Innsbruck – Bolzano – Verona	351
Sidetracks U: The Alps by bus	357
39. **The Arlberg route**	
Zurich – Feldkirch – Innsbruck – Salzburg – Vienna	358
Sidetracks V: Night train perspective	367
40. **Over the Bernina Pass**	
Zurich – Zernez – St Moritz – Tirano – Milan	368
41. **The classic Gotthard route**	
Basel – Lucerne – Gotthard – Locarno – Stresa – Milan	373
Sidetracks W: Through the Simplon	380

42. Following the Glacier Express
St Moritz – Andermatt – Brig – Zermatt   381

43. Swiss lakes and mountains
Zurich – Lucerne – Interlaken – Montreux – Lausanne – Geneva   386
SIDETRACKS X: TO THE TOP OF EUROPE   394

Italy and the Adriatic   395

44. Habsburg connections
Vienna – Semmering – Graz – Ljubljana – Trieste   396
SIDETRACKS Y: RAILWAYS AND WORLD HERITAGE   404

45. From the Riviera to Florence
Nice – Monaco – Sanremo – Genoa – Cinque Terre – Pisa – Florence   405

46. Tuscany and Umbria
Verona – Bologna – Florence – Siena – Orvieto – Rome   412

47. North Italian cities
Genoa – Milan – Cremona – Mantua – Verona – Venice – Trieste   419

48. South to Sicily
Rome – Naples – Messina – Taormina – Siracusa   427

49. By rail and ship to Greece
Venice – Bologna – Rimini – Bari – Patras – Athens   434

50. From the Danube to the Adriatic
Budapest – Lake Balaton – Zagreb – Split – Ancona   442
SIDETRACKS Z: THROUGH ALBANIA   449

GAZETTEER   450

A country-by-country guide to exploring Europe by rail in alphabetical order

Albania	451
Andorra	451
Austria	452
Belarus	453
Belgium	454
Bosnia and Herzegovina	455
Bulgaria	456
Croatia	457
Cyprus	458
Czech Republic	459
Denmark	460
Estonia	462
Faroe Islands	463
Finland	463
France	465
Germany	467

Great Britain	469
Greece	471
Hungary	472
Iceland	474
Ireland	474
Italy	475
Kosovo	477
Latvia	477
Liechtenstein	478
Lithuania	478
Luxembourg	479
Malta	480
Moldova	480
Monaco	481
Montenegro	481
Netherlands	482
North Macedonia	484
Norway	484
Poland	486
Portugal	488
Romania	489
Russian Federation	491
San Marino	492
Serbia	492
Slovakia	493
Slovenia	494
Spain	495
Sweden	497
Switzerland	499
Turkey	500
Ukraine	502
Vatican City (Holy See)	503

REFERENCE SECTION — 504

A word on place names	504
City links: travel times between principal cities	505
Tickets and passes	510
Know your apps	524
Planning overnight stays	525
Cruise trains	527
When a train is not a train	528
A–Z of travel in Europe	529
Index	534
Postscript	544

A word of welcome

It is perfectly possible to explore Europe in a sustainable way which does not wreck the planet. Just take the train. Travelling by rail is a chance to see Europe's varied landscapes and make the most of the journey. You'll meet interesting people along the way and overall your journey will be more eco-friendly than if you fly. On your first trip, you'll most likely try and go too far and too fast. Slow down and enjoy those serendipitous discoveries which come with exploring Europe by rail on an unhurried itinerary.

For over 30 years, successive editions of *Europe by Rail* have shaped travellers' plans, encouraging readers to travel slowly, tread lightly and treasure that sense of adventure which comes from **making a real journey**. Long before slow travel became so fashionable, early editions of this book were highlighting the merits of making time for fine journeys.

With tips on ticketing, fares, rail passes and accommodation, *Europe by Rail* has become the definitive guide to exploring the continent by train. This **18th edition of the book** highlights the rich and intriguing possibilities that are there for the taking, be it for a handful of short trips or for a more extended tour.

This 18th edition is published at a time of great uncertainty. We've endured a terrible pandemic, closely followed by war in eastern Europe. These events, set against a backdrop of resurgent nationalism, have dimmed the affirming flame of pan-European collaboration. Some may be tempted to stay at home, but it is at times like this that we *should* venture out. **Travelling by train is convivial** in a way that is rarely encountered on planes and has never been a feature of car travel. We have swapped stories with passengers on trains in Spain and Bulgaria, we have been on trains marooned in deep midwinter snow in Scandinavia and we have shared snacks and life stories with strangers on night trains that slipped in the dark past silent factories in unnamed towns. We love that **sense of community and solidarity** which underpins rail travel. The train is a great unifier, linking people and places divided by frontiers.

Over the years, we have criss-crossed Europe by train, making fast journeys on sleek expresses and slow meanderings on remote branch lines. We have taken slow trains through Belarus and even slower trains through Bohemia. For this 18th edition of the book, we have **improved our coverage of France and Poland**. And we have removed routes in the western Balkans where cross-border rail connections are currently so woeful.

Despite these cutbacks, there has never been a better time to explore Europe by rail. Trains are back in fashion and the great rail renaissance is introducing new possibilities. Long abandoned lines are being reopened, and there's now **huge demand for overnight journeys** in comfortable sleeping cars. Is it not a matter of wonder that one can board a night train in Salzburg and alight next morning in Warsaw, Paris or on Italy's Cinque Terre coast? Or travel from Zagreb directly to Zurich? This really is just like teleportation.

Back in 2022, Europe marked a special anniversary: 50 years of Interrail. The **Interrail pass** has since 1972 been a potent force in fostering mutual understanding between Europeans. We know that many readers of this book, be they young or old, will be using Interrail passes (either traditional paper passes or the excellent new mobile pass). Interrail (along with a sister scheme called Eurail – for those not resident in Europe) remains in our view the best ticketing option for those intent on following some of the longer journeys in this book. Exploring Europe by train with an Interrail pass is an **intergenerational cultural practice** which has shaped many Europeans' understanding of their home continent.

THE JOURNEY OR THE DESTINATION?

With the development of Europe's first railways, people were suddenly on the move, with the restless English often leading the way. The guidebook market blossomed as early rail travellers packed a **Baedeker guidebook** before embarking on a new journey. In travelling by train around Europe, it is still possible to rediscover the sheer joy of the journey itself.

So in *Europe by Rail* we put the journey at the centre. We present **50 rail routes** that between them cover the full gamut of European rail travel. There are routes where trains speed across great plains, routes where slow trains dawdle from one village to another and there are routes where trains traverse harsh tundra and great mountain ranges. In addition to our 50 routes, we offer 26 mini-features (called **Sidetracks**); these are bite-size teasers which invite you to reflect on rail-related themes or venture into regions not covered by our 50 routes.

Travel by train across Europe and you will inevitably be struck by the sheer **variety of our continent**. Our 50 routes reflect that mix. We include some high-speed hops, where you can cover a lot of ground fast. But we also highlight slow trains that follow less-frequented rail routes. It is on such journeys that the texture and detail of European life is most easily appreciated, whether it be in the changing landscapes beyond the carriage window, the architecture of villages you pass through along the way or in the faces and accents of fellow travellers with whom you share a railway carriage. If you have a choice of fast or slow services, always opt for the slow train.

Try an overnight journey too. Few experiences compare with opening the blinds of the **night sleeper** in the morning to find a fragile blanket of morning mist over a foreign landscape. You can read more about night trains on pages 22 to 24.

Classic destinations like the Rhine, Switzerland and the northern shores of the Mediterranean no longer command attention to the exclusion of other parts of Europe. The routes in this book will take you far beyond the

Arctic Circle and on mountain railways across the Pyrenees and the Alps. We shall lead you from eastern Europe to the Irish hills, from Balkan byways to the Baltic and the Bay of Biscay.

Taking time

Some readers might try and undertake a dozen or more of these routes within a month. We would just sound a note of caution. That way madness lies. Better to focus a little, and take time to stop off here and there along the way. Don't travel every day. Enjoy the change of pace by making two-night stops rather than moving on each morning to somewhere new. Branch out from main rail routes and choose slower trains on at least some parts of your journey to discover the **joys of slow travel**. You can get some inspiration by reading our *Manifesto for Slow Travel* at www.slowtraveleurope.eu.

Rethinking our relationship with travel is no mere luxury. It's now an absolute necessity to save our home planet. Across much of Europe, people are **switching from air to rail**. Train travel is often modestly priced, generally very comfortable and appeals to the pieties of a new generation of environmentally aware travellers. The train comes with green credentials.

Practicalities

Travel light if you possibly can. Heavy luggage and trains do not make good companions. Think about **what apps you'll need** for your smart phone (see our thoughts on this on p524), bearing in mind that access to good maps and **timetable information** will smooth your journey. Try Eurail's *Rail Planner* app for starters. It's incredibly useful and hugely compelling. You may want to consult the *European Rail Timetable (ERT)*, a regularly updated compendium which is a masterpiece of compression (see www.europeanrailtimetable.eu). ERT also publish a useful **rail map of Europe**, but for more detail look to Mike Ball's wonderful *European Railway Atlas* series (www.europeanrailwayatlas.com). This guidebook, good maps and reliable timetable data are three great assets in the rail traveller's armamentarium.

The best way to get started is to read "How to use this book" (pp14-15). You will find useful maps on the inside front cover and inside back cover showing the routes in this volume (numbered 1 to 50). And you may like to know that we have a website to accompany this book at www.europebyrail.eu. There you'll find **more detailed maps** of our 50 routes.

Enjoy the ride.

Nicky Gardner and Susanne Kries
Berlin Wannsee, Germany (September 2024)

Over fifty years of Interrail

In 1972, there was a flurry of new **postage stamps** as countries across Europe and beyond marked the half-centenary of the International Union of Railways (UIC). Belgium and Romania stepped up to the mark. So did many other nations, among them diminutive Monaco with a handsome commemorative issue showcasing trains that surely never ran on Monaco's limited rail network – all 1.7 km of it. The stamps have been consigned to philatelic history, but not so another initiative sponsored by UIC to mark its fiftieth anniversary. UIC's European members launched a remarkable rail pass designed to give young Europeans the freedom to roam the continent. **That pass was called Interrail**.

Interrail created a travel revolution. For eight months from 1 March 1972, any European resident up to 21 years old could buy a one-month Interrail pass valid in 21 countries. In that debut year, initially conceived as a one-off experiment, 87,000 passes were sold to young people who headed off to explore, along the way demonstrating an enviable ability to sleep almost anywhere. It was **such a success** that Interrail became a mainstream offer, still going strong after 50 years. These days, travelling with an Interrail pass is no longer a privilege of youth.

In truth, Interrail didn't come from nowhere. A similar pass for overseas visitors to Europe had been around since 1959. It's called Eurail. The credit for

Interrail milestones

- **1972** Interrail launches as a one-month, second-class pass for under-21s, valid in 21 countries.
- **1976** Age limit increases to 23. East Germany drops out of the scheme but Romania and Morocco join.
- **1979** Age limit increases to 29 and a new senior pass is offered including a first-class option.
- **1989** First restricted offer of passes for people of all ages, initially only trialled in Nordic countries.
- **1994** Now that there are 29 participating countries, zonal passes are introduced covering separate parts of Europe.
- **1998** 'Not just for youths with smelly socks': Interrail opens to all residents of Europe.
- **2007** One-country Interrail passes are introduced.
- **2010** New youth-adult-senior pricing structure, with wider availability of first-class passes.
- **2015** New family offer with children under 12 travelling for free with an adult.
- **2018** *DiscoverEU* programme starts, offering complimentary passes to 18-year-olds.
- **2019** Interrail and Eurail schemes effectively converge, while still retaining distinct brand identities.
- **2020** Cautious launch of very first mobile passes.
- **2021** Mobile passes are chosen by 96% of travellers purchasing Interrail.
- **2022** Europe celebrates 50 years of Interrail with discounts of 50% on some passes.
- **2024** Interrail's sister scheme Eurail marks its 65th birthday.

getting Eurail launched must go largely to an unassuming Frenchman called **Pierre Le Bris** who from his base in San Francisco worked closely with the French national rail operator SNCF and the US-based Rail Europe agency. Le Bris realised the difficulties that Americans visiting Europe had in booking train tickets in advance. His canny idea was to liberate these visitors by letting them use a rail pass which afforded a real freedom to roam.

Rail Europe sold the first Eurail passes in 1959 and before long the company was very purposefully shaping itineraries that showcased European cities and landscapes, helping create in the American imagination an idealised view of a Europe which swept from Paris through the Rhineland, the Alps and the Riviera to northern Italy. In 1971, a heavily discounted **Eurail pass** for students was introduced. The post-68 beat generation was on the move, guitars in hand, and they came in their thousands, keen to explore not merely the canonical sights that featured in the Rail Europe posters but also eager to take in places off the beaten path. But **young Europeans** were quick to question the logic which underpinned Eurail.

"Why," they asked, "should young Americans and other overseas visitors get a great value rail pass to explore Europe, while we who live here on the continent cannot benefit from this offer?"

The pressure was on, and it was no surprise when in 1972 the national rail administrations of 21 countries **launched Interrail**: a product which was geared to European residents and actually covered an even larger area than Eurail.

Few could have imagined how a modest initiative would develop so successfully, profoundly shaping European travel and our shared understanding of our common European home. The Interrail scheme is still **a collaborative programme** of Europe's national rail operators. In the early days it was restricted to young people, but today's passes are equally popular with families and retirees. The Interrail pioneers of 1972 are now aged around 70, and many are still venturing out with their passes – most of them now using the new mobile versions of Interrail. A half century of travel induces many rose-tinted memories, and older readers of *Europe by Rail* have shared with us their early **Interrail adventures**. Many suggested that Interrail isn't the same as in the early days. Europe celebrated 50 years of Interrail in 2022. Let's take a look at how things have changed during half a century of this remarkable rail pass.

Myths of long-lost halycon days

Some maintain that today's supplements (when using Interrail or Eurail) undermine the benefits of a pass. While we agree, we also need to put the record straight. There was never a time in the early days of Interrail when Interrailers could just hop on any train without bothering about reservations. It is part of **Interrail mythology** that there was a great moment in history when the pass cost hardly anything and one could travel on any train.

The truth is that Interrail always came laced with all sorts of restrictions. The entire *Trans-Europe Express* (TEE) network was simply out-of-bounds to pass holders in 1972. This was not a question of having to pay a supplement. TEE was a **complete no-go area** for Interrail travellers. Prime-time departures from Zurich to Munich (on the *Bavaria*), Hamburg (the *Helvetia*) and Paris (*L'Arbalète*) were barred to pass holders. The same applied to sensibly timed morning trains from Milan to Geneva (the *Lemano*), Nice (the *Ligure*), Lyon (the *Mont Cenis*) and Munich (the *Mediolanum*).

France was as difficult for the **Interrail pioneers** as it can still be today. The fastest trains on key routes from Paris to the provinces (eg. on the lines to Toulouse and Clermont-Ferrand as well as on services to Alsace and the Rhône Valley) were all first-class only and thus not available to Interrail pass holders. Even more annoyingly, Interrail was barred on some regional services where alternatives were slow or circuitous. For example, on the only Rapide of the day from Nantes and Tours to Lyon Interrail was not valid. Perversely, or so it seemed to pass holders, SNCF would not accept Interrail on the sole daily direct train from Bordeaux to Grenoble.

Many trains on prime routes to the **Adriatic resorts** of what was then Yugoslavia were barred to holders of Interrail passes. So pass holders could not use the *Marjan Express* from Zagreb to Split, the *Arena* from Zagreb to Pula or the fastest trains from Zagreb to Rijeka. Similarly, the *Sarajevo Express* from Belgrade to Sarajevo was a no-go zone for holders of an Interrail pass.

The secret of rail pass success: taking the slow train

The early users of Interrail passes worked around a tangle of restrictions. Barred from premium services, they took slower options. And they did not complain. Free was free and they rejoiced at being able to travel from Norway to Italy without having to pay a cent beyond that initial outlay for an Interrail pass. That is still perfectly possible today. Nothing has changed except the horizons of a new generation of travellers where high-speed and long-distance are seen as virtues in their own right.

As Interrail turns 50, now is perhaps the time to **rediscover the slow trains** which, being free of supplements and restrictions, are perfectly suited to Interrail. If you want to speed across France on a TGV, the option is there, but you'll need to book a seat and pay a supplement. That means committing yourself to a particular itinerary, whereas Interrail is all about having the freedom to explore. Interrail is about flexibility, stopping off on a whim, and savouring the serendipitous discoveries and diversions that come with Slow Travel. One of our favourite writers, an early exponent of **Slow Travel**, is **Théophile Gautier**. "What charm can there be in a journey when one is always sure to arrive," queried Gautier in 1843.

Perhaps Interrail's fullest potential is yet to be realized. It's **a gift** which allows us to escape the rush of modernity and to rediscover a slower Europe.

How to use this book

The best guidebooks, and we really hope this is one of the best, both **inspire and inform** in equal measure. At the heart of this volume are 50 rail routes which criss-cross Europe. The **full-colour map** on the inside front cover shows most routes. On the inside back cover you'll find our Scandinavia map and an enlargement of the wider Alpine region showing our routes there in more detail. These maps allow you to plot longer itineraries across the continent (eg. Lisbon to Stockholm or Dublin to Athens).

Fifty routes

The main part of this book (between p49 and p449) describes the 50 routes featured in *Europe by Rail*. A **full list of these routes** appears in the table of contents and, in another format, on pages pp16–17. In the latter version, we give the length of each route in kilometres and the travel time.

Each route kicks off with our personal appraisal using a **star rating** (one to three stars with three being the best), and a note of the countries through which the route passes. We also give the **length of the route** (in kilometres) and the rough amount of time that you'll be spending on trains if you follow each leg, as we describe it, right through to the end of the route. Bear in mind that there will often be faster ways of getting from the start to the end of the route – and we usually highlight such options where they are available. But our aim in this book is to showcase the most interesting and scenic options – and those are not necessarily the fastest. You'll find a URL to an online map for each route next to the length of each journey.

Every **route description** includes a simple **sketch map**, showing principal places along the way, with an adjacent table giving route details and the general pattern of rail services along that route. You'll need additional timetable information of course, and for that we heartily recommend Eurail's *Rail Planner* app and the respective **websites or apps of rail operators** along your route (for more information see p524). The *Rail Planner* app is a gem as you don't need to be online to access timetable data.

A route may very occasionally depend on a leg being undertaken by **bus or boat**. On the route sketch map we indicate that by the use of a 🚌 symbol or a ⛴ symbol. Although the route sketches are schematic, they are all aligned with north at the top of the page. The red numbers found on many sketch maps show where the route in question intersects with other routes described in this book. Of course no one dictates that you must follow our routes in their entirety. You can pick and choose, switching from one to another where they intersect, and sometimes branching out on your own to explore territory beyond our recommended routes. Indeed, we very much hope that following a few routes in this book will give you the confidence to **start creating your own itineraries**.

SIDETRACKS, CITY LINKS AND MORE

Our **Sidetracks** mini-features, 26 of them in all, might also encourage you to strike out independently. These are not strictly routes, but rather bold leaps. Some will lead to offshore islands (such as Sardinia or Mallorca), others will take you well beyond the regular tourist trails, even to places like Albania and the Outer Hebrides, where you'll be hard pushed to make good use of an Interrail pass. Sidetracks also cover topics such as railways and world heritage, carriage design and grand stations.

So 50 routes, all with a number and a name, and 26 Sidetracks, each with an identifying letter (from A to Z). Cast an eye again at those **full-colour maps** of the routes (on the inside covers at either end of the book) and you'll see that letters appear on those maps too, giving an indication of the area to which particular Sidetracks relate. Some Sidetracks are less geographical in character, exploring a rail-related theme rather than a place, so for those there's no corresponding pin on the full-colour maps. If you want to get an overview of rail travel in Europe on a country-by-country basis, turn to our gazetteer on pp450–503. That **country gazetteer** also includes key facts on each country such as the currency and languages used, time zone, etc.

Following the overview table of our 50 routes (on pp16–17), we give a wealth of advice on how best to **plan your itinerary** (pp18–20), on cross-city station changes (p21), on **night trains** (pp22–24) and on key shipping links (pp29–32). Tucked away towards the back of the book, after the country gazetteer, you'll find some real nuggets of information. Our list of **city links** (pp505–509) shows travel times on direct trains between principal European stations. We also have sections on cruise trains (p527), on **fares, tickets and passes** (pp510–23) and an **A-Z of travel facts** (pp529–33).

We hope that this book will guide and inspire. Never let yourself be too constrained by it. You can dip in and out of routes. We don't expect readers to follow them slavishly. You will surely need other resources. On page 10 we mentioned Eurail's wonderful *Rail Planner* app. You may find it helpful to consult the *European Rail Timetable* (ERT). The *Rail Map Europe* (also published by ERT) will help keep you on the right track as you travel around the continent by train. Find out more at www.europeanrailtimetable.eu. We also like Mike Ball's *European Railway Atlas*. Read more about it on p222.

At some places in this book, we use short links (eg. www.ebrweb.eu/1) to represent a URL. Some of these lead to **online maps of the 50 routes** (read more on p544). We use these short links purely to abbreviate an otherwise cumbersome URL. Finally, we know that some would-be travellers never leave home because they are overwhelmed by the burden of planning and expectation. Don't be waylaid by the notion of the 'perfect itinerary'. There is no such thing. And if you do need assistance in booking a trip, the team at **Byway Travel** (see p511) will certainly be pleased to help.

Overview: The 50 routes

Our **50 journeys** include some which are short and sweet and others that are long-haul adventures. **Route 15** and **42** are both less than 300 kilometres long. Yet they are as different as chalk and cheese: one is a wonderful rail cruise along the Mediterranean coast, the other is a fine transect by train through the Swiss Alps. At the other extreme we have some long-haul adventures. Five of our routes each extend to more than 1,400 kilometres.

Our table (below and opposite) shows the countries covered, the overall travel time and the length of each route. Note that the **travel time** quoted below does not make any allowance for breaking a journey or any overnight stops along the way. It's just an indication of how long you'll spend on trains (or ferries) if you follow the route, as we describe it, from end to end.

No.	From–to	countries	distance in km	travel time
1	London – Penzance	England	491	5h30
2	London – Kyle	England, Scotland	1,047	12h
3	Amsterdam – Mallaig	Netherlands, England, Scotland	1,132	28h30
4	Rotterdam – Killarney	Netherlands, England, Wales, Ireland	1,194	26h30
5	London – Galway	England, Wales, Ireland	1,006	18h
6	Lille – Amsterdam	France, Belgium, Netherlands	368	6h
7	Lille – Cologne	France, Belgium, Germany	357	3h
8	Amsterdam – Lausanne	Netherlands, Belgium, Luxembourg, France, Switzerland	1,020	12h30
9	Cologne – Zurich	Germany, Switzerland	611	7h30
10	Cologne – Berlin	Germany	612	6h
11	Hannover – Magdeburg	Germany	302	9h
12	Berlin – Salzburg	Germany, Austria	943	10h
13	London – Marseille	England, France	1,347	13h40
14	Paris – Geneva	France, Switzerland	747	8h40
15	Marseille – Nice	France	229	3h
16	Paris – Cherbourg	France	434	4h15
17	Paris – San Sebastián	France, Spain	1,030	16h
18	Paris – Barcelona	France, Spain	1,039	13h
19	Caen – Valence	France	949	12h
20	Geneva – Barcelona	Switzerland, France, Spain	856	12h

No.	From–to	countries	distance in km	travel time
21	Barcelona – Cádiz	Spain	1,265	12h
22	Barcelona – Málaga	Spain	1,136	6h
23	San Sebastián – Santiago de Compostela	Spain	1,260	9h
24	Santiago de Compostela – Seville	Spain, Portugal	1,101	13h
25	Amsterdam – Stockholm	Netherlands, Germany, Denmark, Sweden	1,661	17h10
26	Fredericia – Stockholm	Denmark, Norway, Sweden	1,425	20h
27	Copenhagen – Bergen	Denmark, Sweden, Norway	1,192	14h30
28	Oslo – Svolvær	Norway	1,450	20h
29	Stockholm – Svolvær	Sweden, Norway	1,735	19h
30	Boden – Stockholm	Sweden, Finland	1,501	23h
31	Hamburg – Warsaw	Germany, Poland	1,178	17h50
32	Nuremberg – Prague	Germany, Czech Republic	560	9h30
33	Hamburg – Budapest	Germany, Czech Republic, Slovakia, Hungary	1,291	13h45
34	Vienna – Constanța	Austria, Hungary, Romania	1,465	23h
35	Vienna – Budapest	Austria, Slovakia, Hungary	781	13h20
36	Berlin – Lviv	Germany, Poland, Ukraine	1,207	15h
37	Dresden – Poprad	Germany, Poland, Slovakia	751	13h25
38	Munich – Verona	Germany, Austria, Italy	434	6h20
39	Zurich – Vienna	Switzerland, Liechtenstein, Austria	845	9h50
40	Zurich – Milan	Switzerland, Italy	415	8h30
41	Basel – Milan	Switzerland, Italy	434	9h40
42	St Moritz – Zermatt	Switzerland	290	8h15
43	Zurich – Geneva	Switzerland	338	7h30
44	Vienna – Trieste	Austria, Slovenia, Italy	576	9h
45	Nice – Florence	France, Monaco, Italy	482	7h50
46	Verona – Rome	Italy	562	6h45
47	Genoa – Trieste	Italy	615	7h30
48	Rome – Siracusa	Italy	858	11h
49	Venice – Athens	Italy, Greece	1,444	28h20
50	Budapest – Ancona	Hungary, Croatia, Italy	1,051	22h40

Planning your itinerary

There is an untold pleasure in just breezing off without having given any real thought as to where you are bound. Some of the finest journeys are those which are least planned. Spontaneity brings its own rewards. But, as you'll quickly appreciate when you read our thoughts on train ticket deals (see pp510–23), spontaneity is often a very expensive luxury. You can save a packet if you book at least some aspects of your journey in advance.

Even if money is no object, a modicum of **advance planning** still makes good sense. Missing the once-a-day train from Cádiz to València may not trouble you at all. Cádiz is, after all, a splendid spot to hole up for a day. Missing the only Saturday departure from a dreary small town in the Balkans, and finding that the next train out is not till Monday, may not be quite so much fun. How much planning *you* need to do for *your* explorations of Europe by train has a lot to do with your **budget** and your **personal psyche**. Do you relish uncertainty? Will you be unduly troubled if you cannot easily find a place to stay overnight? How will you feel if there is another wave of coronavirus infections? Only you can answer such questions.

Two key planning tools are the *European Rail Timetable* (ERT) and the celebrated *Man in Seat Sixty-One* website (www.seat61.com) which is a goldmine of great advice. A good website for **checking train times** across much of Europe is www.bahn.de. But bear in mind that the database upon which this website draws is very incomplete when it comes to Spain, parts of the Balkans, Ireland and eastern Europe. We also rely a lot on Eurail's Rail Planner app, but that too has its data gaps.

Solo travel

The question of whether you travel alone is one that is ultimately a matter of personal choice. Solo travel can be immensely rewarding. The lone traveller is far more likely to strike up conversation with locals and fellow travellers. But an extended solo journey takes a certain grit and resilience, especially when all does not go quite as you might hope. There are times when being able to **share experiences** with a friend or partner can help make a journey take on new meaning. Bear in mind, too, that accommodation costs are heavily stacked against the single traveller.

Beware the packed itinerary

By far the biggest mistake made by first timers embarking on a vacation exploring Europe by train is to bite off far more than is feasible. With so much on offer, it is all too tempting to say "Let's just throw in Venice. And Florence. Perhaps we should have an afternoon in Paris too."

Sketch out your **first tentative itinerary** and then halve the number of places you intend to visit. A two-night stop is hugely more rewarding than

Seven steps to perfect planning

Let's assume you have the basics. You'll need a valid passport, or ID card for travelling in regions where an identity card suffices. Remember that Britain no longer accepts ID cards for entry. And how about visas? Check the small print of visa rules. Most of Europe has a fairly benign visa regime, but it's easy to get caught out. The UK still demands visas for visitors from many countries. Beyond these bureaucratic essentials, here are our **seven golden rules** for trip planning.

Prepare an outline budget with estimates of accommodation, food and travel costs, including seat reservation fees and travel supplements for rail pass holders. Add allowances for incidentals. Include entrance fees to galleries and museums, left-luggage charges, plus coffees and cocktails.

Tune your expectations to match your budget. A gondola ride across the Grand Canal in Venice costs just a couple of euros. But if you wish to be serenaded on a private gondola, expect to pay upwards of €100. Grand French clarets will not cost any less in a fine Bordeaux restaurant than at home. Even modest fare may test your wallet in Europe's more expensive countries such as Norway.

Consider money matters. Do you have contactless, cash point (ATM) and credit cards to support your journey? Check in advance what currencies you'll need at each stop on your itinerary. Use contactless payment where possible and plan where you'll pack cash to minimise the risk of loss or theft.

Think about luggage at the outset. A small amount, never more than you can comfortably carry yourself, can be a wonderful asset. More just becomes a terrible burden. We know travellers who have survived long tours around Europe without a portable ice bucket and a miner's lamp. For us, a corkscrew and appropriate plug adaptors are essentials. There is no such thing as a universal packing list to suit all, but http://upl.codeq.info is a good start. And it's fun to play with.

Buy insurance early. While it is a sound principle never to travel with something that you would be desperately sorry to lose, things do go astray. And medical cover is essential. If you are resident in any of the 30 or so European countries participating in the EHIC scheme, you should obtain a free European Health Insurance Card before leaving home. You should review whether it provides adequate cover, and you may consider top-up medical insurance.

Weather watching makes sense. Check out what you can expect along the way. Bear in mind that an itinerary which includes both Arctic Norway and the Greek islands will traverse several climate zones. Remember that places blessed with a wonderful climate may still turn out to have terrible weather on the week you visit.

Be app savvy by downloading and familiarising yourself with all the key travel apps you'll need while travelling (see also p524). Be it online maps of rail networks or target cities, selected public transport apps for checking schedules, real time running information and fares, it's best to have these apps all conveniently located together on your device. Start by downloading Eurail's rail planner app and using the 'my trip' function to sketch out an itinerary – even if you are not planning on using a rail pass.

having just one night in a new city. Three nights is even better. If you opt for a fortnight of one-night stays, each morning setting off for a new city, Europe will collapse in a mishmash of blurred memories. Similarly, **long travel days** take their toll as do several consecutive nights of overnight travel. There will be times when a ten-hour haul by day will allow you to cover a lot of ground. And it may be good fun, especially if you follow a route that takes in some great scenery. But if you have several such long days on the trot, the appeal of train travel will surely wane.

Careful planning can make a long travel day much more enjoyable. If you must make a ten-hour journey in a single day, then why not break it up into two legs of five hours each, and schedule **a decent-length break** at a midway point. A brisk walk or a relaxed lunch (or both) will leave you refreshed for the second stretch of the journey.

The plane question

This book is all about exploring Europe by rail. It's not about flying. We all need to cut our carbon footprint. But very exceptionally, there may be itineraries where a **leg by plane** could make sense, whether at the start or end of your itinerary, or to shift quickly from one part of Europe to another in the middle of a long trip.

Before you start booking many sectors by plane, just consider what **alternatives** might be available. A long overnight journey by train or by boat may usefully bridge a gap. For example we've combined a week exploring Italy with a subsequent week in Spain by taking a ship between the two countries. If you must fly, bear in mind that **early bookers** bag the cheapest fares. Don't just focus on the discount airlines. Close to the travel date, you may find that so-called budget carriers are even more expensive that the traditional full-cost airlines.

Urban or rural?

What kind of Europe are you eager to discover? A Europe full of **cosmopolitan flair**, such as you might encounter in Paris, Dublin and Milan, or a quieter, more rural Europe where the locals may even still have time for and interest in the visitors who come their way?

If you stick to premier-league tourist destinations, you'll probably have a ball, but you'll see places that are not always typical of the countries in which they are located. The wonderful thing about travelling by train is the European rail network can take you to backwaters frequented by few tourists. So make time for some of the small towns and branch lines that we mention in this book and you will be handsomely rewarded. And allow time for slow trains that dawdle through the countryside, stopping off here and there along the way.

Crossing Cities

On many European itineraries, you'll find yourself needing to **change stations within a city** to continue your journey. Be it in London, Paris, Madrid or Milan, or indeed many other cities, a cross-city transfer between stations is often suggested by journey planners as the obvious and fastest option.

But there are some **nuanced choices** to be made here. We personally never mind a stroll through a foreign city in the middle of a long travel day. But others, especially when travelling with children or heavy luggage, may feel differently. There are often alternative routes which **avoid the cross-city interchange**. Travellers from London bound for provincial cities across France may find it easier to change in Lille rather than Paris. On some routes across Spain where a change in Madrid was once inevitable, there are now a small number of direct trains offering routes like Santander to Alicante or Valencia to Burgos, which obviate the need for a trek across Madrid.

But is a trek across Madrid such a bad thing? Or a walk across London or Paris? In **London** we have often walked from Waterloo station to St Pancras (about 45 minutes on foot). In **Paris**, it's an interesting one-hour hike from the Gare du Nord to the Gare de Lyon. Many interchanges on foot are much shorter. From the Gare du Nord in Paris to the Gare de l'Est is just ten minutes on foot. The short hop from Queen Street to Central in **Glasgow** takes under a quarter of an hour. So, if you don't have much luggage, a transfer on foot is often much less hassle than using buses, trams or the metro.

And bear in mind that taxis may not be the fastest in city-centre traffic. Better perhaps to walk and take time to stop off in a city centre park, where half an hour just watching the world go by might seal a lasting impression of a city which is no more than a brief stopover on a longer itinerary. We have twice in spring and summer 2024 enjoyed **recuperative stops in Parisian parks**.

In some cities, urban rail routes may conveniently **link major rail termini**. In Berlin, for example, there are good S-Bahn links between major stations. In London there is the new **Elizabeth Line**, running west to east under the city, linking Paddington with Liverpool Street in under 15 minutes. There is also the Thameslink route which runs south from King's Cross / St Pancras to emerge from the underground for a dramatic Thames crossing at Blackfriars. Interrail passes are valid on the routes mentioned in this paragraph.

For plotting city-centre transfers, be they on foot or **using local public transport**, we often rely on the excellent *Citymapper* travel app which now covers more than 60 urban areas across Europe. This app, available for both Android and iOS devices, offers both walking and public transport options for navigating cities.

Night trains

It is very likely that, sooner or later on your explorations of Europe by train, you will end up taking an overnight service. Here we offer a few thoughts on what to expect. The first important distinction to make is between a **regular train** that just happens to run through the night and a proper **night train**. The first kind of train is, we feel, generally to be avoided. Yes, we have done it, but just take our word that the overnighter from Sighetu Marmaţiei to Cluj-Napoca is not a lot of fun. Following a rural route through northern Romania, this train has few creature comforts and even our considerable enthusiasm for slow trains waned after several hours aboard. If you must travel by night, then make sure that the train you choose is equipped for overnight travel. Many Romanian overnight trains are. We just opted for the wrong one. What's true for Romania applies equally elsewhere. In Germany, ICE 699 makes an overnight journey of over 12 hours from Hamburg to Munich. It has only regular seats, so is best avoided.

At their best, Europe's night trains are superb. They offer various **grades of sleeping accommodation**. Top of the range are luxury sleepers with en suite facilities. You'll only find these on a small number of trains,

NIGHT TRAIN OPERATORS

Germany, so strategically positioned at the heart of Europe, once offered a fine network of night train services. That is less true nowadays as budget-conscious Germans seem happy to sit up all night in seats. The few remaining Deutsche Bahn CNL night trains disappeared in late 2016, with Austrian operator ÖBB stepping in to pick up many former CNL routes. These run under ÖBB's new *Nightjet* banner. It is thus still possible to travel in the comfort of a sleeper on overnight trains to, from and within Germany. Trains leave Berlin and Hamburg every evening for Zurich, Vienna and Basel. *Nightjet* trains also link Munich and Vienna with Rome, Milan and the Cinque Terre coast.

You will find **useful domestic night train links** within many European countries. It is always worth checking if a night train can usefully complement daytime travel on some of the journeys described in this book. There are excellent Czech night trains, night trains across Austria, from Helsinki to the north of Finland, from northern Italy to Sicily and from one corner of Poland to the other. Overnight services leave Oslo and Stockholm each evening, all bound to far-flung corners of their respective countries.

France is a little unusual in that its overnight trains entirely within France have no sleeping cars, so a couchette is your best option. But here too *Nightjet* provides a model of good practice by offering proper sleeping cars on its thrice-weekly routes from Paris to Salzburg, Vienna and Berlin. Prior to the COVID-19 pandemic, Europe's most distinctive night trains ran from Russia to cities in central and western Europe including Paris, Genoa, Prague and Vienna. As long as there is war in eastern Europe, Russian trains are unlikely to be seen in the European Union. Meanwhile, there are now **new market entrants** responding to rising demand for overnight trains: RegioJet and European Sleeper are both expanding their offer.

Check our **city links list** (on pp505–509) where the letter 'N' behind the destination in a city pair indicates that those two cities are linked by a direct night train.

and they are not cheap or you can opt for regular sleeping compartments designed for one or more passengers (but usually bookable as a single for an extra charge) or couchettes. The latter are a down-market version of a sleeper. A normal compartment by day converts to simple bunk beds by night. Some night trains also convey carriages with **reclining seats**, thus affording a little more comfort than a normal seat, but still not great for a 12-hour overnighter. In 2024, Austrian operator ÖBB introduced a new option on some of its *Nightjet* services. New carriages now include sleeping pods which offer much greater privacy than a couchette.

While only the most demanding travellers really need the luxury of the very poshest **sleeping compartments** (some of which may include minibars and flat screen TVs), it is worth trading up to a regular sleeper if you can possibly afford it. They are much more comfortable than **couchettes**. Remember you are saving a night's hotel or hostel accommodation and your appreciation of your destination in the morning will be vastly more positive if you have enjoyed a good night's sleep in crisp linen sheets.

Couchettes usually have four to six places per compartment. They are basic, but adequate. Bear in mind that a full six-berth couchette may be no fun in midsummer heat. Sleepers are usually air-conditioned and typically have one to four berths per compartment. **Sheets and towels** are provided, and generally beds are made up for you. Russia, Belarus and Ukraine are rare exceptions. In those countries, the carriage attendant (called a *provodnik*) gives you the sheets, and you make your own bed. Help is always available for the elderly or less agile.

A shared **two-berth** sleeper compartment usually provides a reasonable measure of comfort. Single travellers booking a berth in a multiple-berth compartment must expect to share with strangers (usually **segregated by gender**). This is a travel experience that, as you move east across the continent, becomes ever more convivial. In Russia, it often involves sharing salami, hard-boiled eggs and life stories with complete strangers. There is no requirement that the stories you tell be true. Some sleeper trains are ideal for **families**. Many Finnish overnight services and the *Caledonian Sleeper* trains from London to Scotland have interconnecting doors between compartments that can be opened to create a larger space for a family.

Especially in central and eastern Europe, a train may include sleeping cars from several different countries. For many night trains, you can check the provenance of sleeping cars and what facilities they have (eg. air conditioning, electric sockets, etc) on **vagonWEB** (www.vagonweb.cz). Choose the English-language version, then select 'composition' and find your service through its train number. Standards may vary widely between the carriages of the various railway administrations. Don't assume that 'east' is bad and 'west' is good. Some of the **most comfortable night trains** we have used are Russian ones.

LONDON CONNECTIONS

Britain **lost its proper night train** to the continent in 1980 with the demise of *The Night Ferry*, a train with comfortable *Wagons-Lits* sleeping cars that provided a direct overnight service from London to Paris and Brussels. For a spell *The Night Ferry* even carried a sleeping car to Switzerland. Travellers from Britain can take Eurostar from London to **Brussels, Amsterdam or Paris**. In Amsterdam you can board night trains which leave every evening for Zurich, Innsbruck and Vienna, and thrice weekly to Dresden and Prague. Alternatively, it is possible to connect in Brussels onto night trains to Berlin or Vienna. There are also **night trains from Paris**. An afternoon journey from London to Paris with Eurostar and aperitifs in the French capital are the natural prelude to an overnight train journey on the Paris to Vienna sleeper (which also serves Salzburg). This train also carries through carriages to Berlin. There are also direct overnight trains from Paris to the Pyrenees, the Riviera and the French Alps. Note that these domestic services in France only offer couchettes rather than sleeping cars.

It also pays to know in advance if there will be a **restaurant car** on your train. It is all too rare these days. Some menus on night trains nicely anticipate the destination. Thus on the journey from London to the Scottish Highlands you can enjoy haggis and neeps for supper and round off the evening with a good malt whisky in the lounge car. On the train from Stockholm to Narvik in northern Norway, a magnificent overnight journey that takes you beyond the Arctic Circle, meat patties made from elk are standard fare on the dinner menu – or at least until the pandemic led to the withdrawal of catering. So be aware that some overnight trains may have no restaurant car. Go prepared! On most Russian trains, tea, coffee and a small selection of drinks and light snacks are available from the **carriage attendant**. In Germany and Austria, the train staff can usually provide drinks, soup and sandwiches on night trains with no restaurant car.

Night trains are of course the stuff of romance. They are a scriptwriter's delight – and a cameraman's nightmare, for the sleeping compartment offers few great panoramas when fixed on **celluloid**. That didn't stop Carol Reed in *Night Train to Munich* (1940) and Alfred Hitchcock in *North by Northwest* (1959) from both having a very good try. The mystery of the night train was forever sealed by *Murder on the Orient Express* (1974), where the accomplished music and superb cinematography that attend the train's departure from Istanbul's Sirkeci station more than compensate for the impish Belgian detective's subsequent difficulty in solving the murder that takes place at some unspecified but decidedly Balkan point along the route. Hercule Poirot will not be on your night train, so the chances are that you'll get a good night's sleep. Try it once, and you'll surely be hooked.

Night trains are suddenly back in fashion, and a number of welcome new routes were launched in 2024. We discuss this theme further in our **Sidetracks** feature on p367.

High-speed rail in Europe

Across Europe, there has been enormous investment in new rail infrastructure over the last 40 years, with the construction and **opening of dedicated high-speed lines** where trains routinely run at 250 kilometres per hour or even faster. These new routes are engineered on very different principles from Europe's legacy rail networks, most of which date back to the 19th century or the early part of the 20th century.

Traditionally, railways followed the warp and weft of the land. The new generation of high-speed lines are still sensitive to the constraints of terrain, but rather less so than with the older, legacy networks. Tunnels cut boldly through mountain ranges and valleys are traversed with great viaducts. With less attention to the dictates of terrain, these new high-speed railways may have **steeper gradients**. Powerful trains are needed to cope with these challenging climbs.

Dedicated networks

Spain has Europe's most comprehensive **network of new-build high-speed routes**, with over 4000 km now in service. France comes second with about 3000 km, followed by Italy and then Germany, which has surprisingly few dedicated high-speed routes, having favoured an alternative policy of **upgrading existing railways** rather than developing completely new railways. Britain's only dedicated high-speed line is the route from London to the Kent portal of the Channel Tunnel, about 110 km in length.

The experience of travelling on dedicated high-speed railways is substantially different from that on a traditional railway. Speed generates its own sensations and brings an inevitable **disconnect from the landscape**. Trains on these new high-speed lines usually stop only infrequently and we find there is less sense of being immersed in the terrain. That said, we have had some utterly memorable journeys on Europe's high-speed railways, including a fine journey on a Eurostar train when we were invited to join the driver up front in the cab for the entire 492-km run from Paris to London.

Making time for journeys

Generally though, our preference is for slower trains where there is a heightened sense of engagement with the landscape. And taking things slowly is very much in vogue with many travellers now espousing the **principles of slow travel** set out in our *Manifesto for Slow Travel* (first published in *hidden europe* magazine in 2009). Throughout this book you will find references to slow travel, often casting the latter in a virtuous light, and thus possibly inviting the reader to infer that there is something less worthy about fast travel. It is interesting that one of the authors of this book is styled by *The Guardian* as that newspaper's 'slow travel expert'.

Good journeys require time, but there are occasions when an itinerary very reasonably relies on a fast leg. Indeed we have routes in this book which make good use of high-speed trains. Examples include the initial stretch of **Route 13** which relies on Eurostar from London to Paris and **Route 22** from Barcelona to the south of Spain. Both those routes illustrate the theatre that sometimes comes with high-speed rail journeys, be it the fractured views of south Essex and north Kent **glimpsed from Eurostar** en route from London to the Channel Tunnel or the sheer drama of gliding through the Sierra Morena on the way to Andalucía.

Memorable high-speed routes

There are some high-speed routes which are truly a delight. We have a soft spot for the new line which cuts south from Erfurt (in eastern Germany) **through the hills of Thuringia** to Bamberg in Franconia. This line opened in December 2017 and it is now used by many German ICE trains including the ICE Sprinter services which dash from Berlin to Munich in just four hours. There are **moments of stroboscopic wonder** along a route which has myriad tunnels and many dramatic viaducts. We catch glimpses of remote villages where rural calm has presumably been shattered by the new railway. We speed by forests and deep valleys on a route where trains reach speeds approaching 300 kph. Many travellers, we suspect, make a mental note that one day they really should return and explore this beautiful region that straddles the former border between the two Germanys which became one country on 3 October 1990.

The new **line has many fine moments**. It may not have the understated beauty of the traditional Saale Valley route from eastern Germany to northern Bavaria, which is still used by local trains as well as occasional Intercity services from Leipzig to Nuremberg. But, as high-speed lines go, that new route from Erfurt to Bamberg gets a big thumbs-up from us.

High-speed in France

France's very first high-speed line from **Paris to Lyon** was completed in 1983, although the southernmost part of this 410-km route had opened two years earlier. More than four decades on, this railway has melded beautifully with the surrounding landscape and the two-hour ride from Paris to Lyon on a TGV or a Frecciarossa is **full of interest**. Of course if you have time, we would recommend following the old main line which lost its trunk route status with the completion of the new high-speed route in 1983. That traditional railway line still has trains running right through from Paris to Lyon and it is described in **Route 14** in this book. But if time is tight, by all means use the high-speed line and you'll discover that it has a charm of its own.

About an hour out of Paris on the high-speed route, the Lyon-bound express train skirts the eastern **flanks of the Morvan hills**, climbing to about 500 metres above sea level and affording excellent views of the terrain, especially on the right side of the train. Heads down and attending to their mobile phones and laptops, the majority of train travellers probably miss ten minutes of rural bliss – for that's all it takes to speed by the Morvan hills. Later in the journey, there's a wonderful section as the train drops down towards the **Saône Valley** with a fine view of the ancient **monastic foundation of Cluny** to the right.

Speeding east from Paris

Another French high-speed line which is very pleasing is the 400-km long route from **Paris to Strasbourg** which was completed in 2016. Again, it may not be a match for the traditional Marne Valley railway which runs east from Paris, and which in its heyday was used by such illustrious trains as the *Orient Express*. These days the only international trains which routinely follow the classic route east from the French capital up the Marne Valley are the Nightjet trains to Vienna and Berlin.

But there is **a quiet drama** around the two-hour journey on a non-stop train from Paris to Strasbourg via the new high-speed line. One slips out of Paris through a litany of forlorn suburbs, leaving the old Marne Valley route at Vaires. As the train gathers pace, we speed by coppice woodland and meadows, and before long we are travelling at over 300 kph. The line sweeps east with distant views of Champagne vineyards. There are **striking viaducts** over the Meuse and the Moselle, two rivers which have lent their names to French *départements*. This is a chance to appreciate European geography as it slips by beyond the carriage window. Later in the journey, the Strasbourg-bound train tunnels under the Vosges at the narrowest point of this mountain range. Emerging from the Saverne Tunnel into **Alsace**, the line drops down towards the Rhine with, on a clear day, views across to Germany's Black Forest far away to the east.

Making time for the Alps

Speed is of course all relative. In mountain regions, we need to rethink our understanding of speed. The German poet **Heinrich Heine** wrote beautifully about how railways reshape our appreciation of space and time. Heine described how the providential spread of the railway annihilated space. "I feel as if the mountains and forests are advancing on Paris," he wrote.

The area of Europe where the need to balance speed with the need to make progress plays out most dramatically is in the Alps. In terms of actual speed, many Alpine rail routes are quite slow. But there are sharp variations. A **Bernina Railway** local train from St Moritz to Tirano (**Route 40**) may average 25 kph. An SOB *Treno Gottardo* train running south from Flüelen to Bellinzona on the classic Gotthard railway (**Route 41**) will average about 60 kph. These are qualitatively different experiences. You get a very different feel for the terrain on these two wonderful Alpine railways. But you could of course dash south through Switzerland towards Italy on one of the express trains which run through the **Gotthard Base Tunnel**, where passenger services routinely run at around 200 kph. This is not the way to see the Alps. It's not merely a question of speed, but also that the tunnel itself, 57 km in length, ensures that the Alps remain entirely invisible.

On many Alpine rail routes, and more widely across Europe, there is a strong impetus to build **deeper, longer rail tunnels** which allow for higher train speeds. These are called 'base tunnels'. The very first in Switzerland was the Hauenstein Base Tunnel which opened in 1916. The most recent is the Gotthard Base Tunnel, opening in 2016. Happily, the original routes that these new base tunnels replaced are still very much in use by regular passenger trains. In **Austria**, new base tunnels are under construction to speed up traffic on the important Semmering (**Route 44**) and Brenner (**Route 38**) routes. In late 2023, a new base tunnel was opened through the Cantabrian Mountains in northern Spain. The **Pajares Base Tunnel** is good for those needing to get to Gijon in a rush, but for those intent on seeing the remarkable scenery of this region it is better to take the one train each day still running via the old line. When travelling in Europe's mountain regions, those prepared to take a slower route often reap big rewards.

High-speed disappointments

We have highlighted some high-speed journeys which we consider particularly appealing. These last two examples from France are not really better than the legacy railways they replaced, but they speed you from Paris to Lyon and Strasbourg respectively, in each case halving the travel time needed via the original route.

So there's a time and place when on some itineraries a high-speed leg makes perfect sense. But for every high-speed route which packs a welcome surprise, there are many which are disappointing. The 42-km line from **Liège to Aachen** means that travellers speeding from Brussels to Germany entirely **miss the fine scenery** of the Ardennes region of eastern Belgium, swapping the valleys which were once home to a thriving textile industry for a long tunnel. Further south, travellers joining fast trains in **Bologna** for the journey to **Florence** should not anticipate glorious views of Tuscan landscapes. Over 90 per cent of the journey is in tunnels. Happily there are alternative, slower routes which do afford fine vistas of the hills.

It's all a matter of horses for courses. Yes, of course there is a place for high-speed in many itineraries. And one day we want to make time to dash from Piedmont to Calabria in a day, with both Italo and Trenitalia offering direct high-speed trains from Turin to the toe of Italy. It would surely be fun. But do **make time for slower journeys** for in our experience they are far more rewarding.

Key shipping links

Why boats and ferries? Isn't this a book about rail travel? Well, yes, but over the years we have found that a day or two afloat is a very fine way of changing the **tempo of a journey**. Just as night trains allow you to cover distance while sleeping, so too do ferries. But it's not just overnight journeys on boats which appeal. In good weather, a day on a comfortable ship can be extremely pleasant. Several of our 50 routes include a **ferry crossing**, the shortest a mere ten-minute hop and the longest extending to about 18 hours.

Looking at the ferry scene in 2024, we cannot recall a time when it has been quite so volatile. Routes come and go in a twinkle. Some old favourites have disappeared, probably for good. P&O's overnight service from Zeebrugge to Hull was axed in early 2021, a victim of **Brexit**. Ironically that route was launched in the year after Britain joined the European Union, and it survived until a year after Britain left the EU.

Many **new routes** are starting. Stena Line has launched a new service from Grenaa (in Danish Jutland) to Halmstad (in Sweden), crossing the Kattegat to link two ports with decent rail connections. Holland Norway Lines launched a new route from Emden (in Germany) to Kristiansand (Norway) in June 2023 which folded three months later.

It's a tough market for new entrants. Two new companies announced routes from **Sicily to Malta** in 2021, bringing competition to Virtu Ferries which have served Malta well for many years. One of the two start-ups never set sail at all, while the other started then stopped a few weeks later.

Be aware that there is an invidious trend to marginalize **foot passengers** – and that hits hard at those making rail-sea journeys. During the pandemic, none of the three ferry operators sailing from Dover to Calais would accept foot passengers. Happily P&O has relented and now permit pre-booked foot passengers on three sailings each day in each direction on that short ferry route. We are pleased to read that for travel in 2025 Brittany Ferries is again accepting foot passengers on routes from Ireland to France and Spain.

Selected routes

In the listings that follow, we highlight just a selection of ferry routes which we have used ourselves or have been recommended by readers of this book. Some are great time savers. The routes from Hirtshals in North Jutland to Norway are examples. Others are included mainly because **they are fun**. An example of the latter is the daytime TT-Line sailing from Travemünde (near Lübeck in Germany). The ten-hour voyage on the *MS Peter Pan* might sound as though it should be bound for Neverland, but it goes to Trelleborg with a stop in Rostock along the way.

The key routes mentioned below have been selected because they link regions of Europe featured in this book (whether in our 50 journeys or in

Sidetracks). But do bear in mind that there's a wealth of other ferries, covering the Scottish islands, the Irish Sea, the Norwegian coast and the Black Sea.

Some routes may not operate year-round; indeed quite a number are **seasonal**. And do check that your preferred route will indeed carry foot passengers. We have included only routes where foot passengers are carried on at least some sailings (as of February 2024). Many routes offer concessions for travellers using **Eurail or Interrail** – just check the operator's website.

Biscay and Western Channel

There are some excellent longer routes which take travellers directly from Spain and France to southern England and the Republic of Ireland.

From	To	Operator	Time
Santander (ES)	Portsmouth (ENG)	Brittany Ferries	24–29 hrs
St Malo (FR)	Poole (ENG)	Condor Ferries	7 hrs
Roscoff (FR)	Plymouth (ENG)	Brittany Ferries	6–9 hrs
Cherbourg (FR)	Rosslare (IE)	Stena Line	18 hrs
Cherbourg (FR)	Dublin (IE)	Irish Ferries	19 hrs

Sicilian escapes

Route 48 is the long-haul south by train to Sicily. You might consider returning to the mainland by boat. Here's a small selection of the many options available.

From	To	Operator	Time
Catania (IT)	Salerno (IT)	Grimaldi Lines	13 hrs
Palermo (IT)	Genoa (IT)	Grandi Navi Veloci	21 hrs
Palermo (IT)	Naples (IT)	Tirrenia	11 hrs
Milazzo (IT)	Naples (IT)	Siremar	18 hrs

Cross-Med sailings

On any longer tour of southern Europe it may make sense to take one of the many Mediterranean shipping services. Don't always think of these journeys as being merely one long leg. There are some good island-hopping opportunities.

From	To	Operator	Time
Barcelona (ES)	Civitavecchia (IT)	Grimaldi Lines	20–22 hrs
Barcelona (ES)	Genoa (IT)	Grandi Navi Veloci	20–22 hrs
Barcelona (ES)	Savona (IT)	Grimaldi Lines	20 hrs
Mallorca (ES)	Toulon (FR)	Corsica Ferries	11–13 hrs

Key shipping links | 31

Adriatic cruises

Train connections are so awful in some parts of the Balkans that for journeys to Albania and Greece it sometimes makes perfect sense to take a ship.

From	To	Operator	Time
Venice (IT)	Pátras (GR)	Anek Lines	32–33 hrs
Bari (IT)	Pátras (GR)	Superfast Ferries	16–18 hrs
Ancona (IT)	Durrës (AL)	Adria Ferries	16 hrs

Short sea sprints

There is a good range of ferry links across the English Channel.

From	To	Operator	Time
Calais (FR)	Dover (ENG)	P&O Ferries	90 mins
Dieppe (FR)	Newhaven (ENG)	DFDS	4–5 hrs
Cherbourg (FR)	Poole (ENG)	Brittany Ferries	4–5 hrs

North Sea crossings

Here are some really useful routes for travellers heading to Britain who fancy arriving on a boat rather than taking the Eurostar train to London.

From	To	Operator	Time
Amsterdam (NL)	Newcastle (ENG)	DFDS	17 hrs
Rotterdam (NL)	Hull (ENG)	P&O Ferries	11–12 hrs
Hoek (NL)	Harwich (ENG)	Stena Line	7–10 hrs

Baltic breezes

Baltic cruise-ferries are some of the finest vessels in European waters. These cross-Baltic routes are among our favourites.

From	To	Operator	Time
Copenhagen (DK)	Oslo (NO)	DFDS	17–18 hrs
Travemünde (DE)	Trelleborg (SE)	TT-Line	10 hrs
Helsinki (FI)	Travemünde (DE)	Finnlines	30 hrs
Kiel (DE)	Klaipėda (LT)	DFDS	20 hrs
Stockholm (SE)	Tallinn (EE)	Tallink Silja Line	16 hrs
Oslo (NO)	Kiel (DE)	Color Line	22 hrs
Nynäshamn (SE)	Gdańsk (PL)	Polferries	18 hrs

Rail-Sail tickets

Historically, some key ferry routes were run by national rail companies or by maritime affiliates of those train operators. One effect of this was that international rail tariffs often included ferries. A train ticket from London to the Rhineland included the ferry crossing, whether from **Harwich to Hoek van Holland** or on the now defunct route from Dover to Ostend. There is an echo of this old way of doing things in some of the excellent value rail-sail fares which combine trains and ferries.

Travelling from Germany to the Alps, the choice is often whether to route around the west side or the east side of **Lake Constance**. But you can also opt for the route *across* Lake Constance, using the ferry from Friedrichshafen to Romanshorn. This ferry route is still fully integrated into rail tariffs.

Similarly, you can use a rail-sail fare from Hoek of Holland to London (or any station in East Anglia), or from any station in Britain to many destinations across Ireland. There are rail-sail tickets to the **Scilly Isles** (using the steamer from Penzance) or from major Scottish stations to islands in the Hebrides and the Clyde. Buy a ticket from **Ankara to Kapıköy**, the easternmost station in Turkey, and your fare will cover two trains and a seven-hour interlude on the ship crossing Lake Van.

Trenitalia sell great-value rail-sail tickets to Elba, just as Deutsche Bahn sell through tickets from any mainland station to some ports in the **North or East Frisian Islands**. You can book a rail-sail ticket from many stations in Denmark through to the island of **Bornholm**; the rail part of the journey slips through Sweden. New market entrants are very aware of the potential of the rail-sail market. RegioJet has experimented with summer-season through fares from central Europe to popular Croatian islands.

Our award for the most creative rail-sail combo goes to rail operator NTV Italo which for a while teamed up with hydrofoil operator Alicost to offer through tickets to the **Aeolian Islands** (Isole Eolie). It sounds like a dream: travel south in the comfort of an Italo train, alight at the appealing small port of Sapri on the Cilento coast and then be whisked over to **Stromboli** on a hydrofoil. Italo and Trenitalia both offer through *Treno+Nave* (rail-sail) fares to Messina in Sicily. Trenitalia also have rail-sail fares to the island of Elba.

★★★

Note on colour feature
Every place included in our colour feature is on or close to one or more of the routes in this book. When a photo is credited to 'hidden europe', it comes from the collection of the authors of this book. All other images, each duly credited to the original photographer, were sourced through www.dreamstime.com.

Europe in colour:
Journeys of discovery

LIÈGE — Santiago Calatrava's fluid design for Liège-Guillemins railway station lies at the heart of a bold urban renewal programme. The station is on **Route 7** and has a mention in **Sidetracks L** in this book (photo © Boarding1now).

Steaming through Scotland! This elegantly curved viaduct at Glenfinnan on the West Highland Railway features on **Route 3**. The route is served by regular diesel trains as well as *The Jacobite* steam special (photo © Miroslav Liska). GLENFINNAN

RÜGEN

The Baltic island of Rügen is easily visited when following **Route 31** in this book. Its fine coastline and mature beech forests are the big draw, but there is a dash of rail appeal in the island's narrow-gauge railway, where steam haulage is still used 365 days a year (photo © Anyaivanova).

A fine combination of old and new at Strasbourg's main railway station. The glass armadillo was added in 2006. Strasbourg makes a good overnight stop when following **Route 8** from the Low Countries to Lake Geneva (photo © Jeff Whyte).

STRASBOURG

JOURNEYS OF DISCOVERY | 35

Lviv

Poprad

ABOVE: The Ukrainian city of Lviv is the end point of **Route 36**. The image shows the eastern side of the main market square, with a fine mix of Rococo and Renaissance architecture. In 1998, the square was inscribed on UNESCO's World Heritage List (photo © hidden europe).

RIGHT: With this new edition, Poprad now features on two routes in *Europe by Rail*. They are **Route 35** and **37**. The Slovakian town makes a pleasing stopover. Our image shows the Church of the Holy Trinity in the town centre (photo © Jaroslav Moravcik).

36 | Europe in colour

Lake Geneva

A regional train to Romont pauses at Grandvaux in Switzerland's Lavaux vineyard region with gorgeous views over Lake Geneva. Smaller places like Grandvaux make perfect overnight stops while exploring Europe by train. Grandvaux is on **Route 8**, and just a short walk down to the lakeshore will bring you to **Route 43** (photo © hidden europe).

Kraków

Serenity in Kraków amid the Renaissance arcades of the Sukiennice (cloth hall). Kraków boasts one of Europe's most celebrated town squares. The Polish city is on **Route 36** and **37** in this book (photo © Tomas1111).

JOURNEYS OF DISCOVERY | 37

BRUSSELS

Brussels' Grand Place rates as one of Europe's finest city squares. Too many travellers just change trains in Brussels, on **Route 7** in this book, without making time to explore. The Grand Place is just four minutes on foot from Centraal Station in the Belgian capital (photo © Jan Kranendonk).

SANTIAGO DE COMPOSTELA

Nearing the end of the pilgrim trail! Sculptures on the hill near Santiago where foot-weary pilgrims get their first view of the town's triple-spired cathedral. Walk if you will, or arrive by train following **Route 23** or **24** in this book (photo © Avictorero).

Lucerne

Few Swiss cities can rival Lucerne when it comes to location. The lakeshore city lies at the intersection of **Route 41** and **43**. It's the perfect place to stop for a couple of nights and perhaps swap trains for boats with an excursion on the lake (photo © Michalludwiczak).

Three Austrian rail routes in this book offer magnificent journeys on very high quality trains. They are **Route 38**, **39** and **44**, respectively covering the Brenner, Arlberg and Semmering railways. Our picture here shows an Austrian Railways Eurocity train on the Brenner route (photo © Leonid Andronov).

Brenner Railway

Journeys of discovery | 39

Warsaw chic at the restored Koszyki market hall in the Śródmieście district of the Polish capital. Warsaw is on **Route 31** and **36** (photo © hidden europe).

Warsaw

Košice

Slovakia's second city Košice made its debut in the 17th edition of *Europe by Rail* and we enhance our Slovakian coverage in this 18th edition. This Košice image shows a remarkable baroque plague column, erected to give thanks for deliverance from an epidemic. The city is on **Route 35** (photo © Peter Lovás).

NANTES

We have better coverage of the Loire Valley in this 18th edition of *Europe by Rail*. Travellers to Nantes (on **Route 17** and not far from **Route 19**) should make time to visit this magnificent mechanical elephant at *Les Machines de l'Île* (photo © Thomas Dutour).

Plan your trip around foodie treats! Slow travel and slow food make natural partners, so think local and eat well while exploring Europe by train. Here's a chance to tickle your taste buds while changing trains in Bologna which is on **Route 46** and **49** (photo © Rosshelen).

BOLOGNA

Bari

The Adriatic port of Bari is on **Route 49**, and is the jumping-off point for ferries to Albania and Greece, plus seasonal services to Croatia. When in Bari, make time to explore the old city and visit the 12th-century Basilica di San Nicola (photo © Mitzobs).

With year-round ferries from France, Scotland and Wales, it is so very easy to reach Dublin. The easy-going vibe of Dublin's Temple Bar district may encourage you to linger in the Irish capital, but do make time to explore beyond Dublin. **Route 4** and **5** in this book will escort you from Dublin to Killarney and Galway respectively (photo © Attila Tatár).

Dublin

Copenhagen

Above: Had you realised that Copenhagen is actually on two islands? They are called Zealand and Amager. So it's no surprise that you find a dash of maritime flair in the Danish capital. Copenhagen is on **Route 25** and **27** in this book (photo © Lukasz Kasperek).

Left: Take time off the rails and linger in some of Europe's finest cities. The arty Parisian district of Montmartre is just a brisk 15-minute walk from the Gare du Nord. The French capital is on **Route 13, 14, 16, 17** and **18** (photo © Outline205).

Paris

Journeys of discovery | 43

Constanța

This Romanian port on the Black Sea coast featured for the very first time in the 17th edition of *Europe by Rail*. That new route remains with some updates for this 18th edition. Follow **Route 34** to reach Constanța and see the crumbling art-nouveau casino on the promenade (photo © Anilah).

Bernina Railway

Autumn colours with the Morteratsch Glacier in the background near Pontresina in eastern Switzerland. This is on the Bernina Railway which forms part of **Route 40** in this book (photo © Yulan).

The Tuscan city of Siena, always a great rival to nearby Florence, preserves many elements of a mediaeval townscape. It is a good place to stop when following **Route 46** south through Italy (photo © Sborisov).

SIENA

LISBON

With just four trains each day entering Portugal from Spain, and none of them running directly to Lisbon, you have to persevere to reach the Portuguese capital by train. But Lisbon rewards those who make the effort. The city is on **Route 24**, newly extended in this 18th edition to continue by bus from Lisbon to Seville in Spain (photo © Altezza).

Journeys of discovery | 45

Trieste

The city at the head of the Adriatic combines Latin style with a dash of Habsburg flair. If pressed to nominate our favourite European city, Trieste might well get our vote. It's gorgeous. See if you agree by taking **Route 44** or **47** in this book, both of which end in Trieste (photo © Freesurf69).

Milan

Milano Centrale is one of Europe's truly great railway stations. Its restrained elegance reflects the emphasis on great public projects in the Mussolini era. Centrale is a place for grand arrivals and grand departures. You'll find it on **Route 40**, **41** and **47** in this book (photo © Alvaro German Vilela).

Vienna can rightly claim to be the rail hub of Europe. It is better connected than any other European capital. But it's much more than just a place for passing through. Our image shows the *Burgtheater*, referred to by the Viennese simply as *Die Burg*. You can reach Vienna on **Route 34**, **35**, **39** and **44** (photo © minnystock).

VIENNA

LÜBECK

The city of Lübeck epitomises Hanseatic style with a dash of modern Baltic flair. Just an hour from Hamburg, Lübeck is an amiable mid-sized city that makes a good stopover for a day or two. It's on **Route 31** in this book (photo © minnystock).

Eliel Saarinen's magnificent design for Helsinki's main station seals this building's status as one of the world's great railway termini. The building's simple austerity is offset by the pairs of giant lamp bearers who attend the station's main entrance. Helsinki is on **Route 30** in this book (photo © Lerka555).

Helsinki

Zweisimmen

Opt for the *belle époque* style of carriages which are used on some of the slower trains from Zweisimmen to Montreux via Gstaad run by the Montreux Oberland Bernois Railway (MOB). Ride this line while following **Route 43** (photo © hidden europe).

48 | Europe in colour

Mussy Viaduct Featured for the very first time in *Europe by Rail*, the *viaduc de Mussy-sous-Dun* is one of the finest early pieces of railway engineering in France. It is on the railway between Paray-le-Monial and Lyon which forms part of **Route 19** in this book (photo © Ricochet69).

The Meeting Place on the concourse of St Pancras station in London has been condemned as pure kitsch. Yet some praise Paul Day's sculpture for capturing the romance of travel. St Pancras is the starting point for **Route 13** in this book (photo © Cowardlion). **London**

Routes

Fifty key rail routes which together capture the very best that Europe has to offer. Our routes cover cities and landscapes from the Arctic to Andalucía, from the Baltic to the Bay of Biscay, from the Atlantic coast of Ireland to the Carpathians. Use our route overview list on pp16–17 to see the specific countries which feature on each of our 50 routes. Or use our index (pp534–43) to identify communities across Europe which feature in our 50 routes or elsewhere in this book.

Discover Britain and Ireland
    Routes 1 to 5   50
    Sidetracks A, B, C

The Low Countries and Germany
    Routes 6 to 12   96
    Sidetracks D, E, F

A taste of France
    Routes 13 to 19   147
    Sidetracks G, H, I

Iberian connections
    Routes 20 to 24   197
    Sidetracks J, K, L

Scandinavia and the Baltic
    Routes 25 to 31   236
    Sidetracks M, N, O, P

Central and Eastern Europe
    Routes 32 to 37   298
    Sidetracks Q, R, S, T

Alpine adventures
    Routes 38 to 43   350
    Sidetracks U, V, W, X

Italy and the Adriatic
    Routes 44 to 50   395
    Sidetracks Y, Z

DISCOVER BRITAIN AND IRELAND
An introduction

Britain created the railway. And the **railway challenged Victorian Britain**. There was 19th-century apprehension about newly emerging industrial landscapes, and the developing rail network had many vocal critics. John Ruskin was one of them. Yet very quickly the railway embedded itself in the national psyche. For writers like **Hilaire Belloc** and **Edward Thomas** the rural railway was the very embodiment of Englishness. In Wales, Scotland and Ireland, the **Age of Steam** transformed cities and the countryside; developments in those countries occasionally even outpaced those in England. Dublin had its first suburban railway before London did.

For many years, Great Britain and Ireland didn't feature in *Europe by Rail*. We rectified that omission with the 16th edition in 2019. We have travelled extensively through both islands by train, taking the pulse of railway life, stopping off here and there in country towns or rural halts. From London to Limerick, Tralee to Tyndrum, we've been there.

Taking time to explore

Beyond the routes presented in this section, you might like to try the railway that runs west from Shrewsbury to Machynlleth then up the coast to Harlech and beyond. It's stunning. In Ireland, there are **many fine journeys** to which we've only been able to allude *en passant*. The line from Coleraine to Derry is unforgettable and might, in a future edition, be a fitting finale to a new route from Dublin to Derry. We also had our sights on a classic Irish rural journey, that from Waterford to Galway via Cahir and Limerick, but in the end there wasn't space.

Train travel in Britain and Ireland is **perfect for visitors** who want to make use of rail passes. Very few trains require advance reservation and you'll not run across those painful supplements which limit pass use in France and Spain. So there is every opportunity to stop off here and there along the way. **Eurail and Interrail passes** are valid throughout Britain and Ireland. There were rumours in 2019 that Britain might no longer accept the two above-mentioned passes. But it is now clear that both will continue to be valid. Great Britain also has its own home-grown pass. It's called **Britrail**. There's also an excellent range of regional rover tickets in Britain which allow one or more days travel within a clearly defined area.

Two of the routes that follow in this section cross the North Sea to reach England from the continent. And there are two routes which cross the Irish Sea. For such journeys, there are tremendous bargains with **rail-sail tickets**, both between Holland and England (or vice versa) or from any station in Britain to destinations in Ireland (and back again). ■

LONDON

While some great European cities – think Vienna, Berlin, Copenhagen or Milan – have a grand central station, London has **a dozen different railway termini**. All date back to the Victorian era. For generations of travellers, these railway stations have been the gateways to a city that has fuelled imperial ambition. Multiracial and multicultural London is a **vibrant world city**, a place which has attracted entrepreneurs and eccentrics, revolutionaries and reactionaries. With a week to spare, one might take in some of the planet's best art collections, exploring bustling local markets and relax in the city's legendary green spaces.

With just a day or two, it's best to focus on the cluster of main sights on the north side of the Thames, broadly between Westminster and the Tower. From Green Park and St James's Park, it's a pleasant wander on past **Trafalgar Square** (for the National Gallery) to **Covent Garden** and Lincoln's Inn, continuing east to the heart of London's business district – known, a little confusingly, as 'the City'.

From there it is but a short hop on to up-and-coming Whitechapel or, closer to the river, the Tower. You may want to venture south of the river into Southwark to visit the **Tate Modern** (www.tate.org.uk) or tickle your taste buds in **Borough Market** (www.boroughmarket.org.uk).

London is a city shaped by its river, so make use of regular boat services, branded as **Uber Boat Thames Clippers** (www.thamesclippers.com), which run downriver from Westminster Millennium Pier (near Big Ben) to Greenwich and beyond. With half a dozen intermediate stops between Westminster and the Tower alone, you're never far from a landing stage.

Arrival, information, accommodation

✈ There are direct **Eurostar** trains to London from Paris, Lille and Brussels. Direct trains from Amsterdam and Rotterdam will be resumed in early 2025. These trains all arrive at **St Pancras International**, a glorious architectural extravaganza of a station (see p148). The Greater London area is divided into six fare zones. Information on travel in London is available at www.tfl.gov.uk. The integrated ticketing scheme accepts **Oyster** and contactless cards. Just remember to touch-in at the start of each journey and touch-out (not necessary on buses) at the end. It's possible to buy tickets at machines for tube and train journeys (not possible for buses), but that's rather expensive. Apart from using the Uber Boat Thames Clippers services, the top deck of one of the iconic, red London buses is a great way to see the city. 🛈 Tourist office: there's a travel information centre at St Pancras station and visitor centres at Liverpool Street station and Paddington station (www.visitlondon.com).

🛏 Located in Spitalfields, not far from Liverpool Street station, **Batty Langley's**, 12 Folgate St, ☎ 020 737 743 90 (www.battylangleys.com) is an elegant and highly regarded hotel in Georgian style. Well west of the main tourist attractions, but conveniently located for both Paddington station and Kensington Gardens, is the friendly **Westbourne Hyde Park**, 51 Gloucester Terrace, ☎ 020 740 250 77 (www.thewestbournelondon.co.uk). If you don't mind the institutional feel of a large chain hotel, then the **Premier Inn London King's Cross**, 26–30 York Way, ☎ 0333 321 1272 (www.premierinn.com) is good value for money and close to King's Cross and St Pancras stations.

Route 1: Following Brunel to Cornwall

CITIES: ★ CULTURE: ★★ HISTORY: ★ SCENERY: ★★
COUNTRIES COVERED: ENGLAND (ENG)
JOURNEY TIME: 5 HRS 30 MINS | DISTANCE: 491 KM | MAP: WWW.EBRWEB.EU/18MAP1

In the beginning there were the graceful classical baths of the Roman Empire. Then came fine cathedrals. But by the late 19th century, **great railway termini** were acclaimed as the representative buildings of the Steam Age. Stations quickly became the unashamed status symbols of any city with ambition. Some echoed the showcase buildings of earlier eras. In New York, Penn Central was inspired by the great Roman baths at Caracalla. While in London, **St Pancras** took a cue from Europe's soaring Gothic cathedrals.

Whichever of the routes you follow in this book, make time for Europe's great railway stations. While some are sadly neglected and others have been the victims of wilful architectural vandalism, such cases are the exception. Many are beautiful places which lift the spirits.

Our very first journey in *Europe by Rail* starts at London's **Paddington station**; it is the unsung star of London's railway termini (for more on the capital of the UK see p51). St Pancras is the most grandiose and architecturally ambitious. Following recent renovations, **King's Cross** may now claim to be the most stately. But Paddington has a light elegance which is utterly charming. Despite its Moorish accents, there is something quintessentially English about Paddington. There are echoes of Paxton's magnificent great glasshouse, built for the Great Exhibition held in London in 1851. Paddington is a fine London home for a railway associated with one great name in 19th-century engineering: **Isambard Kingdom Brunel**. He was the driving force behind the **Great Western Railway**, the legendary GWR. In Victorian England, it was often suggested that the initials GWR stood for God's Wonderful Railway.

Paddington is the perfect place to embark on a journey which takes in some of the finest countryside in southern England. And this is a **London** station which has forever been associated with pleasure. Some termini were always, and still are, stations for commuters. Others suggested trade and commerce. But Paddington was for holidays. So, join us as we climb aboard one of the Great Western Railway trains **bound for Cornwall**.

SUGGESTED ITINERARY

It's a shade under 500 km from **London to Penzance** and the fastest GWR trains take just over five hours for the journey. It's the quick and easy way to get from the capital to Cornwall. There is also the *Night Riviera* sleeper service from London to Penzance.

This is a route which serves some of the most delightful towns in south-west England, including a bevy of fine coastal resorts – some of them not actually on the main line, but reached by minor rail routes which branch off from our route to serve ports and villages on the coasts of **Devon and Cornwall**. So in the description that follows, we highlight points

Route 1: Following Brunel to Cornwall | 53

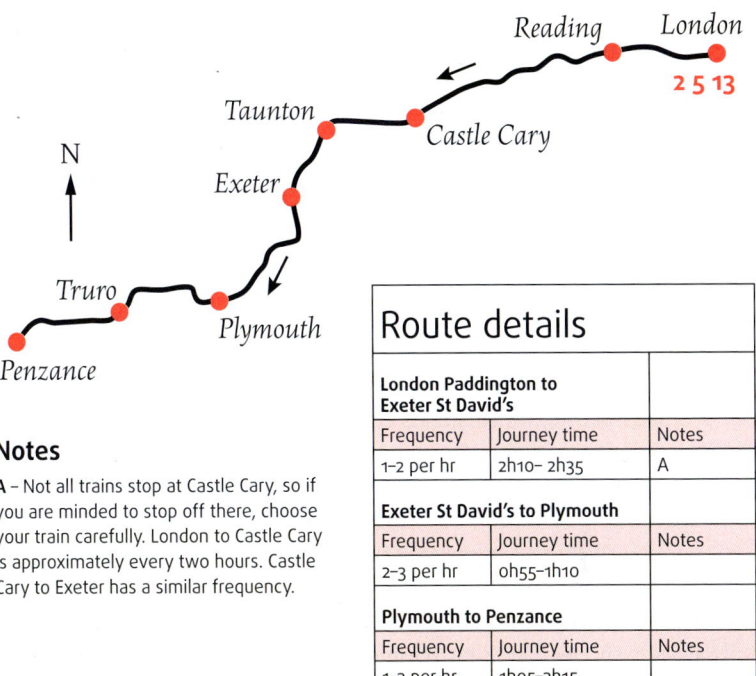

Notes

A – Not all trains stop at Castle Cary, so if you are minded to stop off there, choose your train carefully. London to Castle Cary is approximately every two hours. Castle Cary to Exeter has a similar frequency.

Route details

London Paddington to Exeter St David's		
Frequency	Journey time	Notes
1–2 per hr	2h10– 2h35	A
Exeter St David's to Plymouth		
Frequency	Journey time	Notes
2–3 per hr	0h55–1h10	
Plymouth to Penzance		
Frequency	Journey time	Notes
1–2 per hr	1h05–2h15	

in the journey where you may want to branch off and explore, stopping off perhaps for a night or two on the coast before returning to the main route.

Our top choices for overnight stops are **Castle Cary**, **Looe** and **St Mawes**. The likeable Somerset market town of Castle Cary has the advantage of being on the main GWR route. It's a good option if you are only able to leave London in the afternoon and want an early antidote to the noise and bustle of the capital. Both Looe and St Mawes are in Cornwall and require a diversion from the main line (see our Sidetracks feature on p58).

Penzance is the end of the line. But those who have followed Brunel's wonderful railway the whole way can venture further by boat on the daily sailing to the **Isles of Scilly**. If you opt to turn round and head back towards London, note that there is an alternative, more southerly, route from Exeter to London Waterloo. It is every bit as beautiful as the GWR route to Paddington. There is also the option of stopping in the cathedral city of Salisbury – always a good choice for an overnight stay. Make time to visit nearby **Stonehenge**, served by a bus link from Salisbury station (www.thestonehengetour.info).

West to Reading

This is a journey packed with interest. Hardly has the train left Paddington than there is an excellent view to the right, looking over the **Grand Union Canal**, towards Kensal Green Cemetery. There lie interred the remains of half a dozen members of the Brunel family, including Isambard Kingdom himself. Brunel was the son of a French cabinetmaker who only narrowly avoided ordination as a priest in his native Normandy (a career move which would surely have altered the later trajectory of railway history).

Wilkie Collins also resides in **Kensal Green Cemetery**. He is remembered more for his novels than his travel writing, but his *Rambles beyond Railways* is a perceptive exploration of Cornish byways. It was written at the time when Brunel's Great Western was colonising Cornwall by building branch lines to the remotest corners of the Royal Duchy.

There's a distant view of lofty **Harrow-on-the-Hill**, then comes the old asylum at Hanwell. The latter was built in 1831 for what in those days were then called 'the pauper insane'. The editor of *The Gentleman's Magazine*, one Edward Cave (who wrote under the pen name Sylvanus Urban) drew attention in 1858 to this landmark on the line out of Paddington. "A plain but handsome structure, which stands cheerily in open country," he wrote. No longer is this open country. London has crept west, a tangled web of streets and housing invading old villages and depriving them of their identity.

Speeding west through **Southall**, our train now crosses the Grand Union Canal. We have a guidebook from 1924 which describes a rural scene "with bridges, barges and ducks all doing their best to make it picturesque." Southall has subtly changed. The ducks are gone and just south of the railway is a spectacular Sikh temple. Signs on the railway platforms at Southall are in both English and Punjabi.

Leaving Southall there is little by way of green landscapes. But it is fascinating. Look out for art-deco style in the EMI factory at **Hayes**, planes closing in on Heathrow and the spiral swirls of motorways to nowhere. Beyond West Drayton lorry parks and container dumps go head-to-head with crazy golf and garden centres. This is magnificent stuff, a social roller coaster of a ride through modern England. But there are touches of antiquity too. **Windsor Castle** is visible away to the south.

Away to the right is **Stoke Poges**, where Thomas Gray penned his *Elegy Written in a Country Churchyard*. Nowadays modern **Slough** obscures what was presumably once a glorious vista over open countryside towards Stoke Poges. But, despite the poet John Betjeman's plea ("Come, friendly bombs, and fall on Slough"), the town looks remarkably spick and span as the GWR train speeds past Slough's elegant railway station. Burnham station is next on the line. It was once called Burnham Beeches, but the word 'Beeches' was suppressed in 1930. Happily the beech woods are still there, though you'll be hard pushed to see them from the train.

Beyond Brunel's famous brick bridge, captured in JMW Turner's painting *Rain, Steam and Speed – The Great Western Railway* (first exhibited in 1844), which escorts our train over the Thames at **Maidenhead**, the train sweeps through a swathe of cuttings with fleeting glimpses of Berkshire villages at points where the embankments are happily lower. To our right there's Ruscombe. That's the village where **William Penn** died in poverty in

1718. The infirm Quaker would most surely have preferred to meet his maker in Pennsylvania.

And so we slow for a first stop in Reading where another famous Quaker, George Palmer, saw the potential of the railway in helping distribute his company's biscuits. Reading gave us the custard cream. **Oscar Wilde** helped seal Reading's fate in his *Ballad of Reading Gaol*. These days this town on the Thames, just where the southernmost ripples of the Chiltern Hills slip down to the river, is part of London's busy commuter belt.

From Thames to Tamar

Leaving the Thames Valley at **Reading**, the GWR takes about three hours to reach Brunel's celebrated Royal Albert Bridge which spans the River Tamar at Plymouth, marking the point where the railway crosses from Devon into Cornwall. We rate this ride from Reading to Plymouth as perhaps the finest three-hour main-line train ride anywhere in England.

West from Reading, the train slips through **Aldermaston**, a Berkshire village which for 60 years has been the focus of Britain's pacifist lobby on account of an atomic weapons research centre located here. Just beyond Aldermaston, **Newbury** marks the end of the electrified route – just extended here in early 2019 – from Paddington. With Newbury behind us, the landscape becomes more assertively rural as the railway follows the Kennet Valley upstream through gentle chalk hills, paralleling the picturesque **Kennet and Avon Canal** for long stretches.

Until 1906, GWR trains from London to Devon took a much longer route via Swindon and Bristol. This new line via the Kennet Valley and Castle Cary trimmed the travel time; it's called the **Berks & Hants Line**, taking that name from two English counties, although oddly the railway line never actually touches Hampshire. Instead it takes in a fine swathe of North Wessex landscapes, seen at their best in the low sun angles of a spring morning or summer evening. Watch out for moorhens by the canal and the bold shapes of huge white horses carved into the **chalk hillsides** (there are three of them on the stretch between Newbury and Castle Cary, none of them anywhere near as ancient as locals would have one believe).

This GWR route to south-west England became an **economic lifeline** for the distant counties of Somerset, Devon and Cornwall. Before the coming of the railway, Cornish labourers emigrated to the Americas; only when Brunel's first trains arrived did those Cornish workers seriously think of looking for jobs in London. And the **GWR**, ever alert to the power of a good marketing campaign, filled its trains by promoting Devon and Cornwall as desirable destinations. For over 100 years, until cheap flights on jet aircraft tempted the sun-starved English to the Mediterranean, 'Glorious Devon' and the 'Cornish Riviera' were brands which lured **millions of holidaymakers** onto GWR trains. With a benign climate and lush vegetation, especially on the south coast of those two counties, there was something deliciously exotic about this far-flung part of England. Sandy coves, seagulls, Devon clotted cream and Cornish pasties sealed the holiday imagination for generations of English families.

It wasn't all one-way trade. New potatoes and early spring flowers from the Isles of Scilly were shipped from Penzance to London by train. Teasel from the Mendips and willow from the Somerset Levels, strawberries from the Tamar Valley and fresh fish from Looe and Brixham all helped fill the freight wagons which brought goods to London.

But we are distracting you. We've slipped by Savernake Forest and the Vale of Pewsey, and already we are in **Somerset**, speeding past Frome and Bruton to reach the market town of **Castle Cary**.

Castle Cary Hints

Castle Cary is one of those solid, handsome country towns where there's nothing exceptional to see, but it's a fine choice for an overnight stay. It's a 20-minute walk into town, gently uphill but very pleasant, on a well-signed footpath. Or take the bus or taxi from the station up to the town centre.

Descriptions of several fine walks around the town are online at www.castle-cary.co.uk or visit the tourist office in the Market House. The thatched-roofed **George Hotel**, Market Place, ☎ 01963 350 761 (www.thegeorgehotelcastlecary.co.uk) is a good choice for an overnight stop. From Castle Cary, there's a pretty branch line which tracks south through **Hardy's Wessex** to Dorchester and the coast at Weymouth.

Just beyond Castle Cary, you'll see in the distance (to the right) the distinctive profile of **Glastonbury Tor**, a place so overburdened with myth and legend – the Holy Grail, King Arthur and more – that it attracts more visitors than it can possibly cope with. The flat terrain traversed by the railway was once marshy country, but now drained and known as the Somerset Levels.

Beyond Taunton, the line skirts a busy motorway south to reach the Devon county town of **Exeter**. The train stops at St David's station, and the city centre is about a 20-minute walk to the south-east. Exeter Central, easily reached by trains from St David's via a line which climbs very steeply, is better placed for the centre. If you wish to stop overnight try the Rougemont Hotel, ☎ 01392 410 237 (all.accor.com) right by Exeter Central.

Exeter connections

Take the train to the coast at Exmouth on the **Avocet Line** or explore Devon's beautiful interior by riding the **Tarka Line** to Barnstaple or the new route to Okehampton which opened in late 2021. If you don't have time to venture further along Route 1, then you can return to London via Dorset and Salisbury – a one-time main line now reduced to secondary status, but with plenty of gorgeous scenery along the way.

In a route that brims with superlatives, it might raise eyebrows to suggest that the stretch beyond Exeter is the very best section of the line to Cornwall.

Sit on the left for gorgeous sea views as the railway runs south beside the Exe Estuary, and then along the coast at Dawlish. It's all too brief, as the railway forsakes the coast at Teignmouth, running inland and skirting the southern edge of Dartmoor to reach **Plymouth**, the last stop in Devon before the train slips over the River Tamar into Cornwall.

Kernow a'gas dynergh: Welcome to Cornwall

Saltash, just west of the **Royal Albert Bridge** and the first station in Cornwall, has multilingual signs welcoming travellers to the county. It's likely that you'll want to stop off here and there on the journey through Cornwall and our Sidetracks feature on the next page gives tips on how to make the most of the branch lines which run down to the coast.

Staying on the train towards Penzance, it's easy to discern the main features of the Cornish landscape. There are deeply incised, wooded valleys with occasional distant views of the coast. At one point (near Par), our route touches the south coast, and then at Hayle it briefly skirts the north coast before flitting over to the south coast again, skirting the half-moon shaped Mount's Bay on the final approach into Penzance.

Penzance

Penzance is an unassuming working town, a place where one senses that the business of everyday life continues in spite of the seasonal crowds of visitors. Wander down the waterfront through Wherrytown to **Newlyn** to discover that fishing is still big business in Cornwall. A little further is the pretty coastal village of Mousehole. M6 runs every 20–30 mins between Penzance and Mousehole via Newlyn.

Arrival, information, accommodation
Just a short walk east of the city centre. Tourist office: just outside the station entrance (www.purelypenzance.co.uk).

Located in two Edwardian merchants' houses, a short walk from the station, the **Hotel Penzance**, Britons Hill, ☎ 01736 363 117 (www.hotelpenzance.com), has rooms with great views over the bay. Or try the friendly **Holbein House** B&B, Alexandra Road, ☎ 07776 306816 (www.holbeinhouse.com). A very cosy option in a quiet sideroad in a former Georgian inn is the boutique **Artist Residence**, 20 Chapel Street, ☎ 01736 365 664 (www.artistresidence.co.uk). The latter is well placed for the ferries to the Isles of Scilly.

Connections from Penzance
Land's End is the obvious excursion from Penzance and A1 will whisk you there in an hour. Contrary to popular belief, it's not the westernmost point on the British mainland. That honour goes to Corrachadh Mòr, a rocky headland on Scotland's Ardnamurchan Peninsula.

But Land's End is fun and worth the bus ride. Ignore the commercial tack and tourist traps and just savour the fresh sea air and awesome views. It's a magnificent counterpoint to Paddington station in London where we started this very first route in *Europe by Rail*.

Sidetracks: Cornish branch lines

West from Plymouth, there are still no less than six minor railway lines branching off from the main **Great Western Railway** (GWR) route to Penzance. The first runs up the Tamar Valley to terminate well inland at Gunnislake in east Cornwall, a one-time mining town in a region with rich deposits of tin, copper, silver and arsenic. Of the other five branch lines, one is a **seasonal heritage railway** linking Bodmin Parkway with Bodmin town centre (www.bodminrailway.co.uk).

That leaves four other routes, all of them connecting the main line with a coastal community. Each of these is a gem. Dedicated baggers of unusual railways could feasibly cover all four in a day, and it needn't be expensive. There's a **Cornwall Rover ticket** valid from Plymouth to all points west which allows one day's travel for just £13.50 (discounts for GB railcard holders). But these four branch railways give access to such interesting places that one could easily spend a whole week exploring Cornwall, relying in the main on rail transport, augmented here and there by ferries and bus services. Moving west from Tamar, the lines that run to the coast are Liskeard to Looe, Par to Newquay, Truro to Falmouth, and St Erth to St Ives. The times in parentheses below give the journey time to each destination from the main-line junction.

If you cover just one of these lines, make it the branch railway to **Looe** (30 mins), which is short but very sweet, dropping down steeply from Liskeard and then following the East Looe River down to the coast. The fishing port of Looe is the perfect place for a first night's stop in Cornwall. If you'd like to stay overnight, **Little Mainstone Guest House**, The Quay, ☎ 01503 262983 (www.littlemainstone-looe.com), on the west side of the river, is a welcoming B&B with great views over the harbour.

Next up, as we move west on the main line, is the branch to **Newquay** (50 mins), which diverges from the Penzance route at Par, a tiny south-coast port which makes a living through exports of china clay. Of the four branch lines to the coast, this one wins hands down for giving views of the sometimes bleak landscapes of the Cornish interior. It's an interesting run, but not entirely pretty.

The next diversion is the short hop from Truro down to **Falmouth** (20 mins), which competes with Penzance as the major urban centre on Cornwall's south coast. It's a pleasant ride and, though Falmouth hardly rates as quaint, it has a lively arts scene and **Pendennis Castle** is not to be missed. The real draw, though, are the villages easily reached by regular ferries from Falmouth. We recommend **St Mawes**, perfectly positioned on the east side of the Carrick Roads with grand views of the coast. A friendly B&B to stay overnight is **Nearwater**, Polvarth Rd, ☎ 01326 279278 (www.nearwaterstmawes.co.uk).

St Mawes is one of those spots you may never want to leave. If you really must leave, add a dash of romance to the moment by taking the boat back to Truro to rejoin the main GWR rail route to the west.

Last, but by no means least of the four branches to the coast, is the short line from **St Erth to St Ives** (10 mins), which gives fine views of some of the best beaches on the north coast before skirting Carbis Bay to reach St Ives. This pretty coastal town can be impossibly crowded in summer, but it's a fine spot to while away a few wet winter days.

Route 2: Cathedrals, castles and glens

CITIES: ★★★ CULTURE: ★★ HISTORY: ★★ SCENERY: ★★
COUNTRIES COVERED: ENGLAND (ENG), SCOTLAND (SCT)
JOURNEY TIME: 12 HRS | DISTANCE: 1,047 KM | MAP: WWW.EBRWEB.EU/18MAP2

If there is one rail journey which has consistently fired the English imagination, it is the ride from **London to the Scottish Highlands**. There are two celebrated paintings by the English artist George Earl, dating from 1876 and 1893 respectively, which both capture the excitement of wealthy Victorians leaving from King's Cross for the grouse-shooting season in the Scottish hills. The platform is packed with well-dressed travellers, surrounded by fishing tackle, hunting dogs – the latter a George Earl trademark – and all the paraphernalia necessary for a few weeks of 'sporting fun' in the Highlands. The poor grouse surely never saw anything very sporting in the escapade.

The hounds are long gone, but there's still a hint of magic about **King's Cross station**. In the *Harry Potter* books, the *Hogwarts Express* departs from Platform 9¾ at King's Cross, so there's usually a line of Ravenclaws and Gryffindors waiting to pay homage at the spot immortalised in JK Rowling's novels. Predictably, in this commercial age, there's a *Harry Potter* shop there too, so it's a handy opportunity to pick up a new wand or a time turner which might always come in useful on your trip to Scotland. Even the most adept wizard cannot magic away the Scottish midges though, so consider packing some midge cream before heading north.

We'll cover over a thousand kilometres by train, travelling **via York, Edinburgh and Inverness** to reach Kyle of Lochalsh on the west coast of Scotland. The journey doesn't end there, for from Kyle it is but a short hop by bus over the bridge to Skye, from where more adventurous travellers may wish to continue by boat to the Outer Hebrides. Along the way, we'll take in several great cathedrals, the Scottish capital and some very fine mountain landscapes including the **Cairngorms National Park**.

RECOMMENDED ITINERARY

This is a route replete with possibilities. With an early start from King's Cross and two changes of train – in Edinburgh and Inverness – it's perfectly possible to travel from King's Cross to Kyle of Lochalsh in a day. But you could do better by stopping off here and there along the way. York and Edinburgh are both good options.

If you are less inclined to linger, then why not book a first-class seat on the **Highland Chieftain** which normally leaves King's Cross for Inverness at midday? On weekdays, first-class passengers are served complimentary meals and drinks. The *Highland Chieftain* follows the route described here, bar for the stretch between Edinburgh and Perth where it routes via Stirling rather than the Forth Bridge and Fife. On a summer evening, the final two hours of the journey, from Perth to Inverness, really are hard to beat. Stay overnight at the Royal Highland Hotel (www.royalhighlandhotel.co.uk), which adjoins the railway station in Inverness, and then you'll be fresh as a fiddle in the morning for the stunning ride west to **Kyle of Lochalsh**.

Another possibility, if time is tight, is to travel by the overnight **Caledonian Sleeper** service from London to Edinburgh or Inverness. Note that all overnight services to Scotland depart from London Euston and follow the West Coast route. The Caledonian Sleeper is an experience in itself. Our feeling is that the night train to Edinburgh departs too late in the evening and gives an uncomfortably early arrival in the Scottish capital. The Inverness train is here the better option – and bacon rolls with fresh coffee at the crack of dawn as the train cruises down the Spey Valley, with great views of the **Cairngorms**, are hard to beat. Note that the Caledonian Sleeper services do not run in either direction on Saturday nights.

North to York

The main **East Coast route** might better have been called the Cathedrals Line. Sit on the right side of the train and you should be able to spot three historic ecclesiastical gems on the ride north – they are at Peterborough, York and Durham. This line from **King's Cross** is the most uncompromising of the main-line rail routes running north from London. It runs in a pretty straight line to York and beyond. Being a late addition to England's railway geography, tempting off-route cities like Nottingham and Leeds had already been 'claimed' by rival companies. The **Great Northern Railway (GNR)** had its eyes set on the North and nothing less. Branch lines to growing industrial cities were all well and good, but the GNR didn't want to risk the great prize of capturing the traffic from London to York and beyond.

Curiously, one of the biggest challenges for the GNR's talented engineers was getting out of London. The capital's leafy northern heights and the easternmost ripples of the **Chiltern Hills** in Hertfordshire were tackled in a series of dramatic viaducts, dark tunnels and deep cuttings which still today add a touch of drama to the first half hour of the run out of King's Cross.

The train north dashes over Welwyn Viaduct, which bridges the Mimram Valley, in an ambitious streak of 40 fine arches, styled in the manner of a Roman aqueduct. Then the railway uses the gentle vales created by two chalkland streams, the Hiz and the Ivel, to reach the River Ouse which it follows north towards **Peterborough**. There's a touch of the Fenlands in the sedge and mere terrain around Peterborough, although the town itself, bar for its remarkable but oddly asymmetric cathedral, is nothing special.

CONNECTIONS FROM PETERBOROUGH

For better views of the **watery Fenlands**, take the trains which run east from Peterborough to Ely, where there's another fine cathedral. These trains continue beyond Ely to Cambridge or Norwich. Connect at Peterborough onto **Route 4** in this book, which runs west via Birmingham to North Wales and Ireland. Or follow Route 4 in reverse to the Essex port of Harwich for ferries to the Netherlands. If you are not in any rush to head north, there is an appealing rural route from Peterborough via Spalding and Lincoln which rejoins the main East Coast line at Doncaster.

From Peterborough, our route north rises very gently to **Stoke Summit**. It was on this stretch of track that in 1938 a London-bound train hauled by

Route 2: Cathedrals, castles and glens

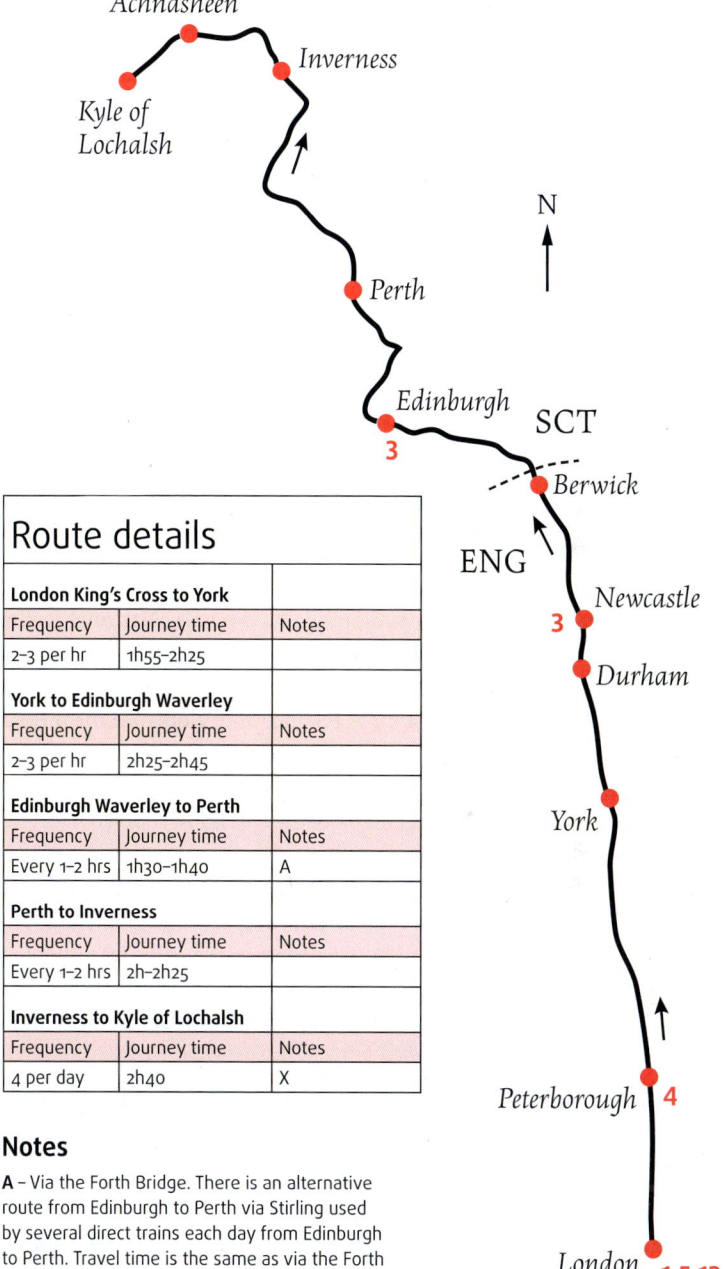

Route details

London King's Cross to York		
Frequency	Journey time	Notes
2–3 per hr	1h55–2h25	

York to Edinburgh Waverley		
Frequency	Journey time	Notes
2–3 per hr	2h25–2h45	

Edinburgh Waverley to Perth		
Frequency	Journey time	Notes
Every 1–2 hrs	1h30–1h40	A

Perth to Inverness		
Frequency	Journey time	Notes
Every 1–2 hrs	2h–2h25	

Inverness to Kyle of Lochalsh		
Frequency	Journey time	Notes
4 per day	2h40	X

Notes

A – Via the Forth Bridge. There is an alternative route from Edinburgh to Perth via Stirling used by several direct trains each day from Edinburgh to Perth. Travel time is the same as via the Forth Bridge route.

X – Only one train on Sundays (or two on Sundays from mid-May to mid-September).

a locomotive called *Mallard* set a **world speed record** for a steam train of 203 km per hour. It's a record that still stands today. This is a line built for speed and modern trains make light of the easy gradients, dashing through Grantham – a town whose great gift to the nation was Margaret Thatcher – and on past the power stations in the Trent Valley around Newark.

Retford and **Doncaster** come and go, with the countryside beyond the carriage window assuming a more industrial demeanour. If you've opted for one of the fast trains, just short of two hours after leaving London the train is already slowing for York.

York (suggested stopover)

York's elegant railway station with its striking curved platforms is a fine introduction to one of England's most interesting cities. **Romans, Vikings and Quakers** have all helped mould York; today it rates as an appealing place to stop off for a night or longer. The **Jorvik Viking centre** gives a splendid introduction to life in York under Scandinavian rule (when York was known as Jórvík; www.jorvikvikingcentre.co.uk). It's not all sepia-tinged romance, so you'll learn a lot about fleas, lice and Viking rubbish. It's fun, educational and not to be missed. In similar vein, make time for the **National Railway Museum** (free entry, check details on www.railwaymuseum.org.uk), which is nowhere near as geeky as it sounds. It's a brilliant romp through the world of trains with as much social history as engineering. Note that the museum is undergoing major renovations with the Station Hall currently being closed. The latter will open again after redevelopment in spring 2025.

York was made for wandering. Explore the city walls, cobbled streets and intriguing pedestrian alleys (locally called snickelways) which cut between buildings, then head for **York Minster**. The great cathedral at York, whose bishop rates second only to that of Canterbury in the Anglican hierarchy, has magnificent stained glass. Take time to experience the calm serenity of this great sanctuary, ideally by taking in a service. Visitors are always welcome. A good choice is choral evensong (usually at 17.30, but at 16.00 on Sundays).

Arrival, information, accommodation

✈ Very centrally located, just west of the mediaeval town centre. 🛈 Tourist office: 1 Museum Street (www.visityork.org). 🏠 Located in a Victorian town house, the **No 21 York**, 21 St Mary's, ☎ 01904 629 494 (www.no21york.co.uk) is a very hospitable B&B within easy reach of the station and just a short stroll from the town centre. Equally well located is the friendly owner-managed **Minster Walk Guest House**, 22 Marygate, ☎ 01904 652 780 (www.minsterwalk.co.uk), housed in a 300-year-old building. Or try **Dean Court Hotel**, Duncombe Place, ☎ 01904 625 082 (www.inncollectiongroup.com); its location close to York Minster is hard to beat.

Connections from York

For a great railway centre, it's no surprise that there's a feast of onward connections from York. For a very fine day out from York, consider taking the 🚌 840 or X40 to Pickering (about 80 mins from York) to pick up the **North Yorkshire Moors Railway** heritage steam line to the picturesque port of Whitby (see www.nymr.co.uk). From Whitby, it is a beautiful journey through moorland wilderness to Middlesbrough, whence there are hourly direct trains back to York. Head west via Knaresborough and elegant Harrogate to Leeds, there to join the **Settle and Carlisle railway** (see box on p73) for a rural ride through the Pennines to connect into **Route 3** in Carlisle. This route via **Harrogate to Leeds** is a very fine run, much nicer than that taken by the fast trains to Leeds, many of which continue to Manchester and Liverpool. From York there are also direct trains to both Hull and Scarborough, the latter featuring an especially nice stretch as the railway follows the River Derwent upstream towards Malton.

York to Edinburgh

From York, our route continues north through the Vale of York in an uncompromising straight line, but now – on a clear day – the broad contours of Yorkshire geography become more evident. The high terrain of the **North York Moors National Park** rises up away to the east, while well west of the vale one can see the Yorkshire Dales, which form part of the Pennine chain, running up the spine of northern England.

There are three great rivers in north-east England – the Tees, Wear and Tyne – and we cross all three of them. Shortly after crossing the River Tees,

THE RACE TO THE NORTH

Cast back 250 years, and those who wanted to get from **London to Edinburgh** would travel by ship or by stagecoach – those who opted for the latter could easily spend a fortnight on the journey. In 1847, the first railway across the Anglo-Scottish border opened for traffic – that was the line running north from Carlisle which is followed by **Route 3** in this book.

Fifteen years later, the main East Coast line from London to Edinburgh opened, ushering in an era of fierce competition between the **West Coast** (from Euston via Carlisle) and the **East Coast** (from King's Cross via York) routes. Each company sought to provide the best service and the shortest journey times – even to the extent that they compromised on safety in the early days of the competition. If you are making a return journey from London to Scotland, you might consider travelling out from King's Cross following the journey described here, and then using the West Coast line through Carlisle for the southbound run. The latter includes an exceptionally fine stretch skirting the eastern edge of the **Lake District** in north-west England.

With the debut of the East Coast line in 1862, the *Special Scotch Express* – a precursor of the famous **Flying Scotsman** – left both London and Edinburgh at 10 each morning, with the 632-km run taking ten hours. Today the fastest train of the day on the East Coast route is the southbound *Flying Scotsman* which leaves Edinburgh at the crack of dawn on weekday mornings and dashes to London in just four hours.

Referring to these key routes to Scotland as the East Coast and West Coast lines is desperately misleading as neither of them hugs the coast. On the East Coast line, described in **Route 2**, you'll not get a first glimpse of the sea until well north of Newcastle-upon-Tyne. On the West Coast line, there's no real coastal scenery, but you do skirt the shores of Morecambe Bay just beyond Lancaster and eagle-eyed observers may get a fleeting glimpse of the Solway Firth as the train crosses the Scottish border.

the route passes through Darlington, home in 1825 to the world's very first public **steam-operated railway**. Just 15 minutes further north, there is (to the right) one of the finest urban panoramas of the entire run as the train skirts the cathedral city of **Durham**. It's matched by two others in the following hour, one at Newcastle as the train approaches the main station with a dramatic bridging of the River Tyne, and then at Berwick-upon-Tweed, where the crossing of the Royal Border Bridge is pure theatre. Our feeling is that the journey from **York to Edinburgh** is best done in one go. There's a real symphonic quality to the route, and it's sad to interrupt that. But we don't want to diminish the charms of Durham, where it's easy to idle away a day or two, or write off the more edgy appeal of Newcastle, which is a major rail hub.

NEWCASTLE LINKS
There is an especially fine railway which runs west from Newcastle-upon-Tyne, initially following the Tyne Valley up to Hexham and beyond and then broadly following Hadrian's Wall west to Carlisle, where one can join **Route 3** in this book. Newcastle is also a good jumping-off point for the continent, with a daily late afternoon sailing from North Shields to IJmuiden on the Dutch coast not far from Amsterdam.

Dashing north from Newcastle towards **Berwick**, we get our first hint of the sea, with especially fine views of the coastal community of Alnmouth and later Holy Island. Heading over the Scottish border, just beyond Berwick, the railway plays cat and mouse with the coast, with tantalising glimpses of cliffs, sandy coves and occasional fishing villages. Approaching Edinburgh, there are good views over the Firth of Forth to Fife while on the left side of the train the great volcanic plug known as Arthur's Seat hoves into view.

Few capital city stations are so centrally positioned as Waverley, the main railway hub in **Edinburgh**. It is set in a valley with the mediaeval Old Town just to the south (ie. your left as you arrive from York) and the neoclassical and Georgian New Town equally close at hand to the north. Alighting from the train at Waverley station is always special; it is as if the city is rising around you on all sides. For our account of Edinburgh with onward connections see **Route 3** (pp74–75). You can follow Route 3 to Scotland's west coast at Mallaig, or return to England by following Route 3 in reverse, taking the old Caledonian main line to Carlisle and beyond.

Highland adventure
In a route which has already had its fair share of superlatives, the best is yet to come. There are two routes from **Edinburgh to Perth**. The more westerly option follows the Forth Valley to Stirling and then north through Strathallan to Perth. It's a fine ride, but we think the eastern route has the edge, if only because it crosses the Forth Rail Bridge – a real *Europe by Rail* magic moment.

Heading west from Waverley, all Perth-bound trains pause at Haymarket (at the western end of the city centre), from where it is about a dozen minutes to the **Forth Bridge**. From the right side of the train, you get a fine view of the bridge on the approach. Once on the bridge, you can see the two road bridges away to your left. The more distant of the two is the new Queensferry Crossing, which opened to traffic in 2017.

Gaining the north bank, the railway skirts the Fife coast before turning inland and then leaving the main line to Aberdeen at Ladybank. This is a more rural route, and the first stretch of single track railway on our journey from London. But not the last for henceforth most of Route 2 is on single-track lines. Almost immediately there's a taste of the hills, as the train cuts through the easternmost outliers of the Ochils. The railway runs through Collessie Den and skirts **Lindores Loch** to reach the shore of the Firth of Tay at the port of Newburgh, where the locals are still very miffed that their railway station was closed in 1955 and trains have never stopped since. From here it's just a few minutes to **Perth**, a handsome station with a complicated layout of platforms.

Perth connections
There are hourly trains running south-west to Stirling and Glasgow or east through the Carse of Gowrie to Dundee and on up the beautiful east coast railway to **Aberdeen**, from where those prepared to venture to rail-free islands can board overnight Northlink sailings north to Orkney and Shetland.

Leaving Perth, the railway traverses pastoral Tay Valley landscapes, with views of the river to the right. Cutting through a short tunnel (the first since Perth), we traverse **Birnam Wood**. No ordinary wood this, for much is made of Birnam in Shakespeare's *Macbeth*. Now the landscape assumes a real Highland demeanour. First stop, but not for express trains which just speed through, is Dunkeld & Birnam, twin towns on either side of the **River Tay**, linked by a striking iron bridge designed by Thomas Telford. The hills close in as the railway climbs up through the valleys of the Tay and the Tummel to reach Glen Garry, along the way stopping at solid, handsome townships like Pitlochry and Blair Atholl. The latter village has one of Scotland's leading stately homes. It's called Atholl Castle.

Cresting the summit of the line at Drumochter, we are now in the heart of the **Grampian Mountains**, amid some of Scotland's remotest terrain. Sit back and relax as the train drops gently down towards Glen Truim and the Spey Valley. The whisky distillery at Dalwhinnie (to the right of the railway) is a reminder that this is the land of *uisge beatha* – the water of life.

All trains stop at the two main **Spey Valley** communities – the first, Kingussie, is as nice a wee town as one could wish. Nothing ever happens here, but it's a pleasant base for tame walks and adventurous hikes. The second stop is at Aviemore, an extraordinary eyesore and a reminder of just how bad town planning was in the 1960s. The town was an oddball attempt to create an Alpine-style resort in the Highlands. Avert your eyes or, better still, let them be drawn to the fine range of hills away to the east. These are the **Cairngorms**, whose summits are – bar for Ben Nevis well away to the west – the loftiest in Britain. This is wild country which in winter has a real hint of the Arctic. Even when spring has come to the Spey Valley, it may still be wild winter on the Cairngorm tops, the late snows sintering into ice and lingering on till summer on shady north slopes. Make time for the Scottish hills and perhaps read Nan Shepherd's *The Living Mountain*, a wonderful piece of nature writing about the author's Cairngorm encounters.

From **Aviemore**, the railway tracks north-west, paralleling the main A9 road towards Inverness, climbing up to Slochd Summit, from where it's downhill all the way to Inverness, with two especially fine viaducts on that descent. The first is at Tomatin where the railway crosses Strathdearn, high above the River Findhorn, and the second is a gracious, gently curved 29-arch viaduct at **Culloden**, close to the spot where in 1745 government forces loyal to England's Hanoverian monarchs brutally snuffed out the Jacobite rebellion, inflicting a blow on Scottish life and culture which is still a sore point in Anglo-Scottish relations. These are thoughts to ponder as, with fine views of Moray Firth to the north, the train drops down into Inverness.

INVERNESS CONNECTIONS
Hourly trains run east on a pleasantly rural railway to **Aberdeen**, a route which never really cuts into the hills, but nonetheless affords great views along almost its entire length. Inverness is also the jumping-off point for the slow but utterly beautiful four-hour ride north to Caithness. Four trains a day (fewer on Sundays) leave Inverness for **Thurso and Wick**, along the way taking in a colourful medley of coastal and moorland landscapes. A highlight is the half-hour stretch between Kinbrace and Scotscalder where the railway traverses an eerily desolate expanse of blanket bog. Tales are told of trains being stranded here for days in winter snowstorms.

By mountain, moors and lochs

Over the past 50 years, timetable improvements have trimmed almost an hour off the travel time from **Inverness to Kyle**, but the journey is as beautiful as ever. This is the only rail route in Great Britain which affords fine views of both the east and west coasts. The train skirts Beauly Firth on leaving Inverness, and then on leaving Dingwall there is a great panorama of **Cromarty Firth** away to the north-east. But those east coast tasters are merely the prelude to a journey which takes in mountains and moorland, forest and glens before a glorious, almost operatic finale as the line skirts west-coast sea lochs on the approach to Kyle of Lochalsh.

The first part of the route out of Inverness has the feel of a very local railway. Three stations between Inverness and **Dingwall**, all closed in 1960, have reopened to passenger traffic in recent years. Beyond Dingwall, the railway swings west and climbs slowly into the mountains. Once past Garve, the hills close in and our train glides past mossy cliffs on the north side of the tracks. In winter, the green moss is eclipsed by cascades of icicles.

The coffee trolley – usually hoisted on board the train at Dingwall – doesn't come a moment too soon. Okay, it's not quite the same as the restaurant car which used to feature on the morning Kyle train as far as Achnasheen, where it was detached and sent back to Inverness with lunchtime duties on the homeward run.

Achnasheen is a place in the wilderness, as indeed are many stations on this rural railway. Two deer look idly on as the train slips by. The station names trip alliteratively off the tongue: Achnashellach, Achnasheen, Achanalt. And soon we are dropping down into Strathcarron, the great glen which drains west to the sea. We speed through **Attadale**, a remote halt where trains stop only on request. The gardens right by the station are an excellent place to break your journey (open daily April–October). From this little fragment of Paradise there are wonderful views of Skye. Not far beyond Attadale is Stromeferry, a delightfully misleading station name for there is no ferry. A three-minute stop is a chance to gulp fresh Highland air, but we are quickly on our way again.

The last twenty minutes down to Kyle offer a tantalising mix of coast, headlands and islands. The sun sparkles on **Loch Carron** and later catches the Crowlin Islands – while all the while there are glorious views north to the rugged Applecross Peninsula. Seals scuttle for safety as we approach Duncraig and all too soon we are pulling into **Kyle of Lochalsh**.

"For those of you who liked it so much that you want to ride back with us to Inverness, we'll be leaving Kyle just after midday," the guard announces. It seems that most of those on board plan to do just that. But for others, Kyle is merely a way station on a longer journey so they alight from the train and head for a waiting bus to take them further into the hills.

Onward from Kyle

Bus connections are well signed at Kyle station. On summer weekdays, buses leave every hour or two from the harbour slipway bus stop (4 mins walk from the station) to cross the bridge to Broadford in **Skye** (services are less frequent on Sundays and in winter). Most of these buses continue to Portree, about 70 mins by bus from Kyle, a pleasant small town which is the hub of Skye life. Just beyond Portree, on Skye's north-west coast, is the port of Uig (regular buses from Portree), whence there are ferries to Tarbert (Harris) and Lochmaddy (North Uist), both in the **Outer Hebrides**.

Broadford is an unlovely introduction to Skye, so there's no reason to stop here other than to change buses if you are heading for the island's beautiful Sleat Peninsula. Occasional buses run from Broadford to Armadale, from where you can take the CalMac ferry to Mallaig to connect into **Route 3**. Check bus and ferry times carefully, and bear in mind that the ferry service over the Sound of Sleat to Mallaig may be disrupted by high winds. By using this bus and ferry connection from Kyle to **Mallaig**, it is possible to combine **Route 2** and **3** in this book to create a marvellous round trip from Edinburgh through the Highlands to Skye, returning to the Scottish capital by an entirely different route.

SIDETRACKS: THE HEBRIDES

Few parts of Europe possess such wild beauty as the **Hebrides**, the complex archipelago off Scotland's west coast. There are about three dozen inhabited islands in the Inner Hebrides, which lie close to the Scottish mainland. And there are around 15 islands in the more distant Outer Hebrides which host a permanent population. The ferry services to the islands are operated by **Caledonian MacBrayne** (CalMac; details on www.calmac.co.uk). These services run from four mainland ports, namely Ullapool, Mallaig, Oban and Kennacraig. In addition, CalMac operates ferries to the islands of Harris and North Uist (both in the Outer Hebrides) from the small port of Uig on the Isle of Skye.

CalMac's comprehensive network of ferry services to, from and between the Hebridean islands offers some of the finest inshore shipping routes in Europe, with superb opportunities for island hopping by scheduled ferry services. Rail travellers often head for **Mallaig**, at the very end of the **West Highland Line** (on **Route 3** in this book), whence there are year-round CalMac services to six different Hebridean islands (five in the Inner Hebrides, plus South Uist in the Outer Isles). The destination list from Oban also runs to half-a-dozen islands ranging from serene Colonsay (in the Inner Hebrides) to beautiful Barra (at the southern end of the Outer Hebrides).

Direct trains from **Glasgow** run to both Oban and Mallaig and at each port it is just a short walk from train to ship. The boats are of different sizes, but on the bigger vessels, travellers will find many creature comforts with a good choice of Scottish fare on offer in the restaurants. All ferries convey cars, but it's also very easy to devise creative itineraries through the Hebrides relying entirely on public transport – be aware, though, that some bus services are infrequent.

These ferries provide **lifeline links** to some of Scotland's remotest communities; they are essential to the economic and social fabric of the region. This has been more than ever the case during the pandemic. And, in a region noted for its wild Atlantic weather, that means being flexible. On a breezy day in November, for example, CalMac advised that gusting winds might cause disruption to the **MS Clansman** as she set off on her scheduled sailing from Oban to Coll and Tiree. A footnote in that CalMac advisory, indicated that "the captain is fine with taking livestock" – it was a nice reminder that the company's vessels are part and parcel of Hebridean life. During late summer and autumn, the company regularly lays on extra sailings to accommodate livestock sales in Tiree and the Uists.

For a first taste of the Hebrides, and with a full week to spare, we recommend sailing out from **Oban to Barra**, then tracking north through the Outer Hebrides to Tarbert on Harris, from where it's just a short hop across to Uig on Skye. One might then enjoy a day or two on Skye before crossing the **Sound of Sleat** on the ferry from Armadale to Mallaig, where one can rejoin the mainland rail network, following **Route 3** in reverse back to Glasgow.

This itinerary requires five ferries in all, with fares for those five boats (in early October 2024) amounting to £36.15 per person. It's a chance to discover island communities with their own distinctive culture, language and stories. **Route 2** and **3** in this book make fine preludes to Hebridean adventures.

Route 3: The rural route to the West Highlands

Cities: ★★ Culture: ★ History: ★★ Scenery: ★★★
Countries covered: Netherlands (NL), England (ENG), Scotland (SCT)
Journey time: 28 hrs 30 mins | Distance: 1,132 km | Map: www.ebrweb.eu/18map3

This route starts on the European mainland and ends in western Scotland. We know that a similar route in recent editions of *Europe by Rail* was popular with European readers wanting to explore the hill country of **northern England and Scotland**. We've tweaked the route for this 18th edition, now introducing a **North Sea ferry crossing** with DFDS. Like every journey in *Europe by Rail*, the route can of course be followed in reverse, perhaps by Highlanders or urbanites from Scottish cities tempted to forsake the plane and travel instead by train and ferry to the continent.

The highlight of this journey from Amsterdam to the West Highlands of Scotland is a railway in the premier league of Europe's scenic lines: the **West Highland Line** from Glasgow to the fishing port of Mallaig by the Sound of Sleat on Scotland's west coast. But we start with a wonderful overnight journey on a DFDS ship. And then we have a rail cruise through northern England and southern Scotland with a stop in Edinburgh.

Itinerary thoughts
We recommend splitting this route into at least two legs. Travelling overnight on the **ship to Newcastle** is always fun, but you may not want to then spend the whole of the following day on trains. Better we think to travel from **Newcastle to Edinburgh** by train, then continue into the Highlands after a night or two in the Scottish capital. There is scope for a wonderful diversion from Carlisle to explore the **Settle and Carlisle railway** when runs south-east up the Eden Valley and over the hills into Yorkshire. For more on that see the box on p73.

Escape from Holland

The ferry route promoted as running from **Amsterdam to Newcastle** doesn't actually do any such thing. It's none the worse for that. On the Dutch side it leaves from the ferry terminal at Sluisplein in the town of IJmuiden on the North Sea coast. On arrival in England, it doesn't sail all the way up the Tyne to Newcastle but docks in North Shields. Purists call it the IJmuiden to North Shields ferry.

The boring way to reach **IJmuiden** from Amsterdam is to take the bus run by Brouwers on behalf of ferry operator DFDS. It costs €10 and you'll find details on the DFDS website at www.dfds.com. A more interesting way of reaching the ferry is to take the train to **Beverwijk**, from where local bus 74 leaves the bus station (turn left as you exit the railway station to find the bus stops) every 30 minutes for the short ride to IJmuiden. If you have time to spare, the Brafoer restaurant just across the road from the railway station in Beverwijk has a pleasant terrace overlooking a lake.

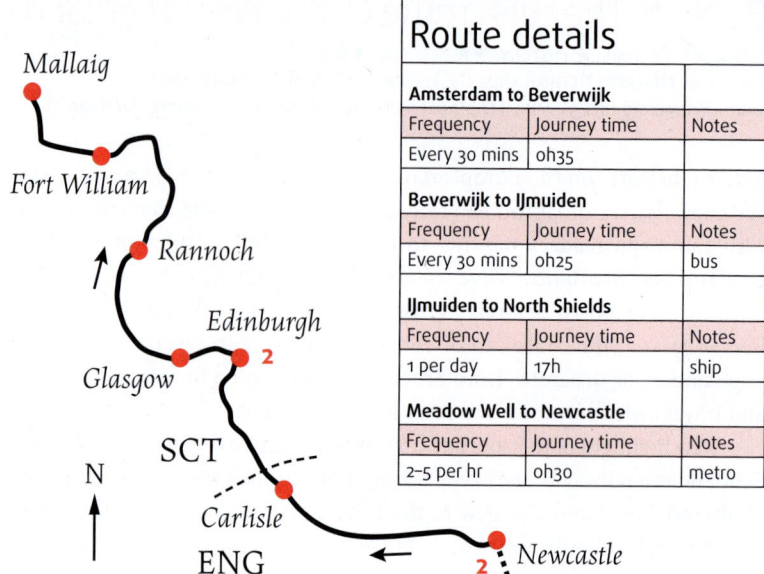

Route details

Amsterdam to Beverwijk

Frequency	Journey time	Notes
Every 30 mins	0h35	

Beverwijk to IJmuiden

Frequency	Journey time	Notes
Every 30 mins	0h25	bus

IJmuiden to North Shields

Frequency	Journey time	Notes
1 per day	17h	ship

Meadow Well to Newcastle

Frequency	Journey time	Notes
2–5 per hr	0h30	metro

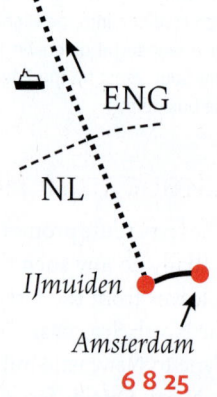

Route details (cont.)

Newcastle to Carlisle

Frequency	Journey time	Notes
1–2 per hr	1h25–1h45	

Carlisle to Edinburgh Waverley

Frequency	Journey time	Notes
Hourly	1h15–1h25	

Edinburgh Waverley to Glasgow Queen Street

Frequency	Journey time	Notes
4 per hr	0h45–1h	E

Glasgow Queen Street to Fort William

Frequency	Journey time	Notes
4 per day	3h45–4h15	X

Fort William to Mallaig

Frequency	Journey time	Notes
3–4 per day	1h25	X A

Notes

A – There are in addition seasonal steam trains (marketed as *The Jacobite*) between Fort William and Mallaig. Special fares apply.
E – Additional slow trains run frequently from Edinburgh to Glasgow.
X – Only two trains per day on Sundays.

Take 🚌 74 to the Oranjestraat stop in IJmuiden, from where it is five minutes on foot due west along narrow Kanaalstraat to the ferry terminal. The Rough Guide dismisses IJmuiden as "eminently missable". We take a more positive view of IJmuiden which we find quite interesting. Amid the cranes and warehouses is a pleasant community with easy access to beaches, sand dunes and fresh fish. Plus IJmuiden features on **UNESCO's World Heritage List** with the island fort in the harbour being part of a wider listing on Dutch water defence lines. Take the little ferry over to the fort for a wander before boarding the DFDS ship to England.

Sailing with Det Forenede Dampskibs-Selskab

DFDS has come a long way since the company was founded by Danish financier **Carl Frederik Tietgen** in 1866. In its early days the company powerfully shaped Russian trade, capturing a big share of the market for shipments between the Black Sea and St Petersburg. There's still a dash of old-school style about many DFDS ferry crossings and the North Sea route from IJmuiden to Tyneside is one of the best.

Board the ship from about 15.00 and take time to explore. Cabins are mandatory, and our advice is to book the best cabin within your available budget. If you can run to one of the poshest commodore deluxe cabins, you're in for a treat. Around 17.00, glasses of bubbly are served in the forward lounge on deck 10 of the *MS King Seaways*. The vessel is one of two smart DFDS cruise ferries which ply this **route to North Shields**. A musical accolade over the ship's PA system marks the moment when the *King Seaways* slips off her mooring and sets sail for England.

This must surely rate as the most stylish way to travel to England. It is a shortcut to Britain which avoids the frenetic hassle of London over the North Sea. With late afternoon departures from both IJmuiden and North Shields and arrival around 10 next morning, the long overnight crossing is **a chance to relax** and indulge in creature comforts. Book one of the posh commodore or commodore-deluxe cabins for stateroom style and enjoy a leisurely dinner in the **North Sea Bistro** which mainstreams on classic European cuisine with tasty staples like sea bass and lamb.

The two vessels on the route, the *King Seaways* and the *Princess Seaways*, are very similar but the *King Seaways* has the edge when it comes to the very best commodore-class cabins, and on that ship there's also the lounge up front on deck 10 for passengers booked in deluxe accommodation.

From the Tyne to the Solway

The route taken by the DFDS ships includes inshore **sailing up the Durham coast** (off the port side) as a prelude to a grand entry through the great breakwaters which mark the mouth of the **River Tyne**. As you enter the river, there's a fine view of the ancient priory and castle at Tynemouth on a headland away to the north.

Then it's just a short cruise up the river through an area with a rich industrial history to the **Tyne Commission Quay** where the DFDS ships dock. Buses outside the terminal shuttle passengers to Newcastle Central railway station (book the bus transfer when making the ferry booking). Or follow our example and walk 25 minutes to Meadow Well station and ride the **Tyne and Wear metro** into the middle of Newcastle.

Newcastle connections

From Newcastle Central station there are direct express trains at least twice each hour running **north to Edinburgh** and south via York to London. There are hourly departures to Leeds, Manchester and Liverpool. Local trains run down the coast to Middlesbrough with occasional services continuing through the **North York Moors** national part to lovely Whitby on the Yorkshire coast.

There are trains at least hourly along the **Tyne Valley railway** to Carlisle, which we follow in the route described here. Newcastle's excellent range of rail services includes direct trains to such far-flung points at Penzance in distant Cornwall or Inverness in northern Scotland, underpinning the value of using **Tyneside as a gateway** on journeys between the continent and Britain.

Our train journey now takes us west from Newcastle, running up the historic Tyne Valley route into the **Northumberland hills**, broadly following the route of Hadrian's Wall to Carlisle.

Leaving Newcastle, the **railway crosses the Tyne** on a dramatic bridge high above the river. We then follow the south bank of the river west to Hexham, a market town with a fine abbey. **Hexham** makes a good stop, and it's worth the uninspiring hike up from the station into town to have a wander. West from Hexham the railway criss-crosses the South Tyne. Just after Haltwhistle the railway breaches the line of **Hadrian's Wall**, cresting a gentle watershed and then dropping down to **Carlisle**. The station has a nice neo-Tudor frontage, but the real star was until recently the traditional station bar on Platform 4 which has unfortunately closed. Nevertheless it is still a very fine station and a pleasant place to watch the comings and goings of trains. Carlisle itself, so strategically placed near the head of the Solway Firth, is well worth exploring.

Carlisle connections

From Carlisle, there's a fast train to London every hour. It's also the starting point for two north of England branch line adventures. The first runs south-east up the Eden Valley. This is the famous **Settle and Carlisle Railway**, which you'll find described in the box on the opposite page. If you yearn for the sea, then hop on the slow train around the **Cumbrian coast** to Whitehaven and Barrow.

If you are Scotland bound, there's plenty of choice with usually at least three trains an hour heading north over the border. Of the two routes to **Glasgow**, the one via Dumfries is slower but has a better mix of scenery.

The Settle & Carlisle Railway

Carlisle marks the northern end of the Settle and Carlisle railway. About eight trains each day leave Carlisle for Settle, a journey that takes about 90 to 110 minutes. This is quite simply **the finest rail route in the Pennines**. That it has survived at all is a miracle. In the early 1980s, when the entire route from Carlisle down to Settle and beyond was slated for closure, **community activism** did not merely save the line but really propelled it to prominence. Long abandoned stations were reopened, and today this railway plays a central role in both local life and tourism in the remote villages which it serves in Cumbria's **Eden Valley and the Yorkshire Dales**. The round trip from Carlisle down to Settle and back will take four to fives hours depending on how long you spend in Settle and we rate it as a must-do trip. It's gorgeous.

From Carlisle, the railway follows the verdant Eden Valley through pastoral landscapes of rare beauty, passing through the market town of **Appleby** (always worth a stop if you have time). Beyond Kirkby Stephen (note that the station is far from the town), we climb steeply to the summit at **Ais Gill**. We skirt Baugh Fell to the right and then stop at Dent, perhaps the loneliest railway station in all of England, perched on a shelf high above the scattered Dentdale dwellings which it serves.

Passing through **Blea Moor Tunnel**, there is is a magnificent, curved viaduct at Ribblehead. The entire route is an ever-changing treat. The stretch from **Ribblehead** down the valley to Settle is real limestone country, with distinctive white stone walls defining the fields, giving way at high levels to barren moorland. **Settle** is a handsome small town, again a good place to pause for a coffee or lunch, its station a characterful reminder of a bygone age of rail travel. You may want to return to Carlisle, but note that all trains continue south to Leeds, so this line can be built into longer itineraries from Cumbria to London.

The railway from Settle down to Leeds is itself very interesting, following **Ribblesdale** and then Airedale. It passes towns like **Bingley** and **Keighley** which were once big players in the global wool trade. And it's well worth making a stop at Saltaire, a UNESCO World Heritage industrial village which oozes architectural ambition and is the legacy of philanthropic paternalism.

Over the border

There used to be two rail routes from **Carlisle to Edinburgh**. The classic Waverley route through the borders to Edinburgh is long gone, although the section from Tweedbank and Galashiels to Edinburgh reopened in 2015. For a dose of **lovely Borders scenery**, the X95 bus leaves from outside the court building on English Street in Carlisle and takes two hours for the run to Galashiels, where you can transfer onto the train to Edinburgh.

Alternatively, stick with us here on Route 3 and take the train on the surviving rail route to Edinburgh, which runs through pastoral Annandale scenery and on over **Beattock Summit**. The route descends into the uppermost part of the Clyde Valley and then veers off to the east, skirting the Pentland Hills to reach the Scottish capital where the trains stop first at Haymarket and then at **Waverley station**. The latter is better placed for the city centre.

Edinburgh (suggested stopover)

Edinburgh is Scotland's major hub of **political and cultural life**, though Glaswegians often assert that their city has the edge over Edinburgh when it comes to the arts and creative industries. Few cities so elegantly undulate over gentle hills as Edinburgh, and walking the city streets is enlivened by occasional views of more significant hills such as **Arthur's Seat** and the Salisbury Crags or, especially in the **New Town** (ie. the area on the low ridge north of Princes Street, the city's main shopping street), glimpses of the Firth of Forth.

Edinburgh has its fair share of annual cultural events, of which the best known is the **Edinburgh Fringe** which takes place in August and started as an antidote to the high-culture Edinburgh Festival: enjoy music, theatre, comedy and performance art. A walk down the **Royal Mile** gets you from the Castle down to the **Scottish Parliament** (www.parliament.scot) by Holyrood Park. You'll pass on the way an array of shops, cafés and the 12th-century **St Giles's Cathedral** – the latter is regarded as the Mother Church of Presbyterianism.

Arrival, information, accommodation

Edinburgh has two railway stations, of which **Waverley** is the more central (and right on Pricess Street). **Haymarket**, in the city's West End area, is connected to the airport (www.edinburghairport.com) by frequent trams which take 25 mins for the ride (buy a ticket before boarding). Tourist office: 249 High Street (www.edinburgh.org).

Be aware that staying in Edinburgh is pretty pricey. The city gets booked up during the Fringe, so plan ahead if you're staying in the summer. An affordable, friendly B&B about 20 minutes on foot south of Waverley is the **Southside Guest House**, 8 Newington Road, ☎ 0131 466 6573 (www.southsideguesthouse.co.uk), well placed for climbing Arthur's Seat. Or stay at **No. 53 Frederick Street**, 53 Frederick Street, ☎ 0131 226 2752 (www.53frederickstreet.com), a centrally located B&B just north of Princes Street. **Six Brunton Place**, 6 Brunton Place, ☎ 0131 623 6405 (www.sixbruntonplace.com), is a cosy B&B in a Georgian town house.

If you want to treat yourself to something special, visit **Valvona & Crolla**, 19 Elm Row. It's an Edinburgh institution. Pick up some Italian deli treats or have a snack in the café. Enjoy fish suppers in the city's trendy **Leith harbour district**.

Connections from Edinburgh

You can connect in Edinburgh onto **Route 2**, following it north into the Highlands. With a short hop over the island of Skye, it's easy to combine Route 2 and 3 into a **perfect round trip** through some of Scotland's finest scenery. Equally, Route 2 can be used to return south from Edinburgh. You can follow it back via the **East Coast line** to York and London. There are departures from Edinburgh at least hourly on that route.

Now it's time for us to head for the hills. There's a vast choice of trains from Edinburgh for the **short hop to Glasgow**. The fastest route is that via Falkirk High. Running west out of Edinburgh, the railway broadly follows two canals (first the **Union Canal** and later the Forth and Clyde) all the way to Glasgow, with good views to the right of the Campsie Fells during the latter part of the journey. It's just a first taste of the hills.

There's a notably steep descent down into the Queen Street terminus in **Glasgow**. One 19th-century guidebook describes it thus: "The immediate approach to the city, dull enough in an artistic sense, is rendered interesting by the famous Cowlairs Incline, the train being lowered by wire ropes along a steep tunnel... which brings us to Queen Street Station."

Glasgow connections

Queen Street is one of two major rail termini in Glasgow. The other is **Glasgow Central**, about a ten-minute walk south from Queen Street, but still on the north bank of the Clyde. Both stations also have low-level (ie. underground) platforms used in the main by suburban services.

Of the two stations, Glasgow Central is by far the more striking with its elegant iron columns, decorated with classical capitals and a remarkable **Edwardian-era booking hall**. It's from here that all trains to England depart, with direct trains to Manchester, Birmingham and London. There are also trains to the Ayrshire coast and Dumfries. Queen Street station serves all trains bound for the **Highlands**.

Loch Lomond, Rannoch and more

There's often a real sense of anticipation surrounding the departure of the **West Highland Line** trains from Glasgow Queen Street. Those in the know grab seats on the left side of the train for the first part of the journey. Modern trains make light of **Cowlairs Incline**, swinging off to the left at the top of the hill and skimming Glasgow suburbs to reach the Clyde near the Erskine Bridge. The first great landmark is **Dumbarton Castle** (on the left), perched on a double-humped rock just by the spot where the waters of the Leven decant into the Clyde.

There are fine views of the Clyde at Cardross, and then the train swings off to the right, climbing up beyond Helensburgh to reach the shores of **Gare Loch**, where the train passes the military base at Faslane which is home to the Trident submarine fleet which carries nuclear weapons. Since 1982, there has been a permanent peace camp here, with protesters highlighting the unwanted presence of a nuclear arsenal in the Scottish hills.

Passing a gentle watershed at the top end of Loch Long, the train drops down towards **Loch Lomond** (on the right), and this is the moment to switch seats, if space permits, to the right side of the carriage. Now there's a real sense of being in the Highlands, with dramatic views across Loch Lomond to the hills beyond.

At **Crianlarich**, the line to Oban branchees off to the left, and carriages for that coastal port are usually detached from the Fort William train at Crianlarich. After that, the railway runs up Strath Fillan and then climbs up onto **Rannoch Moor**, a bleakly evocative landscape of **peat bogs**. "A wearier-looking desert man never saw," in Robert Louis Stevenson's words. We see it more positively: a tinted mosaic of purple-black bog, heather-clad hillocks and the glint of sun on distant lochs.

Like many stations along the line, that at Rannoch has a Swiss-chalet style with Arts and Crafts affectations. Then comes the most remote part of the route. It is not for nothing that just outside **Corrour station**, the railway line runs through snow sheds that prevent drifting snow from blocking the line in winter.

They are not always successful, and many are the times when blizzards prevent the trains from crossing the moor to Corrour where, quite improbably, there is a really **cosy café** on the station platform. Do check in advance that it's open (usually from late March till the end of October) before alighting from the train (www.corrour.co.uk; ☎ 01397 732 236) as this is not a spot you'd want to be left stranded. North from Corrour, the line gently descends, slipping by Loch Treig to reach Glen Spean and then skirting the north flank of Ben Nevis to reach Fort William.

FORT WILLIAM CONNECTIONS
If you are on a tight schedule and with time only for the briefest glimpse of the Highlands, Fort William might be as far as you'll get. It's worth remembering that Fort William has a *Caledonian Sleeper* **night train** (daily except Sat) direct to London.

If you are eager to see **Loch Ness** (with or without its monster), then hop on Scottish Citylink 🚌 919 or 920 to Inverness, a two-hour journey which runs along the shores of Loch Ness (sit on the right side of the bus for loch views). 🚌 918 runs twice daily (not Sun) down to **Oban**, offering brilliant coastal views along the way. Again, take a seat on the right side of the bus. In Oban you can connect onto trains back to Glasgow or CalMac ferries to the **Inner and Outer Hebrides**.

Jacobite country

No one forgets the ride on the final stretch of the West Highland Line from **Fort William to Mallaig**. This is a railway which has been propelled to prominence by the Harry Potter films and the steam train, called *The Jacobite*, which plies the route from late April to October (details on www.westcoastrailways.co.uk). The steam train is very pricey (over £30 for a single journey from Fort William to Mallaig), but the scenery is just the same if you stick to the regular Scotrail train. The best scenery is on the left side.

Leaving Fort William, the train swings west to cross the **River Lochy**. Shortly thereafter, just after the halt at Banavie (where trains stop only on request), there's a fine view to the right up **Neptune's Staircase** – that's the name of the great series of locks, constructed by Thomas Telford and opened in 1820, which allows boats to gain elevation and follow the Caledonian Canal north to Loch Ness.

The railway runs along the north shore of Loch Eil then, just after a short tunnel, there's a moment of real drama as the line crosses **Glen-**

finnan Viaduct, with a tremendous vista south down towards Loch Shiel. A memorial, visible from the train, recalls the historic importance of Glenfinnan; it was here that in 1745 the Jacobites gathered to launch their campaign to reclaim the British crown for the Stuarts.

Slipping on through Lochailort, the railway makes real contact with the coast, with gorgeous views over the **Sound of Arisaig**, before running north to Mallaig.

Mallaig

Mallaig is a pleasant wee port which can be busy when the **steam train** is in town. Most of the visitors on *The Jacobite* stay just a couple of hours. Mallaig deserves more. It's a place for fish & chips, seagulls, and just enjoying a pint or two by the quayside, watching the fishing boats come and go.

Cast back 150 ydears and Mallaig was an important **herring port**. It was the commercial valve of the humble herring which encouraged entrepreneurs to extend the West Highland railway from Fort William to Mallaig, reaching the west coast port in 1901. Mallaig boomed during the herring season following the arrival of the railway, the townscape much enlivened by the 'herring girls' who arrived in Mallaig to work all hours gutting and packing the herrings.

The herring trade is long gone but Mallaig still has **an active fleet**, landing the fish catch from inshore waters. These days there's a buoyant trade in shellfish. There's a pleasant 3-km **circular walk** up onto the hills above the east side of the bay, best made in the evening when you have a fine view west over the harbour with the setting sun dipping down behind Skye's Sleat peninusula. It is a good moment to reflect on how far we have come from Amsterdam and IJmuiden.

ARRIVAL, INFORMATION, ACCOMMODATION

≥ The station is well placed for the harbour and the western part of Mallaig. Walk down Station Road to get to the 🛈 visitor centre (www.road-to-the-isles.org.uk). ⛴ The **Springbank Guest House**, Eastbay, ☎ 01687 462 459 (www.springbank-mallaig.co.uk) is a comfortable B&B, located on the bay and with good views across to the harbour. ✘ For a good fish supper, head for the **Terrace Restaurant** (in the West Highland Hotel, ☎ 01687 462 210) or the **Cornerstone Restaurant** on Main Street (☎ 01687 462 306).

ONWARD CONNECTIONS

There's a fine range of waterborne adventures from Mallaig. There are year-round ferries to **Eigg, Muck, Canna and Rum** – collectively known as the Small Isles – and also to Inverie on the Knoydart Peninsula. That journey to Inverie can be done as a day trip; it's a wonderful opportunity to experience the rugged beauty of Knoydart.

The car ferry shuttles over to Armadale on **Skye**, from where you can travel on by bus via Broadford to Kyle (on **Route 2**). The *Lord of the Isles* sails from Mallaig to Lochboisdale in the Outer Hebrides (weather permitting, daily in summer and irregularly in winter). Details and timetable at www.calmac.co.uk.

Route 4: Across England and Wales to Ireland

CITIES: ★★ CULTURE: ★★ HISTORY: ★★ SCENERY: ★★
COUNTRIES COVERED: NETHERLANDS (NL), ENGLAND (ENG), WALES (WLS), IRELAND (IE)
JOURNEY TIME: 26 HRS 30 MINS | DISTANCE: 1,194 KM | MAP: www.ebrweb.eu/18MAP4

Beurs metro station in the busy heart of **Rotterdam** is the improbable starting point for this journey which takes in four countries and ends in south-west Ireland on the edge of the country's first national park. The contrasts between start and end points couldn't be sharper. Along the way, we take in ferries across the **North Sea** and the **Irish Sea** and some nicely rural rail routes through England, Wales and Ireland.

ITINERARY OPTIONS
It's a route that is best spread over four days, with the first night on the **boat to Harwich**, and then overnight stops in **Chester** and **Dublin**. The journey from Harwich to Chester, as described here, takes about seven hours. Assuming you use the overnight boat from Holland, you'll have an early arrival in Harwich, so you may want to stop off here and there on the journey to Chester. Bury St Edmunds, Cambridge and Stamford are all good options.

You'll need the yellow-themed Route B from **Rotterdam Beurs metro station** for the 14-stop ride to Hoek van Holland. This line to Hoek opened in autumn 2019, replacing the erstwhile rail route to the port. Happily, most of the journey is above ground, and it's a ride to make you think. It's odd to depart on such an ambitious journey on a local metro tram. There's a melancholy born of leaving the continent without having properly said one's farewells. There is no such thing as a grand exit via **Hoek van Holland**.

Along the way, the metro slips past the shadows of quiet villages gobbled up by the city. There are echoes of the last psalms recited in the synagogue at Maassluis. And there are the voices of Jewish children. Thousands upon thousands of them who, in the months prior to the outbreak of the Second World War, travelled by special *Kindertransport* trains to Hoek van Holland, there to board the ship for the crossing to Harwich and new lives in England.

The Stena Line **ship to Harwich** is extremely comfortable. We favour the overnight boat, which doesn't leave till late evening, but foot passengers can normally board from about 18.45 – and we're the ones there at the front

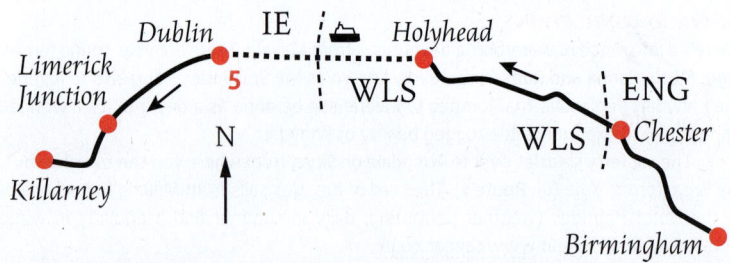

of the line when they open the gate. It's worth boarding early. Take a picnic supper, or for onboard dining choose between the very reasonably priced self-service cafeteria or the more upmarket Metropolitan restaurant.

It's often so placid that one barely notices the short hours as the ship slips over to England. Indeed there were occasions when we awoke to find that we were already quayside in **Harwich** without having even realised that we'd left Hoek van Holland. Foot passengers disembark about 06.45 for a bleary eyed encounter with the uniformed representatives of *Border Force* – men and women with padded shoulders, lots of gear, working on the front line of defence in the war against outsiders. It is a depressing mark of what Britain has become, not helped by the fact that Harwich is not pretty.

Route details

Rotterdam Beurs to Hoek van Holland

Frequency	Journey time	Notes
2–3 per hr	0h35	

Hoek van Holland to Harwich

Frequency	Journey time	Notes
2 per day	7h–9h30	

Harwich to Cambridge

Frequency	Journey time	Notes
Every 1–2 hrs	1h55–2h30	A

Cambridge to Birmingham New Street

Frequency	Journey time	Notes
Hourly	2h40–2h50	

Route details (cont.)

Birmingham New Street to Chester

Frequency	Journey time	Notes
Hourly	2h15	B

Chester to Holyhead

Frequency	Journey time	Notes
Hourly	1h35–2h	

Holyhead to Dublin Port

Frequency	Journey time	Notes
5–7 per day	2h15–3h15	

Dublin Heuston to Killarney

Frequency	Journey time	Notes
Every 2 hrs	3h20	C

Notes

A – There are only occasional direct trains. It is usually necessary to change at Manningtree and Ipswich.

B – Alternate trains require a change at Shrewsbury.

C – Most journeys from Dublin to Killarney require a change of train in Mallow.

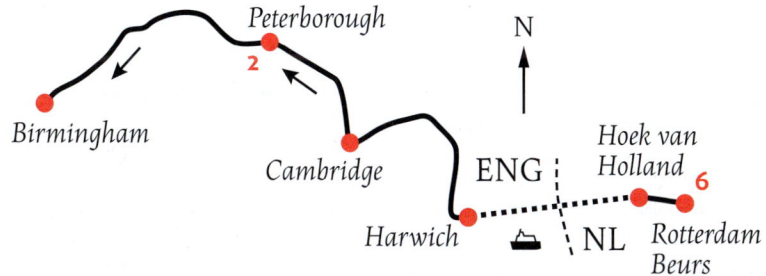

Emerging from that brush with bureaucracy into the soulless terminal building, you may want to grab a coffee at the Quayside Café which is anything but quayside, but one level up an escalator from the railway platforms. It's also a chance for a first encounter with the **bacon roll**, a cholesterol-laden morning fix upon which the English rely to supercharge their arteries. Yet, despite all this, there's something really nice about being up bright and early with a fine train journey ahead.

Westward across England

There's a direct train to Cambridge which connects nicely with the overnight boat. At other times you may need to change at Manningtree and Ipswich. Sit on the right of the train from **Harwich** for pleasing views of the River Stour, with the moorings and maltings at Mistley. Then, skirting lowland landscapes which so inspired the English artist **John Constable**, the train heads north into Suffolk.

It's an excellent run across Suffolk towards Cambridge with frothy meadowsweet, wild roses and willowherb aplenty by the tracks. Along the way, all trains stop in **Bury St Edmunds** where the magnificent St Edmundsbury Cathedral is good enough cause to pause for an hour or two. Bury has some appealing Georgian architecture and some decent cafés.

If this is your first time in England, Bury St Edmunds is a place which can easily win your heart over. The town centre is about ten minutes on foot south of the station. Some trains run directly from Bury St Edmunds to Ely and Peterborough, but sometimes it's faster to route via Newmarket and Cambridge.

Beyond Bury St Edmunds, the landscape becomes less intimate, with large, **rolling fields**, which give way to grassland and paddocks at Newmarket, where the local economy is driven by horse breeding and racing. **Cambridge** station is inconveniently placed for the city centre, but fortunately there are buses aplenty into town from the station forecourt. Look out for 🚌 1 or 3 which leave every five to ten minutes (single fare no more than £2).

The journey north from Cambridge runs through **marshy Fenland** countryside to Ely (where the direct line from Bury St Edmunds rejoins from the right). The cathedral town of Ely takes its name from the local eels which were once common; major drainage projects in the Fens have tamed a landscape which was once a reedy wilderness of meres and tidal creeks. From Ely, you'll see a great swathe of Fenland landscape as the train continues to March and **Peterborough**.

Peterborough links
This major railway centre on the East Coast main line – that's the principal line from London to Edinburgh – is the place to connect into **Route 2** in this book (see p59). It's under four hours from Peterborough to the Scottish capital.

Our westward journey continues, skirting a tip of Lincolnshire, with all trains pausing in the market town of **Stamford** where the handsome mock-Tudor style railway station is just a taste of what this lovely market town has to offer. It's a ten-minute walk from the station to the town centre, which is on rising ground north of the River Welland. West of Stamford, the railway enters hillier terrain and England's smallest county, Rutland, from where it's an easy ride on through less interesting scenery to Leicester and **Birmingham**, where all trains from the east terminate at New Street station.

England's second city was born early in the railway age, and grew rapidly through a preoccupation with profit and industry. Entrepreneurial spirit was more important than civic beauty, and it's said that Queen Victoria would ask for the window blinds to be lowered as the royal train passed through Birmingham. These days Birmingham has spruced itself up, and the city has enviable drive and energy. Imposing squares and canals dominate the modern cityscape, but you can still feel the pulse of a more industrial Birmingham in the **Jewellery Quarter**, just north of the city centre.

BIRMINGHAM STATIONS AND CONNECTIONS
From the railway platforms at **Birmingham New Street** station, head upstairs to the newly refurbished concourse for a dash of contemporary style. The city centre's second station is **Moor Street**, much more intimate than New Street, and magnificently refurbished in Edwardian style. It is the starting point for the excellent Chiltern route to London Marylebone and Stratford-upon-Avon. All other long-distance trains from Birmingham leave from New Street with regular departures to Bristol and Devon, Carlisle, Edinburgh and Glasgow, Oxford and the south coast.

From Birmingham New Street there are two rail routes to Chester – one via Crewe and the other via Shrewsbury. We strongly recommend the latter; it's far more scenic. Edging out of Birmingham, the train parallels a canal through urban terrain, eventually reaching more open country beyond Wolverhampton with views south to the Wrekin and other **Shropshire hills**. Soon we are rolling into **Shrewsbury** where, if you have an hour to kill, the ornate station facade is worth a look, and it's an easy walk into the town centre which has a feast of Georgian and timber-framed buildings.

Sit on the right for the one-hour ride from Shrewsbury to Chester. The railway dips into Wales north of Gobowen, crossing the River Ceiriog to reach Welsh territory. Just to the right of the railway there's a fine view of **Chirk Aqueduct** which carries the Llangollen Canal over the Ceiriog Valley. Beyond Wrexham, the railway crosses back into England, running north across the River Dee, passing Chester racecourse to reach the town's station.

Chester

The handsome walled city of Chester, so proud of its **Roman origins**, is located on the north side of the River Dee. With Merseyside just a stone's throw away to the north, and much of the city's hinterland in Wales, Chester often struggles to assert a regional identity. But with its largely traffic-free central area it's a great place for an overnight stop. Explore the curious **Chester Rows** (a shopping area with elevated walkways in a row of late-mediaeval buildings), check out the Gothic cathedral and explore the city walls. If you are spending a couple of nights in Chester, you might consider a visit to vibrant **Liverpool**, just 45 minutes away on frequent local trains.

ARRIVAL, INFORMATION, ACCOMMODATION

⇌ Just a 10-minute walk, north-east of the city centre. 🄸 Tourist office: at the Town Hall (www.visitcheshire.com).

🛏 The highly regarded **Stone Villa Chester**, 3 Stone Place, ☎ 01244 345 014 (www.stonevillachester.co.uk) is convenient for the station and only a short stroll away from the city centre. Or try the centrally located and welcoming **Grosvenor Place Guest House**, 2 Grosvenor Place, ☎ 01244 324455 (www.grosvenorplacechester.co.uk). More upmarket is the elegant **Chester Grosvenor**, Eastgate, ☎ 01244 324 024 (www.chestergrosvenor.com), a listed building with a black-and-white timbered facade in the heart of the city.

To the Celtic world

If you stay overnight in Chester, you'll not need an early start to reach the afternoon boat from Holyhead to Ireland. Even the slowest trains take only two hours. If you are inclined to stop off along the way, the small town of Conwy is a nice spot to spend a couple of hours.

Leaving Chester, the train slips into **Wales** in the most unromantic manner amid a maze of power lines and factories. But it gets better with the good views to the right across the salt marshes that rim the Dee Estuary.

WELSH WALES

Crossing the **Vale of Conwy**, there is a sense of entering a more **elemental Wales** – a country whose very nature is shaped by rock. **Route 4** merely skims the north coast, and you need to cut inland to really get a sense of Welsh Wales. That's the part of the country where, mainly in more rural areas, the Welsh language is still spoken. This distinct cultural territory extends west from Snowdonia into the Llŷn Peninsula, and south through Merioneth into Ceredigion.

Llandudno Junction is a spot to embark on a journey into the Welsh hills. There's a branch railway which runs south up the Vale of Conwy to reach the slate-strewn town of Blaenau Ffestiniog, where you can join the narrow-gauge **Ffestiniog Railway** (www.festrail.co.uk) down to the coast at Porthmadog. From there, it's a fine run south along the Cambrian coast line, crossing the **Mawddach Estuary** at Barmouth. If you don't mind some longish bus journeys, you can work your way south through deeply rural countryside to join **Route 5** at Llandovery, Carmarthen or Fishguard. It's a chance to see Methodist chapels and remote villages in the hills and a chance to touch the life and spirit of a distinctive culture which has always been undervalued by the English. But beware: one dose of Welsh Wales might be enough to have you hooked for ever. If you are tempted, the book to read in preparation for this cultural expedition is **Jan Morris'** *Wales: Epic Views of a Small Country*.

Then, if you avert your eyes from the dreary ribbon development along the coast, we slowly reach the hills. Approaching **Llandudno Junction**, the great limestone headland of Great Orme rears up to the right, and beyond Conwy there are fine vistas of the hills of Snowdonia to the left, with the island of Anglesey visible across the Menai Strait.

The finest part of the journey from **Chester to Holyhead** is the section from Conwy to just beyond Bangor where the train crosses the Britannia Bridge to reach Anglesey (Ynys Môn). The first station on the island, served only by local trains, is a 58-letters long, tongue-twisting Welsh place name often shortened to Llanfair PG – an enigmatic abbreviation hinting at the linguistic challenges which lie ahead. From here, it's an easy cruise over rough pasture and gorse heath until on the right you'll spot the abandoned aluminium smelter which announces arrival in **Holyhead**.

The railway station has been rudely separated from the town by the security paraphernalia that surround the port. By way of mild recompense, there's a dramatic new footbridge leading from the station into town, nicely embellished with a Welsh inscription which translates as "Pass this way with a pure heart." You'll need it to discern any beauty in run-down Holyhead.

Stena Line and Irish Ferries compete on the **shipping route to Dublin**, the latter offering a choice of a traditional cruise ferry or a catamaran. You'll most likely find that the early afternoon Irish Ferries sailing works well. It's usually operated by the *MS Ulysses*, a traditional vessel with an excellent club-class lounge. It's worth paying the modest supplement for the upgrade. From that lounge, you'll have grand views on a clear day, initially of the Welsh hills slipping away to the east and later, as you approach Ireland, of the **Wicklow Mountains**. Whichever crossing you opt for, buses meet the ferries to carry foot passengers into town.

Dublin (suggested stopover)

The Irish capital is quite simply phenomenal. Few other European cities have quite the buzz and flair of Dublin (which is known as Baile Átha Cliath in Irish). The **River Liffey** flows from west to east through the centre of town, decanting into Dublin Bay, with the city itself split predictably into **Northside** and **Southside**. The latter is stylish and arty, all the more so following the smartening up of the **Temple Bar** cultural quarter, while life on the north bank of the Liffey is that little bit more edgy. But we mustn't generalise, for the Irish President's offical residence (Áras an Uachtaráin) is in Northside – set in **Phoenix Park**, a wonderful open space just west of the central area and open to the public. This huge park – plenty of monuments, meadows and deer – is a great place to relax.

In Southside, to the east of Temple Bar, is the main **Trinity College** campus, extending from College Green east to Pearse station. You can wander freely through the grounds of Trinity, and the *Book of Kells* exhibition is definitely worth a visit. From the campus, it's a short walk to the **National Gallery** (www.nationalgallery.ie), from where it's easy to explore Merrion Square, the grandest of the city's Georgian squares. The entire area from **Merrion Square** down to Fitzwilliam Square is delightful. But by now you'll have walked your socks off so make for St Stephen's Green, a Victorian-style park which is a great spot to just watch Dubliners come and go.

Arrival, information, accommodation

Dublin Connolly, on the north bank of the River Liffey, is the departure point for the cross-border *Enterprise* train service to Newry and Belfast, as well as commuter and DART suburban trains – the latter stop at two Southside stations, Tara Street and Pearse, both of which are more convenient for many Dublin districts south of the Liffey (eg. Trinity College and the Georgian quarter around Merrion Square and the Temple Bar area). The other main station, **Dublin Heuston**, is well west of the city centre, just on the south bank of the Liffey and serves main-line trains to the County Mayo outposts of Ballina and Westport, Kilkenny and Waterford, Cork and Galway. Heuston and Connolly stations are connected by the red **Luas tram line** (www.luas.ie). Buy tickets from the machine at each stop (valid for 90 mins; zonal tariff). Tickets for the bus can be purchased on board (cash allowed, but exact fare only; see www.dublinbus.ie). Tourist office: 3 Palace Street, Barnardo Square and 14 Upper O'Connell Street (www.visitdublin.com).

Brace yourself for Dublin hotel and B&B prices! Booking ahead will help you save on your accommodation costs. Some more affordable options can be found south-east of the city centre – try for example **Pembroke Hall**, 76 Pembroke Rd, ☎ 01668 99 93 (www.pembroke-hall.ie), a welcoming guesthouse in a quiet neighbourhood. Or opt for **Mespil Hotel**, 50–60 Mespil Road, ☎ 01488 46 00 (www.mespilhotel.com), right on the Grand Canal. Convenient for both Heuston station and Phoenix Park is the highly regarded **Ashling Hotel**, 10–13 Parkgate Street, ☎ 01677 23 24 (www.ashlinghotel.ie).

Dublin connections

The contentious **inner-Irish border** is 100 km north of Dublin. Trains from Dublin Connolly leave for Belfast, Sligo and the east coast route to Wexford and Rosslare, which we'll follow in **Route 5**. For great seafood and coastal walks, take the half-hour ride on the DART out to Howth. It's a splendid spot to spend a summer evening. For a good **full day out by train** from Dublin see the box on p94.

Dublin Port has, apart from the direct ferry links to Wales, a year-round shipping link with Cherbourg in France (where you can connect onto **Route 16**), following it south via Caen (where you can join **Route 19**) and on to Paris. Irish Ferries now accept foot passengers on all sailings on this route, which is now primarily operated by the *WB Yeats* cruise ferry, augmented in the peak season with extra sailings using the *James Joyce*. Both are very fine ships. For an interesting summer season way of returning to Britain, consider using the Isle of Man Ferries seasonal service from **Dublin to Douglas** on the Isle of Man, connecting there onto onward sailings to Heysham or Liverpool.

Kerry bound

The Irish county most conspicuously associated with **Romantic ideas** about the picturesque and the sublime is Kerry. And if there is one spot in Kerry which has above all fired the Romantic imagination it is Killarney. Every tour of Ireland must perforce take in Killarney (ideally with a big pinch of salt these days). The town itself is very pleasant, a little too dominated by shamrock tack perhaps, but the real draw are the gorgeous landscapes of County Kerry which are all around Killarney.

These are thoughts to ponder as you wait at **Dublin Heuston**, a handsome station in Corinthian style, for the train to the far south-west of Ireland. Originally known as Dublin Kingsbridge, the station was renamed in 1966 to recall Seán Heuston, one the of republican rebels who was executed by the British after the **Easter Rising**. Heuston was himself a railway clerk. As the train slips out of Dublin to the west, it passes through Kilmainham where Heuston was shot on Sunday 7 May 1916.

Picking up speed, the train passes through unassuming suburbs to reach open country with good views of the **Wicklow Hills** well away to the left. The grassy heathlands around Kildare are premier-league territory for Irish horse breeders. Curragh is the name of the heath and also of the racecourse which you'll see to the left of the train.

Beyond **Kildare**, the landscape becomes slightly hillier, with a fine view of the Barrow Valley at Monasterevin. Passing through Port Laoise, the forested Slieve Bloom Mountains edge closer and then, just a little later, the Galtee Mountains hove into view on the left. Most trains stop at **Limerick Junction**, one of those strange spots which is never a destination in its own right, but a place where all travellers in Ireland end up eventually.

LIMERICK JUNCTION

This station in the middle of an area often known as West Tipp – the nearest town is Tipperary away to the south-east – is really a curiosity, and one celebrated by train enthusiasts for the oddity of its railway operations. **Two main lines cross here**, and transferring trains from one line to the other requires some shunting to and fro. It was made more complex by the fact that until late 2019 the station had only one main platform. It is a place for changing trains. There are frequent connections to **Limerick City**, where the station is called Limerick Colbert, being named after Cornelius Colbert, another of the Easter Rising leaders shot by a firing squad at Kilmainham gaol in May 1916. From Limerick Colbert, five trains a day (four on Sun) run north through County Clare to Galway, where you can connect onto **Route 5** in this book.

Limerick Junction is also the starting point for the rural route to Waterford, which follows the **Suir Valley** for much of the way. We rate this as the finest rural rail ride in Ireland, but it requires careful planning, as there are only two trains a day (not Sun) in each direction. This line features in the itinerary described in the boxed text on p94.

From Limerick Junction, it's just 30 minutes through rich dairy-farming country, often colloquially known as the **Golden Vale** (or Golden Vein), to Mallow in County Cork. There our route turns to the west, following the Blackwater Valley up to Rathmore. Sit on the left for gorgeous views both on the approach to Rathmore and then on to Killarney. This is one of the most famous vistas in Ireland with Mangerton Mountain to the left, grading westward into the great ridge of **MacGillycuddy's Reeks**.

The train rolls slowly down to **Killarney**, which marks the end of Route 4. We have come a long way from that metro station in Rotterdam where our journey started.

Killarney

Nowhere is Irish culture more packaged and sold than in Killarney. This is not new. In the late 18th century, Killarney had already claimed status as the gateway to the exquisite mountain landscapes of County Kerry, and tourism was given a further boost by the **arrival of the railway** and Queen Victoria. The contours of the Killarney experience have hardly changed in 150 years: waterside walks, high tea, and excursions by pony traps (locally called jaunting cars) into the hills. The hucksters and heather-toting colleens, who attracted the opprobrium of late Victorian writers, are still there. But cut through the shamrock haze and Killarney is very special. You just have to ignore the commerce.

Make time to wander through the town of course, but the real draw is **Killarney National Park**, the nearest parts of which are within walking distance of the city centre. If you can stay a day or two, perhaps renting bicycles or venturing out on local buses, you begin to get a feel for a landscape shaped by glaciation and a big dose of Irish mythology. It's an easy half-hour walk from the centre of Killarney out to Ross Castle. Plenty of local Killarney companies offer half-day and longer trips to the Gap of Dunloe and other beauty spots, but do check prices carefully before committing. There are also year-round one-day bus trips around the Iveragh peninsula – this is the famous **Ring of Kerry** route (www.theringofkerry.com).

Arrival, information, accommodation
✈ Right on the eastern edge of the city centre. 🛈 Tourist office: Beech Road (www.killarney.ie).

🚌 The Victorian-era **Great Southern Killarney**, East Avenue Road, ☎ 064 663 80 00 (www.greatsouthernkillarney.com), right by the railway station, is a great place to stay in Killarney. We certainly enjoyed it (and the good news is that they do a lot of discounting). Just a 5-minute walk south of the city centre is the very friendly **Algret House B&B**, 80 Countess Grove, ☎ 064 663 23 37, in a quiet neighbourhood. An equally good option in the same direction is **Killarney Lodge Guesthouse**, Countess Rd, ☎ 064 663 64 99 (www.killarneylodge.ie).

Killarney connections
When the train pulls up at Killarney station, the buffer stops ahead seem to make it clear that this is the end of the line. But Irish trains are cunning. The train in fact reverses out of the station, then branches off to the north, running on to **Tralee**. The latter is a pleasant wee town, dominated by the Slieve Mish Mountains to the south, and the natural jumping-off point for excursions to the Dingle Peninsula.

There are buses aplenty from Killarney. Bus Éireann Expressway service 🚌 40 runs east to Cork, Waterford and Rosslare (on **Route 5**), connecting in all three places with trains back to Dublin.

Sidetracks: Irish questions

Dún Laoghaire, on the south shore of Dublin Bay, was the traditional port for the city of Dublin. In the heyday of **Ireland's Railway Age**, Dún Laoghaire went by the English name of Kingstown, a colonial imposition recalling King George IV's visit to Ireland in 1821.

Kingstown was more than merely a port through which thousands of travellers passed en route to and from Dublin. It thrived on sea trade and became one of the most desirable of Dublin suburbs. The "gaiety of life around the jetty" and "the rippling of the sleepless tide" – as the writer GW Powell remarked – combined to make the port a charmed spot.

So it's no surprise that, when it came to building **Ireland's first passenger railway**, the route selected was between Dublin and Kingstown. The line opened in December 1834. Dublin thus had a working suburban railway even before London – the first passenger service in the English capital, a line to Deptford, did not open until 1836.

In Ireland, as across the water in Britain, there was uncertainty about the preferred track gauge for the emerging rail network. How wide apart should the lines be placed? The initial **Dublin to Kingstown line** was built to 1,435 mm gauge – that is the measure used for most railways in Britain and much of western and central Europe today. Yet it was an Irish one-off. Elsewhere around the island, railways were being built to much wider or much narrower gauges. By the start of the 20th century, Ireland had Europe's most extensive **network of three-foot-gauge railways** (914 mm). From the Glens of Antrim and remote valleys in Donegal to the rugged Dingle Peninsula, Ireland's three-foot network crisscrossed the land. Just imagine what fine tourism assets these could be today had they survived. The last to close was the West Clare Railway; that was in 1961.

Ireland eventually settled on one rail gauge, and it was a peculiarly Irish solution. No other country in Europe uses the 1,600 mm gauge which is now the norm for all railways in Ireland, both north and south of the border. That's even wider than the Russian gauge, where tracks are spaced further apart than those in central and western Europe.

The tussle over track gauge was as nothing compared to the friction caused by the **partition of Ireland** in 1921. A new frontier cut rudely across the landscape, placing new bureaucratic burdens on hard-pressed rail operators. In the ensuing years, most cross-border routes closed. Only that between Dundalk and Newry survived; it is still used today by the *Enterprise* trains from Dublin to Belfast which cross the outer edge of the EU as they speed north.

You can ride the route of Ireland's very first railway, which has long since been changed to the Irish 1,600 mm gauge. That line from Dublin to Kingstown – now happily renamed Dún Laoghaire – is one of the busiest in the country. It's used by **DART commuter services** running south from Dublin and also forms part of the next route in this book. And these days Dún Laoghaire station is called Dún Laoghaire Mallin, an homage to Michael Mallin. He was a quiet man – a silk weaver, devout Catholic and committed socialist. Mallin was executed by the British for his involvement in the 1916 **Easter Rising**.

88 | DISCOVER BRITAIN AND IRELAND

Route 5: West to Europe's Celtic fringe
CITIES: ★★ CULTURE: ★ HISTORY: ★ SCENERY: ★★
COUNTRIES COVERED: ENGLAND (ENG), WALES (WLS), IRELAND (IE)
JOURNEY TIME: 18 HRS | DISTANCE: 1,006 KM | MAP: WWW.EBRWEB.EU/18MAP5

One of the great things about Galway, we were told when we visited in 2019, is that the Irish city doesn't have a working airport. It closed in 2011, and since then visitors have been forced to travel to Galway by road or rail. Most Galway-bound travellers fly in via Dublin or Shannon; this route shows that you could do better. It's perfectly possible to travel from **London to Galway** in a day by the rail-sea route via Holyhead. But Route 5 is the way to do it if you want to see some of the finest scenery in England, Wales and Ireland along the way. It's a chance to **savour a journey** for its own sake.

ITINERARY SUGGESTIONS
Route 5 is best spread over three travel days, with overnight stops in **Llandovery** and **Wexford**. If you are minded to take longer, the possibilities are endless. How about extra stops in Oxford, Hereford and Dublin? Or make time for one of the small Shropshire towns on this route. Ludlow is a good choice. If you are pushed for time and simply cannot follow our meandering route, then leave London Paddington at 07.48 (daily except Sun) and, with a change of train in Swansea, reach Fishguard in time to join the afternoon **boat to Ireland**.

Chilterns and Cotswolds
Our route kicks off with the short hop from **London to Oxford**. Choose between the Thames Valley route from Paddington (which follows **Route 1** to Reading) or the Chiltern line from Marylebone. We think the latter has the edge, and diminutive Marylebone – the London terminus from which all Chiltern trains depart – is a characterful starting point. Look out for the white lattice arch of the new **Wembley Stadium** as the train speeds out

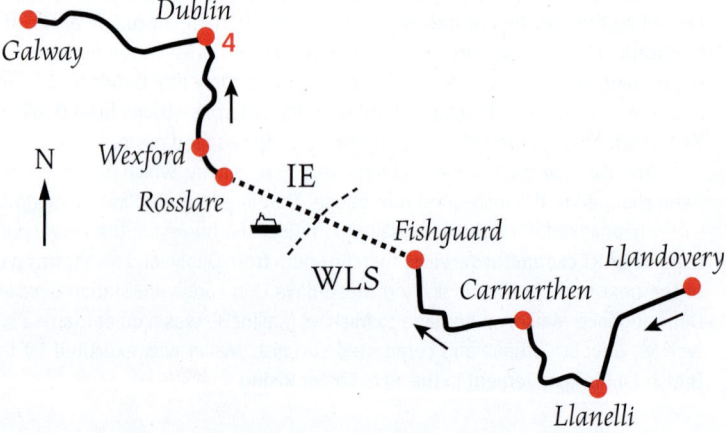

ROUTE 5: WEST TO EUROPE'S CELTIC FRINGE | 89

toward leafy London suburbs and the beech woods of the Chiltern Hills. There's a brilliant stretch just beyond High Wycombe where the railway cuts through beech woods and fine chalk downland, dropping down to reach the Vale of Aylesbury at Princes Risborough. All trains to Oxford stop at **Bicester Village**, which has become a popular shopping Mecca for overseas visitors to Britain. Yep, you read that right. People make day trips from London to go shopping in Bicester where all the top brands have staked a claim to retail space. Announcements at Bicester Village station are made in English, Mandarin and Arabic.

Beyond Bicester, the railway skirts damp Otmoor to reach **Oxford**, stopping first at Oxford Parkway and then at the city-centre station (simply

Route details

London Marylebone to Oxford		
Frequency	Journey time	Notes
2 per hr	1h15–1h30	A
Oxford to Hereford		
Frequency	Journey time	Notes
Every 1–2 hrs	2h–2h40	B
Hereford to Craven Arms		
Frequency	Journey time	Notes
Every 1–2 hrs	0h35	
Craven Arms to Llanelli		
Frequency	Journey time	Notes
5 per day	3h05–3h15	X

Route details (cont.)

Llanelli to Fishguard Harbour		
Frequency	Journey time	Notes
3–4 per day	1h15–2h05	C
Fishguard Harbour to Rosslare Harbour		
Frequency	Journey time	Notes
2 per day	3h30–4h	
Rosslare Harbour to Dublin Connolly		
Frequency	Journey time	Notes
3–4 per day	2h55–3h15	
Dublin Heuston to Galway		
Frequency	Journey time	Notes
6–8 per day	2h20–2h35	

Notes

A – Additional trains, also 2 per hr, run from London Paddington to Oxford.
B – There are 3 or 4 direct trains per day on this route. Where there's no direct train, change at Worcester Foregate St or Great Malvern.
C – Some journeys require a change of train at Carmarthen.
X – Only twice daily on Sundays.

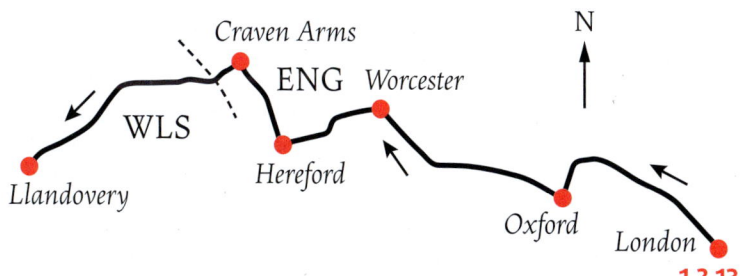

called Oxford). The station belies the grace of the city it serves. The city centre, with the main colleges, is just an eight-minute walk to the east. Make for St Giles, Broad Street, Radcliffe Square, the High Street and Christ Church Meadow (in that order) and you'll begin to see what makes Oxford so special. Note that the colleges have limited opening for public visits.

Our route then tracks broadly north-west from Oxford following a deeply rural railway which winds through **gentle Cotswold landscapes**. There are neat fields, limestone cottages roofed with local slates and in spring and summer a feast of lineside wild flowers. The railway follows the Evenlode Valley upstream, just beyond Kingham passing through the now abandoned station at Adlestrop where one hot June afternoon in 1914 a train from London, carrying the then unknown poet **Edward Thomas**, stopped. Thomas recalled the moment in a poem (called *Adlestrop*) which touches some very English sensibilities about rural life. There's an added poignancy that Thomas was killed in the First World War (at the Battle of Arras in 1917). Adlestrop may have gone, but some local stations on this line survive.

Tunnelling through the Cotswold ridge by Chipping Campden, the railway drops down into the **Vale of Evesham**, so swapping the pastoral scenes of the Cotswolds for one of England's most productive horticultural regions. From soft fruits to summer cherries, from asparagus to Brussels sprouts, this really is a premier-league area for market gardening.

Evesham occupies a plum spot within the neck of a meander on the River Avon, and there's an especially good view of the river as the train leaves Evesham, bridging the river with houseboats bobbing below. Then it's just a few minutes across the vale to **Worcester** on the River Severn, where there are two stations: Shrub Hill and Foregate Street, the latter much better placed for the centre.

Sit on the right beyond Worcester for great views of the Malvern Hills as the train approaches the sedate town of **Great Malvern** where, if you've an hour to spare, there's a pleasant café on the London-bound platform. Cutting through the hills in a tunnel, the train then rolls west into Herefordshire with its distinctive black-and-white timber-framed houses set harmoniously amid the hills and woods. **Hereford's** compact town centre is a delight, and remembered most notably for its fine cathedral, where the star treasure is a mediaeval map of the world (called the *mappa mundi*). The town also has much pleasing Georgian and Victorian architecture.

Connections from Hereford

All trains arriving from Oxford and Worcester terminate at Hereford. Even though this is still England, train services on the north-south main line through Hereford are all run by Transport for Wales (TfW or *Trafnidiaeth Cymru*). Hourly trains run north to Manchester, flying the Welsh flag all the way. There are also direct services to Chester and **Holyhead**, thus giving a convenient connection onto **Route 4**. The early evening TfW train from Hereford to Holyhead offers (Mon–Fri only) a really excellent business-class service where the real perk is an excellent dinner served along the way. The accent is very much on locally sourced food. TfW also run south from Hereford to Cardiff with many services continuing to Swansea and beyond.

The Heart of Wales

From Hereford, it is just a short hop north through beautiful Marches countryside to **Craven Arms**. The agreeable market town of Ludlow is an appealing intermediate stop with a good choice of accommodation. A central yet quiet option just off Broad Street on Valentine's Walk is the elegant Townhouse Ludlow, ☎ 01584 877 143 (www.townhouseludlow.co.uk). At Craven Arms, we turn decisively west and make for Wales. If you find yourself with a long connection time at Craven Arms, consider changing instead at Church Stretton (which is just nine minutes north of Craven Arms). It does of course mean backtracking, but Church Stretton, enviably set among the **Shropshire Hills**, is much the nicer place to while away an hour or two.

There are few better ways of approaching Wales than on the **Heart of Wales line** (*Rheilffordd Calon Cymru*) which we rate as one of Europe's finest rural rail rambles. Just four trains a day (less on Sundays) run the full 146 km from Craven Arms to Llanelli. These trains start their run in Shrewsbury and then pause in Church Stretton before turning off onto the Heart of Wales railway at Craven Arms.

Like the Settle and Carlisle line (described in the box on p73), the Heart of Wales railway is a good example of a rural rail route which not merely survives, but really thrives, because of local community involvement in promoting their local railway.

It's a brilliant ride in any weather. We've done it on a clear summer day but also in less clement weather, with mist shrouding the hills and sheep fading into the fog. We start by tracking south-west towards the Teme Valley which we follow upstream to **Knighton**. The village is on the south bank of the river in Wales, but here the railway and Knighton station are still on English soil. Bridging the river just after Knighton, the train enters Wales, skirting the northern edge of Radnor Forest to reach the Victorian spa town of Llandrindod Wells.

Travel on this line is always fun. Usually it's just a single railcar on the route, and the train guard, who also sells tickets, is often on first-name terms with the regular passengers. Many of the stations are served only on request. "I've never once had anyone ask us to stop at Sugar Loaf," says the guard as we slip through that tiny wayside station, which is on the most dramatic section of the line as the railway cuts through the hills between the Irfon and Tywi valleys. **Llandovery** is the first place of any size, and it's a good choice for an overnight stop. It has the feel of a traditional Welsh market town, with painted stucco buildings with slate roofs and deep eaves.

We can recommend the King's Head, 1 Market Square, ☎ 1550 720 393 (www.kingsheadllandovery.co.uk) or the New White Lion, 43 Stone St, ☎ 01550 720 685 (www.newwhitelion.com).

Leaving Llandovery, it's a pleasant run down the **Tywi Valley**, with fine views up towards Black Mountain to the left. You'll see Llandeilo's bright colour-washed cottages to the right, and then the train cuts through the hills to reach a more industrial landscape and a tidal estuary which escorts us down to **Llanelli**. It's here that one must change trains for Fishguard, but if there's no good onward connection you may prefer to stay on the Heart of Wales train till Swansea, which is just 20 minutes down the line. It'll mean backtracking, but that's never an issue if you are using a rail pass.

It's just 90 minutes from Llanelli to **Fishguard**, but what a ride. Sit on the left for the best views. We pass Pembrey Burrows – a huge area of sand dunes now largely afforested – beyond which are the long, silky sands of Cefn Sidan beach. We then follow the **Tywi Estuary** upstream through salt meadows towards Carmarthen. The train now heads decisively west, traversing good farming country to reach Pembrokeshire. Only on the final approach to Fishguard is there any great change in the landscape, and it's quite a dramatic one, with barren, rock-strewn hillocks as the train follows the fast-flowing Western Cleddau upstream, cutting between hills to reveal a fine view of Fishguard Bay ahead.

At Fishguard Harbour, the second of the two stations in Fishguard, the train pulls up alongside the quay from where the Stena Line ships leave for Ireland. The terminal itself is a fairly spartan affair.

The Fishguard to Rosslare **ferry service** relies on the MS *Stena Europe* being used for most sailings. Although almost 40 years old, she's a comfort-

FISHGUARD FACTS

The west side of the bay, where the ferries come and go, is Goodwick. Fishguard (Abergwaun in Welsh) itself is the small town which sits on a distinct hill away to the east (you'll see it to the right from the train). If you want the boat to Ireland, then stay on the train until **Fishguard Harbour**. For anywhere else, alight at Fishguard & Goodwick, which is in Goodwick village. It's a 15-minute walk east to Fishguard, but there are also buses. If staying overnight, make for Fishguard itself, where Manor Townhouse, Main St, ☎ 01348 873 260 (www.manortownhouse.com) offers stylish rooms, the best of them with stunning sea views.

Fishguard is the end of the railway, but there are excellent bus connections. Venture to the very tip of **Pembrokeshire** by taking the bus to St Davids. 🚌 T11 follows the main road, but the less-frequent 🚌 404 is a better choice, as it detours via Strumble Head with better views of the coast. 🚌 T5 runs hourly up the coast to Aberystwyth, where there are good connections onto the 🚌 T2 for **Bangor** (where you can connect onto **Route 2**). This is really only a journey for dedicated bus travellers. Fishguard to Bangor takes about eight hours. The one-way fare is £13. Travel on this route was free at weekends for a couple of years – but it seems that this amazing concession will not be available in 2025. Perhaps too many people took advantage of it!

able vessel. For a small premium, upgrade to the Stena Plus lounge which is often a haven of quiet on an otherwise busy ship.

It's worth noting that there is an alternative ferry link from south-west Wales to **Rosslare**, with Irish Ferries sailing from Pembroke Dock. This alternative Welsh departure point is served by direct trains from Swansea, Llanelli and Carmarthen. The train to ship transfer is not as slick at Pembroke Dock, which is why we favour the Fishguard route.

Céad Míle Fáilte: Welcome to Ireland

A notice inside the **ferry terminal** at Rosslare welcomes new arrivals to Ireland. "Céad Míle Fáilte" — a hundred thousand welcomes. It's an odd precursor to the soul-destroying walk between fierce metal barriers to the railway station. Worry not! Ireland does get better than this. The station was moved from the quayside to its new less convenient location in 2008 — a mark of how undervalued foot passengers are on the ferries.

Rosslare connections

If you are heading west, bear in mind that the Expressway 🚌 40 (operated by Bus Éireann; www.buseireann.ie) runs from just outside the ferry terminal to Waterford and Cork, with good connections onto the Irish rail network in both those cities. The bus that connects with the early morning boat arrival in Rosslare runs right through to **Killarney** to connect onto **Route 4** in this book. Rosslare to Killarney costs €28 and takes just over six hours.

The train from Rosslare Europort station runs to Dublin. It's far too fine a route to travel in darkness. So, unless it's a long summer evening, if you arrive off the afternoon boat from Fishguard, you may want to stay overnight close to Rosslare and then continue next morning. **Wexford**, just 20 mins around the bay by bus or train from Rosslare Harbour, is the obvious choice. It's an amiable small town, just perfect for a first night in Ireland. Clayton Whites, Abbey St, ☎ 091 22 311 (www.claytonwhiteshotel.com) is a decent hotel with a good, contemporary feel and a convenient location, less than 10 minutes on foot from the station

The railway through the centre of Wexford is one of the most extraordinary we know. The trains run at walking pace along the streets that mark the waterfront. Arriving from Rosslare, you'll have **Wexford Harbour** on your right and a row of shops to your left as the train inches past parked cars to reach O'Hanrahan station at the far end of Wexford's busy central area. The station is named after Michael O'Hanrahan, executed by the British for his role in the **Easter Rising** in 1916.

Ireland's East Coast

Many things may strike you on your first journey on any Iarnród Éireann (Irish Rail) train. **Irish Gaelic** is still very much used in the on-board

Dublin day out

Any trip to Ireland should venture beyond Dublin. If you are not staying with Route 5 on to **Galway**, then here's a thought. For those who enjoy seeing something of the countryside by train, we think that the Dublin – Limerick Junction – Waterford – Kilkenny – Dublin circuit makes a very fine first taste of Ireland beyond the capital. With a 08.00 start from Dublin Heuston, follow **Route 4** to Limerick Junction (see p85), changing there onto the beautiful Suir Valley line to reach **Waterford** by late morning. That city is worth a stop, but also plan to spend three or four hours in Kilkenny, which is by far the most atmospheric of Ireland's mediaeval cities. **Kilkenny** lies just 35 mins north of Waterford on the main line back to Dublin. This entire circuit requires five-and-a-half hours on trains; that's a lot, but it takes in some glorious scenery, and you get to spend some time in two fine cities: Waterford and Kilkenny. It's a perfect trip for a midsummer day, when you can expect great views along the **Barrow Valley** on the evening journey back to Dublin.

announcements and on many trains there's a very sociable, even communal, feel. Travelling by train in Ireland is invariably fun and on most trains they even manage to have the tables perfectly aligned with the windows, so allowing unimpeded views of the passing scenery. And on the run from Wexford up to Dublin, the best of that scenery is all to the east, so grab a seat on the right side of the train.

It's a grand ride north from Wexford, following the tidal lower reaches of the **River Slaney** upstream to Enniscorthy with a panorama to the distant Blackstairs Mountains away to the north-west. Continuing on through Gorey to Arklow, where that Irish word Fáilte is rendered in patterned tile work on a wall by the station platform, the railway then turns inland, plunging deep into the **Wicklow Hills**. This is the most beautiful part of the journey, as the railway follows the wooded Vale of Avoca.

Returning to the coast at Wicklow, the train then hugs the coast as it runs north through small coastal communities which these days are among the most desirable places to live in the Dublin commuter belt. The section of the railway through the cliffs at Bray Head, originally engineered by **Isambard Kingdom Brunel**, really rates as one of Europe's finest sections of coastal railway. Then it's an easy run on through Dún Laoghaire into Dublin. The train from Rosslare and Wexford stops first at Pearse station in Dublin and then continues over the River Liffey to terminate at Dublin Connolly. For more on **Dublin**, and on connecting trains, see p83.

To the wild Atlantic coast

It's a short ride on the Luas Tram red route (single fare €2.10) from Connolly to **Heuston station** for the onward train to Galway. For the first 70 km out of Dublin, the Galway train follows the main rail route to Cork and Killarney (also part of **Route 4**), swinging off right at Portarlington to cross the River

Barrow and enter County Offaly. Much of the single-track route to Galway has a very rural feel. Timetabling has to be slick with many heavy timber trains using the route. We slip over the **Grand Canal** at Tullamore and then, approaching Clara, a town with strong Quaker connections, lush pasture land gives way to rougher terrain. **Athlone** has a nice enough position by the Shannon at the southern end of Lough Ree but it is perhaps a shade pretentious for the locals to refer to Athlone as the Irish Athens. However, there's a great view of the classical, if rather bland, green-domed parish church to the left as the train crosses the Shannon.

Then it's pancake-flat to **Ballinasloe** and then gorse hedges and limestone walls as the railway crosses slightly higher land to reach Athenry, beyond which the grass gets ever greener as we speed west to Galway. The last stretch into Galway is very memorable with fine views to the left over **Galway Bay** to the wild hills of County Clare beyond.

Galway

Galway is one of our favourite Irish cities. Chilled and laid-back, it is the perfect place to spend a few days. The town itself is appealing, and it's a good base for day trips to **Clifden** or the **Aran Islands**. The station is right by **Eyre Square** where the petite statue of Galway-born writer Pádraic Ó Conaire is a natural focal point.

Amble west though the pedestrianised city centre, where traditional Irish music is a staple, to the banks of the turbulent River Corrib. Take time to let the Guinness settle and, when you've had your fill of city flair, walk out along the windy causeway to **Mutton Island**.

Arrival, information, accommodation

Just off the southern end of Eyre Square (it's also where all buses depart). Tourist office: Forster St. (www.galwaytourism.ie).

The **Park House Hotel**, Forster Street, ☎ 091 564 924 (www.parkhousehotel.ie) close to Eyre Square is an excellent place to stay in Galway, with discounted rates if you stay for a few days. Equally well located is the **Skeffington Arms Hotel**, Eyre Square, ☎ 091 563 173 (www.skeffington.ie) which is a Galway institution next to the lively Skeff Bar. The friendly **St Jude's Lodge** B&B, 24 College Road, ☎ 091 569 100 (www.galwayguesthouses.ie) is handy for the station and just a few minutes away from the city centre.

Fresh fish is available everywhere. We especially enjoyed The Seafood Bar @ Kirwan's, Kirwan's Lane, ☎ 091 568 266 (www.kirwanslane.ie) in Galway's Old Town, which has a good selection of wines by the glass.

Galway connections

There's a very useful local rail route which runs south through County Clare to **Limerick** and Limerick Junction, where you can connect into **Route 4** to **Killarney** and onto the fast trains to Cork.

Galway is the gateway to the beautiful Connemara region, easily reached by taking 419 to Clifden. Bus Éireann service 64 runs north via Sligo and Donegal to **Derry**, the latter more than five hours away to the north.

THE LOW COUNTRIES AND GERMANY
An introduction

In the heyday of the **Grand Tour**, affluent young Englishmen (and they were almost always men!) set out to complete their education by exploring the continent. The goal was usually Italy, but the first staging post was invariably the **Rhineland** – and that meant passing through the Low Countries along the way. It's no surprise that when **Thomas Cook** wrote his very first travel guide in 1873, this was the region on which he focused. He bundled the German Rhineland in with the Low Countries. We do just the same here, also including a number of other routes which extend across Germany towards Berlin and Bavaria.

This is generally excellent territory for holders of rail passes (such as **Eurail and Interrail**), as very few trains require advance reservation or supplements. With just some rare exceptions like Eurostar trains, you can roam at will throughout the Netherlands, Belgium, Luxembourg and Germany. If you venture into nearby areas of France (as **Route 8** does in this section) then you'll never need to bother about advance reservations or supplements as long as you stick to regional trains (ie. TER services) and avoid TGVs.

There is a really classic journey in this section of *Europe by Rail*. That is **Route 9** which follows the Rhine upstream from Cologne and then continues through Heidelberg and the **Black Forest** to Switzerland. With the development of the railways in the 19th century it was this itinerary which pulled the crowds. More than a century and a half later, it's still a fine journey, though today often missed by travellers who make haste to get to the Alps.

Many routes in this section showcase railways where Deutsche Bahn's smart ICE services are commonplace. But, to catch a sense of the landscape, it's better to stick to slower trains. In **Route 11**, there's a chance of a real slow travel experience, as we explore the Harz Mountains, taking advantage of the network of **narrow-gauge railways** which serve that region. Prussia, Bavaria and many other territories in Germany once had very extensive networks of *Kleinbahnen* (literally 'small railways', often constructed to a narrower gauge than the main routes). Almost all these minor routes have disappeared, but the Harz network is a chance to recapture an earlier spirit of rail travel.

Make time too for smaller communities and don't just focus on the big cities. Our most memorable stopovers have all been in lesser places. Harlingen, Delft and Middelburg are among our **Dutch favourites**; all three are easily reached by train. In Germany, places like Goslar and Quedlinburg (both on **Route 11**) may be more rewarding than big cities.

Other journeys you may want to explore include **Route 25, 31, 33** and **37**. All combine Germany with other countries, extending north into Scandinavia, east into Poland or south-east to Hungary. ∎

Route 6: Through Flanders to Amsterdam

Cities: ★★★ Culture: ★★ History: ★★ Scenery: ★
Countries covered: France (FR), Belgium (BE), Netherlands (NL)
Journey time: 6 hrs | Distance: 368 km | Map: www.ebrweb.eu/18map6

We like this route. Of course, we like all the routes in this book, but we *especially* like this one. It's short and sweet, taking in a **feast of fine cities** as well as, especially in the early stages, some **engaging rustic landscapes**. It's not a route where you need ever bother about advance booking and, if you are travelling with a Eurail or Interrail pass, there are no supplements to pay on any trains you'll use in taking this journey.

The Huguenot leader **Henri de Rohan** remarked that "he who expects any good to come from living in a land which lies lower than the sea, that in winter is a vast layer of ice and in summer a swamp, must go to Holland." So in this journey, we'll follow Henri's advice and take the train **to Holland**. Our journey starts in Flanders, in the great city of Lille – once home to many Huguenots who variously moved to Switzerland, Prussia and eastern England to escape religious persecution. Read more on Lille on p104.

Recommended itinerary
This journey is split into a number of shortish legs; any of the cities along the way are worthy of a stopover. If you like the buzz of big cities, then Antwerp and Rotterdam are good options for **overnight stops**. But our top choices would be two smaller communities, namely Bruges (in Belgium) and The Hague/Den Haag (in the Netherlands).

Hourly trains run along the entire length of Route 6, even at weekends. You can follow the route with just three **easy changes of train**, viz. at Kortrijk, Bruges and Antwerp. You can of course cut corners and use high-speed trains to skip parts of our recommended journey. And if all you want to do is to dash from Lille to Amsterdam, Eurostar trains will get you there in about three hours. But of course you'll miss all manner of good things along the way.

You can tell that Route 6 has promise when you arrive at **Lille Flandres** station to start the journey. It's an elegant old-style terminus. The Flandres suffix was added to the name in 1993 when the nearby Lille Europe station was opened. While the latter is brash, bold and cosmopolitan, Lille Flandres has a homely, regional feel.

The cross-border rail route to **Kortrijk** (Courtrai in French) is run by the Belgian national rail operator SNCB. The train heads north through industrial edgelands, **crossing into Belgium** just beyond Tourcoing. At Kortrijk, it is always necessary to change onto another regional train for Bruges. At one level, there is something very ordinary about these **Flemish landscapes** — but that prosaic quality is exactly what inspired the artists who lived and worked in the region. Whether it be a line of poplars with a ruined cottage or a lone Bruegelesque tree by a waterway, the everyday scenes of this region were a source of wonder for some of Europe's most celebrated artists.

Notes

A – Most journeys require a change of train at Breda.
B – All trains from Den Haag Centraal to Amsterdam stop at Leiden Centraal 12 mins after leaving Den Haag.
X – On all journeys from Lille Flandres to Bruges, a change of train at Kortrijk is necessary.

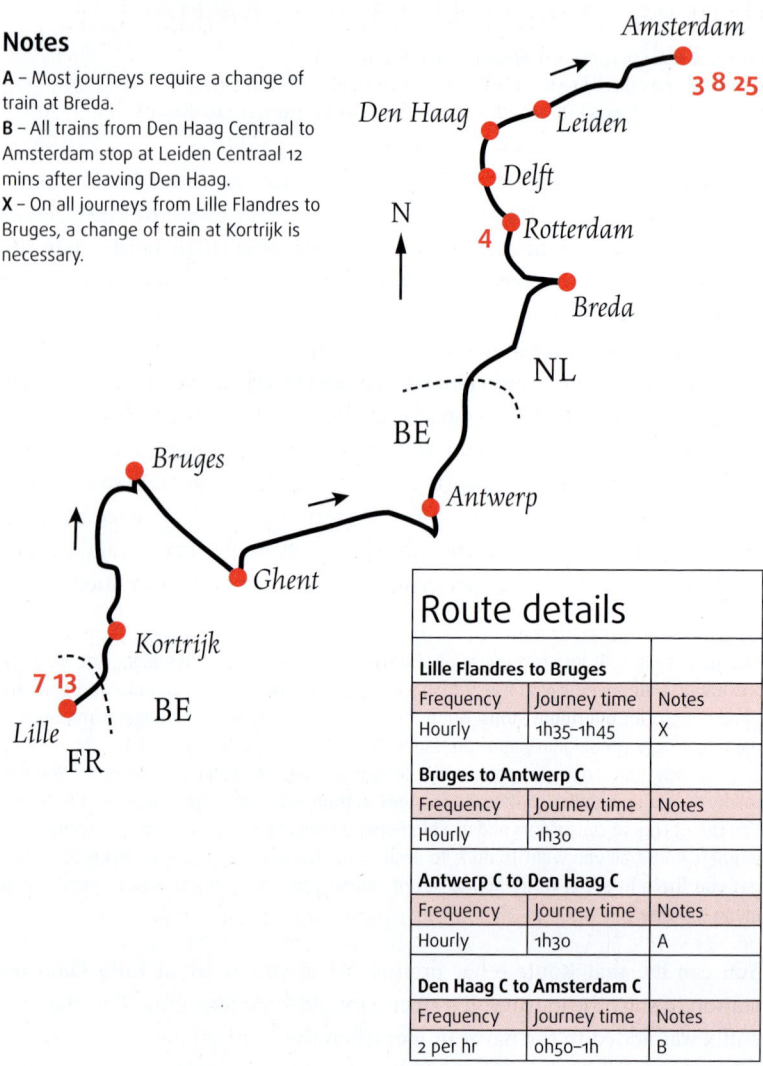

Route details

Lille Flandres to Bruges		
Frequency	Journey time	Notes
Hourly	1h35–1h45	X
Bruges to Antwerp C		
Frequency	Journey time	Notes
Hourly	1h30	
Antwerp C to Den Haag C		
Frequency	Journey time	Notes
Hourly	1h30	A
Den Haag C to Amsterdam C		
Frequency	Journey time	Notes
2 per hr	0h50–1h	B

Bruges (Brugge) – (suggested stopover)

A powerful trading city 500 years ago, Bruges became an economic backwater and the industrial age largely passed it by. Located **in the heart of Flanders**, Bruges is one of northern Europe's most impressive surviving mediaeval cities. A **boat trip** on the extensive and pretty canal system is a good introduction to the town, with frequent departures from quays along Dijver which, along with Groenerei and Rozenhoedkaai, provide some of the vintage views of Bruges. **Markt**, Bruges' large, lively and impressive main square, is surrounded by guild buildings, many of which have been converted into restaurants and bars. The Burg, the other main square, features the **Heilig Bloedbasiliek** (Basilica of the Holy Blood), with an early 12th-century stone chapel below a 16th-century chapel. Bruges' historic centre was inscribed on the UNESCO World Heritage List in 2000. Dijver is the central canal and the road that parallels it (scene of a weekend antiques and flea market) is home to several museums. **Groeningemuseum** (closed Mon) houses a fine collection of Flemish art from the 15th century to the present. Preparatory planning for the new exhibition hall and art complex BRUSK next to the Groeningemuseum started in late 2023.

Don't forget to take a walk around the walled religious village of the **Begijnhof**. The houses where Beguine nuns lived, as well as other single women or widows who opted for living within the community, are neatly arranged near the **Minnewater**, a tranquil, swan-populated lake.

Arrival, information, accommodation

✈ A 20-min walk south-west of the centre; buses stop in front. A single ticket for €2.50 is valid for 60 mins. Text DL to 4884 (includes a €0.15 opertor charge) or pay with a contactless card on the bus. To the right as you leave the station is a branch of the tourist office.
🛈 Tourist office: Markt 1 (www.visitbruges.be).

🛏 Right on the canal in the heart of the Old Town, the **Guesthouse Bonifacius**, Groeninge 4, ☎ 050 49 00 49 (www.bonifacius.be) is a very welcoming option. A comfortable and friendly place is the **Huis't Schaep**, Korte Vuldersstraat 14, ☎ 050 34 06 30 (www.huishetschaep.be), which is conveniently located for both the station and the city centre. Or try the **Hotel Fevery**, Collaert Mansionstraat 3, ☎ 050 33 12 69 (www.hotelfevery.be), a short walk north of the market square.

Connections from Bruges

Note that in online journey planners, the city's name is usually rendered in its Dutch form, Brugge, rather than the French toponym Bruges, which we use in this book as that French version has wider currency among English speakers. Bruges has excellent connections with **the coast**. Ostend and Knokke are both about 20 minutes away. You can connect in either with the **Belgian coastal tramway**, a rather surreal route which extends the entire length of the Belgian coast. Read more in our **Sidetracks** feature on p103. There are three trains per hour from Bruges to Brussels, where you can connect onto **Route 7** to Germany, and an From Bruges there is also an hourly train to Liège, to connect into **Route 8** to Luxembourg, Alsace and Switzerland.

From Bruges, it's a pleasant ride east **across Belgian Flanders** to Antwerp, along the way passing through **Ghent** (Gent in Dutch), an agreeable Flemish university city, rich in culture and very lively during term time. The 12th–17th-century guild houses along the Graslei quay and the old houses by the Kraanlei quay provide two of the city's classic views. The main station, Gent-St-Pieters, is south of the city centre.

Belgium's second city, **Antwerp** (Antwerpen/Anvers) has an extensive old Flemish quarter, a rich Jewish heritage and is at the cutting edge of diamonds and fashion. Nowhere else in Belgium is so thoroughly dedicated

> ## The back-door route to Holland
>
> Travellers heading north from Bruges into Holland have an alternative to that described in Route 6. Instead of looping east through Antwerp, take the hourly bus to **Breskens**, a port on a sliver of Dutch territory on the south side of the Westerschelde Estuary. Bus 42 leaves from Stand 7 outside Bruges railway station. The bus connects perfectly with a **ferry to Vlissingen**, from where trains run every half hour to Rotterdam and Den Haag. This route affords fine views of watery Zeeland landscapes. **Middelburg** (seven minutes from Vlissingen on the train) is wonderful, one of the nicest Dutch towns we know.

to being cool. Even the moment of arrival is something special. The trains from Bruges always arrive on the uppermost level of Antwerpen Centraal station, usually on Platform 1. This is **one of Europe's great railway stations**. The platforms are on three levels and your onward train to Rotterdam and Den Haag will leave from the lowest level. But take time to look around the station and this famously tolerant city on the River Schelde. Antwerp hit the headlines in 2011 with the opening of the **Museum aan de Stroom**, Hanzestedenplaats 1 (www.mas.be; closed Mon) in the Eilandje district of the city's old port. It is dedicated to the city's connections with the world. Just take underground lines 3/5/9/15 to 'Linkeroever' from Centraal station, alighting at 'Meir'. The Royal Museum of Fine Arts (KMSKA) closed for major renovations in 2011 and reopened in September 2022.

North into Holland

The hourly Intercity train service from Brussels and Antwerp to Amsterdam is often called the *Beneluxtrein* or in Belgium sometimes the *Amsterdammer*. It is a hop-on and ride service, unlike the competing and faster Eurostar (ex-Thalys) trains which speed across the border. But its very flexibility is what makes the *Beneluxtrein* so popular. It's the best option for the cross-border hop from Antwerp, changing at Breda for Den Haag. It is a largely urban route, but you'll still see those **staples of the Dutch landscape**: windmills, canals and glasshouses. Parts of the route really are below sea level, crossing reclaimed land which relies on dykes for protection.

Rotterdam was virtually flattened in the Second World War, but much of its modern architecture is strikingly innovative (**Lijnbaan** was the European pioneer of shopping precincts, for example). Situated at the delta of the rivers Rhine, Maas and Waal, **Europoort** is the world's largest container port. Rotterdam Centraal is located on the northern edge of the centre (on the city's blue metro line).

Long famed for **Delftware porcelain** and birthplace of the artist Vermeer, **Delft** is an elegant town with old merchants' houses lining the canal. It has a number of porcelain factories where you can watch production;

the oldest is De Koninklijke Porceleyne Fles (Rotterdamseweg 196), but more central is Aardewerkfabriek de Candelaer (Kerkstr. 13). **Nieuwe Kerk** (New Church) houses the huge black-and-white marble mausoleum of Prince William, and its 109-m spire provides great views.

Den Haag – (suggested stopover)

Den Haag (The Hague) is the **administrative capital** of the Netherlands and a pleasant town, spread over a wide area of parks and canals and centred around the **Binnenhof**, home of the Dutch parliament, just a short walk from the station (or take trams 2/3/4/34 to 'Spui' and walk from there). Most of the city's palaces can be viewed only from the outside. An exception is the huge **Vredespaleis** (Peace Palace), Carnegieplein 2 (tram 1, 🚌 24), which houses the International Court of Justice and the Permanent Court of Arbitration. It's a strange architectural mishmash, with a display of items donated by world leaders (guided tours need to be pre-booked at www.vredespaleis.nl). Make time to visit the seaside town of **Scheveningen** (tram 11), which is effectively part of Den Haag. The pretty fishing port which inspired 17th-century Dutch artists is still there, but nowadays surrounded by all the commerce and attractions which sustain Scheveningen's reputation as a great place for sun, sea and sand.

Arrival, information, accommodation

✈ Centraal (CS) is a 7-min walk from the centre and serves most Dutch cities. Fast services for Amsterdam and Rotterdam use HS (Hollands Spoor) station (1 km south). Centraal and HS are linked by frequent trains and by tram 9 or 17. 🛈 Tourist office: at Centraal station (www.denhaag.com). There is an excellent bus and tram network. A rechargeable or single-use OV-chipkaart is required to travel on public transport (available at the station). 🛏 Very comfortable is the privately run **Paleis Hotel**, Molenstraat 26, ☎ 070 362 46 21 (www.paleishotel.nl). Just a short walk from the city centre towards the beach in Scheveningen is the **Hotel Pistache**, Scheveningseweg 1, ☎ 070 221 09 10 (www.hotelpistache.com), which offers apartments for 2-6 people. Or try the friendly boutique hotel **La Paulowna**, Anna Paulownaplein 3, ☎ 070 450 0091 (www.lapaulowna.com) which also has a good restaurant.

Birthplace of Rembrandt, **Leiden** has a mediaeval quarter, centred on the vast Pieterskerk, plenty of student haunts and some excellent museums, covering archaeology, local history and art. In the Boerhaave, Lange St Agnietenstr. 10, is an **anatomical theatre**, complete with skeletons and displays of early medical paraphernalia. The university, founded in 1575, includes the world's oldest botanical gardens.

Amsterdam

Amsterdam has always been a city that has attracted outsiders, whether tourists, philosophers, immigrants or hippies. **Romantic and laid-back**, what makes Amsterdam so special is its combination of a beautiful setting with a **vibrant and youthful street life** that reflects Dutch society's culture of tolerance.

Yes, the red-light district and the 'coffee shops' will not be to everyone's taste, but thankfully Amsterdam is much more than just sex and smoking, and if you give yourself the time to explore you will discover a city that is home to marvellously varied **museums and galleries**, as well as leafy parks and a network of canals lined with elegant gabled brick houses that rivals Venice in its beauty. The **Van Gogh Museum** at Museumplein 6 (www.vangoghmuseum.nl) houses the largest collection of works by the Dutch painter in the world (tram 2/5/12 from Centraal to 'Van Baerlestraat').

The city centre is wonderful for walking, and there is a series of **signposted walking routes** to help you find your way. It is useful to grab one of the maps from the tourist office, as Amsterdam's layout can be confusing; bear in mind that *gracht* means 'canal' and that the centre follows the horseshoe shape dictated by the **ring canals**. The entire central area of the city was inscribed on the UNESCO World Heritage List in 2010.

Arrival, information, accommodation

✈ Centraal is the terminal for most trains and a 5-min walk north of Dam (the central area). ✈ Amsterdam Airport Schiphol (www.schiphol.nl) is about 14 km south-west of town. Transfers by train to/from Centraal are the cheapest: at least every 10 mins 06.00–24.00 (hourly 24.00–06.00); journey time is about 15 mins.

ℹ Tourist office: at Centraal station (www.iamsterdam.com). You can cross Amsterdam's central canal hub on foot in about an hour and walking is a pleasant way of getting around. Regarding regular public transport, the **tram** is the easiest and the most popular option. The network (www.gvb.nl) covers the city centre, with 14 lines running until 00.30. Buy a rechargeable or single-use OV chipkaart at GVB ticket machines or service desks. **Metro** lines (51, 53 and 54) run between Centraal Station, Nieuwmarkt and Waterlooplein, the city centre stops most likely to interest visitors.

Otherwise just do as the locals do and get on your **bike**. MacBike (four locations, including Centraal Station), www.macbike.nl, is open daily and prices for bike rental start at €10.80 per day, although the longer period you book, the cheaper the daily rate becomes.

🛏 Amsterdam is a popular destination. So book well ahead, especially when visiting at weekends and in summer, and don't expect to find anything really cheap. Located in a 17th-century canal house, **The Hendrick's Hotel**, Prins Hendrikkade 139, ☎ 020 260 30 00 (www.thehendrickshotel.com) is a very comfortable and well regarded option close to Centraal station. A good B&B with strikingly quirky interiors is the **Barangay**, Herenstraat 26, ☎ 062 504 54 32 (www.barangay.nl), also close to the station. Or try the stylish boutique hotel **Maison Elle**, Anna van den Vondelstraat 6, ☎ 020 722 06 46 (www.maisonelle.fr) in a quiet neighbourhood just by the Vondelpark and not far from the Van Gogh Museum.

Amsterdam Connections

You can connect here into two other routes in this book. **Route 8** runs south through the Ardennes region of eastern Belgium to Luxembourg and beyond. **Route 25** runs through Germany and Denmark to Sweden. There's a wide choice of direct trains from Amsterdam Centraal station, including regular departures to Berlin and Cologne. New sleepers now link Amsterdam with Zurich, Innsbruck and Vienna.

Sidetracks: Coastal Tramway

Belgium's Coastal Tramway (*Kusttram*) is the **world's longest tram route**. And it confers on Belgium the distinction of being the only country on the planet where the entire coastline can be surveyed in a single tram ride. From the French border near **Plopsaland** to the dune landscapes of **Knokke** on the Dutch border it is about 70 kilometres, and the Coastal Tramway takes in the entire coast, with about 70 tram stops along the way.

The first section of Belgium's Coastal Tramway was opened in 1885, with most of the existing route being completed by the First World War. The extension south from the coast at De Panne to serve the theme park of Plopsaland and the railway station at **Adinkerke** was opened only in 1998.

The tram links into the Belgian national railway network at each end of its route (viz. at De Panne station in Adinkerke at the western end and at Knokke-Heist station at the eastern end). It also stops outside the rail stations at **Ostend** and **Blankenberge**.

Some countries are best understood by their coastlines. **Paul Theroux** in *The Kingdom by the Sea* came to terms with Britain by exploring its coastline. Some authors even invented coastlines for landlocked countries. Didn't **Shakespeare** in *The Winter's Tale* make reference to travelling by ship to Bohemia? But no one needed to invent the Belgian coast. It is magnificent, all 145 minutes of it.

The tram ride is one of Europe's most engaging pieces of cinema. Rattling down the main street of De Panne, cutting through the forest at Koksijde, speeding along the coastal promenade east of **Middelkerke**, lurching through the streets of Oostende and slipping past back gardens on the final run into Knokke.

All Belgian life is captured in this run along the coast, from gnomes at Plopsaland to a hundred tearooms where people linger for hours over a coffee or a Leffe beer. Kings, mainly called Leopold and occasionally Albert, make cameo appearances in **showpiece monuments** along the way. The backdrop changes dramatically by the minute: one moment a feast of classical colonnades and now piles of containers arranged like **avant-garde art** as the tram skirts the edge of the docks. You get glimpses of art nouveau villas, Gothic town halls, geometric art deco, and heaps of monstrous modern concrete. As a perfectly framed piece of cinema, the journey is utterly engaging. The best 145-minute distraction anywhere around the North Sea.

De Haan is easily the most attractive of the communities along the coast. Until the coastal tram arrived in 1886, De Haan was a poor seaside village, populated by shrimp fishermen and their families. It was just a scattered collection of huts, regarded with disfavour by folk in neighbouring villages who judged De Haan to be the haunt of scoundrels and thieves. After the arrival of the tram, De Haan developed into a select coastal resort – one that was later to number **Albert Einstein** among its visitors.

The coastal tram is very **modestly priced**. A day pass which allows you to travel the entire length of the route, hopping on and off at will, is just €7.50. Trams operate from before 05.30 until about 23.30 – every 10 to 20 minutes during the day and every 30 to 60 minutes in the evening.

Route 7: From Hauts-de-France to the Rhine

Cities: ★★★ Culture: ★★ History: ★★ Scenery: ★
Countries covered: France (FR), Belgium (BE), Germany (DE)
Journey time: 3 hrs | Distance: 357 km | Map: www.ebrweb.eu/18map7

Lille and Cologne are two cities with very **strong regional identities** within their respective countries, but they could scarcely be more different. With a historical legacy dating back to the Romans, Cologne makes great play of its long-standing importance as an ecclesiastical and cultural centre. Lille is altogether more downbeat. Coal mining eclipsed textiles as Lille's economic mainstay in the 19th century, bringing with it a new politics of dissent. Lille is radical while Cologne is conformist.

This is one of the shorter journeys in this book. We include it because of its importance for travellers heading from London or Paris to eastern Belgium and the Rhineland. **Route 13** from London to Marseille via Paris passes through Lille. When the **high-speed line** from Lille into Belgium opened in 1997, it transformed the geography of the Flanders region.

This route, and other new lines from Brussels running east towards Germany, have brought Lille and Cologne much closer together.

Itinerary and tickets

The journey is so short that it can easily be accomplished in a morning. There are however two cities which cry out for a stopover. They are **Brussels and Aachen**. So you could use this journey as the basis for a more thorough exploration, but we give only a brief introduction to intermediate cities on this route. If you are no great fan of the fast trains used on this journey, it is possible to make the entire trip from Lille to Cologne on slow trains using legacy railway lines which quite closely parallel the route described here. The journey by slow trains requires four changes of train (at Tournai, Brussels, Welkenraedt and Aachen), and takes over five hours – that's two hours more than the fast option we commend below, which requires just an easy change between high-speed trains in Brussels.

This journey illustrates the perversity of **railway ticketing in Europe**. Two high-speed rail operators compete on the Lille to Brussels leg (Eurostar and SNCF). Two quite different companies compete with fast services between Brussels and Cologne (Deutsche Bahn and Eurostar). Tickets on these routes are normally limited to a specific operator. None of these operators offer through tickets from Lille to Cologne. This is one of those cases where an independent ticket retailer like Rail Europe (www.raileurope.com), might be the best bet if you are keen to book from Lille right through to Cologne in a single transaction. If you have an Interrail or Eurail Pass, and want to avoid supplements altogether, you'll need to use the slower services mentioned in the preceding paragraph.

Flanders

The largest city in French Flanders is too often underrated. Lille is good for more than merely changing trains. **Flemish touches** are everywhere, whether in the exuberant architecture on the Grand Place or in the Flemish flavours on the menus, which include leek tart (*flamiche*), waffles and

Route details

Lille Europe to Brussels Midi		Brussels Midi to Cologne Hbf	
Frequency	Journey time	Frequency	Journey time
13 per day	0h35–0h50	11–12 per day	1h50–2h

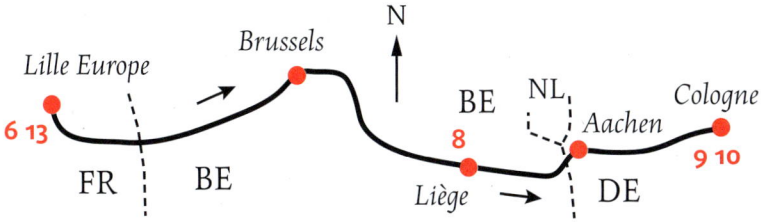

potjevleesch. Central Lille is very easy to explore on foot, and lies just a ten-minute walk west of **Lille Europe** station (which is where all Eurostar trains and most TGVs stop). There is a second, much older station called **Lille Flandres**, which is even more convenient for the city centre. That station is used by a small number of TGVs and most local trains. If you want to avoid the high-speed line and take a slow train to Belgium, then you'll depart from Lille Flandres. Our recommended journey for Route 7 starts at Lille Europe.

You'll find a higher level of security at Lille Europe than at most other French stations. If you are travelling to Brussels on a Eurostar train, you'll need to arrive at least 45 minutes prior to the advertised departure time. If your journey to Brussels is on a SNCF TGV train, then 10 minutes suffice.

The journey between Lille and Brussels illustrates how **high-speed rail travel** has transformed this part of Europe. In 1990, there were just five trains each day from Lille to Brussels. Today there are a dozen or more each day. The fastest services take just 34 minutes and at peak times pull crowds of cross-border commuters. The journey starts by running south from Lille to the **Frétin Triangle**, where Brussels-bound trains turn decisively east and cross into Belgian territory. For one stretch just beyond Enghien, the railway parallels a motorway, the train easily outpacing even the fastest-moving cars. All too soon, the pace slows as the train leaves the fast line and follows the Senne Valley into the centre of Brussels.

The Belgian capital

As the administrative hub of the European Union, and with residents who can trace their origins around the world, **Brussels** is an exceptionally cosmopolitan city. It may not be regarded as the most glamorous or romantic of Europe's capitals – after all, its two most famous monuments are a statue of a urinating boy and an outsized 1950s atomic model – but take time to explore and you will find some **great art galleries**, abundant greenery, a majestic central square, and many excellent restaurants. The city is officially bilingual and so street and station names appear in two versions (e.g. French Rue Neuve is Dutch Nieuwstraat).

The main rail route through Brussels runs just east of the city centre, partly underground, but here and there above the surface for long enough to afford some tantalising views of the city. The fast trains from Lille Europe all arrive at **Brussels Midi** (Zuid in Dutch) and serve no other station in the city. But from Midi it is just four minutes on frequent local trains to Centraal station, from where it's a short walk down to the **Grand Place** – the magnificent square which is the hub of Brussels life. Read more on Brussels stations in our 'connections' section below.

Hotel prices are high in Brussels but they are often greatly discounted on Fr, Sat and Sun nights. If you decide to stay overnight in the Belgian capital, the Novotel Brussels off Grand Place, 120 r du Marché aux herbes, ☎ 026 20 04 29 (https://all.accor.com) is in a good location between Centraal station and the Grand Place.

Connections from Brussels

Brussels is a **major hub for international Eurostar trains**, with direct services to England, the Netherlands, Germany and France. These services serve only **Brussels Midi**. Similarly, all direct TGVs to France stop only at Midi. The same applies to the European Sleeper night train to Berlin and Prague. Deutsche Bahn ICE trains to Germany and ÖBB Nightjet services to Berlin and Vienna stop at both Midi and Brussels Nord. All other international trains make three stops in Brussels, viz. at Midi, Centraal and Nord.

So if you are taking the hourly Intercity *Beneluxtrein* to Rotterdam or Amsterdam, you can board at any of the three stations. The same applies to the Intercity trains to Luxembourg and to the frequent trains to most destinations within Belgium. These include direct services to Bruges and Ostend, Antwerp, Liège and Verviers, Mons, Namur and Charleroi. Trains to **Brussels Airport** also serve all three stations in the Belgian capital.

The Eurostar and Deutsche Bahn trains from Brussels to Cologne all follow the same route. They dash across the flatlands of Brabant to reach Liège (Luik in Dutch and Lüttich in German), an industrial city that sprawls along the west bank of the River Meuse.

In Liège, all trains stop at **Guillemins railway station**, a stunning piece of design by Santiago Calatrava. The building is best appreciated from the road outside rather than from the platforms, but on a sunny day the play of light and shade on the platforms is quite seductive. The station is a reminder that Liège is a city which has always had strong railway connections. Read more in our **Sidetracks** feature on p235.

Connections from Liège

You can connect at Liège Guillemins with **Route 8** in this book, which follows a lovely line south through the Ardennes to Luxembourg and beyond. There is a useful hourly train to Maastricht, just 33 minutes from Liège on the other side of the Dutch border.

A new **high-speed line** from Liège to Aachen opened in 2009, thus marking the end of a slow dawdle through the hill country of eastern Belgium to reach the Germany border. Nowadays, the fast trains dive through tunnels and miss the best of the scenery. Of course, you can if you wish still follow the old line via Verviers to Aachen. There are hourly trains on this route, all requiring a change of train at Welkenraedt.

Into Germany

A frontier town close to the point where the borders of Belgium, the Netherlands and Germany converge, **Aachen** (formerly known as Aix-la-Chapelle) was already a great city 1,000 years ago when Emperor Charlemagne enjoyed the thermal springs here and made it the capital of his empire.

The **Aachener Dom** is the oldest cathedral in northern Europe and inspiring more for its historical associations than for any great beauty. You can see Charlemagne's gilded tomb and the imperial throne. Nowadays, in a post-Schengen Europe largely free of border controls, Aachen thrives as the main city in the three-country Euregio district. The quirky **Dreiländerpunkt** (three-country point) on the edge of town is worth a visit in fine weather. Take 350 from the railway station in Aachen to Vaals Busstation from where it is a 10-minute uphill walk. From Aachen, it is just 40 minutes on the fastest trains to Cologne.

Cologne (Köln)

During the Second World War, nine-tenths of what was Germany's largest **Altstadt** (Old Town) was flattened by bombing, and the quality of reconstruction has been patchy. But there's much to enjoy, in the cathedral, churches and museums, and Kölners themselves have an irresistible verve, exemplified in the city's pre-Lent carnival, reaching its peak on Shrove Tuesday. The **twin spires of the Dom** (cathedral), one of the world's greatest Gothic buildings, soar over the Rhineland capital, and greet the visitor arriving at Cologne's main station. Climb the tower for a splendid view of the city, the River Rhine and a largely industrial hinterland. Lively Cologne has a large Turkish minority. The city boasts **excellent beer** (look for the local *Kölsch*).

Roman traces include remnants of the original 5th-century city wall. The excellent **Römisch-Germanisches Museum** holds many of the finds of the ancient town. You can see the famous Dionysus Mosaic which dates from the 3rd century AD through a large window on Roncalliplatz next to the dome. The museum's permanent exhibition, however, is currently on display in the Belgisches Haus, Cäcilienstrasse 46. By the 13th century, Cologne was a thriving metropolis of 40,000 people, protected by Europe's longest city walls – a 6-km rampart pierced by 12 massive gates. Within the original city wall stand a dozen Romanesque churches, Germany's finest such architectural concentration. The most striking are Gross St Martin, overlooking the Rhine in the Altstadt, and St Aposteln.

From 321 until 1424, the city was home to one of the most important **Jewish communities** in Germany. The remains of a mikvah (a Jewish ritual bath) dating from 1170 are preserved under a glass pyramid in the middle of the square of the City Hall. Nearby, the **Museum Ludwig** (closed Mon) houses 20th-century works including those of Kirchner, Beckmann and Dix and an excellent collection of pop art (Warhol, Lichtenstein and more). The outstanding **Wallraf-Richartz-Museum**, with superb 14th- to 16th-century paintings by the Cologne school and an excellent café, is at Martinstr. 39, about a 10-min walk from the Dom. For information about all these museums, and more, check out www.museenkoeln.de. The Kwartier Latäng – around Rathenauplatz and Zülpicher Strasse – and the Südstadt are good places to chill out.

Arrival, information, accommodation

⇌ Köln Hbf, centrally placed, right by the cathedral with a huge shopping centre, left luggage, information desk, currency exchange and service point. ✈ Flughafen Köln–Bonn, south-east of the city (www.koeln-bonn-airport.de). S-Bahn trains take 15 mins and run every 20 mins, direct to Köln Hbf. 🅸 Tourist office: Kardinal-Höffner Pl. 1 (www.cologne-tourism.com), by the Dom. The comprehensive public transport system includes U-Bahn (underground), S-Bahn (surface suburban trains), trams and buses (see www.kvb.koeln).

⇌ A good-value option also close to the station is the small, family-run **Hotel Domstern**, Domstr. 26, ☎ 0221 16 800 80 (www.hotel-domstern.de). Or stay at the **Eden Hotel Früh am Dom**, Sporergasse 1, ☎ 0221 27 29 20 (www.hotel-eden.de) within sight of the cathedral. The **Hotel Drei Kronen**, Auf dem Brand 6, ☎ 0221 258 06 92 (www.hotel-drei-kronen.de) is a good option not far from both the railway station and the Old Town with views of the River Rhine. ✗ A typical Cologne dish is *Sauerbraten*, a 'sour roast', with beef soaked in vinegar and stewed, served with *Kartoffelklösse* (potato dumplings) and apple sauce. *Blootwoosch* (black pudding) makes a snack served with mustard on a bread roll, known as 'Cologne caviar'. A dish that sounds like half a chicken (*Halve Hahn*) is actually just a cheese roll. Many pubs (*Brauhäuser*) offer local beer and good-value food.

Connections from Cologne

You can connect in Cologne onto two other journeys in this book: **Route 9** runs up the Rhine Valley to the Black Forest and Switzerland, while **Route 10** crosses the flatlands of northern Germany to Berlin.

A **high-speed line** running south-east from Cologne (opened 2002) has transformed the railway geography of the Rhine-Main region. The fastest ICE trains now dash to Frankfurt in just an hour, with some trains continuing to Stuttgart and Munich. Looking north, there are fast trains from Cologne to Hamburg, from where **Route 25** will take you on into Scandinavia.

Sidetracks: Creature comforts

We never pass through Liège without thinking of **Georges Nagelmackers** – a name which for devotees of comfortable rail travel immediately evokes a dose of nostalgia. Georges Nagelmackers was **born in Liège in 1845** into an affluent banking family with interests in the then flourishing Ardennes iron industry. The young Nagelmackers, deciding banking was not for him, trained as an engineer. As a young man he travelled to America, returning to Liège in 1868 to run the family ironworks. But he was distracted by trains, possibly a result of growing up just outside Liège where the main railway line from Brussels to Cologne and Berlin cuts across the corner of the family estate at Angleur.

While in America, Nagelmackers had travelled in George Pullman's saloons, which offered greater comfort than that provided in the regular carriages of the railway companies. Nagelmackers built upon the **Pullman principle**, but took it a stage further. In his purpose-built carriages Nagelmackers offered not just a Pullman-style open saloon, but separate compartments with proper beds. And thus it was that on 1 October 1872, at an office in Liège, the **Compagnie Internationale des Wagons-Lits** was founded. Among the very first services to use Nagelmackers' new *Wagons-Lits* carriages was that from Ostend through Brussels and Liège to Cologne and Berlin. Within ten years the *Wagons-Lits* Company had a fleet of over a hundred carriages, providing **sleeping cars** for many of the continent's premier railway companies.

Despite competition from George Pullman, who attempted to emulate in Europe his successes across the Atlantic, Nagelmackers' concern flourished through successive **waves of innovation**. It may seem extraordinary nowadays, but in the late 1870s, fully a half century after train travel had been invented, no one had thought of providing hot food to passengers on the trains.

Nagelmackers sensed a market opportunity, and before long *Wagons-Lits* passengers were being served both luncheon and **dinner on board** his trains. With plush upholstery, even an occasional Gobelin tapestry, polished mahogany and crystal glasses, Nagelmackers ensured that his clients had **all the very best en route**. His most stylish carriages were reserved for the premium routes: Paris to the French Riviera, the *Nord Express* to Berlin and Riga and the *Rome Express*. In 1883, Wagons-Lits pioneered what became the most famous named train of them all: the *Orient Express*.

Nagelmackers' concern for comfort was not restricted just to the rails. The company also **opened fine hotels** at spots served by its trains; the first two were the Avenida Palace in Lisbon and the Riviera Palace in Nice. By the time Nagelmackers died in 1905 the midnight blue and gold railway carriages of his mobile empire reached as far afield as Siberia, Iberia and the Bosphorus. You could ride in *Wagons-Lits* comfort all the way to Manchuria.

Today, the departure boards at the main railway station in Liège (called Liège-Guillemins) are a little tamer than once they were. Long gone are the through sleeping cars to Copenhagen, Vienna and Moscow. For many years, Belgium had no night trains. But in January 2020, **night sleepers returned to Liège** with the launch of a new *Nightjet* service to Vienna. Georges Nagelmackers can now rest more easily in his grave.

Route 8: From the Netherlands to Lake Geneva

CITIES: ★★ CULTURE: ★ HISTORY: ★ SCENERY: ★★
COUNTRIES COVERED: NETHERLANDS (NL), BELGIUM (BE), LUXEMBOURG (LU), FRANCE (FR), SWITZERLAND (CH)
JOURNEY TIME: 12 HRS 30 MINS | DISTANCE: 1,020 KM | MAP: www.ebrweb.eu/18MAP8

This route describes a journey which draws upon a wealth of railway history. In spring 2016, the last direct Eurocity trains from the **Low Countries to Switzerland** slipped quietly from the pages of the *European Rail Timetable*. *Iris* and *Vauban* – those were the names of the twice daily Eurocity services which pottered south through Luxembourg and Strasbourg to Basel – were unloved and neglected in recent years. But they were a good reminder that, in the last century, the route south via the **Ardennes and Alsace** was a popular choice for Swiss-bound travellers from the Low Countries and, for that matter, from England too.

Picture the scene. Fifty years ago on a summer morning at Amsterdam Centraal station. Families bound for holidays in the Alps and the Mediterranean are climbing aboard train D315: the 10.24 to Basel and beyond.

The journey to Basel stayed entirely west of the Rhine, traversing Belgium, Luxembourg and France along the way. The through trains have gone, but the railways are still there. **Regular regional trains** – all offering a high level of comfort – still ply the entire route. So let's hop aboard and make tracks south, following a route which will lead us all the way from Amsterdam to the shores of **Lake Geneva**.

RECOMMENDED ITINERARY

Route 8 is an antidote to the modern fad for high-speed trains. You can travel end-to-end on services which don't need to be booked in advance; it's a chance to rediscover **the joy of travelling spontaneously**. If you are using a Eurail or Interrail pass, you'll not need to pay any supplements or bother making seat reservations. This is a route which could easily be spun out over a full week, so why not think of stopping off at three cities along the way: **Maastricht, Nancy and Strasbourg** would be our top choices. Luxembourg and Berne would be good additional overnight stays.

The railway heads south-east from **Amsterdam** (more on p101) to Utrecht, paralleling the Rijnkanaal, a waterway opened in 1952 to provide a direct link between the River Rhine and the port of Amsterdam. Tree-lined canals encircle the historic heart of Utrecht; it's not a major tourist destination but we rather like it – and it's a good choice if you are keen to stay in this part of Holland but want to avoid pricey Amsterdam hotels.

Running south from Utrecht, crossing the River Lek and the River Waal, the countryside changes slowly in **Noord-Brabant**. No longer is it quite so pancake flat and the geometric rigour of fields in the Amsterdam area gives way to a less orderly landscape. Crossing the **River Maas**, the train reaches **'s-Hertogenbosch** (often called Den Bosch); always worth a stop if

Route 8: From the Netherlands to Lake Geneva

Route details

Amsterdam Centraal to Maastricht

Frequency	Journey time	Notes
2 per hr	2h20–2h30	

Maastricht to Liège-Guillemins

Frequency	Journey time	Notes
Hourly	0h35	

Liège-Guillemins to Luxembourg

Frequency	Journey time	Notes
Hourly	2h40	C

Luxembourg to Nancy

Frequency	Journey time	Notes
Hourly	1h35–2h	A

Nancy to Strasbourg

Frequency	Journey time	Notes
Every 1–2 hrs	1h30	

Strasbourg to Basel SNCF*

Frequency	Journey time	Notes
1–2 per hr	1h20	B

Basel SBB* to Berne

Frequency	Journey time	Notes
2 per hr	1h	

Berne to Lausanne

Frequency	Journey time	Notes
2 per hr	1h5–1h15	

Notes

A – Some journeys may require a change of train in Metz.
B – Some journeys may require a change of train in Mulhouse.
C – Every two hours at weekends.
***** – The SNCF (French sector) and the SBB (Swiss sector) stations at Basel/Bâle are adjacent.

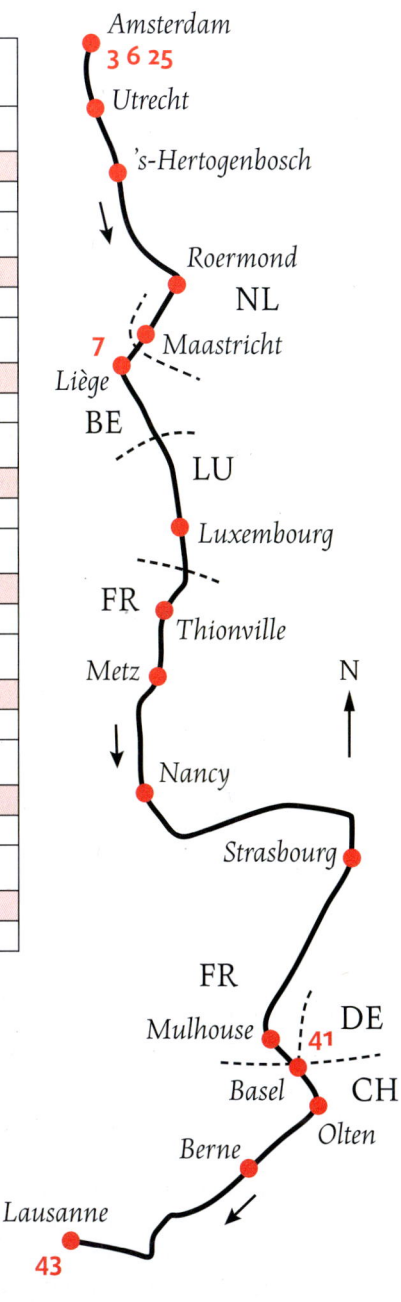

only to take a peek at the town's magnificent market square. There is no reason to pause at the industrial town of Eindhoven, but if you take a couple of hours out at **Roermond**, you'll discover that this southernmost province of the Netherlands – called Limburg – is a world apart from Amsterdam and the North Sea coast. Roermond has a strong Catholic heritage, and that still inflects many aspects of Roermond life.

Maastricht (suggested stopover)

Step off the train in Maastricht and you may wonder if you really are still in the Netherlands at all. The city has a distinctly 'southern' feel. Tucked into a mildly hilly corner of the Netherlands, the provincial **capital of Limburg** is a busy university town. With its **lively squares**, distinctive stone houses and arty boutiques, it really is most appealing. You can get a great view from the tower of **Sint Janskerk**, next to huge Sint Servaasbasiliek (see the 11th- and 12th-century crypts).

As Roermond, this is a largely **Catholic town**. At Museumkelder Derlon, there are *in situ* remnants of Roman Maastricht, while centuries-old fortifications abound in and around the city, notably at Fort Sint Pieter. **St Pietersberg Caves** are the result of centuries of excavation of marl stone, which have left a labyrinth of more than 20,000 passages; you can visit two sections (see www.ebrweb.eu/caves for details).

Arrival, information, accommodation

A 10-min walk east of the centre. Tourist office: Kleine Staat 1 (www.visitmaastricht.com; closed Mon). Just a 5-min walk from the station and conveniently close to the city centre, the hotel-cum-restaurant **Alex Maastricht**, Stationsstraat 17a, ☎ 043 206 51 11 (www.alexmaastricht.nl) has a nice modern and welcoming feel. Or try the **Maison Haas Hustinx**, Vrijthof 20, ☎ 043 852 43 53 (www.haashustinx.nl), which is equally central and close to Sint Janskerk. For spacious, individually designed rooms and a touch of art, head for the **Hotel Dis**, Tafelstraat 28, ☎ 043 321 54 79 (www.hoteldis.nl), just south of the city centre.

Through the Ardennes

From Maastricht, our route follows the River Maas (Meuse in French) upsteam over the Belgian border to **Liège** (see p106), where you can connect onto **Route 7**, running east to Cologne or west via Brussels to Lille. You will need to change trains in Liège; that's a good chance to see the station which is quite magnificent – a building without evident facades and a monumental roof which dips and curves and then soars skyward.

Down on the platforms, the trains come and go: a red Eurostar bound for Paris, a sleek silver ICE heading for Frankfurt-am-Main and the occasional Intercity to Luxembourg. That's the train we want, so climb on board and enjoy the ride on one of **Europe's finest rural rail routes**.

Today's hourly trains from **Liège to Luxembourg** are usually formed of a rake of four Belgian carriages, three second class and one first, all comfy Intercity stock from the 1980s. The electric locomotive at the head of the train works through to Luxembourg. Long gone are the days when there was a change of engine at the border.

Leaving **Liège-Guillemins station**, the line immediately crosses the River Meuse – eyes left for a superb view downstream – and then tracks south up the Ourthe Valley. Twenty minutes out of Liège, the train pauses at Rivage before turning east into the hills. The scenery becomes ever more dramatic as the train climbs slowly into the **Belgian Ardennes**. About 75 minutes into the journey, the train stops at **Gouvy**, the last station before the border with the Grand Duchy of Luxembourg. At 466 metres above sea level, Gouvy is the highest station on the 160-km route from Liège to Luxembourg. The journey south from the border through tilted hill country to the city of Luxembourg is a sheer delight with a medley of **castles, gorges and waterfalls**. If you are minded to break your journey, **Clervaux** is a good place to stop. It's a hike from the station into the town centre, but you'll be rewarded by a world-class photographic exhibition (called *The Family of Man*) at Clervaux Castle (closed Mon & Tues).

One of Europe's smallest capitals, **Luxembourg** is a pleasant place to pass a day or two. The city was founded in Roman times and is dramatically sited on a gorge cut by the **rivers Alzette and Pétrusse**. It falls naturally into three sections: the old centre (north of the Pétrusse Valley and home to most of the sights), the modern city and station (south of the gorge), and Grund (the valley settlement), reachable by deep escalators or lifts from the central part of town. Descending to Grund ('the ground') is like entering a different, darker city, and it is this area that houses most of Luxembourg's racier nightlife.

Connections from Luxembourg

Hourly trains from Luxembourg slip over the German border to Trier, and then continue down the **Moselle Valley** to Koblenz, where you can connect into the next route in this book; follow **Route 9** south up the Rhine Valley to the **Black Forest** and Switzerland. Read more on the Moselle Valley in our **Sidetracks** feature on p125. Luxembourg has long had direct TGVs to **Paris**, and there is also a fast bus link to Lorraine TGV station is France, connecting there with a wider range of TGV services. From Luxembourg there are two useful direct TGVs each day to the **Rhône Valley**, both running via Mulhouse to Dijon, Lyon and Avignon. Closer to hand, there are frequent cross-border local trains to Metz and Nancy.

The train ride into the city of Luxembourg from the north may have seduced you into thinking that the **Grand Duchy** consists entirely of lush green valleys and striking castles. Travelling south to the French border, you see a more industrial side of Luxembourg. The **steel industry**, once so important in southern Luxembourg and adjacent areas of Lorraine (in France), has declined, leaving the region with significant economic challenges. Over the border, the first French town of any size is **Thionville**. This is not the prettiest introduction to France, but it's nonetheless an interesting ride up the Moselle Valley through **Metz** to Nancy.

Nancy

The French city of Nancy is a little off the beaten track. But it deserves to be better known. Those who visit are universally impressed by its **striking architecture** which sweeps from elegant 18th-century classicism to art nouveau.

Nancy's pre-eminent position in architecture and the decorative arts has earned it a place on UNESCO's World Heritage List. The star of the show is the **neoclassical place Stanislas** in the middle of the city. It is locally referred to just as Stan. Its entire south side is taken up by the palatial Hôtel de Ville. Behind is the pl. d'Alliance, and to the north, through the **Arc de Triomphe**, the 15th-century pl. de la Carrière. A good overnight option in the historic Old Town is the Hôtel de Guise, 18 r. de Guise, ☎ 03 83 32 24 68 (www.hoteldeguise.com), about a 15-min walk from pl. Stanislas.

Territorial reforms in France in 2016 nudged Lorraine and Alsace into a single mega-region (which also assimilated the Champagne-Ardenne region to the west of Lorraine). Nancy, the proud capital of Lorraine, lost out to Strasbourg in the bid to be top dog in the new order.

Nancy may be miffed, but there's still an excellent train service running **east to Strasbourg**. It's a pleasant old-style main line, once used by the *Orient Express* and still used today by a once-daily TGV in each direction, though nowadays all other long-distance trains use a new high-speed line to Strasbourg which opened in summer 2016. But the regional TER services from Nancy still use the old route to Strasbourg which meanders delightfully through the **Vosges hills**, paralleling the canal which links the River Marne with the River Rhine.

Strasbourg (suggested stopover)

The old capital of Alsace, once a mere fishing village, has grown into a **most attractive city**, successfully combining old with new. The town is best known today as the seat of the European Parliament, housed in an imposing new building on the city outskirts. The prettiest area of town is **Petite-France**, where 16th- and 17th-century houses crowd around narrow alleys and streams. The river is spanned by the picturesque **Ponts Couverts**, a trio of mediaeval covered bridges with square towers.

The **Cathédrale Notre-Dame** is a Gothic triumph with a carved west front. Highlights include the 13th-century Pilier des Anges (Angels' Pillar) and the 19th-century Horloge astronomique (astronomical clock), which

Exploring the Vosges

To see something of the beautiful wooded hills behind Strasbourg (called the Vosges), take the local train which runs up the **Bruche Valley** to Saint-Dié-des-Vosges, from where you can continue to Épinal in the upper reaches of the **Moselle Valley** before cutting south to Belfort. This is one of those lovely branch-line escapades which take time but are unfailingly rewarding.

strikes at 12.30 each day. The tower, a 332-step climb, provides a marvellous city view.

Arrival, information, accommodation

Pl. de la Gare, 10-min walk to the centre. Tourist office: 17 pl. de la Cathédrale (www.visitstrasbourg.fr). Conveniently located close to the station is the **Monopole Métropole**, 16 r. Kuhn, ☎ 03 88 14 39 14 (www.bw-monopole.com). Or try the elegant and good-value **Gutenberg**, 31 r. des Serruriers, ☎ 03 88 32 17 15 (www.hotel-gutenberg.com), or the stylish and more upmarket **Rohan**, 17–19 r. du Maroquin, ☎ 03 88 32 85 11 (www.hotel-rohan.com), both close to the cathedral. There are plenty of cafés and *winstubs* (traditional Alsatian restaurants) near the cathedral, on r. des Tonneliers and in the Petite-France quarter.

Connections from Strasbourg

From Strasbourg it is just a short hop over the River Rhine to Offenburg, where you can connect with **Route 9** (running north to Cologne and south through the Black Forest to Zurich). German ICE trains are now regularly seen in Strasbourg; they are used on the Paris to Stuttgart and Frankfurt routes. SNCF's smart TGVs are also used on those same routes across the German border. There's a once-daily TGV to Munich and direct Nightjet services to both Vienna and Berlin.

Strasbourg has TGVs to **Paris** and a good range of **provincial cities across France**, including Nantes and Bordeaux, and Lyon and Marseille. International destinations, beyond those already mentioned in Germany, include fast TGVs to Brussels and hourly regional trains to Basel.

The journey south from Strasbourg keeps well west of the River Rhine and you'll not see the river at all. To the right of the train, the Vosges mountains nudge ever closer and south of Sélestat there are especially fine views of the hills with some of Alsace's finest vineyards on their lower slopes. From the train, it's easy to pick out some of the most distinguished wine-making villages in the region, such as Riquewihr and Hunawihr.

Unlike their colleagues to the east of the river in Germany, who work with similar soils, Alsatian winemakers prefer strong, dry wines which are the perfect match for the bold flavours of the local cuisine. **Colmar** is a good place to stop and try those classic Alsace wines. It is the nicest small town on this route. Beyond Colmar there is no particular reason to stop until Basel.

Into Switzerland

Wedged into the corners of Switzerland, France and Germany, **Basel** (Bâle in French) is a big, working city (the second largest in the country after Zurich).

It has long been a crossroads for European culture. The main station, Bahnhof SBB, is a 10-min walk south of the city centre (5 mins by tram from the front of the station), and handles Swiss and main-line German services.

A separate adjacent station, Bâle SNCF, hosts French regional trains. Both stations evoke the heady old days of train travel. For a spell there were even direct overnight trains from here to London (shipped on a ferry across the Channel).

The town's **mediaeval centre** is on the south bank, in Grossbasel. Kleinbasel is the small modern area on the north bank.

Connections from Basel (Bâle)

Basel offers a greater choice of **international rail services** than many European capital cities. All trains mentioned here leave from the main SBB station. TGVs dash to Paris in just three hours. There are fast trains to Berlin and Hamburg, and to Milan via either the Simplon or Gotthard Base Tunnel routes. You can also connect in Basel onto **Route 41** which runs south into Italy via the old Gotthard railway.

The main rail route from Basel to Berne makes a dog-leg to the east, picking up a high-speed line from **Olten to Berne**. It's not particularly special, and if you want a prettier alternative you might consider taking the route via Delémont which cuts through splendid Jura landscapes. Basel to Berne via this routes requires just a single change of train (at Biel / Bienne). It takes one hour more than the faster Basel to Berne route through Olten.

One of Europe's more relaxed capitals, **Berne** is rightly fêted as a wonderfully appealing city. Its **handsome Old Town**, tucked into a big meander of the River Aare, features on the UNESCO World Heritage List. The Alps are often visible in the distance, though the immediate rural hinterland of the city is unremarkable.

It is little more than an hour from **Berne to Lausanne**. Don't expect dramatic views of the distant Alps until the very end. The appeal of most of this route is in the pastoral beauty of the landscape closer to hand. The line climbs to the Vauderens Tunnel and drops down gently through the **Lavaux vineyards** (see p391) towards Lake Geneva. Near **Grandvaux**, a wonderful vista over the lake opens up, on clear days affording views of Mont Blanc. This is one of **Europe's great arrivals** by train. For travellers of yesteryear arriving in Lausanne on the prestigious *Rheingold Trans-Europe Express* (first class only with every creature comfort), this descent into Lausanne was the highlight of the entire run from Amsterdam. However humble the train you choose for the final leg of this route, the arrival in Lausanne will still surely be a moment to remember.

At **Lausanne** (see p391) you can connect into **Route 43** to Geneva (with the option of joining there **Route 20** to the south of France and Spain). Or follow **Route 43** in reverse from Lausanne back to Zurich, a journey that takes in one of the finest mountain rail routes in the Alps.

Route 9: Exploring the Rhine Valley

CITIES: ★★ CULTURE: ★ HISTORY: ★★ SCENERY: ★★
COUNTRIES COVERED: GERMANY (DE), SWITZERLAND (CH)
JOURNEY TIME: 7 HRS 30 MINS | DISTANCE: 611 KM | MAP: WWW.EBRWEB.EU/18MAP9

This is one of Europe's classic rail journeys, as the route south from Cologne hugs the River Rhine and then, once past Koblenz, follows the **dramatic Rhine Gorge** upstream. Moving over the imperceptible divide from northern into southern Germany (read more on the *Weißwurstgrenze* on p138), we leave the Rhine Valley and continue through the **Black Forest** into Switzerland. Once in Switzerland, at Schaffhausen, our route takes in one of Europe's most celebrated waterfalls en route to our final destination in Zurich.

No other journey in this book quite so perfectly recalls the wholesale changes in travel patterns which took place in the early and mid-19th century. The end of the **Napoleonic Wars** heralded a wholly new era in travel – one where many people travelled purely for the sake of it. The restless English were in the vanguard of this movement and many looked to the Rhine as a easy-to-reach continental destination. The liberalisation of steamer traffic on the river, coupled with the completion of new railways stretching from the Belgian coast to Cologne, encouraged the more monied classes from London and the Home Counties to take short breaks to see the **mediaeval castles** and **Rhine landscapes** which poets and artists had helped inscribe on the Romantic imagination.

Clutching their Murray guides, the English sallied forth in the first clear example of international mass tourism in Europe. The extension of rail networks throughout Germany, and the advent of all-inclusive tour arrangements of the kind pioneered by **Thomas Cook**, served only to augment the flow of travellers. By the mid-1870s increasing numbers of visitors were pushing well beyond the Rhine Gorge into central Germany, the Black Forest and the Alps. Thomas Cook pioneered his *Tourist Handbooks* series, which described routes rather than merely places, in much the same way as we do in this book. The very first Cook *Handbooks* covered railways in the territory traversed by Route 9.

There are railways on both sides of the River Rhine from **Cologne upstream to Mannheim**. Our journey here follows the left bank of the river, that is, the west bank, which generally offers a better choice of trains than the east bank.

Suggested itinerary

Our starting point is **Cologne**, which is nowadays just a short hop on regular high-speed trains from Amsterdam, Brussels and Paris. Travellers from Britain can leave London on a morning departure on Eurostar and, with just one change of train in Brussels, be in Cologne to start Route 9 by early afternoon.

Route details

Cologne Hbf to Koblenz Hbf

Frequency	Journey time	Notes
4–5 per hr	0h55–1h40	

Koblenz Hbf to Mainz Hbf

Frequency	Journey time	Notes
2–4 per hr	0h50–1h30	

Mainz Hbf to Mannheim Hbf

Frequency	Journey time	Notes
2–3 per hr	0h40–1h20	

Mannheim Hbf to Heidelberg Hbf

Frequency	Journey time	Notes
4–6 per hr	0h15–0h20	

Heidelberg Hbf to Karlsruhe Hbf

Frequency	Journey time	Notes
1–2 per hr	0h35–0h50	

Karlsruhe Hbf to Singen

Frequency	Journey time	Notes
Hourly	2h45–3h	

Singen to Schaffhausen

Frequency	Journey time	Notes
4 per hr	0h15–0h20	

Schaffhausen to Zurich HB

Frequency	Journey time	Notes
2–4 per hr	0h40–1h	

There are no **compulsory seat reservations** on any of the trains on this route. Holders of Interrail and Eurail passes can thus follow the entire route without paying a cent in supplements. This is, therefore, a journey well suited to spontaneous travel. Cheap tickets, valid only on regional trains, are available for all but the final leg from Schaffhausen to Zurich. Read more on these slow travel deals in the box on p140.

Heidelberg is the obvious place for an **overnight stop**. If you decide to travel from Cologne to Heidelberg in a day, we especially recommend using one of the two morning

Eurocity trains which run up the Rhine Valley from Cologne. These two trains (EC7 and EC9 respectively) are both formed of very comfortable Swiss carriages; both trains have excellent restaurant cars.

A **Swiss panorama carriage** (first class only) was routinely included on the EC9 (and EC8 in the northbound direction) until mid-July 2024. We hope it will return in the 2025 timetables. It is a two-and-a-half hour journey from Cologne to Mannheim, where you'll need to change for a connecting train to Heidelberg, just a dozen minutes away.

If the weather is good and time no object, think of doing part of the **journey by boat** up the Rhine; the best place to do this is definitely between Boppard and Bingen. Holders of Eurail and Interrail passes receive a 20% discount on the regular fares on most scheduled boat services (*Linienfahrten*) on the Rhine and the Moselle.

In his *Tourist Handbook* of 1873, Thomas Cook remarked on the extraordinary amount of traffic to be observed on the River Rhine as the traveller heads south from **Cologne** (see p107) to Bonn. He noted in particular the timber rafts on which entire families had built simple shelters. Modern German officialdom brooks no such improvisation, but the river still bustles with traffic today. The stretch immediately upstream of Cologne towards Bonn wins no prizes for beauty.

With its small-town atmosphere, it is hard to believe that **Bonn** was still a capital city just 25 years ago. Packed with students and top-notch cultural attractions, Bonn is a lively stopover for a day or two. All the central areas are walkable, and the pubs near the river do a roaring trade at night.

Deprived of its capital city status, Bonn now makes the most of its musical connections, of which Beethoven is the biggest. The **Beethoven-Haus-Museum**, where the composer spent the first 22 years of his life, is at Bonngasse 20 and contains his instruments and a rather sad collection of ear trumpets testifying to his irreversible decline into total deafness.

Upstream from Bonn, the landscape perks up as we pass **Königswinter** with its seven hills of which the most striking (though actually the lowest of the seven) is the Drachenfels, the "castled crag" promoted to stardom by Byron in *Childe Harold's Pilgrimage*. Byron sailed up the Rhine in spring 1816.

Koblenz is a name intimately associated with travel: it was here that Karl Baedeker started publishing his famous guidebooks to Europe in 1823, taking advantage of the first of the great wave of visitors then discovering the Rhine.

The Moselle and Rhine rivers meet in Koblenz at the **Deutsches Eck** (the German Corner), marked by a massive, heavy-handed monument to Kaiser Wilhelm I. The pleasant gardens that line the banks of both rivers combine to provide an attractive 8-km stroll. **Ehrenbreitstein** (across the Rhine, ferries in summer) is dominated by an enormous fortress, begun in the 12th century, but grown to its present size during the 16th century. An incline elevator, opened in 2011, grants barrier-free access to the fortress. From the left side of the Rhine, a cable car leads from Koblenz up to the plateau. As well as providing a superb panorama, the fortress contains two regional museums and a youth hostel. A big firework display (the most important of the 'Rhein in Flammen' series) is staged here on the second Saturday in August. The Moselle Valley is of course a tempting diversion, and it is followed in part by trains running up the valley to Trier and beyond. Read more on the Moselle in our **Sidetracks** feature on p125.

The Rhine Gorge

English travellers in the 19th century always travelled with their sketch pads, recording Rhenish landscapes with varying degrees of artistic competence. Not all were as good as **JMW Turner** who visited in 1817. No castles or crags were more frequently sketched than those which line the 60-kilometre stretch of the river between Koblenz and Bingen.

In the space of just 25 years, from 1825 to 1850, the number of travellers taking boats along this stretch of the river increased 30-fold, most of these tourists anxious to discern a rich mediaeval past in the time-worn villages which line the banks of the Rhine. The lure of myth has not quite faded, and today even regular users of the railway still crane their necks to catch a glimpse of the slaty summit of the **Loreley** above Sankt Goarshausen on the east bank. The drama of the Rhine castles may have faded, but this is still a tremendous ride.

Our favourite villages along this stretch of the river are **Boppard** and **Oberwesel** on the west bank and Lorch on the east bank. These, and most other villages on both banks, have railway stations served by local trains. At almost every village, there are ferries over to the opposite bank of the river.

The mood of the landscape changes dramatically beyond **Bingen** as the railway runs through flat terrain to **Mainz**, a city which stands centre stage in German history as the place where Gutenberg invented printing. Our route continues south, still with occasional glimpses of the Rhine through Worms to Mannheim (where a change of trains is often necessary). Beyond Mannheim, we follow the River Neckar to Heidelberg.

Heidelberg (suggested stopover)

Heidelberg's romantic setting, beneath wooded hills along the banks of the **River Neckar** and overlooked by castle ruins, makes it a magnet for tourists and moviemakers. Expect packed streets in the summer high season. The town has a long history and is home to Germany's oldest university, founded in 1386, but there's little that's ancient in the centre, as most of it was rebuilt in the 18th century following wholesale destruction by Louis XIV's troops in 1693. The city's most famous sight is the part-ruined **pink sandstone castle**, high above the town. From its terraces, you get a beautiful view over the red rooftops and the gently flowing river.

Many fine old mansions are scattered around the **Altstadt** (Old Town). The buildings around Marktplatz include the Renaissance Haus zum Ritter and the 14th-century Heiliggeistkirche (Church of the Holy Spirit). Universitätsplatz, which has the **Löwenbrunnen** (Lion Fountain) in the centre, is the location of both the 'old' and 'new' universities. Until 1914, students whose high spirits had got out of hand were confined to the special students' prison round the corner in Augustinerstr. 2. Incarceration was regarded as an honour and self-portraits are common in the graffiti on the walls. Highlight of the summer is the castle festival, when opera, theatre and dance performances are staged outdoors in the cobbled courtyard.

Across the river, over the **Alte Brücke**, the steep Schlangenweg steps zigzag up through orchards to the Philosophenweg (Philosophers' Path). This is a scenic lane traipsing across the hillside, so-called because the views allegedly inspired philosophical reflection.

Arrival, information, accommodation

⇌ Heidelberg Hbf, 10-min walk to the edge of the pedestrian district; or 25 mins to the heart of the Old Town (or 🚌 32).

🛈 Tourist office: Willy-Brandt-Pl. 1, directly in front of the station (www.heidelberg-marketing.de). Accommodation booking service. Guided walking tours of the Altstadt (Old Town) in English (Thur, Fri & Sat at 10.30, Apr–Oct) from the tourist information on Neckarmünzplatz (€12). A network of buses and trams serve the pedestrianised Altstadt, where a funicular ride saves the 300-step climb up to the castle. It's also possible to tour by bike; rentals available from Eldorado, Felix-Wankel-Str. 1 (www.eldorado-hd.de), particularly pleasant for exploring the banks of the Neckar.

🛏 Heidelberg is a prime tourist destination, so the later you book during the summer, the further from the centre you will find yourself. Located right at the Alte Brücke in the Old Town is the comfortable **Holländer Hof**, Neckarstaden 66, ☎ 06221 60 50 0 (www.hollaender-hof.de). Also in the Old Town, in a quiet side street, is the **Backmulde**, Schiffgasse 11, ☎ 06221 53 66 0 (www.gasthaus-backmulde.de), which has a good restaurant and 26 individually furnished rooms. More upmarket is the chic and stylish **Arthotel**, Grabengasse 7, ☎ 06221 65 00 60 (www.arthotel.de), which has spacious rooms.

✕ The Altstadt is very touristy and its restaurants lively with a student atmosphere. Many spill out onto the traffic-free streets. This is also the nightlife hub. You are spoilt for choice along Heiliggeiststr. and Untere Str.

The Black Forest

From Heidelberg, it is a short run south to **Karlsruhe** where the most interesting sight is the palace built in 1715 by Margrave Karl Wilhelm; it is an enormous neoclassical pile with extensive formal gardens. From the tower, you see clearly how he designed the entire city to radiate out from it like a fan and Karlsruhe's grace derives from that ambitious urban plan.

Directly across from the north entrance of the Hauptbahnhof (mind the trams) and right next to the tourist office is the **Zoologischer Stadtgarten**. Much more than a regular zoo, it offers expansive parks and is a wonderful place for walks. There is a boating lake and, in season, outdoor cafés and a blaze of flowers.

CONNECTIONS FROM KARLSRUHE
Fast trains run non-stop to Strasbourg where you can connect onto **Route 8**. There's a very useful direct TGV to Lyon and Marseille, affording a connection in both cities to the French routes featured in this book. TGV and ICE trains dash to Paris. There are frequent services up the **Rhine Valley** to Freiburg and Basel. Some of these trains to Basel continue to other destinations in Switzerland (eg. Chur, Interlaken or Zurich). One daytime train goes as far as Milan. Karlsruhe has direct trains to Berlin and Hamburg, Stuttgart, Munich and Nuremberg.

Some of the **trams** which depart from the station forecourt are shape-shifters, morphing magically into trains once they escape the city. Pick of the bunch is the S8 (called Murgtalbahn) which makes a two-hour journey up the Murg Valley to the Black Forest town of **Freudenstadt**, from where you can take a connecting train to rejoin Route 9 at Hausach (just north of Triberg).

Just south of Karlsruhe, **Baden-Baden** is the European spa town par excellence. Ever sniffy about modernity, the locals kept the railway at a distance and the station is inconveniently far away from the town. Almost oppressively elegant and full of visitors dripping with money, Baden-Baden is a throwback to an earlier age.

But it has a compelling appeal, and nowhere else in Germany offers the same opportunities for people watching (or even snaring a rich, aged spouse). The city has snob appeal and everything is overdone, but it's all the more fabulous for that. You half expect to bump into the Russian tsar or a Hungarian countess as you stroll into the casino.

Beyond Baden-Baden, our route turns into the hills following the **Schwarzwaldbahn** (Black Forest Railway) through glorious wooded hills towards the Swiss border. **Thomas Cook** travelled the route just after it opened in 1873 and remarked on the unusual density of red waistcoats, velvet breeches and cuckoo clocks.

The waistcoats and breeches have slipped from fashion, but the cuckoo clocks are still everywhere, most particularly in **Triberg**, where you'll find fabulous displays of Black Forest kitsch. Known for the purity of its air, this touristy spa town is actually very pleasant; it's been a centre for **cuckoo**

DANUBIAN DIVERSION
Running south from the Black Forest, many travellers are surprised to discover that the **source of the River Danube** lies so far west (and so close to the Rhine). Lovers of rural railways (and Danube hunters) can easily follow much of the course of the river through southern Germany and beyond. You need to leave Route 9 at **Immendingen**, from where a delightful railway follows the Danube down to Ulm. From there, continue via Donauwörth (where you cross **Route 12**) to Regensburg, where you can connect into the Vienna-bound ICE trains which broadly follow the Danube downstream via Passau and Linz.

clock production since 1824, when Josef Weisser started his business in the *Haus der 1000 Uhren* (House of a Thousand Clocks). You can also enjoy **Germany's highest waterfalls** in Triberg. The waters of the River Gutach plunge in seven steps 163 metres into the valley. The main entrance to the waterfalls is easy to reach from the centre of town.

The summit of the *Schwarzwaldbahn*, at over 800 metres above sea level, is about a dozen kilometres beyond Triberg, after which the railway drops down into the **Danube Valley**. The railway parallels the youthful river, here no more than a stream. At **Singen**, it is always necessary to change trains. Running west from Singen, the train slips through Gottmadingen where the station starred in political history. It was here that in 1917 Lenin – en route from Switzerland back to Russia – changed trains, boarding the famous sealed carriage in which he was forced to remain for the long journey across German territory to the Baltic island of Rügen.

All trains stop at **Schaffhausen**, a Swiss town which unusually, though not uniquely, is located on the right bank of the River Rhine, hemmed in by German territory. The one big reason for stopping here is the famous waterfall, that great obstacle to shipping on the Rhine which has been turned into a lucrative economic opportunity. Schaffhausen thrives on tourists intent on getting soaked by the spray from the Rhine. Thomas Cook underplayed the appeal of the spot: "At the outset, let me warn the tourist not to build his hopes too high," wrote Cook in 1873. "They are not equal to Niagara," he continued. Maybe not, but the **Rhine Falls at Schaffhausen** are extraordinarily beautiful, and the town itself, likeable rather than picturesque, has a useful range of onward connections. The two stations nearest the falls are called Schloß Laufen and Neuhausen am Rheinfall, the latter being possibly a shade better placed. The stations are on opposite banks of the river. Both are served by half-hourly local trains from Schaffhausen.

From Schaffhausen it is less than an hour on to Zurich – criss-crossing the **Swiss-German border** a number of times along the way – with a tremendous view of the Rhine Falls to the left just after leaving Schaffhausen. Note that some slower trains from Schaffhausen to Zurich, viz. those routed via Winterthur, do not give the same splendid view of the falls.

Schaffhausen connections

Hourly trains run west to **Basel**, sticking to the right bank (ie. the German side) of the River Rhine. Sit on the left for best views of the river. There's a lovely minor route that runs east along the left bank (ie. the Swiss side) of the Rhine to Kreuzlingen and beyond. It's possible to continue right through to Bregenz in Austria, returning to Schaffhausen by train via **Lindau**. This three-country tour is a grand circuit of Lake Constance.

There is an integrated road-rail ticketing scheme covering the entire **Lake Constance** area. For longer journeys, the Bodensee Ticket undercuts regular fares (for more information see www.bodensee-ticket.com). With a bit more time, you might consider setting out from Schaffhausen to explore Lake Constance by boat. Schaffhausen to **Konstanz** takes 4hrs 40mins, from where it's about another four hours by boat on to Bregenz in Austria.

Zurich (Zürich)

Switzerland's largest town is a classical city with a **contemporary edge**, preserving its architectural and cultural heritage, yet surprising the world with the latest innovations in art and architecture, fashion, shopping and design. Most of Zurich's sights fall within a compact, walkable area on either side of the Limmat River, which bisects the city centre. Next to the Hauptbahnhof on Museumstrasse is the **Swiss National Museum** (www.nationalmuseum.ch; closed Mon). In autumn 2021, the **Kunsthaus Zürich** (www.kunsthaus.ch; closed Mon) opened its highly anticipated extension. Located on the Heimplatz, the museum is not only a place for art, but also for experiencing it.

The ancient hilly **Niederdorf district** to the east is a veritable labyrinth of old, cobbled lanes brimming with trendy bars, cafés and quirky shops. Here you will find the Romanesque **Grossmünster**, the city's cathedral and the birthplace of the Swiss Reformation. Climb the tower for the best views over the city. To the west, the **Altstadt** (Old Town) contains many of the city's finest historic buildings, and broad, leafy **Bahnhofstrasse** counts among the world's most sophisticated shopping boulevards. The trendy former industrial quarter of Zurich West reflects the city's radical change in recent years, while the lake, with its beautiful grassy parks and waterfront promenades, is framed by majestic, snow-capped mountains.

Arrival, information, accommodation

Zurich Hauptbahnhof (HB) is on the west side of the River Limmat, leading out onto Bahnhofstrasse, the city's main shopping street. Zurich Airport is 10 km north-east of the city centre (www.flughafen-zuerich.ch). There are 10 to 13 trains an hour from the rail station, taking approx. 12 mins. The centre of Zurich is small enough to explore on foot. All buses and trams, run by VBZ Züri-Linie (www.ebrweb.eu/zuri), leave the terminal outside the HB frequently. Buy your ticket from machines at stops before boarding or online. Tourist office: at the Hauptbahnhof (www.zuerich.com).

Staying in Zurich is not cheap. However, if you are design conscious and enjoy a relaxed and friendly atmosphere you might like the **25hours Hotel Langstrasse**, Langstrasse 150, ☎ 044 576 52 55 (www.25hours-hotels.com), located not far from the main station. The stylish **St Josef**, Hirschengraben 64/68, ☎ 044 250 57 57 (www.st-josef.ch), is between the station and the university. Just a few steps from the Bahnhofstrasse, the friendly **Townhouse** boutique hotel, Schützengasse 7, ☎ 044 200 95 95 (www.townhouse.ch), has rather memorable wallpaper.

Zurich connections

The Hauptbahnhof in Zurich is the place to connect onto **Tatra diversions, 40** and **43** in this book. All three offer great opportunities for **exploring the Alps** by train. There are half-hourly trains to Geneva, where you can connect onto **Route 20**. ÖBB Railjet trains speed east to Vienna, Budapest and Bratislava. Night trains run to Amsterdam, Berlin and Hamburg, as well as to Ljubljana, Zagreb, Vienna, Graz and Budapest. Eurocity trains run south from Zurich via the Gotthard Base Tunnel to Milan.

SIDETRACKS: RHINE VERSUS MOSELLE

Travellers who progress up the Rhine Valley from Cologne face a big decision at **Koblenz**. Most continue up the Rhine and indeed that is just what **Route 9** does. But you might forsake the Rhine in favour of the Moselle, following the lesser river upstream towards Trier and Luxembourg (where you can join **Route 8** in this book). **Mary Shelley** commended a Moselle excursion as a device to enhance still more "the prouder and more romantic glories of the Rhine." The Moselle landscape, Shelley suggested, possesses "an inferior beauty".

We disagree. The Moselle's lazy sinuous course, occasionally rocky and wild, sometimes densely hung with forests and often gently clad with vines, makes for one of the most seductively beautiful waterways in Europe. The **Moselle** might well lay claim to being the **most European of rivers**. It crosses boundaries; its management is a model of international cooperation, and it even has, on its west bank (in Luxembourg territory), a village whose name is now known through the continent: **Schengen**. The eponymous treaty was signed in 1985 on the *MS Princess Marie-Astrid* which bobbed mid-stream in the Moselle just at the point where the German, French and Luxembourg borders converge. The village of Schengen is nearby.

The **Moselle villages** boast a high density of timber-framed buildings. There are mighty fortresses too. Some, like the ruins of **Grevenburg** above Traben-Trarbach, hint of former glories. The grandest are secluded, like Burg Eltz, hidden away in a tiny side valley above Moselkern. And then there are the enigmatic silhouettes, like **Burg Thurant** above Alken with its double keep. Did one side of the family fall out with the other, one wonders! There are fabulous town gates, like the Roman **Porta Nigra** in Trier, the decorative Brückentor in Trarbach and the elegant Graacher Tor (Graach Gate) in **Bernkastel**. But this is no mediaeval landscape preserved in aspic for the traveller's camera. The Moselle was and is an **industrial river**. The ironworks at Alf were opened in 1824, and with the opening of the river to steamers in 1839, the Moselle quickly developed into a great industrial thoroughfare. True, the boatbuilders who once populated the banks of the river have long since turned to other trades. The Romans brought walnuts and vines to the valley, and two millennia of careful cultivation have given the Moselle region a premier position in **European viticulture**.

It takes less than two hours to reach either Trier or Traben-Trarbach from Koblenz. The latter involves an easy change of train at Bullay. Opt for **Traben-Trarbach** if you want to catch the flavour of a classic Moselle wine town. Trier is less evidently connected to the Moselle than Traben-Trarbach, but offers a big dose of history and culture. The Porta Nigra is one of the most impressive Roman structures north of the Alps. Sedate **Trier** was the birthplace of Karl Marx, and the house where he was born at Brückenstr. 10 has a superb exhibition on his life and work.

There are excellent **boat services** along the Moselle with seasonal services running mainly from Cochem and Bernkastel. There are also interesting cross-border journeys on the Moselle. Our favourite is the Sunday sailing (summer only) on the *MS Princess Marie-Astrid* from Trier to Schengen. Read more details on www.entente-moselle.lu.

Route 10: Across northern Germany

CITIES: ★★ CULTURE: ★ HISTORY: ★★ SCENERY: ★
COUNTRIES COVERED: GERMANY (DE)
JOURNEY TIME: 6 HRS | DISTANCE: 612 KM | MAP: WWW.EBRWEB.EU/18MAP10

This is one **big leap across Germany**, west to east, but let's not beat about the bush. The main rail route linking Cologne with Berlin will hardly inspire you with fine scenery. A sleek ICE train leaves Cologne Hauptbahnhof (Hbf) hourly for the German capital and the journey takes about five hours. There's a delicate beauty to the landscape here and there, particularly around the Weser Hills and in the watery **flatlands of western Brandenburg**. Ultimately this is a journey where few will be spellbound by the scenery beyond the carriage window.

RECOMMENDED ITINERARY
The particular itinerary we describe here is a variant of that followed by the direct ICE trains from Cologne to Berlin. We leave the fast main line at Hannover, favouring instead the old line via Helmstedt. That's the route taken during the **Cold War years** by the **transit trains** which linked West Germany with West Berlin. The only through train from Cologne to Berlin which still follows this precise route in the 2024 timetables is the overnight ICE 100 train between the two cities (which is a no-frills affair with just seats and no sleeping cars). You'll always need to make a couple of changes of train along the way to follow this itinerary by day. You can transform this rather prosaic journey into a real adventure by combining it with **Route 11**, which describes a modest detour through the Harz Mountains.

Our journey starts at **Cologne** Hauptbahnhof (see p107 for more on the city), and almost immediately there is one of the route's best moments as the train crosses the Hohenzollern Bridge over the River Rhine. Look behind you for great views of the Cologne riverfront with its cathedral and splendid Romanesque churches. The run north to Düsseldorf takes in a number of industrial communities, not always pretty, but interesting in their own way.

Too often derided as being too commercial and industrial, **Düsseldorf** has moved quite upmarket, its transition exemplified by the Königsallee (generally termed the 'Kö'), one of the most elegant shopping streets in Germany. The city has a substantial Japanese population, who appear to have learnt the art of drinking beer in the same quantities as the German natives – especially the local 'Alt'. Most of the areas of interest are along the Rhine, itself spanned by the graceful **Rheinkniebrücke** (bridge) with the Rhine Tower prominent on the skyline. Marked by the Schlossturm, all that remains of the original 14th-century castle, the **Altstadt** (Old Town) is small and walkable. One of the most attractive corners is the Marktplatz (Market Square), brimming over with outdoor cafés and restaurants.

The city is also the birthplace of **German punk**. Along with Hamburg and Berlin, Düsseldorf nurtured the nascent punk culture, most notably at the Ratinger Hof, which is still an important music venue in the Old Town.

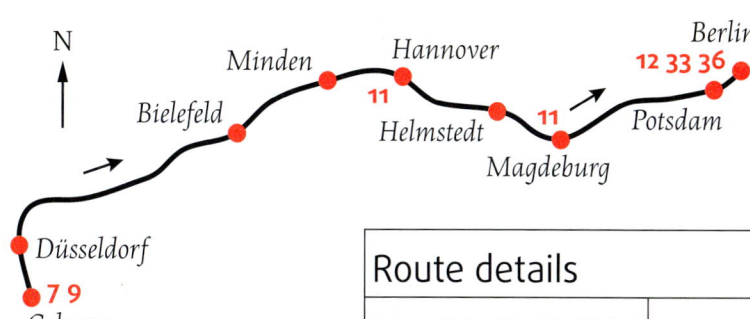

Route details

Cologne Hbf to Düsseldorf Hbf		
Frequency	Journey time	Notes
3–5 per hr	0h25–0h40	
Düsseldorf Hbf to Hannover Hbf		
Frequency	Journey time	Notes
1–2 per hr	2h35–3h	
Hannover Hbf to Magdeburg Hbf		
Frequency	Journey time	Notes
Hourly	1h20	H
Magdeburg Hbf to Potsdam Hbf		
Frequency	Journey time	Notes
Hourly	0h55–1h20	
Postdam Hbf to Berlin Hbf		
Frequency	Journey time	Notes
5–9 per hr	0h25–0h40	

Notes

If you are heading for Berlin and are pressed for time, bear in mind that there are fast ICE trains direct to Berlin from Cologne and Düsseldorf (hourly from both cities, travel time about 4 hrs 30 mins). These Berlin-bound express trains use the new high-speed line which runs east from Hannover to Berlin via Wolfsburg (where there is a fine view of the Volkswagen factory which you can admire as you ponder the ethics of a company which said its cars were less polluting than they in fact were).

H – Only alternate trains between Hannover and Magdeburg stop at Helmstedt.

To the Weser and beyond

The main rail routes running north-east from Düsseldorf skirt once **heavily industrialised valleys** (the Ruhr, Wupper and Emscher). Much of this area has been creatively rescued from its industrial past with impressive new green landscapes. The route then opens out onto the **Westphalian Plain**. You can detour via the fine old cities of Münster and Osnabrück, both with a rich religious history: Münster Catholic and Osnabrück more mixed. The fastest ICE trains speed east on a more southerly route through Bielefeld, a town which is so uncharismatic that Germans often question whether it really exists at all.

The scenery perks up beyond **Herford**, as the train follows the Werre Valley down towards the Weser. Suddenly, and all too briefly, there is a glorious view of the Weser meadowlands and Wiehen Hills. This is the **Porta Westfalica**, the ancient gateway to Westphalia – the historically Prussian province which the railway is now leaving. In the Romantic imagination, the gentle ripples of hills here were magnified into mighty mountains, but even

40 YEARS AGO: THE D243 TO BERLIN

Cast back over 35 years and Germany was still divided, the western states occupied by American, British and French forces; the east, called the German Democratic Republic, stood shoulder to shoulder with the Soviet Union in comradely solidarity. The **Iron Curtain** divided the country. Special transit trains linked West Germany with West Berlin.

Imagine yourself standing on the platform at Cologne Hauptbahnhof in the chill of a March morning in 1985. The first hints of spring are in the air and just a stone's throw away, the great Gothic cathedral looks splendid. But now all eyes are on the train pulling into your platform. This is the D243, an overnight service from Paris which stops briefly in Cologne just after six in the morning and then continues to Berlin. It is one of many **lifeline rail services to West Berlin** in the Cold War years. The passengers at Cologne climb onto the train, taking their seats in the East German (Reichsbahn) carriages for the eight-hour journey to Berlin. Some make for the Mitropa restaurant car where breakfast is already being served.

Travel across the inner-German border between the two German states wasn't easy. There were complicated **border formalities**, with the *Trapos* (the East German transport police) and their dogs carefully checking the train as it entered the territory of the German Democratic Republic. The French couchette carriages and sleeping cars from Paris were removed from the D243 when it stopped at Hannover around ten in the morning. Only the first and second-class seated carriages from Paris continued right through to West Berlin – along the way passing without halt through a medley of East German towns.

In this 2024 journey for *Europe by Rail*, we follow exactly the same route as that taken by the D243 from Cologne to Berlin. The **Mitropa restaurant car** is gone too, as is that slightly antiseptic smell which was a feature of East German railway carriages. The fierce fences which once divided Germany have disappeared. Nowadays Europe finds other uses for fences which so cruelly hinder mobility.

---

without the hyperbole it's all very fetching. Away to the north (ie. on the left side of the train), you cannot miss the huge monument to Kaiser Wilhelm I on the Wiehen Hills. From April to October, there are river cruises on the Weser which depart from **Minden** (details on www.mifa.com). Just half an hour after crossing the River Weser, your train is approaching Hannover, the capital city of the German state of Lower Saxony.

With over half a million residents, **Hannover** is a major centre for education, commerce and culture. It has many fine historical buildings and some world-class landscape gardens. The city certainly deserves a brief stop and the key sights can be seen within a couple of hours. From the station, Bahnhofstraße leads to the **Kröpcke piazza**, in the heart of the largely reconstructed Altstadt; the Kröpcke clock is the most prominent rendezvous point in town. The high-gabled, carefully restored Altes Rathaus is a splendid edifice with elaborate brickwork. Alongside is the Marktkirche, with 14th- to 15th-century stained glass and a bulky tower that is the city's emblem. An absolute must-see are the **Royal Herrenhäuser Gardens**, 10 mins by urban rail line 4 or 5 from Kröpcke (station: Herrenhäuser Gärten) – four once-royal gardens, two of which are the English-style landscaped

Georgengarten and the formal Grosser Garten with spectacular fountain displays in summer. The Herrenhäuser Gardens are often acclaimed as the finest early baroque gardens in Germany.

Connections from Hannover
You can join **Route 11** here. It's a good option for Berlin-bound travellers who have time to detour into the **Harz Mountains** and see some real forest wilderness. As the largest rail hub in Lower Saxony, Hannover offers plentiful onward connections. There are two or three trains each hour north to Hamburg, the fastest taking just 75 minutes to reach the great port city on the Elbe. Southbound you can choose from hourly departures to Frankfurt-am-Main, Nuremberg and Munich. Trains to Stuttgart and Basel both leave every two hours.

Closer to hand, there are hourly trains to **Goslar** and Bad Harzburg, both in the Harz Mountains. Another **regional route** runs south-west to Hameln – that's the Hamelin of pied piper fame. The real gem though, when it comes to the local lines radiating from Hannover, is the minor route which runs north via Soltau to Buchholz (from where it is but a short hop on to Hamburg). Trains for **Buchholz** depart hourly (every two hours at weekends) from Hannover Hauptbahnhof; it's a fine two-hour journey which takes in the Böhme Valley and skirts the great Lüneburg Heath. Flat lands, you'll discover, can indeed be winsomely beautiful.

A tale of two Germanys

German unification in 1990 spawned a number of major rail infrastructure projects to improve communications across the former border between the two German states. The most important of these came to fruition in 1998 with the opening of a new fast line from Hannover to Berlin. Trains now dash between the two cities in just 100 minutes. That's the way to go if you are pressed for time. Along the way, you'll get a great view (left side of the train) of the **Volkswagen factory** at Wolfsburg. It's just one of many striking buildings in a city which has some first-rate architecture.

But we'll stick to the old main line, the one once followed by the transit trains to West Berlin, which runs south-east from Hannover through Braunschweig and cuts through pleasant beech forests to reach **Helmstedt**, the last town on the former territory of West Germany. It's a pleasant place with some fine examples of late 16th-century Weser Renaissance-style architecture – well east of the area where that architectural fashion flourished.

During the Cold War, Helmstedt benefited from its position close to the **East German border**. Trade was good with border hoppers often stopping in Helmstedt to stock up on goods which were less readily available in the German Democratic Republic. Helmstedt was a busy crossing point for road traffic too. The border post where eastbound travellers left West Germany was known as Checkpoint Alpha.

Border antics and the sorrows of living in a divided country are recalled in the **Zonengrenz-Museum** (literally Zonal Boundary Museum) in Helmstedt. It is in a villa just a five-minute walk north of the station at Südertor 6 (closed Mon).

Nowadays, many fast trains speed through Helmstedt without even stopping. It is just six minutes on a local train from Helmstedt to Marienborn, which was the entry point into East Germany. The Berlin-bound transit trains and all other eastbound expresses used to stop at **Marienborn** for checks by the East German authorities. Nowadays this is no more than an inconsequential country railway station, served only by the hourly local trains from Braunschweig to Magdeburg.

The border between the two German states may have gone but, if you take time to explore smaller communities in the eastern part of the country, you'll still find very different attitudes compared to the west. And, as the train rattles east towards **Magdeburg**, you'll notice a string of quiet villages where it looks as though the clocks may have stopped 30 years ago. Magdeburg is always worth a stop, if only to take a look at the city's remarkable cathedral. The city's position on the navigable **Elbe** gave Magdeburg's traders a mighty boost in the Middle Ages; the city was an important player in the Hanseatic League. Today the Elbe is a mixed blessing. The city has on a number of occasions suffered catastrophic flooding and the last of them were in 2013.

Connections from Magdeburg
At Magdeburg, you can connect onto **Route 11** and follow it (in reverse direction) through the **Harz Mountains** back to Hannover. Regional Express trains run north to the attractive city of Wittenberge every hour or two, from where it is just a short hop to Hamburg. Fast double-deck Intercity trains run direct to Leipzig and Dresden, where you can connect with **Route 33** to Prague and Budapest.

Brandenburg and Potsdam

From Magdeburg, Deutsche Bahn's red double-decker Regional Express (RE) trains run hourly to Berlin. Grab a seat on the upper deck as the train cruises east through the Brandenburg flatlands towards the German capital. Brandenburg is the name of the German state which entirely surrounds Berlin; the capital has the status of a state in its own right. All Berlin-bound RE trains from Magdeburg stop at the town of **Brandenburg**, which gave its name to the eponymous state. With a watery setting on the Havel, Brandenburg is an appealing mid-sized town. The nicest areas are around the cathedral, well north of the station.

The next town of any size is **Potsdam** which nudges up so close to Berlin that you might be inclined to see it as no more than a suburb of the German capital. But that's to mistake the historical importance of Potsdam – it was the home of the Hohenzollern family and the hub of imperial power – and the city's status today as the capital of Brandenburg, the largest state in eastern Germany. Potsdam is an absolute 'must see'. The town centre has been superbly restored with two areas especially worthy of a visit. In the very centre is the **Dutch quarter**, a neat area of high-gabled houses with a fabulous mix of small shops and cafés. After wandering through the Dutch quarter, walk north to **Alexandrowka**, once home to the city's Russian community. With its wooden houses, orchards and serenity, Alexandrowka gives a real sense of being a Russian village. There is a delightful Russian café at Alexandrowka Haus 1 (closed Mon).

But Potsdam has of course a real trump card in its **array of palaces and gardens**. The great writer on parks and gardens, Charles Quest-Ritson, lavishes praise on Potsdam in *Gardens of Europe*: "Sanssouci Park is by far the most beautiful, exciting and rewarding garden in Germany and, in my view, the world… It is a series of stupendous palaces and gardens joined together by Peter Joseph Lenné's brilliant, fluid, landscaping." Go judge for yourself. Fast trains link Potsdam and Berlin in less than half an hour. We find Potsdam so beautiful, so exceptional, that we think it worth stopping off there for a night or two. Indeed, some travellers prefer to stay in Potsdam and use it as a base for day trips to Berlin. A good area of town to stay is on or around the **Luisenplatz** close to Potsdam's Brandenburg Gate and the Sanssouci Gardens. Try the Hotel Am Luisenplatz, Luisenplatz 5, ☎ 0331 97 19 00 (www.hotel-luisenplatz.de), or the MAXX by Steigenberger Sanssouci Potsdam, Allee nach Sanssouci 1, ☎ 0331 90 910 (www.maxxhotel.com).

Berlin

Rich history, fabulous art, **alternative culture** – all in the broadest sense – combine to make the city of Berlin a destination that is a little out of the ordinary. The city's turbulent past and cosmopolitan citizens are its main draw; at every corner a piece of modern history plays out in front of you – whether it's the intrigue of the Cold War or the violent trauma of Nazism, it's all represented here.

But Berlin is more than just wars and destruction. Berlin is a city that is always evolving, never stagnant. If you have time to visit just one museum, make it the **Jewish Museum** on Lindenstrasse 9–4 (U-Bahn: Hallesches Tor). Berlin's hottest complex of boutiques, galleries, bars and cafés is the area around **Hackescher Markt**. For a more edgy urban feel head for Schönhauser Allee. The city's latest attraction, the **Humboldt Forum,** opened in July 2021 on the site of the former Hohenzollern city palace as both an exhibition and a space for events.

Rail travellers will most likely enter the city through the **Hauptbahnhof**, a stunning glass-and-steel construction. Indeed, it can be said that Berlin as a city only truly came of age in the era of the railways, and its rich history in this regard is reflected in some wonderful railway architecture, including the Hamburger Bahnhof, now converted into a museum of modern art, the red-brick **Oberbaumbrücke** lifting the elevated U-Bahn tracks across the River Spree, and the ruined facade of the Anhalter Bahnhof.

Also worth searching out is the small memorial by Friedrichstraße station. It shows the two sides of the railway's role during the Nazi era in Germany, from the evacuation of 10,000 Jewish children to England in 1938 on the one side, to the many others who were **deported by train** to the concentration and extermination camps of the Third Reich on the other.

For a cheap sightseeing trip, avoid the tourist buses and take 🚌 100 from Alexanderplatz to Zoo Station. Travelling along Unter den Linden and through the Tiergarten, the bus takes in most of central Berlin's sights at a fraction of the cost.

Arrival, information, accommodation

🚆 Berlin's impressive **Hauptbahnhof** (Hbf) is the city's main railway hub. Note that the railway platforms are not all on the same level, so changing trains, particularly if you are unfamiliar with the station, might take a while. Avoid tight connections. The other stations served by various long-distance services and night trains are **Ostbahnhof** (Ost), **Südkreuz**, **Gesundbrunnen** and **Spandau**. Some regional trains may also serve **Zoologischer Garten** (Zoo), **Lichtenberg** or the newly opened regional rail platforms at Berlin Ostkreuz.

✈ Few cities have had such a tortured relationship with their airport(s) as Berlin. The sparkling new airport (**Berlin Brandenburg International** or simply **BER**) finally opened in autumn 2020 – more than eight years late. **Tegel** (TXL) airport has now closed. The former **Schönefeld** airport (SXF), just ten mins on a shuttle bus from BER and now branded as BER Terminal 5, temporarily closed in 2021 and may never reopen. The main part of BER is about 20 km south-east of the city centre, reached by regional trains to **BER Terminal 1-2** station (4 per hr, some branded FEX) from Berlin Hbf in 30 mins, stopping at Berlin Ostkreuz on the way. The one-way fare is €3.80. Airport information at www.berlin-airport.de.

🛈 Berlin infostores – located at the Hauptbahnhof, BER Airport, the Brandenburg Gate and at the Humboldt Forum – offer city information and accommodation services (www.visitberlin.de). Berlin's efficient public transport system combines buses, trams, underground (U-Bahn) and surface trains (S-Bahn). Tickets can be obtained on station platforms, from machines on the trams, or from bus drivers and are valid on all means of transport mentioned.

🛏 Berlin has some wonderful hotels and, although prices are creeping up, the German capital remains surprisingly reasonable. Hotels in Mitte are best placed for the majority of Berlin's sights, and a recommended option in the area is the stylish and friendly **Circus Hotel**, Rosenthaler Strasse 1, ☏ 030 200 039 39 (www.circus-berlin.de). A no-frills but functional and cheap alternative is the **EasyHotel**, Rosenthaler Strasse 69, ☏ 030 400 065 50 (www.easyhotel-berlin.de), which is in an good location. If you want to treat yourself, the **Casa Camper**, Weinmeisterstrasse 1, ☏ 030 200 034 10 (www.casacamper.com), has brought their extremely popular boutique hotel concept to Berlin from Barcelona.

Connections from Berlin

Berlin is a **major rail hub** with direct trains to Dresden, Prague, Kraków, Warsaw, Leipzig and Munich. The very fastest trains to Munich now take just four hours. Berlin has a superb choice of regional services with direct trains to the **Baltic towns** of Rostock and Stralsund, Kostrzyn in Poland and Cottbus in Lusatia.

Berlin also has a number of **night trains**. Snälltåget and SJ compete on the route to Stockholm. European Sleeper run thrice weekly to Amsterdam and Brussels, facing competition from Nightjet on the latter route. Nightjet introduced a Paris route from Berlin for 2024, although it has proved famously unreliable. There are also direct night sleepers to **Basel and Zurich** as well as direct night trains to Vienna and Budapest.

Route 11: Steaming through the Harz Mountains

Cities: ★★ Culture: ★ History: ★★ Scenery: ★★★
Countries covered: Germany (DE)
Journey time: 9 hrs | Distance: 302 km | Map: www.ebrweb.eu/18map11

The figures quoted for end-to-end journey time and distance for this route exclude the side trip on the steam railway from Drei Annen Hohne to the summit of the Brocken and back.

Every day, thousands of travellers speed across northern Germany on the main rail routes from Cologne or the Ruhr region towards Berlin. The previous route in this volume describes one such journey. It covers a lot of ground at speed, but it's hardly a great rail adventure.

Yet so often in Europe, even just a modest diversion from the main line can transform a prosaic run into something very special, and nowhere is that better illustrated than in journeys **across northern Germany**. You can cut off to the south of the main railways which link Hannover with Berlin to discover the glorious landscapes of the Harz Mountains, a region which boasts Europe's finest network of **narrow-gauge steam railways**. Even if you are not a train buff, the scenery alone justifies an **excursion into the Harz region**. Moreover, the Harz steam trains always go down a treat with children and families.

The entire journey relies on **private rail operators**, rather than the Deutsche Bahn. Interrail, Eurail and other passes are accepted from Hannover as far as Wernigerode and again from Quedlinburg to Magdeburg. For the journey on the Harz narrow-gauge rail routes from Wernigerode to Quedlinburg, rail passes are not recognised and separate tickets must be purchased. There are useful passes allowing unlimited travel on the Harz narrow-gauge network (for fares and rover tickets see www.ebrweb.eu/3).

Recommended itinerary

You could follow this entire journey, from Hannover to Magdeburg via the Harz Mountains in one long day. But it deserves much more time. We suggest making at least two overnight stops along the way. **Drei Annen Hohne** and **Quedlinburg** are good choices.

The best of the scenery is on that part of the journey served by the Harz narrow-gauge trains. Note that there are only very limited services on this network in late autumn, with some routes usually closed completely for a spell between early November and mid-December. Trains to the **summit of the Brocken** are always steam operated, but bear in mind that services may be disrupted by heavy snow or high winds.

We think that this is a route best tackled in the months from May to October inclusive – and, in our view, the Harz Mountains region is at its loveliest in spring or early autumn, so if you can travel in May or October you are in for a treat. Arrange your journey so that the section from Drei Annen Hohne to Quedlinburg is on a Thursday, Friday or Saturday when there is a much better choice of steam-operated services. On other days, diesel railcars operate far more trains on the **Selke Valley railway** to Quedlinburg. Quite apart from the allure of steam, the railcars used on the Harz network just aren't very comfortable. The timetables for the Harz narrow-gauge network are online at www.ebrweb.eu/hrs. They clearly indicate whether **diesel railcars** or **steam trains** are used on particular services.

The Low Countries and Germany

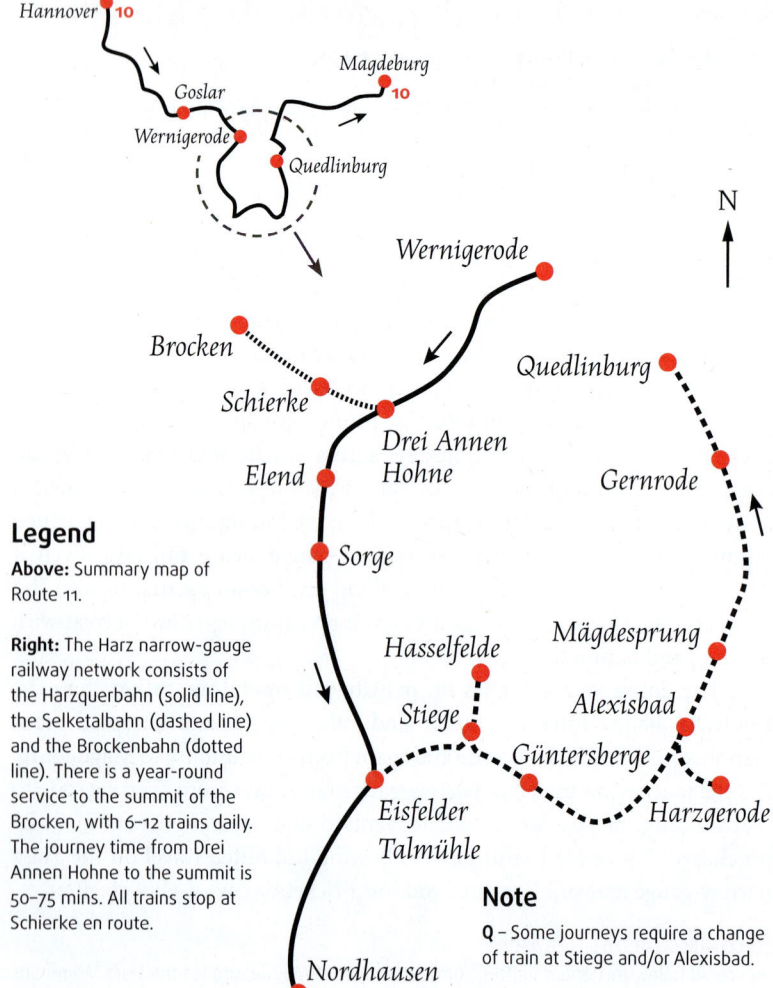

Legend

Above: Summary map of Route 11.

Right: The Harz narrow-gauge railway network consists of the Harzquerbahn (solid line), the Selketalbahn (dashed line) and the Brockenbahn (dotted line). There is a year-round service to the summit of the Brocken, with 6–12 trains daily. The journey time from Drei Annen Hohne to the summit is 50–75 mins. All trains stop at Schierke en route.

Note

Q – Some journeys require a change of train at Stiege and/or Alexisbad.

Route details

Hannover to Goslar

Frequency	Journey time	Notes
Hourly	1h10	

Goslar to Wernigerode

Frequency	Journey time	Notes
Hourly	0h35	

Wernigerode to Drei Annen Hohne

Frequency	Journey time	Notes
6–9 per day	0h40	

Route details (cont.)

Drei Annen Hohne to Eisfelder Talmühle

Frequency	Journey time	Notes
4 per day	1h10	

Eisfelder Talmühle to Quedlinburg

Frequency	Journey time	Notes
4 per day	2h15–3h15	Q

Quedlinburg to Magdeburg Hbf

Frequency	Journey time	Notes
Hourly	1h10–1h20	

Towards the hills

The journey starts at **Hannover** Hauptbahnhof, from where blue-and-yellow trains operated by erixx leave hourly for Goslar. The landscape is initially unremarkable, but soon there are tantalising glimpses of the hills away to the south-east.

All trains pause at **Hildesheim**, a mid-sized town that's worth a stop. It's a busy town, at first glance quite uninviting, but wander into the centre (a 10-min walk south from the main station) and you'll discover a very handsome central area, with two spectacular churches – both inscribed on UNESCO's World Heritage List. Hildesheim is one of northern Germany's best-kept secrets.

From Hildesheim, it is just a short hop on the *erixx* train to **Goslar** which boasts a well preserved mediaeval centre full of half-timbered houses. It owed its prosperity to silver and lead mining in the Middle Ages. At its heart is the **Marktplatz**, presided over by the Rathaus and Marktkirche. It is all very fine, but in our view a shade too touristy. Quedlinburg (further east on this route) offers the same architectural feast but without the crowds. But Goslar is a good jumping-off point for hikes into the hills to the south.

From Goslar, our route continues with a train run by Abellio across the former border between West Germany and East Germany to **Wernigerode**, another historic half-timbered town, notable for what might well be the finest town hall (Rathaus) in all Germany. That, and the extravagant castle, justify a stop. It is here in Wernigerode that the fun begins, as the journey south into the mountains is on the **narrow-gauge Harzquerbahn** (Trans-Harz Railway).

Exploring the Harz Mountains

Trips on the **Harz region steam trains** will appeal to those inclined to savour the ride as much as the destination. You'll have time aplenty to enjoy the journey on trains which chug through woodlands and valleys, for the average speed is only about 25 kilometres per hour.

The network formerly extended into the western Harz, but the routes that ran through West Germany were axed between 1958 and 1963 after harsh cost-benefit analyses which failed to appreciate the potential of the railways as shared community assets. The German Democratic Republic saw the value of **rural railways** in a region that lagged far behind the West in terms of levels of car ownership.

This network (see sketch map on p134) includes a celebrated mountain railway, with steam trains climbing to the highest point in the Harz Mountains which is called the **Brocken**. At 1,141 metres the Brocken is the greatest elevation in northern Germany.

Drei Annen Hohne (suggested stopover)

Drei Annen Hohne is a good base for exploring the region. This railway junction is also the starting point for the branch line (called the **Brockenbahn**) to the summit of the Brocken, an excursion we've made several times. We've found journeys around dusk by far the most memorable. Travelling at that time you'll have the advantage of a completely empty train on the uphill journey, but it does mean that you'll not have much time at the summit before catching the last train back down to Drei Annen Hohne.

Arrival, information, accommodation

Drei Annen Hohne is just a small community with a handful of houses, large car parks and a lovely station building that houses a ticket office and information centre for the Harzquerbahn and a café. The hotel **Der Kräuterhof**, ☎ 0394 558 40 (www.hotel-kraeuterhof.de), is a good place to stay and ideally located just behind the station. Ask for a room with a view of the station to watch the trains go by. The hotel has a restaurant.

The Selke Valley

Whether or not you include the Brocken excursion, our main route follows the **Harzquerbahn** south from Drei Annen Hohne. The start is stunning, as the railway weaves through varied Harz landscapes.

We rate the 29-km stretch from Drei Annen Hohne to Eisfelder Talmühle as one of Europe's finest short train journeys. At **Eisfelder Talmühle**, the main station building houses a decent bar and restaurant if you are minded to break the journey. It is at this station that you switch from the Harzquerbahn to the **Selketalbahn** (Selke Valley railway) for the onward journey to Quedlinburg.

The Selketalbahn traverses landscapes of delicate beauty with many fine opportunities for lineside photography if you are tempted to stop off. The nicest of the many small communities along this line is **Alexisbad**, a small spa town where life is as leisurely as the pace of the trains which stop at the local station. Beyond Alexisbad, the railway drops steeply down from the hills to **Gernrode** on the North German Plain, from where it's just a few minutes across flat country to Quedlinburg.

Quedlinburg (suggested stopover)

The railway station in Quedlinburg is in a wretched state of decay and gives no hint of the beauty of all that waits in the centre of town, just a 12-minute walk north-west of the station. This is one of northern Germany's most engaging small towns. With its remarkable ensemble of **mediaeval buildings**, Quedlinburg knocks spots off the Bavarian competition, yet it still seems undiscovered by non-Germans despite its UNESCO World Heritage status.

Arrival, information, accommodation

The station is a 12-min walk south-east of the main square. Tourist office: Markt 4 (www.quedlinburg-info.de). The hotel **Zum Bär**, Markt 8–9, ☎ 03946 7770 (www.hotelzumbaer.de), is located right on the main square and offers good rooms in a historic building. Other good options are the friendly **Hotel Domschatz**, Mühlenstr. 20, ☎ 03946 70 52 70 (www.hotel-domschatz.de), close to the castle in a quiet location just a 7-min walk from the main square and the **Hotel am Hoken**, Hoken 3, ☎ 03946 525 40 (www.hotel-am-hoken.de), next to the town hall on the main square.

Connections from Quedlinburg

If you want to return to Wernigerode without having to retrace the route by train through the Harz Mountains, there is a useful direct bus from Quedlinburg to **Wernigerode**. Bus service 230 leaves hourly (every 2 hrs on Sat & Sun) from the bus stop by the railway station, and takes about 55 minutes to reach Wernigerode.

On Friday, Saturday and Sunday afternoons, rail operator Abellio runs a great-value express train from **Quedlinburg to Berlin**. The one-way fare (just pay on the train) is €16. This train is marketed as the *Harz-Berlin Express*. Note that rail passes (Interrail, Eurail etc.) are not accepted, nor are Deutsche Bahn train tickets.

To the Elbe Valley

From Quedlinburg, our journey tracks north-east across the plain to **Magdeburg** to rejoin **Route 10** in this book. There is nothing to detain you on the short run from Quedlinburg to Magdeburg, but the latter is definitely worth a look. Approaching Magdeburg from the south, on the train from Quedlinburg, you get little sense of the city's riverside location. But Magdeburg's historical influence and commercial affluence derives entirely from its position on the **River Elbe**. From the main station, it is a 10-minute walk east along Ernst Reuter Allee to the west bank of the river. Take time to wander through the centre and see the city's showpiece Gothic cathedral.

Connections from Magdeburg

Magdeburg is a **major railway junction**. You can follow **Route 10** in this book east to Berlin or west to Hannover and beyond. There are departures at least hourly in both directions. Regional trains leave every hour for Erfurt in Thuringia. Fans of **Bauhaus architecture** and design may be tempted by the hourly trains to Dessau, which is less than an hour away. Read more on Dessau on p141. There are also regular direct trains from Magdeburg to Halle and Leipzig, with some services continuing beyond Leipzig to Dresden.

East German steam

Apart from the Harz region, there are a number of other narrow-gauge steam railways in eastern Germany. You might want to explore the **Rügensche Bäderbahn** which runs through lovely beech woods on the island of Rügen. Also on Germany's Baltic coast, another classic steam outing is the **Molli-Bahn** to Heiligendamm and Kühlungsborn, mentioned on p292 in this book. In Saxony, steam still runs year-round on a line which climbs into the hills behind **Zittau** and on another at **Radebeul** in the Elbe Valley near Dresden.

Route 12: From Berlin to the Alps

Cities: ★★★ Culture: ★ History: ★★ Scenery: ★★
Countries covered: Germany (DE), Austria (AT)
Journey time: 10 hrs | Distance: 943 km | Map: www.ebrweb.eu/18map12

This long journey from **Berlin to Bavaria** and on across the Austrian border to **Salzburg** takes in some very fine German cities (including Leipzig, Weimar and Munich) and some decent countryside – of which the two highlights are the hill country of Thuringia in the middle of the route and the Chiemgau area of Upper Bavaria. The latter gives a grand finale to the journey on the approach to Salzburg.

Route 12 is one of two in this book which lead travellers from northern Germany to the Alps. The other is **Route 9** from Cologne to Zurich via the Rhine Valley and the Black Forest. Both these routes are ideal components in longer itineraries extending from **northern Europe to the Mediterranean** (or vice versa). As you travel the length of Route 12 there is a real sense of swapping cool and practical Prussian restraint for the more easy-going southern pieties.

This route takes in both halves of Germany, viz. the former German Democratic Republic (DDR) and the western part of the country. That erstwhile political division slips slowly into history. Not so the **north-south culinary divide**. Our journey starts in undisputed *Currywurst* territory – although the traditional Berlin curried sausage is not a snack of great antiquity. In the late 1940s American soldiers added ketchup and British forces threw in curry powder and Worcester Sauce to give a much-needed kick to Berlin's anaemic pork sausages. Few Berliners would give shelf space to a Bavarian white sausage (*Weißwurst* in German), any more than lads from Munich would resort to a *Currywurst*.

Route 12 breaches the **Weißwurstgrenze**, that never quite defined but universally acknowledged frontier which will forever separate Prussia from Bavaria, north from south, Protestants from Catholics. Our journey traverses various sausage territories. In Weimar and Erfurt, look out for the famous grilled *Thüringer*; as you move south don't miss the spicy *Würzburger* and the finger-sized *Nürnberger*. Having sucked on mushy *Weißwurst* in Munich, you'll be all set to tackle the celebrated Salzburg *Bosna*, served in a roll much like a hot dog.

Itinerary notes

The beauty of rail travel in Germany is that seat reservations are never compulsory on daytime trains, and there are no supplements for those travelling with Eurail and Interrail passes. So this is a good route for just **hopping on and off at will**. You have a choice of fast services (ie. Intercity or ICE) and slower trains for most legs of the route. It's a journey which could so easily be spun out to a week or more. If you can afford just **three overnight stops**, we would opt for Weimar, Würzburg and Munich.

ROUTE 12: FROM BERLIN TO THE ALPS | 139

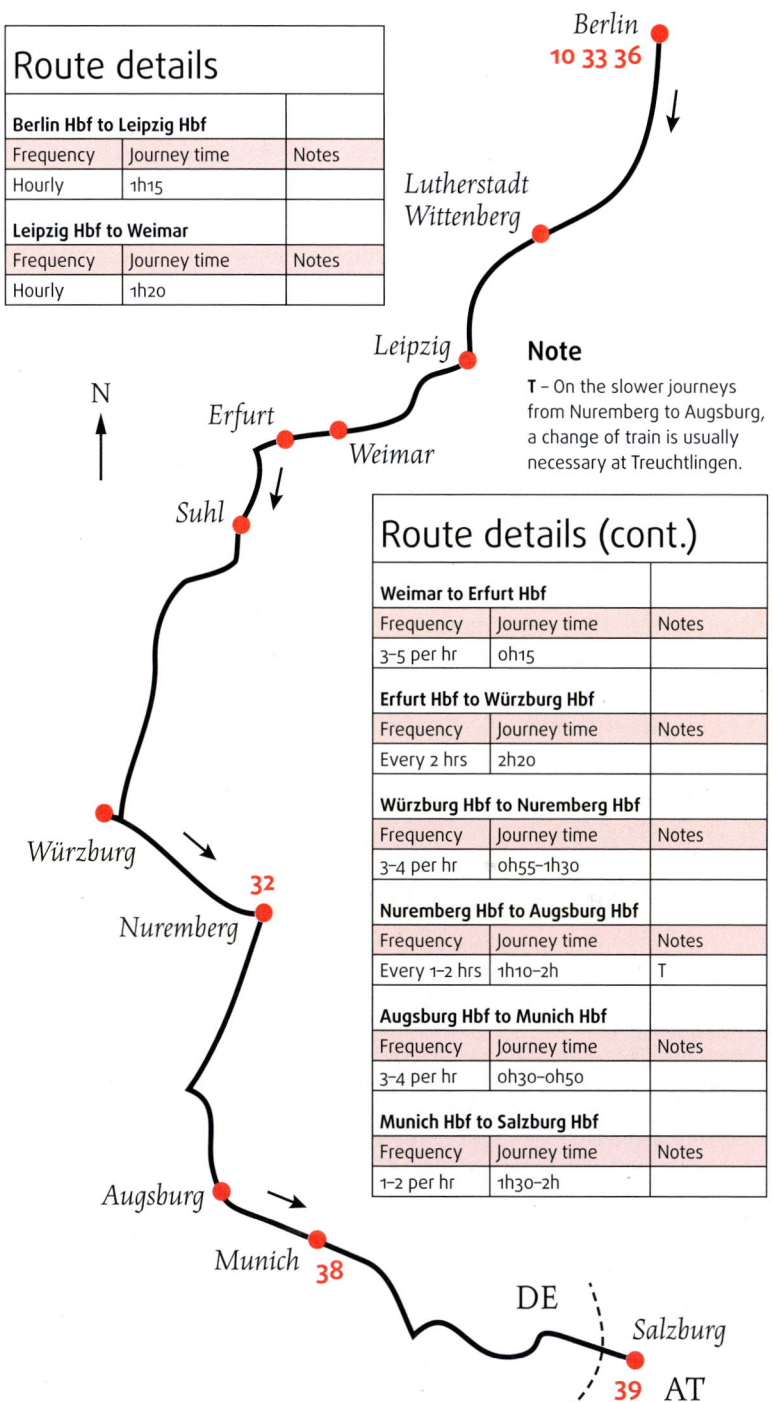

Route details

Berlin Hbf to Leipzig Hbf

Frequency	Journey time	Notes
Hourly	1h15	

Leipzig Hbf to Weimar

Frequency	Journey time	Notes
Hourly	1h20	

Note

T – On the slower journeys from Nuremberg to Augsburg, a change of train is usually necessary at Treuchtlingen.

Route details (cont.)

Weimar to Erfurt Hbf

Frequency	Journey time	Notes
3–5 per hr	0h15	

Erfurt Hbf to Würzburg Hbf

Frequency	Journey time	Notes
Every 2 hrs	2h20	

Würzburg Hbf to Nuremberg Hbf

Frequency	Journey time	Notes
3–4 per hr	0h55–1h30	

Nuremberg Hbf to Augsburg Hbf

Frequency	Journey time	Notes
Every 1–2 hrs	1h10–2h	T

Augsburg Hbf to Munich Hbf

Frequency	Journey time	Notes
3–4 per hr	0h30–0h50	

Munich Hbf to Salzburg Hbf

Frequency	Journey time	Notes
1–2 per hr	1h30–2h	

The countryside between **Berlin** (for more on the German capital see p131) and Leipzig is largely uninspiring, but dotted away here and there are a few interesting towns. Pick of the bunch is **Lutherstadt Wittenberg**, served by many of the fast trains en route from the German capital to Leipzig. In 2017, the town celebrated the 500th anniversary of the Reformation. It was in 1517 that **Martin Luther** pinned his famous theses to the door of a church in Wittenberg.

This handsome small town is worth a visit not merely on account of its Luther connections and the inevitable memorials to the reforming pastor, but also as a chance to see a former East German town that is a little off the beaten track. The **Haus der Geschichte** (House of History) at Schlossstr. 6 gives rich insights into everyday life in the German Democratic Republic from 1949 to 1989.

Leipzig has been a cultural centre for many centuries, famous particularly for its music: numerous great 19th-century works were premiered at the **Gewandhaus**, Augustuspl. 8. The original building is long gone, but the current Gewandhaus is a very fine piece of DDR architecture from 1981. Second only to Vienna for its **musical tradition**, the city was the home of Bach, Mendelssohn and Schumann.

The Gewandhaus Orchestra, Opera House and the Thomanerchor (St Thomas's Church Choir), which was conducted by Bach for 27 years, have a world-class reputation. Take a stroll around the **pedestrianised centre**, where many long-neglected buildings and arcades are fast acquiring rows of smart shops, restaurants and offices. Yet Leipzig retains some of the grace of an old European city.

SLOW TRAVEL DEALS IN GERMANY

Germany has some amazingly good deals for rail travellers prepared to avoid the fastest trains (generally those with an ICE, IC or EC prefix) and stick only to **local or regional train services**. This is a train category called *Nahverkehr* in German. Many of these regional trains make quite long journeys, with many routes extending to well over 300 kilometres. Since May 2023, a mere €49 purchases a full month of unlimited travel on *Nahverkehr* – though there is talk of increasing the price. It's a truly exceptional deal.

Regional tickets covering each German state (or two or more adjacent states) are called **Ländertickets**. For example, the **Bayern Ticket** gives unlimited travel in Bavaria for a day; it costs €29 for one person or €69 for a group of five (for more details see www.ebrweb.eu/5). There is a useful one-day pass valid for nationwide travel. The **Quer-durchs-Land Ticket** (QdL) is priced from €46 for one to €82 for five travellers; it can be used on Mondays to Fridays after 09.00 or anytime at weekends. You can see just what a bargain the QdL ticket is by looking at its potential use in Route 12. It is just possible to travel from Berlin to Salzburg using only *Nahverkehr* services, precisely following Route 12, in a single day. That journey takes 16 hours. Make that trip with the QdL ticket, which is valid beyond the Austrian border to Salzburg, and the one-way fare for one person would be €46 – and there's **no need to pre-book**. Prices correct as of autumn 2024.

Bauhaus architecture

Lutherstadt Wittenberg is a good jumping-off point to visit **Dessau**, the UNESCO World Heritage city that is so popular with fans of 20th-century architecture, but curiously unknown among a wider public. Dessau is the **Bauhaus town** par excellence. Trains from both stations at Wittenberg run at least hourly to Dessau, about 40 mins distant. The main Bauhaus building is just a 4-min walk from the back entrance of Dessau Hauptbahnhof. Catch it on a good day, and the glass curtain facade looks superb against a blue sky.

Other Bauhaus highlights include the **Meisterhäuser** (Masters' Houses), a 20-min walk from the station. These classic Bauhaus buildings were once the homes of the architects, artists and designers who brought such revolutionary impetus to the Bauhaus movement. The roll call of illustrious residents includes Paul Klee, Wassily Kandinsky and Walter Gropius. Don't miss the **Kornhaus Restaurant** (www.kornhaus-dessau.de), a classic piece of Bauhaus style, on the bank of the Elbe. Take 🚌 10 or 11 from Hauptbahnhof directly to Kornhaus. The new Bauhaus Museum (www.bauhaus-dessau.de) which opened in September 2019 in time for the centenary celebrations of the Bauhaus school, is also on those bus routes. There is no need to return to Lutherstadt Wittenberg to continue your journey, for Dessau is served by direct local trains to Leipzig.

In 1989, the mass demonstrations and candlelit vigils in Nikolaikirche, Nikolaikirchhof 3, were the focus for the city's peaceful revolt against the East German state authorities. The Stasi 'Power and Banality' Museum, Dittrichring 24, in the former **Ministry of State Security**, reviews the apparatus of State surveillance and control.

On the edge of the **Innenstadt** (city centre), a 10-min walk to the middle, Leipzig's station is an attraction in its own right, and is one of Europe's biggest and most impressive. Built in 1915, it has in the last two decades been refurbished. If you are minded to stay in Leipzig, the Townhouse Leipzig, Thomaskirchhof 13/14, ☎ 0341 496 140 (www.vagabondclub.com) is in a great location just opposite the Thomaskirche in a listed building. Very convenient for the station is the modern and comfortable Seaside Park Hotel Leipzig, Richard-Wagner-Str. 7, ☎ 0341 985 20 (www.parkhotelleipzig.de).

The **high-speed line** from Leipzig to Erfurt opened in late 2015, so the fastest trains bypass Weimar, but we think it's worth taking the old line which follows the River Saale and then the Ilm upstream to Weimar – along the way passing the first large vineyards on this route.

Weimar (suggested stopover)

Smart shops, pavement cafés and a lively Onion Fair, which takes over the town for the second weekend in October, are outward signs of Weimar's vitality. But, famously, Weimar is steeped in German culture, having been the home of two of the country's greatest writers, **Goethe and Schiller**, as well as the composers **Bach, Liszt and Richard Strauss**, the painter **Lucas Cranach** and the philosopher **Nietzsche**.

Weimar was also where the pre-Nazi Weimar Republic was founded. The entire town centre, with its wide tree-lined avenues, elegant squares and fine buildings, is designated a historic monument. Architecture fans should not miss Weimar's Bauhaus connections. Look out for the **Haus am Horn** (Am Horn 61), a modernist prototype of Bauhaus demeanour that relieves the tedium of Weimar's baroque mansions.

The baroque mansion where Goethe lived, **Goethehaus**, Frauenplan 1 (closed Mon), displays furniture, personal belongings and a library of 5,400 books. A stroll across the little River Ilm in the peaceful **Park an der Ilm** leads to the simple Gartenhaus, his first home in town and later his retreat. Goethe himself became a tourist attraction: people travelled from afar to glimpse the great man. In the **Marktplatz** a plaque marks the house in the south corner where Bach lived when he was leader of the court orchestra. The Liszthaus (closed Tues), on the town side of the park at Marienstr. 17, is the beautifully maintained residence of the Austro-Hungarian composer Franz Liszt. He moved to Weimar in 1848 to direct the local orchestra and spent the last 17 summers of his life here.

Ten kilometres north of Weimar is the memorial museum and site of **Buchenwald concentration camp**, a grim reminder of the horrors of the Nazi regime during the Second World War (closed Mon, easily reached by 🚌 6 from Goetheplatz and the railway station; see www.buchenwald.de).

ARRIVAL, INFORMATION, ACCOMMODATION

✈ A 20-min walk north of the centre (🚌 6/7). 🛈 Tourist office: Markt 4 (www.weimar.de). City tours daily at 10.00 and 14.00 for a fee of €10 (in German). 🍴 Close to the Markt, the highly regarded **36 Pho Co** hotel, Kaufstr. 2/4, ☎ 03643 600 1701 (www.pho-co-weimar.de) has individually designed rooms with Asian flair. The owners also run a Vietnamese restaurant opposite. Located on the edge of the Old Town and close to the Park an der Ilm is the **Hotel Amalienhof**, Amalienstraße 2, ☎ 03643 54 90 (www.amalienhof-weimar.de) with a more traditional ambience. The centrally located **Hotel Erbenhof**, Brauhausgasse 10, ☎ 03643 494 40 (www.hotel-am-frauenplan.de) is good value for money.

Just 25 kilometres beyond Weimar, **Erfurt** has shot to prominence as a tourist attraction, with its substantial variety of attractive old buildings from mills to monasteries, much spruced up since German unification. A flight of 70 steps leads up to Dom St Marien, the hilltop Gothic cathedral beside the Domplatz, a large marketplace and useful tram stop.

An array of decorative buildings surround **Fischmarkt**. To the west is Krämerbrücke, a 14th-century river bridge lined with old houses and shops, best seen from the river itself. In the 15th century, Erfurt was noted for its altarpieces and a superb example can be seen in Reglerkirche, Bahnhofstr.

CONNECTIONS FROM ERFURT

New **high-speed railway lines** have given Erfurt added prominence as a rail hub. The new fast line to Halle and Leipzig has brought Erfurt within two hours of Berlin. In late 2015, a new non-stop service to Frankfurt-am-Main was launched. In late 2017, a new 190-km long fast line from Erfurt to Bamberg in Bavaria opened.

Long gone are the days when Erfurt had direct night trains to Warsaw and Moscow. But the city is still served (albeit not every night) by a direct **Nightjet to Paris**. There are twice-daily fast trains to Vienna. Closer to hand, there's a useful local service running north to Nordhausen, giving a link onto the **Harz narrow-gauge network** described in **Route 11**. By far the prettiest of the local lines spanning out from Erfurt is that via Suhl to Würzburg, which is followed by Route 12.

The next leg of our journey, from **Erfurt on to Würzburg** reveals just how unhelpful online journey planners can be. Most websites will suggest taking a fast ICE and changing at either Fulda or Bamberg to reach Würzburg. You could do very much better by sticking to regional train services which take a more direct route through the hills.

True, it'll take 20 to 30 minutes longer but you'll be rewarded by some fabulous scenery. **Gently rounded hills**, dense forests and folded valleys are the landscape themes in a region which is home to lynx and wolves. As you travel through this part of Thuringia, you'll see small villages which evoke images of mediaeval Europe.

Leaving Erfurt, the regional train to Würzburg crosses gently undulating terrain to reach Arnstadt, a beautiful small town which makes much of its Bach connection: the composer spent four productive years there. Pausing at Plaue, the railway then cuts through the **Thüringer Wald** (Thuringian Forest) nature reserve – relying part on deep cuttings and tunnels, but there are stretches with good views.

Beyond the hills, the train stops at **Suhl**, an improbably large place given its relative remoteness. It greatly expanded in the 1960s as an important administrative centre in East Germany. It is, to be frank, quite an eyesore. The railway then tracks south-west through pleasant countryside, partly forested, to cross the former border between East Germany and West Germany and reach the first stop in Bavaria at Mellrichstadt. From there, it's a easy run south to Schweinfurt and Würzburg.

Würzburg (suggested stopover)

Würzburg is a university town where in autumn the **Winzerfest**, a traditional annual harvest festival, celebrates the (justly famous) Franconian wines – one of the most celebrated of the local vineyards rises up by the station.

The rebuilt domes, spires and red roofs are seen at their best from the terrace battlements of **Festung Marienberg**, an impressive white fortress on a wooded hill above the River Main. Converted to baroque style in the 17th century, little remains inside, though the **Museum für Franken** (www.museum-franken.de, closed Mon) displays a large collection of works by Franconian artists, including superb 16th-century woodcarvings by one of the city's most famous sons, Tilman Riemenschneider. The Festung is best reached by 🚌 9 (from Apr–Oct) in just a 16-min ride. Otherwise it is a 40-min walk.

The marketplace is notable for the **Marienkapelle**, a 14th-century church with more Riemenschneider carvings, and the richly decorated 18th-century Falkenhaus, which houses the tourist office. The town's main sight is the massive sandstone **Residenz** on the eastern edge of town. Built as the new palace of the prince-bishops in the 18th century by Balthasar Neumann, it has been given World Heritage Site status. Statues line the roof facade, symbolising the Church's wealth and power. The rooms are sumptuously decorated with frescos and sculptures by leading artists of their day, including the Venetian master Tiepolo. **Evening bevvies** aplenty in and around Sanderstrasse, popular with students.

Arrival, information, accommodation

🚆 Würzburg Hbf, at the foot of vineyards on the northern edge of the town centre, a 15-min walk. 🛈 Tourist office: in the Falkenhaus, Marktplatz 9 (www.wuerzburg.de).

🛏 There is no shortage of hotels. Just two minutes from the cathedral, the friendly, owner-run **Hotel Franziskaner**, Franziskanerplatz 2, ☎ 0931 356 30 (www.hotel-franziskaner.de) is a good option right in the centre of the Old Town. Or stay at the very centrally located **Hotel Alter Kranen**, Kärrnergasse 11, ☎ 0931 35 18-0 (www.hotel-alter-kranen.de) right on the bank of the River Main.

It is a hop of just a hundred kilometres from Würzburg to Nuremberg, cutting through the gentle **Steigerwald Hills** which lie to the south of the Main Valley. The poet Henry Wadsworth Longfellow had mixed feelings about **Nuremberg** (Nürnberg), calling it "a quaint old town of toil and traffic." Nowadays the city of **Lebkuchen** (a speciality Advent gingerbread) is trying to cast off its associations with Nazi rallies and war trials.

Heading north from the station, you immediately enter the **Old Town** with its impressive Stadtbefestigung (city wall). Beyond the Schöner Brunnen (Beautiful Fountain), the spacious **Hauptmarkt** (market square) makes a perfect setting for one of Germany's liveliest Christmas markets.

Hitler's mass rallies were held in the vast **Reichsparteitagsgelände** (in the Luitpoldhain, in the south-eastern suburbs), a huge area with a parade ground, stadium and the shell of a massive congress hall that was never completed. One of the remaining parts, the **Zeppelin grandstand** (S-Bahn line 2 to Frankenstadion) hosts an exhibition called *Faszination und Gewalt* (Fascination and Violence). If you've used this book to plan your travels to Nuremberg, chances are you will be interested in the **DB Museum** (Verkehrsmuseum Nürnberg), just five minutes from the station at Lessingstr. 6 (www.dbmuseum.de; closed Mon). The major exhibits are managed by German national rail operator Deutsche Bahn and give a good account of German railway history. A second exhibition focuses on other aspects of communication and includes an excellent display of old post coaches. For a note on Nuremberg's identity as a central European city, see p299.

Connections from Nuremberg
You can connect in Nuremberg onto **Route 32** to Prague. Nuremberg is a major hub on Germany's ICE network, with fast trains to most principal German cities, among them Hamburg, Cologne and Munich. The latter is just an hour away on the fastest trains. There are also direct trains to Vienna

---

If you can resist the temptation of taking the fast train to Munich (see our connections from Nuremberg above), then there's much to be seen on the 'old' Nuremberg to Munich line which runs via **Augsburg**. It runs south through pleasant Franconian countryside, crossing the River Danube at Donauwörth and then following the Lech Valley upstream to Augsburg.

Just a stone's throw from Munich, Augsburg nowadays is overshadowed by its larger Bavarian neighbour. But there was a time when Augsburg was respected as one of the largest and most influential centres in all Europe. Be it as a hub for finance and trade, in its social programmes to alleviate poverty or as a centre of Jewish life and culture, Augsburg towered above its rivals. The key to this were two families, the **Welsers** and the **Fuggers** who, in the early 16th century, dominated Augsburg life. The Fuggerei (enter from Jakoberstrasse; tram route 1) is a bold social housing experiment founded by Jakob Fugger. There is a predictably imposing cathedral on the hilly north side of the city centre, and, just a stone's throw from the Hauptbahnhof (on Halderstr. 8), one of Germany's most remarkable **synagogues**.

King Ludwig's castles

Many visitors to Bavaria feel compelled to make an excursion to the royal castles at Füssen, the most famous of which was built at preposterous expense by King Ludwig II. The easiest way of getting to **Neuschwanstein** and **Hohenschwangau** is to take a train to Füssen, an attractive old town beneath the mountains, served by direct trains from both Augsburg and Munich. The journey from Augsburg is rather shorter.

Hohenschwangau and Neuschwanstein are within walking distance of each other (involving a modest climb). Tudor-style Hohenschwangau, built in the early 19th century by **Maximilian II**, was an attempt to recreate the romantic past and was adorned with Wagnerian references by his son, **King Ludwig II**. Ludwig then surpassed his father by building the fairy-tale neo-Gothic Neuschwanstein on a rocky outcrop high above. It might be read as a clever postmodern fantasy, but the great majority of visitors perceive Neuschwanstein as a **Disneyesque** dive into mediaeval Germany. Hohenschwangau, a real castle which was a family home, has been upstaged by an utter fabrication which was never completed – hence the throne room without a throne, and doorways leading to suicidal drops.

Neuschwanstein is really best seen from a distance. If you've a head for heights, the best vantage point is the Marienbrücke, a bridge spanning a huge gorge. The really sad thing is that Germany has real mediaeval castles aplenty, yet it is a fake castle that pulls the crowds.

Munich (suggested stopover)

The less you know about Munich (München), the easier it is to define. Right – it's the **Oktoberfest** city, full of ruddy-cheeked people in lederhosen singing 'ein prosit, ein prosit' with foaming steins raised. But after a few trips – or even a few days – you'll soon discover that Munich is more than just beer. Munich is **affluent and stylish**, with a world-class cultural scene, superb museums, and some of Germany's best restaurants. Join students, artists, musicians and Munich's young crowd on the city's left bank. Schwabing is north of the centre, and a good way to get there is to take the U-Bahn to Münchner Freiheit.

Try Bavarian specialities or pick up the makings of a picnic from around the world at the **Viktualienmarkt** – one of Europe's finest produce markets, right in the heart of the city. Exit Marienplatz to the east and then walk around the corner. Munich's **Lenbachhaus** by the Königsplatz houses the world's largest collection of works by the avant-garde **Blue Rider group** and further 20th-century art (www.lenbachhaus.de; closed Mon).

Munich's location is also a huge asset, with easy access to lakes and mountains, and superb transport connections to Italy, Switzerland, Austria and destinations further south as well as the rest of Germany.

ARRIVAL, INFORMATION, ACCOMMODATION

🚆 München Hauptbahnhof (Hbf), about 1 km due west of Marienplatz in the city centre is the city's main railway station; ✈ Franz Josef Strauss Airport, 30 km north-east of Munich city centre (www.munich-airport.de). S-Bahn lines S1 and S8 run every 10 mins from the rail station via the Ostbahnhof and city centre to the airport, taking 40 mins.

ℹ The main tourist office is at Marienplatz 8 (www.muenchen.travel). For a walking tour with a knowledgeable English-speaking guide, try **Munich Walk Tours**, ☎ 089 24 23 17 67 (www.munichwalktours.de), which also cover Dachau, a brewery tour, a cycle tour and a Third Reich Tour.

🛏 Finding accommodation is rarely a problem except during the city's biggest tourist attractions, the annual Oktoberfest beer festival (mid Sept–early Oct) and Fasching, the bacchanalian carnival that precedes Ash Wednesday. The biggest choice of hotels is around the rail station in streets like Schillerstr. and Senefelderstr.; it's a rather drab area but handy for the centre. A mid-range one is the **Leonardo Hotel München City Center**, Senefelderstr. 4, ☎ 089 551 540 (www.leonardo-hotels.com). A comfortable option not far from the city centre is the **Admiral**, Kohlstr. 9, ☎ 089 21 63 50 (www.hotel-admiral.de). Or try the **Cocoon Hauptbahnhof**, Mittererstraße 9, ☎ 089 54 80 18 99 05 (www.cocoon-hotels.de) with its Alpine-themed design, just a short walk from the station.

It is just 150 kilometres from Munich to Salzburg, but what a journey! Sit on the right side of the train for fine views of the Alps as you approach **Salzburg** (more on the city on p363). Closer to the railway, and on both sides of the train, are the delicate landscapes of the **Chiemgau**. It is a stunning end to a journey which started on the banks of the River Spree in Berlin and ends by the Salzach near the Austrian-German border.

A TASTE OF FRANCE
An introduction

How might one best get a taste of France by train? There is, to be sure, a real thrill in being on a high-speed train as it storms out of a rail tunnel for a **first encounter with France**. Perhaps you are emerging from the Channel Tunnel to find the grey skies of Calais. Or possibly you are on a sleek Spanish train which has dived under the Pyrenees through the Perthus Tunnel and dashes out into sharp southern sunshine after a subterranean crossing of the border **from Spain to France**. You might be slipping quietly over the French frontier on a local train through the Jura hills or on one trundling through German vineyards to enter Alsace at Wissembourg.

Whatever way you arrive in France, and particularly if you arrive by train or boat rather than by plane, there is **a sense of occasion**. To get the most out of your rail travels around France, it is important to cut off the high-speed lines and explore lesser rail routes.

The first French high-speed railway was opened in 1981 – that was between Paris and Lyon. Four decades on, the country has almost 3,000 km of high-speed lines, known in France as *lignes à grande vitesse* (LGV). That's a magnificent achievement, one which has enhanced regional connectivity and reshaped the geography of France. But, let's face it, those **LGV routes** were certainly not designed for sightseeing.

Life beyond the high-speed routes

Happily, France still has a very extensive web of traditional railways, quite apart from the modern LGV network. Several routes in this book all rely on these non-high-speed lines which criss-cross the country. We have included **some of our favourites**, but there were many potential candidates. Would that there had been space to include the 277-km long *ligne des Causses* from Béziers to Neussargues or the 'old' line from Paris to Mulhouse via Troyes and Belfort. Whenever we have the time, that's still our preferred route for journeys from the French capital to Basel (Bâle) and the northernmost cantons of Switzerland.

Whereas, almost without exception, seats must be reserved in advance for trains using high-speed routes, you can travel with much more spontaneity if you stay off LGV routes. Some, but by no means all, Intercités trains require seat reservations. And the entire **TER network** of regional trains is there for you to roam at will. None of these trains need advance reservation.

When you are planning longer-distance journeys through **rural France**, it is worth bearing in mind that services may be thin. The idea of easily memorised regular-interval departure times has never quite caught on in France. So check those schedules carefully! ■

Route 13: From London to the Mediterranean

Cities: ★★ Culture: ★★ History: ★ Scenery: ★★
Countries covered: England (ENG), France (FR)
Journey time: 13 hrs 40 mins | Distance: 1,347 km | Map: www.ebrweb.eu/18map13

This first journey to France in *Europe by Rail* kicks off with an exquisite piece of theatre. It starts at **London's St Pancras station**, as inspiring a space as any cathedral. Great train stations have their own energy, each with its own shades and shadows. At St Pancras there is a bluish tinge to the light which picks up the blue of the soaring ironwork in William Barlow's dramatic train shed. Take time to linger at St Pancras, a station rescued from dereliction through a superb restoration. Then join us for a **fast run to Paris** on Eurostar. We continue south from the French capital on a route which takes us to the shores of the Mediterranean. For lovers of rural landscapes, that journey from Paris to southern France is much superior to the more usual route along high-speed lines. We follow an old main line for the entire route from **Paris to the Mediterranean**, cutting through the mountainous Massif Central region. From the French capital to Clermont-Ferrand we follow the *ligne du Bourbonnais*, then we ride the *ligne des Cévennes* – one of Europe's finest railways – on to Nîmes.

Itinerary options
Paris, of course, demands a stop. It is then perfectly possible to complete this journey in a day, leaving Paris after breakfast and arriving in **Marseille** by 19.40. But there's such a feast of scenery on this route that we recommend also breaking the journey at **Vichy**.
   You might consider taking one of the slightly slower trains for the first leg from Paris to Nevers. This route takes in one of the nicest stretches of the Loire Valley, and it's a pity to dash through on a fast express which does not stop between Paris and Nevers. After a leisurely lunch in Nevers, you could then continue to Vichy for an overnight stay. Next day, the journey continues via **Clermont-Ferrand** to Marseille. Should you only leave Paris in the afternoon, Nevers is also a good choice for an overnight stop.

The commuter crowds are long gone, and St Pancras has settled into the quiet rhythm of a spring day when all the trains are running to time. The first corks have been popped at the station's pretentiously long champagne bar, and oysters and quail eggs are being served to those who know a *blanc de blancs* from a *blanc de noirs*. The area just north of the station, once a maze of sheds and sidings, coal dumps and grain stores, has been reclaimed, but happily not entirely tamed. **Camley Street Park**, tucked into land between the railway and Regent's Canal, is a sanctuary just a stone's throw from the platforms at St Pancras. It is a place to listen to reed warblers and watch a lively siskin searching for seeds. There is hazel, willow and silver birch.
   On the other side of the railway tracks, headstones are stacked neatly around an old oak tree. They were placed there when graves were moved in Victorian times to allow the **Midland Railway** to build its line into St Pancras.

Route 13: From London to the Mediterranean | 149

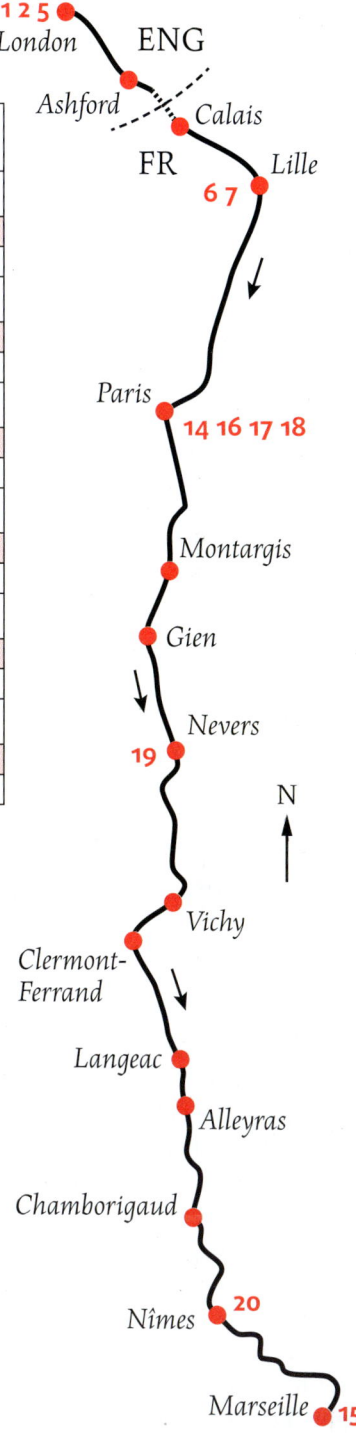

Route details

London St Pancras to Paris Nord

Frequency	Journey time	Notes
Hourly	2h20–2h30	

Paris Bercy to Nevers

Frequency	Journey time	Notes
Every 1–2 hrs	2h10–2h40	

Nevers to Vichy

Frequency	Journey time	Notes
Every 2–3 hrs	1h	

Vichy to Clermont-Ferrand

Frequency	Journey time	Notes
Hourly	0h30–0h35	A

Clermont-Ferrand to Nîmes

Frequency	Journey time	Notes
2–3 per day	5h–5h30	B

Nîmes to Marseille St Charles

Frequency	Journey time	Notes
Every 1–2 hrs	1h10–1h30	

Notes

A – Frequent trains run between Vichy and Clermont-Ferrand in the morning and late afternoon rush hours on Mondays to Fridays.
B – Services on the *ligne des Cévennes* from Clermont-Ferrand to Nîmes are very prone to alterations due to engineering work on the line.

The **numbers in red** adjacent to some cities on our route maps refer to other routes in this book which also include that particular city.

A young trainee architect named **Thomas Hardy** helped clear part of the cemetery; he of course changed profession and become a celebrated writer. Just as St Pancras station, after a long period of decline, changed course and reinvented itself as London's gateway to the continent.

From the Thames to the Seine

"I have little doubt that British Railways will do away with St Pancras altogether," said the poet **John Betjeman** in 1952. "It is too beautiful and too romantic to survive. It is not of this age." But, despite decades of corporate neglect and vandalism, St Pancras has indeed survived and a huge statue of the poet, hand on hat, now stands on the station concourse. The rejuvenation of St Pancras station and the surrounding area is indeed a wondrous thing.

The journey on **Eurostar** from London to Paris is one of many moods and changing landscapes. Within a minute or two of departure, London is eclipsed by darkness. Watch for tantalising shadows at Stratford, then a burst of sunshine as our train, picking up speed now, storms out of the London tunnels onto the Thames marshes. This is a busy, fractured world of overhead pylons, silt lagoons and container parks: the melancholic edge-lands where the capital blurs with Essex.

Eurostar dives under the **River Thames**, emerging in moments into industrial north Kent, which quickly transforms into a green and pleasant land. The **Medway Viaduct** is a gem; the train speeds over the river where once the Dutch tried to attack the English fleet. The view up the Medway Valley (to the right of the train) is one of delicate beauty.

The rail route dances with the ancient Pilgrim's Way, coasting past orchards and oast houses, and within half an hour of leaving London we are approaching the **Channel Tunnel**. Emerging from the tunnel after 25 minutes, the first glimpses of France at Calais do the country no favours. But industry quickly gives way to an expansive rural landscape. Brick villages sit squat in Flanders fields.

Speeding south-east towards Lille, the town of **Cassel** stands bold and clear on a rare hill away to the left. Just beyond **Lille**, our Paris-bound train turns sharply to the right, now heading decisively south towards Picardy. We dash through a landscape once full of sandbags and barbed wire, now scattered with war cemeteries that burst with poppies. The ashen face of death, drenched by hopeless rain and shrapnel scarred, has been replaced by a quiet beauty, broken only by the whoosh of the fast trains that speed by on their way to Paris.

This is territory defined by its rivers. We cross the Scarpe, the Somme and the Oise. The first clear hint of approaching Paris is the line of planes away to our left descending into Charles de Gaulle airport. Suddenly, to the right, there is a tantalising glimpse of the River Seine.

The Gare du Nord

Our journey on Eurostar ends at the Gare du Nord. Each of the principal railway stations in Paris has its own character. Saint-Lazare is for artists (think Manet and Monet) while the Gare de Lyon has the lure of the sunny south of France. The Gare de l'Est is the place where there are meetings and greetings as the thrice-weekly night train from Vienna arrives. But the Gare du Nord is a place apart, a station where the routine comings and goings are unexceptional. It is in a part of Paris full of moral and sexual hazards – hardly changed from the days of *L'Assommoir* except that the downtrodden working-class French residents of **Émile Zola's day** have been replaced by migrants from across the world.

If, like us, you need to pause after such a fast train journey, then make for the courtyard of **Lariboisière Hospital**, as close to the Gare du Nord as the canalside wilderness at Camley Street is to St Pancras. No wilderness or warblers here, but an elegant and quiet space surrounded by neoclassical colonnades. It's a good spot to ponder your onward journey, for Paris is just the beginning, as the French capital is the starting point for five journeys described in this book.

Paris (suggested stopover)

Paris has always held great allure – it's been a byword for **style, glamour and romance** since railway tourism began and the English started to go there for weekends in the 19th century. **Baron Haussmann** transformed the city for Napoleon III, sweeping away many of its crowded slum quarters and replacing them with tree-lined boulevards too wide to barricade. Today, these stately avenues of elegantly matching, shuttered buildings and imposing monuments form the framework of much of modern Paris.

The Île de la Cité in the River Seine, scarred by the fire which so terribly damaged **Notre-Dame** Cathedral in April 2019, is still the heart of the city. Students traditionally hang out in the Latin Quarter on the Left Bank, so-called because studies at the Sorbonne were originally in Latin. The once seedy area around the Bastille has shaken off its revolutionary past to become one of the city's trendiest nightspots with a multitude of bars and restaurants. Older quarters such as **Le Marais and Montmartre** remain warrens of picturesque old streets.

Apart from traditional museums such as the Louvre, Paris has a galaxy of fine modern museums. Check out Citéco (all about economics and money), the Fondation Louis Vuitton (contemporary art) and Musée Yves Saint Laurent (fashion history). Rail history buffs might be interested in the fact that the home of one of Paris' most famous museums – **Musée d'Orsay** – is a grand structure that was built as a train station for the World's Fair in 1900.

Arrival, information, accommodation

🚆 There are seven main rail stations in Paris, each has its own métro stop; all except Montparnasse and Gare de l'Est are also served by express RER trains. Take advantage of the efficient and well coordinated public transport system, made up of the métro and buses of RATP (Régie Autonome des Transports Parisiens) and RER (Réseau Express Régional) trains. RER trains run about 06.00–00.30, consisting of five rail lines (A, B, C, D and E), which are basically express services between the city and the suburbs. 🛈 Tourist office: Hôtel de Ville, 29 r. de Rivoli (www.parisinfo.com) and at Gare du Nord. The **Batobus** (www.batobus.com), is a water-bus (without commentary) and a good way of seeing Paris from the Seine. The Batobus stops at the Eiffel Tower, Musée d'Orsay, St-Germain-des-Prés, Notre-Dame, Jardin des Plantes, Hôtel de Ville, the Louvre, Place de la Concorde and Invalides.

🛏 Cheaper accommodation is getting harder to find anywhere near the city centre, and if you're on a tight budget, you may have to stay out of the centre. We can very much recommend the comfortable **Hôtel du Jeu de Paume**, 54 r. Saint-Louis-en-l'île, ☎ 01 43 26 14 18 (www.jeudepaumehotel.com), which is on the Île Saint-Louis in the middle of the Seine, just a few minutes' walk away from Notre-Dame. The location could not be better – but it has its price. The **Hôtel Langlois**, 63 r. Saint Lazare, ☎ 01 48 74 78 24 (www.hotel-langlois.com), is a lovely place full of character and well worth the price-tag. A good option in Montmartre in a quiet street is the boutique **Hôtel des Arts**, 5 r. Tholoze, ☎ 01 46 06 30 52 (www.arts-hotel-paris.com).

The ligne du Bourbonnais

Our onward journey south from the French capital starts at **Paris Bercy** station, which sadly wins no marks for grace and charm. If you opt for one of the Intercités trains which runs non-stop to Nevers, you'll need to reserve a seat in advance. These fast trains all continue beyond Nevers to Vichy and Clermont-Ferrand. The slower Intercités trains to Nevers make nine intermediate stops; they do not require advance reservation.

The main *ligne du Bourbonnais* runs south from Paris; it was promoted in the mid-19th century by the PLM; that's the same company which ran the line from Paris to Lyon and Marseille (the initial stretch of which is on **Route 14** in this book). We rate the *ligne du Bourbonnais* as the most interesting of the great arterial routes radiating from Paris. It has been much improved and was electrified right through to Clermont-Ferrand in 1990.

The train dashes south through the forests of **Fontainebleau**, then cruises up the Loing Valley through Montargis, cresting a gentle watershed and dropping down to reach the Loire Valley at Gien. For the next 75 km, the railway hugs the east bank of the river – sit on the right for the best views. Watch out for the great **aqueduct at Briare**, parts of which were designed by Gustave Eiffel. It carries a canal over the Loire. A little later you'll see the celebrated wine village of Sancerre perched on a hill on the far bank of the river, and shortly thereafter the train cuts through the chalky vineyards where flinty Pouilly Fumé is produced.

The first city of any size on the run south from Paris is **Nevers**. It's a fine provincial centre, with a strong porcelain tradition. It's one of those unsung towns which are instantly appealing. Look out for the cathedral and the ducal palace. If you are tempted to stay overnight, and are not looking for anything fancy, the Hôtel de Clèves, ☎ 03 86 61 15 87 (www.hoteldecleves.fr) at 8 r. Saint-Didier is perfectly adequate; it's just a 5-min walk from the station. From Nevers, it is just under an hour on the train south to Vichy.

Vichy (suggested stopover)

If you want to break your journey to the south, Vichy is a good choice. This sedate spa town is best known for its role from 1940 to 1944 as the de facto capital of that part of France not under German occupation. If you are looking for a place with a buzzing nightlife, Vichy probably isn't for you. But it's **quirky and interesting** and, with a wide choice of hotels and some fine parks and promenades, it makes a great overnight stop.

Arrival, information, accommodation

✈ Pl. de la Gare, a 10-min walk east of the city centre. 🛈 Tourist office: 19 r. du parc (www.vichy-destinations.fr). 🛏 A good-value option is the centrally located **Arverna Citotel Vichy**, 12 r. Desbrest, ☎ 04 70 31 31 19 (www.arverna-hotels-vichy.com). Budget options include the **Biarritz**, 3 r. Grangier, ☎ 04 70 97 81 20 (www.hotelbiarritz-vichy.com), just 5-min from the town centre, and the **Hôtel DeGrignan**, 7 pl. Sévigné, ☎ 04 70 32 08 11 (www.hoteldegrignan.fr), with its central and quiet location.

Connections from Vichy

There are direct trains running east from Vichy to Lyon to connect into **Route 14**.

Through the Auvergne

Already in Vichy you have a sense of the hills closing in. Our route now tracks south through **Clermont-Ferrand**, where a change of train is always necessary. The city is the centre of the French rubber industry and birthplace of Michelin tyres; it's built of a dark volcanic stone, and wins no prizes for beauty. But the centre has an absorbing maze of little lanes and alleys, dominated by the hilltop Gothic cathedral.

Connections from Clermont-Ferrand

Our recommended route south from Clermont-Ferrand follows the *ligne des Cévennes* south-east via the Allier gorges to Nîmes. But there are alternatives. There is the once-daily IC *Aubrac* train south via **Millau to Béziers**. It follows the *ligne des Causses*, a single-track railway which cuts through very wild terrain.

Running south from Clermont, the scenery becomes ever better. There are glimpses of magnificent **Romanesque churches** and mediaeval red-roofed villages – some of the latter with that haunting run-down look which makes one wonder if they have been purposefully placed as follies for the benefit of artists and passing train travellers.

Beyond **Langeac** you travel through the spectacular Allier gorges amid the wild, volcanic scenery. You'll glimpse fierce chasms and chaotic rock-strewn slopes as the train cuts through sparsely populated territory which lies well beyond the usual tourist trails. If you are tempted to stop off, consider an overnight stay in **Alleyras** where the Hôtel Le Haut-Allier (www.hotel-lehautallier.com; just 2 mins on foot from the station) has reasonably priced rooms and a much acclaimed restaurant.

Further south, after a stop at La Bastide-Saint-Laurent, the train skirts the eastern flank of Mount Lozère, running for long stretches through tunnels. After that comes the highlight of the journey: the magnificent **viaduct at Chamborigaud**. Then it is mainly downhill all the way to Nîmes.

Nîmes boasts several superb Roman buildings. Les Arènes, seating 23,000 in 34 elliptical tiers, is a well-preserved Roman amphitheatre. It still stages concerts, theatrical events and bullfights (open daily, though not in the morning). **Maison Carrée**, a well-preserved 1st-century temple, is now an exhibition centre. Next door is the futuristic Carré d'Art, a contemporary art gallery designed by Norman Foster (closed Mon). To the west, reached by a bridge from Quai de la Fontaine, is the 18th-century Jardins de la Fontaine which features a romantic Temple of Diana.

The onward journey from **Nîmes to Marseille** is richly varied and, despite flattish terrain, actually very interesting. The line to Marseille via Arles is served by both fast Intercités and slower regional (TER) trains, the latter making half a dozen more stops. Leaving Nîmes to the south-east the railway to Arles crosses the high-speed railway. There is a remarkable new railway station, a bold piece of modern architecture, though only the TERs stop here. It's called Nîmes-Pont-du-Gard which is very misleading as the famous Pont-du-Gard Roman-era aqueduct is 15 km away to the north.

Crossing the Rhône at **Tarascon**, the railway turns south, following the left bank of the river down to the historic city of Arles, where the well-preserved Roman arena pulls crowds of visitors. Continuing across rich meadowland interspersed with forest, the railway then skirts the Étang de Berre lagoon to reach the northern suburbs of Marseille – not always pretty but a reminder that the city of pastis and bouillabaisse is also a major industrial centre.

Arriving in Marseille

Marseille is an **earthy Mediterranean city** and hectically vibrant, with a great music scene and superb fish-based cuisine. The busiest port in France, it's a melting pot of French and North African cultures. Marseille's grubby, rough-and-ready character appeals to some, while others will want to move on swiftly – though watch this space, because big regeneration schemes are changing the city, especially in the northern dock areas.

Full of small restaurants and street cafés, the **Vieux Port** (Old Port) is the hub of Marseille life and is guarded by the forts of St-Jean and St-Nicholas on either side of its entrance. From the quai des Belges, the main boulevard of La Canebière extends back into the city. Across the port from the steep narrow streets of **Le Panier** – the oldest part of Marseille – rises Notre-Dame de la Garde, an impressive 19th-century basilica that is Marseille's most distinctive landmark (take 🚌 60 – it's a steep uphill climb otherwise). The golden Virgin atop the church watches over all sailors and travellers; the interior is full of mementos of the disasters the Virgin is supposed to have protected people from. In Dumas' novel of the same name the Count of Monte Cristo was imprisoned in Château d'If on one of the little Îles de Frioul just outside the harbour; it can be visited by boat on the **Frioul-If-Express** (www.lebateau-frioul-if.fr). The **Musée des civilisations de l'Europe et de la Méditerranée** (www.mucem.org; closed Tues) right on the seafront by Fort Saint-Jean is a highlight on Marseille's cultural circuit.

The central (Vieux Port) area is walkable. Elsewhere, use the métro and buses, both run by RTM (Régie des Transports de Marseille; www.rtm.fr). After 21.00 the normal bus routes are replaced by a 12-route evening network called Fluobus, centred on Canebière (Bourse).

ARRIVAL, INFORMATION, ACCOMMODATION

🚆 Gare St-Charles, pl. Victor Hugo, is the main station, a 20-min walk north-east of the Vieux Port (Old Port): head down the steps and straight along blvd. d'Athènes and blvd. Dugommier to La Canebière, then turn right; or take the métro, direction La Timone, station Vieux Port/Hôtel de Ville. Facilities include left luggage, open daily 08.15–21.00. ⛴ Ferries connecting Marseille with Corsica, Sardinia and North Africa all berth at the Gare Maritime ferry terminal, just north of the Old Port; follow r. de la République. ✈ Marseille–Provence Aéroport (www.marseille-airport.com); at Marignane, 25 km north-west of the city. 🚌 91 runs between the airport and St-Charles railway station at least every 20 mins, taking 25 mins. 🛈 Tourist office: 11 La Canebière (www.marseille-tourisme.com).

🛏 Small and cosy, the **Pension Edelweiss**, 6 r. Lafayette, ☎ 09 51 23 35 11 (www.pension-edelweiss.fr), is a 2-min walk from the station. Also close by St-Charles is the retro-style B&B **Casa Ortega**, 46 r. des Petites Maries, ☎ 06 80 62 53 21 (www.casa-ortega.com). If you want great views of the Vieux Port and and are willing to pay for it consider the **Hotel La Résidence du Vieux-Port**, 18 quai du port, ☎ 04 91 91 91 22 (www.hotel-residence-marseille.com). ✘ The harbour and the streets leading from it are lined with Mediterranean and fish restaurants: Cours Julien is good for trendier, international fare, and more elegant restaurants are found along corniche Président J F Kennedy.

CONNECTIONS FROM MARSEILLE

Marseille is a major rail junction and the starting point for some of the most scenic lines in France. **Route 15** runs east along the Riviera to Nice. Our top choice for rural routes is the slow train to **Briançon**.

Beyond Aix, it continues round the hills of the Lubéron (the subject of Peter Mayle's book *A Year in Provence*), and then through increasingly dramatic limestone scenery as you enter the foothills of the Alps. Beyond **Gap**, you're really into the **Alps** proper. The end of the line is at Briançon, more than four hours from Marseille.

Route 14: Paris to Geneva – the slow way

Cities: ★★ Culture: ★ History: ★ Scenery: ★★
Countries covered: France (FR), Switzerland (CH)
Journey time: 8 hrs 40 mins | Distance: 747 km | Map: www.ebrweb.eu/18map14

Slow travel is all about taking time for a journey. Prior to the advent of Europe's high-speed railways, all rail travellers took things slower than is the norm today. They had little choice. For the sun-starved English heading south, the natural route was always to cross the English Channel and travel south via **Paris to the Rhône Valley**, many then continuing down to Provence.

Fifty years ago, travellers from London to the Rhône Valley, the French Alps or western Switzerland might have started their journey by climbing aboard one of the blue-and-gold **Wagons-Lits sleeping cars** that every evening left London Victoria station for Paris. The entire train was shipped on a ferry across the Channel. Eleven hours to Paris, changing stations there, and with time for a late breakfast at the stylish *Le Train Bleu*, a *belle époque* restaurant at the Gare de Lyon, before boarding a mid-morning train for their onward journey.

Let's recreate part of that journey using the 'old' line out of Paris, the one which was superseded in autumn 1981 by the opening of the first section of the high-speed line from Paris to Lyon. As high-speed railways go, the Paris to Lyon route is actually very attractive. Part of its appeal is that it doesn't tussle with the landscape in the way that some new-build high-speed routes do. There are no tunnels.

When we last rode the route (in summer 2024), we were struck by the fine views of the wild Morvan massif. There's a very strong sense of topography as the railway climbs gently to its summit at almost 500 metres above sea level. And the descent into the Saône Valley is full of drama, passing Taizé and the ancient abbey at Cluny.

Here we take a different route, using a regional train to travel from **Paris to Burgundy**, then on to Lyon and Geneva. The classic line south from Paris (via Sens and Dijon), which we describe here, is dubbed the **Paris-Lyon-Méditerranée** (PLM) route. PLM was the company which introduced to the route such celebrated luxury trains as the *Côte d'Azur Rapide* and *Le Train Bleu* – names which evoke the romance of travel in a bygone era.

Back in 1966, the crack daytime express on the PLM route which we'll follow out of Paris was called **Le Mistral**; its train number, TEE 1, signalled its status as the flagship of the then newly created Trans-Europe Express network. With first-class only seating, two restaurant cars and air-conditioned carriages (a rarity in those days), *Le Mistral* was a train of real distinction, attracting the **rich and famous**. By the 1970s, the amenities on board had expanded to include a bookstall and a hairdressing salon.

Route 14: Paris to Geneva – the slow way | 157

Notes

A – Some journeys by TER services from Paris to Dijon require a change of train at Laroche-Migennes.
L – Léman Express L2 service.
S – All trains from Paris Bercy to Laroche-Migennes and Dijon stop in Sens about 60 to 70 minutes after leaving Paris.
X – Occasional journeys require a change of train in Aix-les-Bains. In addition to the direct trains from Lyon to Annecy, SNCF also operate an occasional non-stop bus between the two cities, taking two hours for the journey.

Route details

Paris Bercy to Dijon
Frequency	Journey time	Notes
7–9 per day	3h–3h20	A S

Dijon to Beaune
Frequency	Journey time	Notes
1–3 per hr	0h20–0h30	

Beaune to Lyon Part Dieu
Frequency	Journey time	Notes
Hourly	1h45	

Lyon Part Dieu to Annecy
Frequency	Journey time	Notes
Every 1–2 hrs	2h–2h15	X

Annecy to Genèva Cornavin
Frequency	Journey time	Notes
Hourly	1h30	L

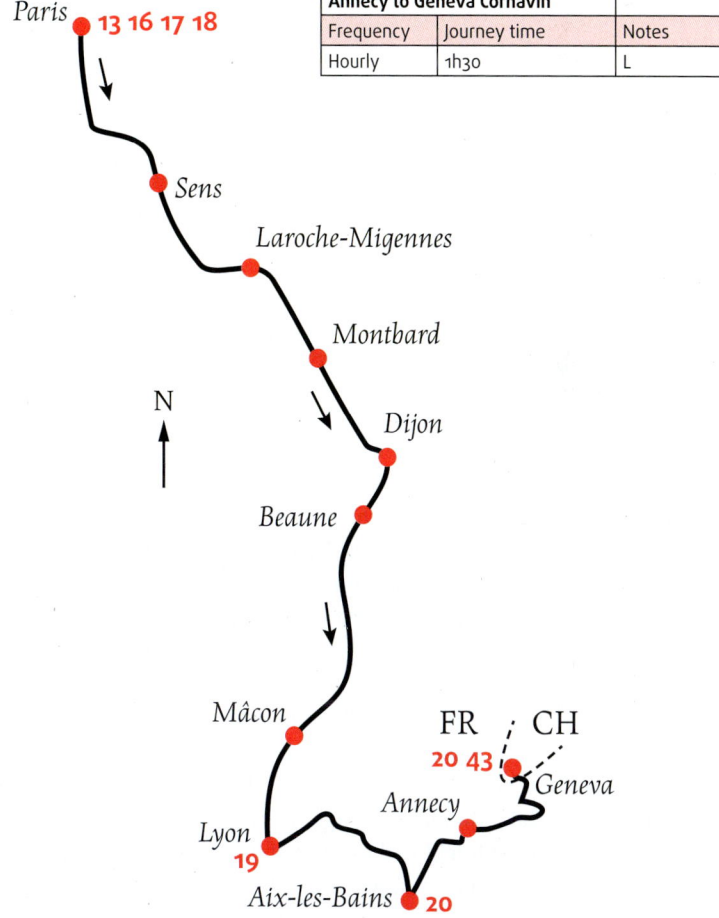

Recommended itinerary

You'll not be able to get your hair styled on the trains which today follow the route once taken by *Le Mistral*. But there are compensations. As we move south along the classic PLM line, the scenery on this route becomes ever better, and the latter part of this journey includes a magnificent ride east from Lyon through a **series of gorges** to reach the lakeshore city of **Annecy** in Savoie, from where it is just a short hop on to **Geneva**.

You can easily complete this journey in a single day. It is possible to do this whole route as described here with just two changes of train, one at **Lyon Part-Dieu** and the other in Annecy. The trains upon which this journey relies are all regional services, where there's no need to pre-book and there are no supplements for holders of rail passes. Consider this, therefore, as a neat alternative to travelling from Paris to Geneva on a fast TGV Lyria train.

This is a journey which might profitably be split into several legs with overnight stops along the way. If pressed to nominate our favourite spots for stopovers on this route, we would opt for **Beaune** and Annecy. If you prefer to stop at places with more of a big-city feel, then Dijon and Lyon are your best bets.

South from Paris

For the journey south from Paris, you'll depart from **Paris Bercy**, an unlovely concrete station which accommodates trains not grand enough to deserve space at the platforms of the nearby Gare de Lyon. If you are keen to push on south at speed, make for the Gare de Lyon from where a TGV will whisk you non-stop to Dijon in just 100 minutes. But far better, if you can possibly afford the time, to take the TER train from Paris Bercy to Dijon – a three-hour journey that gets more interesting with every mile that passes. In recent years, five trains per day on the classic Paris to Dijon route have been extended to Lyon, a move by SNCF that surely pleases PLM purists.

If you shun the TGV and take the slower TER from Paris Bercy to Dijon, you will quickly discover why artists like **Millet** were so taken by the landscapes south-east of Paris.

The train skirts the forests of **Fontainebleau**, broadly following the Seine upstream as far as Montereau and then the Yonne Valley up to Sens – a town where we paused in 2021 and were surprised to discover how it really had, in all sorts of positive ways, the feel of the French provinces. Still in the Parisian hinterland, yet a community that is proud of its historic links with Burgundy, **Sens** turns its back on the capital and looks south towards Dijon and the cities of Burgundy. The town has a particularly fine centre with striking **half-timbered houses**, an engaging Grande Rue (less grand than the name implies, more a quaint alley) and a wonderful covered market. We were surprised to find a local beer called Thomas Becket, evidently named after the English martyr who spent many years in exile in Sens prior to returning to Canterbury where he was murdered. Savour this beer in one of the cafés by the cathedral then take a wander through the lovely **Parc du Moulin à Tan**. Not in its first youth, but right in the centre of town, the Hotel l'Esplanade, 2 blvd. du Mail, ☎ 03 86 83 14 70, is good for a one-night stay.

The TER train from Paris to Sens may be slow in comparison with the TGV, but it still sets a cracking pace on this first part of the journey from the capital. Beyond Sens, the pace slows with the train making more frequent stops and the hills around becoming ever more emphatic. The train pauses at Joigny, another pleasant small town. Then, after passing under the main high-speed line from Paris to Lyon, and now following the Armançon Valley, the train passes through **Tanlay** and **Ancy**, both small towns boasting exceptional châteaux.

The area through which the train passes just beyond Montbard is the heartland of ancient Gaul. To the right of the train you'll see **Mont Auxois**, where Julius Caesar defeated the Gallic tribes in the Battle of Alésia. 20 minutes later the train cuts through a long tunnel and drops down steeply into the Ouche Valley to reach Dijon.

Dijon is a good introduction to Bourgogne (Burgundy), the region of France that is so intimately associated with the fine wines of the same name. The city's grandest building is the strikingly elegant **Palais des Ducs et des États de Bourgogne**, best viewed from the pl. de la Libération. The building reflects the great wealth of the Dukes of Burgundy and now serves as the town hall, also housing the **Musée des Beaux-Arts** (closed Tues, free entry). This is a superb collection of paintings, sculptures and tapestries.

Connections from Dijon

TER trains run north to **Nancy**. There is a regional rail route to **Troyes**, an engaging market town in the heart of Aube en Champagne (2 hrs 20 mins from Dijon, often with a change of train in Culmont-Chalindrey). From Troyes you can continue north-west to return to Paris. In fact, for travellers wanting just a quick taste of provincial France, the triangular route Paris – Dijon – Troyes – Paris is a fine introduction, and one even more enhanced if, while in Dijon, you take time to ride south to Beaune and back. As high-speed lines go, the one that runs east from Dijon through the Franche-Comté region, passing near (but not through) **Besançon** and **Belfort** en route to Mulhouse, really is a fine journey. Sit on the right for good views of the lowest ripples of the Jura. In **Mulhouse** you can connect onto **Route 8** in this book.

Wine country

The entire route south from **Dijon to Lyon** takes you through or close to some of France's most celebrated vineyards, producing wines that north of Lyon are generally classified as Burgundy and Beaujolais. Beyond Lyon, as one continues south, are the various **Rhône appellations**. Tucked away within these general categories are some small properties that have world-class reputations. And nowhere is that more true than on the 20-minute train journey from Dijon to Beaune, which skirts the **Côte de Nuits**. The vineyards to the right of the train produce some of the most expensive wines in the world, among them the grands crus from Chambertin, Vosne-Romanée and Corton.

Beaune (suggested stopover)

Beaune is a charming old town of cobbled streets and fine mansions. The **magnificent Hôtel-Dieu**, r. de l'Hôtel-Dieu, with its flamboyant patterned roof of colourful geometric tiles, was originally built in the 15th century as a hospital for the sick and needy. Inside, don't miss the 15th-century Polyptych of the Last Judgement, its nine oak panels showing sinners tumbling to an unpleasant fate. This building, with its lovely courtyard, is the centre of the prestigious Côte de Beaune and Côte de Nuits wine trade; many local **caves** (wine cellars) offer **dégustations** (tastings). The old ducal palace houses a fine museum dedicated to wine: Musée du Vin, 24 r. Paradis (closed; €4).

ARRIVAL, INFORMATION, ACCOMMODATION

⇌ Av. du 8 Septembre, east of town, just outside the old walls. 🛈 Tourist office: in the Hôtel-Dieu (www.beaune-tourism.com).

🛏 A nice option in the centre is the family-run **La Maison de Maurice**, 8, Rue Edouard Fraisse, ☎ 03 80 20 84 93 (www.lamaisondemaurice-beaune.com). They also arrange wine tastings. Or try the highly regarded **Le Central** boutique hotel, 2, rue Victor Millot, ☎ 03 80 24 77 24 (www.lecentralbeaune.com). Right by the station is the friendly **Hôtel de France**, 35 Av. du 8 Septembre 1944, ☎ 03 80 24 10 34 (www.hoteldefrance-beaune.com), which has a very reliable and competitively priced restaurant.

Lyon (population approx. 1.5 million), at the junction of the Saône and the Rhône, has a lovely old centre, with a hive of charming streets and some truly amazing restaurants; it's rated as one of France's gastronomic high points, and as you might expect from a major university city, there's a lively buzz about the place.

The two rivers divide the city into three parts. On the west bank of the Saône is **Vieux Lyon**, the Renaissance quarter, while on the east bank of the Rhône is the modern business sector, with its high-rise offices and apartment blocks. **Lyon's Part-Dieu station**, where you change trains when following the old PLM route from Paris to Marseille, is in this modern quarter. The station is part of a major urban redevelopment project dating from the 1980s. It's functional, but nothing more. You'll not get a sense of 'old' Lyon if your sole encounter with the city is a quick change of trains at Part-Dieu. Well west of Part-Dieu, between the Rhône and the Saône, lies the partly **pedestrianised city centre**, dating largely from the 17th and 18th centuries. It runs from pl. Bellecour, where the tourist office is located, north to the old silk quarter of La Croix-Rousse.

Lyon is famous for its **traboules** – covered passageways between streets – that once served as shortcuts for the silk traders, protecting their precious cargoes from the weather. Most traboules are in Vieux Lyon and La Croix-Rousse. Just across Pont Galliéni over the Rhône from Perrache station is the poignant **Centre d'Histoire de la Résistance et de la Déportation**, 14 av. Berthelot (closed Mon & Tues).

Connections from Lyon

Part-Dieu station in Lyon is a major rail hub. The further flung international destinations are **Frankfurt-am-Main**, **Barcelona** and **Milan**, the latter route closed since August 2023 due to a landslide, but expected to reopen in the first half of 2025. When it does reopen, there will be a choice of French TGVs or Italian Frecciarossa trains on this key route through the Alps to the Susa Valley in Piedmont.

For travellers wanting to continue south to Avignon and Marseille, there's a choice of a high-speed line or the more scenic route down the **Rhône Valley**, the latter the southward extension of the PLM railway which we have followed from Paris to Lyon. Follow that Rhône Valley line south past some of the regions finest wine appellations (like Côte Rôtie and Hermitage) to Valence where you can connect into **Route 20** and follow it all the way to Catalonia. There's a twice-daily cross-country Intercités train from Lyon via Bourges to **Nantes**. Regional trains run south-west to Saint-Étienne for onward connections to Le Puy. Of the routes running east towards the Alps, the most scenic is that via Ambérieu to Aix-les-Bains, which we follow on this route, but the more southerly line via La Tour-du-Pin to **Chambéry** is also pleasant.

East to Savoie

The first half hour on the train out of **Lyon towards Annecy** is unexceptional, barely improving after you escape the tangle of motorways that hold Lyon

The Mont-Blanc Express

A local railway runs up the **Arve Valley** from La Roche-sur-Furon as far as Saint-Gervais-les-Bain. The valley itself has surprisingly dense settlement, but it's not all tourist-related. The town of **Cluses** for example, once renowned for its watchmakers, is these days a manufacturing hub for precision machine tools. Many of the places in side valleys are year-round resorts, some of these (like Megève) had a pioneering role in the development of Alpine tourism. This is **premier-league skiing country**. The standard-gauge tracks end at Saint-Gervais-les-Bains, where we switch to a narrow-gauge railway for a journey often marketed as the *Mont Blanc Express* – a real misnomer as the 56-km journey from Saint Gervais to Martigny in Switzerland proceeds at a leisurely average speed of 22 km per hour.

Slow it may be, but this is an absolutely brilliant ride. Beyond **Chamonix**, a town thoroughly dedicated to mountaineering which holds an illustrious position in the history of Alpinism, there are superb views of the **Argentière Glacier** and the Mer de Glace to the right (weather permitting). The train from Saint Gervais runs as far as Vallorcine (1,260 metres above sea level) and the last place of any size on French territory. It's an easy cross-platform change of train onto the waiting Swiss variant of the *Mont Blanc Express* at Vallorcine.

The Swiss portion of the journey is enlivened by trilingual announcements (French, German and English), highlighting the history of this railway and aspects of the passing landscape. The train cuts by **great cliffs**, twisting and turning with a feast of panoramic views. On the final, steep descent towards Martigny, there's a tantalising glimpse to the right of the fierce ravine cut by the River Trient as it cascades down from the High Alps.

This 'back-door route' into Switzerland from **Saint-Gervais to Martigny** generally runs hourly. In Martigny, there are excellent onward connections to Brig and Montreux.

in their clasp. But it really picks up beyond **Ambérieu-en-Bugey** with the railway following two dramatic gorges (locally called *cluses*) to reach the heartland of Savoie. For a brief stretch, running down the east side of the Lac du Bourget, our route overlaps with **Route 20** (read more on that lakeshore railway on p200). **Aix-les-Bains**, the principal town on the shores of Lac du Bourget is a well-established and well-heeled spa town; it is the epicentre of the Riviera des Alpes (as the Aix region rather pretentiously styles itself). Taking the waters in Aix is a tradition that goes back to Roman times. The town is extremely pleasant with some gorgeous *belle époque* architecture and a welcoming, laid-back feel. Our train from Lyon reverses direction in Aix, and then runs north to Annecy.

With its lakeshore setting, **Annecy** is the most instantly appealing of the cities of Savoie. The heart of the old city has a slightly Italianate feel and is a 15-min walk south-east of the railway station. The waters of two rivers, the Thiou and the Vassé, decant here into **Lake Annecy** and in a two-hour walk you can take in all the main sights and still have time for coffee. Annecy is most definitely worth a stop, but do be aware that it can very full in midsummer. If you are tempted to stay overnight, we can recommend the Hotel Atipik, 19, Rue Vaugelas Annecy, ☎ 04 50 52 84 33 (www.atipikhotel.fr), conveniently located between the station and the Old Town.

The railway from Annecy runs north-east through open **Savoie countryside** to reach an isolated railway junction at La Roche-sur-Furon, perched on a shoulder of flat land above the Arve Valley. It's the point to change trains if you are tempted to strike deeper into the **Alps** (see box on previous page). Otherwise, you stay on the train which drops down towards Geneva.

This final part of the journey is engagingly downbeat, as it slowly becomes clear that our train from Annecy has shifted from being a rural train service into a humble urban shuttle, serving all stations as it runs along the newly built urban railway that links the city of **Geneva** (see p392) with its suburbs on French territory. This line is part of the wider *Léman Express* network, opened in December 2019, which has reconnected Geneva with communities in France on the south shore of **Lake Geneva**.

You'll not notice the French-Swiss border which is crossed when the train is in a tunnel between Annemasse and Chêne-Bourg stations. Switzerland, although not part of the European Union, is a member of the Schengen area, so border formalities are minimal. From that first station in **Switzerland**, it is several stops on to Genève Cornavin, the city's main rail hub. Much of that final stretch is underground, but the train does emerge into daylight to cross the River Arve and then the Rhône – the latter quite a dramatic moment as the train runs over a viaduct. We slipped out of Paris from an unfashionable, lesser terminus, and we equally arrive in Geneva without great fanfare.

Sidetracks: Exploring the Jura

The communities of the **Jura hill country** in Switzerland have always punched above their weight. A lucrative watchmaking industry might not seem to be a natural springboard for revolution, but the communitarian and anti-state instincts of the Jura watchmakers powerfully shaped the development of European anarchism. Politics apart, this is a region of rare beauty where the meadows and forests have the demeanour of a serene parkland in mid-summer but can be austere and snow-swept in winter. The introduction in late 2018 of trains from the Belfort area of France via **Glovelier to Delémont**, capital of the canton of Jura, helped open up the Swiss Jura to cross-border rail travellers. Then in December 2021, after a sustained closure for rebuilding, the cross-border railway at **Col-des-Roches** reopened with the reinstatement of through trains from Besançon to La Chaux-de-Fonds. There are just three trains a day.

That local railway from **Besançon** into Switzerland climbs gradually to a summit at Avoudrey, then dips down to cross the River Doubs in Morteau, before climbing again to the Swiss border at Col-des-Roches. There is a real sense of entering Switzerland by stealth on this remarkable railway which cuts across the grain of the Jura landscape.

Our favourite Jura railway links these two cross-border routes, running from Glovelier (on the line from Belfort to Delémont) south-west to **La Chaux-de-Fonds**. The railway between Glovelier and La Chaux-de-Fonds was opened in stages between 1892 and 1910. But it was not until 1953 that the first passenger trains ran through from one end of the line to the other. The railway was initially constructed by two different companies and at two different gauges, viz. with standard-gauge track from Glovelier to Saignelégier, continuing as a metre-gauge line down to La Chaux-de-Fonds. In the early 1950s, the initial stretch from Glovelier was converted to narrow gauge, paving the way for through trains over the entire route. Today, the 51-km line is the longest route operated by **Chemins de fer du Jura** (CJ), a company with strong local values which offers bus and rail services throughout the Jura region. Electric trains run at hourly intervals over the line, with an end-to-end journey of just over two hours (hardly a fast dash — the average speed is under 25 kph).

For visitors to the region, the rail journey from Glovelier to La Chaux-de-Fonds is a fine introduction to **Jura landscapes**. The line climbs steeply from Glovelier over the hills to a remote platform at Combe-Tabeillon, where the direction of travel reverses. It's a spot so tucked away that it's rare for anyone to alight or join the train there, but the five-minute stop is a chance to hear birdsong. The line then follows Jura ridges for much of its length, **traversing mountain meadows** before dropping down steeply to run through the streets of La Chaux-de-Fonds to terminate at the town's main station, where there are onward connections to Neuchâtel and back into France on that delightfully rural branch line to Besançon. Visitors to the Swiss Jura can ride the railway from Glovelier to La Chaux-de-Fonds without paying a cent. Public transport throughout the entire Jura canton is free for holders of a **Jura-Pass** — which comes for free for visitors staying at most hotels, guest houses and hostels in the region.

Route 15: Exploring the French Riviera

CITIES: ★★ CULTURE: ★★ HISTORY: ★ SCENERY: ★★
COUNTRIES COVERED: FRANCE (FR)
JOURNEY TIME: 3 HRS | DISTANCE: 229 KM | MAP: WWW.EBRWEB.EU/18MAP15

The train journey east from **Marseille** towards the Italian border is superb, a trip that rates alongside the Rhine Valley (**Route 9**) or some of our Swiss mountain routes as a true European classic. We have travelled this route a dozen times or more, and the most memorable journeys have all been at low sun angles. So this is an ideal journey for a summer morning before the crowds are up and about. The route has a grand, almost **cinematic appeal** when seen from the comfort of a TGV, but suddenly becomes more intimate when you experience it from one of the slower TER services which stop off at lesser stations en route. If you want to use TER trains throughout, you'll need to make a couple of changes of train along the way. Many trains on this route are **double-deckers**, so grab a place upstairs and on the seaward side (ie. on the right as you leave Marseille), sit back and enjoy the view.

The stretch of coast east of **Toulon** became the haunt of British aristocrats in the 19th century, heralding its new status as a sophisticated playground for the famous, beautiful or just plain rich. Grand hotels and casinos sprang up to cater for the incomers' tastes. Although parts of the **Côte d'Azur** have declined into untidy sprawls, there's still an engaging mix of ostentatious villas, pretty waterside towns and fine beaches. **Cannes** and Juan-les-Pins are hot spots for nightlife, while **Nice** is large, cosmopolitan and still pulls the crowds from far and wide. Behind the coast the land rises abruptly and you're in a different world, with rugged mountains and ancient perched villages. Much of that mountainous hinterland is difficult to reach without a car.

SUGGESTED ITINERARY
This route is so short that it's by no means necessary to make an overnight stop. Indeed, part of the appeal of this route is the visual drama of the journey as it unfolds. That said, there are a number of very appealing places along the way, so if you are inclined to break your journey, take your pick from the various communities mentioned below.

The **TER services** on this route do not require advance reservation, nor do the much faster regional services which are branded Intervilles. The latter, unlike the regular TERs, have both first and second class seating. Do note that TGV trains require seat reservations. The Thello trains from Marseille to Nice (and onward to Italy) no longer run.

From Marseille to Toulon

The initial part of this route, running out from **Marseille** (p154), is dismal. The views are dominated by motorways and the low-slung aluminium sheds which seem to have become the favoured architecture for the periphery of French cities. But suddenly the train emerges from a long tunnel near Cassis

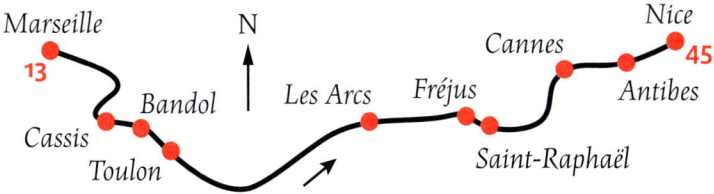

Route details

Marseille St-Charles to Toulon		
Frequency	Journey time	Notes
2–3 per hr	0h45–1h05	A, B
Toulon to Les Arcs-Draguignan		
Frequency	Journey time	Notes
Hourly	0h40–1h05	B
Les Arcs-Draguignan to Cannes		
Frequency	Journey time	Notes
Hourly	0h40–1h	B, C
Cannes to Nice-Ville		
Frequency	Journey time	Notes
2–3 per hr	0h25–0h45	B

Notes

A – Local trains from Marseille to Toulon all stop at both Cassis and Bandol. Those local trains generally run every half hour from Mondays to Fridays and hourly at weekends.
B – Occasional trains on this leg of the journey are TGVs rather than TER trains. Advance reservation is necessary to use these TGV services.
C – Only occasional trains stop at minor stations mentioned in the text (viz. Agay and Le Trayas).

to give a tantalising glimpse of the Mediterranean – a hint of what is to come.

Centred around a pretty fishing harbour ringed with restaurants and an easy day trip from Marseille by train, **Cassis** makes a handy base for seeing the spectacular *calanques*, rocky inlets that cut into the limestone cliffs just west of the town. The station is 4 km out of Cassis, but a small shuttle bus (called *La Marcouline*) runs into town at least hourly. Cassis is a lovely spot in the winter, when the crowds stay away. And winter is the season for the local delicacy of sea urchins, which go down a treat with the dry white wine of the region. Cassis was a one-time haunt of the **Bloomsbury set**, so you could stop off for a few weeks and follow Virginia Woolf's example, quaffing white wine and smoking cigars.

East of Cassis the railway drops down to the coast and skirts the **vineyards of Bandol** – which produce some stunning rosé wines. Bandol was once very popular with the literary crowd – the New Zealand writer Katherine Mansfield wrote some of her best work here – but nowadays the writers have been replaced by the yachting set. Bandol is very much larger than Cassis and lacks the appeal of the latter. But it does offer an oddball excursion by boat to the **Île de Bendor**. This small island has been owned by the Ricard family (makers of pastis) for over 60 years and the island is nowadays a tribute to alcohol. There's an excellent small museum on wines and spirits (www.euvs.org; summer only, closed Wed).

The busy **port of Toulon** is the largest town on this stretch of coast. If you have travelled from Marseille on the stopping train, you'll need to change here for the onward journey to Nice. There's not a lot to detain you in Toulon but, if you have an hour or two to spare, wander down to the traffic-free quayside (curiously named **quai Cronstadt** after the Russian naval base near St Petersburg) where there are fine views over the port and several good seafood restaurants.

Connections from Toulon

There are local trains from Toulon which follow a branch line to **Hyères**, one of the most venerable resorts on the Riviera coast. It caught the attention of English travellers long before the railway from Toulon to Nice was built. Ease of access and a benign climate swept Hyères to popularity, and the roll call of distinguished visitors includes Queen Victoria, Tolstoy, Turgenev and Robert Louis Stevenson.

From Hyères, there are ferries (year round, but not daily in winter) to the islands in Hyères Bay; this small archipelago is known as the **Îles d'Hyères** or the Îles d'Or. Three of the islands have permanent settlements. Head for Port-Cros, reached in an hour by ferry from Hyères port, for wonderful woodland walks.

Skirting the Maures

It is one of the surprises of this journey from Marseille to Nice that the railway doesn't hug the coast beyond Toulon. And that makes the route all the more interesting. When railway engineers planned the railway east of Toulon, the prospect of following the rugged coast of the **Massif de Maures** was just too daunting. So the railway follows a more northerly course, passing *behind* the mountains and only regaining the coast at Fréjus. A modern motorway parallels the railway.

This **diversion inland** offers the chance to see a very different side of Provence, in winter often very green and lush, but parched in the summer months. Sit on the right side of the train for fine views of the forested Maures hills. The highest point, **La Sauvette** (779 m), is visible from the train.

The TER trains on this route serve a number of appealing villages. If you are in no hurry, think of stopping off. But check onward train times carefully, as there are some mighty gaps between trains at the smaller stations. A good choice for a stop in this area is the small town of **Les Arcs** in the Argens Valley because all TER, Intervilles and Intercités trains stop there, plus a handful of TGVs each day. It's a 20-minute walk from the station up into the centre of the village which is very pretty. If you're ready for the hike, we can recommend Le Château d'Argens, ☎ 04 94 99 51 10 (www.chateaudargens.com) as a good choice for lunch or an overnight stay.

Connections from Les Arcs
The full name of the station is Les Arcs-Draguignan, which misleadingly suggests that Draguignan is close to hand. Passengers bound for Draguignan travel by bus (TED bus ligne 5), which departs at least hourly from the station forecourt. It's a 20-min journey.

The Esterel Coast

Beyond Les Arcs, the railway follows the Argens Valley down to the coast at **Fréjus**. The ancient Roman port of Fréjus and the modern beach resort of Saint-Raphaël fuse to form one urban area, though each has its own identity and its own station. **Saint-Raphaël** is the upmarket end and the main transport hub, with spacious beaches and a tiny Old Quarter. Fréjus-Plage is a strip of bars, restaurants and a giant marina lying between the sea and Fréjus town.

The high point of the entire journey comes after Saint-Raphaël when, for 20 minutes, the train cruises around the coast of the **Esterel Massif**. The red volcanic hills tumble down to the sea, and the terrain is so rugged that the creeping urbanisation so prevalent elsewhere on the Côte d'Azur has been kept at bay.

Apart from the frequent fast trains which use this railway, there are half a dozen local services each day which serve eight intermediate stations between Saint-Raphaël and Cannes.

If you take one of these stopping trains, you'll get more chance to appreciate this marvellous stretch of coast. As the train runs through **Le Dramont** (east of Saint-Raphaël), you'll see a small island dominated by a Saracen-style tower. The island is called the **Île d'Or** (not to be confused with the Îles d'Or in Hyères Bay mentioned earlier). The name is misleading, as the island is not gold but tawny-red in colour.

A local doctor, Auguste Lutaud, won the island in a bet in 1909, and promptly set about creating his own micro-nation, issuing stamps and coins with inscriptions in Latin and Arabic (but not French). Lutaud styled himself *Roi de l'Île d'Or* (King of the Golden Isle). The French state soon reasserted its authority over the island as an integral part of France.

If you'd like to break your journey along the Esterel coast, we suggest a stop at either Agay or Le Trayas. **Agay** is much the larger of the two but, by Riviera standards, it's still a small resort. The town clusters around a lovely horseshoe-shaped bay. The Villa Matuzia, ☎ 04 94 82 79 95 (www.matuzia.com), just a 5-min walk from the station via r. Agathonis, offers excellent Provençale cuisine and has a couple of fairly basic rooms (closed Mondays and Tuesdays).

While Agay is sheltered and serene, the station at **Le Trayas** is in an altogether wilder location. It's a great spot to watch the waves crash on the rocks on a stormy day. Beyond Le Trayas, the landscape becomes tamer as the railway skirts the **Golfe de Napoule** to reach Cannes.

Cannes

Cannes is more than merely the world's glitziest **film festival** (see box below). Surprisingly, perhaps, it's perfectly possible to enjoy Cannes without spending a fortune. Make for **Le Suquet** (also called Vieux Suquet or the Vielle Ville), the compact but charming hilly Old Town, where the daily market, cafés and castle panorama sum up the good life on the Riviera. Look out for **cinematic murals** around town tracing the history of the silver screen from Buster Keaton to Charlie Chaplin and Marilyn Monroe. In summer, relax at the beach cafés along **La Croisette**.

Escape from Cannes

Off Cannes, the **Îles de Lérins** are an antidote to chic. Île Sainte-Marguerite is the larger of the two, and boasts the better beaches. At the north end, Fort Sainte-Marguerite was commissioned by Richelieu and enlarged by Vauban in 1712. It is the legendary home of the mythical **Man in the Iron Mask**, made famous by the author Alexandre Dumas. There are daily ferry departures from the quai Laubeuf (close to r. du Port). It's worth venturing further beyond Sainte-Marguerite to the Île Saint-Honorat, home to a large community of Cistercian monks. After the worldly pleasures of Cannes, it is the perfect place to enjoy some sacred solitude.

Springtime in Cannes

Travel writer Lisa Gerard-Sharp, who contributed to several early editions of Europe by Rail, lives in the hills above Cannes. Here she reflects on the appeal of the Riviera community she calls home. Find out more about Lisa at www.lisagerardsharp.com.

May is when the Mediterranean scene wakes up. The *beau monde* dons dinner jackets and descends on Cannes for the **film festival**. Woody Allen dusts down his old jokes: "Eternity is a long experience, especially towards the end." The wrong film always wins but posing Cannes still looks the part. And the Med works its magic – even when the super-yachts exhaust their supplies of smoked salmon and starlets. After the motley crew decamps to Monaco for the Grand Prix, the Riviera is yours once more, from the art trails to the **Michelin-starred restaurants**. Life has moved on since Queen Victoria visited on the royal train, bringing down her own Irish stew to be sure of decent food in France.

The Cote d'Azur is full of Cezanne scenery and Picasso panoramas. But in Provence the food can be as painterly as the art, especially in the hands of masterchefs. Somewhat surreally, Cezanne's peaches can look juicier than the real thing. But when the tastes of *pistou*, *ratatouille* and *bouillabaisse* trump the art, that's when you really love the Cote d'Azur.

"Cannes is for living, Monte Carlo for gambling and Menton for dying" was the Victorian mantra – and Cannes is still living it up. Boosted by the gleaming **Palais des Festivals**, the city is promoting its cuisine as well as its cultural side. On both fronts, style tends to triumph over substance. Still, with its art deco dining room, La Palme d'Or's movie star looks are matched by Michelin-starred Mediterranean cuisine. But once the season starts, fine dining loses out to the beachside bars. On **La Croisette**, Le Baoli Beach is made for posing. More welcoming are the brasseries in the steep and sinuous Old Town. L'Enoteca is typical; it's a cosy haunt with live jazz and good for local staples such as rabbit in red wine sauce.

The branch railway running inland from Cannes to **Grasse**, now so much more reliable after a major uprade, offers an inviting excursion possibility from the coast. Grasse is an appealing inland resort town, famous for its many parfumeries.

The penultimate station on the line, just south of Grasse, is **Mouans-Sartoux** (all trains to and from Grasse stop there). It's a handsome small town (pop. 10,000) with a strong commitment to the arts.

Along the Côte d'Azur

The railway follows the coast for much of the way from Cannes to Nice, veering inland only to avoid the great headland which juts south from Antibes. Just before **Cap d'Antibes**, the TER trains pause at **Juan-les-Pins** where the Côte d'Azur's summer season was invented in 1921. Until then, the Riviera had been primarily a winter destination. Juan has sandy beaches (many are private, but there is still some public space), bars, discos and, in July, the Riviera's most renowned jazz festival, **Jazz à Juan**. It is worth exploring the footpath around the coast of Cap d'Antibes.

The biggest boats in the northern Med may moor in **Antibes**, but the likeable old town is a pretty unpretentious place, with a relaxed atmosphere and a lively bar and restaurant scene. Take a walk along the port, and don't miss the **Musée Picasso**, looking over the sea from its home in the Château Grimaldi. Picasso worked here in 1946 and this excellent museum displays some of his most entertaining creations from that period (closed Mon).

Nice

Nice has been the undisputed queen of the Riviera ever since the 19th-century British elite began to grace the elegant seafront **Promenade des Anglais**. In those days Nice was Nizza and part of the Kingdom of Sardinia. The city was ceded to France in 1860. Hotels such as the **Negresco** capture the old Riviera style and are still as luxurious and imposing as ever, and not excessively expensive for a snack or a drink to sample how the other half lives.

Nowadays you are more likely to hear Russian voices around the salons and promenades once so favoured by English visitors. Standing apart from the belle époque hotels and villas, **Vieux Nice** (the Old Town) is the true heart of the city and, with its green Ligurian-style shutters, seems more Italian than French. There are wonderful outdoor markets, countless cafés and restaurants, and many of Nice's liveliest bars.

Nice boasts some of the best museums in France. Most open 10.00–18.00, are closed on Tuesdays and are easily accessible by local bus. Best of the bunch is the **Musée Matisse**, 164 av. des Arènes de Cimiez (www.musee-matisse-nice.org), wonderfully set in a 17th-century villa amongst the Roman ruins of Cimiez. It houses Matisse's personal collection of paintings (🚌 5/16/18/33 exit at 'Arènes / Musée Matisse'). Next door **Musée et Site Archéologiques de Nice Cimiez**, 160 av. des Arènes de Cimiez (closed Tues), exhibits the copious finds dug up while excavating the Roman arenas in Cimiez (🚌 5/18/33 to 'Arènes'). Matisse and fellow artist Raoul Dufy are buried in the nearby Couvent des Frères Mineurs. Also in Cimiez, the **Musée National Marc Chagall**, 36 av. Dr Ménard, is a graceful temple to Chagall's genius – beautifully lit to display his huge biblical canvases (🚌 5; closed Tues).

In the centre of town, the **Musée d'Art Moderne et d'Art Contemporain**, Place Yves Klein (www.mamac-nice.org), is a white marble cliff rising above the street and filled with striking pop art (🚌 8/12/15; closed Mon). On summer nights, Nice parties till long after midnight, thanks to its many Irish-style pubs and live music venues, though younger visitors often gravitate to the beach.

Arrival, information, accommodation

🚆 Nice-Ville, av. Thiers. Frequent services to all resorts along the Côte d'Azur. A 15-min walk to the town centre. ⛴ Corsica Ferries (www.corsica-ferries.co.uk) offer crossings to Corsica and Sardinia. ✈ Nice-Côte d'Azur, 7 km west of the city (www.nice.aeroport.fr). Take tram line 2 into the centre – it runs along Promenade des Anglais; change at 'Jean Médicin' onto tram line 1 to Gare Thiers which is the stop for Nice-Ville railway station.
ℹ Tourist offices: 5 Promenade des Anglais (www.nicetourisme.com) and at the railway station. See Lignes d'Azur (www.lignesdazur.com) for bus and tram information.

🛏 Try the highly rated **Villa Les Cygnes**, 6 av. du Château de la Tour, ☎ 04 97 03 23 35 (www.villalescygnes.com). A good value option is the centrally located **Le Grimaldi**, 15 r. Grimaldi, ☎ 04 93 16 00 24 (www.le-grimaldi.com), which is only a 10-min walk from the railway station. Set slightly above the town in Cimiez, the belle époque **Hôtel du Petit Palais**, 17 av. Émile Bieckert, ☎ 04 93 62 19 11 (www.petitpalaisnice.com), offers great views of Nice. It is also very convenient for the Matisse and Chagall museums.

🍴 Something of a culinary paradise, Nice is influenced by its neighbour, Italy, and by the Mediterranean. Specialities are *pissaladière*, a Niçois onion tart garnished with anchovies and olives, *socca*, a traditional lunchtime snack of flat bread made from crushed chickpeas, and of course *salade niçoise*.

The Old Town is best for eating out – particularly the warren of streets running north from Cours Saleya and the cathedral. North of the Old Town, pl. Garibaldi boasts the best shellfish.

Nice Connections

There are excellent onward connections beyond Nice. French TER trains shuttle east along the coast at least hourly to Monaco and Menton, most of these services continuing over the Italian frontier to Ventimiglia. This latter journey is described as **Route 45** in this book. From Ventimiglia there are onward connections to Genoa and Milan. A very pretty minor line runs north-east from Nice, serving **Sospel** en route to Breil-sur-Roya, whence there are onward connections to Cuneo in Italy.

For lovers of great scenery, there is a superb route through the hills to **Digne-les-Bains**. This narrow-gauge rail line is privately operated and holders of Interrail and Eurail passes cannot travel for free but receive a 50% discount on the regular fare. From Digne, you can travel south-west by express coach to the TGV railway station at Aix-en-Provence, or take the local bus to Veynes. From Veynes there are TER trains to Valence in the Rhône Valley and north to Grenoble.

Route 16: The Seine Valley and Normandy

CITIES: ★★ CULTURE: ★★ HISTORY: ★★★ SCENERY: ★★
COUNTRIES COVERED: FRANCE (FR)
JOURNEY TIME: 4 HRS 15 MINS | DISTANCE: 434 KM | MAP: WWW.EBRWEB.EU/18MAP16

This route takes in some of the finest townscapes and countryside in **Normandy**. It is one of the shorter adventures in this book. If you are in a hurry, you can get a fast train from Paris to Cherbourg in just over three hours – though the direct trains by-pass the city of **Rouen**, which is one of the high points of the route. The route via Rouen, which follows the River Seine downstream from Paris, is much prettier than the direct line.

When using an Interrail or Eurail pass, it is possible to complete this whole journey without paying any supplements by using the slower TER trains, which are however infrequent on some legs (especially the final stretch to Cherbourg). If you use the faster Nomad services, then there is a mandatory €1.60 reservation fee for pass holders (in both first and second class). The reservation-free slower trains are second class only. Nomad trains on Route 16 can be recognized by their four-digit train number starting with a 3.

From **Cherbourg** you can continue by ferry (see p30), so this journey offers an unusual routing from Paris to southern England or the Republic of Ireland. Check onward ferry times carefully as off-season services are sparse.

If time is tight, and you can allow yourself just a single overnight stop along this route, make it at **Bayeux**. It's a smallish town, but Bayeux has an intimacy which makes it easy to catch the spirit of Normandy – a part of France where regional identity finds full expression in the countryside and small towns much more than in the big cities.

The Seine Valley

The Paris departure point for trains to Normandy is the **Gare Saint-Lazare**. This is the Paris railway station which more than any other attracted the attention of French artists in the 1870s. In 1877, Monet made 11 paintings of his favourite Paris station. Saint-Lazare had already featured four years earlier in Édouard Manet's celebrated painting *The Railway*. The smoke and steam which so inspired both Manet and Monet are gone, but the Gare Saint-Lazare still has shifting patterns of colour and light.

The ride to Rouen is defined by the valley of the **River Seine**, with the train crossing the river on a number of occasions during the 140-km journey. For the best views, sit on the right of the train. At one point, there is a glorious panorama across the River Seine to the village of **Giverny** on the far bank of the river. Monet was so taken with that perspective from the train that he returned to Giverny and rented a house there. His one-time home, studio and gardens now pull the crowds from far and wide (open

A TASTE OF FRANCE

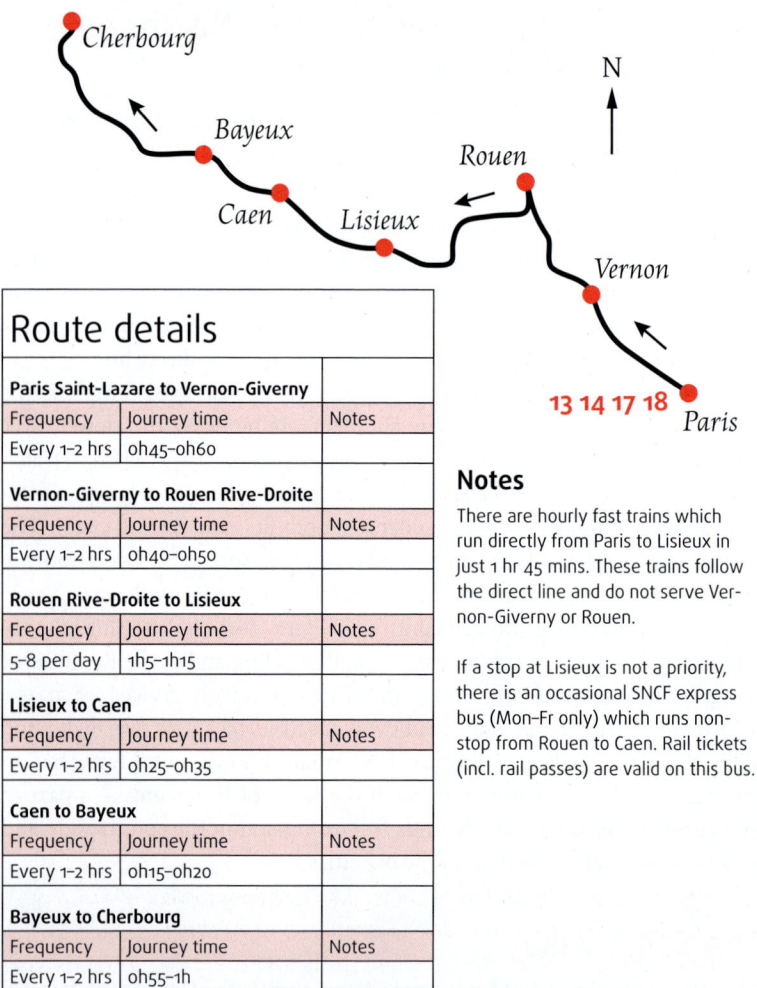

Route details

Paris Saint-Lazare to Vernon-Giverny		
Frequency	Journey time	Notes
Every 1–2 hrs	0h45–0h60	
Vernon-Giverny to Rouen Rive-Droite		
Frequency	Journey time	Notes
Every 1–2 hrs	0h40–0h50	
Rouen Rive-Droite to Lisieux		
Frequency	Journey time	Notes
5–8 per day	1h5–1h15	
Lisieux to Caen		
Frequency	Journey time	Notes
Every 1–2 hrs	0h25–0h35	
Caen to Bayeux		
Frequency	Journey time	Notes
Every 1–2 hrs	0h15–0h20	
Bayeux to Cherbourg		
Frequency	Journey time	Notes
Every 1–2 hrs	0h55–1h	

Notes

There are hourly fast trains which run directly from Paris to Lisieux in just 1 hr 45 mins. These trains follow the direct line and do not serve Vernon-Giverny or Rouen.

If a stop at Lisieux is not a priority, there is an occasional SNCF express bus (Mon–Fr only) which runs non-stop from Rouen to Caen. Rail tickets (incl. rail passes) are valid on this bus.

daily April to October, www.ebrweb.eu/giv). There is a useful shuttle bus link to Giverny from the station at Vernon on the south bank of the river.

From Vernon-Giverny, it is a short hop downstream to **Rouen**, the principal city in Upper Normandy. You'll arrive at Rouen Rive-Droite station, from where it is a 15-minute walk south to the city centre where the star turn is the famous **Cathédrale Notre-Dame**, the subject of another series of Monet paintings. An example of his work showing the western facade can be seen at the attractively restored **Musée des Beaux Arts**, pl. Verdrel (closed Tues). The old city centre, restored after war damage, has many colourful half-timbered buildings. At the end of the main street, in pl. du Vieux Marché, a 20-m cross by the church marks the spot where **Joan of Arc** was burned at the stake in 1431. La Tour Jeanne d'Arc, r. Bouvreuil (closed Tues), is the only remaining tower of the castle where Joan of Arc was imprisoned just before her execution.

CONNECTIONS FROM ROUEN
Dieppe, reached in about an hour from Rouen by train is an attractive coastal town. Its flint and sandstone château is perched on the lofty white cliffs rising high above the shingle beach. The harbour is a lively area, lined with seafood restaurants. In the streets behind, a busy Saturday market draws crowds from far and wide. From Dieppe, there is still a useful direct DFDS ferry to **Newhaven**.

To Lisieux and beyond

The TER train from Rouen to Caen crosses pretty Normandy countryside (with fruit orchards and flowers aplenty in season). The most notable community along the way is **Lisieux**, a place that would barely feature on the tourist map were it not for Saint Thérèse of Lisieux, a 19th-century mystic and nun whose life and work has had an extraordinary influence well beyond Roman Catholicism. Thérèse spent the last nine years of her life in the **Carmelite convent** at Lisieux, so sealing the future fate of the town as a destination for pilgrimages. Make of it what you will, but it's definitely worth a stop. The devotional industry surrounding Thérèse of Lisieux was given a further boost in late 2015 with the canonisation of both her parents; few families can claim such an abundance of sanctity (www.ebrweb.eu/lis). Beyond Lisieux the railway passes through Caen, but there is no good reason to linger. It's best to press on to Bayeux.

Bayeux (suggested stopover)

The first town liberated by the Allies at the end of Second World War, Bayeux escaped any damage to its fine mediaeval centre, dominated by the spires of the magnificent Cathédrale Notre-Dame. The world-famous **Bayeux tapestry** is a 70-m long embroidered linen illustrating the Norman Conquest of England. It is thought to have been commissioned soon after the Battle of Hastings by the Bishop of Bayeux from an Anglo-Saxon workshop run by monks. The historical explanations, film shows and displays in the Centre Guillaume-le-Conquérant in rue Nesmond, where it is housed, interpret the scenes very thoroughly, but it is worth hiring a multilingual audio-guide as you walk round. The **Musée Mémorial de la Bataille de Normandie**, blvd. Fabian Ware, is one of the best museums in the area covering the Normandy campaign of the Second World War.

ARRIVAL, INFORMATION, ACCOMMODATION
Pl. de la Gare, a 10- to 15-min walk south-east of the centre. Tourist office: Pont Saint-Jean (www.bayeux-bessin-tourisme.com). The **Reine Mathilde**, 23 r. Larcher, ☎ 02 31 92 08 13 (www.hotel-bayeux-reinemathilde.fr), is located over a popular brasserie in the Old Town while the **Hôtel d'Argouges**, 21 r. Saint Patrice, ☎ 02 31 92 88 86 (www.

hotel-dargouges.com), is an upmarket option in an 18th-century building. The centrally located **Le Bayeux**, 9 r. Tardif, ☎ 02 31 92 70 08 (www.hotellebayeux.com), is a former coaching inn.

Connections from Bayeux

TER trains run direct from Bayeux to Coutances and the port of **Granville**, in our view one of the finest spots on the coast of Normandy. The upper part of the town is a fortified citadel. From Granville there are year-round ferries to the Archipel de Chausey, the only part of the Channel Islands under French jurisdiction. From mid-April to December, there are also direct ferries (but not always daily) from Granville to **Jersey**.

From Bayeux, it is a pleasant one-hour journey by train north through the **Cotentin Peninsula** to Cherbourg. The landscape is unchallenging, a mix of coppice woodland and pasture known locally as *bocage*. Although you are never far from the sea, the coast is curiously invisible from the train.

Arriving in Cherbourg

Essentially a commercial and military port, **Cherbourg** played a key role in the Battle of Normandy. It was liberated by American troops three weeks after the landings on Utah Beach and used as a deep-water port. Hilltop **Fort du Roule**, overlooking the town and port, has a museum commemorating the Allied liberation of Cherbourg and the Cotentin Peninsula. A worthwhile recent attraction is the **Cité de la Mer**, housed in the former transatlantic ferry terminal, a grand art deco building. Its exhibits cover the theme of underwater exploration, and include Europe's largest aquarium plus a de-commissioned nuclear submarine (www.citedelamer.com).

Arrival, information, accommodation

🚆 Av. Jean-François Millet at the south end of Bassin du Commerce (harbour); ⛴ The Gare-Maritime ferry port is north-east of the town centre; 🚌 8 runs between the two. 🛈 Tourist office: 14 quai Alexandre III (www.normandie-tourisme.fr).
🛏 The area north of the tourist office offers some cheap lodging options. Try the **Hôtel de la Renaissance**, 4 r. de l'Église, ☎ 02 33 43 23 90 (www.hotel-renaissance-cherbourg.com), with views of the sea; or the **Hôtel Ambassadeur**, 22 quai de Caligny, ☎ 02 33 43 10 00 (www.ambassadeurhotel.com), old-fashioned but comfortable, with views of the harbour. Just off the main square, the **Croix de Malte**, 5 r. des Halles, ☎ 02 33 43 19 16 (www.hotelcroixmalte.com) is a modernised option.
🍴 Lots of glass-fronted restaurants line the quayside road; there are cheaper options in the streets behind, where vestiges of the Old Town survive around pl. Centrale.

Connections from Cherbourg

There are useful **cross-channel ferries** to the south coast of England, with a seasonal service to Poole and an occasional link to Portsmouth; note that foot passengers are only carried on the Portsmouth route on selected sailings.
Brittany Ferries offer thrice-weekly direct ferries to **Rosslare** in Ireland. Happily the Irish Ferries sailings to Dublin, which were in the past reserved for car travellers, are now all available for foot passengers. Irish Ferries use the lovely *WB Yeats* cruise ferry all year round on this route, with additional summer sailings relying on the *James Joyce*.

Sidetracks: Carriage design

Rail travel is generally very safe. But that was not the perception of Parisians in 1861 after poor **Monsieur Poinsot** was found dead in a railway carriage compartment at the Gare de l'Est. By the time Poinsot's mutilated body was discovered, the murderer had long fled, presumably having alighted at one of the stations where the train from Mulhouse had stopped on its journey to Paris.

The fate of Monsieur Poinsot made French travellers think twice about buying a train ticket. Before long, Gallic panic over the **dangers of train travel** spread to England, when a particularly gruesome compartment murder took place in London. English trains were designed on the same lines as those in France, with first-class accommodation being in separate compartments, each accessed by a door directly from the railway platform. There was in those days no connection at all between adjacent compartments.

This design was the norm across Europe for first class, in contrast to North America where the open-plan saloon car was more common. **Wolfgang Schivelbusch**, in his marvellous book *The Railway Journey*, suggests that on European trains well-to-do travellers enjoyed the privacy and style associated with travel in a horse-drawn coach on a highway. The first-class **railway compartment in Europe** imitated the coach, but Schivelbusch notes that the design of the American railroad car was inspired by the open saloons on the riverboats which plied the young nation's waterways.

"That only two cases of murder," writes Schivelbusch, "were able to trigger a collective psychosis tells us as much about the compartment's significance for the nineteenth century European psyche as does the fact that it took so long to become conscious of the compartment's dysfunctionality."

That **dysfunctionality** lay not merely in the compartment's appeal for assassins. There were surely many instances of lavatorial distress; no surprise perhaps that, when a train arrived at an intermediate station after a particularly long non-stop leg, there was often a communal rush for the station toilets.

The victim in the London murder was an unfortunate Mr Briggs; his assailant was a German villain named Franz Müller. The railways responded by introducing a small glazed peephole between compartments. These peepholes were called **Müller Lights**. Many a courting couple surely bemoaned the resulting loss of privacy. Before long, railway companies installed communication cords which passengers in distress could pull to alert the train crew to an emergency. But a German railway engineer, Edmund Heusinger von Waldegg, devised a more radical approach to mitigating the dangers of travel in compartments. He suggested an **internal corridor** down one side of each carriage, allowing passengers and train staff to move from compartment to compartment. It did not entirely erode the intimacy of the small compartment but now afforded a new sense of safety and security. It also paved the way for the introduction of on-board facilities such as toilets and restaurant cars.

European carriage design has moved on, with the open-plan saloon now much preferred by most travellers. Trains with individual compartments linked by a connecting corridor are now increasingly rare. Read more on carriage design in **Sidetracks O** (on communal carriages in Russia) on p287.

Route 17: The Loire Valley and Atlantic coast

Cities: ★★★　Culture: ★★★　History: ★★　Scenery: ★★
Countries covered: France (FR), Spain (ES)
Journey time: 16 hrs | Distance: 1,030 km | Map: www.ebrweb.eu/18map17

The 19th-century English lawyer and explorer **Charles Packe** knew western France like the back of his hand, criss-crossing the region on journeys to and from his beloved Pyrenees. But he bemoaned how slow the trains were. Over 12 hours in 1862 by the fastest express from Paris to Bordeaux, and 20 hours with the slower trains. Today's traveller can speed from **Paris to Bordeaux** in little more than two hours, thanks to a new high-speed line from Tours to Bordeaux which opened in mid-2017.

Route 17 is for those less inclined to hurry. It is a leisurely amble through some of Atlantic Europe's most **striking cultural landscapes**: the Loire Valley, Aquitaine and the Basque region. The entire journey can be completed without once resorting to a high-speed service. That's a great advantage for travellers who share our affection for travelling more spontaneously. You can follow this entire route without needing to make a single advance reservation. This route takes in **several superb cities**, notably Chartres, Angers and Bordeaux. It also features several important **coastal resorts**, among them La Rochelle, Biarritz and San Sebastián.

Suggested itinerary
If you are in a rush to get to the **Basque region** and beyond, you can always hop on a fast TGV from Paris to Bordeaux, and join the latter part of this route for the journey beyond Bordeaux. Or you can skip the first part of journey by speeding from Paris to Angers on a high-speed TGV. In an ideal world, if time is no object, you could spin this journey out to a full week, with stops along the way in Chartres, Angers, La Rochelle, Bordeaux and Biarritz. Angers and Bordeaux have more than enough to justify a two-night stay. If you can afford just a couple of **overnight stops**, we recommend you make them at Angers and Bordeaux.
　　　　Bear in mind that througout 2024 (and on into 2025), engineering work on the railway between Hendaye and San Sebastián means that only a limited number of trains are running across the French-Spanish border. Your best bet for this leg is the **Metro Donostialdea tram**.

From Paris to the Loire
The regional rail route from Paris to Angers in the **Loire Valley** always requires a change of train in Le Mans. The TER services to Le Mans leave from Montparnasse station in the French capital. The fast TGV trains which run direct to Angers leave from the same station. The TER route tracks west past Versailles and the forests of Rambouillet, then follows the gentle Eure Valley upstream to **Chartres**, where it is definitely worth stopping for a couple of hours to see the superb Gothic cathedral. It is an easy 10-min walk east of the railway station. The **Cathédrale Notre-Dame** is especially known for the quality and brilliance of its 13th-century stained

Route 17: The Loire Valley and Atlantic coast | 177

Route details

Paris Montparnasse to Chartres

Frequency	Journey time	Notes
Hourly	1h–1h20	B

Chartres to Le Mans

Frequency	Journey time	Notes
Every 2 hrs	1h20	B

Le Mans to Angers St Laud

Frequency	Journey time	Notes
Every 1–2 hrs	0h40–1h10	B

Angers St Laud to Nantes

Frequency	Journey time	Notes
Hourly	0h40	

Nantes to La Rochelle

Frequency	Journey time	Notes
5 per day	1h45–2h05	

La Rochelle to Bordeaux St-Jean

Frequency	Journey time	Notes
8 per day	2h20–2h50	

Bordeaux St-Jean to Hendaye

Frequency	Journey time	Notes
6–10 per day	2h30–2h45	

Hendaye to Amara-Donostia

Frequency	Journey time	Notes
2 per hr	0h35	A

Notes

A – The leg from Hendaye to San Sebastián (Donostia in the local Basque language) is best done using the *Metro Donostialdea* (MD) trams.

B – If time is tight, consider taking a TGV from Paris to Angers. It takes just 95 mins.

glass, dazzling even on the dullest of days, and the wealth of carved stone, notably around the west doorways.

From Chartres the TER rail route continues west, cutting through the southernmost corner of Normandy. This area, known as **La Perche**, has idyllic rural landscapes; the area's quiet beauty is best appreciated in the low sun angles of a summer evening. Sit back and enjoy the view; before long you'll be rolling into the station at **Le Mans** where you change trains. The railway from Le Mans follows the Sarthe Valley downstream all the way to Angers. There are some very pleasant **riverine landscapes** as the railway skirts the Fôret de Pincé just beyond the small town of Sablé-sur-Sarthe.

Angers

Angers is an attractive wine-producing town dominated by the massive striped walls of the 13th-century **Château d'Angers**, whose 17 towers now reach only half of their original height. The moat has been converted into formal gardens. Inside is a series of great 14th-century tapestries known as the *Tenture de l'Apocalypse* (the Apocalypse of St John). As well as wine, Angers produces the liqueur Cointreau. Visits to the distillery museum on blvd. des Bretonnières, Saint-Barthélemy-d'Anjou, ☎ 02 41 31 50 50, are by appointment only (reached via 🚌 11).

From the station it is just a 7-min walk north along r. Marceau to the château. The cathedral is just a few steps beyond the château.

Arrival, information, accommodation

🚆 Angers-Saint-Laud, about a 10-min walk south of the centre, or take 🚌 2. 🅸 Tourist office: 7 pl. Kennedy (www.tourisme.destination-angers.com). 🛏 A warm welcome awaits you in **L'Oisellerie**, 5 r. de L'Oisellerie, ☎ 06 42 43 70 32 (www.loisellerie.com), a B&B located in a 16th-century timber-framed building in the centre of Angers. Or try the B&B **Les Chambres de Mathilde**, 27 r. Hanneloup, ☎ 06 11 71 18 50 (www.chambres-de-mathilde.com), with spacious and comfortable rooms, just a short walk from the city centre.

Saumur excursion

Occasional TER trains run from Angers (taking 25–35 mins) to **Saumur**, with its famous cavalry riding school (the Cadre Noir). The 14th-century château was originally a fortress for Louis I. It later became a country residence for the Dukes of Anjou, then a state prison, and now houses two museums. **Vineyards** surround the town, and mushrooms are grown in the caves that riddle the local hills, making good use of by-products from the riding school. Saumur is on **Route 19**.

The Atlantic Coast of France

From Saint-Laud station at Angers it is just a short hop down the Loire Valley to **Nantes**. Regular TER trains ply the route, and there are occasional trains branded InterLoire (IL). Neither TER or IL services require advance reservation. Sit on the left for good views of the **River Loire**.

Nantes is a place first and foremost to change trains, but if you have an hour or two to spare, you may want to walk west from the station to the nearby Château des Ducs, where you can wander without charge through the moated gardens and climb the ramparts.

CONNECTIONS FROM NANTES
Nantes was historically part of Brittany and that's reflected in the rail timetables. There are direct trains to Lorient and Quimper, with connections in Quimper for Brest. Travellers heading to the north **coast of Brittany** can use the regular services from Nantes to Rennes, where there are good connections to Saint Malo.

Closer to hand there are local services from Nantes to nearby places on the coast. One excursion we especially like is to **La Baule-Escoublac**, a resort town which deftly manages to combine Breton charm with Riviera style.

The leg from Nantes to La Rochelle is the trickiest part of this entire route. Several trains each day run south from Nantes as far as **Luçon**, but there are just five trains which run beyond Luçon to La Rochelle.

La Rochelle is a popular sailing centre. The town is elegant and striking, built in bright limestone, with gracious old squares, a fine town hall and arcaded Renaissance houses. Life focuses on the old harbour, which has some excellent fish restaurants. Two mediaeval towers preside over the harbour entrance, once linked by a protective chain. La Rochelle is a springboard for boat trips and island visits, notably to the **Île de Ré**, connected to the town by a 3-km toll bridge, offering beaches and quiet picnic spots. It's reachable by bus, but best explored by bike.

From La Rochelle you have a choice of TER and Intercités trains, none requiring advance reservation, for the ride south to Bordeaux. Sit on the right for good views of the coast on the initial stretch from La Rochelle. Leaving the coast at **Rochefort**, the railway follows the River Charente upstream before tracking south through increasingly forested country to reach Bordeaux. You cross the two great rivers which have shaped the region on the approach to Bordeaux: first the Dordogne and then the Garonne.

Bordeaux (suggested stopover)

Set on the **Garonne River** just before it joins the Dordogne, Bordeaux is a busy, working city with an 18th-century core of monumental splendour surrounded by industrial gloom. A massive recent revitalisation programme has restored the handsome old centre and made it more pedestrian-friendly.

Above all, the city is the commercial heart of one of the world's greatest wine-growing areas, surrounded by revered appellations such as Saint-Émilion, Graves, Médoc and Sauternes. The **Maison du Vin de Bordeaux**, opposite the main tourist office, arranges courses, tours and tastings. Most of Bordeaux's main sights lie within easy walking distance, but a high-tech tram network is also in place.

Best of the city's historic buildings include the neoclassical Grand Théâtre, on pl. de la Comédie, the **Musée National des Douanes**, housed in the 18th-century Customs House, and the elegant place de la Bourse. The **Musée Mer Marine** (www.mmmbordeaux.com), located in the historic port area, opened its doors to visitors in June 2019 (closed Mon).

Arrival, information, accommodation

≋ Gare St-Jean, r. Charles Domercq, about 2 km south-east of the centre (tram line C runs from Quinconces to the station). ✈ Bordeaux-Mérignac, 12 km from the city (www.bordeaux.aeroport.fr). Tram A takes 35 mins to the city centre. There are buses at least once an hour to Gare St-Jean. 🛈 Tourist office: 12 cours du XXX Juillet (www.bordeaux-tourisme.com).

🛏 Near the centre, r. Huguerie is a good place to look for budget accommodation. Good mid-range options are the friendly and central B&B **La Maison Odeia**, 12 Impasse des Tanneries, ☎ 06 70 33 60 05 (www.lamaisonodeia.com) or the cosy B&B **Chez Dupont**, 2 r. Cornac, ☎ 06 95 15 77 37 (www.chez-dupont.com) opposite the restaurant of the same name. If you want to splash out, try the stylish **Le Boutique Hôtel**, 3 r. Lafaurie de Monbadon, ☎ 05 56 48 80 40 (www.hotelbordeauxcentre.com), set in an 18th-century town house in the heart of the city. ✘ The quartier St-Pierre is a bustling district filled with boutiques and cafés, and pl. du Parlement is a good place to look for restaurants. Take in the *guingettes* (waterfront seafood stalls) along quai des Chartrons.

Connections from Bordeaux

One very good reason for coming to Bordeaux is to visit the great wineries in the surrounding countryside. There are bus tours (ask at the tourist office), but also a local rail line to Lesparre and Le Verdon, with en route stops at places with names suggestive of great claret (Margaux, Pauillac, Ludon, Moulis-Listrac, etc.).

Bordeaux is a **major rail interchange**. There are regular services to Toulouse, some of which continue to Marseille. There are excellent connections to Angoulême, Périgueux and Limoges. A very scenic branch line runs from Bordeaux up the Dordogne Valley to Bergerac and **Sarlat**. The ride to Sarlat and back, a round trip of 336 km, makes an excellent one-day excursion from Bordeaux. Allow time for a leisurely lunch in Sarlat, which has an appealing Old Town. On hot summer days, join the Bordeaux crowds who escape to the beach by taking the local train to Arcachon, just 50 mins away on the Côte d'Argent.

The two-hour train journey from Bordeaux to **Biarritz** reveals a landscape not usually associated with France – a seemingly endless sandy pine forest. The smart set have been coming to Biarritz since the splendid beaches and mild climate were 'discovered' in the mid-19th century by such visitors as Napoleon III and Queen Victoria. Although less grand now, it is still a fairly upmarket coastal resort with nice beaches, great surfing and a casino.

The route south from Biarritz hugs the coast. The little town of **Saint-Jean-de-Luz**, halfway between Biarritz and the Spanish border, deserves a look. All trains stop at Saint-Jean. If you can avoid the high-season crowds, this bustling fishing port is a fine place to linger.

The train journey across the border to San Sebastián requires a change of train at **Hendaye**. It was at this station that Hitler met Franco in October 1940. It is the only remarkable thing about an otherwise unlovely place.

The onward journey to San Sebastián is with the frequent **Euskotren** tram service, which is often referred to by the name of the service operator Euskotren. MD does not accept rail passes, but the fare from Hendaye to San Sebastián costs €2.75. An alternative is to take one of the few French trains that continue from Hendaye over the bridge to **Irún** in Spain, where you can change onto a regular Renfe train to San Sebastián (less frequent than MD but rail passes are accepted). If you opt for the tram, you'll find the tram stop in the forecourt of Hendaye station. Bear in mind that the Basque language is the norm here, so note that the Basque name for San Sebastián is Donostia. For the city centre, buy a 2-zone ticket to Amara-Donostia.

San Sebastián (Donostia)

San Sebastián is an **elegant resort**, with tamarisks gracing the promenade which runs along a crescent-shaped bay. Formerly a whaling and deep-sea fishing port doubling as a stopover for pilgrims en route to Santiago de Compostela, San Sebastián really came into its own in the mid-19th century as a fashionable health resort.

Take time to wander the streets of the Old Town, or *parte vieja*, which lies at the foot of **Monte Urgull**. Although mainly rebuilt in the 19th century, it retains a characterful maze of small streets, tiny darkened shops and bars, arcaded plazas like the **Plaza de la Constitución**, which used to serve as a bullring, and churches such as the beautiful baroque Basilica de Santa María del Coro. Fishing is still much in evidence, with the daily catch on show on stalls in the **fish market**.

The **Museum of San Telmo**, 1 Plaza Zuloaga (closed Mon), occupies a former Dominican monastery and includes a striking new pavilion which blends neatly into the cityscape. At the far end of the quay you'll find the **Naval Museum** (closed Mon) and the renovated Aquarium. For superb views, climb Monte Urgull itself, topped by a much rebuilt fort (the Castillo de la Mota). Standing proudly near the top of the hill is the statue of the Sagrado Corazón (Sacred Heart), which watches over the city.

Arrival, information, accommodation

Renfe: Estación del Norte, Paseo de Francia. Cross the ornate María-Cristina Bridge, turn right, and it is a short walk through the 19th-century area to the Old Town. **Euskotren**: Estación de Amara, Plaza Easo. Tourist office: at Boulevard, 8 (www.sansebastianturismoa.eus).

Head for the Old Town: hidden amongst the narrow streets are many *pensiones*. Try **Pensión Amaiur**, C. 31 de Agosto Kalea 44, ☎ 09 43 42 96 54 (www.pensionamaiur.com), which offers spotless, comfortable rooms, or **Casa Nicolasa**, C. Aldamar 4, ☎ 09 43 43 01 43 (www.pensioncasanicolasa.com). A friendly place in a quiet location is **Pensión Iturriza**, Campanario 10 2°, ☎ 06 06 32 87 83 (www.pensioniturriza.com).

There are many good backstreet tapas bars — try monkfish kebabs, stuffed peppers and wild mushroom vol-au-vents. Two excellent markets: La Bretxa, on Alameda del Boulevard, and San Martín, near the cathedral on C. Loiola. For the best small restaurants, try the Old Town and the fishing harbour at the north end of Playa de la Concha.

Route 18: To the Pyrenees

Cities: ★★ Culture: ★ History: ★ Scenery: ★★
Countries covered: France (FR), Spain (ES)
Journey time: 13 hrs | Distance: 1,039 km | Map: www.ebrweb.eu/18map18

With the opening in 2013 of the Perthus Tunnel through the eastern Pyrenees, two great cities, Paris and Barcelona, moved closer together. You can now board a train in Paris and be in the Catalan capital less than seven hours later. The route taken by those fast TGV trains is actually far from direct; they dash south through Burgundy and the Rhône Valley, skirting Avignon and then broadly follow the coast west through Languedoc and Roussillon towards the Pyrenees.

The journey we describe here is a more direct, but very much slower, route from **Paris to Barcelona**. It runs south-west from Paris, crossing the Loire at Orléans and cutting through the Dordogne to reach **Toulouse**. We then follow the Ariège Valley up into the Pyrenees, crossing into Spain just east of Andorra, and then dropping down to the coast at Barcelona.

The highpoint of the journey is of course the **Pyrenees**; our route follows the only railway still in use which really crosses the mountains – as opposed to tunnelling under them (as the new Perthus Tunnel does) or hugging the coast and skirting around either edge of the mountains (as **Route 17** and **Route 20** in this book do).

The route we follow is a more traditional approach to the Pyrenees and northern Spain, one much favoured by travellers of yesteryear. Prior to the French Revolution this was the *route royale* from the capital to south-west France. With the coming of the motor car, the old royal road morphed into **Route Nationale 20**, the principal road artery from the French capital to Spain. The rail journey described here criss-crosses that highway more than a dozen times.

Itinerary and tickets

If you don't mind taking the first train of the day from **Paris Austerlitz to Toulouse Matabiau** (in autumn 2024 timed for 06.28 except Sun), it is easily possible to cover this route in its entirety in a long day. It would be better, we think, to break the journey. Cahors is a good choice for an **overnight stop**. If you want to spread the journey over three days, then Cahors and Foix are good places for stopovers.

On most evenings, there is a direct **overnight train** from Paris to Latour-de-Carol. It follows the route described here. Like all French night trains, it doesn't have sleeping cars, only a choice of couchettes and reclining seats. Although the train offers no great luxury, the delight of awakening on a bright spring morning as the train heads up the **Ariège Valley** into the mountains more than compensates for any modest overnight discomfort. On those nights when this train runs, it is a sensible way of travelling from Paris to northern Spain. Arriving in **Latour-de-Carol** just after nine in the morning, there's time to savour clear Pyrenean air before joining the onward train to Barcelona.

In our experience, it is simply impossible to buy a through ticket to Barcelona (or anywhere else in Spain) via Latour-de-Carol. This is because the line on the Spanish side

ROUTE 18: TO THE PYRENEES | 183

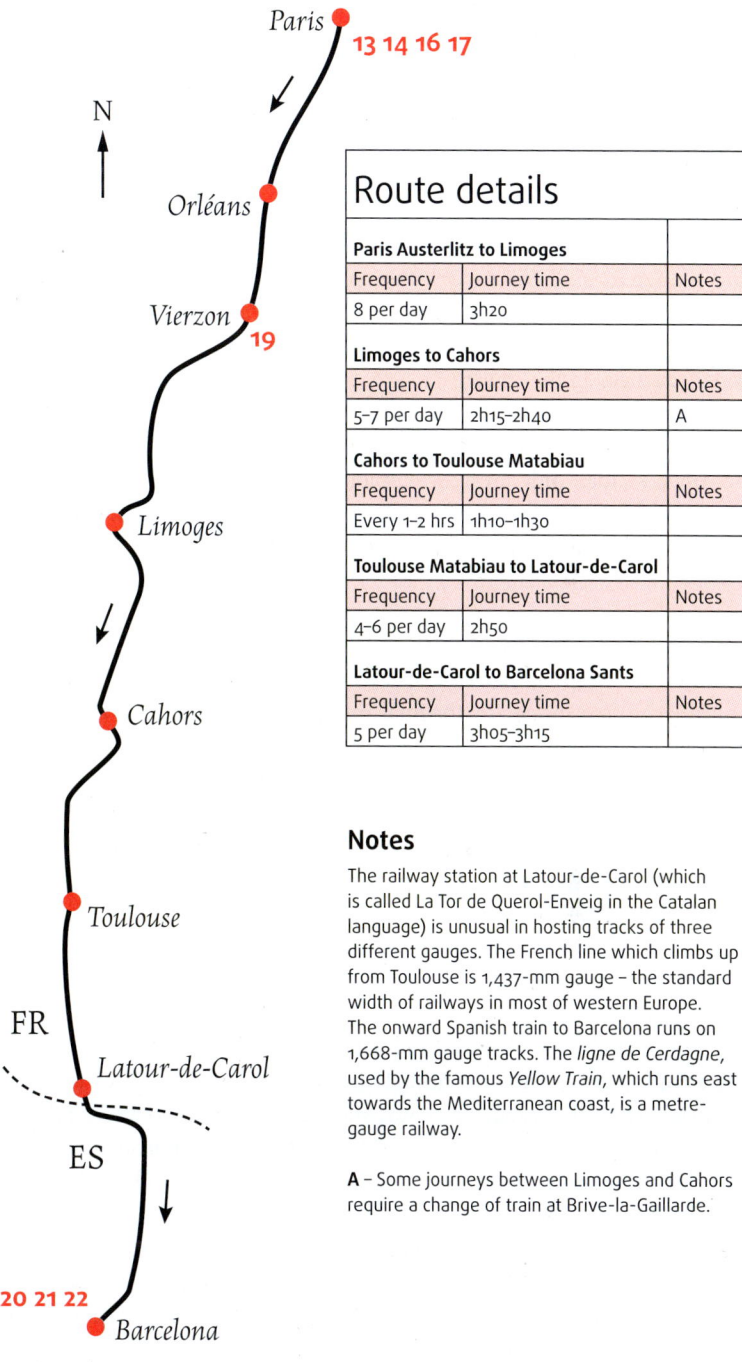

Route details

Paris Austerlitz to Limoges		
Frequency	Journey time	Notes
8 per day	3h20	

Limoges to Cahors		
Frequency	Journey time	Notes
5–7 per day	2h15–2h40	A

Cahors to Toulouse Matabiau		
Frequency	Journey time	Notes
Every 1–2 hrs	1h10–1h30	

Toulouse Matabiau to Latour-de-Carol		
Frequency	Journey time	Notes
4–6 per day	2h50	

Latour-de-Carol to Barcelona Sants		
Frequency	Journey time	Notes
5 per day	3h05–3h15	

Notes

The railway station at Latour-de-Carol (which is called La Tor de Querol-Enveig in the Catalan language) is unusual in hosting tracks of three different gauges. The French line which climbs up from Toulouse is 1,437-mm gauge – the standard width of railways in most of western Europe. The onward Spanish train to Barcelona runs on 1,668-mm gauge tracks. The *ligne de Cerdagne*, used by the famous *Yellow Train*, which runs east towards the Mediterranean coast, is a metre-gauge railway.

A – Some journeys between Limoges and Cahors require a change of train at Brive-la-Gaillarde.

of the frontier, part of the **Rodalies de Catalunya** network, is not integrated into the wider European rail ticketing system. So if you are following this route, just buy a ticket to Latour-de-Carol, which is the last station in France before the border. SNCF's website (www.sncf-connect.com) sells a full range of French tickets (including the night train from Paris to Latour-de-Carol). However, the ticket for the final hop from **Latour-de-Carol** (the station is called La Tor de Querol–Enveig in Catalan) to Barcelona can only be purchased at Latour-de-Carol. The one-way fare is €12 (in autumn 2024).

The railway from Paris to Toulouse was one of France's first *grandes lignes*; the section from Paris to Orléans opened in 1840. Until the advent of dedicated high-speed railways in France (the Paris–Lyon line opened in 1981), the railway we follow south from Paris on Route 18 was one of the most advanced in the country.

In 1967, the **premium trains** between Paris and Toulouse (branded *Le Capitole*) became the first in Europe to be timetabled to run at 200 kilometres per hour – albeit only for a 100-km long stretch near Vierzon. The fastest trains sped from Paris to Toulouse in just six hours. Half a century later, no train on this line comes close to matching the performance of *Le Capitole*.

From Paris to the Dordogne

From **Paris** (see p151) to Orléans, the railway traverses unremarkable agricultural country, though on the final approach to the Loire city, the line cuts through the edge of the Forêt d'Orléans, the former royal domain which is now the largest national forest in metropolitan France.

In **Orléans**, the train stops at Les Aubrais, a station north-east of the city centre, from where a local train shuttles into the central station. Orléans predictably makes much of its associations with **Jeanne d'Arc** (Joan of Arc, the Maid of Orléans), who saved the town from the English in 1429. Her statue takes pride of place in the spacious pl. du Martroi, and the nearby Maison de Jeanne d'Arc, pl. du Général de Gaulle, is a reconstruction of her lodgings with a museum recounting her life and the events of 1429.

From Orléans, the railway tracks due south to **Vierzon**, where it crosses the River Cher, and then continues on through slightly hillier terrain to Limoges, where the grandiose railway station is a feast of fine interior design. It certainly showcases Limoges' position in the French porcelain industry. Administrative capital of the Limousin region, **Limoges** is a large industrial city. Its delightful mediaeval centre is a web of dark, narrow streets filled with half-timbered houses, small boutiques, and antique and china shops.

Surrounded by well-maintained botanic gardens – and overlooking the River Vienne – is the Gothic **Cathédrale de St-Étienne** (St Stephen's). Limoges was a centre of the Resistance during the Second World War. The **Musée de la Résistance et de la Déportation** at r. Neuve Saint-Etienne traces some of the Resistance operations.

ROUTE 18: TO THE PYRENEES | 185

The scenery really picks up south of Limoges as the railway weaves through the valleys of the **Dordogne**, with superb views of crags, lush valleys and perched villages. The route crosses the **River Lot** at Cahors, a town tucked into a bend of the river.

Cahors (suggested stopover)

An important Roman base in a tortuously winding valley, Cahors is famed for its **red wine**, which at its best rivals some of the Bordeaux *crus*. Its major monument, frequently depicted on wine labels, is the 14th-century Pont Valentré, a six-arched fortified bridge with three towers, west of the centre (reached via r. du Président Wilson). **Gallo-Roman remains** dot the town, and well restored 15th-century houses cluster around the cathedral. Cahors may be short on big sights, but we rate this small town for its uncomplicated charm. It's a lovely place to spend a night on a long rail journey.

ARRIVAL, INFORMATION, ACCOMMODATION

✈ A 6-min walk west of the centre. 🛈 Tourist office: Villa Malbec, pl. François-Mitterrand (www.cahorsvalleedulot.com). ⛴ For a special treat, the **Hôtel Terminus**, 5 av. Charles de Freycinet, ☎ 05 65 53 32 00 (www.terminus-1911.fr), is a beautifully restored station hotel dating from the 1920s. Also recommended for its great value for money is **Hôtel Jean XXII**, 2 r. Edmond Albe, ☎ 09 87 75 77 48 (https//hotel-jeanxxii.com). Right on the River Lot and covenient for the station is the Best Western Plus **Hotel Divona**, 113 Av. André Breton, ☎ 5 65 21 18 39 (www.divona-hotel-cahors.com) with great views of the Pont Valentré. ✖ At night, head out to one of the cafés and restaurants on blvd. Léon Gambetta or r. Nationale.

Beyond Cahors the railway, still loyally following Route Nationale 20, skirts the edge of the dry **Causse de Limogne** and then runs down the Garonne Valley to Toulouse.

Now a lively university city and cultural centre, **Toulouse** is one of France's largest cities, not consistently attractive, but lively, assertive and with economic muscle based on high-tech industries, space research and aviation. The pinky-red brick of many of the grandiose town houses has earned the city the epithet of the **Ville Rose**. Many of the main attractions are in the Old Town, centred on pl. du Capitole, dominated by the 18th-century **Le Capitole** (town hall). The superb St Sernin Basilica is the sole survivor of an 11th-century Benedictine monastery established to assist pilgrims en route to Santiago de Compostela.

The main railway station in Toulouse is named after the Toulouse district in which it is located: Matabiau. It is a splendid early 20th-century building by the Canal du Midi, about a ten-minute walk north-east of the city centre.

CONNECTIONS FROM TOULOUSE

Toulouse Matabiau station is an important hub for rail services in south-west France. Local trains shuttle west through the hills to Lourdes and Pau or down to the Mediterranean coast at Narbonne which is on **Route 20** in this book. Bordeaux (on **Route 17**) is just a couple of hours away. There are regular direct services to Marseille with onward connections to the French Riviera (**Route 15**).

There are direct TGV trains to Paris as well as three daily direct TGVs to Lyon which route south via the coast to Montpellier and Nîmes before running north via Valence to Lyon. Toulouse to Lyon takes four hours. Sadly the direct AVE to Barcelona, suspended during the pandemic, has not been reinstated.

Through the mountains

The first part of the run south from Toulouse is unexceptional, but suddenly the railway cuts through a distinct ridge of hills called the **Montagnes du Plantaurel** to reach **Foix**, a town well deserving of an overnight stop. It's one of those unsung but perfect-looking French towns. If you would like to stay, try the Hôtel Lons, 6 pl. Georges Dutilh, ☎ 05 34 09 28 00 (www.hotel-lons-foix.com).

The hillsides tilt ever sharper as the railway climbs the **Ariège Valley**, especially beyond the spa town of Ax-les-Thermes. Tight curves and tunnels are the prelude to arrival at Andorre-L'Hospitalet station. Despite the promise in the station name, there is no bus to Andorra! But see the gazetteer (p451) on how best to get to Andorra.

The train continues south through the Puymorens Tunnel to reach **Latour-de-Carol**, from where the narrow-gauge *Train Jaune* (Yellow Train) runs east to Villefranche-de-Conflent. This is a very scenic diversion along a mountain railway which has been threatened with closure. Facilities are sparse at Latour-de-Carol, but the station is in a wonderful mountain location at 1,230 m above sea level. The village of **Enveitg** (Enveig in Catalan) is a seven-minute walk from the station; just follow the grandly named Avenue de la Gare Internationale.

Latour-de-Carol is in a sunny oasis of fertile soils in an otherwise rather wild region. This great depression is known as **Cerdanya** on the Spanish

Travellers in the Pyrenees

The Pyrenees mountain chain is one of the world's most emphatic national boundaries, a great wall of snow-capped peaks separating France from Spain. Yet the Pyrenees have never quite sparked the **collective travel imagination** in quite the same way as the Alps. Swinburne and de Carbonnière, respectively English and French 18th-century travel writers, both played up the dark and forbidding aspects of Pyrenean landscapes. Swinburne climbed the **Pic du Midi**, mistakenly thinking it was the highest mountain in the Pyrenees, though it is 500 metres less lofty than **Aneto**, which at 3,404 metres really is the highest summit. He wrote of the "horrible view" and "rude and barren mountains". Early accounts of Pyrenean journeys always had a dark, almost Gothic, character. It is no surprise therefore that, even with the coming of the railways, the wider travelling public never engaged with the Pyrenees, generally preferring to linger in the foothills, seeking out the sedate pleasures of towns like Pau and Ax-les-Thermes.

side and Cerdagne on the French side of the frontier. Not a lot of folk head for Cerdanya as a primary destination, but many pass through en route to ski slopes, mountain resorts and of course Andorra.

The entire Cerdanya region is one of Europe's deliciously ambiguous **border zones**. The area juggles three languages with dexterity: Catalan, French and Spanish, not to mention a handful of dialects. And the international frontier meanders across the region without reference to natural features. The very permeability of the border drains energy from communities on the French side. The French village of **Bourg-Madame** is notably down at heel, while neighbouring **Puigcerdà** on the Spanish side of the border is a hive of activity. Easily the most curious of the villages in Cerdanya is **Llívia**, a place which is Spanish through and through and yet is located in a little parcel of Spanish territory entirely surrounded by France.

From Latour-de-Carol, the R3 regional train service runs down through beautiful Catalonian countryside, increasingly more Mediterranean in demeanour, to Barcelona.

Barcelona

This may be 'officially' Spain's second city after Madrid, but Barcelona is the **capital of Catalonia**, and its real sense of regional pride, energy and style make it a capital city to rival any in Europe. Over the past two decades it has become one of Europe's most visited destinations, and every year millions of travellers and tourists descend on Barcelona to marvel at the modernist architecture of Antoni Gaudí, explore the museums and galleries devoted to the likes of **Picasso** on C. Montcada 15–23 (www.museupicassobcn.cat) and **Miró** in Parc de Montjuïc (www.fmirobcn.org), promenade along the wide boulevards of the Eixample, or get lost in the narrow streets and alleyways of the old Gothic Quarter (Barri Gòtic). **La Rambla** is the most famous boulevard in Spain and the hub of city life for locals and visitors.

Beyond the art and the architecture, Barcelona has plenty more to divert you. There are few better places in Europe to eat out, whether you find your dinner in tiny backstreet tapas bars and the food stalls of the **Boqueria market**, or restaurants helmed by award-winning chefs.

The summer months can be very crowded, especially around famous landmarks such as **Gaudí's Sagrada Família** (see box on the next page), and those crowds are a tempting target for the city's pickpockets and bag-snatchers, who have given Barcelona a sadly justified reputation for petty crime. None of this should put you off, however, as Barcelona would be a highlight on any tour, and a perfectly wonderful destination in its own right. Cosmopolitan, prosperous and confident, Barcelona has been forward-looking ever since it hosted the Olympic Games back in 1992 and is firmly established as one of Europe's truly great cities.

A TASTE OF FRANCE

ANTONI GAUDÍ

For many people, Gaudí alone is sufficient reason to visit Barcelona. He designed many of its most characteristic buildings; throughout the city mansions, parks, schools, gateways, lamp posts and sculptures provide a constant reminder of his genius. Particularly striking are **Casa Milà**, with its extraordinary rippling facade devoid of straight lines and right-angled corners, and **Casa Batlló**, an imaginative example of the fusion of architecture with the decorative arts of the époque.

Gaudí's most emblematic structure is the still unfinished **Temple Expiatori de la Sagrada Família**, the city's iconic church that he spent over 40 years creating, personally going out into the street to raise funds among the passers-by to facilitate its construction.

ARRIVAL, INFORMATION, ACCOMMODATION

The main station is **Estació de Sants**, Plaça dels Països Catalans, about 3.5 km from the Old Town (metro: Sants-Estació), for suburban, regional and international trains as well as those to the airport. Estació d'Autobusos Barcelona Nord, Carrer d'Alí Bei 80 (www.barcelonanord.barcelona; metro: Arc de Triomf) and next to Sants station. Aeroport del Prat is 12 km south-west of the city (www.aena.es). RENFE trains run every 30 mins to and from Estació de Sants, taking 20 mins, and Estació Passeig de Gràcia (27 mins). The Aerobús bus service runs every 5–10 minutes from Plaça de Catalunya to the airport. Metro line 9 connects the airport with Zona Universitària. Tourist office: Plaça de Catalunya 17-S and next to the cathedral (www.barcelonaturisme.com). Once in town, the metro service will get you around quickly and easily. The major operator is TMB (www.tmb.cat). It has eight colour-coded lines, and trains are designated by the name of the last stop. There are single tickets valid for just one journey on a bus or metro and travel cards for 2–5 days. Tickets and cards can be purchased at TMB vending machines. The Hola Barcelona Travel Card is valid on the entire public transport in the city. It is activated when first using a bus, metro or tram. Zone 1 covers entire Barcelona (airport is outside that zone).

Barcelona has as wide a range of hotels as any major European city, but be aware that prices are fairly high compared to the rest of Spain. In the summer it is worth reserving in advance, or at the very least, arriving early in the day. There are many reasonably priced *pensiones*, particularly in the areas just off La Rambla in the Raval neighbourhood. Well located close to the Rambla is the cosy and comfortable **Forget Me Not Plus**, Rosellón 198, principal, ☎ 935 32 16 49 (www.forgetmenotbarcelona.com). Boutique-style at boutique prices, the **Casa Camper**, C. Elisabets 11, ☎ 933 426 280 (www.casacamper.com), is worth treating yourself to. The **Olivia Balmes Hotel**, C. Balmes 117, ☎ 932 144 163 (www.oliviabalmeshotel.com), is a good option in the Eixample district.

CONNECTIONS FROM BARCELONA

Barcelona is the perfect jumping-off point for explorations deeper into Spain. You can choose between **Route 21** and **Route 22** for itineraries which lead south to Andalucía. There are **direct high-speed trains** from Barcelona to Madrid, Seville, Málaga and Granada. A slower route cuts through the hills to Bilbao. There is an excellent cross-country service, leaving Barcelona at 09.05 for daytime journeys to Vigo and other cities in Galicia in north-west Spain.

Barcelona's port offers a good range of shipping connections with sailings to Tangier, Sardinia and several Italian mainland ports, among them Genoa, Savona and Civitavecchia. The latter is of course very convenient for Rome. **Overnight ferry journeys** like these are, like night trains, a creative way of covering a long distance while sleeping.

Route 19: From Normandy to the Rhône Valley

Cities: ★★ Culture: ★★ History: ★★ Scenery: ★★
Countries covered: France (FR)
Journey time: 12 hrs | Distance: 949 km | Map: www.ebrweb.eu/18map19

Over successive editions of *Europe by Rail*, we have always been aware that our French routes are very Paris-centric, mirroring the reality of life in a country where economic, social and cultural capital is disproportionately concentrated in Paris. This route is for those who love **provincial France** and don't want to struggle with the crowds of Paris.

On our bookshelves in Berlin, we have a classic social geography text from the middle of the last century. Written by **Jean-François Gravier**, and titled *Paris et le désert français* ('Paris and the French Desert'), the book is a powerful manifesto for the French provinces, with the railways taking some of the blame for Paris' super-dominance of French affairs. So, in the spirit of combatting *la centralisation ferroviaire* (Gravier's phrase), **this new route** for the 18th edition of *Europe by Rail* **avoids Paris** to explore parts of provincial France which have not featured in recent editions of this book.

Our route starts in the Normandy region of north-west France, includes the beautiful **Loire Valley**, then routes via Lyon to reach the Rhône Valley. In Lyon, you can cut off to the east to Savoie and Switzerland. Or you can stick with us for longer, taking the train down the **Rhône Valley** to Valence, where you can connect into **Route 20** for onward travel to western Provence, south-west France and Spain. For travellers starting from southern England, it's easy to connect into this route by using one of the Western Channel ferry routes to northern France, whether to Cherbourg, Ouistreham (on the coast near Caen) or Saint-Malo.

On our journey across France, we shall cross (and often re-cross) many of **France's great rivers**: not just the lovely Loire and the mighty Rhône, but also the Sarthe, Cher, Allier and many more. And that's appropriate, for France is a nation defined by her rivers. When the current system of *départements* was created in 1790, replacing the provinces of the *Ancien Régime*, it was decreed that the new territorial units should be named after geographical entities. Rivers were an obvious choice. And that's still true today. Most of France's *départements* take their names from local rivers, some of them not at all well known to those who live outside France, eg. the Aube, Yonne and Nièvre. All three rivers have lent their names to *départements* to the south-east of Paris. So hop aboard for this **watery meander** across rural France.

Recommended itinerary

You'll almost certainly want to spend a night or two in **Normandy**, which is well covered in **Route 16**. For a stop on or near the Loire, you may consider Angers, Saumur or – if you

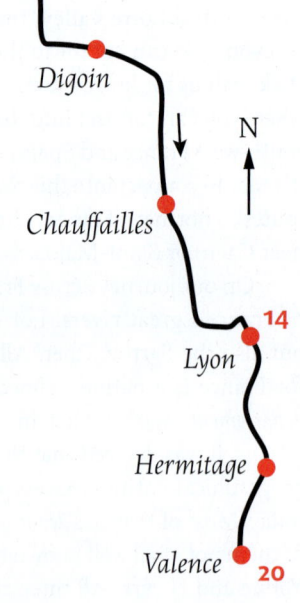

Notes

C – Additional fast trains run 4–6 times daily from Angers Saint-Laud to Saint-Pierre-des-Corps which is a mainline station on the outskirts of Tours.
S – All direct trains from Angers to Tours serve Saumur. Most also stop at Langeais.
T – Additional fast Intercité trains run thrice daily from Saint-Pierre-des-Corps (on the outskirts of Tours) to Bourges.
X – A change at Nevers is sometimes necessary. Additionally, there are thrice-daily Intercité trains from Bourges to Lyon which take a less scenic route via Roanne.

Route details

Caen to Le Mans		
Frequency	Journey time	Notes
5–7 per day	1h40–2h15	

Le Mans to Angers Saint-Laud		
Frequency	Journey time	Notes
Every 1–2 hrs	0h40–1h10	

Angers Saint-Laud to Tours		
Frequency	Journey time	Notes
4–10 per day	0h55–1h25	C S

Tours to Bourges		
Frequency	Journey time	Notes
5–6 per day	1h45	T

Bourges to Lyon Part-Dieu (via Chauffailles)		
Frequency	Journey time	Notes
2 per day	4h	X

Lyon Part-Dieu to Valence Ville		
Frequency	Journey time	Notes
Hourly	1h10	

prefer a smaller community – **Langeais**. Bourges and Lyon are other places along this route where an overnight stay (or longer) makes sense. You will in any case need to make at least one night along the way; it's too long a trip to reasonably complete it in a day. It's a journey which can be done almost entirely by local trains if you have time, with **no need for seat reservations** and no supplements for travellers using Interrail passes.

Southern Normandy

The railway station in **Caen** is a striking 1930s building, one which you'll either love or hate. It's certainly better since a major renovation a few years ago. Regional trains run south to Le Mans, slipping through bucolic Normandy countryside past apple orchards, plump cattle and striking half-timbered farmsteads. And some grand chateaux too, nicely serving as prep for the even grander palaces and castles of the Loire Valley. About 25 minutes after leaving Caen, you'll see the lovely **Château de Vendeuvre** to your left.

Most trains stop at both Argentan and Alençon, two mid-sized towns which were for centuries fierce rivals in the lace industry. This is a pretty rural route which is still not electrified, so these days it is something of a railway backwater. South of Alençon, the countryside becomes less engaging as we follow the Sarthe Valley south to **Le Mans**, an industrial city known worldwide for its association with motor racing. The famous Le Mans 24-hour race still takes place in June each year.

From Le Mans, our routes follows the Sarthe Valley south-west to Angers, following the line also used by **Route 17** in this book. But while Route 17 turns downstream at Angers (following the Loire to Nantes), this route follows the Loire upstream.

Beside the Loire and the Cher

Angers is well worth a stop, most particularly to see the castle, which from the exterior looks frankly hideous but inside is a remarkable haven of calm with beautiful gardens and an exhibition hall displaying one of the world's most historic tapestries. Read more on p178.

From Angers, our route follows the Loire **upstream to Tours**, using rail routes which are served by regional trains (TERs). There are inconvenient gaps in the timetable in the middle of the day. You'll have glimpses of the Loire aplenty from the train, but to appreciate the real beauty of the landscape and riverside towns you'll need to break your journey here and there. Two places along this line which we especially like are Saumur and Langeais. In **Saumur**, a handsome castle perched on a crag presides over this most amiable of towns; it's a lovely spot to wander and a good base for heading out to explore local vineyards, timeworn villages and the former troglodyte dwellings for which the Loire is so well known. **Langeais** is smaller than Saumur and is quite simply a fine place to while away a summer day. By the station is a simple memorial to the enforced deportations from Langeais in August 1944. Then wander by the picture-perfect town hall and main street up to the castle. If you are minded to stop overnight try the friendly B&B La vie voyage, 96 rue Anne de Bretagne, ☎ 07 72 32 95 24 (www.lavievoyage.com), well located for both the station and the Old Town.

East of Langeais, just after the enigmatically named station Cinq-Mars-la-Pile (where the *pile* is a remarkable, slender tower dating back to the Roman era), we cross the Loire for the first time. And what a crossing! There's a touch of drama here, especially at times of flood, as the bridge is at the point where the waters of the Cher decant into the Loire. From this bridge, it is just a few minutes into **Tours** where you will often need to change trains (but see the box below). For its modest size, Tours is remarkably lively. In just a couple of hours you can see the main sights, taking in the cathedral quarter and the busy *vieille ville* around **Place Plumereau** (locally dubbed Place Plum).

Beyond Tours, following the Loire upstream means making a big loop to the north through Orléans, a fine city indelibly associated with Joan of Arc. If you want to detour via Orléans, you can pick up this route again in

Fast or slow from the Loire to Lyon

From **Angers**, as indeed also from other lower Loire towns like Nantes and Saumur, you have many choices when it comes to rail travel to Lyon. There are one or two daily TGVs or thrice-daily Intercité trains – all direct trains but the TGVs and the Intercité services take completely different routes from each other. There is also the option of **using entirely regional trains** (TER services). Our route as described here assumes you use the regional trains, which will require at least one change of train along the way. If you travel straight through without stopovers, then that one change will normally be at Tours, but on some itineraries there may be additional changes, whether at Bourges, Nevers or elsewhere.

For **good scenery**, the slower option using TER trains wins hands down. No question! The Intercité trains follow the same lovely route as the TERs as far as the upper Loire, but take a faster though less scenic route on via Roanne to Lyon. The **TER trains are more adventurous**, abandoning the valley and taking to the hills, traversing the westernmost part of Beaujolais to reach Lyon. Following the route taken by the Intercité and TER trains from Angers via Saumur and Tours, the last stop before the two routes diverge is Moulins. Note that these Intercité trains from Nantes, Angers and Saumur to Lyon do not have mandatory seat reservations for holders of Interrail and Eurail passes, but it is nonetheless worth reserving as these trains are prone to overcrowding during the holiday season. It's only €1.60 and you can reserve on www.raileurope.com. No seat reservations are necessary for travel on the TER trains.

The TGVs leave the Loire Valley at Angers or Saumur, looping north through Paris' southern suburbs and then dashing south along France's **very first high-speed line** to Lyon. That route was opened in 1981, and as high-speed lines go we actually rate it highly, but that TGV routing from the Loire to Lyon elides all the good things which make this new route in *Europe by Rail* so rewarding. Seat reservations are mandatory on all TGV trains in France.

Nevers, and it only adds a couple of hours to the overall journey time. But there is good reason for sticking to the route described here, and **following the Cher Valley** upstream from Tours. This is a lovely rural line and it's a chance to stop off and see the **Château de Chenonceau**, which is perhaps the finest of the set-piece châteaux of the Loire region, although it's not actually by the Loire. It is the waters of the River Cher which drift slowly through the château's **arched foundations**. Fortunately there is a dedicated railway station called Chenonceaux about 30 minutes by train along the Cher from Tours (and there's a curious tale to tell around that extra x on the name of the station compared with the almost eponymous château). Plan your visit carefully and check opening times at www.chenonceau.com.

Continuing east from Chenonceaux station, the railway follows the River Cher upstream. Most trains stop at Gièvres, an out-of-the way railway junction also served by the metre-gauge **Chemin de Fer du Blanc-Argent** (CFBA). That this **narrow-gauge route** has survived at all is surprising. What's even more remarkable is that this line is fully integrated into SNCF's national rail network, one of only three metre-gauge routes in France which enjoy that distinction. The other two are respectively in the Pyrenees (the route followed by *Le Train Jaune*) and the Alps (running up the Chamonix Valley from Saint-Gervais-les-Bains). CFBA trains runs both north and south from Gièvres. The route south to Valençay, just 20 minutes by train, can be combined with a visit to the **Château de Valençay**. It's not quite a Chenonceau, but it is pretty magnificent.

Beyond Gièvres, our route leaves the Cher Valley, tracking south and east through the ancient Duchy of Berry to reach Bourges. On the train to Bourges, we chatted with a local family who assured us that Bourges' *lentilles vertes* (green lentils) are the best in France.

Bourges to Lyon

Bourges is the former capital of long-lost Berry, the French province which slipped from the map of France in the territorial reforms that introduced *départements*. Bourges is a fine city, good for more than just lentils. It makes a perfect one-night stop; we recommend the Hotel d'Angleterre, 1 Pl. de 4 Piliers, ☎ 02 48 24 68 51 (www.bestwestern.fr). Take time to explore the remarkable cathedral and the **watery Marais district** which provides green space right by the city centre.

From Bourges, there are a couple of TERs each day which take the **scenic route to Lyon**, usually around 7.30 in the morning (requiring a change in Nevers) and then a later direct train at 13.52. Times are correct for autumn 2024 but may of course change. To verify that your preferred train takes the scenic route (rather than the more southerly route through Roanne) check that the train stops at Paray-le-Monial.

Our journey from Bourges runs **east across flatlands**, then crosses a heavily wooded area to regain the River Loire (last seen near Tours). There's a splendid view of Nevers to the right as we cross the Loire – and you get to see it twice as the train reverses in Nevers. We follow the **Ligne du Bourbonnais**, also used by **Route 13**, south to Moulins-sur-Allier then branch left along a single-track rural route through Paray-le-Monial which initially seems unexceptional, but then develops into something very special.

At Digoin we leave the Loire Valley for the very last time, running alongside the Canal du Centre to **Paray-le-Monial**, an unassuming but lovely small town with a must-see basilica. Then the railway climbs into the hills, as fields of Charolais cattle give way to forested ridges with fine views of adjacent valleys. There are dramatic viaducts as the railway crosses deep valleys, the most notable of which is the elegant **Viaduc de Mussy** just after the long-abandoned station at Mussy. Many of the intermediate stations on this line have been closed, but those which remain do good business serving remote communities in the hills. These are the westernmost ripples of the uplands which, away to the east, host the vineyards of Beaujolais. Here, though, vineyards are rare, and the **landscape has a wilder touch** with stands of Douglas fir, great sweeps of broom, and here and there heather moors.

The best of the scenery is just after the station stop at Chauffailles, at 440 metres above sea level the highest still-used station on this railway. The summit of the line (at 525 metres) is 10 km south of Chauffailles and marks the boundary of two *départements* with riverine names: Loire and Rhône. From here it is downhill most of the way to **Lyon**, mainly following the River Azergues, which the railway crosses ten times (yes, we've counted!), until we reach the River Saône which we parallel down to Lyon. For more on Lyon, including a note on the excellent range of connections from that city, see p160.

Cruising the vineyards of the Rhône

From Lyon, the final section of our route follows the right bank of the River Rhône **downstream to Valence**, a journey of 105 km served by regular TER trains, mainly leaving from Lyon Part-Dieu station but with some additional trains starting at Lyon Perrache. Leaving the city, we pass factories and oil refineries, power stations and sewage works. But better things lie ahead, for running south to Valence we pass some of **France's most celebrated vineyards**.

Escaping from a tangle of motorways and industrial parks, we slip through Seyssuel where ambitious young winemakers are buying up land amid rumours that its wines could offer all the finesse of the well-established *appellations* just slightly further south. All trains pause at Vienne, a riverside town which boasts a galaxy of Roman-era monuments. The next stretch

Route 19: From Normandy to the Rhône Valley | 195

> ### Vintage views from the train
>
> The wine theme in the final part of this new route in *Europe by Rail* prompts us to reflect on how railways and wine make natural partners. It may be the bottle on the table over dinner in a dining car. **James Bond** opted for 1982 Château Angélus on the train to Montenegro in *Casino Royale*. Or it may be enjoying fine vistas of vineyards from the train. The energetic expansion of rail networks in the 19th century opened up new markets. The **Rioja area** of northern Spain shot to prominence when a new railway was constructed, connecting the wine estates by the Rio Oja and the Rio Ebro with the busy port of Bilbao.
>
> Today, taking the train along the Ebro Valley through Haro is still a wonderful introduction to the Ebro wine region. Other wine areas well suited to exploring by train include **Tokaj**, the Moselle Valley and of course Burgundy where the names of stations on the line south from Dijon recall a litany of fine *crus*.

of railway affords good views across to the **vineyards of Côte-Rôtie**, where Syrah grapes (with a dash of spicy Viognier) produce some the northern Rhône's most sought-after red wines. There's a tantalising view across the river to the turreted **Château d'Ampuis**, home of the Guigal family who have worked so tirelessly to bring the wines to global prominence. Then, also on the far bank of the river, there are glimpses of Condrieu, home to some of France's most delectable whites – all made from the Viognier grape.

A few minutes on, and now there are much prized vineyards rising up above the railway on the east bank. Signs mark the precious parcels of land owned by illustrious winemakers like Chave, Chapoutier and Jaboulet. There's a neck-craning view of a chapel high on a slope above the railway. Not any chapel but the one which dominates a vineyard in Hermitage known as **La Chapelle**, associated with legendary red wines which develop gently over decades in the bottle.

Soon we cross the fast-flowing **River Isère** and just a few minutes later we arrive in **Valence** where the elegant design of Valence Ville railway station recalls the architectural idiom of the Grand Trianon at Versailles. Coming from the north, it's the first town which embodies the energetic vitality of the scented south of France. It's a good place to draw breath and consider just how far we have come. You may have taken just a couple of days to follow this route, or you may have spun it out a fortnight or more. We have covered a lot of terrain, but there is still more of France to come. You may travel further south, joining **Route 20**, which runs further down the Rhône Valley towards the Mediterranean and then west through Occitanie to Spain. Or, if the mountains beckon, then join Route 20 running north-east to Savoie. Valence Ville station is also the starting point for one of **France's most scenic regional railways**, with twice-daily trains taking just over four hours to reach **Briançon**, a mountain community which often styles itself as Europe's highest city. Its striking position and handsome fortifications have earned it a place on UNESCO's World Heritage List.

Sidetracks: France without Paris

France's main-line rail network follows a hub-and-spoke pattern with all main lines radiating out from the **Parisian hub**. Travellers making journeys between provincial cities in France will often follow dogleg itineraries through Paris, invariably with a change of stations in the capital, because it is either faster or cheaper (or both) than taking slower cross-country trains. Sometimes there are simply no viable options other than travelling via Paris.

There are a few direct TGVs which **loop around the edges of Paris**, along the way affording glimpses of parts of the capital and its local hinterland rarely seen by visitors. The once-daily TGV from Le Havre and Rouen to Marseille is a gem in this respect. It slips around the west and south sides of Paris, passing freight yards and following lines used by no other long-distance passenger trains. Other TGVs which take in Parisian edgelands include the direct TGVs from Rennes and Nantes to Lyon, and Nantes and Bordeaux to Strasbourg.

A high-speed line boldly sweeps around the east side of Paris, serving dedicated stations at Aéroport Charles de Gaulle and Marne-la-Vallée – Chessy. This fast route by-passing Paris is called the **LGV Interconnexion Est**. It carries direct trains from Brussels and Lille to the Rhône Valley, Provence and Alsace.

For travellers from England wanting to avoid a cross-city transfer in Paris, the *LGV Interconnexion Est* is a godsend, allowing passengers to switch at Lille Europe station from a Eurostar onto TGVs bound for Lyon, Marseille, Nantes, Rennes, Strasbourg and many other provincial cities across France.

Elsewhere across France, you'll find **occasional cross-country TGVs** which go nowhere near Paris, but they are few and far between. There are once-daily direct trains from Nice to Nancy, from Toulouse to Lyon and from Metz to Montpellier. Trade down from TGVs to France's humbler *Intercité* (IC) trains and the cross-country network is still sparse. But there are three especially useful cross-country IC routes which don't serve Paris at all. These three routes are Marseille to Bordeaux, Nantes to Bordeaux and Nantes to Lyon. The latter could be used to follow part of **Route 19** in this book.

But the **gaps are extraordinary**. Try travelling from Bordeaux to Lyon. It's easy if you don't mind travelling via Paris, switching stations from Montparnasse to the Gare de Lyon in the French capital. The total journey, allowing ample time for that interchange in Paris, runs to about 5 hrs 15 mins. But the cross-country connections are abysmal, involving multiple changes of train and much longer travel times. An independent rail operator called **RailCoop** had plans to launch direct trains between Bordeaux and Lyon in 2024. It was an imaginative initiative run as a cooperative venture, which sadly folded in late 2023.

For those with time on their hands, it is possible to navigate across France relying entirely on **regional train services**. These are generally known as TERs and it's perfectly possible to devise itineraries which steer well clear of Paris using these regional rail routes. Indeed, some of our most memorable travel days with Interrail passes have been using TERs on long, straggly itineraries across rural France. Lovely as the French capital may be, it can be fun to experiment with cross-country routes that **defy the French railway geography** which so resolutely relies on Paris as a central hub.

IBERIAN CONNECTIONS
An introduction

It is now over 30 years since Spain's first high-speed rail route opened. That 1992 line from Madrid to Seville marked the start of the transformation of the Spanish rail network. Just a generation later, Spain now has Europe's most extensive network of **high-speed railways** with almost 4,000 route kilometres now in use. The experience of travelling on a high-speed train in Spain is quite special so it's appropriate that we include one long high-speed hop in this book. That features as **Route 22** (Barcelona to Málaga).

Sadly, rail links between Spain and Portugal have taken a dive. The closure of the route from Salamanca to northern Portugal in 1985 was a tragedy, though much of the route on the Portuguese side of the border survives. It makes a fine **excursion up the Douro Valley** from Porto (see p231). The more recent closure of other cross-border rail routes, running west from Cáceres and Badajoz respectively, were further blows. But two trains each day from Badajoz into Portugal have been reinstated. Improvements in services on the route from Vigo to Porto are of course very welcome and that cross-border link features in **Route 24** (which runs south from Santiago de Compostela through Porto to Lisbon).

Traditional rail routes

The **legacy rail network in Spain**, which existed well before the recent spate of high-speed lines, much of it dating back to the second half of the 19th century, offers many fine opportunities for explorations by rail and **Route 21** and **23** both rely entirely on those traditional lines. If you have time to follow just one route in this section, we recommend **Route 21** which cuts right across Spain from Barcelona to Cádiz, taking in an extraordinary variety of landscapes along the way.

There are of course many other routes which were candidates for inclusion. If you can find time to explore the line from **Zaragoza to València**, you're in for a treat. All the more so if you make an overnight stop at Teruel where you'll find some of the finest *mudéjar* architecture anywhere in Aragon. Another wonderful Spanish diversion is the long rail route which runs west from Santander all the way along the north coast to Ferrol. This 12-hour journey follows one of Europe's finest coastal rail routes.

For this 18th edition, we have connected **Route 24** and **21** to create an Iberian circuit. Direct buses from Lisbon to Seville take about seven hours for the journey. But **more adventurous travellers** might prefer to travel by train through southern Portugal from Lisbon to Vila Real de Santo António from where it's just 10 minutes on a ferry to Ayamonte in Spain, where you can pick up a bus for the short hop on to Seville. ■

Route 20: From the Alps to Catalonia

CITIES: ★★★ CULTURE: ★★ HISTORY: ★★ SCENERY: ★★★
COUNTRIES COVERED: SWITZERLAND (CH), FRANCE (FR), SPAIN (ES)
JOURNEY TIME: 12 HRS | DISTANCE: 856 KM | MAP: WWW.EBRWEB.EU/18MAP20

The train journey from **Geneva to Barcelona** is one of the finest excursions in this volume. It is a good practical way of covering a lot of ground, but it also takes in a wonderful medley of landscapes. This journey could reasonably form the basis for a multi-day trip, stopping off here and there along the way. It relies entirely on local or regional trains. If time is of the essence, you can dash from Geneva to Barcelona by high-speed train in under eight hours, with just one change of train along the way (the fastest connection each day requires a change at Valence TGV). That high-speed alternative follows the route described here only between Nîmes and Perpignan, so although you'll still get good views of the **Languedoc coast**, you'll miss out on most of the scenery which makes this journey so interesting.

The cities at either end of the route are, at first sight, as different as chalk and cheese. The lakeshore city of Geneva is Switzerland's most **liberal and cosmopolitan city**; when it comes to culture and design, Barcelona would always claim to be more cutting-edge. But there are similarities between the two cities; neither is a capital, yet both punch well above their weight on the world stage. Both Geneva and Barcelona are semi-detached from the countries to which they belong. Geneva only became part of Switzerland in 1815; almost entirely surrounded by French territory, the **République et Canton de Genève** is still proudly independent, and the disposition of political power in Switzerland tolerates (or humours) Geneva's free-spirited approach to the Swiss national project.

In Barcelona, notions of secession are altogether more serious. The Spanish region of **Catalonia** (Calalunya in the local Catalan language) has spawned its own energetic brand of nationalism and Barcelona had led the rallying cry for complete independence from Spain. Madrid's mean-spirited clampdown on Catalan protesters has quelled that movement.

Recalling the Catalan Talgo

It is no surprise that, throughout the 20th century, other than in times of war, there were direct trains linking Geneva with Barcelona. Until 1969, that always meant a quick change of train at Portbou on the French-Spanish border. Until the 1990s, most rail routes in Spain were built to the wider **Iberian-track gauge** and passengers had to switch from a French to a Spanish-gauge train. From June 1969, a little technological magic made it possible for passengers to board the Catalan Talgo train in Geneva and ride right through to Barcelona. Axles that shifted in width allowed the train to

ROUTE 20: FROM THE ALPS TO CATALONIA | 199

Route details

Geneva Cornavin to Aix-les-Bains

Frequency	Journey time	Notes
6 per day	1h10–1h25	A

Aix-les-Bains to Valence Ville

Frequency	Journey time	Notes
Hourly	2h10–2h30	

Valence Ville to Avignon Centre

Frequency	Journey time	Notes
Hourly	1h20–1h30	R

Avignon Centre to Perpignan

Frequency	Journey time	Notes
Every 2 hrs	3h20	

Perpignan to Collioure

Frequency	Journey time	Notes
Hourly	0h25	

Collioure to Figueres

Frequency	Journey time	Notes
Every 2 hrs	1h15–1h40	C

Figueres to Barcelona Sants

Frequency	Journey time	Notes
Hourly	1h50–2h10	V

Notes

A – Additional connections are available via Annecy (following Route 23).

C – This leg requires a change of train at Portbou.

R – The journey time refers to the regional trains serving this route. There are some additional TGV services between these stations which are faster. These TGV trains require advance reservation.

V – Additional fast trains run from Figueres Vilafant station to Barcelona Sants in just one hour.

slip easily from French to Spanish-gauge tracks at the border. Fifty years ago, the Catalan Talgo took under ten hours for the journey from the shores of Lake Geneva to the heart of Catalonia.

The route taken by the Catalan Talgo in those days was a superb transect across France, taking in the **Savoy Alps** and then following the **Isère Valley** down to the Rhône. Later the train was rerouted via Lyon but in this journey for *Europe by Rail* we follow the **classic Catalan Talgo route**. Back in 1972, the through train from Geneva to Barcelona was one of Europe's premium services. It carried only first-class carriages and a special supplement was required to use the train. Lunch was served in the air-conditioned restaurant car between Chambéry and Avignon; passengers could enjoy early evening tapas and a glass of wine as the train crossed the French-Spanish border.

The style of yesteryear has gone. The notion of trains which only carry first-class passengers is almost unknown in Europe these days. But the same scenery is still there for the taking and today's travellers with time on their hands can follow the precise route taken by the Catalan Talgo 50 years ago. This journey now relies entirely on trains where there's **no need to book in advance**. The journey from Geneva to Barcelona by this route requires three changes of train along the way. Those changes are at Valence Ville, Avignon Centre and Portbou. And it's a mark of how rail travel has changed that these days all four trains carry only second-class seating.

Recommended Itinerary

It is perfectly possible to follow this route in a day. It'll take about 12 hours. But this journey is too good to hurry. Make at least **one overnight stop** along the way. Ideally two. When it comes to places for those stopovers, our top choices would be Avignon and Collioure. As an alternative to Avignon, you may consider the Rhône Valley town of Valence (see p201) which gives a slightly shorter journey on the first day.

Two other cities on the journey feature on our must-see list, and for very different reasons. For a dash of **belle époque style**, the spa town of Aix-les-Bains is something quite special. Even if you are not into steamy, sulphurous spa treatments, Aix is a beautiful spot to relax. Another very worthwhile distraction is in the Catalan town of **Figueres** where the egg-topped Salvador Dalí Museum is a piece of theatre in itself.

Through the Alps

From **Geneva** (more on which on p392), the TER train (a French regional express) to Aix-les-Bains and Valence cuts through the western suburbs of the city and follows the right bank of the Rhône downstream to the French border. Within a dozen minutes of leaving Geneva, you are already in France. At **Culoz**, the train crosses the Rhône and takes to the hills.

Almost immediately, there is one of the highlights of the entire journey as the train runs along the east shore of the **Lac du Bourget**. This lakeshore railway line has long been a favourite for posters and advertisements proclaiming the merits of rail travel in France. The winning combination of lake and mountains is enhanced by the way in which the railway line hugs the very shore of the lake. At one point, as the route cuts around the **Baie de Grésine**, there is the brief but tantalising illusion of the train even crossing the lake with water on both sides. After stops in **Aix** and **Chambéry**, the railway crests a low col to reach the Isère Valley, which it follows for almost 140 km downstream through Grenoble to Valence.

CONNECTIONS FROM AIX, CHAMBÉRY AND GRENOBLE
Connect in Aix into **Route 23**. At Aix-les-Bains or Chambéry for TGVs to Paris. At Chambéry for Frecciarossa or TGV services to Turin and Milan. At Grenoble for regional trains to Lyon and Gap, and for TGVs to Paris

A few minutes short of **Valence**, the train stops at a new station located at the point where the Grenoble to Valence railway crosses the high-speed rail route from Paris to the Mediterranean. The station itself is a striking glass structure with platforms on two levels. From the TGV station, it is just ten minutes on the regional train to the city centre station which is called Valence Ville. In Valence, there is a palpable sense of having reached the south of France – a region known in French as the **Midi**. Valence Ville railway station marks the end of the line for the regional express train from Geneva. You need to change trains here for the onward journey south.

CONNECTIONS FROM VALENCE
At Valence TGV for fast TGVs to Barcelona, Marseille, Nice and Paris. At Valence Ville for occasional TGVs to Paris, and for regional train services to Lyon, Avignon and Marseille.

Leaving Valence, and heading south towards Avignon, there are fine views across the River Rhône, with peach and apricot orchards giving way to the volcanic hills of the Ardèche region. The railway follows the east bank of the river south through **Montélimar**, once famed for its nougat, but now sadly bypassed by most travellers making for the south. The next major city is **Orange**, which had a population of some 80,000 in Roman times and several sites from the period are still in existence. The **Arc de Triomphe** is the third largest Roman arch to have survived, and was originally in fact a gate to the ancient walled city. Dating from about 25 BC, it is a majestic three-arched structure decorated with reliefs honouring the victories of Augustus and the setting up of Arausio (Orange) as a colony. Orange's most famous sight is its Roman theatre, dating from the 1st century AD.

Avignon (suggested stopover)

In 1305, troubles in Rome caused the Pope to move his power base to Avignon. Wealth flowed into the town – and remained after the papacy moved back to Rome 70 years later. The city walls, built to protect the papal assets, still surround the city and enclose just about everything worth seeing here. Jutting from the north-western section is **Pont Saint-Bénézet**, the unfinished bridge famed in song ("Sur le pont d'Avignon"). It is inevitably a tourist trap (€5), but it does have a museum and a restored rampart walk leading up to the **Rocher des Doms** garden, with great views over both the bridge and the nearby district of Villeneuve-lès-Avignon. Take the steps from the gardens down to the Romanesque cathedral, **Notre-Dame des Doms**, dating from the 12th century and containing the tombs of Pope John XXII and Pope Benedict XII.

Adjacent is the most photographed sight in the city, the huge **Palais des Papes** (Papal Palace), boasting a 45-metre-long banqueting hall where cardinals would meet to elect a new Pope. In appearance it's more like a fortress than a palace and is still the most prominent landmark in the city. It houses a collection of Renaissance treasures that has now made the building into an art museum (€12). Contemporary art is to be found at the Collection Lambert, 5 r. Violette (closed Mon). In the middle of the Rhône lies **Île de la Barthelasse**, a favourite picnic island, with its own summer swimming pool. Place de l'Horloge is popular for its street entertainment and outdoor cafés.

Arrival, information, accommodation

≽ Avignon-Centre, just outside Porte de la République gateway in the city walls. Local trains connect Avignon Centre with Avignon-TGV station, 4 km south of the city on the bank of the River Durance. 🅱 Tourist office: 41 cours J. Jaurès (www.avignon-tourisme.com). 🛏 Head into the Old Town, where you'll find a large number of reasonably priced pensions and hotels in the backstreets a few minutes away: try the **Galante**, 20 r. Garlande, ☎ 04 90 80 08 85 (www.hoteldegarlande.com), which is central and comfortable. Right in the heart of the Old Town, just a short walk away from the Papal Palace, the highly regarded B&B **Le Limas**, 51 r. du Limas, ☎ 06 69 00 60 37 (www.le-limas-avignon.com) is set in a quiet side street. Or try **Hôtel Boquier**, a friendly, good-value option and centrally located, 6 r. du Portail Boquier, ☎ 04 90 82 34 43 (www.hotel-boquier.com).

Connections from Avignon

Avignon has two main railway stations. Avignon Centre is in the middle of town. Avignon TGV is way out of town and served by shuttle trains from Centre. The TGV station has **high-speed trains** to Perpignan, Barcelona and Madrid, as well as services to Paris and Nice, Mulhouse, Strasbourg and Luxembourg and also to Baden–Baden and Frankfurt-am-Main in Germany.

Avignon Centre also has direct TGVs to Paris, which are slower than the fast trains from Avignon TGV station but via a more interesting route, with the Paris-bound TGVs following the Rhône Valley north all the way to Lyon. Avignon Centre has regular local trains to Marseille and to Carpentras, the latter good for access to the Vaucluse region.

Into Languedoc

Moving on from Avignon, too many travellers head out to the TGV station on the southern outskirts of the city, from where a sleek Renfe **AVE train** whisks passengers with breathless speed and considerable comfort to Spain. The Madrid-bound AVEs dash from Avignon TGV to their first stop on

Spanish territory in less than three hours. These fast trains make just four intermediate stops in France before diving under the **Pyrenees** through the Perthus Tunnel, which opened to passenger trains in late 2013.

For this journey, we'll pass on the express and instead take the local train which runs all the way from Avignon Centre to **Portbou** in Spanish Catalonia with 22 stops along the way. It is a train used mainly by travellers making short hops between local stations. When we used this service, we were joined by shoppers on their way to Nîmes, students heading off later than they intended to lectures at the university in Montpellier, a small group of Catholic priests bound for a diocesan function in Perpignan and a young artist following in the footsteps of Matisse to Collioure.

Crossing the River Rhône at **Tarascon**, the train heads west across flat terrain to **Nîmes** (see p154), the city which invented denim and now courts controversy for its devotion to bullfights.

Connections from Nîmes

From Nîmes, local trains trundle south towards the **Rhône delta**; the line skirts salt pans, serving the fortress town of Aigues-Mortes on the way to the fishing port of Le Grau-du-Roi (50 mins from Nîmes). Both communities are interesting in their own way. The line gives glimpses of Camargue landscapes and some memorably ugly suburban sprawl.

Several trains each day run north from Nîmes into the **Cévennes**, with three of these services running the full length of the beautiful *ligne des Cévennes* to Clermont-Ferrand. This line is described (from north to south) as **Route 21** in this book.

From Nîmes, it is just a short hop on to **Montpellier**, a university city which is assertively high-tech, young and trendy. The main attraction is that it's simply a fun place to be. It styles itself as a *cité intelligente*, though Montpellier is not as relentlessly modern as the promotional blurbs might suggest. In June 2019, **MoCo Montpellier Contemporain** (www.moco.art) – a multi-site project and exhibition centre dedicated to contemporary art – opened near Saint Roch railway station. The **Vieille Ville** (Old Town) mixes cobbled streets with many 17th- and 18th-century mansions. Northwards lies the **Jardin des Plantes**, France's oldest botanical garden.

Beyond Montpellier, the railway dances between the hills and the sea, skirting salty lagoons and serving Sète and Agde. There are solid towns like **Béziers**, with its cathedral perched on a low ridge above the River Orb. At certain times of the year, advertisements for upcoming bullfights on station platforms are a reminder that the cultural border between **Languedoc and Catalonia** is more a matter of the mind than a line on any map. At the Gare de Perpignan, the station which so inspired **Salvador Dalí** (see box on next page), there are bilingual station signs, Perpinyà in linguistic alliance with Perpignan.

Perpignan is the principal city of French Catalonia. Catalonia's national circle dance, the sardana, is performed to music a couple of times a week in summer in the mediaeval place de la Loge, Perpignan's main square

God, Dalí and Perpignan

In 1965, Salvador Dalí completed his celebrated painting *La Gare de Perpignan*, which now hangs in the Museum Ludwig in Cologne. Dalí's artistic homage to Perpignan is a surrealist adventure, but it was not Dalí's first brush with the railway station at Perpignan. Two years earlier he had a powerful vision that marked out Perpignan station as a **pivot of the cosmos** which offered a unique perspective on the universe.

"On 19 September 1963, standing on the railway platform at Perpignan," he wrote in his diary, "I had a precise vision of the constitution of the universe." Clairvoyance slips easily into paranoia in the world of Salvador Dalí, but his vision has certainly helped place Perpignan on the map. Dalí regularly paced the platforms of the station, taking photographs and measurements; in 1966 he concluded that the measurements of the earth (and indeed the **weight of God**) are mirrored in the structure of Perpignan station.

Just as Shakespeare did his bit to promote Verona, so Dalí has turned out to be a great commercial asset in promoting Perpignan. Perhaps there are many travellers who, like us, make wholly unnecessary changes of train in the city merely to savour the surreal moment of being at one with the cosmos.

In appreciation of Dalí's enthusiasm for Perpignan railway station, the city council renamed the square in front of the station. **Place Salvador Dalí** is a good spot to reflect on the railway station's cosmic claim to fame. The building itself is a handsome example of a style of station that was often built in southern France, but no other station in the region has a statue of Salvador Dalí balanced on the roof. There are Dalíesque references aplenty in the colour scheme, which evokes something of the spirit of Catalonia. A sign inside the station welcomes travellers to the "Gare de Perpignan: Centre du Monde." It might more properly claim, à la Dalí, that it is the "centre cosmique de l'univers."

From the Gare de Perpignan it is just 23 minutes on a high-speed train to **Figueres**, the Catalan town where Salvador Dalí was born in 1904 and died in 1989. But the slow route around the coast was the one used in Dalí's day, and that is the onward journey to Spain described in this section of this book.

---

and still the hub of the city's life. The imposing Citadelle, to the south, guards the 13th-century **Palais des Rois de Majorque** (Palace of the Kings of Mallorca). It's a reminder that the Kingdom of Mallorca once included extensive mainland territories north of the Pyrenees.

Rattling south from Perpignan, the train returns to the sea and hugs the Côte Vermeille on the run south to the Spanish border. This is a remarkable stretch of railway, once used by many main-line services, but since the opening of the Perthus Tunnel relegated to lesser status.

Connections from Perpignan: Le Train Jaune

Perpignan is the starting point for a remarkable rail adventure which leads high into the Pyrenees. A number of TER trains each day run west from Perpignan into the hills. At Villefranche-Vernet-les-Bains, passengers change onto the narrow-gauge *Train Jaune* (Yellow Train) which negotiates the steep gradients and sharp curves of the 63-km long *ligne de Cerdagne*. In good summer weather, open carriages are used on this mountainous route.

The line terminates at Latour-de-Carol-Enveitg, which is on **Route 18** in this book. It is possible to connect there with SNCF trains running north to Toulouse and Catalan local trains down to Barcelona.

Collioure (suggested stopover)

Collioure on the **Côte Vermeille** makes an excellent overnight stop. This one-time fishing village – now an important centre for summer tourism – lies on a knob of land between two bays, overlooked by a 13th-century château. Matisse, Braque, Dufy and Picasso all discovered Collioure, and artists still set up their easels here. The domed church steeple looks distinctly Arabic.

Arrival, information, accommodation
✈ 400 m west of the centre. 🛈 Tourist office: pl. du 18 Juin (www.collioure.com).
🛏 **Hôtel Madeloc**, 24 r. Romain Rolland, ☎ 04 68 82 07 56 (www.madeloc.com), has a pool in a garden setting, but is pricey (as are other options); open Feb–Nov. Or try the Hotel Restaurant **La Frégate**, 24 Av. Camille Pelletan, ☎ 04 68 82 06 05 (www.fregate-collioure.com) well placed on the edge of the city centre and also convenient for the station. Only a few minutes walk from the centre is the very welcoming B&B **Villa Miranda**, 15 r. du Pla de les Forques, ☎ 04 68 98 03 79 (www.villamiranda.fr).

Across the Border

Beyond Collioure, the railway slips past a dozen capes and bays, each one a little more tantalising than its predecessor. The line runs through neat vineyards at Banyuls and just after **Cerbère** crosses the border into Spain.

The first station on Spanish territory is **Portbou**. It is a world apart from the mass tourism which defines most of the Costa Brava. Portbou has a real sense of isolation, and it's a pleasant spot to stop for an hour or two. You will in any case always need to change trains at Portbou. Continuing south, the railway all too soon cuts inland to Figueres, where the much-visited **Teatre-Museu Dalí** (www.salvador-dali.org, closed Mon except in Jul&Aug) is the main attraction, honouring the town's most famous son. Whether you consider Dalí a genius or a madman, the museum is likely to confirm your views of the Surrealist artist. Appropriately enough, it's a bizarre building, parts of which Dalí designed himself (including his own grave), a terracotta edifice sporting giant sculpted eggs.

The principal town between Figueres and Barcelona is **Girona** with a mediaeval Old Town on the east side of the River Onyar, connected by the **Pont de Pedra** to a prosperous new city in the west. From the bridge you can see the **Cases de l'Onyar** – a line of picturesque houses overhanging the river. In the heart of the labyrinthine Old Town is the Gothic cathedral. Check out the Banys Àrabs (Arab Baths), Romanesque with Moorish touches and dating from the 13th century. In the narrow streets of El Call (the old Jewish quarter) is the Bonastruc ça Porta Centre, which contains the **Museum of Jewish Culture** (entrance from C. de la Força 8).

From Girona, it's an easy run south to **Barcelona**. The railway enters the Catalan city through its unexciting northern suburbs and terminates in subterranean gloom at the Estació de Sants.

Sidetracks: Mediterranean islands

There are over **100 populated islands** in the Mediterranean, but regular scheduled trains on just four of them. The largest and most populous of these islands is of course Sicily which features on **Route 48** in this book.

The railways of Malta and Cyprus are long gone. The former industrial railways of Ibiza and Crete, respectively serving salt pans and mines, never carried regular passenger traffic. The horse-drawn passenger tram at Karlovasi on the Greek island of Samos closed in 1939. The three Mediterranean islands apart from **Sicily** where you will find well-used year-round passenger trains are Mallorca, Corsica and Sardinia.

The Mediterranean is defined by its sea coasts, its rugged peninsulas and its islands, the latter dubbed 'continents in miniature' by the French historian Fernand Braudel. So why not take time to explore at least some of the islands? There are **excellent ferry services**, and not just the obvious short hops from nearby mainland ports. Useful longer overnight crossings include Barcelona to Porto Torres (Sardinia) and Toulon to Alcúdia (Mallorca).

You may care to follow in the footsteps of English writer **DH Lawrence** and his wife Freda who made a midwinter journey to Sardinia. Sensibly, they took care to make bacon sandwiches and prepare a thermos of tea before setting out from their Sicilian home in **Taormina**. First they took the train to Messina ("dreary, dreary hole" wrote Lawrence), and then journeyed by train along the north coast to Palermo.

DH Lawrence wrote a wonderful account of their travels, crossing by ship from Palermo to Cagliari and spending nine days exploring **Sardinia**, much of the latter by train. *Sea and Sardinia* was published in 1921 and remains a classic piece of travel writing. It is witty, insightful and tells us as much about Lawrence as it does about Sardinia. Take a copy if you branch off from Route 48 and head by train from Messina to Palermo for the ferry for Sardinia. The trains on Sardinia are not much faster than in Lawrence's day. It still takes over five hours to travel from Carbonia to Porto Torres.

From Sardinia, it is but a short hop by ferry to **Corsica** where the island's **narrow-gauge trains** still have a certain antique charm. Ajaccio to Bastia takes almost four hours. The finest stretch of Corsica's metre-gauge rail network is the run from Ajaccio up past Vizzavona to Corte. It features superb mountain scenery and crosses Gustave Eiffel's Vecchio Viaduct. Over on **Mallorca**, there are railways from the island capital at Palma to Sa Pobla (52 mins), Manacor (59 mins) and Sóller (55 mins). Trains leave from the transport interchange on Plaça d'Espanya in Palma. The train trip to Sóller is by far the most scenic of the three options. The **Ferrocarril de Sóller** (Sóller Railway), funded through profits from the citrus trade, was built through difficult terrain and quite transformed access to remoter parts of Mallorca. Sóller station is improbably grand for somewhere in the outback, and the town itself a happy maze of little lanes where you can still just imagine what life on this beautiful island might have been like before it was engulfed by tourists. From Sóller a tram runs down to the old fishing village of Port de Sóller. The return from Palma to Port de Sóller, covering train and tram, is €32.

Route 21: Historic Spain

CITIES: ★★★ CULTURE: ★★ HISTORY: ★★ SCENERY: ★★
COUNTRIES COVERED: SPAIN (ES)
JOURNEY TIME: 12 HRS | DISTANCE: 1,265 KM | MAP: WWW.EBRWEB.EU/18MAP21

Spain's high-speed rail network was inaugurated in 1992 with the opening of a fast link from Madrid to Seville. Since then, the network served by super-fast trains (known as Alta Velocidad Española or AVE services) has been progressively extended. With a little planning you can enjoy a Catalan breakfast in Barcelona, stop off for a leisurely lunch in Madrid and still be in Málaga in time for tapas. **Route 22** in this book describes that fast route south from Catalonia to Andalucía.

Not everyone favours such speed, and Route 21 is a **real slow travel experience**. When the early Scottish traveller **Henry David Inglis** headed south from Madrid to Andalucía in 1830, he bemoaned the fact that the regular stage carriage took merely a week – too fast, he felt, to really do justice to the landscapes along the way. The old roads to Andalucía all converge on a single natural defile that strikes a huge gash through the mountains. The **Sierra Morena** may not tower to great heights, but the rugged demeanour of these mountains creates a formidable barrier to travellers bound for the south.

Despeñaperros is the name given to the great gorge that was, for travellers of yesteryear, the pre-eminent gateway to Andalucía. For men like Henry Inglis and others who ventured to Andalucía in the first half of the 19th century, the seductive beauty of the gypsies of Andalucía was presaged in the cruel beauty of Despeñaperros. This was, and still is, a place with fierce relief, great black rocky walls and wild torrents – everything that was needed in fact to appeal to the **Romantic imagination**.

If you take the modern high-speed line south to Andalucía described in **Route 22**, you'll find it slices through the Sierra Morena like butter. You'll hardly notice the hills. But if you have a few hours to spare why not take the old rail route that runs through the gorge at Despeñaperros. It's the route we describe here. This is truly one of **Europe's finest rail journeys**, and it's a creative way of linking Barcelona with southern Spain.

SUGGESTED ITINERARY

There is a once-daily direct Intercity train from Barcelona to Andalucía which follows precisely the route described here – so following the coast down to **València**, and later using the **Despeñaperros gorge** to reach Andalucía. For years it terminated in Seville, but since August 2021 it has been extended to Cádiz. If that seems too much of a long haul for one day – it takes just over 13 hours – try splitting the journey up into bite-size chunks. València, Córdoba and Seville all make rewarding stopovers. Along the early and closing sections of the route, there is a wide choice of trains. It is only between **Alcázar de San Juan and Córdoba** that you are restricted to just one train each day.

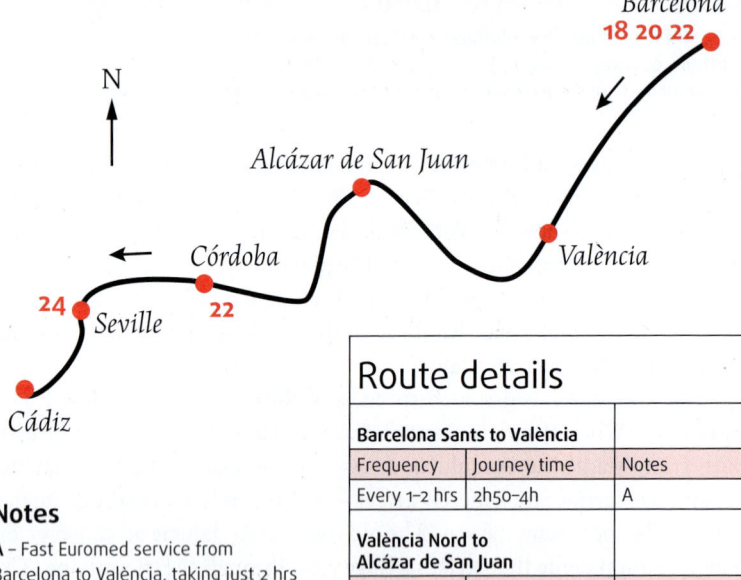

Route details

Barcelona Sants to València		
Frequency	Journey time	Notes
Every 1–2 hrs	2h50–4h	A
València Nord to Alcázar de San Juan		
Frequency	Journey time	Notes
3–4 per day	2h40–4h	B
Alcázar de San Juan to Córdoba		
Frequency	Journey time	Notes
1 per day	3h15	C
Córdoba to Seville Santa Justa		
Frequency	Journey time	Notes
1–2 per hr	0h45–1h25	
Seville Santa Justa to Cádiz		
Frequency	Journey time	Notes
Every 1–2 hrs	1h30–1h45	

Notes

A – Fast Euromed service from Barcelona to València, taking just 2 hrs 50 mins, terminate at Joaquín Sorolla station. The slower IC trains (including the *Torre del Oro*) and regional trains all run to València Nord.

B – Some journeys between València and Alcázar require a change of train at Albacete.

C – The sole direct train is the *Torre del Oro*. There is also a late morning option requiring a change of train in Jaén. It takes over 5 hrs (Jaén, not mentioned in the main text, is on a branch line to the south of this route).

Leaving Barcelona

The Catalan coast south-west of Barcelona (p187) is known as the **Costa Daurada**. It is not all beautiful, yet tucked away in the ugly urban sprawl are some interesting spots. But we have to be patient to see the sea. For the first part of our journey out of Barcelona, our route follows a longish stretch of high-speed line, the last 65 km of which only opened in 2020. That new route ends beyond **Cambrils**, where the railway finally gains the coast, skirting mile after mile of golden beaches – and some fabulously tacky resorts.

A highlight is crossing the **watery flatlands** that blend into the delta of the **Ebro** (Spain's largest river). Despite one or two fine sights, such as the fortified coastal city of Peñíscola, there is no real reason to linger en route to València.

València (suggested stopover)

València is Spain's third city and the **home of paella**. It is a large, modern metropolis, with an enviable capacity for reinvention. València is in the forefront of style and fashion, and sees itself as the natural capital of the entire Levante region. At its heart there's a bustling **atmospheric Old Town** with two mediaeval gateways (Torres de Serranos and Torres de Quart), pleasant squares, characterful run-down backstreets, crumbling baroque mansions and a handful of other historic landmarks. The sizeable student population ensures that there's no shortage of nightlife.

Santiago Calatrava's stunning **City of Arts and Sciences** (www.cac.es), is the city's top attraction and a symbol of the 'new' València. It's a gleaming, white, futuristic entertainment complex which encompasses an excellent hands-on science museum, a vast aquarium, an arts centre and a planetarium. The port and beach area were dramatically revamped for the 2007 America's Cup and València is fast becoming one of the Med's most fashionable hot spots.

The Old Town, which contains the main sights, is easily covered on foot. Two towers preside over the **Plaça de la Reina**: the baroque spire of Santa Catalina and the Miguelete, which is the bell tower of the cathedral; climb the spiral staircase to the top for a good view. València's key building is its cathedral, a mixture of styles ranging from Romanesque to baroque. The city's finest building is the Gothic **Llotja de la Seda**, Plaça del Mercat (closed Mon, €2 entry fee), a legacy of the heady days of the 15th-century silk trade, while the nearby **Mercat Central** is a vast art nouveau market hall.

In summer, many cafés and bars in València offer *orxata*, a sweet milky drink made from *chufas*, or earth almonds, traditionally eaten with bread sticks (either chewy, sweet *fartons*, or more brittle *rosquilletas*).

TORRE DEL ORO OR GARCÍA LORCA

The **once-daily train** from Barcelona to Andalucía has an illustrious history. For 70 years, there has been a morning departure from Barcelona which follows this route to Andalucía. Fifty years ago, the journey from Barcelona to Seville took 22 hours. Now it takes just half that time and extends beyond Seville to Cádiz. These days the train is called the *Torre del Oro*, taking its name from the watchtower and prison in Seville built by the **Almohad Caliphate** in the early 13th century. That's the same name as the train bore in the late 1980s. But for many years from late 1989 the train was named in honour of the radical Andalusian poet and playwright García Lorca.

Ten years ago the *García Lorca* was Spain's most interesting train; apart from the main portion bound for Seville, it carried through carriages to Málaga, Granada, Almería and even Badajoz, close to the Portuguese border in the Extremadura region. It still makes sense to use the *Torre del Oro* from Barcelona to reach all these destinations, but nowadays a change of train is necessary. The recent **reversion of the train name** from *García Lorca* to *Torre del Oro* is interesting. Metaphors of surveillance and detention are perhaps more in keeping with modern pieties than theatre and poetry.

Arrival, information, accommodation

🚆 València is slightly complicated when it comes to train stations. The *Torre del Oro* train which forms the backbone of Route 21 stops at **Estació del Nord**, which has a magnificent tiled entrance hall – it's definitely worth a look. Most other fast trains from Barcelona, as well as the swift AVE service from Madrid, serve **Joaquín Sorolla** station (linked to Nord by a free bus service). Trains to Cuenca and Aranjuez leave from Nord. As a rule of thumb, most 'interesting' trains run to and from Nord. 🛈 Tourist office: Pl. del Ayuntamiento 1 (www.visitvalencia.com) and a branch at Joaquín Sorolla station.

🛏 Good budget areas are around Pl. del Ayuntamiento and Pl. del Mercado. The **Venecia Palazo Centro**, Pl. del Ayuntamiento 3, ☎ 96 352 42 67 (www.hotelvenecia.com), is an excellent value hotel. The **Antigua Morellana**, C. d'En Bou 2, ☎ 96 391 57 73 (www.hostalam.com), is friendly and well located close to the central market. Well located on the edge of the Old Town and just a 5-min walk from Nord station is the modern and comfortable **Sorolla Centro**, Convento Santa Clara 5, ☎ 96 352 33 92 (www.hotelrhsorollacentro.com).

Connections from València

Trains run **down the coast** to Alicante, with some continuing to Murcia and Cartagena. Preliminary work has just started on a new rail link from Murcia to Almería, which will provide a new connection from the Spanish Levante into eastern Andalucía. Until, then you can bridge the gap in the rail network by taking a bus. ALSA (www.alsa.es) serve the Murcia to Almería route. The journey takes three to four hours.

There is a very fine **rural rail route** running inland from València to Zaragoza via Teruel. Fast trains to Madrid via the new high-speed line take less than two hours to reach the capital. Note that the old line to Madrid via Requena closed in summer 2022. València has excellent ferry links with the Balearic Islands. Our pick of the many routings available is the Saturday night sailing from València to Maó (Mahón) on the island of Menorca. It's a 15-hour crossing. In fine weather, this is a wonderful route. For more on Mallorca and other Mediterranean Islands, see our **Sidetracks** feature on p206.

La Mancha

The three-hour stretch of the journey beyond València takes in a region of Spain well off the beaten track. You trade the lush landscapes of the coast for the arid interior. The first place of any size is **Xàtiva**, which looks uninspiring from the train but in fact has a delightful Old Town. The railway then turns decisively west, passing the distinctive Moorish castle at Almansa perched on its limestone crag. Olive groves and red soils are the keynote themes, as the train skirts the southern edge of the **Cordillera de Montearagón** and comes to rest in the ultra-modern station at Albacete-Los Llanos – where you can connect onto the high-speed network with the fastest AVEs running to Madrid in just 90 minutes.

After **Albacete**, the train runs through dusty small towns and crosses the Záncara Valley to reach Alcázar de San Juan. This is Don Quixote country; you'll spot several clusters of windmills from the train.

Alcázar connections

The *Torre del Oro* train from Barcelona to Andalucía reverses direction at Alcázar de San Juan. This is an important railway junction. **Aranjuez**, a verdant oasis of green, is just an hour away to the north. The *Torre del Oro* connects in Alcázar with a direct train to Merida and Badajoz. The run to Badajoz takes almost six hours.

There is also a connection at Alcázar into the train to **Almería** which, like the *Torre del Oro*, follows the Despeñaperros route. You can identify trains via Despeñaperros from the timetable as services that stop at both Alcázar de San Juan and Linares-Baeza (half a dozen daily services in each direction).

The finest part of the entire journey is the two-hour stretch beyond Alcázar de San Juan. The train lopes south through great vineyards towards the Sierra Morena. Cast back to before the construction of the railway and **Despeñaperros** was the haunt of *banditti* who would waylay innocent travellers as they ventured south to Andalucía.

It is tamer nowadays, but still by far the most interesting rail route for those heading for Andalucía. South of Despeñaperros, you emerge into a land of dense olive groves and huge oleanders on the platforms of railway stations. Suddenly there are lush colours and Moorish architecture, and scenes outside the carriage window that seem to be taken directly from paintings by Murillo and Velázquez.

The first stop in Andalucía is **Vilches**, its neat blue-and-white station building a cool antidote to summer sun. The railway then follows the Guadalquivir Valley down to Córdoba – a city which, with its striking mosque-cum-cathedral, is simply not to be missed (read more on p219).

Connections from Córdoba

You can connect in Córdoba into **Route 22**, following it south to Antequera and Málaga or north to Madrid and Barcelona. The train service from Córdoba to Granada has been much improved in recent years with seven direct trains each day, the fastest taking just 92 minutes, although others take close to two hours. It is now very easy to make a day trip from Córdoba to Granada to visit the **Alhambra**.

From Córdoba the *Torre del Oro* continues down the **Guadalquivir Valley** to Seville, through a landscape increasingly dominated by orange groves. The train stops at Santa Justa station, a dramatic piece of architecture which opened just before Seville hosted the 1992 World's Fair.

Seville (Sevilla) – (suggested stopover)

Of all the Andalusian cities, Seville has the most to see. The **capital of Andalucía**, it's a romantic, theatrical place, with a captivating park, a gigantic cathedral and two very important fiestas: the Feria de Abril and the processions of Holy Week. **Columbus** set out from Seville to discover the New World, and *Don Giovanni, Carmen, The Barber of Seville* and *The Marriage of Figaro* were all set here.

Most places of interest are in the **Barrio de Santa Cruz**. A pleasant place for a stroll, it lives up to the idealised image of Spain; white-and-yellow houses with flower-bedecked balconies and romantic patios. The focal point is the Giralda, a minaret that has towered over the Old City since the 12th century and which now serves as a belfry to the cathedral. Built by the Almohad rulers 50 years before Ferdinand and Isabella's Christian Reconquest, it consists of a series of gentle ramps designed for horsemen to ride up; it's in excellent condition and worth climbing for the views.

The cathedral is the largest Gothic structure in the world, simply groaning with gold leaf. The **Sacristía Mayor** houses the treasury and Sacristía de los Cálices contains Murillos and a Goya. A huge memorial honours Christopher Columbus (who may or may not be buried here!).

The **Alcázar** (www.alcazarsevilla.org) was inspired by the Alhambra of Granada, but has been marred by later additions. Within is the Salón de Embajadores, where Columbus was received by Ferdinand and Isabella on his return from the Americas, and there are also shady, interconnected gardens separated by arched Moorish walls. The neighbouring **Casa Lonja** contains a collection of documents relating to the discovery of the Americas.

The **Museo de Bellas Artes** (closed Mon, free for EU nationals), Pl. del Museo 9, has a collection of 13th–20th-century Spanish paintings, second only to that of the Prado in Madrid.

Arrival, information, accommodation

Estación Santa Justa, Av. de Kansas City; 15-min walk from the centre. 32 goes from the station to Plaza de la Encarnación; City buses: C1 and C2 are circular routes around the town. Many buses pass through Plaza de la Encarnación, Plaza Nueva and Av. de la Constitución (for information see www.tussam.es). San Pablo Airport, 12 km east of town. Express buses (EA) take 35 mins to the centre.

Tourist office: at the station (www.visitasevilla.es). During Holy Week and the April Fair accommodation is very difficult to obtain and must be pre-booked. On the whole, staying in Seville tends to be expensive. Just a short walk from the centre of Seville is the very welcoming and comfortable B&B **Casa Alfareria 59**, C. Alfareria 59, ☎ 954 341 317 (www.casaalfareria59.com). A nice and comfortable hotel in a quiet area, a 20-min walk from the town centre across the bridge at Av. Cristo de la Expiración, is the **Monte Triana**, C. Clara de Jesús Montero 24, ☎ 954 343 111 (www.hotel-montetriana.com). Or try the upmarket **Amadeus**, C. Farnesio 6 & C. San José 10, ☎ 954 501 443 (www.hotelamadeussevilla.com), right in the Old Town with wonderfully decorated public spaces that fit with the hotel's name. Seville is probably the best place to sample such typical Andalucían dishes as *gazpacho* (chilled tomato and pepper soup) and *pescaíto frito* (deep-fried fish). The liveliest bars and restaurants, frequented by students, are in Barrio de Santa Cruz.

Connections from Seville

Connect here onto **Route 24**, following it in reverse to Lisbon and beyond. This first leg on that route depends on the express bus services from Seville to **Faro**, most of which continue to Lisbon. You can link into the Portuguese rail network in either Faro or Lisbon.

A rural rail route runs north from Seville to the **Extremadura** region. Services are sparse, but you can take a direct train from Seville to both Merida and Cáceres, with one train each day continuing right through to Madrid, taking just under eight hours to reach the Spanish capital. We rate this back-door rural journey from Seville to Madrid as one of the finest train rides in the Iberian peninsula.

Jerez de la Frontera

Just before you reach Cádiz on the train from Seville you pass through the station for Jerez. This town has given its name to **sherry** and the bodegas are the town's main attraction; it's also home to Spanish brandy. Here you will find such familiar names as Harvey, González Byass and Domecq. Most **bodegas** offer tours (varying prices, reservations necessary for some; many close in Aug) that finish with a tasting. Sherry also appears in the local cuisine; try *riñones al Jerez* (kidneys in sherry sauce).

From Seville, it is just another 100 minutes down to the coast at Cádiz. It's an interesting run, passing **Jerez de la Frontera** and approaching Cádiz through a strange landscape of salt lagoons. For a more romantic approach alight from the train at El Puerto de Santa María and take the ferry across to Cádiz.

Cádiz

Like Venice, that other once-great naval city, Cádiz is approached by a **causeway** and all but surrounded by water. Its tight grid of streets, squares and crumbly ochre buildings exudes an atmosphere of gentle decay. It's all the better for that, and really comes into its own during the carnival in February and in the evening, when the promenaders come out and the bars open. Colourful tiling is a feature of the pavements, parks and even the **Catedral Nueva** (New Cathedral), which was rebuilt, like much of the rest, in the city's 18th-century heyday. However its origins go back to 1100 BC when the city was founded by the Phoenicians; the port was of vital importance at the time of the conquest of the Americas (which was why Sir Francis Drake attacked it). You can get a panoramic view of it all from **Torre Tavira**, both from the top of the tower and in the camera obscura below, via a mirror and lens on the roof.

There's always been fish aplenty on the Cádiz table and the residents of Cádiz are quick to remind British visitors that fried fish was a Cádiz staple centuries before it was even dreamt of in Britain. It was Sephardic Jews who took the idea from Spain to Britain.

Arrival, information, accommodation

The main station is at Pl. de Sevilla. Tourist office: Av. 4 de Diciembre de 1977 (www.cadizturismo.com). A friendly, small hotel in the Old Town not far from the station is **Hotel Argantonio**, C. Argantonio 3, ☎ 956 211 640 (www.hotelargantonio.es). The stylish **El Armador Casa Palacio**, C. Ancha 7, ☎ 620 073 345 (www.elarmadorcasapalacio.com), is well located near Pl. San Antonio in a lively street. A peaceful option in a refurbished convent located in the Old Town is **Convento Cadiz**, C. Santo Domingo 2, ☎ 956 200 738 (www.hotelconventocadiz.net).

Connections from Cádiz

Cádiz is, quite literally, the **end of the line**. You can go no further by train. But our **Sidetracks** feature on the next page has a few words about boat connections from Cádiz.

Sidetracks: South from Spain

Route 21 and 22 end in a region deeply influenced by settlers from North Africa. In its heyday (in the 8th and 9th centuries AD), the Muslim caliphates and emirates collectively known as **Al-Andalus** covered a much larger area than modern Andalucía, extending beyond the Iberian peninsula and the Pyrenees to Septimania, the region of south-west France around Narbonne. This veil of Moorish settlement gave Arab mariners control of much of the western Mediterranean and the Strait of Gibraltar.

Morocco and Spain have for 40 years discussed a possible rail tunnel linking Europe to Africa. Don't hold your breath. If it comes to pass, the first trains from Madrid to Marrakesh won't be running before 2040. So meanwhile it's the boat, and you are spoilt for choice. From **Málaga** (on **Route 22**), there are excellent links to Melilla, one of two autonomous Spanish cities on the North African coast which, along with some other tiny fragments of Spanish territory on the Moroccan coast and some inshore islands, are all that is left of África Española.

Melilla wins no prizes for beauty, but it is a curious political oddity (as indeed is Gibraltar on the European side of the water). From Melilla it is a short walk south across the Moroccan border to Beni Enzar railway station, which has direct daytime and overnight trains to Casablanca, almost 700 km away.

More common jumping-off points for Africa, each with shorter crossings than from Málaga, are **Algeciras** and **Tarifa**. If you are bound for Tangier, Tarifa is the best bet, for services from there go to Tangier city rather than the out-of-town port (shown in timetables as Tangier Med). The crossing from Tarifa takes one hour (see www.frs.es for the timetable). From Algeciras, there are frequent crossings to **Ceuta** (the second Spanish city in North Africa). As in Melilla, you can walk into Morocco, along the way seeing the fierce fences that surround this little outpost of Europe in Africa to deter migrants who judge that Ceuta or Melilla might be an easy route into the European Union.

There is one port that, in terms of its historic status as a great mercantile centre, quite eclipses anywhere we have yet mentioned in this Sidetracks feature. And that is **Cádiz** (on **Route 21**).

During more than 500 years under Moorish rule, Cádiz was very bound into Mediterranean and North African trade, but since the Spanish settlement of the Americas, Cádiz has set its sights on the Atlantic. That is reflected in modern shipping schedules, for Cádiz has no scheduled service to the African mainland. But the town has something special for those with a dose of sea fever, viz. a ferry to the **Canary Islands**. It takes 31 hrs to Lanzarote, 40 hrs to Las Palmas de Gran Canaria, 48 hrs to Santa Cruz de Tenerife, and 64 hours to Santa Cruz de La Palma.

It used to be possible to continue beyond the Canary Islands to either Madeira or to El-Aaiún on the African mainland, but these routes no longer run. You can however return from the Canaries by a completely different route to the European mainland, using the weekly Naviera Armas sailing back to **Huelva** (www.navieraarmas.com).

Route 22: High-speed Spain

CITIES: ★★ CULTURE: ★★ HISTORY: ★★ SCENERY: ★★
COUNTRIES COVERED: SPAIN (ES)
JOURNEY TIME: 6 HRS | DISTANCE: 1,136 KM | MAP: WWW.EBRWEB.EU/18MAP22

The preceding route in the book, from Barcelona to Andalucía via the Despeñaperros gorge, is a very fine journey if you have plenty of time. Now, in Route 22, we present an alternative which relies entirely on **high-speed lines**. Our journey as presented here was made possible with the completion of the new fast line from Barcelona to Madrid in 2008. While our natural inclination is to avoid high-speed lines, this route for *Europe by Rail* really plugs a gap – and it's an enjoyable run, **full of quiet drama**, with some fine views across expansive Spanish landscapes.

No other country in Europe, not even France, has used high-speed rail to transform the relationship between regions as effectively as Spain. Twenty years ago, there were six daytime trains from **Barcelona to Madrid**. A journey time of seven to eight hours was normal. Today, there are 30 trains from Barcalona to Madrid on a typical weekday, the fastest taking just two-and-a-half hours to reach the capital. The geography of Spain has been reshaped by the railway.

SUGGESTED ITINERARY
You can dash from Barcelona to Málaga on an sleek high-speed train in less than six hours. But **Madrid** and **Córdoba** are too good to miss. Why not spend at least a night in each? Even if you are very pushed for time, you should at least stop for a few hours in Córdoba to view the Mezquita, which ranks alongside Granada's Alhambra as one of the grandest Moorish designs in Spain.

Slip on board the AVE in **Barcelona** (more on the city on p187) – having booked a window seat in advance – and relax as Spain slips by beyond the window. This is pure cinema. At one level this is a route which transcends geography, but it is also one constrained by the landscape. Having thought you were heading inland, there is suddenly a fleeting glimpse of the sea from above **Tarragona**. The railway then sneaks round the edge of the hills above Montblanc. By now the AVE is at full speed, sweeping east to the Ebro Valley. Some trains stop at **Zaragoza**, a city with a brace of fine cathedrals and a stunning Moorish fortress-palace called the Aljafería. The railway then follows the **River Jalón** upstream, cutting through the hills beyond Calatayud and coasting down to Madrid.

Madrid (suggested stopover)

Madrid occupies a location at the very centre of Spain, and deliberately so. In 1561 **Philip II** chose the city as his capital to avoid inflaming regional

216 | IBERIAN CONNECTIONS

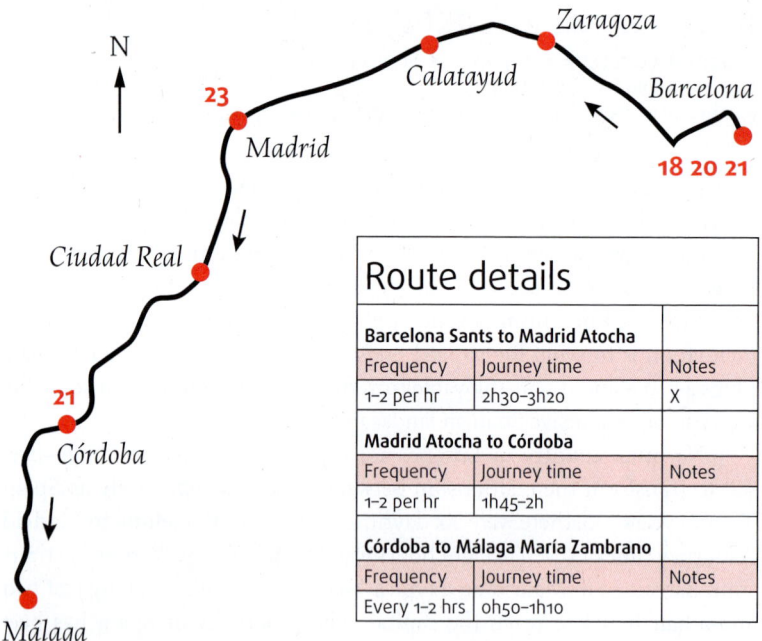

Notes

Thrice-daily AVEs run directly from Barcelona to Córdoba without stopping in Madrid (although their route does take them through the suburbs of the Spanish capital). Two of these three trains continue to Málaga. The fastest journey time from Barcelona to Málaga on a direct train is six hours. Independent operator iryo also has twice-daily direct trains from Madrid to Córdoba.

X – These days there's real competition on the route from Barcelona to Madrid. Renfe is the main operator, using smart AVE trains on the route. SNCF launched a low-cost Ouigo service in May 2021 and Renfe responded with its budget Avlo trains. In November 2022 a new operator called iryo (partly owned by Trenitalia) joined the competitive fray with its *iryo* branded services.

jealousies. Beyond the mediaeval **Old Quarter**, the majority of Madrid was built from the 19th century on, and much of the city is given over to relentless, drab high-rise buildings. But its charm is not necessarily its architecture. What Madrid is good at is its street- and nightlife, with the smart, fun-loving Madrileños taking their evening *paseo* along **Calle del Carmen** and **Calle de Preciados**; thereafter the city keeps going late into the night.

The other main attraction of the city is the fine collection of museums. The **Prado** (www.museodelprado.es) is one of the world's great art galleries, and you could spend days exploring the collection in order to feel that you have done it justice. It celebrated the bicentenary of its opening in 2019. Elsewhere, the **Centro de Arte Reina Sofía** (www.museoreinasofia.es; closed

Excursions from Madrid

Few European capitals offer such a feast of wonderful days out by train as Madrid. Top of many visitors' lists is the palace-cum-monastery complex at **El Escorial**. As Europe's largest Renaissance building, the sheer scale of the place is daunting, to an extent that makes the gardens seem no more than a weak sideshow. A number of late 16th-century buildings arranged around a vast quadrangle are open to visitors (not Mon). A visit to El Escorial is a great reminder of **Spain's fabulous wealth** in its heyday as an imperial power. Part of the appeal of El Escorial is its setting on the edge of the Sierra de Guadarrama. El Escorial is easily reached on *Cercanías* line C8A, which runs hourly from Madrid Atocha (journey time 70 mins) or from Chamartín (taking 55 minutes). Reservations are not necessary on this rail route. Suburban rail route C3 runs in the opposite direction all the way to **Aranjuez**, normally every half hour, taking 45 minutes from Atocha and slightly more from Chamartín. Aranjuez is another wonderful palace and garden complex, but here the gardens definitely have the edge. The palace is closed Mondays, but the gardens are open daily.

Our third suggestion for a day trip from Madrid is to take the train to **Toledo**. Avant trains leave hourly from the main-line platforms at Atocha station, taking just 33 minutes for the 75-kilometre journey to Toledo. This is a rail route where you always need to reserve seats in advance. A palpable **sense of history** pervades every street and alley in the UNESCO-listed walled city of Toledo, which is perched on a hill with the Rio Tajo forming a natural moat on three sides. Even the railway station communicates a strong sense of **Toledo style**: look out for the colourful tiles and Moorish design. The heavily buttressed cathedral is renowned for its stained glass, delicate carvings and fine art collection: El Greco, van Dyck, Goya, Caravaggio and more. In Toledo's Jewish quarter, there are two spectacular synagogues.

Few other European cities can quite match Toledo in so brilliantly juxtaposing Muslim, Jewish and Christian heritage. It is an **incomparable cityscape**. No surprise, perhaps, that it can be busy. You might want to consider staying overnight for in the evening, once the day trippers have gone, Toledo is very special. A good, central hotel is the Santa Isabel, C. Santa Isabel 24, ☎ 925 25 31 20 (www.hotelsantaisabeltoledo.es).

Tues) houses a superb collection of modern art, including a masterpiece of anti-war painting: Picasso's *Guernica*. The **Royal Palace** and its gardens are worth exploring, as is the lovely green space of the Retiro, Madrid's biggest park just a short walk from the city's art museums. For train buffs, there is the **Railway Museum** (www.museodelferrocarril.org), located in the city's former Delicias station. More than anything though Madrid is a place where you can simply enjoy the atmosphere – on the city streets, in its many squares, or at the counter of a tapas bar.

There's a maze of quaint old streets to explore heading south and west from the city's principal square of the **Puerta del Sol**. Particularly picturesque is the Plaza de la Villa halfway down the Calle Mayor. The arcaded rectangle of **Plaza Mayor** is at the heart of the Old Town, a place to stroll around or have a coffee in the sunshine. The Plaza Mayor is close to the Puerta del Sol, and therefore is not only in the heart of the city, but a few steps away from Point Zero, from where all distances in Spain are measured.

Arrival, information, accommodation

🚄 **Puerta de Atocha** Station (metro: Atocha Renfe), just south of the city centre, is Madrid's terminal for high-speed trains to the south (Córdoba, Málaga, Seville and Valencia) and north-east (Zaragoza and Barcelona). The magnificent original 19th-century building now shelters tropical gardens. However, most trains to the north-west and north of Spain and those to France via Irún/Hendaye and the overnight train to Lisbon, depart from Madrid's other main station, **Chamartín–Clara Campoamor**, C. de Agustín de Foxá (metro: Chamartín), in the suburbs, 8 km north of the centre.

✈ Madrid Barajas Airport (www.aeropuertomadrid-barajas.com), 12 km north-east of town, is served by suburban trains (Cercanías line C1), running every 30 mins (06.00–23.30) from terminal T4 to Chamartín (15 minutes), Atocha Cercanías (29 minutes) and Príncipe Pío (41 minutes), serving all stations en route. Metro line 8 runs into central Madrid in 13–15 mins. Public transport: With services every 5 mins (06.00–01.30) and colour-coded lines, the metro, which marked the centenary of its creation in 2019, is easy to use. Tickets are loaded onto a contatless, reloadable Public Transport Card (TTP), which you can purchase at ticket machines (www.metromadrid.es). The EMT city bus system is comprehensive, efficient and the same price as the metro. ℹ Tourist office: within the Casa de la Panadería on Plaza Mayor (www.esmadrid.com).

🛏 If you'd like to stay close to Atocha station, then the **Only You Hotel Atocha**, Paseo Infanta Isabel 13, ☎ 914 09 78 76 (www.ebrweb.eu/d) is a stylish and comfortable option. A wonderful place to rest your head is the **Palacio San Martín**, Pl. San Martín 5, ☎ 917 01 50 00 (www.ebrweb.eu/c), a 19th-century palace converted into a hotel with stunning views from the rooftop restaurant. Just a short walk from the Plaza Mayor and the Puerta del Sol, the **Mayerling**, C. del Conde de Romanones 6, ☎ 914 201 580 (www.mayerlinghotel.com) is a good, comfortable option.

Connections from Madrid

As the country's major rail hub, Madrid has direct trains to all major cities in Spain. The city's only international departure is an AVE which departs daily at 13.25 for the eight-hour ride to Marseille. Direct trains to **San Sebastián** or **Irún** (five daily) give onward connections to Hendaye in France. The overnight trains to Portugal and France have sadly been withdrawn.

South to Andalucía

Remember when leaving Madrid for the south that **Atocha** station is more like an airport than a railway station. Passengers boarding high-speed trains need to be at the station well in advance. Luggage is routinely scanned and only passengers with valid tickets can go to the platforms. The stretch of this route from **Madrid to Córdoba** was opened in 1992 as Spain's first high-speed railway. It's interesting to see how, thirty years later, the railway has settled into the landscape.

Running south from Madrid, there is a glorious view of **Toledo's honey-hued townscape** in the distance. Just south of **Ciudad Real** (where some trains stop), you'll see one of Europe's most extraordinary architectural follies: a disused airport, complete with its own abandoned railway station. Beyond Puertollano, the landscape changes dramatically as the railway cuts through the **Sierra Morena**. This 100-kilometre stretch is nothing short of superb – perhaps Europe's best new-build railway.

All too soon, the train pulls into **Córdoba**, where the star attraction is undoubtedly the Mezquita, the grandest and most beautiful mosque ever built in Spain. Córdoba is laden with history; the city boasts one of the largest mediaeval townscapes in Europe, and certainly the biggest in Spain, offering a harmonious blend of Christian, Jewish and Moorish architecture.

The huge **Mezquita** was founded in the 8th century by Caliph Abd al-Rahman I and was enlarged over the next 200 years. At the foot of the bell tower, the delicately carved Puerta del Perdón leads through the massive outer walls to the **Patio de los Naranjos** (Courtyard of the Orange Trees), a courtyard with fountains for ritual cleansing. Inside the mosque, the fantastic forest of 850 pillars, joined by two-tiered Moorish arches in stripes of red brick and white stone, extends over a vast area. After the Moors departed, the Christians added the cathedral within the complex, incongruous but stunning, and blocking out the light that was an integral part of the design.

If you are minded to stay overnight in Córdoba, you can try the style-conscious Viento 10, C. Ronquillo Briceño 10, ☎ 957 764 960 (www.hotelviento10.es) in a quiet area, a 15-min walk to the Old Town. A good central budget option is the Carpe Diem, C. Barroso 4, ☎ 957 476 221 (www.hotelcordobacarpediem.com), not far from the Mezquita.

Málaga had to wait until 2007 for the high-speed line from Madrid to Córdoba to be extended to the coast. The railway crosses the **River Guadalquivir** west of Córdoba and then gradually climbs into the hills which form a western extension of the **Sierra Nevada** range. Reaching 400 metres near Antequera (where there is a new station for high-speed trains), the line then drops down steeply through several tunnels to reach the coast at Málaga.

In the Andalusian city, all trains terminate at the stylish modern María Zambrano station, named in honour of the distinguished Andalusian-born philosopher who suffered greatly under the Franco regime.

Málaga

The sixth largest city in Spain and a **busy working port**, Málaga at first sight isn't pretty, with high-rise modern apartment blocks built up within close range of a dismal-looking canalised river. But the centre is a hundred times more cheerful and resolutely Spanish in character, with a tree-lined main boulevard, dark back alleys, an atmospheric covered market and traditional shops and bars where Spanish (not holidaymakers' English!) is very much the first language.

Málaga's past is most evident in the area near the port. The long, shady walks of the **Paseo del Parque** are overlooked by the **Alcazaba**, a fort built by the Moors on Roman foundations; it has the character of the Alhambra in Granada, albeit on a smaller scale, and the views extend over the city to the coast. Its neighbour, the **Gibralfaro castle**, is of Phoenician origin, reconstructed later by the Moors, and offers even better views.

Just off the Paseo is the **cathedral**, set in a secluded square and built between the 16th and 18th centuries. Close by, in Calle San Agustín, is the city's star attraction, the **Museo Picasso** (www.museopicassomalaga.org), where you can admire over 150 of the master's works in a 16th-century palace. Picasso was born in Málaga in 1881 and you can visit his birthplace, now the **Museo Casa Natal**, on the Plaza de la Merced 15, with works of art and personal effects. Plaza de la Merced is the city's liveliest and most attractive square with several good bars and restaurants.

Fans of contemporary art might also like to visit the **Centro de Arte Contemporáneo** on Calle Alemania (www.cacmalaga.eu). It has a small permanent collection of art and is highly regarded for the quality of its temporary exhibitions.

ARRIVAL, INFORMATION, ACCOMMODATION

≉ María Zambrano station, Explanada de la Estación, a 20- to 30-min walk from the centre of town. 🚌 3 goes to Alameda Principal and Paseo del Parque near the centre. Local trains for the coastal resorts leave from here as well (at a different level). Note this coastal rail route is also served by another more centrally located station, Centro Alameda. ✈ 8 km from the city. There is a tourist office in the main hall. Trains to Málaga run every 20 mins, taking about 15 mins. 🛈 Tourist office: Pl. de la Marina 11 (visita.malaga.eu).

🛏 There is a good choice of hotels, including a small parador set in the gardens of the Gibralfaro castle (🚌 35 from Paseo del Parque) above the town. In high season, central Málaga is lively at night (all night); the only solution is to ask for a room away from the street, or buy earplugs. Well located fo the Alcazaba, the port and the Paseo del Parque is the **Hotel MS Maestranza**, Avda. Cánovas del Castillo 1, ☎ 952 213 610 (www.hotelmsmaestranza.com). Close to the Old Town is the highly regarded modern and comfortable **Icon Malabar**, C. Tomás Heredia 13, ☎ 95 260 67 03 (www.iconmalabar.com). A good central option in the Old Town is the **Hotel del Pintor**, C. Álamos 27, ☎ 952 060 980 (www.hoteldelpintor.com). ✖ There are several good restaurants around the cathedral, especially along C. Cañón. Seafood and gazpacho are good bets. Paseo Marítimo and the seafront in Pedregalejo are the best areas for seafood restaurants.

CONNECTIONS FROM MÁLAGA

A frequent train service runs west from Málaga (Centro–Alameda and RENFE stations) along the **Costa del Sol**, connecting the city with its airport and the busy resorts of Torremolinos, Benalmádena and Fuengirola.

There is a not-to-be-missed regional rail route which runs north-west from Málaga, more or less paralleling the new high-speed line from Málaga to Córdoba, but hugely more exciting as it takes in the **El Chorro Gorge** – this stretch of railway is where the dramatic final scene of the film *Von Ryan's Express* was filmed. You can ride the El Chorro line by taking any Media Distancia (MD) train from Málaga bound for Seville. There is also a high-speed service from Málaga to Seville, but these Avant trains do not use the El Chorro route. If a train from Málaga takes over an hour to reach Antequera, then you know it takes the El Chorro line. Finally, there is a daily ferry, usually departing late evening from Málaga to **Melilla**, one of the fragments of Spanish territory on the north coast of Africa. It's a useful link if you are making for Morocco. See also Sidetracks K on p214.

Route 23: Not quite the pilgrim route to Santiago

CITIES: ★★ CULTURE: ★★ HISTORY: ★★ SCENERY: ★★
COUNTRIES COVERED: SPAIN (ES)
JOURNEY TIME: 9 HRS | DISTANCE: 1,260 KM | MAP: www.ebrweb.eu/17map23

Santiago de Compostela (or just plain Santiago to most) has been the goal for millions of pilgrims over many centuries, walking the various routes from France and across northern Spain that have come to be collectively known as the Camino de Santiago or the **Route of St James**. Even for those of no or little faith, that long walk is a remarkable adventure.

Until 2020, Spanish rail operator Renfe ran the *Camino de Santiago* train, which broadly followed the route of the **ancient pilgrim trail**. Changing patterns of train services, in part prompted by the opening of new high-speed lines has necessitated a rethink of this route for this 18th edition of *Europe by Rail*. Beyond Burgos, our new route tracks further south, now running via Zamora rather than León. **San Sebastián** (Donostia in Basque) stands on the coast below the green, rainy foothills of the Pyrenees in the Basque province, the region of Spain known to the assertively independent Basque people as **Euskal Herria**. Conquered by neither the Romans nor the Moors, the Basques suffered appalling repression during the Franco period and their language was banned. Several decades of agitation by the *abertzale* followed up by ETA action have secured for the Basque people a measure of autonomy.

From the Basque region, we cut through the hills, reaching **Burgos** and **Valladolid**, two engaging cities which lie on the great *meseta* (high plain) of Castilla y León (formerly known as Old Castile). It is dusty country. By contrast, **Galicia**, comprising Spain's north-west corner, is lushly verdant and intricately hilly, with a coastline buffeted by Atlantic gusts and characterised by fjord-like scenery.

ITINERARY THOUGHTS

This is a route well suited to being done in a day. There is something about the way in which the **landscape changes** – from hills to plains and then hills again – which creates its own drama. The once-daily direct train from San Sebastián to Santiago de Compostela recalled the name of the traditional pilgrim trail. Perhaps realising that pilgrims shun creature comforts, that train was a spartan affair. Its loss is probably not greatly mourned. These days it's better to take a more southerly route. It's a strange quirk of the Spanish timetables that it is sometimes actually quicker to **travel via Madrid**. This detour allows travellers to catch the early afternoon direct AVE train from Madrid to Santiago de Compostela. That train dashes non-stop from Madrid to Zamora in little over an hour. But it does mean travelling all the way down to Madrid then back north again, covering the 135 km from Olmedo Junction to Madrid in both directions. Bizarre, but that's how it is.

If you have a psychological aversion to such backtracking, you can avoid it with some extra changes and a long wait at **Medina del Campo**. For real diehards who want to avoid any hint of high speed, there is still one slow connection per day via the route once followed by the old *Camino de Santiago* train, making one or more changes along the way and using the line which runs west from León into Galicia. There is just one surviving daily

222 | IBERIAN CONNECTIONS

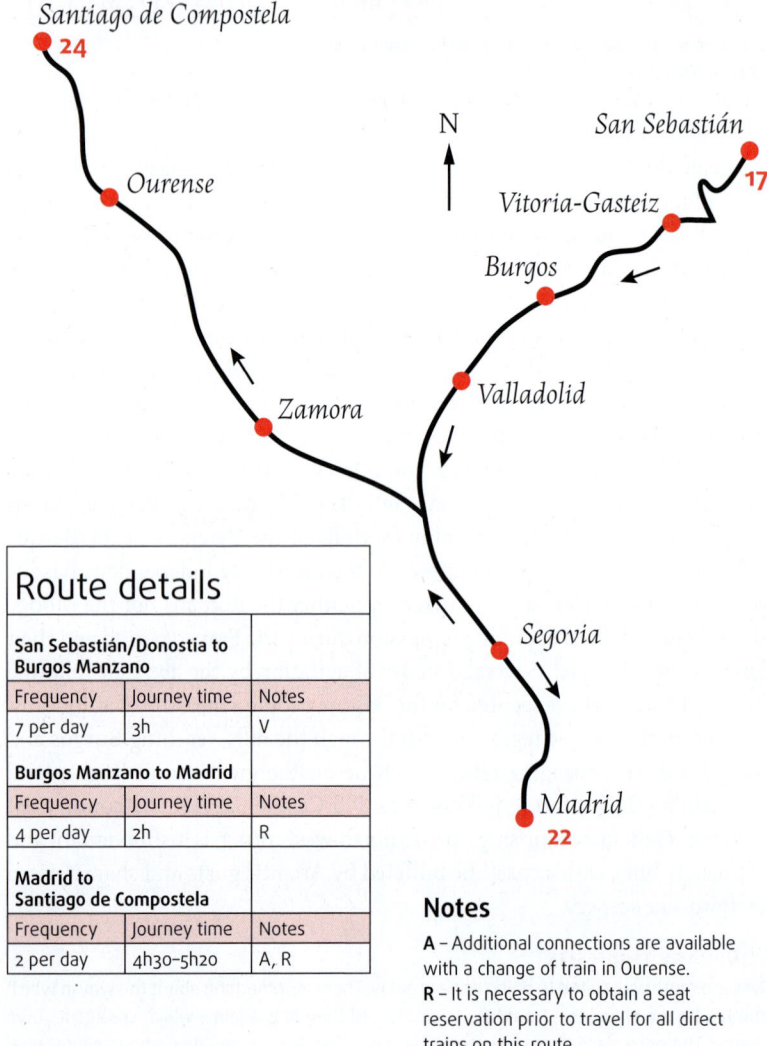

Route details

San Sebastián/Donostia to Burgos Manzano		
Frequency	Journey time	Notes
7 per day	3h	V

Burgos Manzano to Madrid		
Frequency	Journey time	Notes
4 per day	2h	R

Madrid to Santiago de Compostela		
Frequency	Journey time	Notes
2 per day	4h30–5h20	A, R

Notes

A – Additional connections are available with a change of train in Ourense.
R – It is necessary to obtain a seat reservation prior to travel for all direct trains on this route.
V – Some journeys require a change of train at Vitoria-Gasteiz.

EUROPEAN RAILWAY ATLAS

If you are looking for better maps of European rail routes to help in travel planning, we can strongly recommend the series of atlases produced by **Mike Ball**. You'll find details of the various products at www.europeanrailwayatlas.com. The one upon which we rely for so much of our work is the *All-Europe Enthusiast Edition*. You can purchase it as a printed book, as a pdf download or a book-pdf bundle. Mike's long-term commitment to producing bang up-to-date railway atlases is legendary, and each new edition of a Mike Ball atlas is a real treasure trove of information.

train in each direction on that route. In the westbound direction the timings are awful, only giving a very late evening arrival into Santiago. Travelling east from Galicia back towards the Basque region, it is much better with departure from Santiago at 07.40 or 08.14 (depending on the day of the week) and changing in **Vitoria-Gasteiz** to give an early evening arrival in San Sebastián.

Although the nature of the journey suggests covering the route in a long day, don't forget that there are **many fine cities** along the route. Should you be minded to stop overnight, we suggest the city of Burgos.

Across the hills to Castile

Heading south from **San Sebastián** (see p181), our route cuts through the green hills of Gipuzkoa, a province where the Basque language and culture still thrive, especially in remoter communities away from main roads. After skirting the **Sierra de Aralar**, the railway cuts south with great views of the Basque region's highest peak, Aizkorri, away to the right of the train. This great limestone massif rises to 1,551 metres.

The next community of any size is the unofficial Basque capital: **Vitoria-Gasteiz**, though Basque speakers tend to refer to it simply as Gasteiz. The almost perfectly preserved centre of this mediaeval hill town has handsomely arcaded squares; at the centre of **Plaza de la Virgen Blanca**, a monument commemorates a nearby battle of 1813 in which Napoleon's army was defeated by the Duke of Wellington. Beyond Vitoria-Gasteiz, the railway traverses easier terrain, crossing the River Ebro at Miranda and tracking south-west to Burgos.

Burgos (suggested stopover)

In mediaeval times Burgos grew rich on the wool trade, and in the 11th century the city became the **capital of Christian Spain** as well as the home of Rodrigo Díaz de Vivar, better known as **El Cid**, the romantic mercenary. During the Civil War in the 1930s, the town again rose to fame as the **Nationalist headquarters**. It was here that Franco formed his Falangist government. Burgos has now grown into a large and busy modern city, but its heart is the atmospheric Old Town around the ruined castle (itself of little interest apart from the views from it). The grand entrance to old Burgos is formed by the **Arco de Santa María**, a fortified 14th-century gateway, altered and decorated in 1536 to pacify Charles V, depicting his figure and those of the founder (Diego Porcelos) and El Cid (whose equestrian statue stands near the Puente de San Pablo). From here, it's a short walk to the bulk of the main attractions, eating places and hotels.

Foremost is the **cathedral**, consecrated in 1260 but not completed until the 18th century, making it the third largest cathedral in Spain (after Toledo and Seville), and also probably the richest. Amidst the splendour of the 19 chapels and 38 altars, dripping in gold leaf, is El Cid's unobtrusive tomb and a grotesque crucifix. Evening sees everyone promenade along the **Paseo del Espolón**, graced with fountains and statues, stretched out along the river, with cafés and restaurants making the most of the atmosphere.

Arrival, information, accommodation

✈ The railway station is called Burgos Rosa Manzano (sometimes still referred to by its former name Burgos Rosa de Lima); it's an assertively modern design in the Villímar district on the very edge of town, about 5 km north-east of the centre. Buses 25 and 43 shuttle into the centre. 🛈 Tourist office: C. Nuño Rasura 7 (http://turismo.aytoburgos.es). 🛏 Located in a former convent a short walk to the cathedral is the **Palacio de Burgos**, C. de la Merced 13, ☎ 947 47 99 00 (www.ebrweb.eu/nhburgos). A simple but comfortable hotel in the Old Town is the **Cordon**, C. la Puebla 6, ☎ 947 26 50 00 (www.hotelcordon.com). The **Mesón del Cid**, Pl. de Santa María 8, ☎ 947 20 87 15 (www.mesondelcid.es) has nice views of the cathedral and square.

Connections from Burgos

Burgos is a **major rail hub**. There are half a dozen daily direct trains to San Sebastián with connections to Hendaye in France, where you can connect onto the French TGV network and **Route 17**. There are regular direct trains to Madrid, some using the **new high-speed**

Spain's north coast by train

Route 23 follows main lines from San Sebastián to Santiago de Compostela. But there is **an entirely different rail route** between the two cities, one that takes very much longer and for much of the journey follows the north coast of Spain. If you follow Route 23 in its entirety, you may feel inclined to use this alternative coastal line for the return journey.

The railway along the north coast is sometimes referred to as the **FEVE line**, recalling the days when a separate company called FEVE ran the metre-gauge railways in northern Spain. FEVE stands for *Ferrocarriles Españoles de Vía Estrecha* (effectively Spanish narrow-gauge railways). Nowadays FEVE is merely an operating division of Spain's national rail operator Renfe.

This excursion is one of Europe's **great narrow-gauge rail journeys**. It extends from San Sebastián along the coast to Ferrol, from where it is a short hop (about 100 minutes) by train to Santiago de Compostela. The narrow-gauge coastal route splits naturally into four stages, viz. San Sebastián – Bilbao – Santander – Oviedo – Ferrol. The one-way fare for the entire run from San Sebastián to Ferrol is about €70. Our **favourite stretch** of this magnificent route is the section between Santander and Oviedo, where the railway cuts a narrow trail between the rugged **Picos de Europa** (to the south) and the dramatic coastline to the north. The small resort town of Llanes in the very middle of this stretch is an immensely tempting spot to alight and linger for a few days.

As well as regular services, a **very smart tourist train** called *El Transcantábrico* plies the narrow-gauge coastal line. Passengers are accommodated in deluxe suites on the train, and the package includes all meals with an emphasis on high quality local fare. The eight-day journey from San Sebastián to Santiago de Compostela makes some use of road transport too, allowing participants in this rail cruise to see key sights across northern Asturias and Galicia. Naturally, **packages** like this are not cheap. The fare in summer 2025 for a couple sharing a cabin is €18,500. For a single traveller requiring sole occupancy of a cabin, the fare is €16,000. We leave you to judge whether that's a wonderful bargain or a downright waste of money.

line and just two each daily taking the mountainous old route via Ávila which skirts the southern edge of the Sierra de Guadarrama and then drops down past El Escorial to reach the Spanish capital – the latter a very fine ride. Other cities in northern Spain with direct trains from Burgos include Salamanca, Bilbao and Barcelona.

Detour via Madrid

On the journey west of Burgos, the train initially runs along the **Arlanzón Valley**, then follows the River Pisuerga down to Valladolid. It's a pleasant enough city with a curiously squat, unfinished cathedral and an elegant railway station called Valladolid Campo Grande. South of **Valladolid** we cross the River Duero (the river which, known as the Douro in Portugal, flows down to reach the Atlantic in Porto) from where it's a high-speed dash south to Madrid. The Spanish poet **Gil de Biedma** penned some poignant lines on the closure of the old railway through Nava de La Asunción. Now the trains are back, these days on a high-speed line which speeds assertively past Nava de la Asunción which you'll see off to the right of the railway. As so often across Europe, the new line brings no benefit to the local community for want of stations. The only intermediate stop on this line is at Segovia-Guiomar, though few trains actually stop there. There is a nice view of **Segovia** away to the left of the railway, then **two long tunnels** (respectively 28 km and 9 km long) lead us into Madrid's northern suburbs where you change trains at Madrid-Charmartin-Clara-Campoamor station. The Clara after whom the station is now named was a pioneering feminist and advocate of women's suffrage in Spain. For more on **Madrid** see p215.

Our route then backtracks, following the same railway back north for 135 km then swinging off left at Olmedo along a new high-speed line to **Zamora**. This very strange arrangement, making a seemingly pointless detour via Madrid, is purely an artefact of the train timetables, though actually it's not without certain merit. We found it interesting to travel the same route in both directions, being struck by how different the landscape seemed when travelling in the opposite direction. It's a shade over an hour from Madrid to Zamora, from where it is two hours on the fastest trains on to **Santiago de Compostela**. Sit back and enjoy a ride which sweeps through the hills with quiet drama, crossing the **River Miño** in Ourense and then cutting through a final ridge of low hills to reach Santiago de Compostela.

Santiago de Compostela

A magnet for millions of pilgrims for the last thousand years, Santiago de Compostela hit the big time when the **tomb of St James** (Sant' Iago, Spain's patron saint) was discovered in 813, supposedly by a shepherd who was guided to the site by a star. Destroyed in 997 by the Moors, the town was rebuilt during the 11th century and began its Golden Age. In the 12th century, the Pope declared it a **Holy City**: for Catholics, only Jerusalem and Rome share this honour. The Old Town (contained within the mediaeval walls) is one of the most beautiful urban landscapes in Europe.

The **Old Town** contains a host of fine churches and monasteries as well as notable secular buildings tucked down the narrow side streets. The **cathedral** (started in 1075) is the obvious centre of attention. To celebrate their arrival in the Holy City, pilgrims traditionally touch the base of the **Tree of Jesse** on the central column, accordingly known as the 'Pilgrim Pillar', and deeply worn down by millions of fingers over the centuries. On the other side of the pillar, facing the altar, is a figure of the **sculptor Mateo**, popularly known as the 'Saint of bumps on the head', as people knock heads with him in the belief that his talent is contagious. The interior is dominated by a silver Mexican altar and a dazzling 17th-century baroque altarpiece. It's a calming space, even when busy, but bear in mind that pilgrims take priority over tourists on major Catholic feasts and solemnities.

Four plazas surround the cathedral, each architectural gems in themselves. On the largest, the pigeon-populated **Praza do Obradoiro**, stand the impressive Hostal de los Reyes Católicos (the former hospital for pilgrims, now a parador) and the classical **Pazo de Raxoi** of 1772 (now the town hall). The Old City is tiny and everything of interest is easily accessible on foot.

ARRIVAL, INFORMATION, ACCOMMODATION

⇌ Rúa do Hórreo, 1 km south of the Old Town. Bus 6 goes into the centre, but it's quicker to walk ✈ 10 km from the centre, bus takes 25 mins. 🚍 Bus station: Estación Central de Autobuses, Praza de Camilo Díaz Baliño, bus 5 runs from Praza de Galicia. There is a good local bus system and route plans are posted at most stops. 🛈 Tourist office: R. do Vilar 63 (www.santiagoturismo.com). From the station turn left up R. do Hórreo to Praza de Galicia.

🛏 During the three weeks leading up to the feast of St James on 25 July, the town is absolutely packed and you should book well in advance. Accommodation ranges from the 5-star **Hostal de los Reyes Católicos**, Praza do Obradoiro 1, ☎ 981 58 22 00 (www.parador.es), a magnificent 16th-century pilgrim hostel built by Ferdinand and Isabella, to an array of small, relatively inexpensive guest houses in both the old and new parts of the city. For budget accommodation in the Old Town, try around Rúa do Vilar and Rúa Raiña. A good mid-range option is the welcoming **Altair Hotel**, R. Loureiros 12, ☎ 981 55 47 12 (www.altairhotel.net). Located in the Old Town close to the cathedral, the **Hotel Rua Vilar**, R. do Vilar 8–10, ☎ 981 51 98 58 (www.hotelruavillar.com) is a good option with comfortable rooms. ✕ There are plenty of budget restaurants around the Old Town, especially on the streets leading south from the cathedral.

CONNECTIONS FROM SANTIAGO

You can join **Route 24** and continue south through Galicia into Portugal. Frequent trains from Santiago de Compostela run north to the coast at **A Coruña**, a lively port with fine beaches. The very best excursion from Santiago will however require you forsake the train in favour of the bus. Six buses daily run west to **Fisterra**, a two to three-hour journey (see www.monbus.es). This takes in some fabulous rural Galician landscapes, ending on the Finisterre Peninsula. From Fisterra village, it is a 30 to 40-minute walk to **Cape Finisterre** – the remote headland which was for many centuries regarded as the very end of the world.

Route 24: The Atlantic coast of Iberia

CITIES: ★★★ CULTURE: ★★ HISTORY: ★★ SCENERY: ★★
COUNTRIES COVERED: SPAIN (ES), PORTUGAL (PT)
JOURNEY TIME: 13 HRS | DISTANCE: 1,101 KM | MAP: WWW.EBRWEB.EU/18MAP24

Cast back to the mid-19th century and overland travel in Portugal was formidably difficult. The opening of the first railway in 1858 heralded a new era in Portuguese communication, giving inland communities access to the country's great ports at **Porto and Lisbon**.

Today, the railway is a fine way to take the pulse of Portugal and this route is designed to do just that. Route 24 is the sole journey in this book which crosses the **Spanish-Portuguese border**, but it is not the only way to reach Portugal by train. Bear in mind that the excellent *Lusitania* hotel train which connected Madrid and Lisbon was suspended in 2020. It is unlikely to be reinstated. Plans to link Madrid and Lisbon with a new high-speed line for daytime trains have stumbled with the Portuguese government refusing to fund the route on their side of the border. Meanwhile, the line to Porto described here and the route running west from Mérida are the only two passenger rail routes from Spain into Portugal.

Route 24 starts in Spain at the lovely pilgrimage city of **Santiago de Compostela**, which lies at the end of **Route 23** in this book. Heading south, the train crosses into Portugal, taking in the beautiful coastal resort of **Viana do Castelo** the port-producing city of Porto and the old university town of Coimbra. We continue south by train to Lisbon. Then, because we don't want to leave you stranded far from any other routes, we suggest a longish hop on a comfortable long-distance **coach to Seville** in southern Spain where you can connect into **Route 21**, which you can follow in reverse to take you to Barcelona.

SUGGESTED ITINERARY
Using the **Celta cross-border train** service, it is now possible to take an early morning train from Santiago de Compostela and be in the Portuguese capital by early afternoon. With a day or two to spare though, you might profitably stop off here and there on the journey south. Porto would be our top choice for an intermediate stop. If you have time for a longer stop in northern Portugal, then you may want to venture inland from Porto to explore the scenic and deeply rural **Douro Valley** (see box on p231). After a stop in Lisbon – definitely a must – head to Seville by bus.

South through Galicia

For more on **Santiago de Compostela** see p225. Train services running south from the city were radically improved in 2015 with the modernisation of the line to Vigo. It is certainly an impressive piece of engineering, and it has trimmed the travel time between Santiago and Vigo, but it'll take a few

IBERIAN CONNECTIONS

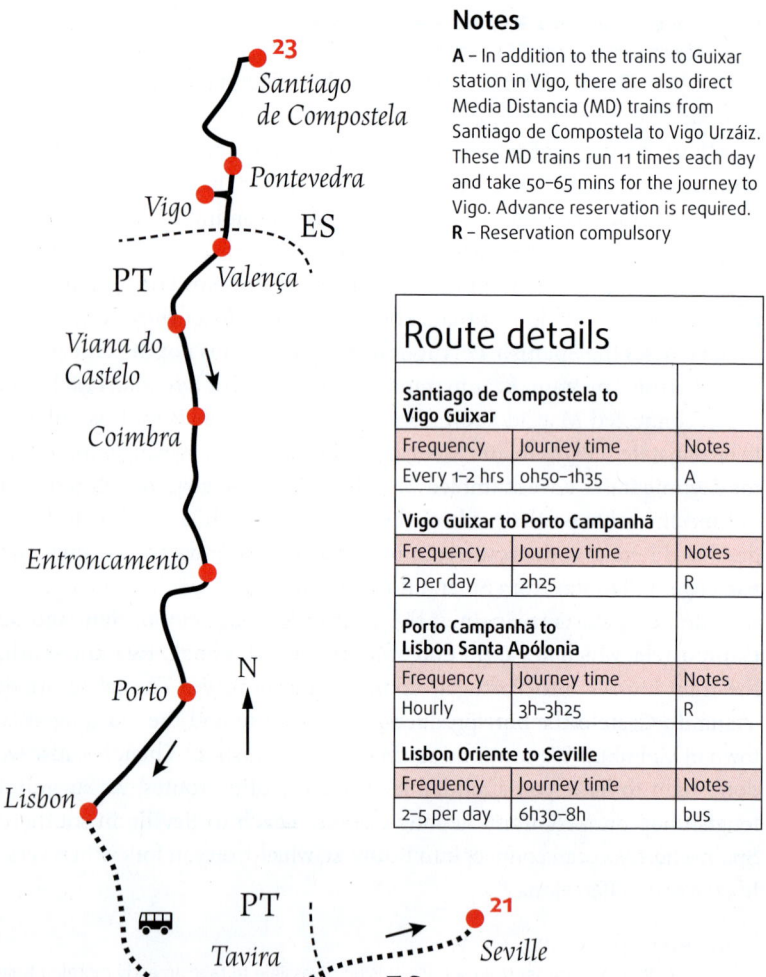

Notes

A – In addition to the trains to Guixar station in Vigo, there are also direct Media Distancia (MD) trains from Santiago de Compostela to Vigo Urzáiz. These MD trains run 11 times each day and take 50–65 mins for the journey to Vigo. Advance reservation is required.
R – Reservation compulsory

Route details

Santiago de Compostela to Vigo Guixar		
Frequency	Journey time	Notes
Every 1–2 hrs	0h50–1h35	A

Vigo Guixar to Porto Campanhã		
Frequency	Journey time	Notes
2 per day	2h25	R

Porto Campanhã to Lisbon Santa Apólonia		
Frequency	Journey time	Notes
Hourly	3h–3h25	R

Lisbon Oriente to Seville		
Frequency	Journey time	Notes
2–5 per day	6h30–8h	bus

RAILWAY STATIONS IN VIGO

Vigo's main railway station is called **Vigo Urzáiz**. It reopened in 2015 after **major refurbishment**, but many trains are still using the temporary station (called Vigo Guixar and located closer to the waterfront) which was constructed to allow trains to still serve Vigo during the Urzáiz closure. As of October 2024, the trains to Portugal still leave from **Vigo Guixar**. If you arrive in Vigo on a fast train from Santiago (ie. one with the prefix MD), then it will run to Urzáiz station. But if you travel from Santiago de Compostela on a slow train (any service taking more than 70 minutes), you'll arrive at Vigo Guixar. If you do need to change stations in Vigo, note that it takes 12 to 15 minutes to walk from Urzáiz to Guixar.

years for the line to settle into the landscape. At the moment, the cuttings and embankments all look a little raw.

Older parts of the route which meandered through the hills have been replaced by dead-straight tunnels. But there are still some good views, especially as the railway bridges major valleys on the run south and at one point (just beyond Padrón) follows the **River Ulla**. Sit on the right for the best views.

The principal town of note between Santiago and Vigo is **Pontevedra** which began life as a port, but its importance dwindled as the old harbour silted up. Although surrounded by a new city, the compact **Old Town** is pretty much intact, with parts of the original walls still visible around a maze of cobbled streets, arcaded squares with carved stone crosses and low houses with flower-filled balconies. **Iglesia de la Virgen Peregrina**, an unusual chapel with a floor plan in the shape of a scallop shell, is situated by the partly arcaded main square, Praza da Ferrería, on the boundary between the Old and New Towns. The railway station is a 12-minute walk south-east of the centre.

When following Route 24, it is always necessary to change trains at **Vigo**. The town is a major fishing port and lies on a beautiful sheltered bay. It's a clamorous, busy place built of grey granite, not immediately attractive except in the old, sloping quarter near the seafront. **Castro Castle**, the ruined fort on a hill just above the town, provides a fine view. The wonderfully unspoilt **Islas Cíes archipelago**, reached by ferry from Vigo from June till the end of September and during the Easter Week, is the main reason for stopping here. Designated a national park, the islands have white sands and rugged hilltops, with enough trails to provide a day's walking on the main two isles (which are joined together by a sandbank).

The Celta train to Portugal

The fortunes of the rail route from **Vigo to Porto** have ebbed and flowed over the last 50 years. Like many rural **cross-border** rail links in Europe, there has been talk of closure including serious discussions in 2012. That the route has survived has been mainly due to the dedicated support of local activists in the Minho region – the portion of north-west Portugal which abuts onto the Spanish border. The line was happily reprieved, with a renewed commitment by the regional authorities in both **Galicia and Minho** to improving services between Vigo and Porto.

In summer 2013, the service was relaunched under the *Celta* brand. It is a name which nicely appeals on both sides of the border, for residents of the Minho and Galicia regions are justifiably proud of their Atlantic heritage, communicated through maritime links along the seaways which connect the major Celtic regions of Europe. Football supporters of **FC Porto** do however have to endure the oft-repeated jibe that the new train service is named in honour of their rivals **Celta Vigo** on the Spanish side of the border. The current timetable shows that the trains maintain a decent pace – indeed, a positive dash compared with the timings of yesteryear. Cast back to 1965, and the morning train from Vigo to Porto took over six hours. Ten years ago, it still took over three hours. Today, trains on this route take little more than two hours.

The first part of the run out of Vigo follows the estuary upstream until the train turns south at **Redondela**, cutting through soft hill country to reach the Minho Valley and the Portuguese border. The last place in Spain is the tiered town of **Tui**, from where there's a road and rail bridge across the Minho to **Valença** in Portugal. Remember to set your watch back by one hour for Portuguese time.

The next stretch of the route is very pleasant as the railway runs beside the Minho down to the coast, following the Costa Verde south to the old fortress town and resort of **Viana do Castelo**, with the beach on one side of the River Lima and the charming little town – noted for its Renaissance and Manueline architecture, which appeared when trade began with the great Hanseatic cities of northern Europe – on the other.

With the exception of Santa Luzia on the top of the **Monte de Santa Luzia** (accessible by funicular from its beautifully restored station on Avda. 25 de Abril; excellent view), all of Viana do Castelo's interesting sights are walkable. The central square, **Praça da República**, has a 16th-century fountain that has been copied all over the region. If you are looking for a quiet place to stop for a day or two, we can especially recommend the *pousada* by the basilica at Santa Luzia.

South from Viana do Castelo, the railway runs inland before returning to the coast at **Porto**. The train terminates at **Campanhã** where the station facade, with its Romanesque windows and imposing station clock, exudes quiet authority. Do take a look and then, if you are heading for the city centre, take the local train which runs four times each hour to **São Bento station** in the very middle of Porto.

Porto (suggested stopover)

Portugal's seductive second city, Porto (sometimes Oporto in English), is spectacularly sited on the steep banks of the **River Douro**. It gives its name to the fortified wine the English-speaking world knows as port (fortuitously invented by two Englishmen who used brandy in an attempt to preserve Portuguese wine).

Get your bearings by climbing the **Torre dos Clérigos**, Porto's symbol, an 18th-century granite bell tower that gives a magnificent view. Below, the characterfully **fading Old Town**, with its pastel shades and changes in level, is strongly atmospheric, notably in the Ribeira riverside area. The **Soares dos Reis Museum** (closed Mon), housed in the Carrancas Palace, is acclaimed for its collection of decorative arts, including Portuguese faience.

For an astonishing temple to money-making, take the guided tour of the centrally located **Palácio da Bolsa** (former Stock Exchange, now headquarters of the Chamber of Commerce, www.palaciodabolsa.com), rather grey and boring-looking from outside but revealing a lavish interior which includes the Arabian Hall, a 19th-century gilded evocation of the Alhambra in Granada. The nearby **Church of Santa Clara** is a fine example of the Manueline style and has a dazzling baroque interior.

The **vineyards** themselves are a long way upriver in the magnificently scenic Douro Valley, but most of the port is aged in the numerous lodges in the district of **Vila Nova de Gaia**, linked to the city centre by the double-decker coathanger-shaped Dom Luís I Bridge; walk over on the top level for dizzying views. Many lodges offer tours with **tastings** and booking is not generally necessary. Some are closed at weekends outside the main season. Lodges usually levy a charge, starting at about €5, but with the option to upgrade if you wish to taste more illustrious wines.

Having visited many of the **lodges**, the three we especially recommend to get a sense of port and its history are those at Taylor's, Ramos Pinto (which has a wonderful small museum on wine) and Graham's, where the guides are especially good and show amazing prowess in many different languages. Moored on the river, small barrel-laden sailing craft (*barcos rabelos*), last used in 1967, serve as a reminder of how the young ports used to be brought downriver from the vineyards.

In Porto, we have a nice instance of a railway station being a sight in its own right. The city's more central station at **São Bento** celebrated in 2016 the centenary of the opening of the current building. With its spectacularly painted glazed tiles (known as *azulejos*), São Bento is one of Europe's truly

Excursions from Porto

Do explore the mountain-backed **Douro Valley** east of Porto, with its many **vineyards** as well as some enchanting places accessible by train. Even if you are pushed for time, consider at least taking the train up the Douro Valley to **Pinhão** and back. It takes two-and-a-half hours each way. Sit on the right for the best views and certainly plan to spend a couple of hours or more in the riverside town which is dedicated entirely to the production, marketing and consumption of port.

North-east of Porto, **Guimarães** was once the Portuguese capital and contains a nice mediaeval core despite the unpromising industrial outskirts. Another excellent outing from Porto is to join pilgrims looking for absolution from their sins in **Braga**, little more than an hour away by train. The real draw in Braga is the monumental **Bom Jesus do Monte** shrine in a wonderful wooded setting on the hills east of the town. Braga rates alongside Međugorje (Bosnia & Herzegovina), Knock (Ireland) and Częstochowa (Poland) in hosting some of the best penitential theatre in Europe.

great railway stations. It may lack the grandeur of other notable stations (see our **Sidetracks** feature on p235), but the elaborate tiling in the main reception hall is something very special.

ARRIVAL, INFORMATION, ACCOMMODATION

🚆 **Campanhã**, Rua da Estação, near the south-east edge of town, serves trains from Lisbon and Vigo (local train or metro to the city centre). **São Bento**, near Praça da Liberdade, handles local/regional services. Frequent connections between the stations, taking 4 mins.
✈ Francisco Sá Carneiro, 11 km outside Porto (www.ana.pt). Metro line E links the airport with the city centre.
🛈 Tourist office: Praça Almeida Garret 27 (www.visitporto.travel). Tickets for Porto's public transport system are sold at STCP kiosks. The city has three tram lines and six metro lines. For information on public transport see www.stcp.pt. The **Museu do Carro Eléctrico** is a vintage tram that tours the city from near the Church of São Francisco (www.museudocarroelectrico.pt; closed Mon mornings). ⛴ 50-min boat trips depart from Praça da Ribeira, touring the River Douro.
🛏 For cheap lodgings, try the central area around Av. dos Aliados. Avoid the dockside Ribeira. Located between the Ribeira and São Bento station in the historic centre is the very welcoming **InPatio** guest house, Pátio de São Salvador 22, ☎ 222 085 477 (www.inpatio.pt). Located right next to the river and well placed for exploring the city is the welcoming **Guest House Douro**, R. Fonte Taurina 99-101 (www.guesthousedouro.com). The **Spot Hostel**, R. de Gonçalo Cristóvão 12, ☎ 224 085 205 (www.spothostel.pt), is a firm favourite on the European hostelling circuit.

Onward to Lisbon

The train journey from **Porto to Lisbon** is an interesting transect from north to south, with a strong sense of entering gentler, sunnier landscapes. The initial stretch south from Porto is close to the coast as far as Espinho, a now rather faded resort which once affected to have an almost Californian appeal. The serious surfers are long gone as Espinho struggles with pollution. Beyond Espinho, the railway turns inland, briefly returning seaward to skirt the eerie salt pan landscapes at Aveiro.

The first major city south of Porto is **Coimbra**, a centre of the Portuguese Renaissance and the seat of one of the oldest universities in the world. Set on a hillside above the **River Mondego**, the town is packed with mediaeval character; in term time it has a lively, youthful air. Coimbra has its own version of the **fado**, a melancholic, monotonous and sentimental chant originally sung by sailors in the 18th century.

From Coimbra, there is an alternative route south along the coast to Lisbon, but the main line takes a more easterly course to reach the **Tejo Valley** at Entroncamento which has a once-daily train to Badajoz in Spain. Our route then follows the Tejo downstream to Lisbon. All trains stop first at Lisbon Oriente station, a striking modern design by **Santiago Calatrava**, with most services then continuing to Santa Apolónia station in the city centre.

Lisbon

The Portuguese capital is a city on a human scale, and its immediately **likeable atmosphere** is the gateway to a rich cultural background. History and politics are inscribed on its soul and written into its unique geography. Get up high on the **Elevador de Santa Justa** and look out over the cobbled, hilly streets and hotchpotch of roofs and alleyways that cover Lisbon's seven hills. At one end of the city you'll see the **Castelo de São Jorge**, towering over an area that forms a powerful historical and architectural reminder of the city's reclamation from the Moors. At the other end of Lisbon, the 1960s Padrão dos Descobrimentos is a monument to its maritime glories.

Located at the mouth of the Rio Tejo (River Tagus), the city has a rich gastronomy influenced both by the sea and by its imperial history. In the streets you'll smell **roasting chestnuts** and freshly baked custard tarts, and in the restaurants they'll serve up salted cod or fresh sardines washed down with young vinho verde wine and fiery after-dinner **ginjinha**. Fado music and other sounds fill the air in the historic **Bairro Alto**. However you like to spend your days and evenings, immerse yourself in Lisbon's enticing atmosphere and you're sure to find something to entertain you.

Arrival, information, accommodation

Santa Apolónia station, on the banks of the Tagus near Alfama, is the main station, handling all international trains and those to east and north Portugal. All trains to and from Santa Apolónia also call at the **Gare Intermodal do Oriente**, where there is an interchange with the metro system. From Oriente take the metro (changing at Alameda) to Rossio or Baixa-Chiado, the main areas for accommodation. **Cais do Sodré** station doubles as the quay for the Tagus ferries and as the station handling the local coastal services. Lisbon Portela Airport (www.ana.pt) is 7 km north of the city, with a metro connection to the city centre (Saldanha). Public transport in Lisbon is cheap and efficient, consisting of buses, trams, the metro and funiculars (*elevadores*) between different levels of the city. Make a point of getting a walking map of the labyrinthine Alfama district. Tickets for single trips on buses operated by Carris cost €2 on board and trams €3 (www.carris.pt), cheaper fares can be obtained by buying and charging a 7 Colinas / Viva Viagem card. The main tourist office is in the Lisboa Story Center, at Praça do Comércio 78–81 (www.visitlisboa.com).

Accommodation is scarcest and priciest at Easter and in summer. The vast majority of cheap places are in the centre of town, on and around Avda Liberdade or the Baixa. In the latter, head for the three squares Praça da Figueira, Praça dos Restauradores and Praça Dom Pedro IV. Based in a former convent, the modern and positively minimalist **Hotel Convento do Salvador**, R. do Salvador 2 B, ☎ 218 872 565 (www.conventosalvador.pt) is a great option in Lisbon's Alfama district. Cheap it may not be, but for the amazing public spaces alone, try the elegant **Hotel Avenida Palace**, r. 1 Dezembro 123, ☎ 213 218 100 (www.hotelavenidapalace.pt), in a great central location. A friendly and quiet guest house in the Bairro Alto district is the **Casa do Bairro**, Beco Caldeira 1, ☎ 913 136 320 (www.shiadu.com/casa-do-bairro).

Connections from Lisbon

Direct overnight trains from Lisbon to Spain and France were suspended in March 2020 and are unlikely to be reinstated. If you want to linger in Portugal, a good day trip by train from Lisbon is to **Évora**, the capital of the Alentejo region. This walled city, with its distinctive whitewashed houses with tile work and balconies, is inscribed on UNESCO's List of World Heritage Sites. Looking south from Lisbon, there are fast trains down to **Faro** on the Algarve, from where there are local trains along the coast, running west to Lagos and east to Vila Real de Santo António, a small town right on the Spanish border. Ferries shuttle over the border to Ayamonte in Spain.

From Lisbon to southern Spain

We know from feedback from readers of earlier editions of this book that many, having reached Lisbon, want to continue to southern Spain. The rail plus ferry route via Faro and Ayamonte, mentioned in the previous paragraph, is a possibility but it's very slow. Or you can travel from Lisbon to Seville entirely by train with changes in **Entroncamento, Badajoz and Mérida**. As of October 2024, that option now runs daily.

So this might be a rare case where it really makes sense to use a **direct bus from Lisbon to Seville**. The direct coaches are operated by two companies, namely Flixbus (www.flixbus.es) and Alsa (www.alsa.es), with each operator offering a journey time of under seven hours for the fastest itineraries. One-way fares can be as little as €17, but around €35 is more the norm. Note that tickets for the Flixbus services tend to go on sale earlier that those for the Alsa buses. Check timetables carefully, as these change by season and even day of the week. The journey is best done with **a midmorning departure**, but that's not always possible.

Whichever company you use, buses to Seville depart from outside Oriente station in Lisbon. The route out of Lisbon usually takes in the remarkable **Vasco da Gama bridge**, which is at this point unusually wide. At a length of over 12 km, this is Europe's longest road bridge, second only to the Kerch bridge linking the Crimean peninsula with mainland Russia. Once away from the Lisbon metropolitan region, the bus covers the **plains of Alentejo**, with huge plantations of cork trees and sunflowers. Ripples of hills interrupt vast fields of wheat further south and just short of the coast, the bus swings east onto the A22 motorway, which is here part of Europe's E1 highway. That makes it sound very grand, which it isn't. You actually see little of the coast, which may be a blessing as this part of the Algarve coastline is densely settled with a string of resorts. All buses pull off the motorway to serve the city of **Faro**, some stopping both in the centre and at the airport. A little further east some buses also pause at **Tavira**, which we rate as one of the most likeable places in the Algarve. If you are not into long bus trips and you want to break your journey, Tavira is the place to do it.

Back on the motorway, it's just another 20 km to the **Rio Guadiana**, where we cross on a bridge into Spain. Remember that Spanish time is one hour in advance of clocks in Portugal. From here the motorway runs due east to **Seville**, where this route ends.

Sidetracks: Grand stations

Even in the earliest days of train travel, railway stations were more than merely functional. In great cities, the principal termini made **bold statements** about style, status and ambition.

On rural rail routes in country areas, the **design of stations** was often equally symbolic though usually more geared to communicating a sense of domesticity and order. Here was the railway as part of the community, sometimes adapting the best of regional **vernacular architecture** to its own purposes and in other cases deploying standard designs which reminded villagers in far-flung parts of the network that they, too, were now connected to 'the centre' – be it a pivot of art and culture or a great centre of **imperial power**. Many rural railway stations in Finland date from the tsarist period and even today look like stage sets for 19th-century Russia while some country stations in south-west Poland – in territory which until 1945 was German – still have echoes of Prussian authority.

Yet it was in Europe's cities that railway stations were at their most opulent and eclectic. The railway reshaped geography and used architectural whimsy to create a kaleidoscope of exotic design. Travellers arriving in **Liverpool** on the world's first passenger railway were greeted by a Moorish Arch. In London the station at **Euston**, with its glorious Doric *propylaeum*, may have seduced some passengers into thinking that they had been magically transported to Rome.

Sadly, both the Liverpool and Euston structures are long gone. But the last 20 years have seen a happy renaissance of interest in early railway architecture. The restoration in London of **St Pancras** has been so beautifully executed that this station attracts many visitors who have no intention of catching a train. It is an exuberant starting point for **Route 21** in this book. Across the continent, many other grand termini have been restored. **Antwerp Centraal** (on **Route 6**) once again looks as splendid as it did on the day it first opened. Its extraordinary main reception hall and bold facade, Mannerist in style, may have a few too many gilded trophies for some tastes, but it is a space that can only be approached with reverence. To these outstanding examples of recent **landmark renovations**, we might add in a handful of other grand termini where a missed connection gives good cause to just sit and look at the extravagant space around you: Leipzig Hauptbahnhof, Milan Centrale, Limoges-Bénédictins, Paris Est and Moscow Kazanskaya all deserve a place on any list of Europe's great stations.

Sometimes it is just one aspect of a station which commands attention: the delicate lattice facade at Porta Nuova station in Turin, the **decorative ceilings** and stained glass at Groningen, the superb tile work at Estació del Nord in València or at **São Bento station** in Porto, the covered plaza and indoor garden in the old part of Atocha station in Madrid and the art nouveau interiors at Vitebsky station in St Petersburg.

Of course, not all of Europe's grand stations are old. Our home city of Berlin has in its Hauptbahnhof (opened in 2006) a very fine modern cathedral devoted to trains. Other modern stations which invite **comparison with cathedrals** are Liège-Guillemins and Lisbon Oriente, both soaring structures designed by Santiago Calatrava. If you find yourself travelling through any of the stations mentioned here, why not stop off for an hour and take a look around?

SCANDINAVIA AND THE BALTIC
An introduction

In this section of *Europe by Rail*, we include seven journeys to and through Denmark, Norway, Sweden, Finland and the Baltic coasts of Germany and Poland. Note that journeys into Russia in this book were removed following Russia's invasion of Ukraine in February 2022. We are, on the whole, travelling here through countries with **efficient and reliable train services**. Even Poland has been playing catch-up with much-needed investment in new trains and network infrastructure.

But what of the **eastern side of the Baltic**? We would in the not too distant future like to include journeys through Lithuania, Latvia and Estonia. The pitiful state of the railways and in particular the paucity of cross-border trains means that it must wait for a future edition. But we are quietly hopeful. 2024 saw the reinstatement of once-daily passenger trains from Lithuania to both Latvia and Poland. You can read more about rail travel in the **Baltic States** in our Sidetracks feature on p297.

It's very pleasing to present in this edition a wonderful route along the Baltic's southern shore. **Route 31** takes in some of the region's most striking **Hanseatic cities**: Lübeck, Stralsund and Gdańsk.

More than in other areas of Europe, journeys by public transport through Scandinavia and the Baltic region often rely upon more than just trains. So in this section of *Europe by Rail* you find routes which require a **short hop on a bus or a boat**. In Scandinavia in particular you'll find perfectly integrated timetables which make it very easy to connect between different modes of transport. Just be aware that Interrail passes will normally not be accepted for free travel on bus or boat links – although in some cases a handsome discount may be available on ferries.

There are many wonderful routes in Scandinavia for which we just couldn't find space in this book. We are great fans of some of the rural railways in central Sweden, particularly those around **Lake Vänern**. You'll get a glimpse of that lovely region if you follow the main line between Oslo and Stockholm which forms the final part of **Route 26**.

There's a classic slow journey much favoured by many devotees of Sweden's railways. It is the **Inlandsbanan** which runs up to Gällivare. It is open to passenger traffic for just nine weeks each year and, for those who love trees, it's hard to beat. Yet perhaps the most celebrated Scandinavian slow journey of all is not a train but a shipping service. If you tire of trains, make time for the **Hurtigruten ships** which ply the Norwegian coast from Bergen all the way to Kirkenes near the Russian border. Two journeys in this volume (**Route 28** and 29) take in the Lofoten Islands, an archipelago often acclaimed as the most scenic stretch of the entire Hurtigruten itinerary. ∎

Route 25: Great maritime cities

Cities: ★★ Culture: ★ History: ★ Scenery: ★
Countries covered: Netherlands (NE), Germany (DE), Denmark (DK) Sweden (SE)
Journey time: 17 hrs 10 mins | Distance: 1,661 km | Map: www.ebrweb.eu/18map25

One of the longer journeys in this book, this route is rich in **maritime character**. Most of the cities along the way have developed through sea trade or their links with the sea, although none is really on an open coast.

Amsterdam, Hamburg and Stockholm, all watery places to be sure, are in protected locations well removed from the sea. Even Copenhagen is sheltered from the open waters of the Øresund by Amager Island. Exports of iron and tar from **Stockholm**, coffee imports into **Hamburg**, the movement of spices, silks and later Baltic grains through Amsterdam, all these and the ubiquitous herring helped create the trade ecosystem of the cities along this route. You'll still find the humble herring aplenty on this journey; it is a staple on the breakfast table in this part of Europe.

We'll visit places shaped by the **Hanseatic League** and feel the sea breeze on this journey through four countries. A highpoint of the journey (literally) is the **Rendsburger Hochbrücke** (Rendsburg High Bridge) on the railway between Hamburg and the Danish border. This extraordinary piece of railway architecture, which bridges the **Kiel Canal**, embodies a compromise between shipping interests and those of the railway magnates.

There was a time when Dutch clippers regularly sailed directly from Amsterdam to the Baltic. No longer. True diehards wanting to travel by sea from the Low Countries to Sweden can opt for the regular cargo vessels which leave Ghent or Zeebrugge (both in Belgium) several times each week for the 32-hour voyage to Göteborg on Sweden's west coast. Operated by DFDS Tor Line, there is space for a few leisure passengers on most sailings.

Recommended itinerary

If you are in a rush, you could complete the journey described here in under 24 hours, leaving Amsterdam late afternoon to travel to Hamburg and there joining the night train to Stockholm (note that this new overnight link, which started in 2021, does not run daily). At the very least we would suggest stops in Hamburg and **Copenhagen** but this is a journey that could easily be spread out over a week or more, with additional stops of a day or two in Bremen, Fredericia, **Odense** or Malmö.

From Amsterdam to Bremen

Who said that the Netherlands are pancake-flat? Watch closely as the Intercity train rattles east from Amsterdam towards the German border and you'll see that beyond **Amersfoort** the landscape rises and falls in gentle ripples. The train crosses the River IJssel just before Deventer and an hour later reaches the border at Bad Bentheim. The prefix 'Bad' in the town's

Route details

Amsterdam Centraal to Osnabrück Hbf

Frequency	Journey time	Notes
Every 2 hrs	3h	

Osnabrück Hbf to Bremen Hbf

Frequency	Journey time	Notes
Hourly	2h15	X

Bremen Hbf to Hamburg Hbf

Frequency	Journey time	Notes
2–3 per hr	0h55–1h30	

Hamburg Hbf to Odense

Frequency	Journey time	Notes
3–6 per day	3h30	A

Odense to Copenhagen H

Frequency	Journey time	Notes
2–3 per hr	1h10–1h40	

Copenhagen H to Stockholm C

Frequency	Journey time	Notes
5–7 per day	5h20	B

Notes

A – It is worth noting that the direct trains from Hamburg to Odense and Copenhagen really can be very full at peak travel times; a seat reservation was mandatory on this route from 1 June to 1 September 2024. New trains on order, due for delivery in mid-2025, will give increased capacity on services from Hamburg into Denmark.

B – There are plenty of additional options by taking a regional train from Copenhagen to Malmö Central, whence there are hourly trains to Stockholm.

X – Using the local trains described on p239.

name reveals its status as a spa town. If brine and sulphur are your thing, Bad Bentheim might be worth a stop.

Running east from the border, the landscape becomes more three-dimensional. The forested hills to the right are the **Teutoburger Wald**. Next stop is the genial university city of **Osnabrück**, where the scale of the late 19th-century station building is a reminder that this is one of the major railway junctions in western Germany. You'll arrive on the lower level of this two-tier station, and you'll need to change trains here for an onward service to Bremen.

Connections from Osnabrück

Osnabrück used to be a paradise for insomniac train spotters. They would gather at all hours of the night to watch the long-distance expresses leaving for Copenhagen, Paris, Warsaw and Moscow.

The departure boards have been tamed, but there's still a good range of connections from Osnabrück. There is a fast train every two hours to **Hannover** and **Berlin**. There are hourly fast trains to **Cologne**, most of which continue up the Rhine Valley to Koblenz, Mainz and beyond. Private rail operator NordWestBahn has an hourly slow train on a scenic line which runs all the way to Wilhelmshaven on the North Sea coast.

The easy choice from **Osnabrück to Bremen** is the hourly Intercity train which usually leaves from Platform 3 (on the upper-level platforms). But there is a much more interesting alternative, namely the slow trains operated by NordWestBahn (which normally leave from Platform 13 on the lower level; see www.nordwestbahn.de). Rail passes are accepted on this privately operated rail service. Trains depart Osnabrück hourly (usually at 24 minutes past each hour) and take 2 hrs 14 mins to reach Bremen Hauptbahnhof.

The **NordWestBahn** trains take in some of the finest countryside in Lower Saxony. Don't expect anything dramatic, but sit back and relax as the slow train to Bremen wends its way through landscapes of delicate beauty. The train wanders past arable land, forests and heath with lots of pretty farms. All too soon, you'll be running into Bremen where the train crosses the River Weser on its approach to the city's Hauptbahnhof.

Bremen is one of Germany's foremost maritime cities. It boasts a rich Hanseatic history and the city's links with the Americas brought great wealth to Bremen. Coffee and cotton were key to the transatlantic trade and many of the **merchants' houses** from the 16th century survive. Together with Bremerhaven, its outer harbour some way downstream towards the mouth of the Weser River, Bremen is one of the Länder (states) that make up Germany, continuing a proud tradition of self-government that dates back to the Middle Ages.

The Old Town, on the north-east bank of the river, is the main area of historical interest. The wide Marktplatz is dominated by the Rathaus (town hall), a 15th-century structure overlaid with a Renaissance facade. It's worth joining a tour to see the splendid interior.

Ticket tips: Amsterdam to Stockholm

This is a journey which can be done remarkably cheaply. Tickets from Amsterdam to Stockholm, using precisely the route described here, can be purchased at www.bahn.de for as little as €60 one way.

The problem is that the period of **validity of international rail tickets** has been progressively attenuated over the last year or two. So whereas in the past a through ticket from Amsterdam to Stockholm could be used over several days, with leisurely stops along the way, now the validity is limited to the travel date shown on the ticket and the following day. For those wanting to make **stopovers** and maintain some flexibility in their travel plans, the reduced validity of international point-to-point tickets has surely prompted many travellers to opt instead for **Interrail or Eurail passes**.

Don't miss the quirky statue of the **Four Musicians of Bremen** on Marktplatz, which recalls a Grimm Brothers' tale. The 11th-century twin-spired St Petri Dom, Sandstr. 10–12, is sombrely beautiful. In the Bleikeller (basement, open Wed–Sun in Apr–Dec) are some ghoulish corpses, preserved from decay by the lack of air.

To the south side of **Marktplatz** is Böttcherstrasse with its eclectic mix of Jugendstil (Germany's version of art nouveau) and art deco. Today it houses cafés and artisans' workshops, making it a fine part of town to wander and feel the relaxed pulse of Bremen life. Bremen has accommodation options to fit all wallets.

Connections from Bremen

Trains leave Bremen twice-hourly for Hannover. If you've tired of northern flatlands and crave some hills, you can escape from Bremen with a direct ICE to Munich. This route runs every two hours and the journey to the Bavarian capital takes under six hours.

There are hourly regional trains to **Cuxhaven**, serving Bremerhaven along the way. Cuxhaven itself is uninspiring, but it's the departure point for boats to **Helgoland**, an extraordinary hulk of red rock in the North Sea which was variously Danish and British, before becoming German territory in 1890 – as part of a deal whereby the German Kaiser relinquished claims on Zanzibar.

Two great trade cities

It'll be no surprise to learn that Bremen and Hamburg are great rivals. Both were key members of the Hanseatic League, and both have privileged status as city states in modern Germany. Berlin is the only other city in the country which is also a German state in its own right.

The train journey from **Bremen to Hamburg** takes less than am hour, speeding you from the Weser to the Elbe – the latter is the river which defines so much of Hamburg life. Along the way, the train to Hamburg passes through Scheeßel, a small town which springs to life in June each year when it hosts the **Hurricane music festival**. Some say it's Germany's version of Glastonbury.

Hamburg (suggested stopover)

Hamburg's long maritime history and its status as **Germany's media capital** means that it has grown to become one of the country's richest, most cosmopolitan and sophisticated cities. It has everything you would expect of a port city – with a multicultural population, red-light district centred on the infamous Reeperbahn and a waterfront of hulking warehouses and storerooms. But the city is much more than that. For a start, Hamburg is surprisingly green, with leafy streets and pleasant parks, and its location on the water provides plenty of opportunities to take boat trips on the **Alster Lakes**. Take a tour of the city's huge harbour with boats leaving from St Pauli Landungsbrücken. It's worth bearing in mind that Hamburg has several ferry routes which are fully integrated into the city's public transport network (and are thus very cheap). A good choice is the hour-long ride on ferry route 62 from the **Landungsbrücken** (Pier 3) to Finkenwerder and back.

As Germany's second largest city after Berlin, Hamburg also offers up a wealth of cultural attractions, including a vibrant and hedonistic nightlife, a fine collection of museums and plenty of events and festivals taking place throughout the year. The city on the River Elbe has a fascinating combination of historic and modern architecture, including many former warehouses now renovated to house some of the city's top cultural and tourist attractions. Among them is the **largest model railway** in the world (www.miniatur-wunderland.com; Kehrwieder 2–4 in Hamburg's Speicherstadt). The **Elbe Philharmonic Hall**, inaugurated in 2017, incorporates part of a brick-built former warehouse. For more on the **Speicherstadt** see p289.

Arrival, information, accommodation

⇌ The **Hauptbahnhof** (Hbf) handles most long-distance trains. It's huge, central and on the U-Bahn and S-Bahn. 🛈 The Hauptbahnhof houses the main tourist office (www.hamburg-tourism.de) and a wonderfully cosmopolitan selection of eateries. Altona station, in the west of the city, is the starting for most trains serving Schleswig-Holstein. **HVV** (Hamburg Transit Authority) run efficient buses, U-Bahn (underground) and S-Bahn, as well as a night bus service to most city districts (www.hvv.de).

🛏 Hamburg has a wealth of mid-range accommodation options, including the boutique hotel **Henri**, Bugenhagenstr. 21, ☎ 040 554 35 70 (www.henri-hotel.com), a 10-min walk from the Hauptbahnhof. The friendly hotel **St Annen**, Annenstr. 5, ☎ 040 317 71 30 (www.hotelstannen.de), is centrally located between the St Pauli district and the Schanzenviertel (yet far enough from the Reeperbahn). For a bit of luxury take a look at **SIDE design hotel**, Drehbahn 49, ☎ 040 309 990 (www.side-hamburg.de).

Connections from Hamburg

You can connect in Hamburg onto **Route 33** to Berlin, Prague and Budapest. There are departures at least hourly from Hamburg Hauptbahnhof to Berlin, Frankfurt-am-Main and Munich. **International departures** from Hamburg include direct daytime trains to Denmark, Austria and Switzerland, plus **overnight services** to Vienna, Innsbruck, Zürich and seasonally also to Stockholm. Closer to hand, there are good links to Germany's Baltic and North Sea coasts with direct trains to the resorts of Westerland on the North Sea island of **Sylt** and to Binz on the Baltic island of **Rügen**. The notion of trains running direct to offshore islands may test your credulity, but Sylt and Rügen are both linked by causeways to the German mainland.

German-Danish borderlands

The entire 600-km long peninsula which juts north from Hamburg is the historic territory of **Jutland**. In mediaeval times Scandinavian influence extended much further south than today.

Yet as the train heads north from Hamburg towards the Danish border, there is a strong sense of entering a different cultural realm. Germany's northernmost state of **Schleswig-Holstein** really has a sense of being a place apart — all the more so if you take time to explore away from the main rail routes. Saxons, Danes and Angles tussled for centuries over the southern part of Jutland. The current line of the border between Germany and Denmark is less than one hundred years old and even today there are Danish-speaking communities on the German side of the border and a vocal German-speaking minority in Danish Jutland.

The Rendsburg Bridge

The bridge over the **Kiel Canal** at **Rendsburg** is one of Europe's most striking civil engineering achievements. Like all great railway bridges, it is best seen from the ground rather than from the train itself. But the experience of travelling by train over the bridge is nonetheless extraordinary. The canal links the North Sea with the Baltic and is thus a major artery for trade. It dates back to the late 19th century; in the early days low-level swing bridges carried the railway over the canal, but that meant that ships had to be stopped to allow the passage of trains.

In 1913 a much higher bridge was opened that is still in use today. But so flat is the terrain in these parts that an elaborate girder structure is necessary for the railway to gain sufficient height to reach the deck of the bridge. The descent on the north side is especially impressive as the train circles in a **grand spiral** over the rooftops of Rendsburg.

Take time to look at the bridge from the canal bank too. It is a 15-minute walk from Rendsburg station down to the canal. A **gondola** hangs from the railway bridge; it shuttles to and fro, ferrying cars and pedestrians across the canal without any charge. It has been out of service following an accident in 2016, when a cargo ship rammed the gondola. The historic gondola was rebuilt and returned to service in spring 2022. There's a pleasant restaurant and café right under the northern end of the bridge by the canal bank (www.brueckenterrassen.de).

Rendsburg's fine suite of technological assets is not limited to the bridge and unusual ferry. There is a **long pedestrian tunnel** under the Kiel

Canal, accessed by escalators which, when the tunnel was first opened in 1965, claimed records as the longest in Europe.

Into Denmark

About 40 minutes north of Rendsburg, the train reaches **Flensburg**, the last stop on German territory before the Danish border. Half a dozen trains each day run right through from Hamburg to Denmark. If you are arriving in Flensburg on one of the regional German trains from Hamburg or from Kiel, you need to allow at least 10 minutes to transfer onto the onward train to Denmark.

Beyond Flensburg, the railway tracks north through dull country, only returning to the coast at **Kolding**, a small port in a lovely setting at the head of Kolding Fjord. If you have an hour to stop, it's a fine first encounter with Denmark, with a very appealing Old Town just five minutes west of the railway station. Just a dozen minutes beyond Kolding the train pulls into Fredericia, another town deserving of a short stop.

Kolding and **Fredericia** are as different as chalk and cheese. While Kolding is a mediaeval jumble (and all the better for that), Fredericia is a well-ordered garrison town dating back to the 17th century. Make time to wander along the grassy ramparts which surround the town; it is a fine walk on a clear, still day. Fredericia has thrived thanks to its strategic position on the narrow strait known as the **Lillebælt** (Little Belt) which separates Jutland from the Danish island of Fyn (often known as Funen in English). If you are tempted to stay overnight in Fredericia, the Hotel Gammel Havn, Gothersgade 40, ☎ 75 92 01 99 (www.hotelfredericia.dk) is a good choice.

Connections from Kolding and Fredericia
Connect in Fredericia onto **Route 26**, which offers a completely different way to reach Stockholm, travelling via Oslo. From Kolding there are regular trains west to Esbjerg with connections at Bramming for **Ribe**, which we rate as the loveliest small town anywhere in Jutland. Fredericia is also the departure point for trains to Struer in west Jutland, for onward connections to Thisted in north Jutland.

Over Fyn to Sjælland

From the old harbour district of Fredericia, you can look south over the Little Belt to the island of Fyn. This narrow stretch of water remained unbridged until 1935, when a truss bridge was constructed. It's still used today by all trains running from Fredericia toward Odense and Copenhagen. Rattling over the bridge, one is immediately struck by the mellow, partly forested, landscapes that await on the far side of the Little Belt. It's not for nothing that **Fyn** styles itself 'Denmark's garden island'. It's a pleasant half-hour train ride across Fyn to Odense, which is by far the largest town on the island

and a place which makes much of its connections with **Hans Christian Andersen**. The Danish author was born in Odense and was by all accounts keen to leave as soon as possible. He managed that when he was just 14. That hasn't prevented Odense from using Andersen as a trump card in their marketing. The pedestrianised city centre is a 10-minute stroll south of the station. Spend a little time in amiable **Odense** and you'll begin to understand why Danes rate as among the happiest people on earth. Wander through the quaint town centre, take a peek at Andersen's childhood home in Munkemøllestræde (closed Mon) and stroll through green parkland by the river. A new museum about the Danish writer opened in June 2021. **Hans Christian Andersens Hus** (www.hcandersenshus.dk) was designed by Japanese architect Kengo Kuma and creatively combines exhibition space with landscape design and architecture.

Rail travellers and train buffs may want to make time for **Denmark's Railway Museum**, located on the north side of the railway station (open daily 09.00–16.00, www.jernbanemuseet.dk). For an overnight stay in the city, check out the Hotel Odeon, Odeons Kvarter 11, ☎ 65 42 05 00 (www.hotelodeon.dk) which is handy for both the station and the Old Town.

Crossing the Storebælt

From Odense, it's just 15 minutes by train to **Nyborg**, the easternmost community in Fyn, and the jumping-off point for the long crossing of the Storebælt (Great Belt) to Sjælland, the largest and most populous of the islands of Denmark. The opening in 1997 of this important rail link dramatically reconfigured Danish geography. It is in fact a two-stage crossing, with first a long box-girder bridge from Nyborg to the small island of Sprogø – an isle which was once used as a place of exile for women of ill repute – whence twin-bore tunnels escort the railway east under the sea to Sjælland.

Emerging back into daylight on **Sjælland**, the train tracks broadly east via Ringsted, from where a new high-speed line which opened in summer 2019 makes for a quick dash to Copenhagen. But some trains still use the old line via Roskilde, a handsome town which was Denmark's first capital.

Roskilde is rich in history, with a magnificent brick cathedral that is the traditional burial place of Danish royalty. The impressive **Viking Ship Museum**, one kilometre north of the centre on the shore of Roskilde Fjord, exhibits the intact remains of five original ships and shows a film about their excavation in the 1960s (www.vikingeskibsmuseet.dk). The famous open-air **Roskilde music festival**, which has done so much to put Roskilde on the map, is held in late June and early July (www.roskilde-festival.dk); it features some of the biggest international rock groups as well as lesser-known Scandinavian bands. Following cancellation during the pandemic, the festival is back on track and the 2025 event will be the 53rd Roskilde festival.

Copenhagen (København) – (suggested stopover)

Copenhagen is a refined and vibrant city of great Renaissance architecture, cobbled pedestrian walks and meandering canals and lakes, with a distinct, easy-going and **friendly atmosphere** that is a joy to take in, especially in the summertime. Cruise boats tour the canals that thread through the historic core, revealing an appealing diversity of open spaces, spires, towers and statuary.

Cycling is encouraged here and the outdoor, almost Mediterranean, feel is compounded by an effervescent street life and excellent nightspots. In spring 2018 a new urban space opened on the city's harbour waterfront. **BLOX** is home to the Danish Architecture Centre and its exhibitions, but also aims to be a meeting and living space for Copenhagen's citizens.

For an evening of mindless pleasure, do not miss the Tivoli Gardens and its stomach-churning rides, giant puppets, kitsch merry-go-rounds and all the fun you would expect of the fair in what is one of Europe's oldest, and best-loved amusement parks. Or have a stroll through **Christiania**, a unique social experiment, and enjoy a picnic on the lakeside, sip on a beer with the curious array of locals and visitors, or just browse through the market stalls.

Arrival, information, accommodation

≥ The main rail station is **København Hovedbanegård** (København H; www.dsb.dk), with an S-train (urban train) station of the same name. Buses to districts in and around Copenhagen stop right outside and the city centre is a 5-min walk away. ⓘ Tourist office: Vesterbrogade 4, opposite the station (www.visitcopenhagen.dk).

Buses, trains and the driverless metro all form part of an integrated system in the Copenhagen area and tickets are valid on all. Most attractions are central, so for a single journey you will probably only need the cheapest ticket, 24 DKK, which covers travel in two zones for 1 hr 15 mins. Or buy a 24-hr City Pass for 80 DKK. Validate your ticket in the machines on board buses and on S-train platforms. Bus tickets can be purchased on board, but train tickets must be bought before boarding the train at one of the automated machines at the station (or download the DOT Tickets App). The M3 City Circle Line opened in autumn 2019 and the first section of the M4 in March 2020. An extension of the latter to Sydhavn is planned to open later in 2024.

⌂ Copenhagen has a wide range of accommodation options, although turning up without a reservation – especially during the summer months – can be risky. **Hotel Absalon**, close to the Centralstation, is a reasonably priced option in Helgolandsgade 15, ☎ 33 31 43 44 (www.absalon-hotel.dk). Basic, but quite affordable are the huge **WakeUp Copenhagen** hotels at Bernstorffsgade 35 and at Borgergade 9, ☎ 44 80 00 00 (www.wakeupcopenhagen.dk). If you are in the mood for something extra special, opt for the **Hotel Nimb**, Bernstorffsgade 5, ☎ 88 70 00 00 (www.nimb.dk), a fabulous piece of stylish escapism just opposite the train station's eastern exit, close to the Tivoli Gardens. If like us you can't afford the room prices, just have a peek around.

Connections from Copenhagen

Take the local train to **Helsingør**, a relaxed small town on the shores of the Øresund with a spectacular castle (called Kronborg Slot), which features centrally in Shakespeare's *Hamlet*. From Helsingør, Scandlines ferries shuttle frequently over the Øresund to **Helsingborg** on the Swedish side, where there is a connection into **Route 27** north to Göteborg and Oslo.

Swedish detours

Travellers with a little time on their hands can take an alternative, more easterly route from **Malmö to Linköping**. It relies entirely on regional trains which do not require advance reservation. The journey kicks off with a 2 hrs 45 mins ride on one of the hourly regional trains from Malmö to **Karlskrona**, a beautiful planned city with great architectural ambition which was once Sweden's premier naval port. It's on the UNESCO World Heritage List. From Karlskrona, continue north via Emmaboda to Kalmar to join a local rail route (trains every two hours) which runs up through **Östergötland** to Linköping, from where it's just a short hop on to Stockholm. Malmö to Linköping via this rural route takes eight to nine hours. Those with an appetite for island adventures may want to venture offshore to visit the Swedish island of **Gotland** (reached by ferry from Oskarshamn and Nynäshamn).

Over the Øresund into Sweden

If you travel **east from Copenhagen** on one of the direct Stockholm-bound trains you need to be at the station 15 minutes before departure; there is sometimes an ID check before you board the train. If you take any other eastbound service from Copenhagen or Kastrup (that's the airport station now increasingly referred to in timetables as CPH Lufthavn) expect a cursory ID check on the train. This may change in 2025, but our advice is still to allow an extra half hour for all journeys between Copenhagen and **Malmö** on local trains on the Øresund route. As of autumn 2024 there are no ID checks on the reverse route, ie. from Sweden to Denmark, but that too could change of course.

Route 25 shares a common stretch with **Route 27** between Copenhagen and Lund (for more on Malmö – including connections from the Swedish city – see p255). Beyond **Lund**, the two routes diverge, Route 27 heading north-west through rolling agricultural land towards Göteborg and our train running north-east through pleasant countryside towards Stockholm. See the box above for an alternative route north to Stockholm.

There are a number of unremarkable small towns, but none that really cries out for a stop until **Linköping**, where the prime attraction is Gamla Linköping, an ambitious museum that seeks to recreate the 19th-century town, much of which was painstakingly relocated piece by piece and rebuilt here. Linköping's **Domkyrka** is one of Sweden's oldest cathedrals, with a 107-m green spire visible from far outside the town, and containing fine stone carvings along the south doorway.

The next place of any size is **Norrköping**, a prosperous textile centre, with a museum celebrating the town's industrial legacy. The cluster of old mills around the River Motala is truly impressive. Beyond Norrköping, the surrounding countryside becomes more densely populated as the train gets closer to **Stockholm** (see p252). The Swedish capital is reached in about 80 minutes on the fastest trains from Norrköping.

Route 26: To the Skagerrak and beyond

CITIES: ★★ CULTURE: ★ HISTORY: ★ SCENERY: ★★
COUNTRIES COVERED: DENMARK (DK), NORWAY (NO), SWEDEN (SE)
JOURNEY TIME: 20 HRS | DISTANCE: 1,425 KM | MAP: www.ebrweb.eu/18map26

This journey makes the perfect introduction to **southern Scandinavia**. We start in Fredericia, a pleasant small town in Danish Jutland, the latter a long peninsula attached to the European mainland. Fredericia is the point at which this current route branches off from the preceding journey in this book (**Route 25**). You can read more about Fredericia on p243.

Our journey runs up **Jutland** to the northernmost city on the peninsula at **Aalborg**. It then crosses a bridge onto North Jutland, an island created in the 19th century when the northernmost part of the peninsula was severed from the rest in a great storm. This is a region of Europe where the sea has long had the upper hand. Then it's a short **hop on a ferry** across the Skagerrak **to Norway** for a train journey through the hills to Oslo. The final leg of our journey takes us east from the Norwegian capital to Stockholm.

The three countries on this journey share a common cultural heritage. Indeed in the 15th century, following the 1397 **Treaty of Kalmar**, they shared a common monarchy. And these days Denmark, Norway and Sweden are all part of the European Economic Area (EEA) and the Schengen zone.

RECOMMENDED ITINERARY

If you are in a rush, you could complete the journey described here in just two days, leaving Fredericia at breakfast time and reaching **Stockholm** in time for dinner the following day. You'll need to make at least one overnight stop along the way, but – and you know what comes next – this route deserves more time. It could easily be spread out over a week or more, with stops in **Aarhus**, Aalborg, **Kristiansand** and Oslo. Along the way, we'll point out one or two smaller places where you might be inclined to stop off, whether for just a few hours or for an overnight stay.

From **Fredericia**, it is just an hour on to Aarhus. Although there are occasional tantalising glimpses of coastal inlets and harbours, the railway stays away from the coast for most of the journey. That said, there is an especially nice stretch near the start as the train sweeps through mature woodland to emerge on the south shore of **Vejle Fjord** which it then follows west with fine views of the cantilever bridge that here spans the inlet. At the head of Vejle Fjord is the neat little harbour town of Vejle, which once mainstreamed on bargain-basement sausages, but nowadays exports improbably large quantities of chewing gum.

Aarhus (suggested stopover)

The main station of Denmark's second largest city doubles as a shopping centre. It gives an oddly consumerist first impression of Aarhus. Yet there's

248 | Scandinavia and the Baltic

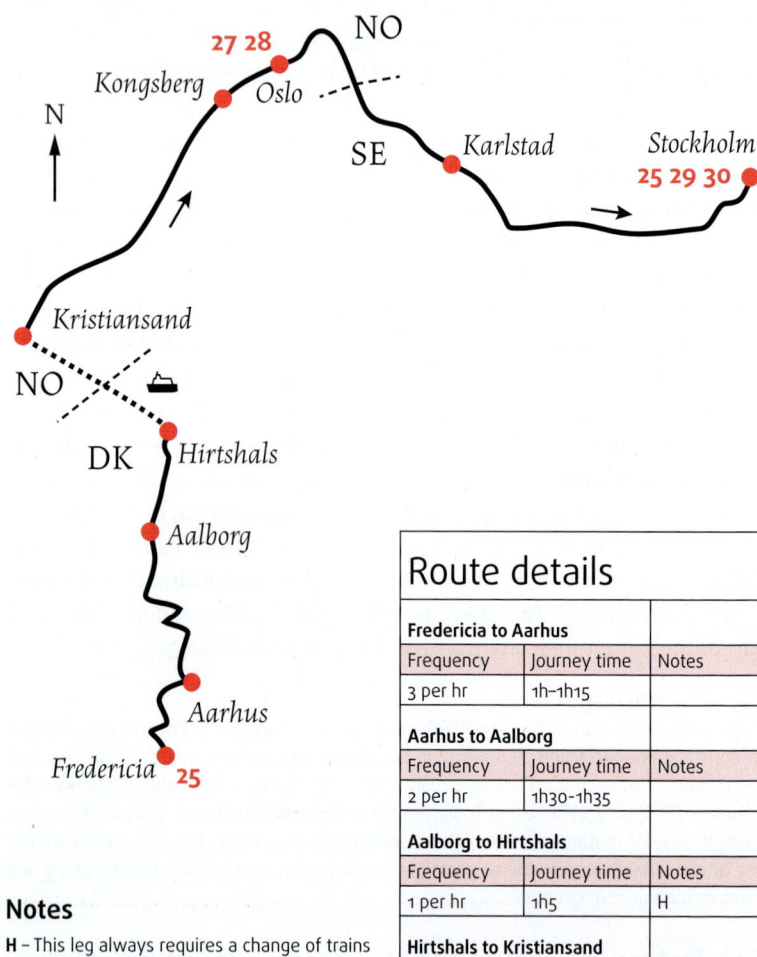

Notes

H – This leg always requires a change of trains in Hjørring.
K – Additional connections are available with a change of train in Karlstad.
S – The journey time and frequency refers to the year-round Color Line shipping service. The summer-season Fjord Line catamaran operates 2–3 times per day and takes 2h15.

The **numbers in red** adjacent to some cities on our route maps refer to other routes in this book which also include that particular city.

Route details

Fredericia to Aarhus		
Frequency	Journey time	Notes
3 per hr	1h–1h15	

Aarhus to Aalborg		
Frequency	Journey time	Notes
2 per hr	1h30–1h35	

Aalborg to Hirtshals		
Frequency	Journey time	Notes
1 per hr	1h5	H

Hirtshals to Kristiansand		
Frequency	Journey time	Notes
2 per day	3h15	S

Kristiansand to Oslo S		
Frequency	Journey time	Notes
5–8 per day	4h30–4h50	

Oslo S to Stockholm C		
Frequency	Journey time	Notes
3–5 per day	5h25–6h30	K

more to the city than shops. Aarhus was European Capital of Culture in 2017 and you'll find culture aplenty in this fascinating port city. Most sights are within easy walking distance. Old Aarhus holds the monopoly on nightspots as well as a few museums, including **Køn**, Denmark's gender museum (www.konmuseum.dk; closed Mon), Domkirkepladsen 5. Aarhus' renowned art museum, **ARoS**, is just a 10-min walk from the railway station at Aros Allé 2 (www.aros.dk; closed Mon).

The city's major attraction is **Den Gamle By**, an open-air ethnographic museum featuring close to a hundred traditional half-timbered Danish homes. About 10 km south of the city, the superb **Moesgård Museum** is home to the 2,000-year-old preserved Grauballe man, discovered in a nearby peat bog in 1952 (www.moesgaardmuseum.dk; closed Mon); take 🚌 18 from Aarhus Park Allé. To pick up a **city bike** from special stands around town, you first need to download the Donkey Republic bike-sharing App. Prices start at 15 DKK (30 mins) and using a bike for a full day costs 100 DKK.

Arrival, information, accommodation

🚆 The station is just south of the centre, buried away in the Bruuns Galleri shopping complex; left luggage lockers available. ℹ️ Tourist office: at Dokk 1, outside the station (www.visitaarhus.com). 🛏️ Just round the corner of the station is the functional but friendly **Hotel Ritz Aarhus City**, Banegårdspladsen 12, ☎ 86 13 44 44 (www.millinghotels.dk). A good mid-range option a short walk from the station in a quiet location is Hotel Oasia, Kriegersvej 27–31, ☎ 87 32 37 15 (www.hoteloasia.dk). If you want to splash out, try the stylish design hotel **Villa Provence**, Fredens Torv 12, ☎ 86 18 24 00 (www.villaprovence.dk), in the heart of the city.

All trains reverse direction in Aarhus and then head decisively inland for the run north to Aalborg. It's best to opt for an **Intercity** train for this leg of the journey, rather than the faster **Lyn** services. The slower services are better for appreciating the quiet beauty of the heath and forest landscapes of Jutland.

There's an especially pretty stretch as the railway winds through woodland just beyond Hadsten. That's just a foretaste of what is to come, namely a glorious few minutes as the train cuts through **Rold Skov**, one of the last remaining areas of true wilderness in Jutland. It's all too brief, and if you want to explore this area a little more, alight at Skørping from where there's ample scope for walks and cycle rides through the region. All Intercity trains stop at Skørping.

Aalborg (suggested stopover)

Herring brought prosperity to this north Jutland town in the 17th century, and the legacy of that boom is the handsome Old Quarter with finely preserved merchants' houses, such as the spectacularly ornate Jens Bangs Stenhus. **Kunsten**, Aalborg's museum of Modern Art, is home to one of the nation's foremost collections of 20th-century art and has a sculpture garden too. The museum is located at Kong Christians Allé 50 (www.kunsten.dk; closed Mon). After the sun goes down, **Jomfru Ane Gade** is the street to hit for restaurants, music and bars (be sure to sample the local spirit, Akvavit). The Aalborg Carnival takes place in late May every year, and throughout the summer open-air rock concerts are held in Mølle Park and in Skovdalen.

ARRIVAL, INFORMATION, ACCOMMODATION

⇌ A short walk south down Boulevarden from the town centre. ℹ Tourist office: Kjellerups Torv 5 (www.enjoynordjylland.dk).

🛏 Opened in 2019 and still a good value option is the **Zleep Hotel Aalborg**, Jyllandsgade 6, ☎ 70 23 56 35 (www.zleep.com). Or try the **Comwell Hvide Hus Aalborg**, Vesterbro 2, ☎ 98 13 84 00 (www.comwell.com). More upmarket is the **Scandic Aalborg City**, Europa Plads 1, ☎ 70 12 51 51 (www.scandichotels.com). All three hotels are on the functional side, but are located conveniently close to both the railway station and the city centre.

North Jutland

Leaving Aalborg, the railway crosses a low girder bridge which spans **Limfjord**, here at its narrowest point, to reach the island of North Jutland. Most trains on this route running north from Aalborg – called the **Vendsyssel Railway** – are bound for Frederikshavn, whence there are ferry links with Stena Line to Göteborg and with DFDS to Oslo. Our journey requires alighting before Frederikshavn at the small town of **Hjørring**, and then taking the local train down to the coast at Hirtshals. If time permits, you might enjoy a walk through Hjørring, the centre of which exemplifies the laidback charm of the communities in North Jutland.

The port of **Hirtshals** boldly styles itself as "a geographical turntable close to some of Europe's best fishing." It's certainly true that Hirtshals has been shaped far more by its maritime connections than by its hinterland. It still is an important port. A small museum in Hirtshals, at Sophus Thomsens gade 6, nicely documents the manner in which fishing has long been an economic mainstay (open Tue, Thu, Sun in Apr–Dec and everyday in July).

Our journey continues with a **short sea crossing** to Kristiansand in Norway. Fjord Line (www.fjordline.com) runs fast catamarans twice daily from early-April to late October, while Color Line (www.colorline.com) has year-round services using very comfortable ships. We find the latter, although slower, preferable to a bumpy catamaran. By far the most exotic departures from Hirtshals are the Smyril Line sailings to the Faroes and Iceland. Read more about this maritime expedition in our Sidetracks feature on p254.

Arriving in Norway

A little over three hours relaxing on the ferry from Hirtshals will leave you well prepared to enjoy **Kristiansand**, a working port and resort town at the southernmost tip of Norway. In summer, the town's pleasant beaches are busy. Much of the town was laid out in the 17th century by Christian IV, after whom it is named. His plan included the **Christiansholm Festning**, built to guard the eastern approach to the harbour; the circular fortress is the major sight with views to match. Forming the north-eastern part of the Old Quarter, Posebyen has many carefully preserved little wooden houses. The fish market on the quay, called **Fiskebrygga**, is a good place to pick up some smoked salmon or prawns for a picnic lunch. If you are minded to stay overnight, the Thon Hotel Parken, Kirkegata 15, ☎ 38 17 20 40 (www.thonhotels.no) is right in the centre, just a short walk east of the station.

KRISTIANSAND CONNECTIONS
This current route of course continues to Oslo, but there's also a railway running north-west from Kristansand to Stavanger. This is a remarkable route, cutting across **wild mountain terrain**. From Stavanger there are onward connections by either bus or boat to Bergen, connecting there into **Route 27**. Be aware that the short-lived ferry links from Kristiansand to Eemshaven (Netherlands) and Emden (Germany) have been discontinued. The company operating these routes folded in late 2023.

If you are expecting a pleasant run along the Norwegian coast from Kristiansand to Oslo, you'll be disappointed. Construction of the 266-km stretch of the **Sørlandet Line** (Sørlandsbanen) from Kristiansand to Kongsberg was only started after the First World War; the route was only completed in 1938. The Norwegian authorities were worried about the risk of invading forces taking control of a coastal railway, so the line was routed inland. Although this did nothing to improve communications to the small towns around the coast, it does mean that the line cuts through lovely wilderness areas.

The nicest town on the journey to Oslo is **Kongsberg**. It grew following the discovery (in the early 17th century) of silver deposits of unique purity in the nearby mountains. Mining remained the town's *raison d'être* for three centuries: most of the mines closed early in the 19th century, but the last one survived until 1957. Just out of town, the disused **silver mines** at Saggrenda (8 km west, 🚌 Vy1 from Kongsberg centre; tours available mid-May to mid-October) take you by train into the mountain to 560 metres below sea level. In the town centre a striking legacy of the silver-boom heyday is **Kongsberg Kirke**, a sumptuous triumph of baroque architecture. Close to Nybrufoss waterfall is the **Norsk Bergverksmuseum** (Norwegian Mining Museum), housed in an old smelting works. Den Royal Mint Museum is an offshoot of the industry and part of the Mining Museum: coin production moved to Kongsberg in 1686 and the National Mint is still here. From Kongsberg, it is little more than an hour to **Oslo** (see p259) where the train terminates at the Sentralstasjon, usually abbreviated as Oslo S.

CONNECTIONS FROM OSLO
Connect in Oslo onto **Route 28** which offers a splendid adventure north via Trondheim then on up the Norwegian coast, crossing the Arctic Circle along the way. Or follow **Route 27**

west to **Bergen** or south to Göteborg and Copenhagen. There are also ferries leaving Oslo early afternoon each day for longish overnight trips to **Copenhagen** and Kiel, respectively operated by DFDS and Color Line.

East to Stockholm

The train journey to Stockholm from Oslo is a reminder that we are a long way north and in fairly inhospitable terrain. Oslo and Stockholm both lie a shade south of the **sixtieth parallel**. On the journey from Oslo to the Swedish border the railway goes beyond 60° N – that's just as far north as the Shetland Islands in Scotland or Cook Inlet in Alaska. Bare rock and forests abound.

Leaving Oslo, we follow the **Glomma Valley** east, continuing on past a string of lakes to reach the Swedish border at the oddly-named community of Morokulien (seen to the right of the train) which rates as one of Europe's more peculiar border communities. The frontier bisects the tourist office. A peace monument unveiled in 1914 is a testament to harmonious relations between Sweden and Norway.

The first major community in Sweden is **Karlstad** (served by all trains on the route), an engaging community with a fine location on the north side of Lake Vänern. Karlstad is well placed for connecting onto the minor railway which runs down the west side of the lake (see also the box on p259). If you are minded to break the journey between Oslo and Stockholm, Karlstad is the place to do it. Beyond Karlstad we follow the **Värmlandsbanan** (Värmland Railway) to Laxå, where we join the Västra stambanan (Western Main Line) for the final run into the Swedish capital. Beyond Flen, the railway passes through serene forests, interspersed with many lakes. This watery approach is good prep for Stockholm itself, a city whose appeal relies heavily on its setting amid myriad lakes and waterways.

Stockholm

Spread over **14 islands** with countless inlets, Stockholm has a stunning waterfront that rivals those of San Francisco and Sydney, and most visitors would probably rate it the most rewarding of the Scandinavian capitals. At its heart is the impressively intact original part of the city, **Gamla Stan**, with an enticing blend of dignified old buildings, cafés, and craft and designer shops; in contrast, the **Djurgården** is a huge natural park where the city comes to swim, canoe, fly kites, visit the zoo and the superb outdoor museum **Skansen** (www.skansen.se), or just admire the views. Stockholm is airy and very much a harbour capital. It's a lovely place to be outdoors in summer (winter can be cosy and romantic, but take warm clothes), whether listening to an outdoor concert or taking a cruise, but there are also plenty of superb indoor attractions, such as the Nationalmuseum and the historic Vasa warship – dredged from the mud and restored to reveal its full 17th-century glory. The **Vasa museum** (www.vasamuseet.se) that houses the ship is located on the island of Djurgården, which can be reached by boat from Slussen (all year round) or Nybroplan (during summer) or by tram no. 7 from the railway station.

Arrival, information, accommodation
≥ **Centralstation** has a bus information/ticket office and good food stalls (train information at www.sj.se). Stockholm City station is located below the T-Central station (for metro services) that is part of Stockholm's central railway station. Stockholm City serves all commuter train services. ✈ Stockholm Arlanda (www.swedavia.se/arlanda) is 45 km north of Stockholm. The **Arlanda Express** rail link (www.arlandaexpress.com), takes 18 mins to Centralstation (every 10–15 mins, daily, 04.20–23.35, then every 30 mins until 00.35).
🛈 Visitor centre is at Centralstation (www.visitstockholm.com).

Storstockholms Lokaltrafik (SL; www.sl.se) runs the excellent bus and metro (T-bana) network. Buy tickets for buses and the T-bana at SL Centers, newsagents, at machines on T-bana platforms or commuter train stations, by contactless card (touch in at SL readers) or the SL App. The zonal fare system was abandoned in January 2017. A smart card system is now in place (SL Access card), but you can also buy a single journey ticket (SEK 39) which is valid for unlimited travel on all SL services for 75 minutes. Note that tickets cannot be purchased on the bus. Validate your ticket before you enter the T-bana or bus, or bypass the machines by buying a pass for free transit within 24 hours or 72 hours. The T-bana has three main lines (red, green and blue). Trains are fast and frequent, 05.00–01.00. Metro stations display a blue 'T' on a white circle. The decor on some lines is among the most imaginative in Europe: walls are moulded to look like caves, are painted in strident colours or hold original murals.

🛏 Staying in Stockholm is certainly not cheap, especially in the city centre. A good-value option right on Gamla Stan and thus not far from Centralstation is the atmospheric **Sven Vintappare**, Sven Vintappares Gränd 3, ☎ 08 22 41 40 (www.hotelsvenvintappare.se), housed in a renovated, early 17th-century building. Another good option on Gamla Stan is the very welcoming **Victory Hotel**, Lilla Nygatan 5, ☎ 08 506 400 00 (www.victoryhotel.se) with a nautical theme. The well located **Story Hotel Riddargatan**, Riddargatan 6, ☎ 08 545 039 40 (www.storyhotels.com), north-east of Gamla Stan offers smart design and arty details – perfect for guests who like their hotel room to be modern and trendy.

Connections from Stockholm
From Stockholm, you can fast-track north on an overnight train to **Swedish Lapland**, which continues over the border to Narvik in northern Norway. This journey is described in **Route 29** in this book. Train services up Sweden's Bothnian coast are much improved. It's now much quicker to head north to **Sundsvall** and **Umeå**. Ten years ago, the journey from Stockholm to Umeå took over ten hours – today it takes just over six hours.

Stockholm offers a good range of **shipping connections**. There are overnight services leaving late afternoon every day for both Helsinki and Tallinn run by Tallink Silja, all making a brief call in the Åland Islands along the way. You have a choice of both daytime and overnight crossings from Stockholm to the Finnish port of **Turku**, all stopping in the **Åland Islands** en route. It will be no surprise to learn that the shipping route from Stockholm to St Petersburg has been suspended. Meanwhile, the Tallink Silja ferry link to Riga has been axed. If you are heading to **Latvia** from Stockholm, take the train to Nynäshamn (82 mins) from where Stena Line offer an overnight ferry to Ventspils.

SIDETRACKS: SLOW BOAT TO ICELAND

As we travel north through Jutland on **Route 26**, we have a sense of going to the very end of the world. With changes of train in Aarhus, Aalborg and Hjørring, we are at last on the branch line which leads to the port of **Hirtshals**. There the *Norröna* is at the quayside, preparing to depart for Iceland. This is just one of many inviting shipping links from Hirtshals. Another is the ferry to Kristiansand, a short sea crossing which forms part of **Route 26**. There is also a very useful Fjord Line sailing each evening from Hirtshals to Stavanger and Bergen. It connects nicely in **Bergen** with the northbound *Hurtigruten* ship to northern Norway. Adventurers can thus travel by boat all the way from Hirtshals to Kirkenes on the Barents Sea coast near the Russian border, with just one easy change of boat in Bergen. That entire journey requires seven nights afloat.

But let's take a closer look at the *Norröna*. The ship's funnel is embellished with a merlin (*smyril* in Faroese). The small bird of prey is common in the North Atlantic region served by **Smyril Line**. The company is based in the Faroes, a scatter of mountainous islands midway between Iceland and the Shetlands. The company's sole ship is called *Norröna*, a name that underlines the vessel's role as an ambassador for the north.

Within an hour or two of boarding the *Norröna*, everyone has found or created a tolerable lair. For some it is the privacy and comfort of a cabin. Following a major refit in 2021, the *Norröna* now has some very upmarket cabins. For others it is a couchette deep in the bowels of the ship or an improvised arrangement of rucksacks and deck chairs on an upper deck. **Wind and waves** are a good prelude to geysers, glaciers and icy tundra wilderness.

Denmark recedes to nothingness, and the *Norröna* is soon alone among the waves. Distant views of oil rigs, supper in the *Munkastova* – a chic onboard restaurant that takes its name from the oldest surviving building in the Faroes. It means 'monk's house', though there's no monastic restraint in the menus where a seven-course dinner runs to over €100. A day out from Hirtshals and a **Shetland outpost** hoves into view on the port side. **Fair Isle** hovers in the mist, ethereal and other-worldly. Many hours later a first glimpse of the east coast of the island of Sandoy signals that the Faroese capital of **Tórshavn** is only an hour or two away. Travellers bound for Iceland can go ashore in the Faroese capital, wander the streets of Tórshavn and explore Europe's smallest cathedral.

Soon the *Norröna* is on her way again, threading a course through the beautiful Faroe Islands. The great ridge that defines **Kalsoy** is on the starboard side, its steep slopes entirely uninhabited. Another night on board, then all thoughts are on Iceland. Eventually the land of elves reveals herself, and soon the *Norröna* is sliding up one of the eastern fjords in absolute silence. On either side of the great loch there are the ruins of long deserted farmsteads while naked crags dominate the skyline. This is for the *Norröna* the very end of her journey to Iceland. She docks in **Seyðisfjörður**.

Note that in winter the leg between Tórshavn and Seyðisfjörður is liable to delay or cancellation.

Route 27: Sampling Scandinavia

Cities: ★★ Culture: ★ History: ★ Scenery: ★★★
Countries covered: Denmark (DK) Sweden (SE), Norway (NO)
Journey time: 14 hrs 30 mins | Distance: 1,192 km | Map: www.ebrweb.eu/18map27

This long route from Copenhagen to Bergen via Oslo is a journey of extremely varied character. It starts with a tame prelude but develops into a great symphony of lakes, snowfields and mountains. Along the way, you have in Oslo a very pleasant (but expensive) capital city.

Suggested itinerary

The **two principal cities** on this journey are Göteborg and Oslo, both certainly deserving of an overnight stop. If you follow this route from end to end, you will in any case need to change trains in those two cities. We really judge this entire journey to be one well worth taking.

If time is tight, you could at a pinch consider taking the **DFDS boat to Oslo**. It leaves Copenhagen every afternoon, sailing overnight up the Kattegat to reach Oslo just before ten the next morning, in sufficient time to catch the midday train to Bergen. If you hate fine scenery, but love **night trains**, you can sleep your way from Oslo to Bergen on a comfortable overnight service which departs every evening except Saturdays.

The first part of the journey from **Copenhagen** is sometimes complicated by the occasional ID checks for travellers using the **Øresund link** from the Danish capital to the Swedish city of Malmö. This stretch of the railway is also followed by **Route 25** in this book, so take a look at p246 to see what we say there about the journey.

Malmö is Sweden's fast-growing third city and a lively place, with plenty of good bars, clubs and coffee houses, and an excellent festival in August. Capital of the Skåne province, the city was part of Denmark for much of the Middle Ages and came under Swedish sovereignty in 1658: even today the Skåne accent has something of a Danish tinge.

Enclosed by a canal that loops round through a park and doubles as the castle moat, the city's well-groomed historic centre dates back to Danish times and features a pair of **fine cobbled squares.** Leaving the station southwards along Hamngatan, you soon reach the large central square, **Stortorget**, presided over by the statue of Carl Gustav, who won Skåne back from Denmark. The square is flanked on the east by the 1546 Rådhuset (town hall), just by Södergatan, the main pedestrianised street. Behind stands **St Petri Kyrka** (St Peter's Church) – Sweden's second-largest church – its whitewashed Gothic interior complementing its baroque altar and mediaeval frescos.

Connections from Malmö

Malmö has a feast of rail connections. The most important is the trunk route which runs north-east to Stockholm. It is followed by **Route 25**. Malmö also has an overnight

256 | SCANDINAVIA AND THE BALTIC

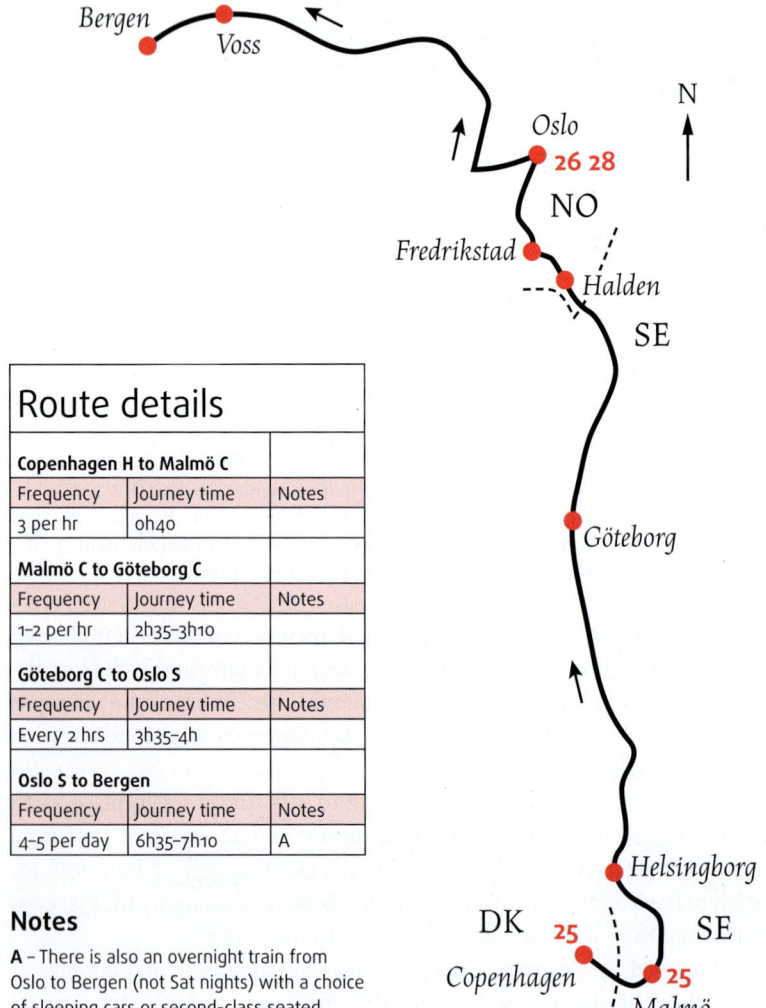

Route details

Copenhagen H to Malmö C		
Frequency	Journey time	Notes
3 per hr	0h40	

Malmö C to Göteborg C		
Frequency	Journey time	Notes
1–2 per hr	2h35–3h10	

Göteborg C to Oslo S		
Frequency	Journey time	Notes
Every 2 hrs	3h35–4h	

Oslo S to Bergen		
Frequency	Journey time	Notes
4–5 per day	6h35–7h10	A

Notes

A – There is also an overnight train from Oslo to Bergen (not Sat nights) with a choice of sleeping cars or second-class seated accommodation. It takes 7 hrs 25 mins.

The **numbers in red** adjacent to some cities on our route maps refer to other routes in this book which also include that particular city.

train (leaving every evening except Saturdays) to Stockholm. Closer to hand, there is an interesting secondary railway which runs through undulating Skåne countryside to **Ystad**, which we rate as one of Sweden's most attractive small towns. From Ystad, it's short hop by ferry to the Danish island of **Bornholm**. Ystad also has several ferries each day to Świnoujście in Poland where you can join **Route 31** in this book. The ferries from Ystad to Poland are operated by Polferries or Unity Line.

Other regional rail links from Malmö run east to the windy east coast towns of **Karlskrona** and **Kalmar**. These two towns, very different from each other, both repay a day trip or an overnight stay. These Swedish links aparts, Malmö also benefits from direct **overnight trains** to Berlin, operated variously by SJ or Snälltåget.

Lund and Helsingborg

From Malmö, it is just ten minutes on frequent trains to the handsome ancient university town of **Lund**, which is one of the most rewarding spots to visit in southern Sweden. A religious centre in the 12th century, much of mediaeval Lund is still visible.

From Lund, the railway returns to the coast and runs north to **Helsingborg**. Don't be put off by Helsingborg's subterranean train station as the city is well worth a stop. During much of the Middle Ages, Helsingborg was Danish and functioned as an important garrison town; the massive fortified keep, the Kärnan, still dominates the place. The bustling port is a pleasant enough base, with an **Old Quarter** to explore. If you decide to get off the train here, you should pay a visit to the rewarding 15th-century Church of St Maria and the entertainingly eclectic **city museum** in Dunkers Kulturhus on Kungsgatan 11 (www.dunkerskulturhus.se; closed Mon outside Jul–Aug).

Connections from Helsingborg
There is a **car ferry** which breezes across the narrowest point of the strait to Helsingør in Denmark, from where there are frequent trains to Copenhagen. Helsingør is a great place to visit in its own right, so this boat trip makes a fine afternoon out from Helsingborg.

Running north from Helsingborg, the railway leaves the historic territory of Scania and crosses into Halland where all but the fastest trains stop at **Varberg**, which made its mark in the late 19th century as a bathing station, attracting many prominent artists.

Göteborg (suggested stopover)

The huge cranes and shipyards that greet visitors arriving at **Scandinavia's biggest port** mask the fact that this is one of Sweden's most attractive old cities, one that grew rapidly when Dutch merchants settled here in the early 17th century. Boat tours take in the best of the waterside views from the old canals, while elsewhere there are atmospheric squares and numerous leafy parks that have earned Göteborg (also called Gothenburg in English) the nickname 'Garden City'. To get your bearings, go up **Skanskaskrapan**

(Skanska Skyscraper) – a striking red-and-white skyscraper, 86 m high, which has a lookout (Göteborgsutkiken; opening hours vary) and is locally referred to as 'lipstick'. It has a small café (June–Aug only) near the top, giving superb views over the harbour. It's situated in **Lilla Bommen**, itself a charming area, with shops and craft workshops. Dominating the whole scene here, however, is the spectacular waterside opera house – its postmodern design is a fine instance of form matching function.

Kungsportsavenyen, usually known simply as 'Avenyn' (The Avenue), is the hub of the city, a 50-m-wide boulevard lined with lime trees, shops and eateries, further enlivened by buskers and ad hoc street stalls. It leads up to Götaplatsen, the city's cultural centre, fronted by Carl Milles' fountain of Poseidon. Just off Avenyn is **Trädgårdsföreningen** (turn right into Nya Allén towards Slussgatan), a fragrant park full of flora and birdsong, speckled with works of art and other attractions.

The city's oldest secular building (1654) is **Kronhuset** (Crown Arsenal; closed Sun), close to Gustaf Adolfs Torg at Postgatan 6–8. Around it is Kronhusbodarna, a courtyard bounded by handicraft boutiques in 18th-century artisans' dwellings. Other good places for browsing are the Antikhallarna antique market in Västra Hamngatan, and Haga Nygata, a renovated historic area of cobbled streets, lined with craft, second-hand, antique and design shops, as well as cafés and restaurants. Opposite, across the water, the **Feskekörka** resembles a 19th-century church, but is actually a thriving fish market (open Mon–Sat). It's a fine place to sample local seafood, either in the restaurants or from the stalls.

Some city museums close on Mondays but open daily in summer. Don't miss Göteborg's **maritime museum** at Packhuskajen next to the opera house (open daily), the **Konstmuseet** (Art Museum; www.goteborgskonstmuseum.se; closed Mon), Götaplatsen, and the Universeum (the National Science Centre), Södra vägen 50.

ARRIVAL, INFORMATION, ACCOMMODATION

⇌ Centralstation, a short walk north-east of the centre. Most buses stop at Nils Ericsonsplatsen, next to the station. ✈ Landvetter Airport is 20 km south-east of Göteborg (www.swedavia.se/landvetter); buses every 12–30 mins, depending on time of day, to Centralstation, taking 20 mins. ⛴ Stena Line (www.stenaline.se), to/from Germany (Kiel), sail from Elof Lindälvs Gata, on the western edge of Göteborg; Stena ships to/from Denmark (Frederikshavn) sail from Emigrantvägen, at the western end of the centre.

🛈 Tourist office: Kungsportsplatsen 2 (www.goteborg.com). The centre's attractions are quite close together, but there's also an excellent tram network (buy tickets in advance at Västtrafik sales outlets or via the ToGo App). ⇌ Not far from Göteborg's cathedral is the comfortable **Hotel Vanilla**, Kyrkogatan 38, ☎ 31 71 16 220 (www.hotellvanilla.com). Just 300 m from Centralstation, **Scandic No. 25**, Burggrevegatan 25, ☎ 31 75 15 500 (www.scandichotels.com), is a good budget option. Located in the station building, the **First G**, Nils Ericsonsplatsen 4, ☎ 31 63 72 00 (www.firsthotels.com), is a quiet mid-range place.

✗ The seafood is excellent, most restaurants clustering along the waterfront. For other types of cuisine, try around Avenyn or in Linnéstaden. The Nordstan complex offers

Lake Vänern rail tour

Göteborg is also the jumping-off point for a wonderful rural rail adventure around **Lake Vänern**, Europe's largest lake outside the Russian Federation. Only two Karelian lakes, Lagoda and Onega, are larger. Travel out from Göteborg to **Karlstad** along the south side of the lake via **Mariestad** (see also p252 in this book), returning on the direct train from Karlstad back to Göteborg which skirts the north side of Lake Vänern. We made this **circular journey** as a day trip a year or two ago; it was just at the time that winter thawed into slushy spring, but the sun shone and we recall it as a journey through landscapes of considerable beauty.

a lot of eateries, including a good supermarket, Hemköp. Try the indoor Stora Saluhallen market, Kungstorget, for a tempting range of goodies.

Connections from Göteborg

From Göteborg, multiple rail operators compete on the busy route to Stockholm. Given Göteborg's port status, it's no surprise to find plenty of **boat connections**. The most interesting are the DFDS Tor Line sailings to Ghent in Belgium and Brevik in Norway. A small number of passengers are accepted on both routes.

There are daily departures each week to Ghent, but services to Brevik only leave Göteborg on Thursdays. Stena Line offer a regular overnight sailing to Kiel. Several ferries a day cross from Göteborg to Frederikshavn on the coast of Danish Jutland (a useful link to connect into **Route 26** in this volume).

At Göteborg, the railway to Oslo tracks inland, passing close to the southwest corner of Lake Vänern before heading north through bleak terrain to the Norwegian border. The first community of any size beyond the border is **Halden**, an old border post on the attractive Iddefjord, overlooked by the star-shaped **Fredriksten Fortress**, a huge 17th-century castle east of the town. Other highlights include the Fredrikshalds Teater, with its fully restored baroque stage, and **Rød Herregård**, a furnished 18th-century manor house with an enviable collection of art.

Cutting down to the east shore of Oslo Fjord, the train stops at **Fredrikstad**, a town still protected by fortified walls. Fredrikstad guarded the southern approaches to Oslo and its Old Town has survived as one of the best-preserved fortress towns in Scandinavia. It's conducive to wandering, particularly around the walls and along the cobbled alleys of **Gamlebyen** (the Old Town) over on the east bank. Fort Kongsten is a pleasant 15- to 20-min stroll.

OSLO (suggested stopover)

Hemmed in by water, forests and rolling hillsides, Oslo is a pleasant and laid-back modern city. It is not a big place – nor is it as architecturally captivating as the other Scandinavian capitals – but it is definitely worth a stop before venturing out to experience Norway's great outdoors. The city has a number of outstanding art museums – with attractions such as Edvard Munch's *The Scream* – as well as great harbour views from the **Akershus Fortress** and a **lively nightlife** scene in the central districts of Grünerløkka and Grønland. The fortress is still used for state occasions and contains the Resistance Museum, which gives a startlingly forthright account of the German occupation of Norway. In **Vikingskipshuset** (Viking Ship Museum) on the Bygdøy peninsula, the well preserved Gokstad, Tune and Oseberg Viking ships, all dating from 800–900, are on display. The **new Munch museum** opened in October 2021 in the city's revitalised harbour district of Bjørvika (www.munchmuseet.no; closed Mon). A further attraction was added when Oslo opened its new national art museum in June 2022 on Rådhusplassen.

Oslo is connected by **ferry** to Germany and Denmark, and you can catch trains via Sweden to Denmark and on to the rest of Europe. Oslo is also the starting point for some spectacular train journeys to the Norwegian fjords, mountains and on to the Arctic, which are also featured as routes in this book.

ARRIVAL, INFORMATION, ACCOMMODATION

The main rail station is the central Oslo Sentralstasjon (known as Oslo S). All long-distance trains stop here, as well as some local services. This modern construction feels more like an airport than a train station, and it is crammed with facilities of every kind. The T-bane (metro) is to the right as you leave the station. There are usually daily sailings to Germany (Kiel) by Color Line (www.colorline.no). DFDS Seaways sail daily to Copenhagen (www.dfds.com) and Stena Line sail to Frederikshavn (www.stenaline.no). Long-distance buses use Bussterminal, which is easily reached from Oslo S by an enclosed walkway. Gardermoen (50 km north; https://avinor.no/flyplass/oslo). Airport express trains take 20 mins to Oslo (www.flytoget.no); buses take 45 mins but are cheaper. There are also direct trains to Lillehammer and Trondheim. Ryanair and Wizz Air flights land at Oslo Torp (www.torp.no), which has bus connections with Ryanair flights (booking not necessary); buses to Oslo Torp leave Oslo's main bus terminal around 3 hrs before flight departure (www.torpekspressen.no) and take 1 hr 40 mins. Oslo's centre is relatively small and outlying attractions are easily reachable on the excellent public transport system (www.ruter.no). Single tickets are valid for 1 hr (plus 30 mins per extra zone). Oslo's metro lines converge at Stortinget and Jernbanetorget (T-bane: Oslo S). Most trams converge at Oslo S and most city buses around the corner on Schweigaardsgate (on Vaterland, by Oslo S). Pre-purchase your ticket at kiosks or Ruter service points or use the RuterBillett App. Ferries to Bygdøy, Hovedøya, Langøyen and other islands in the Oslo Fjord leave from the Rådhusbrygge. Visitor centre: right next to Oslo S in Østbanehallen (www.visitoslo.com).

Very centrally located is the boutique hotel **Christiania Teater**, Stortingsgata 16, ☎ 21 04 38 00 (www.christianiateater.com), housed in a former theatre. For a good budget option try the **Citybox Oslo**, Prinsensgate 6, ☎ 21 42 04 80 (www.citybox.no), just a 10 min walk from Oslo S station. Head for the **Saga Hotel Oslo**, Eilert Sundts gate 39, ☎ 22 55 44 90 (www.sagahoteloslo.com) if you are looking for a smaller hotel. It's a friendly and stylish place in a quiet area not far from the Royal Palace.

CONNECTIONS FROM OSLO

You may wish to return to Copenhagen by ship and there is also a useful daily ship to Kiel in northern Germany. You can connect in Oslo onto two other routes in this book. Follow

Route 28 north through Norway to beyond the Arctic Circle. You can also take **Route 26** in reverse to Kristiansand for boat connections to Danish Jutland, or follow that same route east from Oslo over the Swedish frontier to end in Stockholm.

Fjells and fjords

The railway from Oslo to Bergen is one of Europe's most remarkable main-line journeys. It climbs to an altitude of over 1,200 metres, crossing a starkly beautiful mountain plateau called **Hardangervidda**. All trains on the route stop at Finse, which at 1,222 metres claims the record as the highest railway station in Scandinavia. Many communities along this route rely entirely on the railway for their links with the outside world – and the **Bergensbanen** (as the line from Oslo to Bergen is called) has served them well, providing reliable service in all but the very worst of winter weather. Snow fences and avalanche protection along long stretches of the railway give a hint of the hazards which are part of everyday life in this region.

For a rail route which has been so showered with superlatives, you might expect the Bergensbanen to be sheer beauty from end to end. In fact, the entire first half is unexceptional. Only beyond the ski resort of **Geilo** (three-and-a-half hours out of Oslo) does the scenery really pick up, switching from prosaic to stunning in a space of just a few kilometres. Now's the moment to forsake your phone or laptop and just focus on the landscape slipping by beyond the carriage window.

At the lonely railway junction at **Myrdal**, a branch railway (called the **Flåmsbana**) cuts north, dropping down steeply to Flåm. The descent offers superb views of towering cliffs, chasms and cascades. There are 16 tunnels on the route, including one where the line makes a 360° turn completely within the mountain. Most trains stop briefly at the spectacular **Kjosfossen waterfall**. This 20-kilometre railway is unashamedly touristy, but still fun. It is often marketed as 'Norway in a nutshell' and is a popular day trip for cruise ship passengers from Bergen. From **Flåm** there is a direct bus to Bergen.

Staying with the main Bergensbanen line at Myrdal, the only place of any size before Bergen is the lakeside resort of **Voss**, where water sports and skiing are the principal seasonal distractions. From there, it is a pleasant run down through gentler terrain to Bergen.

Bergen

Norway's appealing second city is the gateway to some of the country's most magnificent fjords. Perched on a peninsula and **surrounded by mountains**, Bergen has meandering cobbled streets lined with gabled weatherboard houses and dignified old warehouses.

The city centres on the waterfront **Torget**, a working fish (and various other things) market open Mon–Sun 08.00–23.00 May–Sept (otherwise Mon–Sat 09.00–21.00, Sun 11.00–21.00). At the centre of the Old Quarter, **Bryggen** contains a fine row of mediaeval houses designated a UNESCO World Heritage Site. When the Bryggens Museum was being constructed, the remains of the original city of 1050–1500 were found and incorporated.

Ole Bulls Plass, south-west of Bryggen, is good for bars, as is the area behind Torget. There are more student-frequented bars and cafés up towards the university. Look out for events at **USF Kulturhuset** (www.usf.no), on an old wharf to the south. You can get almost everywhere on foot in Bergen, but take the **Fløibanen** (funicular) from the centre up Mt Fløyen (320 m), for a panoramic view. At the top there's scope for pleasant picnics and walks in the woods.

Arrival, information, accommodation
✈ Strømgaten, a 10-min walk east of the centre; walk straight ahead down Marken and keep going. ⛴ Most ferries and local boats leave from Strandkaiterminalen and Skoltegrunnskaien. Hurtigruten leaves from Nøstegate. 🛈 Tourist office: Strandkaien 3 (www.visitbergen.com).

🛏 Advance booking is recommended since Bergen is often chock-full of tourists and conference-goers. Located on top of a hill in the vicinity of the university is the friendly and quiet family-run **Hotel Park**, Harald Hårfagresgate 35, ☎ 55 54 44 00 (www.hotelpark.no). If you are looking for a good budget option, try the clean and friendly **Marken Gjestehus Hostel**, Kong Oscars gate 45/Tverrgaten, ☎ 55 31 44 04 (www.marken-gjestehus.com) well located between the station and Torget. Just opposite Bryggen and overlooking the harbour and bay, the **Clarion Hotel Admiral**, C. Sundts gate 9, ☎ 55 23 64 00 (www.nordicchoicehotels.com), is a good choice.

Connections from Bergen
The **quaysides at Bergen** still appeal to lovers of ferries, even though some of the more interesting sailings have slipped from the schedules. No longer does the P&O ship *St Clair* weigh anchor at two on a Sunday morning (as she did in summer 1996) for the voyage to Aberdeen via the Shetland Islands. Sadly, Bergen nowadays has no direct ferry links to Britain. The Bergen to Newcastle route was axed after 140 years in service.

But the town still has a feast of Scandinavian connections. **Fjord Line** depart every lunchtime for Stavanger and Hirtshals, where you can first join **Route 26** and then **Route 25** and follow them in reverse to Hamburg and Amsterdam. The cruise south from Bergen to Stavanger is a fine trip for a summer afternoon; it takes about six hours. From Stavanger you can return east to Oslo by either daytime or overnight train.

Fjord Line also now offer a **daily sailing** from Bergen to Langesund; it takes 24 hours, but is another good option for travellers returning to Oslo who don't want to retrace their outward train journey. There are bus and train connections from Langesund via Porsgrunn to Oslo.

Bergen's most distingushed shipping link is of course the **Hurtigruten** service which departs every evening and runs north all the way up the Norwegian coast to far beyond the Arctic Circle. After six nights on board and over 30 stops along the way, the voyage ends at the **Barents Sea** port of Kirkenes. This is one of Europe's finest coastal journeys – and it runs year-round route.

Route 28: North to the Lofoten Islands
CITIES: ★ CULTURE: ★ HISTORY: ★ SCENERY: ★★★
COUNTRIES COVERED: NORWAY (NO)
JOURNEY TIME: 20 HRS | DISTANCE: 1,450 KM | MAP: WWW.EBRWEB.EU/18MAP28

If you follow just one Norwegian route in this book, make it this journey from Oslo to beyond the **Arctic Circle**. This long ride north nicely reveals the variety and scale of Norwegian landscapes. The appeal of this journey beyond the Arctic Circle is undoubtedly the scenery and the real sense of remoteness that you encounter along the way. Townies may get jittery with such **vast expanses of wilderness** and begin to yearn for concrete (of which there is plenty in some of the townships of northern Norway). In midsummer you will experience perpetual daylight, but this is a journey for winter too, when the subdued, sometimes even ethereal, character of very short days bring a special quality to the landscape.

The scene outside the carriage window evolves from gentle and bucolic pasturelands near Oslo to breathtakingly **dramatic fells and lakes** in the northernmost reaches. This is territory inhabited by reindeer and by the **Sámi** (the more common term Lapp is considered a shade derogatory) – the Nordic region's indigenous inhabitants. The journey ends with a short trip on a boat from Bodø to Svolvær on the **Lofoten Islands**.

SUGGESTED ITINERARY
The journey from Oslo to Bodø is best spread over two full days, with an intermediate stop of one night (or more) in **Trondheim**. There are direct overnight trains from Oslo to Trondheim (departures every evening except Saturdays) and also from Trondheim to Bodø (every night). Yet the scenery on this route is too good to be missed in sleep.

But here's an idea for a **midsummer journey**. You can leave Oslo on the early afternoon train which arrives in Trondheim about three hours before the overnight train to Bodø leaves. So you'll have ample time for dinner. After a meal, join the night train north – but don't even think of sleeping for in mid-summer dusk will morph into dawn and you can savour the real beauty of the northern night. You'll arrive in Bodø in good time to have a look around and then join the afternoon boat to the Lofoten islands.

Lake Mjøsa and beyond
For a relatively small capital, Oslo's main station has a remarkably large number of railway tracks. Arrive in good time to find the right platform. You may want to consider taking regional train services for the first part of the journey north, only changing onto the main-line service to Trondheim at Hamar or Lillehammer.

Shortly after the airport (served by all trains), the slower services pause at **Eidsvoll**, a small town known to every Norwegian as the place where Norway's first constitution was hammered out, way back in 1814. It's

264 | SCANDINAVIA AND THE BALTIC

Route details

Oslo to Trondheim		
Frequency	Journey time	Notes
3–5 per day	7h–8h	C
Trondheim to Bodø		
Frequency	Journey time	Notes
1 per day	9h55	B, D
Bodø to Svolvær		
Frequency	Journey time	Notes
2 per day	3h25–6h	

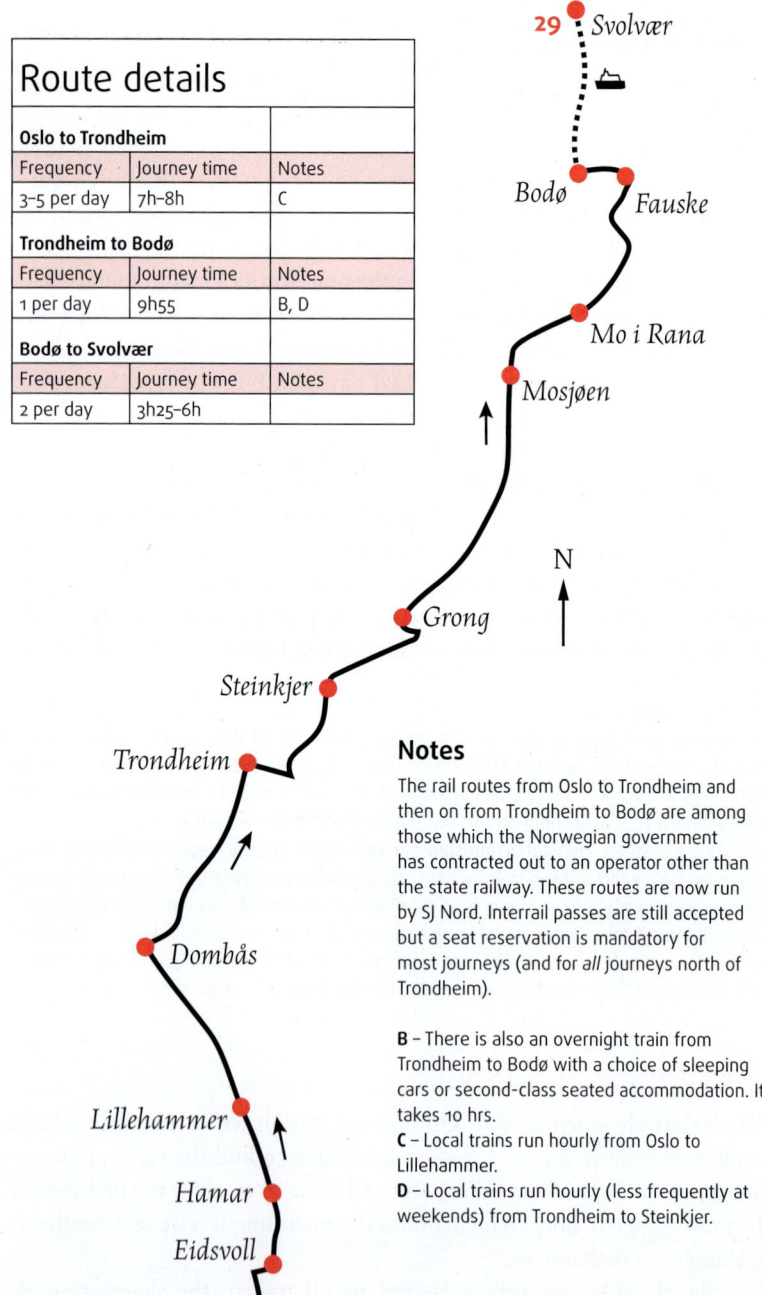

Notes

The rail routes from Oslo to Trondheim and then on from Trondheim to Bodø are among those which the Norwegian government has contracted out to an operator other than the state railway. These routes are now run by SJ Nord. Interrail passes are still accepted but a seat reservation is mandatory for most journeys (and for *all* journeys north of Trondheim).

B – There is also an overnight train from Trondheim to Bodø with a choice of sleeping cars or second-class seated accommodation. It takes 10 hrs.
C – Local trains run hourly from Oslo to Lillehammer.
D – Local trains run hourly (less frequently at weekends) from Trondheim to Steinkjer.

a pleasant small town; the centre is reached by a footbridge from the station which leads over the River Vorma.

Running north from Eidsvoll, the railway also bridges the Vorma, and then hugs the east bank of **Lake Mjøsa**, which is by a long chalk Norway's largest lake. For a closer look at this beautiful region, we suggest taking a three-hour boat trip from Eidsvoll to Hamar. A remarkable heritage paddle steamer (the *DS Skibladner* built in 1856) plies the route in mid-summer. It has an excellent, though pricey, restaurant (see www.skibladner.no).

At the northern tip of Lake Mjøsa lies **Lillehammer** which is both a major skiing centre and an appealing lakeside town, typified by winsome wooden houses that cling to the hillside. It hosted the 1994 Winter Olympics and many of the facilities can now be visited – and in some cases used.

Into the hills

Running north from Lillehammer, the railway parallels the E6, the main highway which extends from southern Sweden to Kirkenes in the far north-east corner of Norway, a distance of 3140 km. Distances can be deceptive in Scandinavia. Whether you travel by rail or road, be prepared for very long hops between settlements. About 30 minutes north of Lillehammer, you'll catch a glimpse of a typical Norwegian **stave church** on the hillside on the far side of the lake.

All trains pause at **Dombås**, junction for the 114-km long branch line to Åndalsnes, a small town at the head of a coastal fjord. The ride to Åndalsnes on the **Rauma Railway** is an epic one, plunging through tunnels, across bridges, past cascading waterfalls and the highest vertical canyon in Europe. Beyond Dombås, the main line to Trondheim changes in character, swapping the soft, green landscapes of the Gudbrand Valley for much harsher terrain as the railway cuts through **Dovrefjell-Sunndalsfjella National Park**. Home to eagles, reindeer and musk ox, this wild area is a foretaste of what's to come as we head north towards the Arctic Circle.

Just after the railway crosses the boundary of the Trøndelag region, the train reaches **Kongsvoll station**, a handsome essay in wood with neat blue shutters and delicate red moldings. If your trip has been too full of city stays, this is your chance to redress the balance. There is an attractive hotel

Two lines to Trondheim

The town of **Hamar** on the east shore of Lake Mjøsa is the starting point for an alternative and rather slower route north to Trondheim via **Røros**. There's a bigger dose of stark wilderness on the Røros route but, if you are following this journey all the way to Bodø, you'll get wilderness aplenty on the run north from Trondheim. However, if your travels merely take you to Trondheim and then back to Oslo, we strongly recommend that you travel out on the main line via **Lillehammer** and then back via Røros.

just a five-minute walk from the station. Kongsvold Fjeldstue has a homely, welcoming feel and there's a good restaurant (open May to early October, ☎ 47 67 06 53, www.frich.no/kongsvold-fjeldstue-2). In June 2020 it changed hands and is now called Frich's Hotel & Spiseri Kongsvold.

Trondheim (suggested stopover)

From Kongsvoll, it's just two hours more to the city which prides itself on being Norway's first capital. Trondheim was founded in 997 by **King Olav Tryggvason**, whose statue adorns the market square, and the city still has strong royal connections. Monarchs are crowned in the cathedral and Trondheim has been the seat of the monarchy since the 12th century. This major university town, with more than 20,000 students, boasts some of the best nightlife in Norway – not quite what you expect at over 63° north. The narrow streets of the compact centre make for a pleasant strolling ground.

Nidaros Domkirke (cathedral), Bispegata, is cavernously Gothic in design, and well worth seeing for its decorative stonework and elegant stained-glass windows. Northwards from the cathedral lies **Torvet** (main square), while further on at the water's edge is Ravnkloa, home to a fish market. From here, hourly boats run, usually mid-May to mid-Sept, to the island of Munkholmen, a monastery-cum-fortress-cum-prison; it's now a popular place for swimming. **Trondhjems Kunstforening** (Trondheim Art Gallery, www.tkf.no), Bispegata 9a, exhibits some of Norway's greatest art, including a few works by Munch. Although the building of the **Nordenfjeldske Kunstindustrimuseum** (National Museum of Decorative Art; www.nkim.no), Munkegata 3–7, is currently closed for renovation, its collection of contemporary arts and crafts is still accessible and displayed at different venues. Other sights include the **Gamle Bybro** (Old Town Bridge), with views of the wharf and its 18th-century warehouse buildings.

ARRIVAL, INFORMATION, ACCOMMODATION

🚄 The train and bus station is just a short walk north of the city centre. 🅸 Tourist office: Nordre gate 11 (www.trondheim.no); entrance from Torvet (market square).

🛏 Centrally located next to the River Nid and not far from the station is the **Scandic Bakklandet**, Nedre Bakklandet 60, ☎ 72 90 20 00 (www.scandichotels.com). If you don't mind the slight cool of a business hotel, then the **Clarion Hotel Trondheim**, Brattørkaia 1, ☎ 73 92 55 00 (www.nordicchoicehotels.com) is a good option just north of the station. Or try the welcoming **Clarion Collection Grand Olav**, Kjøpmannsgata 48, ☎ 73 80 80 80 (www.nordicchoicehotels.no) well located close to the Olavshallen concert hall.

CONNECTIONS FROM TRONDHEIM

If the lure of the North means less to you, there is a useful escape route running east from Trondheim into Sweden. Twice daily diesel railcars climb up into the hills on the **Meråker Railway**. They cross the Swedish frontier and connect in Storlien with Norrtåg electric trains to Östersund and Sundsvall. At **Sundsvall**, you can join a fast train to Stockholm. The entire cross-country journey from Trondheim to Stockholm via this route takes 10 hours. At

Boats from Trondheim

If you have had enough of trains by the time you reach Trondheim, bear in mind that the city is a major port-of-call on the **Norwegian coastal shipping service**. A southbound Hurtigruten boat sails at 9.30 each morning, taking 29 hours to reach Bergen. The northbound vessel leaves just after midday, bound for Bodø (24 hrs), Svolvær (33 hours) and a medley of other northern ports on its way around the top of Norway to the Russian border.

Closer to hand, smart cyan-and-white twin-hulled **Kystexpressen catamarans** speed twice or thrice daily down the coast from Trondheim to Kristiansund, a west-coast port city which is not to be confused with Kristiansand on the south coast. The catamaran journey from Trondheim to Kristiansund takes three-and-a-half hours.

Östersund, you can connect in summer onto the seasonal *Inlandsbanan* trains which run north to **Gällivare** in Swedish Lapland.

The Arctic Circle and beyond

One of the most remarkable rail trips we have made in Europe was a June overnight journey from Trondheim to Bodø. Yes, the sun did set, but only just, and the light had a peculiar quality all of its own. Since then, we have made this same journey by day in deep mid-winter and it was every bit as engaging as on the first occasion. This line is called **Nordlandsbanen**.

Here is an instance where the journey is the thing. There is no particular reason to break the ten-hour journey from Trondheim to Bodø. The towns along the way are unprepossessing and it comes as a surprise that they are quite industrial.

The journey starts by skirting Trondheim Fjord, taking two hours to reach **Steinkjer**, a small town which lies at the very head of the longest arm of the fjord. Beyond Steinkjer, the railway takes to the hills, traversing increasingly desolate country. The train may stop here and there at country halts, and you may notice the great variety of station buildings: a neat pastel-green building in Grong, bold fiery red at Harran and a startling shade of flamingo pink at **Mosjøen**, where the stark rurality of this part of Norway is suddenly interrupted by the sight of an aluminium smelter which relies on copious supplies of water from the adjacent fjord.

An hour beyond Mosjøen is **Mo i Rana** (usually dubbed Mo for short) which has a steel works. In terms of scenery, we rate the stretch beyond Mo as the finest of the journey. Here the railway skirts the **Saltfjellet–Svartisen National Park**, along the way going to within five kilometres of the Swedish border and shortly thereafter crossing the **Arctic Circle**. For more on this magic line of latitude which seems to exert so strong a pull on travellers' imaginations, see p273 in **Route 29** in this book.

We now run back down towards the coast. The train drops down through Saltdal to reach the shores of Skjerstad Fjord, on the north shore of which lies the small town of **Fauske**. You can take the express bus to Narvik from here, to connect with the Ofoten Railway to northern Sweden. For passengers bound for Bodø, this is a last glimpse of the E6 highway, before the train turns west and hugs the fjord on the way to its final destination.

After such a remarkable journey, a trip so rich in landscape and scenery, the railway station at **Bodø** comes as something of a let-down. It is an uninspiring piece of 1960s architecture.

Bodø (suggested stopover)

Bodø is a busy little port and departure point for ferries to the Lofoten Islands. The Domkirke (cathedral) is notable for its unusual detached spire, while the **Norsk Luftfartsmuseum** (Norwegian Aviation Museum), Olav V gata, has a fine collection of **civil and military aircraft** from various eras (www.luftfartsmuseum.no).

ARRIVAL, INFORMATION, ACCOMMODATION
✈ Centrally located, 300 m east of the tourist office. 🛈 Tourist office: Tollbugata 13, by the waterfront (www.visitbodo.com). ⛴ Hurtigruten cruises and ferries to the islands leave from quays on the road near the station. 🚍 Long-distance bus station is on Sjøgata close to the tourist information centre.

🛏 The welcoming **Skagen Hotel**, Nyholmsgata 11, ☎ 75 51 91 00 (www.skagen-hotel.no), offers a complimentary light supper and afternoon waffles. Or try the **Thon Hotel Nordlys**, Moloveien 14, ☎ 75 53 19 04 (www.thonhotels.no) in a quiet area close to the marina. The **Scandic Havet**, Tollbugata 5, ☎ 75 50 38 00 (www.scandichotels.com), has great views over the harbour.

By boat to Lofoten

From Bodø, it is 130 kilometres across the open waters of the Vestfjord to the port of **Svolvær** on the Lofoten Islands. This great open bight is part of the Norwegian Sea and in a south-westerly gale the water can be very choppy. If you are a nervous sailor or like your creature comforts, the best bet is the northbound **Hurtigruten ship**, which leaves Bodø just after three every afternoon. It makes one stop on the way to Svolvær; that's at Stamsund. On a summer evening there is no nicer way to arrive in Svolvær.

There is a another departure from Bodø, usually at 18.00, but later on Sundays. This service is operated by a **fast ferry**, taking three to four hours for the crossing. The boat will normally make between three and seven intermediate stops, so you'll catch a glimpse of some remote coastal communities along the way.

Arrival in **Svolvær** (see also p274) marks the end of an extraordinary journey. You'll surely want to spend a day or two exploring the Lofoten Islands, but rather than retracing your outward route from Oslo, why not think of following **Route 29** in reverse all the way to Stockholm?

Route 29: Night train to Narvik
CITIES: ★ CULTURE: ★ HISTORY: ★ SCENERY: ★★★
COUNTRIES COVERED: SWEDEN (SE), NORWAY (NO)
JOURNEY TIME: 19 HRS | DISTANCE: 1,735 KM | MAP: WWW.EBRWEB.EU/18MAP29

No ifs, no buts! This route showcases one of Europe's great train journeys. There is a once-daily direct train from Stockholm which runs north to **Swedish Lapland**, crossing the **Arctic Circle** and continuing over the Norwegian border to Narvik. That's a journey of about 1,500 kilometres; it takes over 20 hours. The service operator has changed twice in recent years. Since December 2020, the route has been run by Vy Tåg AB. The train is often promoted under the name **Norrlandståget**.

While we normally encourage travellers to linger over journeys and stop off along the way, the very character of this route suggests a different strategy. The overnight journey to Swedish Lapland is worth doing in one long hop. Most places of real interest lie beyond **Kiruna** – in the final three hours of the journey.

The departure time from Stockholm may vary by season and day of week; it's usually about six in the evening. You can board the train about four to five hours later in **Sundsvall**. Some travellers prefer taking an early afternoon fast train to Sundsvall, then enjoy a wander around this handsome city before joining the night train later in the evening.

The nature of this route demands a different approach in our description. So, just for once, we use a more narrative style to present the journey from Stockholm to Narvik.

From Stockholm to Boden

The adventure of the overnight train to Lapland is to a good degree all in the imagination, for in truth the first dozen hours of the journey are mainly a matter of watching the birch trees get smaller and the snow get deeper. Or eating and sleeping. But that's not to belittle the experience of travelling so far north, a journey which starts in the rather prosaic surroundings of **Stockholm Central** station. While city commuters make haste for home, another kind of passenger makes for the *Norrlandståget*. There are people wearing fur hats and sheepskin coats, soldiers on their way to one of the bases in the far north and families with skis. Some travellers opt for the comfort of the sleeping cars; those of a hardier disposition may book an ordinary seat. Few of those climbing aboard the night train to Narvik don't share in the communal **sense of adventure**.

The train rattles north through Stockholm's suburbs, pausing at Arlanda Airport and the university town of **Uppsala** to pick up passengers. Then suburbs give way to country, with forests, pulp mills and a tantalising

Just for foodies

The **bistro service** on the *Norrlandståget* was suspended during the pandemic but in earlier times it featured tempting shrimp sandwiches. There were the tasty elk burgers with tatties and lingonberry sauce, though if you spot elk through the train window you may think differently about this menu option. This really is a journey which cries out for a good restaurant car. Let's hope that a full meal service is reinstated before long.

If you are tempted by our idea of joining the overnight train in **Sundsvall** (see the introduction to this route on p269), make time for dinner at *Saffran*, a wonderful restaurant just a five-minute walk from the station at Nybrogatan 25 (☎ 060 17 11 07; www.saffran.nu; closed Sun & Mon). With a fine **choice of tapas** for all tastes, a relaxing meal at *Saffran* could be a great prelude to the overnight train journey.

---

glimpse of the sea just beyond Skutskär. This is the route north followed by **Lenin** on the evening of Good Friday 1917 on his long journey back from exile in Switzerland to a Russia on the brink of revolution. Lenin was engrossed in the Russian newspapers he had picked up in Stockholm; most travellers making the journey today, even those who have travelled north many times before, are **spellbound by the scenery** slipping by beyond the window.

Moving north, the train enters a land which might have been slumbering for years. The train pauses. No one boards or alights, and nothing stirs in the churchyard that lies beside the tracks. Just a distant church, a pale shade of pink that catches the dipping sun, and the gravestones in this village of the dead. "Saliga äro de vilkas väg är ostraffilg," reads the inscription on one of the stones. "Happy are those whose way is perfect." That seems as good a motto as any for this long ride north. There is a jolt as the train starts to move again.

Pines and birch trees with a tumble of lichen-covered granite boulders poke up through the last remnants of winter snow. Every now and again, glimpses of lakes in the evening sunshine. Dusk settles, but seems to linger forever. Night never really comes. Just a dreamy bluish twilight. Time for some hours of sleep with an occasional twitching of the curtain to glimpse the rocks and the trees, and see the birches sink ever deeper into the snow.

Overnight, little changes. More rocks and forests. But the trees have thinned out, the birches have shrunk and the snow has become deeper. The **lakes have frozen**. Dawn comes before anyone awakes. Those who stir in the small hours stare out into the dim of the northern night and might glimpse moose, deer or a fox.

In early morning, some travellers are already up and about and there is a smell of fresh coffee. Those who curl under blankets begin to move. After hours of gently sliding through rocks and trees, the train slithers to a halt in **Älvsbyn**, a place where winter snow has been bulldozed into neat piles. Men in fur coats chat on the platform, their breath making a hoary mist that hangs steady in the still air. A white van speeds up to the train and

ROUTE 29: NIGHT TRAIN TO NARVIK | 271

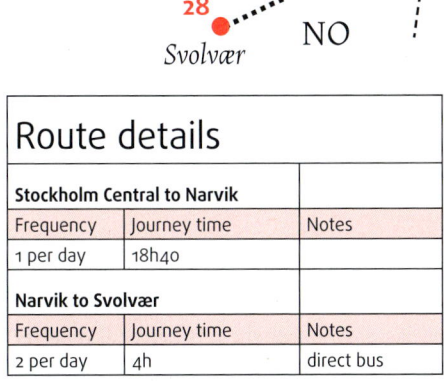
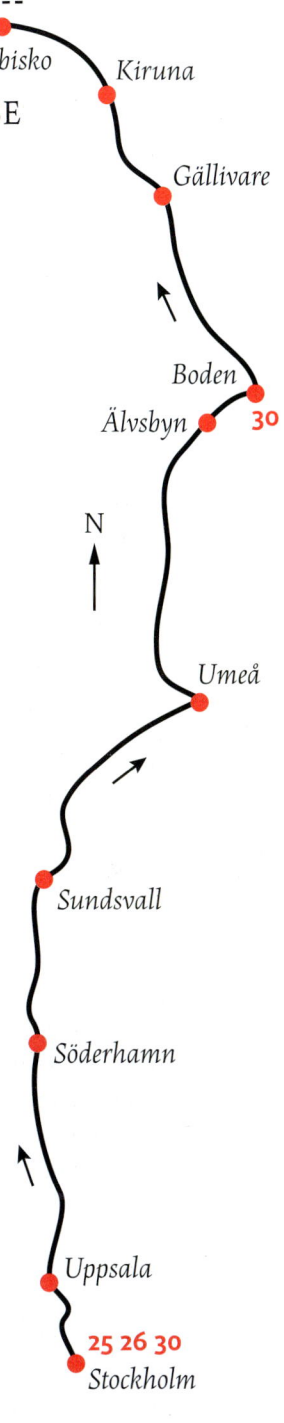

Route details

Stockholm Central to Narvik		
Frequency	Journey time	Notes
1 per day	18h40	
Narvik to Svolvær		
Frequency	Journey time	Notes
2 per day	4h	direct bus

Notes

It is now feasible to make the entire journey north from Stockholm by day. In the autumn 2024 train timetables, a departure from Stockholm at 06.22 (daily except Sundays) gives an arrival in Boden at 16.56 with one change of train (with a one-hour wait) in Umeå. Continuing from Boden next day, a train leaves at 11.15, reaching Narvik at 18.38.

Additional local trains are now running on certain days on the cross-border stretch between Abisko and Narvik, operated by Arctic Train.

delivers the morning newspapers. Within a few minutes, folk on board are browsing the *Norrländska Socialdemokraten*, one of those old style dailies which speak to local values in this land of rocks and trees. There is news of the spring thaw, adverts for flights that hop over the Arctic Circle and obituaries for men and women who lived long lives and never left their northern homeland.

The train jogs on through the forest and soon arrives in **Boden** (where there is a connection onto the next route in this book, which follows Lenin's April 1917 route on over the border into Finland). A longer stop at Boden gives passengers the chance to emerge from their sleeping compartments and taste the bitter cold of a clear northern morning. A man wearing a Stetson stands on the station platform. A handful of soldiers alight from the train. Others sit in a jeep beside the tracks. Boden is a Swedish military outpost. A bastion, that during the cold war years reminded the Soviet Union that Sweden was prepared to defend its borders – even in the far north.

Here there is a **festival of shunting**, for some carriages are bound for Luleå on the coast, while the other half of the train will head even further north, across the Arctic Circle to Narvik.

From Boden to the Norwegian coast

Whoever thought of building a railway over the mountains to Norway? It is an extraordinary route. The train takes about seven hours from **Boden to Narvik** – and with every mile that passes, the scenery gets better and better. Seven hours of some of the most beguilingly beautiful landscape in Europe. Placid to begin with, to be sure, with more rocks and forest, but by now the birch trees have thinned out.

Now there is the anticipation of the **Arctic Circle**. How odd it is that we ascribe such significance to a particular line! Old hands can ignore this arbitrary rite of passage. "But it's not arbitrary at all," protests a bespectacled student standing in the corridor. "The Arctic Circle is a loxodrome, the precise line of which is determined by the obliquity of the ecliptic."

Reindeer obviously understand all about loxodromes and the obliquity of the ecliptic. No sooner has the train passed a sign that marks the line of the Arctic Circle (well, the current line, because it is moving north) than there is a first encounter with a small herd of **reindeer** standing around rather aimlessly in the snow.

A little reception party waits at **Gällivare** to greet travellers who alight onto the snowy platform. From Gällivare the railway runs through formidably bleak terrain to reach **Kiruna**. The railway route from Kiruna through the mountains of Swedish Lapland and over the Norwegian border to Narvik was built just over a hundred years ago. Valuable deposits of iron ore were found in the hill country of northern Sweden in the 17th century. Pioneer miners used to drag sledges laden with the valuable ore over the mountains to the ice-free waters of the Norwegian coast.

In the late 1880s the Norwegian railway engineer **Ole Lund** marked out possible routes for a railway, and English investors provided the capital – on the condition that the marine terminus of the railway on the Ofot Fjord should be named after the then English monarch. Hence Victoriahavn. The company went bankrupt and English aspirations to create an Arctic monument to their queen were quickly eclipsed as Swedish and Norwegian financiers moved in to finish the task. **Victoriahavn** was renamed Narvik, and the entire route across the mountains to the Norwegian port was completed in 1902.

The wandering Arctic Circle

As the train crosses the Arctic Circle near the appropriately named hamlet of **Polcirkeln**, the driver usually gives a loud blast on the engine's horn. The Serbian climatologist **Milutin Milanković** calculated how variations in the tilt of the earth's axis – a sort of astronomical wobble – cause the Arctic Circle to move around. Fortunately, the good folk in Polcirkeln recognise that visitors are not satisfied with being told that the Arctic Circle is somewhere nearby, but want to see the exact line. So they have obliged by erecting signs that show where the Arctic Circle was in 2005 and 2015, and also exactly where it will be in 2025. Just now, it seems, this elusive line of latitude is heading north at a rate of about a metre a month.

The railway traverses some of Europe's wildest country. For travellers today, enclosed in the cosseted comfort of the train, it is difficult to imagine the hardships endured by the navvies who for a dozen years laboured to build the railway line. Ole Lund oversaw construction work on the Norwegian section of the line. It would be, he said, a perfect piece of engineering. Lund's daughter, Hanna, meticulously documented many of the ballads sung by the navvies as they carved out the route of the railway. A young Swedish railway worker, **Manne Briandt**, who later became an accomplished musician in his own right, studied the navvies' songs on the Swedish section of the building project. That work by Hanna and Manne became an important milestone in Scandinavian ethnomusicology, and much of the atmosphere of those early days on the **Ofoten railway** is captured in recordings of the *Rallarviser* (Ballads of the Navvies).

There is a lyrical quality to these northern landscapes, ever more so as the railway skirts the shoulders of mountains and creeps up narrow valleys where the hillsides tilt ever sharper. For over 50 kilometres the train runs along the south shore of **Torneträsk**, a magnificent glacial lake which is frozen for more than half the year. Black dots on the ice mark the spots where fishermen have carved holes in the ice and cast their rods in the hope of catching tonight's supper.

In **Abisko**, nowadays a major resort on Torneträsk, most of the passengers alight. As the railway heads up into the hills at the western end of Torneträsk lake, there is a little cemetery beside the tracks with the remains of the navvies who died in the construction of the Ofoten railway. Simple white crosses poke up through the snow. Some died in accidents; others perished from typhus.

At **Riksgränsen**, a station that balances on the very border of Norway and Sweden and the highest point of the route, several skiers alight. The train tunnels through deep snow, and then begins the long and winding descent to the Ofot Fjord. Avalanches and landslides play havoc with the line, and the route has been rebuilt many times. Away to the right there is a glimpse of the old **Norddal bridge**, which once carried the railway but now stands protected as a national monument. Views then of the great fjord in the distance, more tight curves and steep drops until, bang on time, the sleek carriages of the night train from Stockholm to Narvik come gently to a halt at their final destination.

You might take some pleasure in noting that on its **approach to Narvik** the train traverses the northernmost passenger rail route anywhere in Scandinavia, reaching a latitude of 68° 27' N. Serious record chasers must go to Russia, though, where passenger trains edge even closer to the North Pole.

Narvik

This small modern port wins no prizes for its architecture, though the setting is magnificent. Narvik was invaded in 1940 by the Germans in a bid to control shipments of iron ore; within days the British destroyed the German fleet and the Allies recaptured the town. The first section of the **Narvik Krigsmuseum** (Narvik War Museum; www.krigsmuseet.no) commemorates the town's important role in the Second World War as well as the work of the Resistance. Narvik's prosperity owes virtually everything to the Ofoten railway line, which transports iron ore from Sweden, then ships it out to sea from town; the **Ofoten Museum**, Administrasjonsveien 3, provides a thorough overview of the industry and its history.

The overnight train from Stockholm arrives in Narvik in sufficient time to connect with the afternoon bus to the Lofoten Islands. If you are tempted to stay in Narvik, we suggest the Breidablikk Gjestehus, Tore Hunds gate 41, ☎ 76 94 14 18 (www.breidablikk.no).

Narvik connections

See our **Sidetracks** feature on p276 for details of connections beyond Narvik to North Cape and Norway's Barents Sea region, the easternmost part of the country which shares a common border with the Russian Federation.

There are twice-daily buses from **Narvik to Fauske** and Bodø, which connect at Fauske into southbound trains to Trondheim (see **Route 28**). These buses leave from the bus station near the AMFI shopping centre, as do the Boreal Transport services to Svolvær.

The bus journey from **Narvik to Svolvær** (Boreal Transport bus route number 300) is truly remarkable. With sub-sea tunnels and magnificent bridges, this new road connection has transformed access to the once-remote Lofoten region.

Svolvær

Svolvær is the islands' main town (pop. 4,500) and located on **Austvågøy**. The spectacular **Lofoten Islands** are a chain of improbably jagged glacially-sculpted mountains that shelter fishing villages, farms, sheep and thousands of birds. This is Norwegian scenery at its best – mild climate, comparatively uncrowded and a sense that you are with nature at its purest. It is excellent terrain for walking, horse riding and cycling (it is possible to hire bicycles), and there are some great boat trips – including to the beautiful cliffside bird colonies of Værøy and to **Trollfjord**. Røst and Værøy support colonies of puffins; both have accommodation.

Don't miss the picturesque fishing village with the modest name of Å, 5 km south of the island of Moskenes, with cottages, an HI hostel (Å Vandrerhjem, ☎ 76 09 12 11) and a campsite. Fishing, caving and hiking trips can all be arranged here.

Arrival, information, accommodation
⛴ Hurtigruten boats dock in the centre at Fiskergata; the bus station where the express bus to Lofoten stops is just a short walk away. Boats to Skutvik and Skorva leave from Svolværveien on the E10.

ℹ Tourist office: Torget 18 (www.lofoten.info). Public transport information can be found on the excellent website of Nordland county at www.177nordland.no. 🛏 The small island of Lamholmen which overlooks Svolvær harbour and is connected to the town by road has two good accommodation options. We stayed at the **Scandic Svolvær**, Lamholmen, ☎ 76 06 82 00 (www.scandichotels.com). Or try the **Anker Brygge**, ☎ 76 06 64 80 (www.anker-brygge.no), which has cosy *robuer* (each with a kitchen) and other hotel accommodation. Despite being in the harbour, both places are quiet and close to Svolvær's centre. They also allow you to watch the comings and goings of the Hurtigruten boats.

Connections from Svolvær
You can connect in Svolvær with the previous journey in this book by following **Route 28** backwards to Oslo. Svolvær is of course on the main **Norwegian Coastal Voyage** route. Hurtigruten boats leave daily, sailing south to Trondheim and Bergen and north to Tromsø and Kirkenes.

An alternative finale: by boat
Route 29 concludes with the long ride on the express bus to Svolvær. But there is an alternative, one we took ourselves and really found a worthwhile detour, as it includes a superb daytime leg on a **Hurtigruten ship**.

Instead of taking the bus all the way to Svolvær, alight at Tjeldsund Kro, whence there is a connecting bus to Harstad. You can check bus times on www.177nordland.no. You'll need to overnight in Harstad; we stayed at the **Thon Hotel** by the harbour (Sjøgaten 11, ☎ 77 00 08 00; www.thonhotels.com). Next morning, take the southbound Hurtigruten boat which leaves at 08.30. The ten-hour trip to Svolvær is in our view the finest stretch of the entire Norwegian Coastal Voyage. It takes in the scenic drama of **Raftsundet** and, if you are lucky, a foray into Trollfjorden.

If you just want to get a taste of Hurtigruten, this daytime sailing from Harstad to Svolvær is the perfect opportunity. There are brief stops at three small ports along the way. All in all, you'll see a greater variety of Lofoten communities and landscapes than if you stick to the express bus from Narvik to Svolvær.

Sidetracks: Norway's Far North

Whether you approach **Narvik** on the direct overnight train from Stockholm or on the bus that runs up the Norwegian coast from Bodø and Fauske, you are sure to have that distinct feeling of having reached somewhere very far from civilisation. Narvik is the end of the line, and the spectacular **Ofoten railway** that runs over the mountains from Sweden (part of **Route 29**) is the northernmost rail journey included among the fifty routes in this book.

End of the line does not mean end of the road, and true adventurers can continue beyond Narvik to explore Norway's two northernmost *fylker* (or counties): **Troms** (or Romsa in the Sámi language) and **Finnmark** (Finnmárku in Sámi). If you are tempted to head north from Narvik, don't underestimate the formidable distances involved.

There is a bus connection from **Narvik to Kirkenes**, the last community of any size in Norway before the border with Russia. The journey takes over 30 hours. That long haul includes a ten-hour overnight stop in Alta, a superbly located but utterly dreary town on Altafjord.

An alternative route north is by the regular coastal shipping service called **Hurtigruten**. Ships operate daily in each direction, but do not serve Narvik. You can board the Hurtigruten boats in **Bodø**, whence it is 66 hrs around the northern Norwegian coast to the Barents Sea port of Kirkenes. If you are in Narvik, your best bet is to take the direct bus to **Tromsø** (4 hrs) and join the Hurtigruten boat there. Tromsø to Kirkenes by ship takes 43 hrs.

Travel right to the furthest reaches of eastern Finnmark and you'll realise that remoteness is utterly relative. Experience those long bus and boat journeys to **Kirkenes**, and now Narvik will retrospectively glow in your memory as a bustling hub of northern life. Kirkenes is further east than Istanbul, while Vardø is further east than the Egyptian city of Alexandria.

Like Kirkenes, **Vardø** is also served by the Hurtigruten boats. The town, located on a small offshore island linked by an undersea tunnel to the mainland, is an important fishing port. "Cod is great," reads a sign by the harbour. But Vardø has a dark secret. in the 16th century, 77 women and 14 men were **condemned as witches** and burned. A new shoreline memorial is a moving tribute to these poor souls. Nowadays there's witchcraft of another kind in the array of electronic gadgetry that sits atop a hill on the mainland. Officials say the **radar facility** is there to keep an inventory of satellites in the heavens above. Locals say the dishes point only at Russia.

For **Russia** really is just over the horizon. Kirkenes will again become a great jumping-off point for journeys into Russia when peace eventually returns to Ukraine. A 15-min drive from Kirkenes harbour and you can be eye-to-eye with a Russian border guard across a wire-mesh fence. If you have a Russian visa, you will again be able to cross the frontier at **Boris Gleb** (Борисоглебскй). As of September 2024, this border crossing between Norway and Russia is closed to tourists. We used this backdoor route into Russia in 2014 and were impressed by the speed with which one could cross the border – just 10 minutes. Direct buses used to run daily from **Kirkenes to Murmansk** in Russia (5 hrs) where you could hop on a train for the 24-hour journey to St Petersburg.

Route 30: A foray through Finland

Cities: ★★ Culture: ★ History: ★★ Scenery: ★★
Countries covered: Sweden (SE), Finland (FI)
Journey time: 23 hrs | Distance: 1,501 km | Map: www.ebrweb.eu/18map30

This is the only journey in *Europe by Rail* which starts and ends in the same country, having along the way made a great loop through quite another country. Our journey commences in **northern Sweden** and ends in Stockholm, but actually the bulk of the rail travel on this wonderful journey is through Finland. We make tracks around the northern edge of the Gulf of Bothnia to reach Finnish territory. On the long journey south through Finland, we take in three great provincial cities – **Oulu, Tampere and Turku** – plus of course the capital Helsinki. But there's more than city streets on this fine trip: you'll see lakes and forests aplenty and learn a thing or two about Finland's history. For devotees of traditional wooden architecture, we suggest **two off-route forays**, one at the start to the Swedish church town of Gammelstad and later in Finland to the port of Jakobstad (in a mainly Swedish-speaking area of the country).

This route comes with a history. Until 2022, *Europe by Rail* featured a journey which routed through Finland to reach Russia. But following Russia's invasion of Ukraine in late February 2022 (and the subsequent cancellation of all passenger rail services across the Finno-Russian frontier), our earlier rendering of the route seemed insensitive to the realities of Russian aggression. We have therefore rewritten this journey so that, after **exploring Finland**, the traveller is then escorted back to Sweden.

But there is still a **dose of Russian history** on this journey. The first part of our route broadly follows that taken by **Lenin** when he returned to Russia in spring 1917, swapping exile in Switzerland for the fiery politics of Petrograd. Pack a copy of Catherine Merridale's excellent *Lenin on the Train* (published by Penguin in 2017). For much of this journey, we shall travel through territory that until 1917 was part of the Russian Empire. So although this journey no longer enters Russia, there are echoes of Tsarist history: the trains in Finland still run on Russian-gauge tracks.

Suggested itinerary

The four **major Finnish towns** on this route are the obvious stopovers, viz. Oulu, Tampere, Turku and Helsinki. Another possibility, which would mean sacrificing both Tampere and Turku, is to travel by overnight train from **Kemi** or **Oulu** to Helsinki and then take a direct overnight ferry to Stockholm. With a journey time of 12 hours from Kemi (10 from Oulu), it's a long enough leg to justify a night in a sleeping car – and Finnish night sleepers really are some of the best around.

Finally, in the latter part of this journey, you may consider stopping in the **Åland Islands**, a self-governing province of Finland which is almost entirely Swedish speaking. This archipelago of over 6,000 islands (of which only 60 are inhabited) is a place to catch sea breezes and reflect on issues of culture and identity.

Notes

B – In addition to the new train service from Boden to Haparanda, there is also an express coach service from Luleå to Tornio bus station. It runs 10 times daily Mon–Fri and less frequently at weekends.

H – Generally, alternate trains stop en route in Hämeenlinna.

X – It is a 10-min walk from the railway station at Haparanda to the new Haparanda / Tornio *resecentrum* (bus station).

Z – Shipping services are offered by Tallink Silja and Viking Line. Each operator offers a choice of daytime and overnight sailings. Daytime crossings stop at Mariehamn while the overnight boats stop at Långnäs in the Ålands.

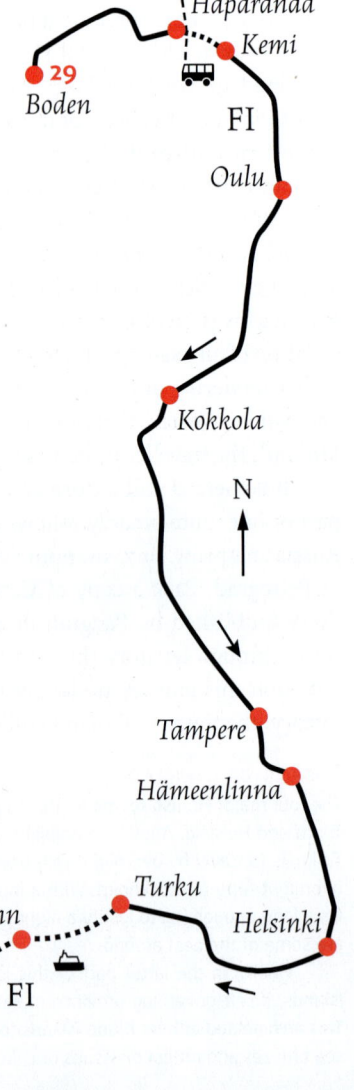

Route details

Boden to Haparanda		
Frequency	Journey time	Notes
3 per day	1h30	B X

Tornio to Kemi (by bus)		
Frequency	Journey time	Notes
2–9 per day	0h30–0h40	X

Kemi to Oulu		
Frequency	Journey time	Notes
7 per day	1h–1h10	

Oulu to Tampere		
Frequency	Journey time	Notes
Every 2–3 hrs	4h–6h	

Tampere to Helsinki		
Frequency	Journey time	Notes
2 per hr	1h35–3h	H

Helsinki to Turku		
Frequency	Journey time	Notes
Every 1–2 hrs	2h	

Turku to Stockholm		
Frequency	Journey time	Notes
4 per day	11h	Z

Getting to Boden

Boden is probably not a town where anyone lingers, although its setting – perched between two lakes – is very pleasant. The town is an **important railway junction** and has a very useful direct overnight train from Stockholm. That overnight journey is described in **Route 29** in this book, to which Route 30 is thus a natural extension.

With recent improvements to the *Botniabanan* (along Sweden's Gulf of Bothnia coast), it is now also possible to travel by day from **Stockholm to Boden** (a journey of 10 hrs 20 mins), with just one change of train in Umeå. There is also a twice-daily link from Narvik. If you need to stay overnight in Boden before joining Route 30, try the Hotell Nivå, ☎ 0921 558 60 (www.hotellniva.se), right by the station.

To the Finnish border

Let's start by just making a little detour. Having come this far north in Sweden, it is at least worth taking a peek at **Luleå** on the coast before heading east. The railway to Luleå follows the east bank of the River Lule from the railway junction at Boden down to the coast. It's just a half-hour journey. Look out on the left for a glimpse of the church town of **Gammelstad**, a purpose-built township constructed to allow worshippers who made long journeys through difficult terrain to attend Sabbath services to stay overnight by the church. As an example of the *kyrkstad* tradition, once widespread in northern Scandinavia, Gammelstad features on UNESCO's World Heritage List. It is easily reached from Luleå by frequent local buses. Luleå itself is a workaday port and industrial city, but it's instantly appealing as a welcome haven in a sparsely populated region.

Now let's head to Finland where we can take advantage of a brand new railway. Lenin travelled all the way to **Haparanda** by train, but the old line carried its last passengers in 1992. Its replacement, following a different route, opened in April 2021. Trains on this route to the Finnish border start from Luleå and pick up passengers in Boden about 25 minutes later. Then it's a delightful run east through forests with just one intermediate stop at Kalix before reaching Haparanda, the last community in Sweden before the Finnish border.

There are plans to reconnect the passenger rail networks of **Sweden and Finland**, but the trains won't run before 2025. The realisation of that project is not made any easier by the fact that Sweden's railways use the standard-gauge common in much of western Europe while Finland's railways were built to the broader Russian gauge. In Haparanda you'll see the enterprise which makes this town tick – the huge branch of IKEA which attracts customers from the entire Bothnia and Barents regions. Until the COVID pandemic it wasn't at all unusual to see vehicles with Murmansk license plates in the car park. Haparanda seems rather proud to host the world's northernmost IKEA.

One senses that Haparanda is no longer the exotic outpost it was when **Thomas Cook**, 150 years ago, commented that those who were really well travelled would surely have set foot in Timbuktu, Samarkand and Haparanda.

Over the River Torne

From Haparanda, you can gaze over the River Torne to Finland. Nowadays one hops with such ease across this border that it's easy to forget that this was once a difficult frontier.

The River Torne marked the border of the Russian Empire, of which the **Grand Duchy of Finland** was a part until 1917. When Lenin arrived in Haparanda early on the morning of 15 April 1917 (Easter Sunday in the Orthodox calendar) on his journey from Switzerland back to St Petersburg, he hired pony-drawn sledges to take his party across the frozen river. It was at Tornio on the east bank that Lenin first touched Russian territory after his long exile.

You can walk over the **border bridge** into Tornio. Don't forget to **advance your watch** by one hour. Summer or winter, Finnish time is always an hour ahead of Sweden. The new bus station is on the Finnish side of the river. No less than six different bus operators compete on the route from here to **Kemi**, so there's a good choice of buses but be aware that there are few evening buses and weekend services (especially on Saturdays) are sparse. The one-way fare is about €7. At Kemi, undistinguished and memorable mainly for the smell of wood pulp, the best thing is to get the first train out of town towards Oulu.

Connections from Kemi

Kemi is a significant railway junction. There's a morning train running north to Pello and Kolari, two small towns buried away in the forests of the Torne Valley. Both lie north of the **Arctic Circle**. Kolari has the distinction of being Finland's northernmost railway station. If you are arriving from Sweden via Haparanda, note that you can walk over the frontier and join the Kolari-bound train at Itäinen station in Tornio.

There are occasional trains from Kemi which follow the **Kemi Valley** upstream to Rovaniemi from where there are onward bus connections to northern Finland and in summer also to northern Norway.

The train journey from **Kemi to Oulu** will be for many travellers a first chance to experience a railway which is thoroughly Russian in design. The line dates from the late-Tsarist period, having been completed in 1903. Although it has been completely modernised — it was electrified in 2004 — there is still a distinct retro ambiance about the route, evident most particularly in the **design of station buildings** (like those at Simo and Haukipudas). It's a pleasant journey through forest and meadows with occasional distant views of the shallow waters of the Gulf of Bothnia away to the right. Along the way, the railway bridges a number of strikingly beautiful rivers with names to match: Simojoki, Iijoki and Kiiminkijoki.

Oulu (suggested stopover)

The railway station at Oulu is a welcoming wooden structure with a nicely retro feel. The city it serves is much more modern. Oulu is one of Finland's **high-tech industry hubs**. A few of the town's older buildings, such as the city hall, recall the 19th-century tar boom – in which Oulu was a world leader. A short walk away is the **Science Centre Tietomaa**, Nahkatehtaankatu 6, an interactive science and technology museum that will appeal to visitors of all ages. There's an assemblage of Sámi artefacts and other local miscellanea at the nearby Pohjois-Pohjanmaan Museo (Northern Ostrobothnia Museum), Ainola Park (closed Mon & Tue, free entrance).

Arrival, information, accommodation

⇒ Rautatienkatu, east of the centre. 🛈 Tourist office: Hallituskatu 36B (www.visitoulu.fi). 🛏 Best Western **Hotel Apollo**, Asemakatu 31–33, ☎ 08 522 11 (www.hotelapollo.fi), is a no-frills option close to the railway station. Or try the stylish **Lapland Hotels Oulu**, Kirkkokatu 3, ☎ 08 881 11 10 (www.laplandhotels.com), not far from the station and close to the cathedral. Centrally located, the **Scandic Oulu City**, Saaristonkatu 4, ☎ 0300 30 84 64 (www.scandichotels.com), is comfortable and reliable.

Ostrobothnia

From Oulu, take your pick from comfortable daytime Intercity heading south or overnight trains with sleeping cars direct to Helsinki. It's a long

Inland from Oulu

If you are Helsinki-bound and are in no great rush, why not consider following the inland route from **Oulu via Kajaani** and Kuopio to the Finnish capital, taking in some deliciously rural countryside along the way. You can travel that entire line in the comfort of a through train. It takes 8 hrs 30 mins and, as of late 2024, leaves Oulu at 07.10 daily except Saturdays. If you are minded to take this alternative route south, myriad possibilities await. You may want to break the journey with an overnight stay at **Kuopio** in Finland's Lake District. An alternative is to take the train only as far as Kajaani, switching there onto the once-daily bus (not Sats) to **Nurmes** for an overnight stay in that delightful township close to the Russian border in North Karelia. Nurmes in 2023 celebrated the 150th anniversary of its founding by Tsar Alexander II. This rural community, perched on a narrow peninsula jutting into the northernmost part of Lake Pielinen, is a perfect spot to spend a day or two. From Nurmes, there are twice-daily trains to Helsinki, always with a change in Joensuu. The two-hour stretch from **Nurmes to Joensuu**, served by Czech-built diesel railcars, takes in some **wonderful Karelian landscapes**, along the way crossing the 30th meridian east of Greenwich four times. This rural line is thus the easternmost passenger railway in the European Union. The railway station at Uimaharju is the easternmost stop along the way. The village lies as far east as St Petersburg.

haul south through the lowlands of Ostrobothnia from **Oulu to Tampere** – almost 500 kilometres and a journey of about five hours. The countryside is not riveting, but it has a serene charm, seen at its monochromatic best in the depths of winter.

From Oulu the railway heads inland, only returning to the coast much further south at Kokkola. Slightly further down the coast is the predominantly Swedish-speaking town of **Jakobstad** (the Finnish name is Pietarsaari), in our view easily the nicest spot on the Ostrobothnian coast. This delightful small town is full of unpretentious wooden architecture – a good place to relax for a day or two, especially in good summer weather when you can explore the beaches along the coast. To reach Jakobstad, alight from the train at Pännäinen, from where there are good bus connections for the ten-kilometre hop to Jakobstad. If you are minded to stay overnight, the Hotel Epoque, Jaakonkatu 10, ☎ 06 788 71 00 (www.hotelepoque.fi), is a good option just a short walk from the Old Town.

Tampere (suggested stopover)

Finland's second city was once the nation's industrial fulcrum, but the atmospheric **red-brick factory buildings** and warehouses have since been converted into museums, galleries and shopping centres, and Tampere (Tammerfors in Swedish) today stands as a surprisingly attractive place, flanked by lakes and graced with abundant green spaces. From the station, Hämeenkatu leads across the **Tammerkoski**, a series of rapids that connect the city's two largest lakes and provide it with hydroelectric energy.

For an entirely different take on faith in Tampere (and more generally in Finland), take a peek at the ornately Byzantine **Orthodox church**, which lies on Suvantokatu just a couple of minutes south of the railway station. It's a wonderful fantasy of domes and turrets in the Russian Romantic style. Although now owned by the Orthodox Church of Finland, it's a reminder of former Russian influence here.

Tsar Alexander I encouraged the Scottish Quaker industrialist **James Finlayson** to develop the mills at Tampere. You cannot miss the former Finlayson factory, now a centre for crafts and artisan works. More on the life of the factory's workers can be found at **Amurin Työläismuseokortteli**, Satakunnankatu 49 (Amuri Museum of Workers' Housing; open June–September, closed Mon). There's a **Lenin Museum** at Hämeenpuisto 28, near the end of Hämeenkatu (www.lenin.fi; closed Mon outside summer). This marks the spot where Lenin met Stalin at the Bolshevik Congress in 1905 – Lenin lived in Tampere after the 1905 revolution. The museum is a remarkable survey of European socialist history as seen from a Finnish perspective. It's worth remembering that after centuries of subservience to Sweden (until 1809), and then 108 years in an ambiguous and often difficult relation with Russia, the Bolsheviks were the midwives of the first truly independent Finnish state.

ARRIVAL, INFORMATION, ACCOMMODATION
≥ A 5-min walk east of the centre. ⓘ Tourist office: Kelloportinkatu 1B (www.visittampere.fi). ⨳ A good budget option not far from the station is the **Dream Hostel and Hotel**, Åkerlundinkatu 2, ☎ 0452 360 517 (www.dreamhostel.fi) that also has apartments. Right by the station is the comfortable **Scandic Tampere Station**, Ratapihankatu 37, ☎ 0300 30 84 32 (www.scandichotels.com). Equally well located is the stylish **Sokos Hotel Villa**, Sumeliuksenkatu 14, ☎ 020 123 46 33 (www.sokoshotels.fi), next to the landmark Torni Hotel.

CONNECTIONS FROM TAMPERE
There are regular fast trains to Helsinki. A very useful cross-country line runs east from Tampere to Pieksämäki. There are connections in Pieksämäki to **Kuopio** and **Joensuu**, the latter a lakeshore town which is a good jumping-off point for exploring Finnish Karelia.

The train journey from Tampere to Helsinki traverses forests and comfortable agricultural country. This region in the south-west is **Finland's farming heartland**. Of the various small towns on the 187 km leg from Tampere to Helsinki, the one we like best is **Hämeenlinna** (often known by its Swedish name of Tavastehus). The town, revered as the birthplace of composer Jean Sibelius, makes a perfect break of journey and certainly deserve a couple of hours or more. All but the fastest trains from Tampere to Helsinki stop in Hämeenlinna. From the railway station, on the east side of **Lake Vanajavesi**, it's a ten-minute walk west over a bridge to reach the delightful Old Town. If you have time, visit the fine late 13th century castle with its beautiful lakeshore setting. It was an important defensive outpost in the borderlands where Sweden and Russia vied for influence. From Hämeenlinna it's just 90 minutes on fast trains (or abour 2 hours on local trains) south through densely settled country to Helsinki.

Helsinki (Helsingfors) – (suggested stopover)

Arrival in Helsinki is something to be savoured. Take time to look around the main railway station. Elien Saarinen's theatrical **art nouveau design** is dominated by the four granite giants that flank the station's main entrance. Look out also for the huge streamlined clock tower, a design element that was later imitated in railway stations in the United States.

Built on a series of peninsulas, Helsinki is first and foremost a city of the sea. It has a gritty, north-meets-east flavour, but in recent years this modern city has become one of the most culturally pulsating capitals in Europe. Helsinki was **rebuilt to a grid plan** in the 19th century when it became capital of the Grand Duchy of Finland. With its public buildings standing proud upon great granite steps, Helsinki's architecture has a distinctly

Russian air – the city itself was originally modelled on St Petersburg. The wide boulevards are lined with cobbles and tramlines and exude a liberating sense of space. Don't miss **Uspenski Cathedral**, the showpiece centre of the Finnish Orthodox Church. Located near the harbour, its golden cupolas and red-brick facade are widely visible.

The real heart of Helsinki is **Kauppatori** (Market Square) and the harbour. Take your pick of the many stalls offering tasty fresh fish cooked to order and then hop on a boat for a harbour tour. If time permits stop off on **Suomenlinna**, a lovely island with that perfect sense of being so near to and yet so far from Helsinki. We have had some of our laziest Helsinki summer days just hanging out on Suomenlinna. Ferries to the island leave twice or thrice per hour from Kauppatori.

Arrival, information, accommodation

Helsinki Central Station, right in the heart of the city. Helsinki-Vantaa Airport (www.finavia.fi/fi/helsinkivantaa) is 20 km north of the city. Trains between the airport and the city centre run every 10 mins Mon–Sat during the day (every 15 mins in the evenings and Sun), taking about 30 mins to Helsinki Central station. Many of the sights are in the area between the station and Kauppatori, and **trams** are a quick way of reaching most of the others. Buy single tickets (valid for 80–110 minutes, depending on selected zones) from blue HSL ticket machines or R-kiosks (www.hsl.fi). 24-hour tickets are also available (buy at ticket machine or the tourist information). Tourist office: at Helsinki Central Station (www.myhelsinki.fi).

East from Finland

Relations between Russia and the European Union have been at an all-time low since 2022. Since Finland joined NATO in April 2023, the relationship between Helsinki and Moscow is especially frosty. Parked up in sidings just north of Helsinki's main station are the sleek **Allegro high-speed trains** which until March 2022 were used on the regular run to St Petersburg. The service was axed in protest at Russia's invasion of Ukraine. While the trains ran, **St Petersburg** was just three-and-a-half hours in Allegro comfort from Helsinki. Now the Russian city seems light years away.

With no trains running across the Finnish-Russian border, and the overnight ferry service from Helsinki to St Petersburg never reinstated after the COVID pandemic, those few travellers still intent on going to Russia have to be quite creative. All flights have been suspended. The **Saimaa Canal** summer cruises on the *MS Carelia* to Vyborg, for so long a good way of getting a visa-free trip to a fascinating Russian city (with a Finnish history), did not run in 2024 and they look unlikely to be reinstated any time soon – not least as the Russian Federation may revoke the treaty which granted Finland permissive use of the Saimaa Canal until 2063. So the only other option is an express bus from **Helsinki to St Petersburg**. Services are still being offered by Lux Express (www.luxexpress.eu) and Ecolines (www.ecolines.net), in each case with twice-daily services. The journey time is scheduled for about eight hours but, as of autumn 2024, Finland's decision to seal its order with Russia means even these buses are not running.

Don't forget that most travellers need a **visa** to enter Russia. Lenin turned up to a rapturous reception in St Petersburg when he arrived without official permission. The Russian authorities won't be so wild if you arrive without the proper papers.

🛏 A short walk west of the train station is the good-value **Hotel Helka**, Pohjoinen Rautatiekatu 23, ☎ 09 61 35 80 (www.hotelhelka.com). Or try the sleekly designed boutique hotel **Glo Kluuvi**, Kluuvikatu 4, ☎ 010 344 44 00 (www.glohotels.fi). Very central and not far from the harbour in a quiet location is the upmarket **Hotel Lilla Roberts**, Pieni Roobertinkatu 1–3, ☎ 09 6824 28 60 (www.lillaroberts.com).

Connections from Helsinki

Helsinki has a tantalising **range of ferry connections**, ranging from short hops over the Gulf of Finland to **Tallinn** in Estonia and longer-distance crossings to Stockholm to a daily service to the German port of **Travemünde** run by Finnlines. In previous editions of *Europe by Rail*, we have included routes leading south from Helsinki, using the boat to Tallinn and then continuing south by train to Latvia (with, in some editions, onward buses to Lithuania and Poland). As the rail connections through the Baltic States are so fragmented these days (see our **Sidetracks** on Baltic Trains on p297), we have withdrawn those routes in this current edition. But things may improve with talk of an undersea rail tunnel from Helsinki to Tallinn, part of a new railway which will run south through the Baltic States to Poland. This bold scheme is called **Rail Baltica**.

From Helsinki we make tracks **west to Turku**. The relocation of the Finnish capital from Turku to Helsinki in 1812 was at the behest of the Russians. It suited the tsar to have the administrative centre of the Grand Duchy closer to St Petersburg, and the move had the effect of diminishing Swedish influence in Finnish affairs. Turku has never quite forgiven Helsinki. That's a fact to ponder as Finnish and Swedish voices intermingle on the two-hour ride from Helsinki to Turku. Running west from Helsinki, the railway passes for a dozen kilometres through an area that until 1956 was leased by the Soviet Union. Trains travelling on this route in those days had dark window blinds which were pulled down as the train traversed that area. We surely would not have been able to resist the temptation to take a peek into another world. For more on **corridor trains** – that's the name for services which criss-cross borders and traverse the territory of another country on a domestic journey – see our **Sidetracks** feature on p349.

Finland's oldest city and its capital until 1812, **Turku** (Åbo in Swedish), is home to the country's oldest university and is a vibrant commercial and cultural centre, with a pulsating nightlife. Turku's much-rebuilt but nonetheless impressive **Tuomiokirkko** (cathedral) is easily spotted by the tower's distinctive face, the result of several fires over the centuries. The cathedral is the seat of the Lutheran Archbishop of Finland and very much the centre of Protestant life in Finland. The **Sibelius Museum**, Piispankatu 17 (www.sibeliusmuseum.fi; closed Mon), displays over 350 musical instruments, as well as memorabilia of the great composer (although he had no connection with Turku itself). The museum also stages music events.

If you want to spend the night in Turku consider staying at the Park Hotel, Rauhankatu 1, ☎ 02 273 25 55 (www.parkhotelturku.fi). This early 20th-century villa has art nouveau galore and offers individually styled rooms in a good central location.

ÅLAND STOPOVER

The two daytime **ferries from Turku to Stockholm** both follow the same route, sailing west through a maze of islands, and eventually following the strait between Föglö (to port) and Lemland (to starboard) to reach the principal island in the Åland archipelago. It's known as **Fasta**, which means 'mainland'. All things are relative in island life. The ship docks at Mariehamn, Åland's closest take on urban living. The peninsula town is instantly welcoming. An afternoon is enough to take in the key sights, which include the **Åland Maritime Museum** (www.sjofartsmuseum.ax) and old maritime quarter. Rent a bike for out of town excursions. For an overnight stay, try the family-friendly Park Alandia Hotel, Norra Esplanadgatan 3, ☎ 018 14130 (www.parkalandia.com) conveniently located in the centre of Mariehamn.

Connections from Turku

The busy port of Turku has plenty of **ferries to Stockholm**, usually with a choice of four daily sailings. It's about an 11-hour crossing, and you can opt for either a daytime or overnight sailing. There is a very useful morning boat to Mariehamn in the **Åland Islands**, a scattered archipelago which is an autonomous region of Finland with strong cultural and linguistic links to Sweden.

From the **docks in Turku**, served by their own dedicated railway station (called Turku satama), comfortable cruise ferries sail west both by day and by night to Stockholm. Our preference is for the daytime sailings offered by both Tallink Silja and Viking. If you want to skip Turku itself, an early start from Helsinki will get you to Turku satama in time to board the ship. This is a route where you are barely out of sight of land and there are glorious views of the **Åland Islands** and then later of the Stockholm archipelago. On most sailings there is an early afternoon stop at Mariehamn, the only community of any size in the Åland Islands. It's a perfect spot to stop off for a day or two, and you may wish to use the opportunity to head out of Mariehamn to explore some of the remoter inhabited islands.

The reason why most boats from Finland to Sweden stop at **Mariehamn** at all is curious. This scatter of islands lies outwith the EU's fiscal regime – a little accounting curiosity that the Åland Islands share with Mount Athos, the tiny theocratic polity on a peninsula that juts into the northern Aegean. These islands really do have a capital in Mariehamn, just as they have their own parliament, flag, car licence plates and their own postage stamps. **Åland autonomy** comes with the privilege of duty free cigarettes, aquavit and snuff – yes, snuff, for the Swedes have an appetite for ground tobacco unmatched by any other nation in Europe. So the Åland Islands, we have found, really make one think about issues of autonomy and identity. These are issues to ponder on the crossing as you enjoy the fabulous smörgåsbord with a dozen varieties of pickled herring.

Our journey ends in **Stockholm**, where you can connect into **Route 25, 26** and **29** in this book. For more on Stockholm, see pages 243 and 244.

Sidetracks: The communal carriage

Russia is currently off-limits for most readers of this book, but the day will surely come when people venture back. Looking just at European Russia, there are some amazing possibilities. How about the direct train from St Petersburg to **Sochi** (Сочи) and **Adler** (Адлер) on the **Russian Riviera**? That's one long Baltic to Black Sea leap, a 51-hour trip on Train 171A. The one-way fare from St Petersburg to Adler (including a sleeping berth in an open-plan carriage) is about €34. There's now a direct daily train from St Petersburg to Sevastopol in the Crimea (38 hrs, €38), a service which like the similar trains from Moscow, is all part of Russia's policy of integrating the Crimea into Mother Russia.

Would prefer to head north? Then make for Ladozhsky railway station in **St Petersburg** (Ладожский вокзал), the newest major station in the city, from where every morning Train 16A departs for **Murmansk** (Мурманск) on Russia's Kola coast. It is a 25-hour journey with some tickets costing under €30 – not bad for a trip way up north into the Russian Arctic.

The cheapest fares quoted here are for the **communal open carriages** where everyone gets a berth but not much privacy. This is third-class travel, cheap and cheerful at its best, though a long journey in a crowded communal carriage may leave you with frayed nerves. Each carriage in this class offers 54 bunks, most of them arranged in bays of four berths apiece. There has been talk of scrapping this **quintessentially Russian style of travel**, but such proposals have not been warmly received by budget-conscious Russian travellers who seem to rather enjoy the convivial mood on board these third-class carriages.

At stations along the route, passengers tumble out onto the platform in search of the roving babushki who sell everything from berries to beer. The third-class carriage was made for sharing. It is a place where food, drink and **life stories are shared with complete strangers**.

The traditional Russian long-distance train has an interior focus. That's true of all classes of travel, but it is especially the case with the communal carriages. Sightlines to the wider world beyond the train are limited. Russia is a country with too much landscape, and the train is thus a retreat from the scenery outside into an **inner sanctuary**. The question is whether the noise and bustle of third class is anathema to inner peace.

Third-class open carriages are not seen these days **within the European Union**. Prior to the pandemic, they were included on trains from Riga to Moscow, St Petersburg and Minsk. But, as of autumn 2024, those services are suspended, as are the direct trains from Vilnius to Minsk and Moscow which also had communal sleeping cars. For some, these old-style communal carriages recalled the heyday of Soviet-era rail travel. Their days are surely numbered.

True devotees of the rails see the new generation of smart Russian trains as almost too comfortable. The **social magic** of the Russian train has traditionally been rooted, like so much of Russian life, in patience, endurance and discomfort. A shared commitment to those values bred solidarity and conversation. These are virtues revealed at their best in the lower travel classes, and nicely exemplified in Dostoyevsky's 'idiot' protagonist as he made his way back to Russia from a Swiss asylum in a **third-class carriage**.

Route 31: Baltic adventure

Cities: ★★ Culture: ★ History: ★★ Scenery: ★
Countries covered: Germany (DE), Poland (PL)
Journey time: 17 hrs 50 mins | Distance: 1,178 km | Map: www.ebrweb.eu/18map31

Let's go in search of the **red brick trail**. This route, first introduced into *Europe by Rail* in 2022, links a number of cities that draw on a common architectural tradition, often known by the German name *Backsteingotik* (brick Gothic architecture). This style was intimately associated with the **Hanseatic League** – a confederation of ports and other cities that in the 15th century dominated seaborne trade and commerce across the entire Baltic region and more widely. From the Dutch coast to western Russia, the *Hanse* lowered barriers to trade and advanced the mutual prosperity of its members. It was an enormously successful northern European trading alliance, one which established enclaves even in ports which were not nominally *Hanse* affiliates. In London for example there was a tightly regulated *Hanse* zone, effectively a tariff-free port, on the north bank of the Thames, recalled to this day in a riverside thoroughfare called Hanseatic Walk.

Hanseatic wealth was evidenced in **showpiece representational buildings** such as town halls, merchants' houses and guildhalls. In their design and construction, many cities of the *Hanse* drew on shared architectural principles, in much the same way that many centuries later the representational buildings of another era – Europe's great railway termini – also drew on a shared understanding of design and aesthetics.

Many of the most celebrated examples of brick Gothic are found in towns close to Germany's Baltic coast – and more widely across the Baltic region in places touched by the Hanseatic League.

This journey broadly follows the Baltic shore of northern Germany and northern Poland, escorting us from **Hamburg to Gdańsk** and Malbork, from where it's just a short ride south to **Warsaw**. This route thus presents a credible alternative to the much faster option from Hamburg via Berlin to Warsaw (following **Route 33** and **Route 36** in this book).

The appeal of the **Baltic journey** described here resides not merely in the superb townscapes; there's some fabulous beaches and wonderful green landscapes, the latter often at their most appealing during spring when the apple blossom is at its best.

Itinerary suggestions

There are many changes of train in the first half of this route. We are sticking mainly to lesser rail routes. But there are opportunities to cut corners by using express services here and there. At the very least, we suggest overnight stops in **Stralsund, Szczecin** and **Gdańsk**, but you could easily extend this journey to a week. If beaches are your thing, then you may want to build in stops at Kühlungsborn (near Bad Doberan), the German part of the island of Usedom or at **Sopot** in Poland.

This is a journey with a particularly fine range of off-route **detours and diversions**, and these give huge scope for an extended holiday shaped around this route. One book to take along for the ride is Paul Scraton's *Ghosts on the Shore: Travels along Germany's Baltic Coast* (published by Influx Press in 2017).

It is perfectly possible to follow the first part of this route from Hamburg to Stralsund in a day, stopping off for just over an hour in **Lübeck** and then having a three-hour afternoon stop in Bad Doberan to visit the Minster and ride the steam railway to the coast and back. With those stops, allow nine hours from Hamburg to Stralsund via this route. If you skip Lübeck and travel directly via Schwerin and Wismar to Bad Doberan, you'll trim a couple of hours off the overall journey time.

We'll be seeing brick Gothic buildings aplenty on this route, many of them dating from the heyday of the Hanseatic League. Brick as a basic building material is truly a feature of **Baltic Europe**. There are few natural sources of granite, limestone or sandstone in the lowlands around the southern and eastern rims of the Baltic. So it was entirely natural that builders turned to the one resource which they did have to hand, namely clay, to create bricks.

Leaving Hamburg

The same applied in **Hamburg**, the starting point of this route. Before you leave, take a peek at Hamburg's very evocative **Speicherstadt district** (on the north bank of the Elbe about a 20-min walk south-west of the Hauptbahnhof). In the mid-1880s, this huge new area of warehouses was constructed to serve the port of Hamburg. The entire complex was built in brick with Gothic affectations. This dash of Wilhelmine nationalism invited comparison between the glorious days of Hanseatic trade and the economic muscle of a newly united Germany. **Kaiser Wilhelm** himself came to Hamburg in October 1888 to lay the foundation stone for a bridge linking the new warehousing area with the city. Speaking to the assembled merchants, he remarked: "You are the ones who spread our ideas and values to the wider world; for this the fatherland owes you a special debt of gratitude." More than 300 years after the heyday of the Hanseatic League, brick Gothic was revived to become part of a German narrative.

Hamburg (see p241) is a city shaped by its history at an important North Sea port. The destiny of Lübeck, just 65 kilometres away to the north-east, has also been forged by the sea, but here the **maritime connections** are Baltic. It's just a short ride on a fast regional train from Hamburg to Lübeck, the latter part of the journey following the River Trave downstream.

Lübeck

Lübeck's 12th-century **Altstadt** (Old Town), on a moated island in the River Trave just a 10-min walk east of the main station (Hauptbahnhof), has been beautifully restored. Between the station and the Altstadt is Lübeck's

emblematic, twin-towered 15th-century **Holstentor**. It's a superb example of the brick Gothic style which secured for the Hanseatic city a proud place on UNESCO's World Heritage List. More generally the Lübeck townscape gives the chance to understand more about the *Hanse*, which relied on the close juxtaposition of mercantile wealth and artisans. So explore the alleys (locally called *Gänge*) behind the smart merchants' houses to access secluded courtyards where once there would have been many busy workshops. These days those courtyards often house cafés. Throughout this route, be it in Lübeck or Gdańsk or somewhere in between, you'll be struck how the art of modern urban living benefits enormously from the legacy of Hanseatic city planning.

Get your bearings by taking the lift up the fifty-metre spire of the **Gothic Petrikirche**; from the observation platform you'll see the Baltic Sea on a clear day. The Marktplatz is dominated by the striking mediaeval Rathaus, typical of Lübeck's affection for alternating red unglazed and black glazed bricks, a trick later copied by the Dutch. Opposite the east wing is **Café Niederegger**, Breite Str. 89, renowned for displays of marzipan (the town's speciality and produced since the Middle Ages).

Connections from Lübeck
There are two lovely rural railways which track north from Lübeck, one leading through the gentle Holstein hills to **Eutin** and **Kiel** and the other leading eventually to the island of Fehmarn, linked to the mainland by a bridge. On **Fehmarn** trains terminate at Puttgarden, whence a modern car ferry runs over the Fehmarn Strait to Rødby on the Danish island of Lolland. This was the route taken until late 2019 by trains which were shunted onto the ferry to reach Denmark. These days the Hamburg to Copenhagen services avoid the ferry and run via Odense (see also **Route 25** in this book). From about 2030, the route via Fehmarn will again be back in favour with the opening of a rail tunnel under the Fehmarn Strait.

East along to the Baltic coast
Leaving Lübeck, the railway loops round the south of the city and almost immediately crosses the River Wakenitz, which until October 1990 marked the

ROUTE 31: BALTIC ADVENTURE | 291

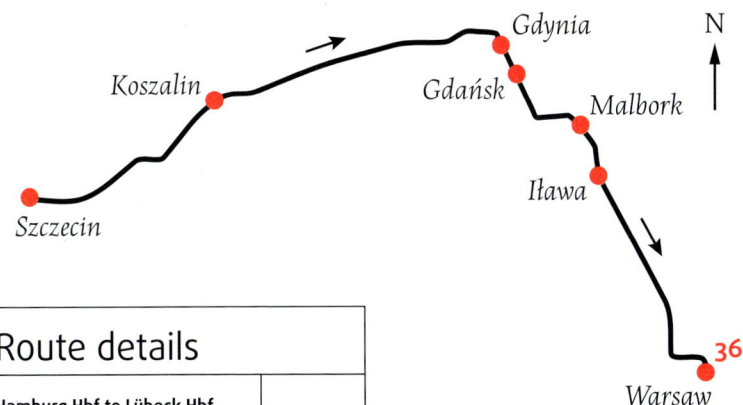

Route details

Hamburg Hbf to Lübeck Hbf

Frequency	Journey time	Notes
2 per hr	0h40–0h50	

Lübeck Hbf to Bad Doberan

Frequency	Journey time	Notes
Hourly	2h30	A

Bad Doberan to Stralsund Hbf

Frequency	Journey time	Notes
Every 2 hrs	1h30	B

Stralsund Hbf to Świnoujście Centrum

Frequency	Journey time	Notes
Hourly	2h20–2h40	C F

Świnoujście to Szczecin Główny

Frequency	Journey time	Notes
Every 1–2 hrs	1h30–2h	F

Szczecin Główny to Gdańsk Główny

Frequency	Journey time	Notes
5 per day	5h–5h20	

Gdańsk Główny to Malbork

Frequency	Journey time	Notes
1–2 per hr	0h30–0h50	

Malbork to Warsaw Centralna

Frequency	Journey time	Notes
Every 1–2 hrs	2h10–3h	

Notes

If you want to skip the early part of this route, you can travel directly from Hamburg to Stralsund, picking up the onward journey there. Fast ICE or IC trains leave Hamburg every two hours, taking about 2 hrs 50 mins for the journey to Stralsund.

A – This journey requires a change of train at Bad Kleinen and in Wismar. This may sound complicated, but these are well-timed connections where the trains usually wait for each other.
B – A change of train is required at Rostock Hbf.
C – A change of train is necessary at Züssow.
F – Allow one hour to transfer from Świnoujście Centrum to Świnoujście station. The ferry between the two stations crosses the River Świna, runs frequently and is free for foot passengers.

border between the two German states and thus the line popularly known as the **Iron Curtain**. The railway runs east through a sparsely settled landscape and with an easy change of trains in Bad Kleinen we reach **Wismar**, another ancient Hanseatic city but a place with far more Swedish influence than Lübeck. If you have an hour to spare, do take a look at the wonderful cobbled market square, just 7 mins on foot from the station. From Wismar it's a delightful ride north to Bad Doberan which definitely warrants a stop.

Bad Doberan happens to boast one of the very finest brick Gothic churches that we'll pass on this journey, so you should definitely make time to visit the Doberaner Münster (as the church is called). So much of the brick Gothic architecture is secular in character, but the Minster at Bad Doberan is a lovely ecclesiastical example.

For those interested in rail travel, Bad Doberan has one of Germany's most photographed branch lines. A **narrow-gauge steam railway**, affectionately known as the Molli, runs from Bad Doberan to the nearby seaside resorts of **Heiligendamm** and **Kühlungsborn**. The ride to the coast starts with the train running through the streets of Bad Doberan. The trip from Bad Doberan to the end of the line and back takes under two hours and the return fare is €16. It's worth it. This is also your first chance to dip your toe in the Baltic.

Back in Bad Doberan, we pick up our main route and continue east, changing trains in **Rostock** to reach Stralsund, a perfect place to stop off for a day or two.

Stralsund

Emerging from Stralsund's Hauptbahnhof, there's little to suggest that this coastal town is very special. It's a **pleasant walk** over the causeway into the compact town centre, where you'll find some of the finest examples of brick Gothic architecture in what was once a key node in the affairs of the Hanse. Don't miss the **Rathaus** (town hall) on the Old Market square. Hemmed in as it is by islands (see box on p293), Stralsund is very protected from the open sea. Enjoy a wander along the quaysides and adjacent streets where you find fish restaurants and cafés aplenty. The **Ozeaneum** on the seafront invites visitors to learn about the sea and marine ecosystems (www.ozeaneum.de).

ARRIVAL, INFORMATION, ACCOMMODATION

≋ Stralsund Hbf is a 15-min walk west of the city centre (or use bus 1 or 4). ℹ Tourist office: next to the town hall on Alter Markt (www.stralsundtourismus.de).

⛵ Right in Stralsund's harbour area and with views on sailing boats and yachts, the owner-run **Hotel Kontorhaus**, Am Querkanal 1, ☎ 03831 28 98 00 (www.hotel-kontorhaus-stralsund.de) is a good overnight option close to the main waterfront sites and a plethora of cafés and restaurants. Or try the welcoming **Altstadthotel Peiss**, Tribseer Straße 15, ☎ 03831 30 35 80 (www.altstadt-hotel-peiss.de), located between the station and the city centre, which is good value for money.

Island excursions from Stralsund

Stralsund is a good base for a couple of days (or more). During the summer season, it's easy to make a day trip by boat to the nearby **Hiddensee**. This car-free island is a haven of quiet, and offers delightful, easy walking. For those less inclined to walk there is a useful electric bus which runs up the island's only road from Neuendorf via Vitte and Kloster to Grieben. A good option is to travel out **by boat** to Neuendorf (1hr 40mins from Stralsund), returning from Kloster (2hrs 40 mins to Stralsund). Find boat times on www.reederei-hiddensee.de and the island bus timetable on www.seebad-hiddensee.de. A day-return ticket from Stralsund to any Hiddensee port is €26 (as of late 2024).

The 'must-do' excursion from Stralsund for anyone with an interest in railways is a day trip to the **island of Rügen** which is linked to the mainland at Stralsund by both a causeway (carrying a road and a railway) and a dramatic modern cable-stayed bridge that carries a new road to the island which is in the premier league of German holiday destinations. But Rügen is sufficiently large that it's usually possible to find peace and seclusion. The finest scenery is in the south-east corner, which is well served by public transport with a good network of boat and bus services.

The real gem though is the **narrow-gauge steam railway** which runs all year from Göhren to Putbus, extending in summer to the south coast at Lauterbach. It's a glorious journey through meadows and mature deciduous woodland (including some very fine stands of beech), beautiful at any time of year but we especially love this route in winter snow. From Stralsund, there's an hourly rail connection to Putbus (changing at Bergen auf Rügen), where you connect with the steam route which is called the **Rügensche Bäderbahn** or, more colloquially, *Rasender Roland*. A one-day rover ticket (€25) allows you to hop on and off steam trains at will.

Do visit **Sellin** with its celebrated white pier (with an excellent restaurant), consider taking the boat from Lauterbach around the south coast to Baabe and perhaps end the day with dinner in stylish **Binz**, from where there's an hourly main-line train back to Stralsund.

Connections from Stralsund

Regular regional trains run south to **Berlin**, augmented by four daily ICEs, of which one normally runs right through to Munich. There is a pleasant local rail route running south from Stralsund to Neustrelitz. Another branch line runs north-west to Barth, a pleasant market town with good onward bus connections to the Darss peninsula. Hourly trains run north from Stralsund over the causeway to **Rügen** (read more on Rügen in the box above).

The port of Sassnitz on Rügen, just 55 mins by train from Stralsund, is a useful stepping stone to other Baltic destinations. From Sassnitz the seasonal (Apr-Oct inclusive) *Skane Jet* catamaran speeds over to **Trelleborg in Sweden** in just 2hrs 15mins (fares and timings on www.frs-baltic.com). In Trelleborg, there are good onward train connections to Malmö where you can connect onto **Route 25** to Stockholm or **Route 27** to Oslo and Bergen. Sassnitz also offers a year-round ferry link with the Danish island of **Bornholm**, running daily in high season and twice weekly in low season (see www.bornholmslinjen.de).

East into Poland

If you are in a rush, it's possible to get from Stralsund to Gdańsk in a day (8 hrs travel, with changes of train in Pasewalk and Szczecin). But there is a far better option, routing via the **Baltic island of Usedom**. It adds three hours or more to the overall travel time, but if you stop off here and there along the way, this Usedom routing inevitably means breaking the journey overnight in Szczecin or, if you don't mind a late arrival in Gdańsk, taking the evening train from Szczecin to Gdańsk.

The first place of any size is **Greifswald**, a pleasant university town with a modest show of brick Gothic. It's a good spot for an hour or two, before moving on. From Greifswald, it's a short hop to **Züssow**, where you'll change onto the branch railway which runs to Świnoujście in Poland. This 90-minute journey from Züssow is extraordinary. At Wolgast, the line crosses on a bridge over the Peenestrom to reach the island of Usedom; the railway the runs east to the farthest extremity of the island which is Polish territory – a fragment of the country connected only by ferry to the rest of Poland. Usedom (called Uznam in Polish) is thus a remarkable geographical oddity: a small island bisected by an international border.

You can see the darker side of Usedom history at **Peenemünde** (on a branch line, served by hourly trains from Zinnowitz), where there's a historical museum on the site of the **Nazi-era rocket research station**, once the largest armaments centre in Europe. It's a sharp contrast to Usedom's stylish beach culture which finds its fullest expression in Heringsdorf and Ahlbeck. You don't see a lot from the train, so it's worth stopping off at either or both resorts.

Two kilometres before the end of the line, the Usedom railway crosses the **German-Polish border**, and the train runs into the minimal **Świnoujście** Central station, from where you'll need to walk east down to the slipway for the ferry over the River Świna to the Polish town's second and much larger railway station for the onward journey through lovely countryside to Szczecin. Like Świnoujście, Szczecin was until 1945 German territory.

Szczecin

Szczecin is certainly a tongue-twister, as much of a challenge for outsiders as understanding the convoluted history of the city. Once part of **Swedish Pomerania**, the city was ceded to Prussia in 1720. Over the ensuing two centuries, the city – called Stettin in German – developed into Germany's premier **Baltic port**. It was a city that built ships, and the busy quays and docks of Stettin sustained Berlin. Cheap freight rates on the railways linking Pomerania with Berlin meant that Stettin merchants had the edge over their rivals in Hamburg when it came to supplying the German capital.

Berliners came by train to **Stettin** to board the steamers that took them to Baltic resorts on the islands of Usedom and Rügen. In 1945, the city was ceded to Poland, and these days no-one could be in any doubt as to Szczecin's Polish credentials. Szczecin is very much more interesting than its industrial suburbs might suggest. Its *Hanse* history is there, but less

Malbork Castle

Malbork Castle (*zamek w Malborku* in Polish) is **Europe's largest brick castle** and a fine example of the brick Gothic architecture of the Baltic region. The castle is widely acclaimed for its antiquity with many writers commending it as the greatest work of mediaeval secular architecture in Europe, and some commenting that its completeness attests to the quality of 14th-century craftsmanship.

Such plaudits gloss over the fact that 200 years ago Malbork Castle was in a woeful state of disrepair; its reconstruction in the 19th century was an important assertion of **Prussian power** in the region. By recalling the alleged mediaeval roots of Germanic power in these eastern territories, Prussia was effectively legitimising its annexation of the Malbork region towards the end of the previous century. After the unification of Germany in 1871, the castle at Malbork was used to give credence not merely to Prussian authority and heritage in the east, but to wider German rights in these territories. Malbork was thus a key staging post in the *Kulturkampf* (culture war) between Germany and its Slavic neighbours to the east.

Malbork Castle was inscribed in 1997 on **UNESCO's World Heritage List**. Poland of course advanced the nomination, walking a political tightrope along the way. Poland identified Malbork's importance "as a sign of the tendency to treat history and its monuments as instruments in the service of political ideologies." The history of this castle reveals sanctity, great violence and a big dose of politics. Such **layers of meaning** could never be discerned in a quick glimpse of the castle from the train. So it's worth taking time to explore. Open daily to the public, but closes mid-afternoon in winter, so a morning visit works best. Allow three hours. The castle is a ten-minute walk from the station.

---

evident than in Stralsund or Gdańsk. The permanent **historical exhibition** in the *Ratusz Staromiejski w Szczecinie* (Szczecin Old Town Hall) recounts very well how German Stettin morphed into Polish Szczecin.

Arrival, information, accommodation

⇌ Szczecin Głowny, a 12-min walk south of the centre. Also of interest is the area about 1 km north-east of the station. 🛈 Tourist office: 20 Żołnierza Polskiego square (www.visitszczecin.eu).

🛏 We can heartily recommend the **Hotel Focus**, ul. Małopolska 23, ☎ 91 433 05 00 (www.focushotels.pl). It is perfectly positioned near the Odra waterfront just a stone's throw from the Maritime Academy and also has an excellent restaurant, with good food at modest prices. Well placed in the Old Town close to the Pomeranian Dukes' Castle is the **Hotel Zamek Centrum**, ul. Panieńska 15, ☎ 091 85 22 777 (www.hotelzamek.biz).

Szczecin connections

As a major rail hub, Szczecin has direct train services to cities right across Poland, including regular services to **Poznań** and Warsaw, both on **Route 36**. There are daytime and night sleeper services to Kraków and Przemyśl, the latter in south-east Poland close to the Ukrainian border (also on Route 36).

Trains to **Berlin** depart every two to three hours, some direct but otherwise with a quick change of train at Angermünde. For devotees of slow trains, there is a fine cross-country route which meanders west through forested western Pomerania and Mecklenburg, taking five hours to reach Lübeck (seven departures each day).

To Gdańsk and beyond

After so much time on lesser routes, there's now the chance to take a big leap east using a faster service from **Szczecin to Gdańsk**. It's a pleasant ride through rolling countryside that – frustratingly for some travellers – never actually touches the coast until the very final section. You arrive into Gdańsk from the north, stopping at the industrial port of **Gdynia** and the seaside resort of **Sopot** along the way.

It was in this part of Poland that *Solidarność* (Solidarity) was born. It was founded at the Lenin shipyards in Gdynia and from that base went to shape Polish resistance to the Warsaw government in the 1980s. The dramatic story of this political movement is told at the **European Solidarity Centre in Gdańsk** (ecs.gda.pl); it's a first-rate museum. Otherwise your time in Gdańsk will probably mainly be spent exploring the city centre district called **Główne Miasto** (Main Town), which is the heart of the old *Hanse* quarter. It's every bit as fine as that in Lübeck.

Arrival, information, accommodation

≠ The main railway station is Gdańsk Główny, a 10-min walk east of the Glowne Miasto.
🛈 Tourist office: ul. Długi Targ 28/29 (www.visitgdansk.com).

🛌 Well placed close to the landmark Crane and the historic part of Gdansk is the comfortable **Hanza Hotel**, ul. Tokarska 6, ☎ 058 305-34 27 927 (www.hotelhanza.pl). Equally well placed close to the yacht marina on the other side of the river is the boutique **Hotel Gdańsk**, ul. Szafarnia 9, ☎ 058 30 01 717 (www.hotelgdansk.com.pl). The **Fama Residence**, Długa 81-83, ☎ 058 506 56 86 (www.famagdansk.pl) is great value for money and very convenient for both the station and city centre.

Connections from Gdańsk

Gdańsk is the jumping-off point for rail trips east into the **Mazurian lake district** with direct trains to **Ełk**. But rail links to the eastern Baltic are difficult. The direct daytime train from Gdańsk to the Russian exclave city of Kaliningrad was withdrawn some years ago, and shows no sign of returning. There is however a useful direct overnight bus to **Vilnius** in Lithuania (which avoids traversing Russian territory). It's run by Polish operator Sindbad and leaves Gdańsk at 19.00 every evening (www.sindbad.pl). Another useful link is the direct overnight ferry from Gdańsk to **Nynäshamn** in Sweden, from where it's just about 80 minutes to Stockholm by train. There you can connect into **Route 25, 26** and **29**.

Heading south from Gdańsk on the towards Warsaw, you have one of those magic moments which can define any European train trip. A glimpse of the monastery of Melk from the train heading towards Vienna (**Route 39**) or the sight of the great basilica at Esztergom as the Budapest-bound train crosses from Slovakia into Hungary (**Route 33**) are but two. But even these two remarkable views are as nothing compared with the view to the south as the train from Gdańsk crosses the River Nogat at Malbork (see box on p295).

Let that image of Malbork linger with you as the train dashes south towards Mazovia and the Polish capital (see p335) where you can connect onto **Route 36**, following it west to Berlin or south to Kraków and on to Lviv.

Sidetracks: Baltic trains

We would love to restore more eastern Baltic routes to *Europe by Rail*. It is not easy. Travelling through Lithuania, Latvia and Estonia, we often hear locals explaining away their abysmal rail services, with particularly poor cross-border links, as a **legacy of Soviet times**. "All lines led to Moscow, and only to Moscow," is a common phrase. That explanation, however, is all too easy.

A key factor in the Baltic countries has been **public attitudes towards the railway**. Train travel was so central a part of the Soviet experience, and remains so important in Russia today, that the post-independence political and cultural elites in the Baltic States turned their backs on the railway in much the same way that anything Russian fell into disfavour. In the new political piety, all eyes look west. That psychological chasm between the Baltic States and Russia was set in stone with Russia's invasion of Ukraine in early 2022.

A new breed of home-grown entrepreneurs catered for the car-less by developing **long-distance bus services**. You'll find some of the most luxurious coaches in Europe in use on routes between major cities in the Baltic region.

Cast back to 1989, and the *Chaika Express* ran from Tallinn via Riga to Vilnius. From Vilnius there were also **direct trains to Warsaw and Berlin**. In the post-independence era of the 1990s, when car ownership in the Baltic States rocketed, the region's railways were left to rot. Many routes closed, and elsewhere the **lack of investment** in infrastructure meant that line speeds were so reduced that buses easily outpaced trains – so giving weight to the view that trains were an outdated relic of the Soviet period.

Various **European Union initiatives** are tempting Lithuanians, Latvians and Estonians back onto the train. The key project here is **Rail Baltica**, an ambitious plan to build a new passenger railway from Warsaw to Tallinn, serving cities in Lithuania and Latvia along the way. This new railway is being built to the standard European gauge (1,435 mm, as opposed to the wider Russian gauge), a decision driven more by politics than by engineering considerations. Having the same width tracks as most other EU countries is of great symbolic importance in the Baltic region.

Rail Baltica's first achievement was the **extension of standard-gauge tracks from Poland** over the border into Lithuania. This line reached Kaunas in 2015, and a special train carried EU officials and the media from Poland to Kaunas. Throughout 2024, there is now a once-daily Intercity (called the *Hańcza*) from Kraków via Warsaw and Białystok to Mockava (just on the Lithuanian side of the border), where there is an easy cross-platform change onto a modern Lithuanian train for the onward journey to Kaunas and Vilnius. Such a minimal service hardly justifies the huge investment in infrastructure. It is, however, a small step in realising the *Rail Baltica* dream. In 2024, another welcome innovation is a daily train from Vilnius to Riga and back.

Advocates of *Rail Baltica* suggest that, when a standard-gauge railway line runs right through to Tallinn, fast daytime trains might dash the 970 kilometres from Warsaw to the Estonian capital in under six hours. Now that would give the operators of luxury coaches a real run for their money.

CENTRAL AND EASTERN EUROPE
An introduction

Of the eight regional subdivisions in this 18th edition of *Europe by Rail*, it is that devoted to central and eastern Europe which has been the most challenging. Over successive editions of the book, we extended coverage east to include three routes to Ukraine, plus new journeys to Belarus and Russia. With a war now taking place in Ukraine, we know things have to change. The pandemic led to the **withdrawal of rail services** over the European Union's eastern borders. Now, with a fully fledged war, these services won't resume for some time. We have removed the sole remaining Russian route. Our Belarusian coverage is gone, as have two of the three journeys into Ukraine which featured in earlier editions of the book. One remains, namely a **journey to Lviv** in the far west of the country and in an area which thus far has mercifully been less targeted by Russian forces. That doesn't mean you should jump on a train to Lviv tomorrow.

While the territories in the former Soviet Union have lost coverage, other regions have been beneficiaries. We now have far better coverage of **Slovakia** and Romania, with new routes through the Tatra region to Košice and our first ever journey to the **Black Sea coast** of Romania. On the downside, the lack of trains across Serbia's borders has meant the loss of one route.

A matter of geography

The very use of terms like central Europe and eastern Europe encourages us to reflect on how geographical horizons change through time. In the heyday of the **Austro-Hungarian Empire**, educated Europeans shared some tacit understanding about where central Europe was. True, they may have squabbled over where its boundaries lay. In the salons of Vienna those inclined to geographical debate questioned frontiers and languages: "Should we include Lusatia and Lodomeria? And what about Podlachia and the Posavina? Are they part of central Europe?"

The Habsburg flame was snuffed over a century ago, and with it died a peculiarly central European zeitgeist. A generation later, in the wake of the Second World War, Europe was split asunder, rent in two by the **Iron Curtain**. A more binary view of Europe gained ascendancy: there was western Europe and eastern Europe. That was the geopolitical reality of the Cold War years. The **quiet revolutions of 1989** and the years thereafter allowed for the re-emergence of central Europe, redeeming a number of countries from the eastern Europe label. They included Czechoslovakia (as it was until 1993), Hungary, Slovenia and other parts of fragmenting Yugoslavia, and a swathe of places with former Habsburg connections. In Chernivtsi (Чернівці) and Trieste there was a sudden recognition of shared history and heritage. ∎

Route 32: Bohemian byways

CITIES: ★★ CULTURE: ★★ HISTORY: ★★★ SCENERY: ★★
COUNTRIES COVERED: GERMANY (DE), CZECH REPUBLIC (CZ)
JOURNEY TIME: 9 HRS 30 MINS | DISTANCE: 560 KM | MAP: WWW.EBRWEB.EU/18MAP32

This route represents our first serious encounter with Central Europe, a geographical notion which has enjoyed a renaissance in recent years. When Europe was divided by the Iron Curtain, during those decades when the continent was so markedly fractured into East and West, there was no space in our imagination for Central Europe. But 'twas not always so: from the mediaeval period until shortly after the demise of the Habsburg Empire in the last century, there was always a region with distinctive geography, culture and traditions which was unmistakably *Mitteleuropa*.

In this journey from **Nuremberg to Prague** we take in spa towns and synagogues, make time for coffee and cake, and explore some deeply rural areas of **Bohemia** – the latter another of those cartographic entities which have always played both real and imaginary roles in the lives of Europeans. Nuremberg is a good spot to embark on our journey, as it is a city which for centuries strongly played the *Mitteleuropa* card (although American occupation after 1945 very firmly 'pulled' Nuremberg westwards). The city has always taken geography seriously; it was here in Nuremberg in the 15th century that **Martin Behaim** created the first globe (his Erdapfel, literally 'earth apple'). Early modern cartographers from the city always placed Nuremburg in the very middle of Central Europe, much to the annoyance of their rivals in Prague and Budapest. This route is your chance to take the pulse of one of Europe's most elusive regions.

ITINERARY NOTES
Even if the social rhythm of spa life has no appeal, you should definitely think of stopping off for a night in either Mariánské Lázně or Karlovy Vary – perhaps even in both as the two towns are very different from each other. The **finest stretches** of the train journey are the section over the German-Czech border and the short hop from Mariánské Lázně to Karlovy Vary.

From Bavaria to Bohemia

The rail journey through the hills east from **Nuremberg** (see p144 for more on the city) into the Czech Republic is superb. The train follows the Pegnitz Valley which narrows as the railway heads towards the low range of hills known as the **Fränkische Alb**. Modest though these 'alps' may be, one tunnel on another railway through the hills – used by trains to Cheb and Bayreuth – is boldly called the Gotthard tunnel, inviting comparison with its Swiss counterpart. Cutting through the valleys of the Naab and the Regen, the railway then climbs up through the **Bayerischer Wald** (Bavarian

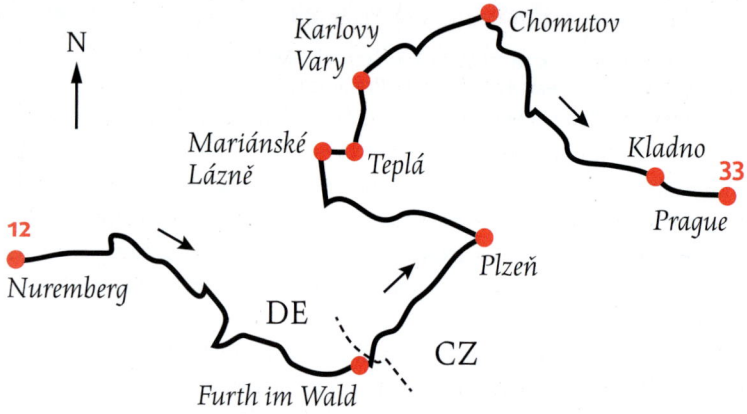

Route details

Nuremberg Hbf to Furth im Wald

Frequency	Journey time	Notes
Hourly	1h55–2h25	A

Furth im Wald to Plzeň hlavní

Frequency	Journey time	Notes
Every 2 hrs	1h10	

Plzeň hlavní to Mariánské Lázně

Frequency	Journey time	Notes
Hourly	1h–1h10	

Mariánské Lázně to Karlovy Vary

Frequency	Journey time	Notes
8 per day	1h15	

Karlovy Vary to Chomutov

Frequency	Journey time	Notes
Every 1–2 hrs	0h50–1h05	

Route details (cont.)

Chomutov to Prague Masarykovo

Frequency	Journey time	Notes
3–4 per day	2h45	C

Notes

A – On most journeys, a change of train is necessary at Schwandorf.

C – On our recommended route from Chomutov to Prague, a change of train is required at Lužná u Rakovníka. There is an alternative route from Chomutov to Prague via Ústi. Trains on this route run every two hours, taking 2 hrs 30 mins. These trains run direct from Chomutov to Prague's main station (hl.n.).

Forest) to reach the Czech border at Furth im Wald. Very few trains run right through. Travellers from Nuremberg normally need to change trains in Schwandorf. Once **over the border**, the train passes through the enigmatically named community of Babylon and then descends steeply towards **Domažlice**, the first place of any size in the Czech Republic. This is Chod country. The Chods were an early version of border guards. They made a decent living by keeping an eye on the borderlands where Bohemia runs up against Bavaria. Imagine a militia armed with bagpipes which kept Bavarian aspiration in check and so secured the independence of Domažlice.

The small towns of south-west Bohemia, many of them just a stone's throw from the border with Bavaria, are a part of Europe that remains well off most tourist trails. Domažlice, a one-time stronghold of **Hussite reformers**, is well worth visiting in its own right, but is also an excellent base for exploring this area (see the box below). The town's nicely elongated main square, lined by arcades, is a place to linger and watch life go by. **Domažlice's museum**, located in the renovated castle, tells the story of the region, explaining the history of the local Chod minority, and making much of a fine collection of bagpipes that ranges from the Magyar duda to the Swedish säckpipa.

Domažlice has two railway stations. The direct trains from Munich, Nuremberg and Prague all stop only at the main station, simply called Domažlice, 1 km east of the centre. Many local trains, including those from Furth im Wald, also serve Domažlice město, a small halt located 500 metres south of the main square.

From Domažlice, it's downhill all the way to **Plzeň**, where you might expect the most striking building to be a brewery. The name of the fourth largest Czech city (often rendered Pilsen in German and English) is synonymous with good beer. The distinctive **golden lager** known as pilsner (or often just pils) has been brewed in the city for about 140 years.

But there's more to Plzeň than beer. From the **main railway station** (hlavní nádraží), walk west over the river into the city centre. This road is called Americká, having previous been called Moskevská. You'll quickly reach the main north-south thoroughfare, which is called Klatovská. Gaze up beyond the tacky shop fronts and there are some remarkable embellishments to the peeling facades of the buildings that line **Klatovská**. For those who pause to look, there's everything from baroque to art nouveau.

Slow train through Bohemia

For devotees of slow trains, Bohemia is well served by a dense network of **rural railway lines**. Some services are still operated by antiquated red railcars which trundle through the forests stopping off here and there at tiny wayside halts. **Domažlice** is a good base for exploring such rail routes. Just a short hop from Domažlice is **Horšovský Týn**, the most attractive small town in the region abutting the border with Bavaria (with a fine sloping main square). Domažlice to Horšovský Týn takes less than an hour, with a change of train at Poběžovice.

If you fancy a **longer rural excursion** and do not mind missing Plzeň, you can cut the corner on Route 32 and travel north on characterful minor railways through Bor to Mariánské Lázně. These lesser rail routes in Bohemia recall an era of rail travel which has long disappeared in western Europe. It is a region to which we return time and time again and, so dense is the rail network, we rarely cover the same ground twice. If, like us, you find yourself addicted to **Bohemian branch lines**, then it's worth exploring the specialist website at www.spravazeleznic.cz where you'll find excellent Czech timetables to download, along with a network map.

But one building outshines any other in Plzeň. It is one of the most impressive pieces of sacred architecture anywhere in Europe: the **Great Synagogue**. It is majestic! In terms of size, it is surpassed in Europe only by the Dohány Synagogue in Budapest. There are too few surviving synagogues in the cities of Central Europe. And even fewer which can match Plzeň's Great Synagogue for its artistry. Pause in the choir loft and gaze over to the **Aron Kodesh** – the Holy Ark in which the Torah scrolls are traditionally kept. It looks peculiarly Indian in style. Touch the cantor's platform which is carved from the finest mahogany. Raise your eyes aloft to the Heavens and ponder the golden stars set in a dome of **celestial blue**.

More's the pity that it's all too rare these days that the Great Synagogue in Plzeň echoes to the chanting of the psalms. One hundred years ago, this was one of the largest *kehillot* in central Europe. During the 19th century, Plzeň's growing Jewish population had consistently outgrown smaller synagogues. The Great Synagogue was triumphantly opened in 1892, its Moorish Revival style eliciting much praise from local citizens of all religious persuasions.

That the building survived the onslaughts of **Nazi Germany** is remarkable. But it emerged from the war in bad shape, and has benefited in recent years from extensive renovation. Now it once again stands proud on the city's principal thoroughfare as a witness to the civic influence and the economic power once wielded by the city's Jewish community.

Spa diversions

Our journey from Nuremberg has thus far been entirely on secondary rail routes, none of them electrified. That changes in Plzeň as we join a main line which runs to the north-west corner of Bohemia, home to some outstanding examples of **European spa culture**. All have their origins in the Austro-Hungarian spa tradition, and all were once favoured holiday destinations for Europe's royalty. These are not places for Bohemian excess. But colonic irrigation is not mandatory, and these three towns are just wonderful places to hole up and relax for a day or two.

Travelling north-west on the main railway from Plzeň, the line follows the beautiful winding **Mže Valley** to Planá – where the station is signed as Planá u Mariánských Lázní. How misleading! This is not Mariánské Lázně – that's another ten minutes up the line.

Mariánské Lázně has a feast of *belle époque* decadence, a lovely Russian Orthodox church and the town is surrounded by some beautiful parks and woodland. There is still all the *fin de siècle* charm of old Marienbad, the hideaway in the hills which once attracted monarchs from across Europe. If you are minded to stay overnight, try the central and comfortable Villa Patriot, Dusíkova 62, ☎ 354 673 143 (www.villa-patriot.cz) which also has a good restaurant.

A TRIO OF SPA TOWNS

The three most famous spa towns of Bohemia, from the smallest to the largest, are (with their old German-language names in brackets): Františkovy Lázně (Franzensbad), Mariánské Lázně (Marienbad) and Karlovy Vary (Karlsbad). Each has its own charm.

Visiting **Františkovy Lázně** means deviating from the route we describe here. It's an easy day trip from either Mariánské Lázně or Karlovy Vary – about 90 minutes by train from either of those towns, in each case normally with a change of train at **Cheb** – where the retro atmosphere of the railway station will evoke a wave of nostalgic memories for travellers who experienced travel in Czechoslovakia in the 1970s and 1980s. Františkovy Lázně is a tiny picture-perfect community with the air of an outdoor sanatorium and a nice line in erotic sculptures. **Fertility treatments** are one of the town's specialisations and this gives Františkovy Lázně a more youthful air than the other spa towns mentioned here.

From Mariánské Lázně, it is an entertaining ride on a branch line to Karlovy Vary. These trains start at the main railway station (simply called Mariánské Lázně), but they also stop at Mariánské Lázně město station, which is much closer to the town centre. It's a **request stop**, so just stand on the platform and stick out your hand, as one might for a bus. The line climbs steeply up through forests to over 700 metres above sea level. It's a fine piece of Habsburg engineering. The stations ooze **faded Habsburg style**, their former German names eclipsed by Czech renderings. The highest station on the line, once Habakladrau, is now called Ovesné Kladruby. Prosau has morphed into Mrázov.

Once over the summit, away to the right of the railway are the imposing twin towers of the abbey church at **Teplá**. The line then runs down the Teplá Valley to Karlovy Vary – through richly varied forests of pine, sycamore, spruce, elm and birch.

The hills rise up steeply on either side of **Karlovy Vary** with the River Teplá running through the heart of the town. The therapeutic qualities of these waters have created a sanctuary which pulls visitors from far and wide. The town was (until the Russian invasion of Ukraine) particularly popular with Russian visitors. They follow a tradition extending back to **Peter the Great**, who first took the waters here in 1711.

In Karlovy Vary, very much larger than the other Bohemian spa towns, the real world intrudes on the pursuit of health and recuperation, and there's a bustle about the place, especially during the **annual film festival** which takes place in July each year. The Hotel Embassy, Nová Louka 21, ☎ 353 221 161 (www.embassy.cz), is extremely friendly and located right in the heart of the spa zone. The excursion up the funicular railway (called the 'Diana') to the viewing tower is a must in Karlovy Vary.

All three spa towns offer good-value hotels, often more geared to long-stay clients nursing their ailments than passing trade, but if space is available casual guests are accepted. Plan for **leisurely days** taking the waters, going for healthy walks, and enjoy afternoon tea and waltzes aplenty! If you really want to catch the spa atmosphere, head for Františkovy Lázně or Mariánské Lázně. If you're uncertain whether you can cope with such unalloyed commitment to healthy living, Karlovy Vary makes for a good compromise. At least there you can sup on something stronger than the spa waters. Try the **Jan Becher Museum** on TG Masaryka 57, which provides an interesting history of the locally produced **Becherovka** spirit, as well as ample opportunity to sample the product itself.

Karlovy Vary connections

With all those **Russian guests** having forsaken Karlovy Vary in 2022, the town's small airport is eerily quiet. It had only flights to and from Russia. The direct trains to Minsk and Moscow have also gone, but Karlovy Vary still has a range of connnections to cities across the Czech Republic. Fast trains run to Prague, just 3 hrs 20 mins away and there is a daily Pendolino service to Ostrava. There is a lovely route north from Karlovy Vary; it runs through the mountains via Johanngeorgenstadt to Zwickau in Saxony, from where it is a short hop east to **Dresden** to connect with **Route 37** to Poland and **Route 33** to either Budapest or Hamburg. Plenty of trains run from Karlovy Vary to Cheb, from where there are three local rail routes across the border into Germany.

From Karlovy Vary, you have a number of options for the onward journey to Prague. There are direct trains which run east to Ústí nad Labem and then follow the Elbe Valley upstream towards the Czech capital. A more interesting route is to cut off to the south at **Chomutov** and taking the old main line through Žatec and Kladno to Prague. The fast trains on this route were axed in 2008, but there are still local services. It's a fascinating journey, passing through a major area of **hop cultivation** (essential for the Czech beer industry). By contrast, you'll see some of the worst industrial dereliction anywhere in central Europe. Towns which were surely never beautiful in the Communist period have decayed even more under capitalism. It's a good reminder that market economics cut two ways. **Prague** (see p309), a city so full of creative energy, is just one face of the modern Czech Republic. The view from Kladno looks rather different.

Connections from Prague

In Prague you can connect with **Route 33** which runs north to Hamburg via Berlin or south to Budapest. Railjet trains run south to Vienna, most of these continuing beyond the Austrian capital to Graz in Styria. There is an especially nice route south from **Prague to Linz** in Austria. It runs via **České Budějovice**, where brewing has been a habit since the 13th century. The town created and still brews the original Budweiser (Budvar) beer. From České Budějovice, it is just a short hop to Český Krumlov, a sererely beautiful (but in mid-summer often busy) south Bohemian town which boasts one of the most-photographed castles in the Czech Republic.

Russian Railways offered direct services from Prague to Minsk and Moscow; they have been suspended since March 2020. There is a good choice of **night trains** with direct services leaving most evenings for Warsaw and Kraków and Zurich. There are direct overnight trains to Poprad (for the Tatra Mountains) and to Košice.

Route 33: Four capitals in a day

CITIES: ★★★ CULTURE: ★★ HISTORY: ★★★ SCENERY: ★
COUNTRIES COVERED: GERMANY (DE), CZECH REPUBLIC (CZ), SLOVAKIA (SK), HUNGARY (HU)
JOURNEY TIME: 13 HRS 45 MINS | DISTANCE: 1,291 KM | MAP: www.ebrweb.eu/18map33

The rail journey from **Hamburg to Budapest** can be completed in a long day. The only direct train between the two cities takes just under 14 hours for a journey of about 1,300 km. It really does take in four capital cities in a day. Travel all the way through if you will, but the great majority of travellers will stop off en route, usually at one or more of the following cities: Berlin, Dresden, Prague or Bratislava. On this journey from the banks of the **Elbe to the Danube**, there is a strong sense of swapping the cultural realm of northern Europe for that of *Mitteleuropa* (Central Europe).

TIMETABLE MATTERS

The **once-daily direct Eurocity** train from Hamburg to Slovakia and Hungary which inspires this route is partially suspended as we go to press with this 18th edition of *Europe by Rail*. It is currently running only between Berlin and Budapest. But fear not! It is likely to be reinstated along the full route from spring 2025, although no date has been confirmed. Throughout the entire route there are in any case regular daytime fast trains between major cities, so this is a perfect journey for making frequent stops along the way. There are also **night train options** for those wanting to sleep their way through central Europe. So a Nightjet leaves Hamburg each evening for Vienna (from where it's just a short hop next morning on to Bratislava or Budapest), and there's a Euronight train with comfortable sleeping cars from Berlin to Budapest.

The Hungaria

The direct train from Hamburg to Budapest is a Eurocity service called the *Hungaria*. Its section from Berlin to Budapest has been a mainstay of the timetables for over half a century; only in late 2015 was it extended to start from Hamburg. Cast back to the **Cold War days**, and the *Hungaria* carried East German families off for summer holidays in Hungary — where Lake Balaton was a favourite destination. It was also the train that transported government officials and party stalwarts carrying fraternal greetings between the Warsaw Pact capitals. The *Hungaria* was much favoured by spies too. In the 1980s, it still carried through carriages from Sweden to Yugoslavia, both non-aligned countries, and the train was a good spot for discreet exchanges of intelligence as it trundled through the central European countryside.

The Europe traversed by the *Hungaria* has been utterly transformed over the last 30 years. The **Iron Curtain** has gone and borders have melted. All four countries on this journey are part of the Schengen group of nations, meaning that it's normally possible to make the entire journey without any passport checks. COVID-19 led to the Schengen resolve being tested, as each country tweaked entry requirements with each new wave of the pandemic,

306 | CENTRAL AND EASTERN EUROPE

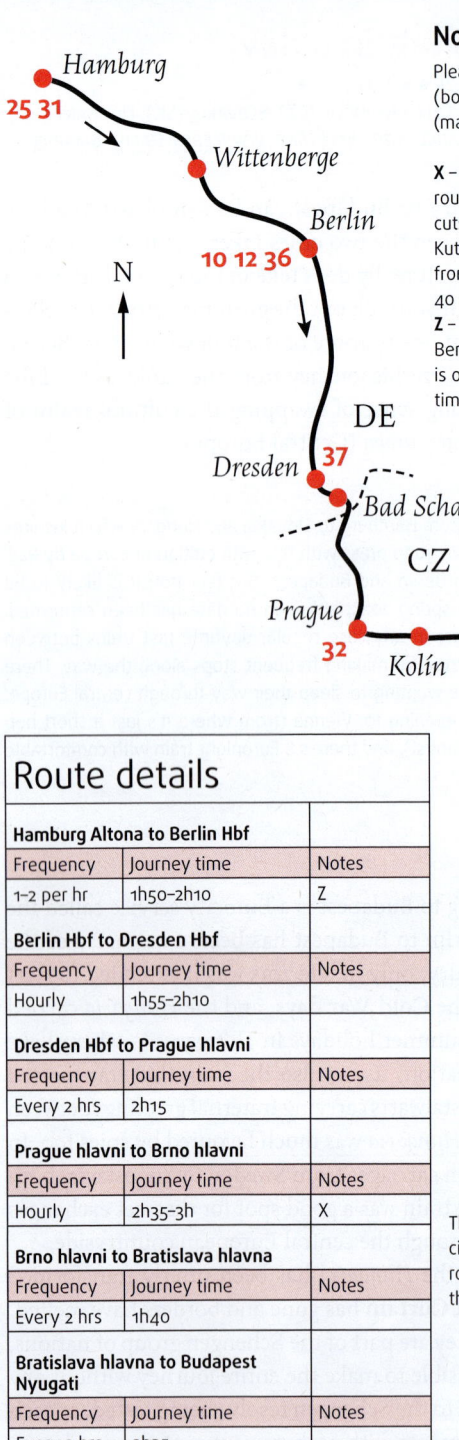

Notes

Please note that 'Hbf' in the route details (bottom left) stands for Hauptbahnhof (main station).

X – There is an alternative, more rural, route between Prague and Brno which cuts the corner south of Kolín, serving Kutná Hora along the way. The travel time from Prague to Brno via this route is 3 hrs 40 mins. Trains run every 2 hrs.

Z – Track work between Hamburg and Berlin means that until spring 2025 there is only one train per hour with a travel time of 2h30 to 2h50.

The **numbers in red** adjacent to some cities on our route maps refer to other routes in this book which also include that particular city.

Route details

Hamburg Altona to Berlin Hbf

Frequency	Journey time	Notes
1–2 per hr	1h50–2h10	Z

Berlin Hbf to Dresden Hbf

Frequency	Journey time	Notes
Hourly	1h55–2h10	

Dresden Hbf to Prague hlavni

Frequency	Journey time	Notes
Every 2 hrs	2h15	

Prague hlavni to Brno hlavni

Frequency	Journey time	Notes
Hourly	2h35–3h	X

Brno hlavni to Bratislava hlavna

Frequency	Journey time	Notes
Every 2 hrs	1h40	

Bratislava hlavna to Budapest Nyugati

Frequency	Journey time	Notes
Every 2 hrs	2h25	

but as of late 2024 there are no significant travel restrictions. The *Hungaria* train which once served three capitals (Berlin, Prague and Budapest) now stops at four. The **velvet divorce** that divided Czechoslovakia gave Bratislava capital city status on 1 January 1993.

The route from Hamburg to Budapest is shaped by two of Europe's great rivers, with the *Hungaria*'s **blue-and-white carriages** following the Elbe Valley (Labe in Czech) on its route south from Germany into the Czech Republic. The latter part of the journey plays cat and mouse with the Danube, never actually crossing the river, but on several occasions running close by the river banks. Indeed at one point, just north of Bratislava, you can look across the river to Austria in the distance.

Across eastern Germany

The *Hungaria*, like almost all trains from **Hamburg** (see p241) to Berlin, departs from Hamburg Altona station. It is in an erstwhile working-class area of the city which has recently seen fractious debates over gentrification. It's worth joining the train here if you have time as the ten-minute journey to Hauptbahnhof (where all trains to Berlin also stop) affords excellent views of the wider Hamburg cityscape.

The train crosses the one-time border between the two German states about half an hour after leaving Hamburg Hauptbahnhof. The open **meadowlands and forests** of this part of eastern Germany possess a rare beauty which is hard to appreciate through the train window. Make a note to come back and explore some time. There is a good network of minor rail routes through the region. Some Hamburg to Berlin fast trains (including the *Hungaria*) stop at **Wittenberge**, from where there is an alternative route via Wittstock to Berlin which traverses beautiful swathes of forest. Trains on this rural line leave Wittenberge hourly (every 2 hrs on Sat & Sun) and take 2 hrs 30 mins to reach Berlin.

If you stay on the main line, less than an hour after Wittenberge you are approaching **Berlin** (see p131) where most trains from Hamburg arrive at the lower-level platforms of Hauptbahnhof station.

Eastern connections from Berlin
Change at Berlin to connect into **eastbound services** to Kraków, Poznań and Warsaw. There are many other direct trains from Berlin to Poland, including hourly services from Berlin Lichtenberg to Kostrzyn which follow the **Ostbahn**, the railway which once ran all the way from Berlin to Königsberg in East Prussia (now Kaliningrad in Russia). There are also occasional direct trains from Berlin to the Polish cities of Bydgoszcz, Gdańsk and Gdynia and to the port city of Szczecin.

All Dresden-bound trains from Berlin pick up passengers at both Hauptbahnhof and Südkreuz stations. There's a remarkable mixture of trains on this route. Very comfortable new double-deck Intercity trains were introduced in 2020, but Czech and Hungarian Eurocity trains also make regular appearances on this line – both with restaurant cars and menus reflecting their respective national culinary traditions. It's an easy run south from Berlin through largely **rural terrain**, with the train crossing the River Elbe on the approach into Dresden.

The capital of Saxony for four centuries, **Dresden** will long be remembered for one of the great tragedies of the Second World War. In February 1945, the city was carpet-bombed by the Allies, and some 35,000 people died. But despite the devastation, the city has risen from the ashes, and is once again a major cultural destination — although still with its difficulties. The **Elbe Valley** is very prone to flooding, and many areas have from time to time been catastrophically inundated. And the city was rightly criticised when it pressed ahead with plans to ruin the Elbe Valley by building a new road bridge through the heart of a UNESCO World Heritage Site. UNESCO responded to such civic vandalism by stripping the city of its World Heritage status — making Dresden the only place in Europe to have been so publicly humiliated. Dresden continues to attract negative publicity for the right-wing rallies organised by the anti-immigrant *Pegida* group.

The baroque magnificence of the city's centre is best appreciated from the raised terraces on the south bank of the Elbe, with views of the **Residenzschloss** (the tower of which gives another good view), and the spire of the early 18th-century Catholic **Hofkirche** (royal cathedral). By the cathedral are the **Semper Opera House** and the **Zwinger**, a gracious complex of baroque pavilions, fountains and statuary. Out of the centre, Dresden is just as interesting. Follow the River Elbe upstream for gorgeous views of villas perched on the hillside on the opposite bank, and within minutes of the centre you are virtually into countryside as you head east. Forests and vineyards aplenty. Further on, **Schloss Pillnitz** was the only baroque building in Dresden to have escaped bombing; entry is free.

Connections from Dresden
There are four direct trains each day from Dresden to Zgorzelec in Poland, with good connections on to Wrocław. This journey forms part of **Route 37** in this book. There is an hourly service from Dresden to Hof in Bavaria with onward connections to Nuremberg, Regensburg and Munich. Leipzig is little more than an hour from Dresden. There is a very attractive route which runs from Dresden to Zittau, briefly cutting through a finger of Czech territory on the approach to Zittau. Some trains continue beyond Zittau to Liberec.

The Elbe Gorge
The stretch of the Elbe Valley upstream from Dresden has the **finest scenery** on this entire journey. Heading south, sit on the left side of the train. You may wish to consider taking slow trains for the cross-border leg from Dresden to Děčín. While the fast services take just 45 mins, the slow trains take twice the time and usually require an en-route change of train at **Bad Schandau**, a

small town in southern Saxony that has become a Mecca for hikers wanting to explore the sandstone hills which tower over the Elbe Valley. A **ferry** across the river links the station with Bad Schandau's small town centre. The train slips across the border into the Czech Republic at **Schöna**. The landscape south towards Prague becomes slowly more industrial, but still full of interest, as the train cruises past Bohemian riverside villages full of timber-framed houses and tottering barns. These landcapes of northern **Bohemia** inspired Smetana's music *Má vlast* (which means 'My Country').

Prague (suggested stopover)

Even in the '70s and early '80s, a steady stream of travellers of all ages were making for Prague (Praha) from the West. Before the Iron Curtain wavered in 1989, Prague was for many Westerners the only glimpse they'd had of life in 'the other Europe'. Three decades on and the stream of travellers has become a flood. During the spring and summer months, Prague is packed. Yet, for all the crowds, the Czech capital has a **very special appeal**.

You'll find architectural styles galore, everything from Gothic to cubist, on both sides of the **Vltava River**, which languidly loops through town. Plenty of parks, a pulsing nightlife and a galaxy of classical music offerings all add to Prague's heady mix. **Václavské náměstí** (Wenceslas Square) is the Czech Champs-Élysées and the biggest and busiest shopping plaza in Prague, as well as being the focal point for political rallies, protests and parades, such as the unrest in 1968/1969 and the Velvet Revolution of 1989. Take the metro to Muzeum and then walk down the length of the square towards the **Old Town**.

Possibly the largest ancient castle complex in the world, **Pražský hrad** (Prague Castle) boasts a magnificently elevated cliff-top position and is crammed with artistic and architectural treasures. Cross the bustling **Karlův most** (Charles Bridge) from the Old Town and walk up through the narrow, picturesque streets. At a hight of 318 m, **Petřín Hill** is covered in eight parks and topped with a 62-m copy of the Eiffel Tower. It offers fabulous views of Prague and the surrounding area. Trams 9/12/20/22 will get you to the start of the funicular up Petřín Hill at Újezd.

ARRIVAL, INFORMATION, ACCOMMODATION

🚆 **Praha hlavní nádraží** (Prague Main Station) is on Wilsonova, not far from the top end of Wenceslas Square. Prague's efficient, fast and clean public transport system is a good choice if you need to speed across town. There are three metro lines and more than twenty tram routes (some running all night). You will need to buy an extra ticket for a large backpack or luggage. Remember to validate your ticket by stamping it once at the outset of your journey in the yellow machines at metro entrances and on trams.

🛈 The main tourist office is in the Old Town Hall (Staroměstská radnice), Staroměstské náměstí 1 (www.praguecitytourism.cz). There is also a branch at Václav Havel Airport and on Wenceslas Square. 🛏 Prague is no longer as cheap as it once was, but there are good-value options throughout the city. Some recommended hotels that might be worth trying include the small, quiet and perfectly located **Hotel Antik**, Dlouhá 22, ☎ 222 322 288 (www.hotelantik.cz). Another reasonably priced option is the **Hotel Jungmann**, centrally located on a quiet square at Jungmannovo náměstí 2, ☎ 224 219 501 (www.hotel-jungmann.cz). The classic art nouveau **Hotel Paris Prague**, ul. Obecního domu 1, ☎ 222 195 195 (www.hotel-paris.cz), is close to all the main sights and worth the financial splurge.

CONNECTIONS FROM PRAGUE

Prague's role as a **rail hub** has, along with cheap beer, propelled the city into the premier league of destinations favoured by young travellers (many of them using Interrail passes). There are **night trains** from far and wide, with direct overnight services to Budapest, Košice, Kraków, Warsaw and Zurich, plus summer-season trains to Rijeka and Split.

Vienna is just four-and-a-half hours away from Prague, with a choice of two operators on that route. As an alternative to the main line south to Vienna, travellers bound for Austria might consider the more rural line through České Budějovice to Linz.

Apart from the obvious main routes out of the city, there are a number of lesser lines which deserve to be better known. **Private operator** ALEX (rail passes are valid) offers a beautiful route to Munich, which cuts through the hill country that straddles the border between Bohemia and Bavaria.

From the Czech capital, the train heads past **Kolín** (from where there is a connection to Kutná Hora, with its mediaeval Old Town huddled around a superb Gothic church), through the **Bohemian-Moravian uplands** to Brno in South Moravia. This is a land of rolling hills, dotted with elegant châteaux and mediaeval castles where many Czech and foreign films are set; if you've time to stop off, you'll discover peaceful nature reserves and areas with karst limestone scenery and underground caves. It's also the main **Czech wine-growing region** (with attractively painted wine cellars dotting the hills).

High-rise blocks and an unmistakably industrial look might tempt you to skip **Brno**, which expanded in the 19th century as a textile-making centre. But the town does have a scattering of good sights (most are closed Mon, and are either cheap or free) within 1 km of the station in the largely traffic-free centre.

The neo-Gothic **Katedrála sv. Petra a Pavla** (Cathedral of Sts Peter and Paul) crowns Petrov Hill, while the 13th-century **Špilberk Castle** was the most notorious prison in the Austro-Hungarian Empire – you can visit the horrifying prison cells (closed Mon Oct–Mar). A little way south-west is the Augustinian Monastery, where in 1865 the monk Mendel studied genetics, breeding pea plants in the garden. Garden and plants remain, and there's also a small museum, the **Mendelianum**, Muzejné 1 (www.mendelianum.cz; closed Mon).

The city's **Old Town Hall** at Radnická 8, is a combination of Gothic, Renaissance and baroque style and displays a 'dragon'; a stuffed crocodile from 1608. Brno's most bizarre sight is the crypt of the **Kapucínský klášter** (Capuchin Monastery) close to the station on Kapucínské náměstí, containing 150 mummified bodies, air-dried since 1650.

Through Slovakia

Beyond Brno, the landscape becomes more subdued as the railway follows the flatlands around the **River Morava**, dropping down slowly to the Danube. For a 200-km stretch, the train cuts through Slovakian territory, along the way passing through the capital Bratislava.

Overshadowed by Prague, it has sometimes been hard for **Bratislava** to make its mark. But the city enjoys a superb location, where the last ripples of the Carpathians reach the Danube. It is midway between Prague and Budapest, and less than an hour by train east of Vienna. Bratislava fans argue that the city has all the merits of Prague without the crowds (for more on Bratislava see p325).

The scenery through the **Danube Lowlands** east from Bratislava is largely unexceptional, so what follows comes as a surprise. Shortly after leaving the last station in Slovakia at **Štúrovo**, there is a magnificent view south across the Danube to Esztergom in Hungary. The vista is dominated by **Esztergom Basilica**, the tallest building in Hungary and an impressive symbol of ecclesiastical power in the Danube town that for 250 years served as capital of Hungary. Seen in the right light, we would really rate that view of Esztergom from Slovakia as one of the finest anywhere on Europe's rail network. Within a few minutes, the train crosses into Hungary (but still does not cross the Danube) and there is a superb stretch with the train running through small **Hungarian villages** surrounded by vineyards. Not many long train journeys across Europe have quite such a rousing finale.

Budapest

Budapest is a **grand city**, and was always the most westernised of the Warsaw Pact capitals. In the two decades since the fall of the Iron Curtain it has demolished many of its communist monuments, while moving others, such as the Liberation Monument, to be reassembled in a statue park. Within a medley of Habsburg and Ottoman influences, Budapest is now a city to indulge yourself, in spas, Hungarian cuisine and the city's thriving cultural scene.

The grey-green Danube splits the city into **Buda**, on the west bank, and **Pest** on the east. Buda is the photogenic, hilly Old Town, with its pastel-coloured baroque residences, gas-lit cobblestone streets and hilltop palace, while Pest is the thriving, mostly 19th-century commercial centre, with the imposing riverside **State Parliament building**, its wide boulevards and **Vörösmarty tér**, the busy main square. Between Buda and Pest, Margaret Bridge gives access to Margaret Island (Margit-sziget), a green oasis and venue for alfresco opera and drama in summer. The city's **Museum of Fine Art** houses the Romanesque Hall which served as a storage space but has now been restored to its original splendour. Szent István Bazilika (St Stephen's Basilica), Mátyás Templom (Matthias Church) and Nagy Zsinagóga (Great Synagogue) are just three lavishly decorative places of worship that reflect the diverse paths of religion in Budapest. Take the **Budavári Sikló** (Buda Castle Funicular) up to the **Halászbástya** (Fishermen's Bastion).

Budapest has excellent rail connections to the rest of central Europe, the Balkans and destinations further east, and if your enthusiasm for railways is unbounded, don't miss the Magyar Vasúttörténeti Park (Hungarian Railway History Park) on Tatai út 95 (www.vasuttortenetipark.hu; closed Mon).

Arrival, information, accommodation

There are three major stations: **Nyugati pályaudvar** (Western Station), designed in 1877 by the Eiffel firm from Paris; **Keleti pályaudvar** (Eastern Station); and **Déli pályaudvar** (Southern Station). All three are fairly central, close to hotels and on the metro: Keleti on lines 2 and 4, Déli on line 2, Nyugati on line 3.

Budapest Airport (www.bud.hu), 16 km east from the centre at Ferihegy. There's a rail service 2–6 times an hour from Ferihegy station, near Terminal 2, to Budapest Nyugati station, taking 25 mins. To get to Ferihegy station from the airport, take the frequent 200E. Airport shuttle 100E connects Deák Ferenc tér with the airport (every 10 mins during the day), stopping at Kálvin tér along the way (buy tickets before bording). The **metro** is fast and cheap and runs 04.30–23.30 (buy tickets from kiosks or machines inside stations; individual tickets or blocks of ten). Tickets must be stamped in the machines at the station entrance. The middle section of metro line 3 is currently being refurbished (bus replacement service is in operation). Detailed information on public transport at www.bkk.hu. Outside winter, **boat services** operate from the southern end to the northern end of Budapest, from Haller utca to Újpest, Árpád út and Rómaifürdő, daily 08.00–18.35. The **funicular** (*sikló*) from the Buda side of the Chain Bridge to Buda Castle runs daily 07.30–22.00. Budapest tourist offices are at Sütő ut. 2 (Deák Ferenc tér) and at Károly körút (www.budapestinfo.com).

Budapest has a wide range of hostels and hotels in all categories, as well as pensions and private rooms. The **Casati Budapest Hotel**, Paulay Ede ut. 31, ☎ 30 638 17 31 (www.casatibudapesthotel.com), is on a quiet street, yet centrally located in Pest. Close to the Danube and overlooking the Parliament building, is the chic and modern **art'otel budapest**, Bem rakpart 16–19, ☎ 1 487 94 87 (www.artotels.com). **Bo18**, Vajdahunyad ut. 18, ☎ 1 783 20 07 (www.bo18hotelbudapest.com), offers comfortable, modern rooms.

Enjoy traditional Jewish-Hungarian fare at the **Rosenstein** restaurant, Mosonyi ut. 3, ☎ 1 333 34 92 (www.rosenstein.hu), close to Keleti station.

Connections from Budapest

You are spoilt for choice when it comes to moving on beyond Budapest. There are direct services to Lviv and Kyiv, Bucharest, Zurich, Ljubljana and Zagreb. There's an interesting direct daytime train (called the *Latorca*) to Mukachevo in Ukraine, a seven-hour journey that crosses into Ukraine at Chop. Budapest is the natural hub for Hungarian domestic rail services, with hourly departures to Debrecen and regular trains to Szeged, Pécs and Győr. All four are fine cities which will repay a visit of a day or two.

Note that direct trains from Budapest to destinations in Serbia are suspended while the railway is upgraded. Reopening is scheduled for mid-2026. During the summer season, there are direct trains to destinations on the **Adriatic coast**, notably Koper, Rijeka and Split. When planning onward journeys, check carefully from which of Budapest's stations your train will depart. You can connect in Budapest onto **Route 34, 35** and **50** in this book.

SIDETRACKS: NAMED TRAINS

Train names can be very **powerful brands**, and some names – such as *Orient Express* and *Flying Scotsman* – were mainstays of the European railway scene for decades. Named trains have inspired art. Thus the luxurious *Train Bleu* which ran overnight from Calais and Paris to Nice in the **heyday of the Riviera** inspired Sergei Diaghilev's 1924 ballet of the same name.

It's been a two-way process. While a train sparked Diaghilev's creative instincts, so art and music have inspired the naming of trains. Until 1987, the daytime train from Hoek van Holland to Basel took its name from *Das Rheingold*, the first of the four operas in Richard Wagner's Ring Cycle. No doubt images of Wagner's Rhine maidens helped **market the train**, which for much of its route ran along the banks of the River Rhine. All good romantic stuff, and perhaps it cheered up passengers from England who found themselves riding the Rheingold through Holland's bleak estuarial landscapes at dawn after a short night on board the packet boat from Harwich to the Hook.

If the train names of yesteryear were impossibly romantic, some of those we have come across more recently are prosaic in the extreme. We made an early morning journey in the Austrian Vorarlberg region a few years ago on a train named after a **brand of Tyrolean ham**. We could never see Diaghilev cooperating with Pablo Picasso, Jean Cocteau and Coco Chanel (as he did in *Le Train Bleu*) to stage a ballet named after a piece of bacon. We note that *Handl Tyrol Speck* quickly disappeared from the Austrian timetables, presumably because the eponymous company terminated the sponsorship agreement. Other **bizarrely named Austrian trains** in recent years have included *A1 Blackberry*, the *Hotel Ibis* and the deeply theological *Licht für die Welt* (Light for the World).

Composers, artists and writers have always been **safe choices** for named trains. You can never go wrong with Chopin, Rembrandt or Goethe. A morning train from Berlin to Prague was for many years called *Carl Maria von Weber*. A later train on the same route was the *Johannes Brahms*.

Mountains and lakes are also sound bets. Shift to more abstract concepts and you get into tricky territory. In the 1980s, the afternoon train from **Prague to Berlin** was called the *Progress*, a name that sounded, well, nicely progressive in Czechoslovakia and East Germany. After the political reforms of 1989, progress became all-too-retro and the train name was quietly dropped.

Other names that initially had a **political edge** to them have however survived. When the *Krasnaya Strela* (Red Arrow) started operating in 1931, it was hailed by Soviet commentators as a great socialist achievement. Curiously, the train's carriages were blue in the early days. Only in 1949 were they changed to red – the shade carefully matched to the same red that dominated the Soviet flag. Both the train name and its distinctive colour have outlived the Soviet Union. Train number 1, the *Krasnaya Strela*, still pulls out of **St Petersburg** at five minutes to midnight every evening, just as it did in the days of the Soviet Union. And the musical accompaniment has not changed either. The station still resounds to Reinhold Glière's *Hymn to the Great City*, the orchestral piece which has signalled the departure of the *Krasnaya Strela* for over half a century. It remains one of Europe's great overnight journeys.

Route 34: To the Black Sea

Cities: ★★ Culture: ★★ History: ★★ Scenery: ★
Countries covered: Austria (AT), Hungary (HU), Romania (RO)
Journey time: 23 hrs | Distance: 1,465 km | Map: www.ebrweb.eu/18map34

Let's go to Transylvania! And ever further. We'll venture to the shores of the enigmatic, stubborn sea which marks the very edge of Europe. This journey will take us from **Vienna to Venus**.

Now we sense your confusion. Trust us. This is a journey to Romania. For travellers from western Europe, most routes to Romania lead through Vienna, which has a fine range of rail links to Romania. That's why Jonathan Harker came this way. Remember Jonathan? He was the diligent young solicitor in Bram Stoker's *Dracula* who travelled by **train to Transylvania** to meet a client. Stoker's novel has lots of geography, and trains play a part. Indeed, the novel opens with a complaint about punctuality with Harker observing that "the further east you go the more unpunctual are the trains."

So let's hope for the best as we venture east, and we'll not get frazzled if trains are delayed or we find ourselves inconveniently stranded at some remote railway junction in Romania – let's just hope that, if misfortune befalls us, it's not at Copşa Mică. You'll understand why in the pages that follow. For months during the pandemic, the trains from **Austria to Romania** were all suspended, but their happy reinstatement in December 2021 has nudged us to research and write this route in 2022. It appeared for the first time in the 17th edition of *Europe by Rail* and is now updated for this 18th edition.

The route starts with an overnight journey through Hungary into Romania. There we'll make time for three Transylvania cities: a few hours (or an overnight stay) in Dracula-themed **Sighişoara**, then visits with an optional overnight stay in magnificent Sibiu and historic Braşov. Jonathan Harker went no further than Transylvania. But our route continues east into

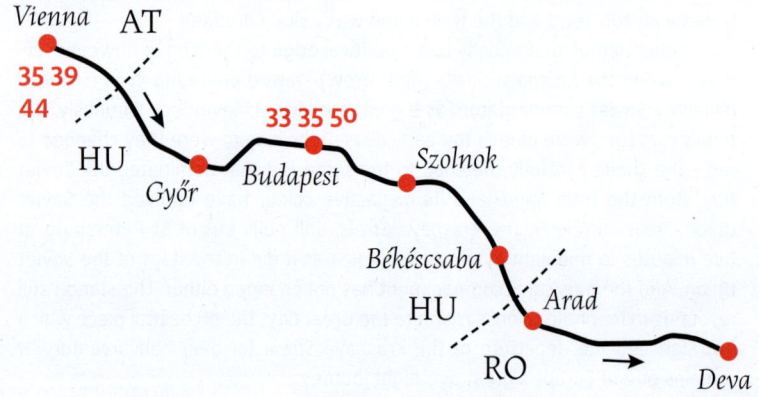

Wallachia, passing through Bucharest and finishing on the **Black Sea coast**, where there really is a string of resorts with planetary names. You can take your pick from Venus, Saturn or Jupiter.

ITINERARY SUGGESTIONS

This new route is one of the longer journeys in this book, and it really makes sense to take the **night train** from Vienna to Romania. Even with that fast start, you'll still want some days to get a feel for Transylvania's cities and mountains, before heading on to the Romanian coast, passing through Bucharest. For the first trip to the country, our inclination might be to skip the capital and head from Transylvania straight for the coast, where the Black Sea port of **Constanța** really is something special.

Notes

C – Two direct trains per day. Other services require a change of train in Mediaș or Copșa Mică.

N – Direct overnight trains. Addtional daytime options (with a change) via Oradea or Arad, generally with an overnight stay in one of those cities or in Cluj-Napoca.

X – The direct night train from Vienna to Romania is called the *Dacia*. It leaves the Austrian capital at 19.42 and picks up passengers in Budapest three hours later.

Route details

Vienna to Sighișoara

Frequency	Journey time	Notes
1 per day	12h35	N X

Sighișoara to Sibiu

Frequency	Journey time	Notes
5 per day	2h05–4h	C

Sibiu to Brașov

Frequency	Journey time	Notes
5 per day	2h45–4h	

Brașov to Bucharest Gara de Nord

Frequency	Journey time	Notes
Hourly	2h20–3h40	

Bucharest GdN to Constanța

Frequency	Journey time	Notes
Hourly	2h10–2h40	

Constanța to Mangalia

Frequency	Journey time	Notes
10–15 per day	1h–1h30	

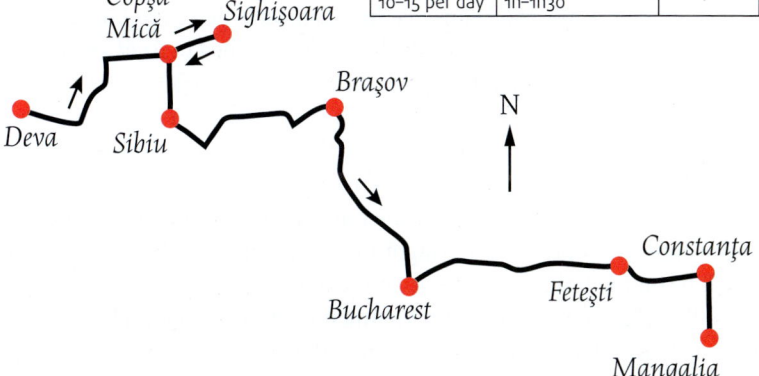

If you don't fancy the idea of a night train, then bear in mind that there are also daytime options from Vienna to both **Arad** and **Oradea** (and an even larger choice of routes and services from Budapest). Travel time in each case is about nine hours. Whether you opt for Arad or Oradea, both very fine cities, there are onward connections next morning to both Sighișoara and Sibiu – with travel times of seven to nine hours.

The beauty of the **Romanian rail network** is its rich topology, so often offering multiple route options on longer journeys. So if you follow the route described here on your outward journey, you'll find plenty of alternatives for the return, possibly detouring via northern Romania to connect into the direct daytime train from **Baia Mare** to Vienna.

Whichever itinerary you opt for, take some books for the road for one can only spend so much time window gazing. The poetry of George Bacovia, who described his native Romania as "a sad country, but one full of humour" is a good start, as are the plays of Eugène Ionesco. Bram Stoker's *Dracula* is good for Transylvania (though Stoker never visited Romania), and a must-see film is Corneliu Porumboiu's *12:08 East of Bucharest*, which reflects on the Romanian revolution with a mildly comic take on the end of the Ceaușescu regime in 1989.

Through the night

Where were we? Ah, yes! **Vienna Hauptbahnhof**. Shall we have supper before travelling? There are many spots to choose from, but we like L'Osteria. It's nothing fancy, but it fills the spot and the food – pasta, pizza and salads – is tasty. There's a screen in the restaurant showing the roll call of destinations. Look, there's the overnight train to the Baltic port of Warnemünde about to go, and over the following 60 minutes night sleeper services will be heading off to Paris, Rome, Amsterdam, Milan, Hamburg and Bucharest.

The 19.42 to Romania carries a **curious mixture of carriages** and passengers. There are Hungarian business people returning to Budapest after a day in Vienna. Then there are the overnighters, passengers like us heading to towns large and small across Romania. The train is actually composed of four portions, all bound for different destinations. Happily, the restaurant car is still there for 2024, albeit just for the Vienna to Budapest segment.

The smart Hungarian carriages only go as far as **Budapest**. Then there is the Romanian segment of the train which later splits into three. The main part of the train runs via Sighișoara and Brașov to Bucharest. A lone sleeping car, also bound for Bucharest, is detached in Arad and takes a completely different route through Romania, running via Craiova to reach the capital. Then there are also carriages to Cluj-Napoca – the latter first appearing only in 2022, which we affect to think might be a historical nod to Jonathan Harker, for he used the train from Vienna to Cluj-Napoca.

So let's join the main part of the train and travel through the night to **Sighișoara**. It's a pleasant overnight journey; long enough to really relax. You'll be on the train until after 10 in the morning. On a summer evening, it's still daylight for the ride from **Vienna into Hungary**, with a late evening stop at Keleti station in Budapest where there's time to stretch your legs and admire the statues of James Watt and George Stephenson on the main facade of the building.

From **Budapest**, it's more than four hours to the Romanian frontier, where chances are you'll stir as border officials wander through the train. Romania became a full member of Schengen in spring 2024, so bringing to an end a rare case of an inner-EU border where the checking of passports or other IDs still took place. Romanian time is one hour in advance of Hungarian time, so watches should be put forward during the night. When we used this service, we were awakened by a nocturnal festival of shunting at Arad, but then we slept right through until about 07.30, nudging back the window blinds to see some Romanian wooden crosses by lineside cottages and in the distance the great citadel at Deva which dominates the **Mureş Valley**.

Welcome to Romania! This is the real charm of the night sleeper. You drift off to sleep and awaken somewhere completely different. The ride from **Deva to Sighişoara** isn't all pretty. The industrial dereliction around Copşa Mică is something to behold. But an hour later we are rolling into Sighişoara, where the main station building with its yellow paint and orange trim looks very welcoming.

Sighişoara (suggested stopover)

Many commentators rave about Sighişoara. "Transylvania's most atmospheric mediaeval town," says the *Rough Guide to Romania*. "The archetypal Transylvanian town," writes Lucy Mallows in her *Bradt Guide to Transylvania*, qualifying that with a remark on the "countless, cheesy Dracula souvenir shops." There you have it. Sighişoara is an absolutely brilliant place to alight from the overnight train from Vienna. There are brooding ramparts aplenty, but it is **fairly Disneyesque**. As Lucy Mallows reminds us "everything looks like a Dracula film set." The disjuncture between Viennese sophistication and Sighişoara's Gothic style will not suit all temperaments. Whatever, it's all a matter of personal taste.

THE APUSENI MOUNTAINS AND CLUJ

There is an **alternative overnight option** to travelling out to Sighişoara, and that's to join the portion of the night train from Vienna bound for Cluj. There are three reasons you might do this. Firstly, it's definitely the way to go for Dracula purists, keen to replicate Jonathan Harker's journey. Secondly, **Cluj** itself repays a short visit. Thirdly, the route to Cluj passes through the beautiful Apuseni Mountains, and the last two hours of the ride into Cluj are magnificent. The best stretch is east of Bratca, which the train from Vienna is due to reach just after 06.30. We can imagine no finer introduction to Romania than **cruising through the hills** on a spring morning. If you do travel to Cluj, there are onward daytime connections to Sibiu and Sighişoara, allowing you to pick up our main route there.

It's a short walk south-west from the station to the compact **walled citadel**, passing the oddly monochromatic Romanian Orthodox Holy Trinity Church and crossing the footbridge over the River Târnava Mare along the way. Once over the river, you'll see the Roman Catholic Church before entering the citadel. **Transylvania** has a wide spectrum of Christian Churches, not to mention other faiths. So, while the Romanian Orthodox Church is the dominant force, there's an admixture of Roman Catholics, Uniates (sometimes called Greek Catholics; see p328 for more on the Uniates), Lutherans, Calvinists and Unitarians. The most striking of the **many churches** in Sighişoara is the Lutheran church built by Saxon settlers; it's known as the Bergkirche (Church on the Hill) and it's memorable as much for the extraordinary covered wooden staircase which leads up to it as for the church itself.

Quite how a lad called **Vlad**, born in Sighişoara around 1430, acquired such a reputation for cruelty that he became known as Vlad the Impaler is a long story. Were it not for Bram Stoker's 1897 novel, which first posited a link between Vlad and vampirism, we probably would never have heard of Vlad, who is widely known in western Europe as **Dracula**. Dedicated fans and would-be vampires can take in Vlad's birthplace. The one thing not to miss on even the shortest stop is Sighişoara is climbing the clock tower, which affords a fine panorama over the town and nearby countryside.

ARRIVAL, INFORMATION, ACCOMMODATION
🚆 A ten-minute walk north-east of the Old Town. 🛈 Tourist office: Octavian Goga Str. 8 (www.romaniatourism.com).

🛏 We think Sighişoara deserves a one-night stay, but we do understand those travellers who, fresh from the night train, wander through Sighişoara for a couple of hours and then enjoy a leisurely lunch before hopping on the afternoon direct train to Sibiu (which, until at least December 2024, leaves at 15.37). If you'd like to stay overnight then the **Casa Savri**, Morii Str. 17, ☎ 0757 073 665 (www.casasavri.ro) is a good choice and convenient for both the station and the Old Town.

The **narrow-gauge railway** which once linked Sighişoara and Sibiu closed in 1963, so these days you need to backtrack by train to Copşa Mică, eerie in its carbon-black dereliction, to reach Sibiu.

The Saxon heritage

The Saxons who settled in Transylvania in the 12th century and thereafter didn't all come from Saxony, but they collectively left their mark with a strong Germanic legacy in the architecture and culture of the region. That is especially evident in Sibiu and Braşov. In terms of allocating time between the two, we think **Sibiu** has the edge, so if you can only afford one overnight stop then opt for Sibiu where the main sights are arranged around three interlinked squares. It's all very walkable. The railway station is a 10-min walk north-east of the centre. Sibiu is a chance to see how sensitive handling of historical themes, in this case the Saxon migrations to Transylvania, can lend real meaning to the cityscape. The topography really helps, but so does the variety. Sibiu is a place where you wander through **dark and twisting alleys** to emerge in the stately, sun-drenched square. When it took its turn as European Capital of Culture, Sibiu played the Saxon card and made no mention of Dracula. As to hotels, we can recommend the Art Hotel, Centumvirilor Str. 2, ☎ 0369 409 360 (www.arthotel.ro), a short walk from the main square.

The 149-km rail journey between Sibiu and Braşov offers the **finest scenery** on this entire route, it's a line plied entirely by local trains, typically taking about four hours and some pausing at over 30 intermediate stations. If you don't want to stop in Braşov, it's perfectly possible to travel right through from Sibiu to Constanţa in a day.

Set among the hills of south-east Transylvania, **Braşov** has a very fine central area that reflects the prosperity of the city in its Saxon heyday. With its showpiece baroque buildings, the heart of the city in and around **Piaţa Sfatului** feels even more Germanic than Sibiu. Too many would-be visitors are put off by arriving in a dreary suburb as the main station is some way from the centre. But bus number 4 from departure stand 3 runs frequently into the Old Town. It's a 10-minute ride. If you want to stay overnight in Braşov, the highly regarded Hotel Bella Muzica, Piaţa Sfatului 19, ☎ 268 477 956 (www.bellamuzica.ro) has a great location close to Piaţa Sfatului and the Black Church.

CONNECTIONS FROM BRAŞOV
Braşov is a good spot to leave this route if you are not intent on going all the way to the coast. There is an entirely different route from here **back to Budapest** via northern Transylvania and Oradea which is served by direct daytime and overnight services, each taking about 15 hours. That same line north from Braşov also has direct trains to many Romanian destinations, including Baia Mare, Târgu Mureş and Cluj-Napoca.

Into Wallachia

Transylvania's coherence as a geographical entity is underpinned by its setting within the mountains. This is especially evident in the first hour of the train journey south from Braşov, as the railway cuts through hills to reach the flatter territory of Wallachia. The railway climbs steeply up the summit at **Predeal**, just 27 km from Braşov and at 1,054 metres above sea level. The line then drops down into the beautiful Prahova Valley, with superb views of rugged peaks to the right. **Buşteni** is the place to stop if you fancy heading into the hills.

Beyond Buşteni, it is downhill through superb scenery to Sinaia, from where it's a short walk from the station to **Sinaia monastery** and stately

Peleş Castle, the latter a late 19th-century royal affection which looks more Bavarian than Balkan. Both are open to the public. The Pensiunea Maria, Octavian Goga Str. 1a, ☎ 0244 312 254 (www.pensiuneamariasinaia.ro) is a good option close to both the station and the park.

Slowly the hills recede, and our route enters the **Wallachian plain**, where we encounter one of the world's earliest commercial oilfields. All trains stop at Ploieşti; this hub of the Romanian oil industry isn't pretty. From here it's about 60 km to **Bucharest**, a city which in the context of this journey is merely a place to change trains. It deserves more of course, and although it's large, often frustrating and chaotic, the Romanian capital has a historic centre, many fine museums and some unexpectedly lovely gardens. Don't judge Bucharest by what you see at the Gara de Nord, where the trains from Braşov arrive and the onward service to Constanţa departs (although one train each day runs right through from Braşov to the coast).

Connections from Bucharest
From the Romanian capital, there is a daily train south to **Ruse** in Bulgaria, where there is a good onward connection (and sometimes through carriages) to Sofia. There are summer season through carriages from Bucharest to **Halkalı** in Turkey (during winter months passengers from Bucharest must change in Ruse and Dimitrovgrad to reach Turkey. There is also a direct **overnight train** leaving Bucharest each evening for Chişinău in Moldova.

East from Bucharest

There is a moment when you might be tempted to dose off as your train rattles over the flatlands east of Bucharest. It's unexciting terrain, yet there is a wistful beauty in this unchallenging landscape. Some of the station buildings you pass are extraordinary. And so are the communities they serve. Take for example the small town of **Lehliu-Gară**. It is the product of Romanian social engineering when, in the late 1980s, the Ceauşescu regime was keen to see unviable rural villages left to wither next to new urban centres created in the countryside. Lehliu-Gară was one of these purpose-built towns.

The railway runs dead straight to **Feteşti**, and this is where things suddenly get extremely interesting. We are about to experience one of historic highlights of European rail transport – a stretch of railway which transformed European travel habits and opened up entirely new horizons for late 19th-century travellers.

Immediately ahead lies the **Danube**, which here bifurcates into two branches about nine kilometres apart. It was a sensible place to try and **bridge** one of Europe's great waterways, and that was eventually done in 1895. It allowed the railway to be extended to the Dobruja region and the port of Constanţa, where passengers could transfer to ships for the onward journey to Asia Minor, the Crimea and other Black Sea destinations. Crossing the second branch of the Danube, which here is the main part of the river, all trains stop at Cernavodă with its unlovely nuclear power plant. From here towards the coast, the railway is paralleled by the **Danube-Black Sea canal**, another pet project of Ceaușescu, but one which has been very successful in smoothing the passage of Danube shipping. This commercial waterway allows vessels to reach the Black Sea without having to navigate the shifting shallows of the Danube Delta. If you are heading for the Delta, the junction at Medgidia is where you'll change onto the local train to **Tulcea**, where the remarkable socialist-era railway station is easily the most adventurous piece of architecture in town. Tulcea is the best jumping-off point for excursions into the watery wilderness of the Danube Delta.

Constanța

Constanța is a **maritime city** of enormous commercial, political and cultural importance in the Black Sea region. It doesn't have the neat charm of Dubrovnik or the elegant nostalgia of Trieste, but it's in the premier league of European cities which have shaped the course of history. Greek, Roman, Byzantine and Ottoman influences underpin Constanța's **rich past**. Like Venice or Lisbon, it's a city that somehow demands a grand arrival. You won't get it.

The place to go on a first visit to Constanța, indeed on any visit to the city, is the **peninsula**. The challenge is to get a city that has turned its back on the sea to rediscover its maritime assets. For more than a decade, the Constanța city administration was dominated by cultural vandals. Happily that's changing, but the city's iconic landmark, the striking **art**

THE PLANETARY RESORTS

Along the Romanian coast **south of Constanța**, there's a string of resorts developed in the 1960s and 1970s to meet demand for budget holidays for workers and their families. Local trains run south from Constanța via Cap Aurora to **Mangalia**, taking 60 to 90 mins for the 43-km journey. Among the resorts are Neptun and Jupiter, both to the north of Cap Aurora; south of that gentle cape towards the Bulgarian border are **Venus and Saturn**.

These purpose-built holiday resorts catered primarily to domestic tourism, with most of the holidaymakers relying on all-inclusive vouchers which covered travel to the coast, accommodation in a fairly basic hotel and some meals. But there were also foreigners who made tracks for the Romanian coast, the great majority of them coming from Warsaw Pact countries.

The **political changes of 1989** and thereafter fundamentally undermined the tourist economy of these coastal resorts in south-east Romania. The voucher holiday all but disappeared and many designs from the 1960s and 1970s haven't stood the test of time. A number of the leading hotels from that period have been abandoned or now have entire wings mothballed. If you visit Jupiter, Venus, or another of the resorts on that coastal strip, it'll be a chance to read history through buildings and recall the days when sun, sea and socialism made natural partners.

nouveau pavilion on the promenade, lies abandoned. Other key buildings are neglected or abused. Feathers were ruffled in 2019 when the dilapidated former Ashkenazi synagogue was used, evidently with the assent of the city council, for a lingerie photo shoot.

That older part of town, the heart of the former Greek city of **Tomis** with narrow streets hemmed in by the sea, reveals the many faces of Constanța and the multiple influences which have shaped the city. Start at **Piața Ovidiu**, presided over by a melancholic statue of the poet Ovid (who spent the last years of his life in exile in Constanța) and check out the Roman mosaics, the striking Mahmudiye Mosque, the Genoese Lighthouse and that mournful beachfront pavilion and one-time casino – the latter a reminder of the days when the **Romanian Riviera** thought it might have the style and panache to rival the French Riviera.

Arrival, information, accommodation

⇌ The trains used to run through to the striking Gara Maritimă on the quayside; the old station is still there, now housing the Port Authority, but the trains are long gone. Passenger trains now drop their passengers at a 1960s-era station 2 km west of the city centre. The city's **public transport** is run by RATC (www.ctbus.ro). Take 🚌 101 from the railway station to 'Poarta 2 Port' (on the peninsula) or 🚌 5-40 to 'Centru'. Single-journey ticket 1.50 Lei (€0.30), 24-hour ticket for all lines 5 Lei (€1). 🛈 There is no tourist office in Constanța, but a number of travel agencies (www.romaniatourism.com).

🛏 The well appointed **Belle Epoche Boutique Villa**, Bulevardul Tomis 16, ☎ 0770 587 357 (www.belle-epoque-villa.ro) has a perfect location on the peninsula close to Piata Ovidiu. Or try the **Hotel Cherica**, Stefan cel Mare 4, ☎ 241 617 174 (www.cherica.ro) which is close to both the beach and the historic centre.

For another take on the Romanian Riviera, ride the local train down to **Mangalia** and back, stopping to explore Saturn, Neptun or Venus (see box on previous page). Ultimately this is a landscape of the liminal, a place where sand, sea and sky merge. It is a region of endless possibilities and of none. Here's a part of Europe where myth and reality mingle – as true here on the shores of the Black Sea as it was in Dracula's Transylvania.

After taking the pulse of life at Venus, hop on the train back to Constanța, and walk by night through the oldest part of the town. Listen for the whispers of Pontic Greeks and Crimean Tatars, catch a fragment of **Ovid's poetry**, hear the commands of Scythian overloads, and watch the ghosts of vessels at anchor in the harbour. There's an Ottoman galley; here's the **Battleship Potemkin**, its mutineers seeking refuge from Russia, and now... do you hear that? Surely that's the *Krymskaya Strela*, the sleek red and white catamaran which once regularly sped between Constanța and Odesa, sometimes even making excursions to Sevastapol. Constanța was once a great hub of Black Sea transport commerce; today it is a disconsolate backwater. We promise you: of all the places we escort you to in this book, Constanța is one which will forever haunt you.

Route 35: Exploring Slovakia

Cities: ★★ Culture: ★★ History: ★ Scenery: ★★
Countries covered: Austria (AT), Slovakia (SK), Hungary (HU)
Journey time: 13 hrs 20 mins | Distance: 781 km | Map: www.ebrweb.eu/18map35

One family dominated the politics and power of central Europe until the First World War. Until the start of the 18th century, the **Habsburg dynasty's imperial power** extended way beyond central Europe. It's easy to forget that Spain was once part of the Habsburg realm. But with the assignment of Spain to the French Bourbons in 1700, Habsburg power was concentrated on two great cities on the Danube: Vienna and Budapest.

This route, first introduced into *Europe by Rail* in 2022, links those two great cities. In the final phase of Habsburg power, **Budapest and Vienna** were the twin centres of political influence and commercial innovation in Austria-Hungary. With an arcane web of law and privileges and a rich medley of cultures and languages, this was a disparate empire. But from about 1840, the **railways assumed ever greater importance** in linking the scattered Habsburg territories.

The first line, linking Vienna with Brno, opened in 1839, and before long the railways extended into the Bukovina and Banat and the remotest corners of Carniola and Carinthia. The pace of development was so fast that the state only narrowly avoided bankruptcy by hastily selling off railway assets in 1850. Even today, some key routes are still sometimes referred to by the old Habsburg names: the Rudolf Railway, the Emperor Franz Joseph Railway, the Empress Elisabeth Railway — each one name-checking a Habsburg royal.

The journey on the main line from Vienna to Budapest is unremarkable. Despite linking two Danube cities, the railway affords few glimpses of the river, though there is a pleasant short stretch around Komárom where the train to Budapest hugs the south bank of the Danube.

Our recommended route from Vienna to Budapest is much more circuitous, making a great loop to the north to skirt the southern flank of the **Tatra Mountains** and along the way taking in Slovakia's two largest cities: Bratislava and Košice. This is a route that explores just one small part of Habsburg Europe, blending Habsburg style with assertive Modernism and along the way taking in some grand mountain scenery.

Itinerary and tickets

The two really obvious stops on this route are **Bratislava** and **Košice**, but there are other candidates. If you like the general antics that surround spa towns, you might consider a night in **Piešt'any** (though it's a pale shadow of the West Bohemian spa towns mentioned in Route 35). This is a route which in its long central section from Bratislava right through to Košice, has consistently fine mountain scenery. If you are tempted to stop off, and this is your first encounter with the Slovakian hills, make that stop in the Tatra Mountains. **Poprad** is the most popular jumping-off point for Tatra excursions, but we think that Štrba is actually a better choice for connecting into the **Tatra tram network**.

324 | CENTRAL AND EASTERN EUROPE

Route details

Vienna Hbf to Bratislava hl.st.

Frequency	Journey time	Notes
Hourly	1h10	

Bratislava hl.st. to Poprad-Tatry

Frequency	Journey time	Notes
Every 2 hrs	3h40–4h20	S

Poprad-Tatry to Košice

Frequency	Journey time	Notes
Hourly	1h10–2h	

Košice to Budapest Keleti

Frequency	Journey time	Notes
Every 2 hrs	3h50	

Notes

The Slovakian part of this route is well served by night trains, with departures from Bratislava every evening for Poprad, Košice and other points in the east of the country. There is also an overnight service from Prague to Košice via Žilina and Poprad.

A small number of trains along the main axis from Bratislava to Košice are run by independent operators Leo Express and RegioJet. Interrail passes are also valid on these trains.

S – All trains, bar for occasional IC services, stop at Štrba about 20 mins before Poprad, for connections to the Tatra Railway.

Interrail and Eurail passes are valid on almost all trains along Route 35. This is a region of Europe where fares are generally fairly cheap. A one-way ticket from Bratislava to Košice costs under €20, so pass-holders should consider whether valuable pass days might better be saved for longer and more expensive journeys, all the more so as seat reservations are mandatory for pass-holders on many longer-distance trains in Slovakia, as also on the leg from Košice to Budapest.

The Marchlands

The two **EU capitals** which are closest to each other are Vienna and Bratislava, so it's no surprise that there are many train services between them. Of the two routes that run east from Vienna to the Slovak capital, the northern one via Marchegg definitely has the edge in terms of scenery, and wins out on another count. Trains on this northern route run to Bratislava's main station (called hlavná stanica or Bratislava hl.st.), rather than terminating in the uninspiring suburb of Petržalka, well away from the city centre on Slovakia's only territorial fragment on the left bank of the Danube. Just note that on the northern route via Marchegg buses replace trains from Marchegg across the border until the start of 2025.

Fast trains via the Marchegg route to Bratislava usually leave from **Vienna's Hauptbahnhof** at about a quarter past each hour. Looping past the distinctive brick buildings of the Arsenal (on the left), the train swings north to cross Prater Park and the Danube to reach a line running east from Vienna. This route to Bratislava opened in 1870, but it's not been continuously in use. During the Cold War years, there were no trains across the Slovak border via this route. But now it's firmly back in business, with electrification and upgrading in progress.

Leaving Vienna behind, the railway crosses the watery **Marchfeld**, the borderlands around the River March (known as Morava in Slovak) which offer fertile soils for growing fruit and vegetables for the nearby cities. The last stop in Austria is at **Marchegg**, which looks nothing special from the train, but the main part of the village, about 3 km away to the north of the station, is sleepy but pretty with a fine palace. Marchegg slumbered through the Cold War and after, then suddenly reawakened in 2022 as the community hosted a major regional exhibition from March to November. Rattling over the River March, the train enters Slovakia, making its first stop in the country at **Devínska Nová Ves** which is one of a number of places in the region to have a substantial Croatian minority. From here it's but a short hop to Bratislava.

Bratislava (suggested stopover)

Overshadowed by Prague, it has sometimes been hard for the Slovak capital to make its mark. But the city is **superbly placed** midway between Prague and Budapest, and is less than an hour by train east of Vienna. Bratislava fans always argue that the city has all the merits of Prague without the crowds. There will not be a lot to detain you in the dreary suburbs, but the **Old Town** (Staré Mesto) is a gem. The main sights cluster within the old city walls on the east side of **Staromestská**. West of that is a prominent hill topped by the rather austere **castle** (Bratislavský hrad). The Danube riverfront is dominated by the modernist **New Bridge** (Nový most) that leads over to the huge Petržalka estate.

The Old Town is full of atmospheric lanes. In and around Ventúrska, Michalská and Panská you'll find excellent **baroque palaces**. Look out for the Mozartov dom (which has only the most tenuous of links with the composer), the rococo Mirbach Palace and the **Pálffyho Palace** that houses part of the Bratislava City Gallery (closed Mon). Noteworthy Gothic structures include the Franciscan church and the striking tower of St Klara's Convent (today not a convent at all but a library).

Climb **St Michael's Tower** at Michalská 22 for a great panoramic view. At the west side of the Old Town stands the Gothic St Martin's Cathedral, nowadays rather hemmed in by Staromestská. Immediately on the west side of Staromestská, under the shadow of the castle, is Bratislava's **old Jewish Quarter**.

The castle itself houses extensive museums. Information on the various exhibitions and locations of the **Slovak National Museum** on www.snm.sk. Bratislava's Old Town is full of bars, cafés and restaurants that spill out onto the streets on sunny evenings, with the highest concentration on Ventúrska.

Arrival, information, accommodation

≽ Bratislava has two main train stations. The chief one, **Hlavná stanica**, is used by almost all trains and is 1.5 km north of the Old Town (tram 1 provides a reliable link). A second station at **Petržalka** (3 km south of the city centre on the south side of the Danube) has fewer facilities, but it is the terminus for an alternative service from Vienna via Kittsee. 🛈 Tourist office: Klobučnícka 2 (www.visitbratislava.com) and at Hlavná stanica.

⨽ Budget accommodation is hard to find in Bratislava. Just a ten-minute stroll from the Old Town is the comfortable **Loft Hotel Bratislava**, Štefánikova 4, ☎ 02 57 51 10 00 (www.lofthotel.sk). Or try the equally central **Danubia Gate Bratislava**, Dunajská 26, ☎ 091 72 32 30 00 (www.danubiagate.sk). Just around the corner of the Old Town and close to the bank of the Danube is the modern **Hotel Avance**, Medená 9, ☎ 02 59 20 84 00 (www.hotelavance.sk).

Connections from Bratislava

You can connect in Bratislava into **Route 33** in this book. Take your pick from the impressive range of **international trains** serving Bratislava. You can travel directly to both Dresden and Berlin. There's choice of both daytime and overnight trains to Warsaw in Poland. Bratislava is also the jumping-off point for journeys to the **Tatra Mountains** and eastern Slovakia. Prague and Budapest are both just a short ride on regular Eurocity services.

There are a number of rail routes from **Bratislava to Košice**. There's the northern route via the Váh Valley and Poprad, and that's the one we describe here. But there are alternative slower options via Zvolen and then either Plešivec or the mountainous line through Brezno. Bear these options in mind if you find yourself making a second journey across Slovakia. Both are extremely beautiful.

Our northern route is the main line between Slovakia's two largest cities. There's a good choice of express and local services, the latter much slower and normally requiring at least two changes of train along the way.

Through the Slovakian Hills

The run out from Bratislava has its fair share of dreary suburbs, but the view is enlivened by the forested ridge of the **Malé Karpaty** (Little Carpathians) away to the left. Leaving the hills and crossing the plain, all trains stop at Trnava, which really is a remarkable walled city, the central area of which is utterly delightful. There's more to come in **Piešt'any**, which has none of the antique charm of Trnava, but cuts a dash on the spa circuit. If you've never stopped at a spa community in central Europe, then spend a few hours or stay overnight in Piešt'any.

For a couple of hours or more beyond Piešt'any, the railway follows the Váh Valley upstream into the hills. You'll slip through **Trenčín** where the undoubtedly impressive castle is offset by some dreadful apartment blocks. Parts of the valley are heavily industrialized, but the attractive hills on the left are the White Carpathians, the summit line of which marks the Czech border.

Púchov and Žilina connections

In a region where lines of communication are shaped by topography, both Púchov and Žilina are important railway junctions. Travelling from Bratislava, **Púchov** is reached first, from where semi-fast trains run every two hours to Prague. A further 44 km up the **Váh Valley**, Žilina offers connections to Ostrava with most trains continuing to Prague.

From Žilina, there's a delightful backdoor route north into Poland, using a local train from **Žilina to Zwardoń**, changing there for an onward service down the Sola Valley towards Katowice. Finally, there's a useful semi-fast regional train running south from Žilina to Banská Bystrica and Zvolen. Both those cities offer alternative routes east to Košice.

Tatra diversions

The small network of rail routes which extends north from Štrba and Poprad into the lower parts of the **Tatra massif** has been critical in supporting tourism in the hills. The Slovakian side of the hills is remarkably populated and there's a well-developed tourist infrastructure (which includes some memorably tacky developments). But there's some fabulous walking and it'd be a real shame when following Route 35 not to at least take a closer peek at the hills. The route we describe here, using the narrow-gauge Tatra Railway from **Štrba to Poprad** is 14 km longer than the main line between the two places. You'll need to buy a separate ticket for this stretch, but the fare is just €2.

The **cog railway** which climbs into the hills from Štrba is locally called the *zubačka*. Trains leave from a separate area of Štrba station, climbing at a gradient of up to 15% to reach **Štrbské Pleso** (at over 1,300 metres) in just 15 minutes, where there's usually five minutes to connect onto the narrow-gauge train to Poprad. The journey time from Štrba to Poprad via this route is 90 minutes. Yet why not take time to stop off along the way? Štrbské Pleso is a good jumping-off point for mountain walks. Of the various communities in the hills, **Starý Smokovec** – halfway between Štrbské Pleso and Poprad – is our favourite and also has the best range of facilities. For a nostalgic dash of old Tatra style, head to the Grand Hotel for tea and cake amid fading parquetry. Suitably satiated, you might then work out any excess calories by a forest walk, and there is an abundance of choice around Starý Smokovec.

The town is also convenient to connect into the cross-border bus service to Zakopane in Poland (a link newly introduced in this 18th edition of *Europe by Rail* as an extension of **Route 37**). An express bus leaves Starý Smokovec daily at 15.58 and takes 1hr 40mins to reach Zakopane (book on www.flixbus.pl). A later evening bus over the border to Zakopane at 19.55 continues overnight all the way to Berlin.

Beyond **Žilina**, the real mountains begin, as our route follows the River Váh up through the Malá Fatra range. This is where the journey gets really interesting. The hills close in but it is still remarkable just how industrialized the valley is. To the south of the railway at Vrútky is the industrial complex which for decades produced tanks, and further up the valley in Ružomberok cotton was once king. Today the entire Váh Valley struggles with a legacy of industrial decline; it's not all pretty, but as we move east the Tatra Mountains become visible away to the north.

The summit of the line, at just over 900 metres, is on the gentlest of cols near **Tatranska Štrba**. This watershed marks the divide between water flowing down the Váh Valley to eventually reach the Black Sea and the Poprad Valley which drains north into the Baltic. The latter seems a little against the odds, given the huge bulwark of the Tatras that here dominate the view to the north. The summit station is simply called **Štrba**, and you'd be foolish not to alight here. From Štrba our main route drops gently down to **Poprad**, just 20 km away to the east, but there's a wonderful little detour which gives a nice taste of the Tatra landscapes. It adds a little by way of time and distance and is described in the box on p327.

Down to Košice

Poprad railway station cuts a dash for those interested in the East Modernist style which found its fullest expression in towns across the eastern part of Czechoslovakia. There is no real reason to stop in Poprad, though it's the jumping-off point for the scenic *Beliansky Expres*, which runs twice daily at summer weekends (1 June to 1 September in 2024) to Muszyna in Poland, for onward connections to Kraków.

Beyond Poprad, the railway gently crests a ridge to gain the **Hornád Valley** which it then follows downstream to Košice. It is altogether less industrialized than the Váh Valley, which we followed from Piešt'any up to **Tatranská Štrba**, but there's still a good smattering of settlements, many with very fine wooden churches – each one capturing the artistic and architectural expression of a region where wood is so valued a commodity. Faith is important in eastern Slovakia. But it's easy to mistake quite what religion dominates in any particular community. There are plenty of Roman Catholics to be sure, but some of the Orthodox-style crosses on churches you'll see from the train are misleading. Although there are Orthodox Christians in the region, there are also many **Uniates** – an intriguing hybrid faith which is linked to the Latin Church and recognizes the authority of the Roman pontiff, yet uses the Byzantine liturgies and favours Orthodox iconography. Uniates are often known as Greek Catholics.

The upper part of the Hornád Valley is the heart of the **Spiš region**, where a federation of some two dozen communities was founded by settlers from Saxony in the late mediaeval and Renaissance periods. Today, these places still have a Teutonic demeanour and pleasing architectural coherence. This is a part of Slovakia where one might easily lay up for a day or two in a small town. If you have time to spare, make for **Levoča**, easily reached by buses (2 to 3 per hour, journey time 20 to 30 mins) from Spišská Nová Ves, the first major station east of Poprad. On the first weekend in July each year, the branch railway to Levoča is reopened for just two days to accommodate the crowds making for a Catholic festival just north of Levoča. That weekend apart, Levoča is a sleepy place, utterly charming with its fetching main square and a clutch of good restaurants. The Hotel U Leva (www.uleva.sk) is far from posh, but it's a nice spot for a night or two. Ask for a room overlooking the market square.

There's an especially fine stretch of the Hornád Valley east of **Margecany**; it's the only part of this entire journey through Slovakia where the railway is not paralleled by a main road. Before long, the train is running into Košice.

Kosiče

Slovakia's second city is a place where myth and reality merge. At one level, Košice has a certain ragged splendour. But is it disingenuous to wax lyrical about a city with high unemployment exacerbated by recent lay-offs in the huge steel works? Košice has its challenges, among them the pressing need to give the city's **Roma minority** a better deal. But the central area of the city, just west of the railway station, is undeniably beautiful. Civic leaders are keen to emulate the success of Kraków and Lviv with an ambitious programme of restoring Habsburg-era and earlier buildings in the central area. The result is a remarkable confection of wonderful buildings ranging from gnarled Gothic and stately fin de siècle styles, mostly gathered within a lens-shaped and very walkable area extending along and on either side of Hlavná ulica – which itself has a lenticular plan, with Kosiče's **striking Gothic cathedral** spanning that road at its widest point.

Košice was in the limelight in 2013 when it was one of Europe's culture capitals, using that opportunity to emphasise that effective urban renewal means more than cleaning old buildings. The city has been a showpiece for culture-led regeneration with strong involvement of Košice's youth and minorities. Walking into town from the railway station, you'll pass **Theatre Romathan** (at Štefánikova 4), home to the Slovakia's leading Roma stage company and also Košice's Roma orchestra. From here it's just a short walk further west to **Hlavná ulica**, that curiously lozenge-shaped main boulevard, which is the main hub for visitors. Head up to the north end of Hlavná ulica and take a peek at the wonderful wooden Greek Catholic church; it's tucked away behind the museum on the north side of Hviezdoslavova.

For us, any spell in Košice is punctuated by frequent visits to the **Café Slávia**, a local institution at Hlavná 63 where locals have gathered for coffee and cake for over a century. It is an extraordinary place, great for people watching with excellent food (and great-value lunchtime specials on weekdays). They also have rooms (see accommodation notes below).

ARRIVAL, INFORMATION, ACCOMMODATION

⇌ Košice railway station is about a 10-minute walk east of the city centre. 🛈 Tourist office: Hlavná 59 in the town hall (www.visitkosice.org).

🛏 A comfortable option in a quiet area within a short walk to all main attractions is the **Penzion Hradbová**, Hradbová 9, ☎ 05 57 29 06 66 (www.penzionhradbova.sk). Equally conveniently situated is the stylish **Boutique Hotel Slávia**, Hlavná 63, ☎ 05 52 86 20 00 (www.kaviarenslavia.sk). Or try the **Boutique Penzion Slovakia**, Orlia 6, ☎ 05 57 28 98 20 (www.penzionslovakia.sk) located between the station and the city centre, where the restaurant serves a decent steak plus traditional Slovakian fare.

South into Hungary

In Habsburg days a main communication artery, the cross-border section of the railway from **Košice to Budapest** has suffered years of neglect. For far too long, just two trains each day ran south on the main line from Košice into Hungary. That changed in December 2021 with the launch of the new Eurocity *Hornád* service, taking its name from the river which runs through Košice, and giving a direct link every two hours to the Hungarian capital.

Running south from Košice, and still broadly following the River Hornád, the railway crosses under the broad-gauge line built in the 1960s to bring Soviet iron ore to Košice steel works, visible well away to the right of the train. In about 20 minutes, the train slips into Hungary where the first stop is at **Hidasnémeti** where the lime-green décor of the station building brings a splash of colour to otherwise drab surroundings.

From Hidasnémeti, it's an easy run south through tame agricultural country to the industrial city of **Miskolc**. Fast trains from Košice usually make five intermediate stops along the way to Miskolc's Tiszai station. There's a great opportunity to try a **roundabout Hungarian route** from Miskolc to Budapest. When the train from Košice arrives at Miskolc Tiszai, there is usually a train to Budapest via Tokaj and Debrecen leaving just a few minutes later. It's a four-hour tour that takes in Hungary's premier wine region. If you make this loop, do pause in **Debrecen** which is Hungary's second city, and a place where Calvinist traditions still run deep. These days it's a stronghold of Viktor Orbán's right-leaning Fidesz alliance. Trains on this route from Miskolc to Budapest run into Nyugati station in the Hungarian capital.

There's nothing to detain you in Miskolc though, and from here the train from Košice runs in express mode, taking just another two hours to reach **Budapest** where the service terminates at Keleti station. For more on Budapest, see our description on p311.

Sidetracks: Carpathian connections

The city of **Košice** in eastern Slovakia is an important way station on **Route 35**. It's is also a natural jumping-off point for exploring the Carpathian region, which is home to one of Europe's most interesting minorities: the **Rusyn people**.

In the closing decades of the **Habsburg Empire**, Carpathian Rusyns successfully asserted their national identity. Rusyn life was interpreted as an essentially rural endeavour. It was intimately linked to the Uniate (sometimes called Greek-Catholic) faith that found a great following among Rusyns. This religion, which deftly bridges two branches of Christianity in Europe (namely, the Orthodox and Roman traditions), is however not peculiar to the Rusyns. At a day-to-day level, it was this religion, a distinctive East Slavic language — seen by many linguists as deeply influenced by Church Slavonic — and the valued status of wooden architecture which emerged as the trinity of virtues which underpinned Rusyn self-awareness.

Stories of rural suffering shaped Rusyn thinking, even though a dash of poetry helped alleviate the burden and that remained even more true in the post-Habsburg period. "We are shepherds, we sing our own liturgy," wrote Rusyn poet **Petr Prodan** in 1941, alluding to the distinctive tradition of unaccompanied singing in their churches.

Bardejov is a good place to aim for to embark on Rusyn explorations. It's easily reached by local train from Košice, with a journey time of about two hours and an en-route change of train in Prešov. Just bear in mind that some of the Rusyn villages are **quite remote**, but local buses run, albeit infrequently, to even the most out-of-the way communities on the Slovak side of the borders with neighbouring Poland and Ukraine.

You may be tempted to venture across those borders and in each case there are interesting options by train. The train from Košice to **Medzilaborce** is a regular year-round service, but on Saturdays and Sundays during the summer, it's possible to continue on over the border into Poland. This line tracks through sparsely populated terrain to give access to a very beautiful part of south-east Poland.

For those keen to head into Ukraine, there are twice-daily fast trains from Košice to **Mukachevo** in Ukraine. The train is called the *Zakarpatia* ('Transcarpathian' in English). This "international express" makes just two intermediate stops on the four-hour journey to Mukachevo – but when we used it, the train consisted of an aged Slovak **red-and-white railcar** of the kind you might expect to encounter on a rural branch line. If political conditions in Ukraine permit, then do consider trying this cross-border link. The very existence of this train has been part of the political project to bind western Ukraine into the European Union's sphere of influence. In 2019, European standard-gauge tracks were extended from the Slovak and Hungarian borders all the way to Mukachevo, so averting the need for trains to switch bogies at Chop (though trains making journeys deeper into Ukraine, like the night train from Vienna to Kyiv, still need to do that). The Košice to Mukachevo trains still stop at Chop, whence a fine rural railway runs north through **Uzhhorod** (Ужгород) and on over Užok Pass towards Lviv. We rate the latter as the finest rail route in the Carpathian region.

Route 36: East from Berlin

Cities: ★★ Culture: ★ History: ★★★ Scenery: ★
Countries covered: Germany (DE), Poland (PL), Ukraine (UA)
Journey time: 15 hrs | Distance: 1,207 km | Map: www.ebrweb.eu/18map36

Route 36 is a journey full of historical overtones. In 1701, the Elector of Brandenburg decided to style himself King of Prussia, thus creating a new monarchy — one with no precedent, but one which developed into a great dominion with its pivots in the twin centres of Berlin and Königsberg (now Kaliningrad in Russia). Our journey starts in Berlin, the city which was Prussia's real political powerhouse.

This route ends in a city whose inhabitants know a thing or two about empire. The first railways to **Lviv** were all planned in Vienna for, after the partition of Poland in 1772, Lviv was part of the **Austrian Empire**, where it remained until the collapse of Habsburg authority at the end of the First World War. Lviv was the capital of Galicia, an Austrian crown land — not to be confused with the region in north-west Spain still known today as Galicia. Between the two world wars, Lviv was part of Poland, then in 1946 it found itself in the Soviet Union. Borders have shifted, empires have come and gone, yet in the cities on Route 36 the echoes of history still inflect everyday life. Especially nowadays in Ukraine.

Between Berlin and Lviv, Route 36 takes in two particularly **fine Polish cities**, Poznań and Kraków — both with magnificent central squares. Not to mention the capital Warsaw too. Like every route in the book, this journey is not just about getting from A to B. It's better to linger and take a few days exploring places along the way. **Kraków** deserves at least a couple of nights. If you want to make an interesting rural diversion, it is an easy journey south from Kraków to visit the Tatra Mountains (that rail excursion is described towards the end of **Route 37**).

Across the border

Our journey starts in **Berlin** (see p131) at the city's glitzy Hauptbahnhof. It is a station which really invites exploration. With trains serving two different levels, there are interesting sightlines, some of them revealing a train where you might not have expected to see one. Trains to Poland normally leave from platforms 11 or 12.

The ageing Polish carriages on the journey to Poznań are comfy, but often crowded. The 19th-century writer **Erasmus Wilson** commented that only Russian princes and English tradesmen travel first class. Our view is that, if you are travelling at a peak time, it might be worth paying the modest extra charge to rub shoulders with princes (or tradesmen) on the ride to Poznań. The train passes through tame countryside, with lots of

Polish steam

Western Poland has been the last area in Europe to retain steam locomotives for scheduled standard-gauge passenger trains. In September 2024, steam haulage was still routinely used on a return run from Wolsztyn to Zbąszynek (Mon to Fri), and on the **Wolsztyn** to Poznań line on Saturdays. It is uncertain how long these steam services will continue.

That the Wolsztyn area has survived as a steam outpost, long after steam haulage disappeared elsewhere in Europe, is the result of cooperation between the Polish railway authorities and **British train enthusiasts**. The latter have provided financial support to ensure that the locomotive depot at Wolsztyn is kept operational. Local Polish staff retain the necessary skills to keep old locomotives in good order. A driving force in the survival of steam at Wolsztyn was Howard Jones, a British rail enthusiast. Howard sadly died in June 2023, leaving a question mark over the future of the venture.

The steam trains seen around Wolsztyn are immensely evocative of a bygone age of European rail travel. The area is often blanketed in winter by deep snow and in such conditions the engines are seen at their best.

forest. Highpoint is the crossing of the **River Oder** into Poland (where that river is called Odra).

Poznań (suggested stopover)

The **capital of Wielkopolska** is one of Poland's most engaging and oldest cities. It was the seat of Poland's first bishop in the 10th century. Its status as a great mercantile centre (it's still an important centre for trade fairs) has contributed to the architectural heritage of its Old Town.

The city's focal point is **Stary Rynek**, a spacious square with gabled burghers' houses and a spectacular multicoloured 16th-century Renaissance **Town Hall**, where at midday two mechanical goats emerge from above the clock to lock horns. Inside is the Chamber of the Renaissance with its beautifully painted, coffered ceiling (1555).

Several churches form an outer ring around the market square. Of those, the baroque **Poznań Parish Church** (Kolegiata Poznańska) at the southern end is dedicated to St Mary Magdalene. The Jesuit College next door, once Napoleon's residence, now hosts Chopin concerts. A short walk north-east of the centre is **Ostrów Tumski**, the oldest part of the city on an island in the River Warta; here stands the cathedral, fronted by a huge but gentle statue of Pope John Paul II.

Arrival, information, accommodation

Poznań Główny is a 10-min walk to the centre or take tram 3. Buy tickets from one of the kiosks at the western exit. All international and domestic trains call here. Tourist office: Stary Rynek 59/60 (www.poznan.travel).

We very much recommend staying at the **Brovaria**, Stary Rynek 73–74, ☎ 61 858 68 68 (www.brovaria.pl), and if you can secure one of the few rooms that overlook the Stary Rynek, then it is worth every złoty. The friendly **City Solei Boutique Hotel**, ul.

CENTRAL AND EASTERN EUROPE

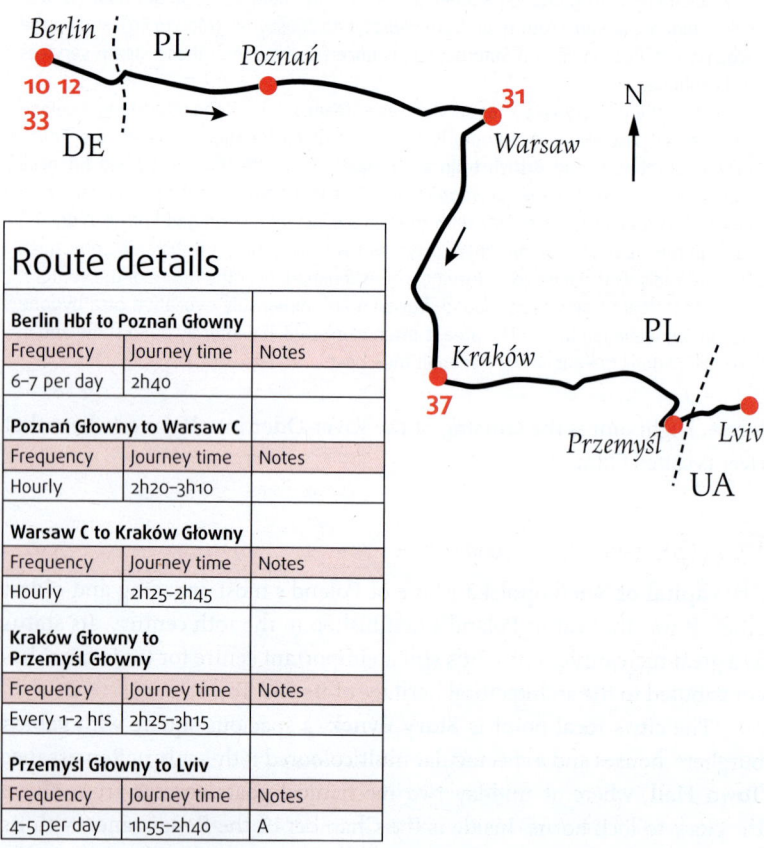

Route details

Berlin Hbf to Poznań Główny

Frequency	Journey time	Notes
6–7 per day	2h40	

Poznań Główny to Warsaw C

Frequency	Journey time	Notes
Hourly	2h20–3h10	

Warsaw C to Kraków Główny

Frequency	Journey time	Notes
Hourly	2h25–2h45	

Kraków Główny to Przemyśl Główny

Frequency	Journey time	Notes
Every 1–2 hrs	2h25–3h15	

Przemyśl Główny to Lviv

Frequency	Journey time	Notes
4–5 per day	1h55–2h40	A

Notes

If you like the idea of travelling from Berlin to southern Poland and western Ukraine, but need a short cut on the full route described here, then help is at hand in the Eurocity trains which provide direct daytime connections from Berlin to Kraków. As of October 2024, these direct trains leave Berlin Hauptbahnhof at 10.52 and 16.52, taking a shade over seven hours to reach Kraków. The morning train from Berlin extends beyond Kraków to Przemyśl.

A – Seek good advice on the wisdom of entering Ukraine at the moment. Check Ukrainian visa and entry requirements before purchasing your train ticket to Lviv. Holders of EU passports, as well as citizens of many other countries (including Canada, the USA and the UK) may enter visa-free for up to 90 days.

Wenecjańska 10, ☎ 512 36 88 18 (www.citysolei.pl), has individually styled rooms and is well located just a short walk east of the Stary Rynek. A modern and stylish option in the old Jewish quarter close to the Old Town Square is the **Puro Hotel Poznan**, Stawna 12, ☎ 61 333 10 00 (www.purohotel.pl).

SIDETRIPS FROM POZNAŃ
From Poznań, there is a very nice rail route which runs north-east to **Gniezno**, a handsome little town which can justifiably claim to have been the first capital of Poland. In a route largely dominated by big cities, albeit very fine ones, a night in Gniezno would make a worthwhile diversion and give a taste of small-town Poland. Trains on this route continue beyond Gniezno to **Toruń**, a wonderful city on the River Wisła with a rich Hanseatic history or to Gdańsk on the Baltic – another city with a proud Hanseatic past (and on **Route 31**).

Another option from Poznań is to go south to **Wrocław**, a university city on the Odra River which is on **Route 37**. There are direct trains to Kraków should you prefer skip Warsaw after having visited Poznań.

As the train leaves Poznań, there is a tantalising glimpse (back to the right of the train) of that city's remarkable Town Hall. Before long you are running through pleasant **Mazovian countryside** on the approach to Warsaw. There are glimpses of rural estates and manor houses, wistfully beautiful meadows and concrete apartment blocks – a very Polish mix. The melancholic, plaintive melodies of the region found expression in **Chopin's music**; the composer was born in Żelazowa Wola, about 45 kilometres west of Warsaw.

Warsaw (Warszawa) – (suggested stopover)
Warsaw, capital of a resurgent Polish nation, is once again punching its weight as a major European city. Straddling the **River Wisła** (Vistula), its location between the old powers of Germany and Russia has ensured that the city has been a victim of history on more than one occasion. After the horrors of the Second World War, the communist period saw the meticulous reconstruction of the city's historic buildings and a rash of new Socialist Realist buildings. Among the latter is the widely visible **Palace of Culture and Science**, Stalin's gift to Poland.

The city's reconstructed **Old Town** is a bewitching network of cobbled streets, church spires and hidden courtyards. Take some time to explore the

WARSAW JAZZ
Although it comes as a surprise to most Western Europeans, jazz has a **long tradition** in Poland. Pre-war dance club bands in Warsaw and other cities got Poles moving to swing-based jazz in the 1930s. In the early 1960s the first Warsaw Jazz Jamboree Festival was staged. In 1992, the idea of the annual **Warsaw Summer Jazz Days** was born (www.adamiakjazz.pl). The festival quickly became an important event on the jazz circuit. Innovation is the watchword and the main location is the awe-inspiring Congress Hall within the Palace of Culture and Science. Even outside the festival season, Warsaw has a vibrant year-round jazz scene.

churches and cathedrals, of which Poland has no shortage, making sure not to miss St John's Cathedral in the Old Town. One of the city's highlights is the **Muzeum Sztuki Nowoczesnej** (Museum of Modern Art) with cutting-edge contemporary Polish art located not far from the Palace of Culture and Science on ul. Pańska 3 (www.artmuseum.pl; closed Mon). There is a further exhibition space called the Museum on the Vistula. **Muzeum Powstania Warszawskiego** (Warsaw Uprising Museum) recalls Warsaw's most heroic moment relived inside one of Poland's finest museums, located on ul. Grzybowska 79 (www.1944.pl; closed Tues). Don't miss **POLIN**, the Museum of the History of Polish Jews, ul. Mordechaja Anielewicza 6 (www.polin.pl; closed Tues).

Warsaw is the hub of modern Polish culture and Poland's centre of academia. The large student and young professional contingent has ensured one of Europe's most happening nightlife scenes. For real Warsaw buzz, explore the area well south of the tourist-focused Old Town. Poznańska and the streets around are where the locals gather. Enjoy **Koszyki Market Hall**, just beyond the southern end of Poznańska, with its eateries, food stalls, trendy bars and a bookshop.

ARRIVAL, INFORMATION, ACCOMMODATION

Warszawa Centralna is the principal rail station at Al. Jerozolimskie 54 in the city centre. Other large stations in the city are: **Warszawa Wschodnia** on the east bank of the River Wisła, and the western suburban station, **Warszawa Zachodnia**, 3 km west of Centralna, opposite the PKS bus station. Warsaw Frédéric Chopin Airport lies 10 km south of the city (www.lotnisko-chopina.pl). Line S2 of Szybka Kolej Miejska (SKM – Rapid Urban Railway) links the airport with Warszawa Zachodnia and Wschodnia. 175 connects the airport with Warszawa Centralna (about a 30-min ride). Or take the KML airport train run by Masovian Railways. Trams and buses operate on a frequent network (www.wtp.waw.pl). Prepaid tickets (from kiosks etc.) are cheaper than paying on the bus. Don't forget to validate your ticket before travel. There are frequent services on Warsaw's two metro lines which run from north to south and east to west through the centre of the city (stations are marked with a red 'M' on yellow background). Covering all public transport, 24 hr tickets are excellent value (available for one or two zones). Tourist office: pl. Defilad 1 in the Palace of Culture and Science (www.warsawtour.pl).

For rail travellers, an excellent choice just a short walk from Centralna station is the very stylish **H15 Boutique Hotel**, ul. Poznańska 15, ☎ 22 553 87 00 (www.h15boutiqueapartments.com). Don't miss the H15's excellent *Signature* restaurant. An upmarket hotel close to the Old Town in a quiet area is the very welcoming **Le Regina**, Kościelna 12, ☎ 22 531 60 00 (www.mamaisonleregina.com). Not far south of the Old Town, the **Residence Diana**, ul. Chmielna 13A, ☎ 22 50 59 100 (www.mamaisondiana.com), is a comfortable and welcoming mid-range option.

EXPLORING BEYOND WARSAW

There is a useful eastbound sleeper from Warsaw departing every afternoon to Kyiv. From Warsaw, there are good rail links to the north-east corner of the country, an area of Poland not much visited by tourists. **Białystok** is the main regional centre, but it's worth cutting off the main routes to explore the Masurian lakeland (where Mikołajki is the best base) and the **Tatar villages** close to the Belarusian border. Kruszyniany and Bohoniki both have traditional wooden mosques and Muslim cemeteries. It's an interesting reminder that Poland has a centuries-long Islamic tradition. Train services beyond **Białystok** are few and far between. The daily direct service from Warsaw via Białystok to Hrodna (Гродна) in Belarus is suspended. There is better news on **links with Lithuania**, with a direct daily train from Warsaw now running again. As of October 2024, this is the 07.50 from Warsaw Centralna to Mockava, a village just inside Lithuania and close to the Polish border. There's a cross-platform connection onto an onward train to **Kaunas** and **Vilnius**, where arrival is at 17.34. This cross-border line was rebuilt at great expense as part of the **Rail Baltica project**. Thank goodness it is now being used, but it's a scandal that there are not more trains.

The Central Trunk Line to Kraków

There surely could not be a less romantic name for a railway than the Central Trunk Line – in Polish *Centralna Magistrala Kolejowa*, often just abbreviated to CMK. This could so easily have been Europe's first modern-era high-speed railway. It was designed to a very high engineering specification with a view to trains running at over 200 kilometres per hour. But in the 1970s, when Poland had no trains capable of achieving such speeds, the Central Trunk Line was used mainly for freight. Not until late 2014 was a respectably fast passenger train service introduced, with **Pendolinos** speeding non-stop between Warsaw and Kraków. The fastest trains are branded **Express Intercity Premium** (EIP); seat reservation is compulsory. The CMK route wins no prizes for scenery, but before long you'll be in Kraków, where you can connect onto **Route 37**.

Kraków (suggested stopover)

Kraków is by far the most **popular tourist destination** in Poland. The city's main square rivals St Mark's in Venice as one of the finest piazzas in Europe. Kraków was once Poland's capital, and, though it lost that status in 1596, much of Polish history has been forged here. After Poland was partitioned, it was briefly an independent city-state, and then became part of the Austro-Hungarian province of Galicia. During the 20th century, Kraków was Poland's pre-eminent city of ideas. Be it in the arts, politics, commerce or in church affairs, the town has always punched above its weight.

Kraków is also an important centre of industry and home to the huge steelworks at **Nowa Huta**, north-east of the city. As a tourist attraction, the Nowa Huta district offers a very different experience from its romantic counterpart, but this fascinating, carefully designed socialist suburb is more than concrete blocks and just a tram-ride away from the beaten path.

The city's main sights are concentrated on the north bank of the River Wisła (Vistula). Focal points are the Old Town Square and **Wawel Hill** with the castle and cathedral within walking distance of each other. The **Old Town Square** (Rynek Główny) is a gem, but to experience it at its best you will have to see it at dead of night or at dawn on a sunny spring morning. No other space in Poland is so utterly dedicated to tourists, and the impact of the square's magnificent architecture is often lessened by the sheer number of visitors. The centrepiece is the **mediaeval cloth hall** (Sukiennice), a fine covered market in 16th-century Renaissance style.

An easy 20-min walk due south from the Old Town Square will bring you to **Kazimierz**, once a separate community outside the walls of Kraków, and later the city's **Jewish quarter**. There are several synagogues and a number of restaurants that proclaim their Jewish credentials (some not as kosher as they may seem).

ARRIVAL, INFORMATION, ACCOMMODATION

⇌ Kraków Główny (main station) is a short walk north-east of the centre. Head left from the station, turn right down Basztowa, enter the large underpass and head for the Planty/Basztowa exit to the right. Główny has services to Oświęcim (for the Auschwitz memorial), Zakopane and Wieliczka, as well as long-distance trains. 🛈 Tourist office: Sw. Jana ul. 2 (https://krakow.travel/).

🛏 If you've travelled around Poland and become used to good-value accommodation, prepare for a shock if you arrive in Kraków in high season. Market rules apply, and prices rocket. Centrally located close to Rynek Główny is the friendly **Hotel Unicus**, Św. Marka 20, ☎ 12 433 71 11 (www.hotelunicus.pl). Or try the **Ascot**, ul. Radziwiłłowska 3, ☎ 12 384 06 06 (www.ascotpremium.pl), a mid-range hotel just outside the Old Town walls. A comfortable option in the Kazimierz district is the **Dada Boutique Home Hotel**, ul. Krakowska 30, ☎ 12 345 09 92 (www.dadahotel.pl). ✗ Rynek Główny and the surrounding streets are packed with restaurants. For premium locations on the Old Town Square, expect to pay premium prices. Make for the small streets around the university to find the best deals. Enjoy excellent Polish-Mediterranean cuisine at the **Farina**, ul. św. Marka 16, ☎ 12 422 16 80 (www.farina.com.pl), close to the Old Town Square.

If you stop at just one place between Kraków and Lviv, make it **Przemyśl**, a small town on the River San just short of the Ukrainian border. Frontier-hopping shoppers have boosted the economy of this **border town** that has a delightful centre just a 5-min walk south-west of the railway station. The **main square** (Rynek) doesn't match up to those in Wrocław and Kraków, but the real draw in Przemyśl are the churches, where you will find western-style Roman Catholicism merging gently into Eastern Orthodoxy. The Uniate (or Greek Catholic) Church bridges the divide and commands a great following in this area of eastern Poland. Przemyśl is a chance to experience another side of Poland before taking a deep breath and leaping over the border into **Ukraine**. Make sure that you have your passport to hand and check that the visa requirements have not changed.

The train journey from **Przemyśl to Lviv** is slow. But in this 98-km ride, you slip between two worlds. Just a few minutes out of Przemyśl, the train enters Ukraine and – however unholy the hour – you'll need to be awake for passport checks. Soon you'll be on the move again, trundling east through busy villages to **Lviv**. For onward journey options from Lviv see p339 and our **Sidetracks** feature on p340.

Lviv (Львів)

If Lviv were just 100 km further west, it would be in the premier league of European tourist destinations. The problem is, that while Poland oozes youthful chic from every cobblestone, Ukraine is embroiled in a war not of its own making. Lviv's attempts to style itself as 'the new Kraków' have yet to bear fruit. While Kraków pulls the crowds, Lviv slumbers.

The two cities share a common history, both having been part of the Austro-Hungarian province of **Galicia**. And both have that same Italianate flair in their central square and some of the surrounding courtyards. The centre of Kraków was the very first place in Poland to be inscribed on the UNESCO List of World Heritage Sites. That was back in 1978. Lviv had to wait another 20 years to receive the same accolade.

Lviv boasts a galaxy of fine churches and civic buildings. 'Must sees' include the **Armenian Cathedral** and the over-the-top baroque St George's Cathedral. The latter was the traditional hub of the Ukrainian Uniate Church which dominates religious affairs in western Ukraine. Following the Orange Revolution, the Archeparchy was transferred to Kyiv.

Above all, Lviv is a fine place just to wander. In good weather the Italian Yard is a spot to linger over coffee; it is a superb Renaissance courtyard. Or watch the sunset from **Vysoky Zamok** (Castle Hill) when the view of the city takes on a dreamy quality. For a more macabre take on life (or death), don't miss **Lychakivsky Cemetery**, a magnificent wooded parkland east of the city full of crumbling memorials to poets, philosophers and soldiers.

ARRIVAL, INFORMATION, ACCOMMODATION

≈ West of the city centre. Trams 1 and 9 get you to the town centre at Rynok Square.
🛈 Tourist office: in the city hall, opposite the Neptune Fountain (www.lviv.travel).

🛏 Lviv is happily very cheap. Even such a venerable institution as the **George Hotel**, Mickiewicz sq. 1, ☎ 032 232 62 36 (www.georgehotel.com.ua), is very affordable. We very much enjoyed staying at the **Swiss Hotel**, 20 Knyazya Romana ul., ☎ 032 240 3777 (www.swiss-hotel.lviv.ua), which is close to the centre and has a wonderful restaurant. Or opt for the **Vintage Boutique Hotel**, 11 Serbska ul., ☎ 032 235 68 34 (www.vintagehotel.com.ua), just a short walk from Rynok Square in the heart of the city.

CONNECTIONS FROM LVIV

Lviv is the **principal rail hub** in western Ukraine with a wide choice of long-distance trains. If you've followed Route 36 right through to Lviv, you'll probably not be looking to return immediately to Poland. But you may want to make tracks south through the hills to **Mukachevo**, less than 4 hrs from Lviv on the fastest trains. With a breakfast-time departure from Lviv, and a change of train in Mukachevo, it is now possible to be in either **Košice** (in eastern Slovakia) or in **Budapest** by early evening the same day. Read more on these links in our *Carpathian Connections* Sidetracks on p331. If leaving under cover of night is more your thing, then the direct night train from Lviv to **Vienna** was made for you. It leaves Lviv daily at 21.00, reaching the Austrian capital late morning the next day. For onward journeys from Lviv through Ukraine to Odesa and Kyiv see the next page. Note that trains from Lviv to Belarus and Russia are all currently suspended.

SIDETRACKS: THROUGH UKRAINE

The **plight of Ukraine**, invaded by Russian troops in February 2022, prompted a serious reappraisal of Ukrainian content in this new edition of *Europe by Rail*. The 16th edition of the book featured three Ukrainian routes, respectively entering Ukrainian territory from Romania, Hungary and Poland. We have retained only the latter, updating it as necessary. We think it's important to say something about what might await travellers when peace and stability return to the region. For now, **Route 36** ends in Lviv. If and when better times come, we would be tempted to include **Odesa** (Одеса) in *Europe by Rail*; the Black Sea port really in a gem and it's easy to reach by train. There is even a direct daily train from Przemyśl in Poland to Odesa, leaving early evening and reaching Odesa late morning the following day. That train is called *White Acacia* (Біла акація), taking its name from one of Odesa's signature trees – which isn't actually an acacia at all, but that's another story. As of October 2024, that direct train from Przemyśl to Odesa continues to run as normal, leaving Przemyśl every evening at 20.28, just as it has every day since the Russian invasion. The men and women of **Ukrainian Railways** have been real heroes in this difficult period.

Quite suddenly the railway station at **Przemyśl** became a hotspot for global news teams. It was here that in the opening weeks of the war the media gathered to witness refugees arriving from Ukraine. And it was from Przemyśl that politicians and activists set off to travel to Kyiv (Київ) to highlight support for President **Volodymyr Zelenskyy** and his wartime government. That the trains have continued to run right through to Kyiv is remarkable. And not just from Przemyśl, but also from Vienna and Budapest.

As and when tourist travel resumes, you'll find that long train journeys are a quintessential part of the Ukrainian experience. After Lviv (Львів), if you've not been seduced by our mention of Odesa's white acacia, then **Kyiv** is the obvious next stop. A daytime Intercity dashes non-stop from Lviv to Kyiv, taking just over six hours for the journey.

There are also **overnight trains** from Lviv to Kiev. Everyone is allocated a sleeping berth on these overnight runs. This may be in a 2- or 4-berth compartment or a specific place in an open-plan carriage with about four dozen bunks. This last type is effectively third class; it is called *platskarty*. We've used it, and it certainly feels safe, but you'd be wise not to leave valuables lying around in what is effectively a dormitory on wheels.

Kyiv certainly deserves a couple of days. The city is set on wooded hills around the River Dniepr and has an altogether grander and more eastern demeanour than Lviv. It boasts impressive squares, graceful boulevards and magnificent churches and museums. Star of the show is the **Kyievo-Pecherska lavra**, in English dubbed the Monastery of the Caves, one of the highest-ranking ecclesiastical foundations in the Orthodox world. It includes a number of churches and a newly rebuilt cathedral. Let's hope that the great churches of Kyiv and the city's other cultural assets survive the Russian onslaught.

To learn more about life in **eastern Ukraine** in these times of civil strife and discord, turn to *In Wartime: Stories from Ukraine* by Tim Judah. This compelling account of how conflict has affected ordinary people is published by Allen Lane.

Route 37: From Saxony to the Tatra Mountains
Cities: ★★★ Culture: ★★ History: ★★★ Scenery: ★★
Countries covered: Germany (DE), Poland (PL), Slovakia (SK)
Journey time: 13 hrs 25 mins | Distance: 751 km | Map: www.ebrweb.eu/18map37

Thirty-five years ago this autumn, some weeks before the 1989 **fall of the Berlin Wall**, Dresden's main railway station was in the news as word spread through the city that special trains carrying migrants to West Germany would stop at Dresden Hauptbahnhof. Those trains were in fact **carrying East Germans** who had spent some weeks camping in the grounds of the West German embassy in Prague. Their wish to move to the West was granted, but the East German authorities insisted that the trains transit Saxony en route to West Germany. Many thousands of **Dresden citizens** gathered at the station, some keen to join a westbound train, others just curious to see comrades deserting their country in favour of a new life in a capitalist state.

Dresden has always been a place for comings and goings. In Europe today, the principal flow of refugees is from south to north. In the last century, different patterns prevailed. In this journey we travel east through the **shatterzones of history**, through territories where tyranny and violence shaped lives and landscapes.

These are places where the past is a foreign country. That's true of Dresden and Görlitz, which a generation ago were still paid-up members of the **German Democratic Republic**. It's true of Wrocław which was for 200 years Prussian and German. Our journey east will take us through the borderlands of three empires: Germany, Russia and Austria-Hungary. Along the way we'll transit the **vanished kingdoms** of Saxony, Lusatia, Silesia and Galicia.

The highlight of this route is the rail journey from **Kraków up to Zakopane**, and we therefore describe that portion of the journey in more detail. Beyond Zakopane, our route concludes with a short cross-border road journey through glorious mountain scenery, slipping from Poland into Slovakia to end in **Poprad** with a connection onto **Route 35**.

Itinerary notes
This journey from Dresden east through Wrocław to Kraków follows a former main-line railway which has been demoted to secondary status. Train services are never fast. On the final leg from Kraków to Zakopane, trains are even slower, but the **beauty of the landscape** as the train creeps up into the hills means that the slow progress is never a burden. Distances are not huge on this route, but even without stops you'd not manage to cover the entire route in a day. **Wrocław** and **Kraków** both deserve an overnight stop. And you'll almost certainly want to spend a day or two in Zakopane. If you want to stop off during the initial part of this route, while still in Germany, then the top choice is most certainly **Görlitz**.

Running **east from Dresden** (see p308), the railway cuts through the Oberlausitz (Upper Lusatia), which is home to the **Sorbian people**. The

342 | CENTRAL AND EASTERN EUROPE

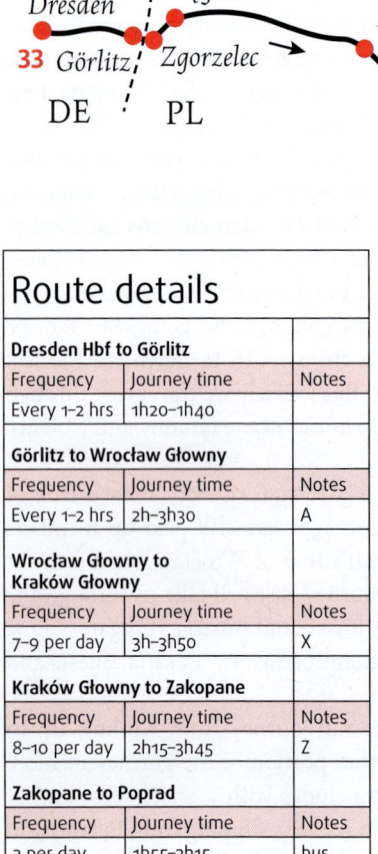

Route details

Dresden Hbf to Görlitz

Frequency	Journey time	Notes
Every 1–2 hrs	1h20–1h40	

Görlitz to Wrocław Głowny

Frequency	Journey time	Notes
Every 1–2 hrs	2h–3h30	A

Wrocław Głowny to Kraków Głowny

Frequency	Journey time	Notes
7–9 per day	3h–3h50	X

Kraków Głowny to Zakopane

Frequency	Journey time	Notes
8–10 per day	2h15–3h45	Z

Zakopane to Poprad

Frequency	Journey time	Notes
2 per day	1h55–2h15	bus

Notes

Train times in Poland change frequently. It makes sense to check timings just prior to travel at www.rozklad-pkp.pl.

A – Journeys from Görlitz to Wrocław always require a change of train in Zgorzelec or Węgliniec.

X – Most direct trains travel via Katowice (shown on our map as a continuous line), others via Częstochowa (shown as a dashed line).

Z – For a real slow travel experience, we strongly recommend taking one of the slower trains from Kraków. Second class only, lots of local colour and more opportunity to savour the passing countryside.

The story of the Neisse Viaduct

Route 37 was only made possible by the decision of regional authorities in Germany and Poland to **reinstate train services** between Dresden and Poland. The trains started running again in December 2015, using the railway viaduct which crosses the River Neisse between Görlitz and Zgorzelec.

There were surely local voices protesting against the construction of the **viaduct across the green valley** of the River Neisse in 1847. But just as viaducts elsewhere have settled into the landscape, so too has the long railway viaduct across the Neisse. History has not always been kind to this structure or to those who travelled over it. During the **Second World War**, many trains running east over the viaduct were bound for the concentration camp at Auschwitz.

In the very final hours of the war, after the unconditional capitulation of Germany had already been agreed, Wehrmacht troops detonated the central spans of the viaduct. Only 12 years later was the railway reopened and by then the five-minute journey from **Zgorzelec to Görlitz** had become an international adventure. For the post-war Potsdam Agreement defined Germany's new eastern frontier along the Oder and Neisse rivers. Under the new order, Görlitz was now the easternmost town in the **German Democratic Republic** and the territory east of the Neisse belonged to Poland.

But slowly the traffic built up, and by 1965 there was even a train carrying through carriages from Paris which trundled over the border at Görlitz on its journey to Kraków. The journey required two nights on board in ordinary seating. There were no couchettes or sleepers running through from Paris to Kraków, so this was surely a trip only for very hardy comrades.

The political and social eruptions of late 1989 ushered in a new era of importance for the old viaduct. Suddenly **all Europe was on the move**. Those who watched the movement of trains across the Neisse Valley could occasionally spot Russian carriages slipping over the border from Poland to Germany. Even the Moscow to Geneva service came this way. This looked like a railway whose hour had eventually come.

The two German states were united in 1990. Poland joined the European Union and was later admitted to Schengen. With no frontier formalities, Görlitz and Zgorzelec moved closer. In 2012 there was a major programme of renovation, funded in part by the European Union, to create a viaduct fit for a new Europe.

That **new Europe** was still on the move, but the new Europeans had discovered discount airlines and coach services with bargain basement fares. The trains were not quite so full; profits dwindled, and the line was closed to passenger traffic. "The market is not large enough," explained officials. We suspect that half a century ago, no one ever hired consultants to evaluate the potential market for rail travel between Paris and Kraków.

It took local protests to get the line reopened. The decision 177 years ago to build a great viaduct across the Neisse Valley was **a visionary leap**. Now that elegant structure, one of central Europe's finest pieces of railway engineering, needs a dose of 21st-century vision. The trains are on the move again, but we desperately need more **creative transport policies** to boost rail travel on Europe's cross-border rail routes.

Sorbs are a linguistic minority which has survived rather against the odds, in some ways helped between 1948 and 1989 by the East German state for whom it was rather convenient to have some home-grown Slavic culture. Sorbian villages, most of them deeply Catholic, are dotted across the region, but the strongest urban presence is in the town known at **Budyšín** (Sorbian) or **Bautzen** (German). Bilingual station signs here, and at other stations along the line, are more than merely a token deference to the linguistic diversity of this region of Saxony.

East through Silesia

Görlitz, right on the Polish border, has one of the finest city centres in central Europe with a dazzling array of Renaissance, Gothic and baroque architecture. The best of the show is on and around the Untermarkt where you'll find courtyards with an almost Mediterranean demeanour. Although nowadays in the German state of Saxony, Görlitz was historically part of **Silesia**. When Germany ceded Silesia to Poland after the Second World War, only those fragments of the province which lay west of the River Neisse remained German territory. Görlitz is thus the only community of any size in modern Germany which can legitimately claim Silesian heritage. But it is a whiff of 1930s central Europe, rather than the specific Silesian link, which has pulled many **filmmakers to Görlitz**, among them Wes Anderson who filmed much of *Grand Hotel Budapest* in and around the city.

If you want to stay, we can thoroughly recommend the Hotel Börse at Untermarkt 16, ☎ 03581 764 20 (www.boerse-goerlitz.de). Rooms in the main building offer a real touch of luxury, but there are also cheaper rooms in an annexe around one of the nearby courtyards.

Crossing the **Neisse Viaduct**, we enter Polish Silesia (Śląsk in Polish). The railway runs east through mixed forest and arable land, pausing here and there at railway stations in such a state of dereliction that it seems barely possible that any train might even stop.

Wrocław (suggested stopover)

Poland's fourth largest city is the **capital of Lower Silesia** and is culturally one of the most interesting oddballs in this part of Europe. Prior to the Second World War, it was a predominantly German city, then known as Breslau, which was ceded under the 1945 **Potsdam Treaty** to Poland. The Germans left, quickly to be replaced by thousands of Polish migrants from the Lwów region. Today Lwów is the Ukrainian city of Lviv, the end point of **Route 36**.

In 2016, Wrocław was one of Europe's two capitals of culture. We rate Wrocław as being almost as good as Kraków, but happily without Kraków's high prices. The central area is compact and easily covered on foot. The city is defined by its river, the Odra, which skirts the northern edge of the city centre. Apart from the **stunning main square** dominated by the magnificent town hall, our favourite part of Wrocław is the ecclesiastical and university district north-east of the centre. Head over Piaskowy bridge onto Wyspa Piasek and then right over the colourful **Tumski bridge** to reach the **cathedral**. Back on the south side of the river, you can easily spend many happy hours exploring the various streets around the central **Rynek** (main square).

One highlight not to be missed is the **Racławice Panorama** in a striking modern building in Słowackiego Park about 1 km east of the Rynek (closed Mon in winter). The panorama was produced for an exhibition in Lwów in 1893 and thus predates the heyday of cinema. Its portrayal of one of the rare glorious moments in Polish military history, the **Battle of Racławice**, where Polish peasants armed with scythes and pitchforks outwitted better-equipped Russian forces, evokes a great sense of reality that must have been truely dramatic when first viewed by late 19th-century Poles who had no experience of media we now take for granted. Today, it still is very impressive. The panorama accompanied the post-war mass movement of **Polish exiles from Lwów** to Wrocław, and is the most tangible expression of the historic connections between the two cities.

Arrival, information, accommodation
≈ Wrocław's main station is a Disneyesque confection about 1 km south of the heart of the Old Town. ❷ The main tourist office is on the central square in the Old Town at Rynek 14 (www.visitwroclaw.eu). ⊨ A good central hotel just a few minutes from the main square is the **Hotel Dikul**, Antoniego Cieszyńskiego 17–19, ☎ 71 796 77 66 (www.hoteldikul.pl). Equally central is the boutique hotel **The Granary**, Mennicza 24, ☎ 71 395 26 00 (www.thegranaryhotel.com), located in a historic building. On our most recent visit to Wroław, we stayed at the welcoming **Jana Pawła II**, Św. Idziego 2, ☎ 71 327 14 00 (www.hotel-jp2.pl). The hotel is a real haven of calm in a busy city, right on Ostrów Tumski.

Connections from Wrocław
There are fast trains to Poznań, to link into **Route 36**, and to Warsaw where you can connect into **Route 31** to the Baltic coast. Of the many regional rail routes which fan out from Wrocław, the most interesting is that to **Szklarska Poręba Górna**, a small town in the Karkonosze Mountains which straddle the Polish-Czech border. This route now extends over the border to Harrachov in the Czech Republic. Wrocław is also the Polish starting point for the **Pociąg do Kultury** (Culture Train) which provides a seasonal direct link (mainly on Fridays and weekends) to Berlin on a special train which highlights cultural links between Berlin and Wrocław. Expect anything from face painting to poetry readings on board the train, which is known as the **Kulturzug** in German. In addition to that special train, there are twice-daily Eurocity trains from Wrocław to Berlin.

Our rail journey from Wrocław broadly follows the **River Odra** upstream to Opole. This is the heart of Silesia, the great industrial region which was variously Polish, Austrian and German before being restored to Poland in 1945. Polish history runs deep here, despite the many empires and armies that have tussled over this territory. The train pauses at **Brzeg** and Opole, both one-time centres of ducal power. In Brzeg, which enjoys a fine setting by the Odra, there's a decent ducal palace, often compared to the Wawel in Kraków. **Opole** is equally appealing, with a nice Old Town and cathedral district north of the station. East of Opole, the rich agricultural lands of the Odra Valley are eclipsed by landscapes of increasing industrial demeanour. This easternmost part of Silesia faces challenges associated with the decline of heavy industry.

Most trains to Kraków continue via Katowice, although occasional services loop further north through **Częstochowa**, a town which plays host to one of Poland's foremost Catholic places of pilgrimage. The crowds are drawn by the celebrated **Black Madonna icon** at Jasna Góra, an uphill walk west of the city centre. For an insight into the many contradictions which underpin modern Polish life, Jasna Góra is well worth a visit. All trains continue to Kraków where you'll almost certainly want to stop overnight. Read more on the city on p337.

Into the hills

Eighty years ago, Poland's prestige *Luxtorpeda* train linked Kraków with Zakopane in less than three hours. In 1936, a *Luxtorpeda* made the run in a record time of 2 hrs 36 mins. The railway is a marvellous piece of **Habsburg engineering**, though no longer in great shape. Some trains these days take almost four hours, although in summer 2024 one daily express train was scheduled to reach Zakopane in just two hours and seven minutes.

Anyone in a hurry to reach Zakopane from Kraków will usually take the bus which runs non-stop and takes two hours. Along the way, you'll catch an eyeful of roadside hoardings while tussling with the traffic. The train is a gentler, greener way to Zakopane. We usually opt for one of the slower trains which make 48 intermediate stops. Yes, 48. We've counted.

Rattling south from Kraków's main station, the train passes **St Nicholas Church** on the right which has a fine Armenian votive cross in its garden. Then to the left is one of the two Jewish cemeteries in the Kazimierz district. Soon we are crossing the **River Wisła** on an impressive bridge with a complex lattice of girders. Until 1846 this meandering river marked the frontier between the Free City of Kraków (Rzeczpospolita Krakowska) and the Austro-Hungarian Empire. We shudder to a stop at **Zabłocie**, where tourists come to see the former enamelware factory featured in Spielberg's epic film *Schindler's List*. The train stops off at many Kraków suburban stations. **Sanktuarium** is the most striking, serving the memorial complex and sanctuary dedicated to the life and work of the late Polish pope, now canonised as St John Paul II. This is a rail route which touches on many places which featured in the early life of the future pope.

Once away from Kraków, much of the route south to Zakopane is single track, albeit liberally sprinkled with passing loops. The beauty of this train journey is the way in which the **train dances with the topography**. Here and there it changes direction, occasionally striking assertively south but more commonly following the warp and weft of the landscape. In places the hillsides tilt ever sharper, but just occasionally the landscape opens out sufficiently to reveal glorious **views of the High Tatras** to the south.

High up on the hills to the right we have a tempting glimpse of the monastery church of **Kalwaria Zebrzydowska** where Pope John Paul II celebrated his last ever Mass on Polish soil. Here the railway cuts through a remarkable World Heritage Site, a pilgrimage landscape which was conceived a sort of substitute Holy Land. This is the most ambitious of Europe's *sacri monti*, and four hundred years after its creation it is still in the care of the Franciscan Bernardines.

We reach the **Skawa Valley**, latterly reshaped by a major new dam project. The railway crosses the river on a bold new bridge and then skirts the reservoir. Twice our train reverses as we make stop-go progress through the Beskid Hills. At **Chabowka** there is a remarkable collection of old steam engines in sidings from where we climb south, cresting a gentle summit and then dropping down to Nowy Targ where Lenin once endured a brief spell in prison.

We always have mixed feelings about the last 20 kilometres of the journey, from **Nowy Targ** up to Zakopane. Increasing numbers of wooden houses are a hint of the feast of vernacular architecture which gives such style to the Polish Tatras. But at this point the railway also parallels the main highway to Zakopane which is lined by billboards and fast food outlets. We cross the 700-metre contour just before Biały Dunajec, the village where **Lenin** once lived. "This is almost Russia," Lenin wrote in 1913 of this area, alluding to the fact that the border of the Tsarist Empire was not far away. Our train pauses at the railway station at **Poronin**, to which Lenin would regularly cycle to collect his post. It was in this village that a landmark Bolshevik congress was held in 1913.

Ahead the distinctive line of the High Tatras marks the southern sky. These are the hills where the young future Pope would regularly roam, following the same paths where Lenin had once hiked while pondering developments back in Russia. For **poets and philosophers**, for future saints and revolutionaries, the railway to Zakopane has long been laced with creative energy and the promise of pure mountain air.

Zakopane

Every Pole knows Zakopane, a resort town in the **Tatra Mountains**. It is the place to which the Kraków intelligentsia came (and still come) to rest and play. With **beautiful late 19th-century villas**, wooden churches, leafy avenues and easy access to Poland's highest mountains, Zakopane is a year-round resort: excellent winter sports, rock climbing and summer hiking.

The imprint of one man is everywhere in Zakopane: **Stanisław Witkiewicz**. At a time when Poland was partitioned between three empires, Witkiewicz promoted a new architectural grammar which spoke to a uniquely Polish identity, drawing upon the vernacular building traditions of the Carpathian region. So here, in what was at the time a remote corner of the Habsburg world, **Polish artists and writers** began to envision an independent Poland, a sovereign state which might determine its own future. A particular fussy style of wooden architecture, with plenty of art nouveau accents, became the hallmark of that emerging national spirit. It is seen at its very best in Zakopane.

As for day hikes from Zakopane, one of the best is to the summit of **Giewont** (there and back takes seven hours); there's also a cable car up to Kasprowy Wierch (1,985 m) from Kuźnice, from where there's a ridge path along the Slovakian border. The less energetic may like to take the modern **funicular railway** from the centre of town to Gubałówka (1,120 m) for excellent views south to the main Tatra range; there are cafés at the top.

ARRIVAL, INFORMATION, ACCOMMODATION
≥ It's a 15-min walk south-west to the town centre. 🚌 Buses from Kraków arrive very close by. 🛈 Tourist office: ul. Chrámcówki 35 (www.zakopane.pl); arranges accommodation and has useful maps. 🛏 Book ahead, especially during the peak winter season. The **Grand Hotel Stamary**, Kościuszki 19, ☎ 18 20 24 510 (www.stamary.pl), has a wonderful central location and an excellent restaurant. It's also handy for the station. Right on Zakopane's main street (pedestrianised) and just a few minutes' walk to the funicular railway is the **Villa Vita**, ul. Krupówki 2, ☎ 18 200 06 00 (www.villavita.pl). Or try the **Sabala**, ul. Krupówki 11, ☎ 18 201 50 92 (www.sabala.zakopane.pl).

Across the Tatras

There is a useful year-round once-a-day **bus link** from Zakopane, with a second daily bus in summer, which cuts through rugged Tatra countryside to Poprad in Slovakia. It is operated by Flixbus. The bus stops along the way at Tatranská Lomnica and Starý Smokovec, both places where you can connect onto the **narrow-gauge Tatra electric trains** (or are they trams?) which serve several resorts on the south side of the Tatras.

In **Poprad**, the main railway station is a faded but still very good example of the distinctive bold style of architecture known as **Slovak East Modernism**. In Czechoslovakia, Slovak architects often had the edge over their Czech counterparts. The station is on **Route 35** in this book. It has trains to Prague, Bratislava and Košice. There is a very useful connection in Košice with the new cross-border daytime services to Mukachevo in Ukraine (mentioned on p331).

Sidetracks: Crossing frontiers

The relationship between **railways and international frontiers** is always fascinating, though often not easy. Railways were the ambassadors of empire, but also served to protect imperial interests. But borders evolve and move, and railways sometimes find themselves transgressing new frontiers.

In the 1870s, **Baron Victor von Erlanger** promoted a railway which ran west from Győr via Sopron to Ebenfurth in Austria. His aim was to export Hungarian grain to Austrian markets. In the days of the Habsburg dual monarchy, Erlanger's railway flourished, but following the **First World War**, his railway was divided by a new frontier separating Austria from Hungary. That wasn't good for business, but worse was yet to come. After the Second World War the *Győr, Sopron and Ebenfurth Railway* (usually abbreviated GYSEV) was bisected by the **Iron Curtain**. Better times arrived for GYSEV when Hungary joined the European Union (of which Austria was already a member) in 2004 and three years later acceded to the **Schengen group of nations**. The fading of borders brought a big boost to business for GYSEV, and the company is now an important independent rail operator in western Hungary. It still plies Baron von Erlanger's original route to Austria.

In many parts of Europe, countries have to negotiate with their neighbours when railways criss-cross frontiers. In some cases, **privileged transit** is arranged on a railway which crosses another country – in much the same way that **Lenin** and his colleagues were given special permission to leave Switzerland in 1917 and travel across Germany in a sealed railway carriage on their way back to Russia. That was a moment of political drama, but dozens of trains across Europe enjoy a less Lenin-like form of privileged transit every day.

Nowadays, fast trains **between Innsbruck and Salzburg** (both in Austria) cut through Bavaria for 115 kilometres between Kufstein and Freilassing. Austrian Railjets running from Innsbruck to Vienna use this transit corridor without stopping on German territory. Authorities which grant such privileged transit may set certain conditions. In the early 1950s, when the Soviet Union still leased the Porkkala district of southern Finland, trains running from **Helsinki to Turku** (a line which forms part of **Route 30** in this book) had window blinds which remained lowered while the train transited the Soviet zone.

Such border-hopping services are called 'corridor trains'. Borders in most of Europe are pretty relaxed these days, but in the past things were not so easy. Special **corridor trains** linking villages in Austria were given permission to transit Yugoslav or Italian territory. The train journey between Bebra and Heringen (both places in West Germany) crossed East Germany (GDR). Trains running north from **Ventimiglia to Cuneo** still transit French territory. In Germany, the railway from Görlitz to Zittau twice dips in and out of Poland. Perhaps the strangest corridor train of all was the Polish local train which in the 1970s and 1980s gave a **visa-free glimpse of Soviet life**. Trains from Przemyśl to Zagórz cut through the Soviet Union for 37 kilometres. For a spell, it was a favourite route with *Solidarność* activists who would throw leaflets from the train in the hope of sowing the seeds of local dissent. Moscow reacted by imposing a 'no open windows' rule.

ALPINE ADVENTURES
An introduction

Many veterans of European rail travel suggest that the sheer joy of exploring Europe by train reaches its apotheosis in the Alps. We agree! Throughout the region, and most particularly in Switzerland and Austria, the traveller is **spoilt for choice** with a dense network of rail routes served by frequent, modern and reliable trains.

Bar for a few services intended **primarily for tourists** – like the *Glacier Express* and *Bernina Express* services – there are no trains in Switzerland where a seat reservation is required for domestic journeys. Much the same is true in Austria. The Alps of course extend across borders into the Savoie area of France, Oberbayern in Germany, the hill country of northern Italy and western Slovenia. In all these areas, you can travel on all local and regional trains without any need to reserve seats in advance.

We include a choice of six Alpine adventures in this section of *Europe by Rail*. Of these, **Route 38, 40** and **41** are all north to south routes over the Alps, ending in northern Italy, leaving you well placed to embark on itineraries which lead deeper into Italy. The other three routes in this section (**Route 39, 42** and **43** respectively) are more in the nature of **Alpine tours** in their own right, rather than being designed to lead beyond the Alps. Pushed to nominate our favourite route in this section of the book, we would opt for **Route 40** – the roundabout journey from Zurich to Milan via the classic **Bernina railway**. Bear in mind that elsewhere in this book, the first part of **Route 44** has real Alpine character. It follows the **Semmering Railway**, one of the finest rail routes through the Austrian Alps.

We are very pleased to make space for the **classic Gotthard line** in this edition of *Europe by Rail*. If you wonder why we don't include the much busier new Gotthard route, it's merely because you don't see much Alpine scenery when travelling through a long tunnel. The new Gotthard Base Tunnel (opened in 2016) is 57 km long. That's a lot of Alpine darkness which is pretty indistinguishable from any other variety of darkness.

A number of other Alpine railway lines cried out for inclusion in this book. We make mention of the **Simplon** in our Sidetrack feature on p380. And by rejigging some of our French content, we have made space for an account (see p161) of the *Mont Blanc Express* narrow-gauge route from Saint-Gervais-les-Bains and Chamonix to Martigny in Switzerland.

Yet still we feel we only scratch the surface of Alpine possibilities. You might want to make time for the fine route which runs west from Lienz into Italy, for the line to Mariazell in Austria and for a real Slovenian gem: the railway which runs south-west from Jesenice through the Julian Alps to Sežana. ■

Route 38: Crossing the Alps

CITIES: ★★ CULTURE: ★ HISTORY: ★ SCENERY: ★★
COUNTRIES COVERED: GERMANY (DE), AUSTRIA (AT), ITALY (IT)
JOURNEY TIME: 6 HRS 20 MINS | DISTANCE: 434 KM | MAP: www.ebrweb.eu/18map38

This route is a very useful fast hop south **over the Alps** from southern Germany to Italian sunshine. But it is also worth doing in its own right for Route 38 packs in an astonishing variety of scenery. **Munich and Verona** could hardly be more different and each city deserves a few days of exploration. Along this route, the Alps change in character almost from one valley to the next.

ROUTE OPTIONS
Innsbruck makes a marvellous overnight stop along the way (where there is a connection with **Route 39**). Should you wish to extend this journey into a longer trip, then Garmisch, Mittenwald and Bolzano all commend themselves as good places to stop off. If you have had many city stays during your explorations of Europe by rail then Mittenwald, with its homely small-town feel, is the perfect antidote to big city blues.

There are direct express trains every two hours from Munich to Verona, but it's worth noting that these services take a completely different route from Munich to Innsbruck than suggested here in Route 38. They loop well east of the **Karwendel Alps** and then approach Innsbruck via the *Unterinntalbahn* (Lower Inn Valley Railway). This route, which gains Austrian territory at Kufstein is not a patch on the journey described below, which is shorter in distance but takes longer than the route via Kufstein.

Beyond Innsbruck, there is no choice of route to Verona, so the regular Railjet trains offer a fast option for the journey over the **Brenner Pass** into northern Italy – though the slow trains which ply the same route are more of an adventure.

Through Upper Bavaria

The journey from **Munich** (p146) to the Austrian border runs entirely through a part of Bavaria known as Oberbayern (Upper Bavaria). The ride south is dominated by the approaching Alps, but don't focus merely on the mountains in the distance.

There are glimpses of lakes, baroque churches, neat farmsteads and half-timbered houses – the latter invariably decorated with the wall murals which are so typical of this region. This local form of vernacular art is called **Lüftlmalerei**; it celebrates religious and moral themes, and often depicts local crafts and agricultural practices. It speaks volumes about a community and its relationship with the land. Critics note that it is also deeply conservative and to non-Catholics even possibly oppressive. Make what you will of this local take on graffiti.

Before long, the train is running up the Loisach Valley, the mountains closing in on either side as you approach **Garmisch-Partenkirchen**. Once two quiet Bavarian villages at the foot of the 2,962-m Zugspitze, Germany's

Alpine adventures

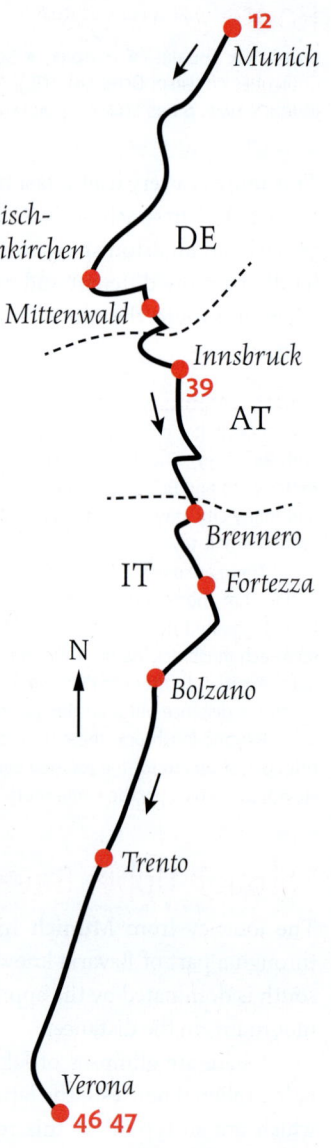

Route details

Munich Hbf to Garmisch-Partenkirchen		
Frequency	Journey time	Notes
Hourly	1h15–1h25	M

Garmisch-Partenkirchen to Mittenwald		
Frequency	Journey time	Notes
Hourly	0h20–0h25	

Mittenwald to Innsbruck Hbf		
Frequency	Journey time	Notes
Every 1–2 hrs	1h–1h10	S

Innsbruck Hbf to Bolzano		
Frequency	Journey time	Notes
Every 1–2 hrs	2h–2h10	T

Bolzano to Verona Port Nuova		
Frequency	Journey time	Notes
Hourly	1h20–1h50	

Notes

M – Most trains from Munich to Garmisch depart from platforms 27 to 36 at Munich Hauptbahnhof. Note that these platforms are a five-minute walk from the main station concourse.

S – On some journeys between Mittenwald and Innsbruck, a change of train may be necessary at either Scharnitz or Seefeld in Tirol.

T – Some journeys on local trains between Innsbruck and Bolzano require a change of train at Brenner/Brennero (on the Austrian-Italian border). Regular Railjet trains run right through from Innsbruck to Bolzano and beyond.

highest mountain, Garmisch and Partenkirchen were officially united to host the 1936 **Winter Olympics**. Though now separated only by the railway line, they retain individual personalities. Partenkirchen is more modern and upmarket while Garmisch has much more of a traditional Bavarian character – the most appealingly rustic part is around Frühlingstraße.

Garmisch is Germany's most popular ski resort, with downhill and cross-country skiing on offer. The **Bayerische Zugspitzbahn** rack railway leaves from its own dedicated station just by the main railway station, with the journey to the summit of the Zugspitze taking 75 minutes. On the way, the train stops at **Eibsee**, an idyllic mountain lake, where you can transfer onto the Eibsee cable car (often crowded) to reach the summit much quicker than remaining on the train.

If summit bagging is not your thing, there are good walks around Eibsee. The seven-kilometre lake circuit is an undemanding but beautiful stroll on an easy path.

Connections from Garmisch
From Garmisch-Partenkirchen, you can cut off to the west on a **beautiful branch railway** which runs through Austrian territory en route to the **Allgäu** region of southern Germany. It is a two-and-a-half hour journey from Garmisch to Kempten, en route passing through the Austrian town of Reutte. From Kempten there are fast trains back to Munich, or you can continue west to Lindau on the shores of Lake Constance.

The Innsbruck-bound railway heads east from Garmisch, cresting a gentle col and dropping down into the Isar Valley. Close to the Austrian border, **Mittenwald** is perhaps the most attractive town in the German Alps, with an abundance of character in its gabled, whitewashed houses, hung with green shutters and sporting creaky wooden balconies.

The town has some of the most elaborate Lüftlmalerei anywhere in Oberbayern, but Mittenwald's main claim to fame is in its violins. **Matthias Klotz** (1653–1743), a pupil of the great Amati, began Mittenwald's tradition of high-quality violin making that continues to this day. If you are tempted to stop overnight you might try the Hotel Alpenrose, Obermarkt 1, ☎ 088 23 92 700 (www.hotel-alpenrose-mittenwald.de) right in the centre.

The Tyrol

The Tyrol (Tirol in German) reveals a medley of influences which mark it out as being palpably different from the rest of Austria. It was an important **Habsburg** *Kronland* (crown land) but the area has also been variously under Bavarian and Italian control.

Our journey beyond Mittenwald cuts through a beautiful part of the Austrian Tyrol, continuing over the Brenner Pass into the region known as South Tyrol, a predominantly **German-speaking region** which was ceded to Italy under the terms of the Treaty of Saint-Germain-en-Laye in 1919. Frontiers are fragile in this part of Europe, and political authority waxes and wanes. The historical development of communities along this route (such as Mittenwald, Innsbruck, Bolzano) has been governed not by distant emperors or kings, but by trade. This has for centuries been one of the most important **trading routes** through the Alps.

Innsbruck (suggested stopover)

The 800-year-old Tyrolean capital on the River Inn is a bustling, amiable Austrian city overlooked by the **Karwendel Mountains** to the north and the Patscherkofel Mountains to the south – making the town an excellent base for walks and other activities in the Alps.

The **Hungerburgbahn** cog railway, which ascends from the Alpenzoo on the edge of the city on to the Hungerburg plateau – a superb place for walks and views – opened in 2007, following the earlier rebuilding of the **Nordkettenbahnen**, which take visitors from the Congress Centre up onto the Hafelekar by cable car (more on www.nordkette.com/en).

Innsbruck's Altstadt (Old Town) is dotted with 15th- and 16th-century buildings, many with elaborate stucco decorations and traditional convex windows to catch extra light on the narrow streets. Its most famous sight is the 15th-century **Goldenes Dachl**, Herzog-Friedrich-Str. 15 (www.goldenes-dachl.at), a roof of 2,657 gilded copper tiles covering a balcony, which Emperor Maximilian I (the subject of an exhibition inside) added in 1500 to the Neuhof, the residence of the Tyrolean princes. The **Stadtturm** (city tower) opposite the balcony offers views across the rooftops to the mountains. Nearby is the Dom zu St Jakob, a striking baroque cathedral.

Near the Hofgarten (court gardens), the revamped **Tiroler Volkskunst Museum** (www.tiroler-landesmuseen.at) concentrates on Tyrolean culture, displaying traditional costumes and wood-panelled rooms. The Tiroler Ferdinandeum, Museumstr. 15 (closed Mon), is more diverse, with beautiful stained glass, mediaeval altars and works by Cranach and Rembrandt.

ARRIVAL, INFORMATION, ACCOMMODATION

Innsbruck Hauptbahnhof (Hbf) is about a 10-min walk south-east of the city centre. Innsbruck Airport (www.innsbruck-airport.com), 4 km west of the city centre (take F from the station).

Tourist office: Burggraben 3, on the edge of the Altstadt (www.innsbruck.info). 24 hr ticket (also for families) for use on trams and buses (www.ivb.at).

Right in the Old Town, the characterful, family-run **Hotel Weisses Kreuz**, Herzog-Friedrich-Straße 31, ☎ 0512 594 79 (www.weisseskreuz.at), is offering something for every budget. Apparently it is where Mozart stayed when his family visited Innsbruck in 1769. The stylish **Hotel Maximilian**, on the edge of the Old Town at Marktgraben 7–9, ☎ 0512 599 670 (www.hotel-maximilian.com), is a good up-market choice. Right in the Old Town, the **Hotel Goldener Adler**, Herzog-Friedrich-Strasse 6, ☎ 0512 57 11 110 (www.goldeneradler.com), offers comfortable rooms in a historic building. ✖ The Altstadt area is generally expensive. **Café-Konditorei Munding**, Kiebachgasse 16 (www.munding.at), is the oldest Tyrolean café and pastry-shop, and serves fabulous cakes.

INNSBRUCK CONNECTIONS
Our journey crosses **Route 39** in Innsbruck, which you can follow east through Salzburg to Vienna, or west through Liechtenstein to Switzerland.

Railjets head from Innsbruck in all directions: east to **Bratislava** and **Budapest**, north into Germany via Kufstein, west to Zürich and south into **Italy**, where the roll call of destinations includes Venice, Verona, Bologna and in summer also Rimini. Much closer to hand, there's a local service, more a tram than a train, which runs up the Stubaital to Fulpmes. Innsbruck also has year-round **Nightjet** connections, with evening departures every day to Amsterdam, Cologne, Hannover and Hamburg. For those who don't mind a departure after midnight, there is also a direct Euronight train to **Zagreb**.

If you decide to stick with Route 38 to Verona, then you will head south over the **Brenner Pass** into Italy. By Alpine standards, the Brenner is a modest affair. No great tunnels as on the Simplon and Gotthard routes and no great heights as on the Bernina. The Brenner route tops out at just 1,370 metres, but what it lacks in height is made up for by the beauty of the landscape.

If you have the time, take slow trains south from Innsbruck, changing at Brennero and usually Bolzano to reach Verona. Once over the top, you can cut off to the east at Fortezza to follow a beautiful branch line back over the border at **San Candido** (Innichen in German) to reach the Austrian town of Lienz, from where there are good onwards connections to Villach and even a daily Railjet to Vienna.

Although in Italy and with street names in Italian, **Bolzano** (Bozen in German) looks decidedly Austrian, with its pastel-coloured baroque arcades and Austrian menu items; for centuries Bolzano was part of the South Tyrol region of Austria. Set beneath Alpine slopes in a deep valley, it's handy for exploring the Dolomites. Pza Walther (named after the poet Walther von der Vogelweide) is the focus of the town's outdoor life.

CONNECTIONS FROM BOLZANO
From Bolzano, there are trains at least hourly up the **Adige Valley** to Merano, where you can connect with a local service, more a tram than a train, which runs west through Val Venosta (Vinschgau in the local German dialect) to Malles. This is a great ride through vineyards and orchards, a joy at any time of year but certainly at its very best in spring. Malles (Mals in German) is the jumping-off point for the bus links to Switzerland and Austria explored in our **Sidetracks** feature on p357. There's an hourly direct bus to Zernez (to connect into **Route 40**) and a less frequent connection via Martina to Landeck (on **Route 39**).

Remaining with the main line south towards Verona, the railway parallels the E45 highway as it runs down the Adige Valley. All daytime trains pause at Trento, a handsome regional centre and a good base for exploring the Dolomites. Beyond **Trento**, the landscape becomes gentler for the final stretch down to Verona.

Verona

Placed on an S-bend of the **River Adige** and best explored on foot, this beautiful city of pastel-pink marble thrives on the story of Romeo and Juliet, but the real attractions are its elegant mediaeval squares, fine Gothic churches and massive a **Roman amphitheatre** – the Arena – which comes alive during the annual opera festival in July and August (ticket office ☎ 045 800 5151, www.arena.it; the cheapest seats are unreserved, so arrive early). Dominating the large **Piazza Brà**, it has 44 pink marble tiers that can accommodate 20,000 people – incredibly, the singers and orchestra are perfectly audible.

Via Mazzini, which leads off Piazza Brà, is one of Italy's smartest shopping streets. This leads to Piazza delle Erbe, which is surrounded by faded Renaissance palaces. Originally the Roman forum, the square is now a daily market. An archway leads to a serener square, **Piazza dei Signori**, the centre of mediaeval civic life, and framed by the 15th-century Loggia del Consiglio and the crenellated Palazzo del Capitano.

Across the river, over the partly **Roman Ponte Pietra**, Verona's best-known bridge, are the remains of the Roman theatre (where plays were performed, as opposed to the amphitheatre, which held coarser public entertainments); although smaller than the amphitheatre, there's rather more to see, as entrance includes admission to the **Archaeological Museum**, housed in an old convent with great views of the city.

ARRIVAL, INFORMATION, ACCOMMODATION

🚆 Stazione Porta Nuova, a 10 to 15-min walk south of the centre (🚌 21/22/23/51/52).
✈ There are two airports: the main one is Valerio Catullo, (www.aeroportoverona.it), with a shuttle bus running every 20 mins to Port Nuova station. 🅸 Tourist office: Via Degli Alpini 9 (www.turismoverona.eu). For information on public transport see www.atv.verona.it.
🛏 Try the friendly and highly regarded **B&B Agli Scaligeri**, Vicolo Ponte Nuovo 2, ☎ 0347 4765089 (www.agliscaligeri.it), well located in Verona's historic centre, west of Piazza delle Erbe. Another good and comfortable option is **Hotel Torcolo**, Vicolo Listone 3, ☎ 045 800 75 12 (www.hoteltorcolo.it), just north of Piazza Brà. Overlooking the Piazza delle Erbe, the central **Hotel Aurora**, Piazzetta XIV Novembre 2, ☎ 045 59 47 17 (www.hotelaurora.biz), is also a good choice.
🍴 For reasonably priced restaurants, look along Corso Porta Borsari, in the streets around Pza delle Erbe or the Veronetta district on the east bank of the Adige. The Pza delle Erbe's food market is also useful.

CONNECTIONS FROM VERONA

From Verona, you can speed south to **Rome** and **Naples** on either a Trenitalia service or on one of Italo's sleek red high-speed trains. The city lies on the main rail axis across the North Italian plains, with regular services running west to Milan and Turin or east to Venice and Trieste.

Verona has direct night trains to Rome, Vienna and Munich. Closer to hand, there is a very **good network of regional trains**; destinations include Bologna, Mantua, Padua, Vicenza and Modena.

Sidetracks: The Alps by bus

The area where Switzerland, Austria and Italy conjoin is one of the most beautiful areas of the Alps. Several railways penetrate this region, but they do not connect in a manner which allows **cross-border train journeys**. So travellers must perforce resort to buses – which is just what we did when exploring this mountainous area a year or two ago.

Bolzano (on **Route 38** in this book) is a good starting point for rural cross-border adventures. First take the train to Merano, a graceful German-speaking spa town in the Adige Valley, which is worth a stop. From Merano, take the **Vinschgaubahn**, a local railway which happily reopened in 2005, to Malles (Venosta). German is very much the *lingua franca* here, and the town is shown on many maps and in timetables by its German name: Mals im Vinschgau.

There are some very tempting local bus routes which start outside the station in **Malles**. Swiss post bus (route number 811) runs hourly from Malles to Zernez via beautiful **Val Müstair** and the Ofen Pass (every two hours in winter). You may want to stop off at the UNESCO-listed Benedictine monastery in Val Müstair (closed Sunday mornings). Most people in the Müstair Valley speak Romansh. The principal village of **Santa Maria**, just west of the monastery, is well worth a wander. The bus from Malles to Zernez in Switzerland takes 95 minutes. In **Zernez**, you are on the Rhaetian Railway network (and on **Route 40** in this book).

Another equally appealing option is bus 273 which runs north from Malles along the east side of the **Lago di Resia** and on over Reschen Pass to Nauders in Austria. From there the bus drops down steeply into the Inn Valley, and terminates at Martina in Switzerland. Buses on this route run hourly all year round (less frequently on Sundays in winter). On the run north alongside the lake, you'll see an **extraordinary spectacle**: an eerily beautiful campanile projecting from the waters of the reservoir. It is a reminder of the fate of the Italian village of Graun which was flooded in 1950, when the valley was dammed to enlarge a pre-existing natural lake – curiously to provide water for Switzerland. The scene at Graun is so striking that you may want to alight from the bus and take a look around.

The journey from Malles to **Nauders** takes 37 minutes; from Malles to Martina takes 48 minutes. This bus route is operated by Servizi Autobus Dolomiti. In **Martina**, bus 273 connects with an hourly Swiss post bus which runs 17 kilometres down the Inn Valley to the Engadine railhead at **Scuol-Tarasp**, from where the Rhaetian Railway has two trains an hour for your onward journey through Switzerland.

If you want to move north into the **Austrian Tyrol**, there are Austrian post bus services from both Nauders and Martina on to Landeck – on the Arlberg rail route – which is featured in **Route 39** of this book.

Our experience is that bus to bus, bus to train and train to bus connections in this region generally work perfectly. Only in severe winter weather, when snow may close even major roads, is there any serious risk of disruption.

Route 39: The Arlberg route

CITIES: ★★ CULTURE: ★★ HISTORY: ★ SCENERY: ★★★
COUNTRIES COVERED: SWITZERLAND (CH), LIECHTENSTEIN (LI), AUSTRIA (AT)
JOURNEY TIME: 9 HRS 50 MINS | DISTANCE: 845 KM | MAP: WWW.EBRWEB.EU/18MAP39

The very mention of the word Arlberg evokes memories of a *belle époque* of continental rail travel. The Arlberg is the rugged mountain region which separates Austria's westernmost province, Vorarlberg, from the Tyrol. The mountains achieve no spectacular heights – there are no summits in excess of 3,000 metres. But the difficult terrain was for centuries an obstacle to travel until the **Arlberg Railway** opened in 1884. It is the principal west to east line through the Alps, a railway noted for its remarkable beauty, and it is the highlight of this route from **Zurich to Vienna**.

The Arlberg railway has long been a major artery for international traffic. One of the many versions of the legendary *Orient Express* took this route, and the modern *Venice-Simplon Orient Express* (VSOE) tourist train still often routes via the Arlberg line on its run from Paris to Venice (the train's name is thus misleading as it really doesn't use the Simplon route from Switzerland to Italy very often).

But no one complains over that detail for, when it comes to the **quality of the scenery**, the Arlberg route knocks spots off the Simplon (more about the Simplon line in the Sidetracks on p380). The Arlberg is, quite simply, the finest mainline rail route **through the Alps**. There are five direct Austrian Railjet trains each day from Zurich to Vienna, with one continuing to Bratislava and another to Budapest. There are also overnight sleeper services from Zurich to Vienna, Budapest, Ljubljana and Zagreb.

The daytime **Railjets** from Switzerland to Innsbruck and beyond are perfectly functional, but they don't quite have the character of the old express trains which plied the route. The Railjets also take a short cut between Innsbruck and Salzburg, slipping through a corner of German territory which is less scenic than the classic line described here.

RECOMMENDED ITINERARY

This is a superb journey to do in a **single day**. Choose your trains carefully. By far the best option is the 08.40 departure from Zurich. It's not a Railjet, but the very comfy Eurocity

Transalpin service with large windows which are perfect for sightseeing. All the better if you have a first-class ticket or rail pass, as there is a very fine Swiss observation car on this train. This particular Eurocity train (EC163) runs to Graz. But with a change of train in Schwarzach-St Veit, you'll be Salzburg by late afternoon and reach Vienna by 18.30, from where it's just an hour on to Bratislava.

If you want to break your journey, there are of course three premier-league cities on this route: **Innsbruck, Salzburg** and **Vienna**. If you favour smaller towns as stop-off points, then Feldkirch is a good choice, with the option of a day exploring the Principality of Liechtenstein. We also recommend Kitsbühel which ticks all the boxes if you are looking for a dose of small-town Alpine fantasy.

Coffee in three countries

Our route leaves Zurich (see p124) heading south-east; the first 90 km out of Zurich parallel **Route 40** in this book (which runs via the Bernina Pass

Route details

Zurich Hbf to Feldkirch		
Frequency	Journey time	Notes
Every 2 hrs	1h40	

Feldkirch to Innsbruck Hbf		
Frequency	Journey time	Notes
Hourly	2h–2h30	

Innsbruck Hbf to Kitzbühel		
Frequency	Journey time	Notes
Hourly	1h10–1h45	W

Kitzbühel to Salzburg Hbf		
Frequency	Journey time	Notes
Every 2 hrs	2h30	X

Salzburg Hbf to Vienna Hbf		
Frequency	Journey time	Notes
2 per hr	2h25–3h	

Notes

The Arlberg Railway stands centre stage on this route. This line through the Vorarlberg and Tyrol can also be built into journeys from south-west Germany to Innsbruck and Vienna. There's a useful morning Railjet from Stuttgart (dep 07.44) and Ulm (dep 09.02) to Feldkirch (arr. 11.12) where you can pick up this route (times correct for autumn 2024).

W – On many journeys a change of train at Wörgl Hbf is necessary.
X – There are additional options requiring a change of trains at Schwarzach-St Veit or Bischofshofen.

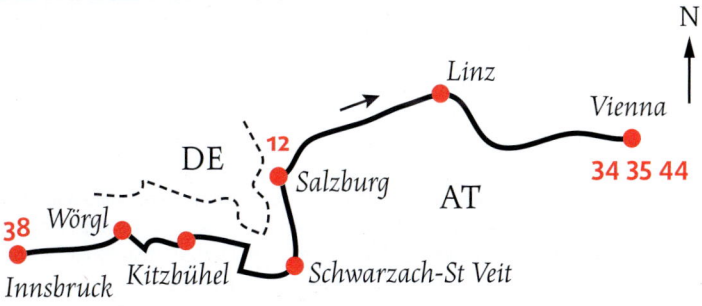

to northern Italy). The train skirts the Zürichsee and then the Walensee, entering an area which **Thomas Cook** describes (in his 1874 Swiss guide) as "the Lancashire of Switzerland." If you follow this route and spot any resemblance at all to Lancashire, let us know! We're inclined to write off Cook's comparison as a bit of wishful thinking. At **Sargans**, the railway turns north, following the Rhine Valley downstream. Until Buchs, the railway stays in Swiss territory, with Liechtenstein on the far bank of the Rhine. At Buchs the train reverses and then crosses the river into Liechtenstein.

If you buy a coffee in the train's restaurant car at **Buchs**, you'll have travelled on the territory of three countries by the time you've drained the cup. The train takes all of nine minutes to traverse mighty Liechtenstein (see also our box above). This is the sole railway which crosses the territory of the principality. Slow trains from Buchs to Feldkirch stop (weekdays only) at three minor railway stations in Liechtenstein. Shortly after crossing the **Austrian border**, the railway line performs a graceful pirouette around the Ardetzenberg to reach the station at Feldkirch.

Even in these days of light-touch borders, **Feldkirch** still has the feel of a border town – a place which is not quite Austrian. If the international community had listened to the locals, it wouldn't be Austrian at all today. In 1919, the people of the **Vorarlberg region** voted overwhelmingly to leave post-Habsburg Austria and become a canton of Switzerland. Their wishes were not granted. The train taking Emperor Charles and his wife Zita to exile in Switzerland stopped in Feldkirch in March 1919 and the unhappy monarch issued a manifesto declaring that he had been illegally deposed. No one in Feldkirch paid much notice.

Interestingly, a plaque at the railway station recalls literary rather than political events. For James Joyce, Feldkirch was the last stop on Habsburg territory as he fled with his family from Trieste to Switzerland in 1915. He

LIECHTENSTEIN

In late 2020, Liechtenstein's citizens turned out in force for a **referendum** and said an emphatic 'Nein' to a proposal to improve the one railway which runs through the country. So the Railjets and Eurocity trains will continue to trundle rather than dash through Liechtenstein en route from Buchs to Feldkirch (see map on p358).

The **Alpine principality** is more than just cowbells and questionable bank accounts. The word on Liechtenstein, rehearsed in so many guidebooks, is that the only reason to go to Liechtenstein is to tick it off on the list of countries you have visited. This is nonsense and a myth perpetuated by those who have spent merely an hour or two in the capital Vaduz. Liechtenstein deserves more.

Liechtenstein's lemon buses reach to every corner of the principality and there are good cross-border services to the railway stations in Sargans, Buchs and Feldkirch. If you have time, consider spending a whole day roaming Liechtenstein by bus. A one-day **rover ticket** for the entire country costs 12 Swiss francs (€11.50).

was nervous that they would not be permitted to leave Austria. Returning to Feldkirch after the war, he recalled that "Over there, on those tracks, the fate of *Ulysses* was decided in 1915."

There are two very good reasons for pausing at Feldkirch. First, it happens to be a very pleasant small town. Second, Feldkirch is by far the best jumping-off point to **explore Liechtenstein** by bus. Although there are bus connections into the principality from Sargans and Buchs, we think the approach from Feldkirch is just much prettier.

Tucked in against the hills, Feldkirch is a place to linger and wander through the nicely arcaded main streets. It is worth climbing up to the Schattenburg, not so much for the contents of the museum now housed in the old fortress, but more for the views. Don't miss **St Nikolaus Cathedral** (Domkirche), with its odd double nave and flamboyant 1960s stained-glass windows. If you want to stay overnight, try the family-run Hotel Bären, Bahnhofstr. 1, ☎ 05522 355 00 (www.hotel-baeren.at), close to the station.

Over the Arlberg

The 160-kilometre stretch of railway from **Feldkirch to Innsbruck** is the best part of this entire route. Time and technology have tamed the mountains. In the early days of the line, specially designed locomotives were needed to cope with the gradients. Today, the trains slide with seeming ease through the mountains, with the fastest trains taking under two hours to travel from Feldkirch to Innsbruck.

The line climbs through **glorious Alpine scenery** to over 1,300 metres, passing under the watershed in a ten-kilometre long tunnel. It all seems too easy, compared with the arduous rigours of travel in the region before the coming of the railway. An early John Murray guide recalls the days when travellers perished in the Arlberg snows, their corpses left to rot by the side of the path with birds pecking at their eyes.

On the west side of the Arlberg, the waters drain to the Rhine and thus eventually to the North Sea. On the east side, the clear mountain streams flow east, joining the Inn and eventually follow the Danube down the Black Sea. Emerging from the **Arlberg Tunnel**, the train stops immediately at St Anton am Arlberg – an upmarket ski resort as full of glitz and gloss as the ultra-modern station building suggests.

Beyond St Anton, the railway follows the River Rosanna downstream through lovely Tyrolean landscapes to the town of **Landeck**, which would hardly warrant a mention, were it not for its key position on the Tyrolean transport network. It's the jumping-off point for buses which follow the Inn Valley up to Nauders, from where there are onward bus connections to the Engadine area of eastern Switzerland and to Malles in Italy. You can read more in our **Sidetracks** feature on p357.

The Inn Valley

Beyond Landeck, the railway follows the valley downstream through Imst, a town which once thrived on the twin industries of mining and breeding canaries, prosecuting the latter with such success that birds from Imst were once delivered on foot to potentates across the Middle East. East from **Imst**, the valley becomes more heavily industrialised on the approach to Innsbruck. You'll find a short description of **Innsbruck**, one of our recommended stopovers on this route, on p354.

Connections from Innsbruck
Join **Route 38** in this book, following it north around the Karwendel Alps to Garmisch and Munich, or south via **Brenner** to Verona. Sticking with the present route towards Salzburg and Vienna, you'll find a choice of two lines to Salzburg. The fastest trains cut through German territory, giving passengers a glimpse of Bavaria on the way to Salzburg. Purists will stick to the classic line which remains on Austrian territory. That's the route we describe below. There are very few direct trains from Innsbruck to Salzburg which follow the traditional line through Kitzbühel and **Zell am See** – so it's usually necessary to change trains at Wörgl and Schwarzach–St Veit.

An Austrian rail cruise

So you opted to stick with our recommended route on the classic line through Kitzbühel to Salzburg! Good for you. You're in for a treat. The initial stretch down the **Inn Valley** to drab Wörgl is nothing special. In Wörgl, we branch off east to follow the 200-kilometre long *Giselabahn* to Salzburg. The railway is named after the second daughter of Austrian Emperor Franz Josef I. The first place of any size is the pleasant old town of **Kitzbühel** which, with its mountain backdrop and tree-lined streets of steeply gabled pastel-coloured buildings, is one of Austria's prettiest and largest ski resorts (though the snow's not that reliable; main season Christmas–Easter). Don't miss the **Kitzbüheler Hornbahn cable car** to the summit of the Horn; near the top, some 120 species of flowers bloom in an **Alpine Flower Garden**, 1,880-m high and open from spring to autumn (free guided tours 11.00 in July and August). The ski elite arrive in January for the Hahnenkamm ski competition, a World Cup leg, down one of the world's trickiest ski runs. If you are tempted to break the journey, try the family-run Hotel Resch, Alfons-Petzold-Weg 2, ☎ 05356 62294 (www.hotel-resch.at), in a good central location.

There are fine views of the **Kitzbühel Alps** as the train climbs east towards the Griessen Pass and then drops down towards the Pinzgau region. Zell am See is a good spot to stop for an hour. Beyond Zell, the railway follows the **Salzach Valley**, eventually turning north for the run into Salzburg.

Connections from the Giselabahn
There are two important railway junctions on the **Gisela Railway** east of Zell. Connect at Schwarzach-St Veit for trains to Villach. This is a very useful link to the Balkans. There is a

good daytime connection from Schwarzach-St Veit to Ljubljana and Zagreb (with an easy change in Villach). At **Bischofshofen**, you can connect onto the beautiful line which runs along the Enns Valley with trains running right through to Graz.

Salzburg (suggested stopover)

Wonderfully sited between the Alps and the lakes of the **Salzkammergut**, Salzburg lies on one of the major trading routes through the Alps. The city's wealth was rooted, as its name implies, in the salt trade. It's a place which has always buzzed with the ebb and flow of ideas and people – though not always with great tolerance. When a good percentage of the population switched allegiance to the Protestant faith, the Catholic authorities promptly expelled them en masse. These refugees found sanctuary in Prussia.

Salzburg is renowned as **Mozart's birthplace**. Much of the city's appearance dates from the 17th century, when many of the old buildings were pulled down and others given a baroque makeover to create Italian-style squares with spectacular fountains. Salzburg's entire **Old Town** (Altstadt) is designated a UNESCO World Heritage Site and much of it is sweetly beautiful, although some find it cloying and the crowds can be oppressive. The **compact centre** is largely pedestrianised; the main shopping street is narrow Getreidegasse, bordered by elegant old houses, decorative wrought-iron signs and mediaeval arcades, which now house jewellery shops or boutiques. Mozarts Geburtshaus, No. 9, where the composer was born in 1756 and spent most of his first 17 years, is now a museum.

On **Mönchsberg** (Monk's mountain), high above the Altstadt, looms the formidable **Festung Hohensalzburg**, Mönchsberg 34 (entry fee), once the stronghold of the Archbishops of Salzburg. Built over six centuries, it's almost perfectly preserved, with early Gothic state rooms, and a 200-pipe barrel organ that booms out once the 7th-century 35-bell carillon of the **Glockenspiel**, Mozartplatz, has pealed (at 07.00, 11.00 and 18.00). The castle can be reached on foot from Festungsgasse behind the cathedral, or by the **Festungsbahn**, Austria's oldest cable railway dating from 1892. Alternatively, the Mönchsbergaufzug (Mönchsberg Lift) operates from Gstättengasse 13 (by Museumplatz) and takes you to the uncompromisingly minimalist contemporary art museum, the Museum der Moderne, from whose café terrace there are great views over the city.

The big event is the **Salzburg Festival**, mid-July to late August. For major performances, tickets must be booked months ahead (www.salzburgerfestspiele.at).

Arrival, information, accommodation

Salzburg Hbf, Südtiroler Pl. 1, 20-min walk from the Old Town (or take 1/3/5/6/25 to Makartplatz or Theatergasse). The station was thoroughly renovated in 2014, but it's still a confusing place. Take care to arrive early if you are boarding a train bound for Germany, as there are occasionally still ID checks prior to boarding the train. ✈ Salzburg Airport, 4 km west of the city (www.salzburg-airport.com), 🚌 2 connects the station with the airport every 10 mins (evenings and Sun every 20 mins), taking about 25 mins for the journey. 🚌 10 runs every 10 mins to the city centre, taking 15 mins.

🛈 Tourist offices: Mozartplatz 5 and at the station (www.salzburg.info). Bus and trolley bus tickets: from vending machines or kiosks; more expensive from driver (punch ticket on boarding). Day passes also available. 🛏 During festivals, it pays to book early as accommodation often gets very scarce. Salzburg is not a cheap place to stay, especially during the summer season. **Hotel Weisse Taube**, Kaigasse 9, ☎ 0662 842 404 (www.weissetaube.at), in the centre of the Old Town, is a friendly and good-value place close to the cathedral and Mozartplatz. Or try the comfortable **The Mozart**, Franz-Josef-Str. 27, ☎ 0662 872 274 (www.themozarthotel.com). For an upmarket option in a great location close to Mozartplatz try the stylish **Art Hotel Blaue Gans**, Getreidegasse 41–43. ☎ 0662 842 491 (www.blauegans.at).

Connections from Salzburg

As befits a major rail hub, there is a wealth of onward connections. You can join **Route 12** in this book at Salzburg, following it in reverse all the way to Berlin. **Munich** is the nearest large city to Salzburg, and there are plenty of cross-border trains. The journey to Munich takes less than two hours. There are direct Eurocity services to Stuttgart, Frankfurt-am-Main and Cologne. Budapest is little more than five hours away on a fast Railjet train. Closer to hand, there are hourly buses to Bad Ischl.

Towards Vienna

The 300-km journey from Salzburg to Vienna is for many visitors from western Europe (who often arrive in Salzburg from Munich) their first taste of rail travel in Austria. In 1873, when Vienna hosted the World Exposition, the fastest run on the route was the lunchtime express from Salzburg, which dashed to the Austrian capital in just under eight hours. Today it takes just two-and-a-half hours on the fastest trains.

The first part of the run out from Salzburg is superb, with the railway following the narrow valley of the **River Fischach** up to Wallersee. The train skirts the shores of the lake before climbing steadily towards the summit of the line at just over 600 metres above sea level – and that barely 20 minutes out of Salzburg. From here it is downhill all the way to the Austrian capital, with the rail route dropping down through the Vöckla, Ager and Traun Valleys to reach the Danube at **Linz**.

Linz, Austria's industrial third city, is gradually reinventing itself with ultra-modern museums and events, such as the **Ars Electronica Center**, Ars-Electronica-Str. 1 (www.aec.at; closed Mon), Europe's first museum dedicated to virtual reality. Facing it across the river, the sleek **Lentos Kunstmuseum**, Ernst-Koref-Promenade 1, glows with changing colours after dark. Hauptplatz blends colourful baroque and rococo facades around the baroque marble Trinity column. In 1938, **Hitler** – who grew up here – stood on the balcony of Hauptplatz 1 (now the tourist office) to inform the Austrians that the Nazis had annexed their country.

Connections from Linz
Linz is the place to connect onto direct ICE trains to many **destinations across Germany**, including Berlin, Hamburg, Frankfurt am Main, Koblenz, Cologne and the Ruhr region. There are direct services to **Prague**, Budapest and Graz, the latter taking a very scenic route through Selzthal. Another fine rural route is that which leads south from the Enns Valley to Steyr and beyond.

Leaving Linz, travellers anticipating an early glimpse of the Danube will be disappointed. When it was opened in 1861, this line was one of the best engineered routes in the **Habsburg Empire**, and part of the line's success was keeping a safe distance from the Danube, so averting the risk of flooding. But there are fine views of the handsome little town of **Enns** just before crossing the river of the same name to enter the province of Lower Austria.

After playing cat and mouse with the little stream called the **Ybbs**, the train eventually plucks up courage to confront the Danube, giving a fleeting view of the **monastery at Melk**. This is one of those great moments of European rail travel where patience is eventually rewarded by something far more uplifting than one might ever have dared to imagine. It is a feast for the eyes and for the soul, so much so that most travellers will hardly notice the tunnels and cuttings that dominate the last part of the run into Vienna.

Vienna (Wien) – (suggested stopover)
Not for nothing does Austria's capital regularly top lists revealing Europe's most liveable city, for Vienna is an enviably **civilised place**, safe and manageable yet rarely dull. The **Altstadt**, or historic core, is traffic-calmed if not entirely pedestrianised, with cobbled streets, old merchants' houses, spacious gardens and hundreds of atmospheric places to eat and drink, though some of the most charming – and least touristy – lie in the districts just beyond the ring. A visit to one of the classic coffee houses for coffee and home-made cake is *de rigueur*. Most sights are on or inside the famous **Ringstrasse**, which encircles the city centre. For architectural splendours of the late 19th century, take trams 1 or 2, passing the neo-Gothic Rathaus (City Hall), Burgtheater, Parlament and Staatsoper. Or admire the lavish state apartments and some seriously glittering crown jewels at the vast **Hofburg** (Imperial Palace) complex, which was once home to the Habsburgs.

The **Albertina Museum** opened a new gallery for modern art at Karlsplatz 5 in 2020, complementing the Albertina's other site at Albertinaplatz 1 where the focus is on graphics and drawings. The most visted attractions in the city are the **St Stephen's Cathedral** (Stephansdom) and **Schönbrunn Palace** in the suburb of Hietzing. There is in our opinion no finer way to spend a summer day in Vienna than exploring the palace's gardens. As the great garden expert Charles Quest-Ritson remarks, the Schönbrunn gardens "are imperial in a way that Versailles can never be, and much less brash."

Art in Vienna

Unrivalled in the art department, Vienna offers a kaleidoscopic palette of Old Masters and new talent. Start off at the **Hofburg**, which showcases glittering jewels and Biedermeier portraits, then head over to the Albertina, with its riot of Rembrandts, Picassos and Warhols, or gaze on the **Kunsthistorisches Museum's riches**, which include works by Velázquez and Caravaggio. Design reaches a peak at the MAK (Museum of Applied Arts), which houses precious Wiener Werkstätte pieces. Visit the Upper Belvedere for great Impressionist works and a fine Klimt collection; or see Hundertwasser's colours make a secessionist splash at **KunstHaus Wien**. For a modern twist to the city's art offerings visit the MuseumsQuartier. Take a trip to the cube-shaped Leopold Museum, which houses an impressive collection of Egon Schiele paintings, or the Kunsthalle Wien where contemporary art comes boldly to the fore. The monolithic **MUMOK** (Museum of Modern Art Ludwig Foundation) gives you a shove into the 20th century with works by Warhol, Magritte and Kandinsky.

Arrival, information, accommodation

✈ A new main station (**Hauptbahnhof**) opened in 2014. **Westbahnhof**, once so important for travellers arriving in Vienna from the west, is now relegated to secondary status although private operator Westbahn still uses Westbahnhof for trains to Salzburg. Some long-distance trains arriving in Vienna now run beyond Hauptbahnhof to terminate at the newly expanded airport station (shown in timetables as Flughafen Wien).

The U-Bahn (underground trains), S-Bahn (suburban trains) inside the city limits, trams and buses all use the same tickets, with transfers allowed. Under-6s travel free, under-15s travel free on Sundays, public holidays and school holidays; photo ID required. You can get a 24 hour (€8), 48 hour (€14.10) or 72 hour (€17.10) rover ticket. Just before travelling, validate (time-stamp) the ticket. 🛈 Tourist office: Albertinapl., corner of Maysedergasse (www.wien.info) and at Hauptbahnhof.

🛏 A comfortable and very central option is **Hotel Austria**, Fleischmarkt 20, ☎ 01 515 23 (www.hotelaustria-wien.at). Close to the new Museumsquartier, **Pension Wild**, Lange Gasse 10, ☎ 01 406 5174 (www.pension-wild.com), has great rooms and is both backpacker- and gay-friendly. In the vicinity of Westbahnhof is the eco-friendly boutique hotel **Stadthalle**, Hackengasse 20, ☎ 01 982 42 72 (www.hotelstadthalle.at).

Vienna connections

Connect in Vienna onto **Route 44**, which takes the Semmering railway through the Alps and leads to Trieste. Vienna is the best-connected city in central Europe when it comes to railways. From the city's impressive new Hauptbahnhof, there are direct trains to Budapest and Warsaw. Ljubljana and Zagreb are each just a few hours away on comfortable Eurocity services. **Railjets** run to Prague and Zurich. There are **night trains** to Bucharest, Rome, Kraków, Berlin, Kyiv, Paris, Amsterdam and Brussels.

Closer to hand, Vienna is the hub for a fine network of regional and local services, many of which cross nearby borders into **Slovakia and Hungary**. This area has benefited enormously from the enhanced mobility afforded by the Schengen Agreement. Trains apart, from Vienna you can cruise up the Danube to Krems an der Donau or speed downstream in just 75 minutes on a catamaran to Bratislava (Mar–Nov).

From Vienna there are two rail routes east to Bratislava. We strongly recommend that you use the more northerly of the two. This route is more rural and beyond **Marchegg** affords good views of the water meadows that surround the Danube.

SIDETRACKS: NIGHT TRAIN PERSPECTIVE

There are interesting things happening in Europe's night train market. Our previous route in this book ends in **Vienna**, a city which has in recent years emerged as the grand hub for Europe's reviving night train network. Berlin and Munich act as key secondary hubs, each securing new routes in 2024. New night train routes were launched from Berlin to Paris and Aachen, plus from Munich to Kraków and Warsaw. The Nightjet between Berlin and Paris signalled the welcome return of a key overnight link between two major European capitals which had not been connected by direct trains since RZD Russian Railways axed its Berlin to Paris sleeper service in March 2020.

In France we have seen the happy revival of night trains retired many years ago. Night trains from Paris to both Nice and Lourdes are back. In 2024, it has again been possible to snooze your way from Paris to Aurillac and Béziers. Brussels returned to **Europe's night-train map** in 2020 with a new sleeper service to Vienna (with operator ÖBB promoting the new service as 'lying not flying'). Amsterdam followed in 2021, and it is now possible to travel in the comfort of a sleeper from the Dutch city to Zürich, Vienna, Innsbruck, Dresden and Prague.

Brussels now even has a choice of two different operators on the important overnight route to Berlin. You can use our City Links tables on pp505–509 to identify selected city pairs which benefit from a direct overnight link.

In 2016 the French daily *Le Monde* proclaimed the death of the night train. "Le train de nuit. C'est fini," read their lament. How wrong they were! Two things have conspired to change **attitudes towards night trains**. The legitimacy of flying as a social norm was hardly questioned a decade ago. No longer can we be oblivious to our **carbon footprint**, and the almost addictive hyper-mobility – often regarded as a symbol of status in the early 2000s – is being challenged. Travellers who might once have flown are having second thoughts. With environmental concerns now tugging at the conscience of every European citizen, the night sleeper is making an irresistible comeback. But there's something else. Attitudes towards **personal space** changed dramatically during the COVID pandemic. Night trains often offer the security of a private compartment, be it a single berth sleeper for a solo traveller, or a compartment with four couchettes for family use. Suddenly, the overnight train has a new competitive edge.

This all sounds like good news. But there are some serious question marks around current trends. Innovation is being driven by some traditional players, notably the Austrian national **rail operator ÖBB**, but there are also a new market entrants like European Sleeper. New and old players alike face challenges in punctuality and reliability. Much-needed improvements to track and signalling are often scheduled for nighttime hours, so overnight trains are often delayed and diverted. Plus there's a chronic shortage of **high-quality sleeping cars**. ÖBB introduced new Nightjet carriages in 2024, so that is easing the pressure, but it's still not clear where all the sleeping cars will come from for the full range of projected services. For now, at least, it pays to check carefully just quite what you are buying when booking an overnight train. An overnight journey in a seat is no substitute for the real creature comforts of the sleeping car. Few travel experiences quite match the joy of a good night train.

Route 40: Over the Bernina Pass

CITIES: ★ CULTURE: ★ HISTORY: ★★ SCENERY: ★★★
COUNTRIES COVERED: SWITZERLAND (CH), ITALY (IT)
JOURNEY TIME: 8 HRS 30 MINS | DISTANCE: 415 KM | MAP: WWW.EBRWEB.EU/18MAP40

The high point of this journey, indeed its entire *raison d'être*, is the Bernina Railway which links the **Engadine** area of eastern Switzerland with the Valtellina region in **Lombardy**. The Bernina is in our view far and away the finest of the three north-south rail routes connecting Switzerland with Italy. Just for the record, the other two are through the Gotthard and Simplon tunnels, each of them routes well woven into the rich tapestry of Alpine transport history. You can read more about the Simplon route in particular in our **Sidetracks** feature on p380.

Of these three main rail links across the Alps from **Switzerland to Italy**, the Bernina is the youngest. Unlike the Simplon and Gotthard routes, it has never echoed to the rumble of distinguished international expresses. It has from the outset been a rural railway carrying only local trains. The fact that it is of a different gauge — much narrower than the standard and thus better suited to a railway line with tight curves in challenging mountain terrain — has meant that long-distance trains linking Europe's great cities have never been able to use the Bernina route.

While the Gotthard and Simplon routes tunnel *through* the mountains, the **narrow-gauge Bernina Railway** (since 2008 included on the UNESCO World Heritage List) climbs high *over* a mountain pass at **Ospizio Bernina**, reaching an elevation of 2,253 metres. If you are heading from Basel or Zurich for Milan or elsewhere in northern Italy, the Bernina route means quite a detour, but it is extra time well spent. Route 40 is special at any time of year, but the Bernina stretch is really at its very best in deep mid-winter.

ITINERARY SUGGESTIONS

This journey can be done in a single day, but we think it deserves more. Why not think of staying **overnight at St Moritz**? The advantage of spreading the journey over two days is that you'll be able to make short breaks, perhaps just an hour or two, at interesting points along the way. With trains every hour or two along much of the route, it's easy to continue your journey on the next train. **Zernez** deserves just such a stop-off. On the Bernina Railway itself, we recommend a short stop at **Alp Grüm**, where the views are stunning. Purists may want to stop instead (or as well) at the highest station at **Ospizio Bernina**. At both these stations, public facilities (in each case a cosy restaurant with rooms for those wanting to stay overnight) are only open from mid-May to early November. At other times of the year, only alight if you have appropriate boots and warm clothing for harsh winter conditions.

Our experience is that the carriages on the **regular local trains** are more fun than the slick observation cars on the trains branded as *Bernina Express*. And no supplement is payable to ride the slow trains routinely used by locals travelling between remote communities along the route. So opt for the slow train, throw open the window, take a deep breath of mountain air and enjoy the ride. It is pure magic.

ROUTE 40: OVER THE BERNINA PASS | 369

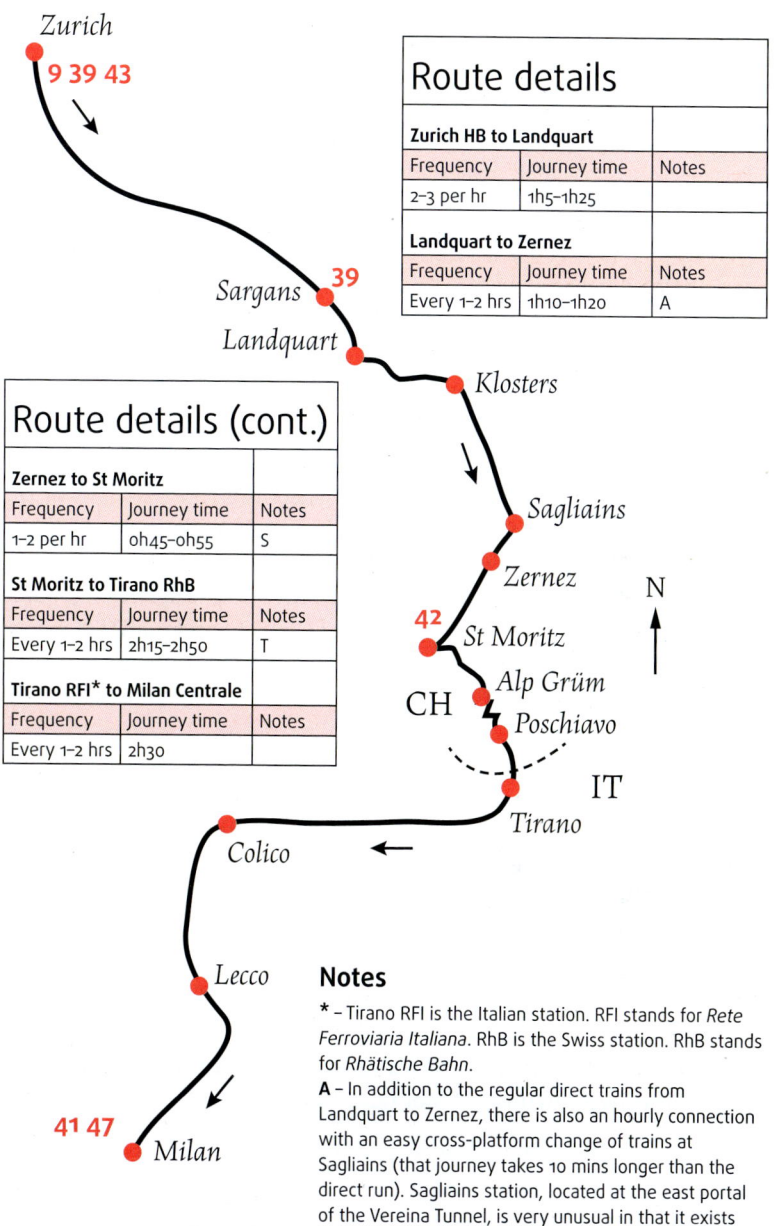

Route details

Zurich HB to Landquart

Frequency	Journey time	Notes
2–3 per hr	1h5–1h25	

Landquart to Zernez

Frequency	Journey time	Notes
Every 1–2 hrs	1h10–1h20	A

Route details (cont.)

Zernez to St Moritz

Frequency	Journey time	Notes
1–2 per hr	0h45–0h55	S

St Moritz to Tirano RhB

Frequency	Journey time	Notes
Every 1–2 hrs	2h15–2h50	T

Tirano RFI* to Milan Centrale

Frequency	Journey time	Notes
Every 1–2 hrs	2h30	

Notes

* – Tirano RFI is the Italian station. RFI stands for *Rete Ferroviaria Italiana*. RhB is the Swiss station. RhB stands for *Rhätische Bahn*.

A – In addition to the regular direct trains from Landquart to Zernez, there is also an hourly connection with an easy cross-platform change of trains at Sagliains (that journey takes 10 mins longer than the direct run). Sagliains station, located at the east portal of the Vereina Tunnel, is very unusual in that it exists purely for the purpose of changing trains. There is no public access to or from the platform.

S – On many journeys a change of train is necessary at Samedan (which is just before St Moritz).

T – Note that there are no evening trains running through to Tirano. The last departure from St Moritz is usually before 17.00 (16.48 in October 2024).

Railways to the Engadine

The Engadine is the name given to the Inn Valley area of eastern **Graubünden**. It takes its name from the Romansh name for the valley: Engiadina. The importance of the **Rhaetian Railway's network** in the economy and social life of this valley cannot be overemphasised. Prior to the coming of the railway, the canton of Graubünden was a Swiss paradox, a mountain fortress which was barely accessible from the rest of the country. The Inn Valley, accessible in winter only from Austrian territory, was a world unto itself. But the arrival of the **Albula Railway** (which is described, travelling north from St Moritz, in the next route in this book) in 1903, ended the isolation of the Inn Valley. The opening of the Vereina Tunnel in 1999 gave the Engadine a second year-round rail link to the Rhine Valley and thus on to the rest of Switzerland.

Through Graubünden

Our journey starts in **Zurich** (for more on the city, see p124), for the first hour running in parallel with **Route 39**. There is a short account of the stretch from Zurich to Sargans on p359. It is at **Sargans**, a stone's throw from the tiny Principality of Liechtenstein, that **Route 39** (to Vienna) and our current journey diverge, as we follow the River Rhine upstream towards the cathedral city of Chur. But, just short of Chur at **Landquart**, we change trains, swapping a main-line Swiss train for a **Rhaetian Railway** narrow-gauge one for the onward journey deep into the mountains of eastern Switzerland.

The red train climbs slowly up the **Prättigau Valley**, lush green pastures slowly giving way to rockier terrain. Just beyond the chic ski resort of Klosters, the line dives into the long Vereina Tunnel to reach the Inn Valley, which it then follows upstream to **Zernez**. If you are tempted to stop for an hour or two, Zernez is a very good choice. This pretty village lies at the heart of the Romansh-speaking area of Graubünden canton. It is the jumping-off point for excursions into Val Müstair, which we rate as one of the most beautiful of all Swiss valleys. The post bus for **Val Müstair** leaves from outside Zernez station. It continues on to Malles in Italy. Read more on border hopping by bus in this area in our **Sidetracks** feature on p357. From Zernez, the railway parallels the River Inn up to St Moritz.

St Moritz (suggested stopover)

Even with competition from the likes of Zermatt, Gstaad and Davos, St Moritz still pretty much leads the way as a **Swiss winter sports resort**, with a breathtaking location and an enviable sunshine record. It is the starting point for the famous *Glacier Express* rail journey, which features as the next route described in this book.

St Moritz divides into **Dorf** (village) on the hill, and **Bad** (spa) 2 km downhill around the lake. A long escalator leads up from the station to St Moritz Dorf. You'll find the main hotels, shops and museums in Dorf (including the Engadine Museum, offering an absorbing look at the furniture and house interiors of the area).

The centre for downhill skiing is **Corviglia** (2,486 m), but even if you're not skiing it's worth the 2-km funicular trip for the views and a glimpse of the 'beautiful people' at play. From there, take the cable car up to **Piz Nair** (3,057 m) for a panorama of the Upper Engadine. **Muzeum Susch** (www.muzeumsusch.ch; Thu, Fri, Sat & Sun 11.00–17.00) with its art exhibitions and experimental performances is only a short rail trip away from St Moritz (50 mins). Located in the remnants of a mediaeval monastery, it opened its doors to the public in January 2019.

ARRIVAL, INFORMATION, ACCOMMODATION

The station is close to the centre of town (St Moritz Dorf). Tourist office: Via Maistra 12 (www.stmoritz.com). Accommodation and food are generally expensive, but less so in St Moritz Bad than in St Moritz Dorf. For great views over the lake, try the **Waldhaus Am See**, Via Dimlej 6, ☎ 081 836 60 00 (www.waldhaus-am-see.ch). Located in St Moritz Bad, the **Hotel Piz**, Via dal Bagn 6, ☎ 081 832 11 11 (www.piz-stmoritz.ch) is a good, functional option. Very handy for the station, the welcoming and comfortable family-run hotel **Houser**, Via Traunter Plazzas 7, ☎ 081 837 50 50 (www.hotelhauser.ch) is a good choice if you want to stay in St Moritz Dorf.

Over the Bernina Pass

You can board the Bernina Railway train in St Moritz, from where it's just ten minutes to **Pontresina**, a small town where creative types once came to relax long before St Moritz became famous (see box on p372).

The 55 kilometres of the Bernina railway from Pontresina to the Italian town of Tirano are almost all above ground. With gradients at over seven per cent, the railway leads passengers from Pontresina up into a high Alpine environment of icy glaciers and rocky moraines before plunging in a great series of loops down into the **Poschiavo Valley** which it then follows south to the Italian Valtellina.

Until the opening of the railway, only the most adventurous visitors to Pontresina contemplated the arduous excursion to **Alp Grüm**, which was commended by **Baedeker** for its restaurant and fine view of the Palü glacier. Now the railway transports tourists from Pontresina up to the front door of the restaurant at Alp Grüm in just forty minutes, and the view is every bit as magnificent as it was in Baedeker's day. The **Palü glacier** has receded a little, and Mr Baedeker might well be bemused by the signs in Japanese on the railway station platform, but otherwise it is much the same. A place for deep snow in winter with gentian, edelweiss and moss campion in summer.

This railway line offers a **kaleidoscope of scenery** from rocky gorges to carefully tended vineyards. The descent into Italy communicates a sense of entering the sunny south.

Changing times in Pontresina

Hans Christian Andersen stayed in Pontresina. So did Richard Wagner. Stefan Zweig was a regular, giving a wonderful account of hotel life in Pontresina in his novel *The Post Office Girl* – one of two Zweig books which influenced Wes Anderson's film *Grand Hotel Budapest*. **Mrs Gaskell** started writing *Wives and Daughters*, her gossipy tale of scandal and intrigue in an English country town, while holidaying – with all her daughters – in Pontresina. But Pontresina's star faded as the **literary crowd** shifted their affections elsewhere. A certain class of English traveller stayed loyal to Pontresina, but that class dwindled and eventually there was no one left to attend the English church there. So in 1974 it was demolished.

Pontresina has slipped out of fashion, but its fate is a nice reminder of how travel fads come and go. That said, the place still has a certain charm, and its setting in the shadow of the **Bernina Alps** is superb. If you are inclined to stay – it's a cheaper alternative to St Moritz – we can recommend the guest house right by the station, ☎ 081 838 80 00 (www.station-pontresina.ch).

In **Tirano**, the train runs through the streets. Traffic waits, not always patiently, as it moves smoothly past shops and houses, then on past the great pilgrimage church of the **Madonna di Tirano**, before coming to a halt at the Rhaetian Railway's own little station just beside the Italian station.

The Bernina trains terminate at Tirano. Walk over to the adjacent Italian railway station for onward services to Milan. The journey first follows the vineyard-clad **Adda Valley**, and then runs down the east side of **Lake Como** and Lake Lecco. Sit on the right for the best views. If your appetite for good scenery has not been entirely satiated by the Bernina Railway, then pause at **Colico**, at the north-east end of Lago di Como and continue by boat to Como.

Even if you stick with the train, you'll still be in for a treat. This is a wonderful ride as the train follows the lakeshore. If you have time to stop, we suggest **Varenna-Esino** as the place to alight (all trains from Tirano stop at that station). From the station it is a seven-minute walk down to the village, following a path along the shoreline.

You'll find that Varenna is picture-perfect, made all the more appealing by the coming and going of ferries serving other communities around the lake. It is worth taking a ride over to **Bellagio** and back; the ferry takes just 15 minutes each way. Although a busy road and railway skirt Varenna, it is still possible to discern in the centre of the village something of the serenity so characteristic of the Lake Como region prior to the advent of major roads and railways.

You'll arrive in **Milan** at Centrale station (read more about the city on p420). In Milan, you can connect onto **Route 47** in *Europe by Rail* which runs in one direction to Verona and Trieste and in the other direction down to the Mediterranean at Genoa. For other direct connections by train from Milan see p422.

Route 41: The classic Gotthard route

Cities: ★★ Culture: ★ History: ★ Scenery: ★★★
Countries covered: Switzerland (CH), Italy (IT)
Journey time: 9 hrs 40 mins | Distance: 434 km | Map: www.ebrweb.eu/18map41

The Gotthard is Switzerland. And Switzerland is the Gotthard. The mountain is intimately linked to **Swiss national identity**. Swiss self-awareness, be it on a social or a political level, is fundamentally underpinned by a shared understanding of the Swiss landscape that includes neat Alpine pastures with cows in attendance, an obligatory mail coach (or modern post bus) and trains. How could we not include the Gotthard railway in this book?

The great **Baedeker** dubbed the route "one of the grandest achievements of modern engineering." But it was more than that. The Gotthard railway acquired a symbolic meaning that captured Swiss technological prowess. In the opening ceremonies for the railway in 1882, Switzerland presented itself as a natural mediator at the heart of Europe and before long Switzerland was being dubbed 'Gotthard nation'. It helped that the railway runs through the very area where representatives of Switzerland's three founding cantons allegedly came together to swear eternal loyalty to each other.

The historic Gotthard railway was sidelined when the **Gotthard Base Tunnel** opened in 2016. That new route slashed timings on the main north-south axis carrying trains from Basel and Zürich to Milan, but it's a long, dark tunnel so passengers miss the best of the Alpine views. For some years after the new Base Tunnel opened the old scenic Gotthard route was relegated to the status of a minor railway. But in spring 2021, with the introduction of through trains every two hours from **Basel to Locarno**, the classic Gotthard railway reacquired something of the status of a main line. And we are delighted to feature this magnificent railway in this 18th edition of *Europe by Rail*.

Our journey starts in Basel, a city which spills over Switzerland's borders into adjacent areas of France and Germany. The route ends in the north Italian city of Milan. Along the way we'll see **Lake Lucerne**, which is a wholly Swiss affair, and **Lake Maggiore**, the waters of which are bisected by the Swiss-Italian border.

Itinerary hints

Choose your travel date carefully and it is very easy to follow this route from Basel right through to Milan in a day. It is essentially an initial long hop on the *Treno Gottardo* from Basel to Locarno, followed by a boat trip down Lago Maggiore to Stresa, from where it's just an hour to Milan on the fastest trains. Two towns worth a stop along the way are **Lucerne** and **Locarno**.

Even if you skip Lucerne, a stop in Locarno makes lots of sense. This lakeside city is so full of pleasant vibes that no one could possibly object to spending a night there. Continuing on the following morning by boat, you'll have time to break your journey in the **Borromean Islands** before continuing to Stresa for the train to Milan.

374 | ALPINE ADVENTURES

Notes

X – Additional options by using a local train to Arth-Goldau and changing there onto the Zürich to Locarno *Treno Gottardo*.

Y – As this reprint of *Europe by Rail* goes to press, it is unclear if the Locarno to Stresa boat service will run in winter 2024/2025.

Z – Faster trains generally run to Milano Centrale, slower services to Milano Porta Garibaldi.

Route details

Basel to Lucerne		
Frequency	Journey time	Notes
2 per hour	1h5–1h15	

Lucerne to Locarno		
Frequency	Journey time	Notes
Every 2 hrs	3h10	X

Locarno to Stresa (by boat)		
Frequency	Journey time	Notes
1–4 per day	1h10–4h	Y

Stresa to Milan		
Frequency	Journey time	Notes
Hourly	1h–1h40	Z

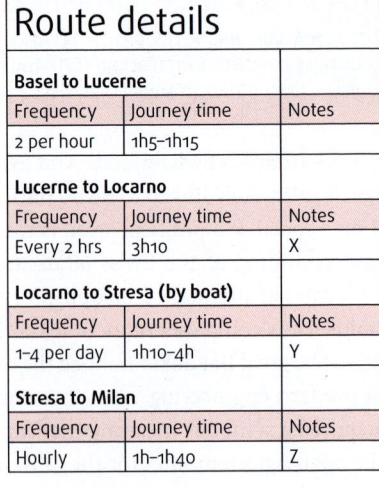

The boat from Lucerne to Flüelen is a classic Swiss lake trip and makes a nice alternative to the train.

From Göschenen it's a short hop by train to Andermatt where you can join **Route 42**.

The pale grey line shows an alternative finale to Route 41, travelling by train from Locarno via Domodossola to Stresa and Milan.

Alternative ending

Locarno to Domodossola		
Frequency	Journey time	Notes
Hourly	1h45–2h	

Domodossola to Milan		
Frequency	Journey time	Notes
Every 1–2 hrs	1h35–2h15	Z

For out-of-season travellers (there's no boat from Locarno to Italy in winter), or others who don't find a convenient onward boat from Locarno, there's a lovely all-year alternative route by train from Locarno, following the narrow-gauge **Centovalli railway** from Locarno to Domodossola in Italy (see the box on p378), changing there onto a direct train to Milan. You'll still get fine views of Lago Maggiore as the railway generally follows the west shore of the lake south from Baveno to Stresa and beyond.

For a **relaxing trip**, think of stopping for at least one night in both Lucerne and Locarno, and for something really special consider having an overnight stop on Isola dei Pescatori in the Borromean Islands. Note that this island goes under the alternative name of Isola Superiore. Now you'll begin to see how a relatively short route, by the standards of this book, has potential to form the basis of a four day or even longer journey.

Into the hills

The Swiss station in **Basel**, formally called Basel SBB, is an engaging spot to embark on a grand journey. It's a station with atmosphere. Fifty years ago, you could board a very posh train called the *Gottardo* at Basel at 7.30 in the morning and travel in air-conditioned comfort through the Alps to reach Milan six hours later. The six-carriage *Gottardo* TEE train carried 168 passengers in open saloons – a seating arrangement that was seen as very

MIND YOUR GOTTHARD

When fast trains were diverted through the **new Gotthard Base Tunnel** in 2016, we feared for the future of the original Gotthard line. It was relegated to secondary status and used almost exclusively by local trains.

No longer did the great expresses tackle steep gradients by the impetuous waters of the Reuss, and later perform elegant pirouettes on the spiral loops at Airolo as, on the south side of the Gotthard, the railway dropped down into the **Ticino Valley**. True, the classic line has its share of darkness for the watershed is crested in a tunnel, but that is a mere 15 km in length. And on that original Gotthard line, there is a real sense of being in the mountains, and that's somehow missing in the prolonged darkness of the new Gotthard Base Tunnel.

So how do you know whether any specific train will take the classic old railway rather than the new Gotthard Base Tunnel route? That's actually quite easy. The only year-round regular scheduled trains to use the old route are those operated by Switzerland's **Südostbahn** (SOB). These trains run every two hours from Basel to Locarno, and every two hours from Zürich to Locarno. The two routes converge at Arth-Goldau, giving an hourly service to Locarno south of that point. There are simply no SOB trains routed via the new Gotthard Base Tunnel. All SOB trains via the classic line are branded *Treno Gottardo*, usually using SOB's distinctive *Traverso* trains.

As a double-check, just ensure that the train you are using stops at **Göschenen**. If it does then you can be sure it's following the old Gotthard railway. There are no trains on the old line which do not stop at Göschenen. There is only one non-SOB train via the old line. It's a seasonal tourist train run by SBB known as the *Gotthard Panorama Express* which runs only during the spring and summer months. It's a first-class only train with a supplementary charge, and there is absolutely no reason to use it. Stick to SOB's lovely *Treno Gottardo* and you'll be just fine.

modern at a time when separate compartments were still the norm on most long-distance trains in Europe (for more on carriage design see p175). The *Gottardo* had a full-service restaurant car where passengers could enjoy a leisurely breakfast as the TEE train rattled by the shores of Lake Lucerne. In those days, trains really did rattle. Even the chic *Trans-Europe Express*.

We can make do with the *Treno Gottardo*, the copper-hued Interregio run by Switzerland's **Südostbahn** (SOB). Their *Traverso* trains are actually extremely comfortable, especially in first class. If you are only travelling as far as Lucerne on the first day, then there are also regular SBB trains on that initial leg of the journey.

Our trip from Basel starts with a small piece of Swiss railway history. When it opened, the **Hauenstein rail route** from Basel through the hills to the Aare Valley at Olten was one of the steepest rail routes in Switzerland. Heavy trains struggled, so a new line was constructed, with a much longer tunnel and at a lower elevation, so obviating the need for the steep gradients. This was Switzerland's first instance of a new base tunnel augmenting an earlier higher route. It opened in 1916, exactly 100 years prior to the Gotthard Base Tunnel. And, just as with the Gotthard, the original, steeper line was left in place and is still used by some trains today.

You'll hardly notice the Hauenstein Base Tunnel; its just 8 km long. But it decants the train into the pleasantly green **Aare Valley** where all trains stop at Olten, from where it's 35 mins on through tame landscape to Lucerne.

Lucerne and its lake

Lucerne once had a very grand railway station, dominated by a giant cupola. Sadly, it was destroyed in a fire in 1971, and replaced by an uninspiring but functional building. Step out to the front and you'll see a ceremonial arch, which is all that remains of the original station. Beyond that arch are the boarding stages for the lake steamers and the bridge which leads over the **River Reuss** into the heart of the old city. Framed in part by city walls, on gently sloping land at the north-west corner of its lake, Lucerne has a superb setting. Baedeker nicely described it as 'amphitheatrical', and there's certainly a touch of drama about Lucerne, especially in the soft light of a spring morning with the sun rising up above the **Rigi**.

With such a strategic location, Lucerne has long been the **transport hub** of central Switzerland. It was from here that early travellers bound for Italy set off by boat for Flüelen at the southernmost tip of the lake, continuing from there on foot or mule over the perilous Gotthard Pass. Those embarking on steamers at Lucerne's piers today surely have in mind nothing more demanding than a **leisurely cruise** on a body of water which, by virtue of its many twists and turns, rates as the most inviting and the most visually dramatic of all Swiss lakes.

Read more on Lucerne on p388. If you are minded to stay overnight, you can try the Waldstätterhof, Zentralstrasse 4, ☎ 041 227 12 71 (www.hotel-waldstaetterhof.ch) which is a good, functional option right by the station.

LUCERNE CONNECTIONS
When it comes to where to go next from Lucerne, you are spoilt for choice. Our **Route 43** escorts you south-west to Interlaken and on via Gstaad to Lake Geneva. For a short excursion into the hills, the 33-km ride up to Engelberg on the *Luzern-Engelberg Express* is fun. In good weather, the **Rigi ascent** makes an utterly beautiful day out: take the boat to Vitznau and then the **rack railway** up to Rigi Kulm.

There are two regional routes starting from Lucerne which we especially like. One is the hourly *Voralpen Express* to **St Gallen**, run by SOB and generally using the same comfortable Stadler *Traverso* trains as are in service on the *Treno Gottardo*. The other is the local service to **Berne** via Entlebuch and Emmental, the latter a vale as celebrated for its striking wooden farmhouses as for its cheese. But this is not just a route for cheese lovers. The line to Berne serves **Trubschachen**. There's not a Swiss kid who wouldn't seize the chance to visit Trubschachen and feast on **Kambly** Bretzeli or the company's crunchy Matterhorns with their milk chocolate and nougat slivers. It's a mark of the power of the Kambly brand that some of the trains along the rail route from Lucerne to Basel carry a special livery celebrating Kambly's contribution to Swiss life. For those who feel able to skip the Emmental and Kambly chocolate, there is a fast Interregio train from Lucerne to Berne, leaving on the hour and taking exactly one hour. This train takes a much less scenic route, looping north of the hills

South to Ticino

You'll be switching seats a lot on the ride south from **Lucerne to Locarno**, such is the quality of the neck-craning scenery on either side of the route. The *Treno Gottardo* runs non-stop from Lucerne to Arth-Goldau, normally taking the route via Rotkreuz rather than the much prettier lakeshore line via Meggen. If you want to use that latter route, there are local trains twice hourly from Lucerne to Arth-Goldau via Meggen, revealing a wonderful panorama south towards the bulky Bürgenstock and east towards the Rigi.

From **Arth-Goldau**, the *Treno Gottardo* skirts the east shore of Lake Lucerne. Just south of Brunnen, there are fine views across the lake to **Rütli**, where legend has it that in 1291 the Swiss Confederation was founded. One hour out from Lucerne, all *Treno Gottardo* services stop at **Flüelen**, at the southern tip of the lake, where the railway station is right by the pier served by the boat from Lucerne.

For a really classy start to this section of the route, why not take the boat from Lucerne down to Flüelen? Boats run hourly in mid-summer, less frequently off-season, taking about 2 hrs 45 mins, with about ten stops at lakeshore communities along the way, normally including Rütli. From Flüelen, now in the confines of the upper part of the **Reuss Valley**, the railway gradually climbs. Too many of the former orchards have been given over to habitations, but with increasing height there's a fine sense of entering a wilderness, with some real drama as the train circles through looping tunnels to gain altitude. Look out for the distinctive Roman Catholic church at Wassen, which you'll see from three completely different angles from the train. The final stop before the tunnel is at **Göschenen**, from where the *Schöllenenbahn* rack railway trains leave twice hourly to climb up steeply to Andermatt (to connect with **Route 42** in this book).

The run through the summit tunnel takes about ten minutes. Emerging into the Leventina district of the **Ticino Valley**, it is immediately evident that there's a more southern demeanour to the landscape. Down through spiral tunnels, the valley slowly loses any Alpine character, with chestnuts, walnuts and vines becoming abundant. From the southern portal of the tunnel, it takes an hour to reach **Bellinzona**, dominated by its three castles (Castelgrande, Montebello and Sasso Corbaro) which have earned this handsome town a place on UNESCO's World Heritage List. It's worth a stop, for this is a town full of atmosphere, and from here the short onward hop to Locarno is easy, with three trains each hour normally taking about 25 mins.

BELLINZONA CONNECTIONS

If all you aimed to do was ride the classic **Gotthard railway**, Bellinzona is the place to turn back. There are fast trains, generally hourly, through the Gotthard Base Tunnel to Zürich

THE CENTOVALLI RAILWAY

Locarno is the end of the line for Switzerland's standard-gauge trains. But it's also the start of the **spectacular metre-gauge railway** that crosses the Italian border to reach the main Simplon Railway at Domodossola. It's a fine run through the mountains. Last time we took the Centovalli train, there were camellias aplenty at both ends of the route, a sharp contrast to the lingering snow in the mountain villages and high valleys served by this extraordinary railway. "Were it not for the train, I'd never leave Verdasio," said an elderly gentleman who stood with us on the station platform as we waited for the slow train back down to Locarno. The *Centovalli Railway* really is a lifeline link for the communities it serves.

You can travel to **Domodossola** from Locarno in just under two hours, but our advice is to stop off along the way. Particularly on the eastern part of the line, so once beyond the Swiss border, trains are very frequent. If you do just hop off on a whim, you'll never have to wait more than an hour for the next onward train. The Swiss villages of **Intragna** and **Verdasio** each deserve an hour or two. Further west Re and Druogno, both in Italy, each warrant a stop. This route offers Alpine rail travel at its best. Interrail tickets are valid, as indeed is the Swiss Pass (even though the western part of the route is in Italy). From Domodossola, you can return north via the **Simplon Tunnel** into Switzerland. Trains generally run every hour or two to Brig, with some trains continuing to Berne or Geneva. For an adventure by road, you can also take Swiss Postbus route 631 from outside Domodossola station over the Simplon Pass to Brig. The 100-minute ride is great fun. Just note that winter snow may disrupt this bus service.

It's an easy run south from Domodossola to **Milan** with slow trains leaving every two hours, and a small number of additional fast services. These trains all route down the west side of Lake Maggiore, giving fine views of the Borromean Islands.

(just 1 hr 40 mins away). If you are heading south to Milan, and just don't have the time to follow our onward route via Lake Maggiore, then Bellinzona is the place to leave the *Treno Gottardo*. There's an hourly fast train to **Milan**, serving Lugano and Como along the way, with some trains continuing beyond Milan to Genoa, Bologna or Venice.

Locarno and Lake Maggiore

The train from Bellinzona arrives in Locarno having travelled through fertile lowlands (called the Piano di Magadino) and along the north shore of Lake Maggiore. Few towns rival Locarno and the neighbouring resort of Ascona when it comes to setting. With a great sweep of the Alps away to the north, Locarno lies on the left bank of the Maggia where its waters decant into **Lake Maggiore**. Ascona is on the right bank of the river. With its bougainvillea and olives, its fig trees and vines, Locarno oozes relaxed, almost Mediterranean style. Locarno life revolves around the gracefully arcaded **Piazza Grande**, a 10-min walk south-west of the main train station.

The must-do excursion is the steep hike (or short funicular ride if you are feeling less energetic) up to the **Madonna del Sasso** above the town. For an overnight stay, we can recommend the pastel blue Hotel Millennium at via nuova Dogana 2, housed in the former customs house right by the quay where the lake steamers come and go.

The boat service from **Locarno to Stresa** is operated by Navigazione Laghi (see www.navigazionelaghi.it for current timetables). The company operates a large fleet of traditional steamers and a small number of hydrofoils. The latter have premium fares, but in our view are much too fast to allow any appreciation of the lake and its surrounding landscapes. The fast vessels dash down to Stresa in just 75 minutes. Locarno to Stresa on the regular ferry can take up to four hours. It is a gorgeous trip with some really appealing stops along the way.

Last time we took this route, we took an early boat from Locarno and stopped off in **Cannobio** for an hour – just enough time to enjoy a coffee on the town's gracious lakefront piazza. Then we continued to the **Borromean islands**, staying on Isole dei Prescatori for a couple of days, where we can thoroughly recommend the Hotel Verbano, ☎ 0323 30 408 (www.hotelverbano.it; closed in winter).

Whether you travel straight down the lake, or linger for a week along the way, Stresa is the place where you'll eventually shift back to rail. It's a bustling wee town that no longer has the lustre that propelled it to popularity in the 1920s. But the lakefront promenade has style, and it's a pleasant 10-min walk to the station, from where the fastest trains to **Milan** take under an hour (for more on the city see p420). The train runs south along the Lake Maggiore shore to beyond Arona, then passing Rho and Milan's exhibition grounds (Fiera Milano) on the approach to the busy capital of Lombardy.

SIDETRACKS: THROUGH THE SIMPLON

Roman Catholic bishops do not normally incline to subterranean exploits. But on a spring Sunday morning in 1905, Bishop Jules-Maurice Abbet skipped his normal duties at the **cathedral in Sion** in Switzerland's Valais canton. Instead of celebrating Holy Mass at his cathedral he travelled deep into the bowels of the Lepontine Alps to bless the **new Simplon rail tunnel**. The Bishop of Sion embraced an Italian bishop deep below Mount Leone at the point where the tunnel crosses the Swiss-Italian border. A small band played the *Marcia Reale* and the *Cantique Suisse* – so appealing to the national sentiments of all present. Bishop Abbet dowsed the tunnel with **holy water** and said nice things about technological progress – perhaps wondering if the new rail tunnel would mean redundancy for the Augustinian canons who offered shelter and succour at the hospice on the difficult carriage road which climbs over the Simplon Pass.

The first trains did not run through the Simplon Tunnel until a year after Bishop Abbet's subterranean excursion. The train service was inaugurated to coincide with the start of the **Milan EXPO** in late April 1906. In those days, it was expected that each new World Fair (or EXPO) would celebrate a particular technological achievement: examples included the Eiffel Tower at the Paris *exposition* in 1889 and the motor car at the Brussels fair in 1897.

The 1906 EXPO focused fair and square on transport and the showpiece achievement associated with the Milan fair was the Simplon Tunnel – when it opened it was the longest railway tunnel in the world. It kept that record for 76 years. The **official medallion** of the 1906 EXPO showed the Italian portal to the tunnel near Iselle. Promotional posters urged Parisians to take the train to the Milan exhibition.

The Simplon route from **Paris to Milan** was faster than the Mont Cenis route. The latter relied on the Fréjus Tunnel which had opened 35 years earlier. Travellers to the 1906 Milan EXPO could leave Paris on a *train de luxe* just after eight in the evening, and by breakfast time the following morning their train was cruising gently through the towns of the Valais: Sion, Visp and **Brig**. The latter was the last station in Switzerland prior to the Simplon Tunnel. Departure from Brig was at 08.40, giving an arrival in Milan just after midday – a total journey time from Paris of slightly over 16 hours.

The **Thello overnight service** from Paris to Venice, sadly withdrawn in 2020, used the Simplon route to Italy – though, as the train travelled through the Simplon Tunnel in the wee small hours, most of those on board were surely unaware that they slept through a medley of Swiss cantons. The Simplon route remains today one of the trunk rail routes **through the Alps**. It is still well used by the direct Eurocity services from Geneva to Milan and Venice as well as by car trains which ferry motorists from Brig through the tunnel into Italy. For a real engagement with Alpine landscapes, it's not our top choice – the Bernina Railway described in **Route 40** gets that prize. But the Simplon is a fast route south, and gives a magical introduction to northern Italy as the train skirts the western shore of **Lago Maggiore** with fine views of the Borromean Islands. **Route 41** joins the Simplon railway at Stresa.

Route 42: Following the Glacier Express

CITIES: ★ CULTURE: ★ HISTORY: ★ SCENERY: ★★★
COUNTRIES COVERED: SWITZERLAND (CH)
JOURNEY TIME: 8 HRS 15 MINS | DISTANCE: 290 KM | MAP: www.ebrweb.eu/18map42

The historical rise of mass tourism in Switzerland has changed our understanding of **mountain landscapes**. In the decades after the Napoleonic Wars, before the railways had extended their networks into remote valleys, travel through the Alps was arduous and slow.

Representations of the mountains in Romantic literature and picturesque art (think Turner and Ruskin) gave travellers some inkling of what to expect. By the mid-19th century, the developing rail network widened possibilities and in 1863 **Thomas Cook** was offering a 16-day excursion through Switzerland which he billed as "fulfilling the wishes of a lifetime, in a pleasant duty never to be repeated."

A century and a half after Cook, with myriad **editions of Baedeker** in those intervening years, the *Glacier Express* is the epitome of the constructed tourist experience. Ruskin's descriptions of the Alps echo down through the generations: "Infinitely beyond all that we had ever thought or dreamed... lost Eden could not have been more beautiful to us." And the marketing men and women have moved in to give the affluent visitor to the **Swiss Alps** an experience which transcends even Cook and Ruskin. Here is a case of what the American historian Rudy Koshar described as externally directed tourism: "You go not where you want to go, but where the industry has decreed you shall go... Tourism requires that you see conventional things and that you see them in a conventional way."

Glaciers and brooding mountain valleys are Swiss staples and the conventional way of seeing them is through the panoramic windows of a train full of other tourists. Indeed, the *only* Swiss train trips sold by thousands of travel agents in North America are packages showcasing journeys on the *Glacier Express* and/or the *Bernina Express*. The routes taken by these trains feature in this book as **Route 42** and **40** respectively

All of which might lead you to wonder why we have Route 42 in this book at all. Until 2016, the *Glacier Express* route from **St Moritz to Zermatt** was not included in *Europe by Rail*. And that, we decided, was an oversight because it is a truly amazing rail journey. It runs through high mountain scenery from the **Engadine to the Valais**. It takes in valleys whose water drain down towards the Black Sea, and it touches the upper reaches of both the Rhine – which flows to the North Sea – and the Rhône, which runs eventually into the Mediterranean.

The important thing to remember about Route 42 is that it's not compulsory to take the tourist train which plies this route. Read more in our itinerary notes on the next page.

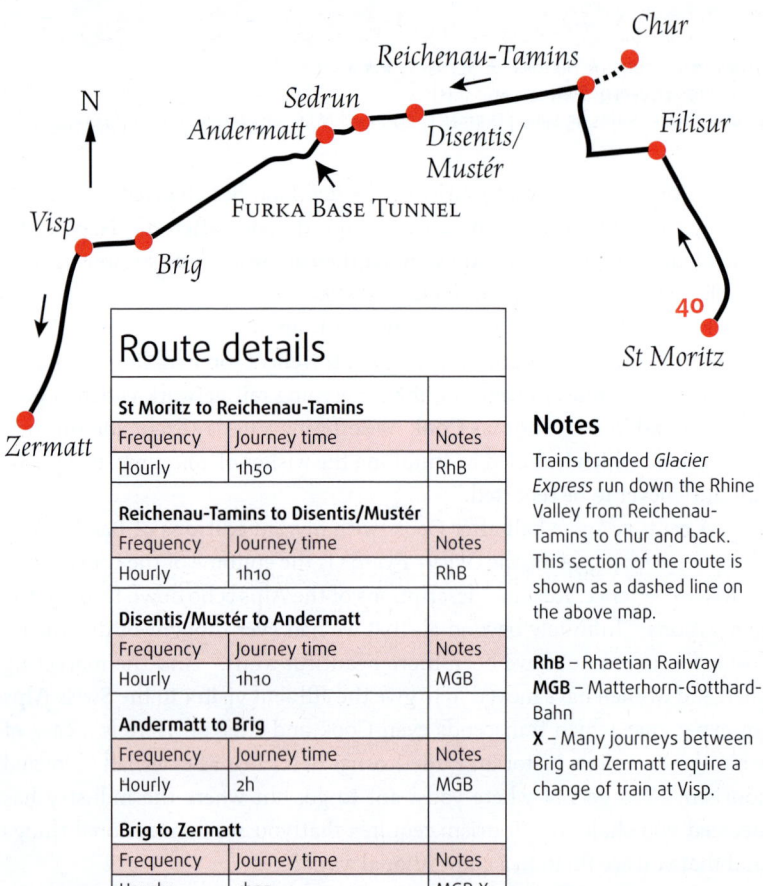

Thoughts on itinerary

The train known as the *Glacier Express* runs year round bar for a seven-week break in the autumn. A supplementary fare is payable; this includes a reserved seat. The one-way fare varies from 191 Swiss francs (second class, low season) to 317 Swiss francs (first class, high season) (€181 to €300). In 2019, a new Excellence Class service was launched under the banner "the most sought-after seats in Switzerland". The 688 Swiss franc (€650) one-way fare includes champagne, a five-course lunch and pampered service.

The *Glacier Express* leaves St Moritz and Zermatt (at either end of the route) each morning and takes just over eight hours to cover the entire 290-kilometre journey. The number of *Glacier Express* trains in each direction increases to three per day in mid-summer. It's a packaged experience with a **rather cinematic quality**.

All that stacks up to an interesting day out, but **there is an alternative**. Why not just take the **regular local trains** which ply the entire *Glacier Express* route all year? There are hourly services along the full length of the route from St Moritz to Zermatt (see table above). You will need to change trains a number of times along the way but trains always connect perfectly – this is Switzerland after all, a country which has refined train connections into a high art. We find that the local trains have far more character than the

Glacier Express. And guess what? Unless you decide to stop off along the way, the journey from St Moritz to Zermatt relying on local trains will not take a minute longer than if you had opted for the *Glacier Express*.

If you use local trains as we suggest, your trains will be run by the **Rhaetian Railway** (RhB) from St Moritz to Disentis/Mustér. There RhB hands over the baton to the **Matterhorn-Gotthard-Bahn** (MGB) which runs the onward trains via Andermatt to Brig and Zermatt. RhB accepts both Interrail and Eurail passes. MGB has historically been rather sniffy about rail passes but happily changed its policy in 2017, so that holders of Interrail and Eurail passes can now travel for free on all MGB trains (except for the *Glacier Express* where a seat reservation fee is still payable by pass holders – as indeed by all other travellers).

Is it worth stopping off? Well, we think it really is possible to overdose on too much fine scenery, and the entire run from St Moritz to Zermatt takes in a vast number of mountains, gorges, meadows and glaciers. Why not break the journey and spend a night at **Andermatt**?

Profile of the route

This journey starts high and ends high. St Moritz, in Switzerland's Engadine region, lies at a breezy 1,775 metres above sea level. Zermatt is only slightly lower. But during the journey we'll dip down twice to about 650 metres, once into the **Rhine Valley** and then later into the Rhône Valley. Between the two, the railway climbs over the mighty **Oberalp Pass**, which marks the boundary of two Swiss cantons: Graubünden to the east (Grisons in French) and Uri to the west. The Oberalp Pass railway station at the summit is the highest point on our journey: 2,033 metres above sea level. The journey thus has a profile shaped like the letter W.

Highlights

On a route which is so full of scenic superlatives, we are not sure that a blow-by-blow account of the journey serves any great purpose. But it's surely useful to say something of the landscapes you'll encounter along the way.

Our journey starts in **St Moritz** (read more on this stylish mountain resort on p370), and initially follows the **Albula Railway** down towards the Rhine Valley. This mountain railway was added to UNESCO's World Heritage List in 2008 (along with the Bernina Railway on **Route 40**). It's a tremendous engineering and architectural achievement, and one which in its design and execution shows great sensitivity to the environment. As visitors, it's easy to forget that this, like other rail routes through the Alps, does not exist purely for the benefit of tourists. These are key links in the local transport infrastructure, all the more so in winter when roads may be blocked by snow. A museum by the station at **Bergün** tells the remarkable story of the Albula Railway (www.bahnmuseum-albula.ch; closed Mon).

If you are using local trains for the journey to Zermatt, the first place to change trains is at **Reichenau-Tamins** station, where an inconveniently

Connections with the *Glacier Express*

The very nature of the *Glacier Express* route, running as it does from east to west across part of Switzerland, means that it intersects several north-south transport arteries along the way. The eastern end of the route in St Moritz is easily reached from either Zurich or Milan, the latter taking in the celebrated Bernina Railway along the way. The **Zurich – St Moritz – Milan** journey features as **Route 40** in this book.

From Reichenau-Tamins it is just a short ride down the Rhine Valley to nearby Chur where you can connect onto regular direct trains to Zurich and Basel. From Andermatt, a mountain railway drops down steeply to Göschenen, just 14 minutes away, giving easy connections into trains on the classic **Gotthard route** running north to Lucerne and south to Locarno. This is not the new Gotthard Base Tunnel line, which opened in December 2016, but the original Gotthard railway.

In Brig, there are good connections north to Berne, Basel and Zurich and south via the Simplon Tunnel to Milan. There is even a direct train from Brig via the Simplon to Venice. For more on the **Simplon route**, see our **Sidetracks** feature on p380.

The fast northbound trains from Brig all use the Lötschberg Base Tunnel which opened in 2007. Happily, the old **Lötschberg pass railway** was not abandoned and that makes a splendid route north via Kandersteg to Spiez, Berne and beyond. There are also connections in Brig or Visp onto the main-line trains down the Rhône Valley to Lausanne and Geneva. Zermatt is very much the end of the line. If you follow Route 42 to its very end, you'll have no choice but to return back down into the Rhône Valley, connecting in Visp or Brig through to your next destination.

---

positioned main road makes it difficult to reach the bank of the River Rhine which is just a few metres north of the railway station. From Reichenau-Tamins, sit on the right of the train bound for **Disentis/Mustér** for the best views of the Vorderrhein; it's not always pretty with scars of huge rockslides, many very ancient, on the north side of the valley.

Beyond Disentis, now on a MGB train, the line climbs steeply towards Oberalp Pass. Look out for the village of **Sedrun** which lies immediately above the north-south Gotthard Base Tunnel which opened to passenger traffic in June 2016. An ambitious plan to build a passenger station on the new link – 800 metres beneath Sedrun – had been shelved. The Swiss authorities even went so far as to give the station a name: Porta Alpina. Had the station been built, it would surely have transformed this remote mountain valley for ever.

The most **dramatic mountain scenery** is in the section of the journey between Sedrun and Andermatt. This sense of desolation in the winter is quite terrifying. Dropping down from the summit, the town of **Andermatt** makes a good overnight stop. It's a place which has moved dramatically upmarket in recent years – helped by substantial investments from the Middle East. The **Chedi Hotel** (which you cannot miss as you walk from the station into town) was the first manifestation of a revolution which has transformed Andermatt from a sleepy mountain village to a high-end resort.

Take a look at the Chedi, Gotthardstr. 4, even if like us you couldn't possibly afford to stay there (www.thechediandermatt.com). Its 'Andermatt-meets-Arabia' design is captivating. There's a good choice of cheaper accommodation. We can recommend the River House, Gotthardstrasse 58, ☎ 041 887 00 25 (www.theriverhouse.ch).

Running west from Andermatt, the railway to Zermatt affords fleeting views of the glaciers away to the north before diving into the **Furka Base Tunnel**, at 15 kilometres by far the longest tunnel on the entire route. Emerging from the tunnel into the Rhône drainage basin it's downhill all the way to **Brig** (Brigue in French), an amiable small town dominated by the Italianate-style **Stockalper Castle**. It is worth wandering up Brig's main street, which is lined by merchants' houses, and taking a look at the arcaded courtyard of the castle. Kaspar Stockalper controlled the Simplon trade from his base in Brig. Today, the town remains an important transport hub (see the connections box on p384).

Beyond Brig, the valley scenery down to **Visp** is unexceptional, but there the line to Zermatt turns south and climbs steeply up into the mountains. It's a **dramatic finale** to a journey full of scenic wonder. Yet the final stretch is not without surreal touches, such as the vast car parks at **Täsch** where even the most determined motorists are forced to abandon their cars and take to the train.

Zermatt

No matter how chic your Mercedes, there's no way you'll be allowed to drive into Zermatt. The only way to Zermatt is by train. It's much to the credit of local planners that the town has not been completely wrecked by mass tourism – and the car-free atmosphere is one of many things which make Zermatt special.

The **Pennine Alps** rise up steeply behind the town, from where on clear days there are superb views of the **Matterhorn** and the Dufourspitze. And you don't need an ice axe and crampons to really get up high. The **Gornergrat mountain railway** climbs up from Zermatt to well over 3,000 metres above sea level.

ARRIVAL, INFORMATION, ACCOMMODATION

✈ The train station is just a short walk south along Bahnhofstr. into the centre of Zermatt.
🅘 Tourist office: Bahnhofplatz 5 (www.zermatt.ch).
🛏 There is no shortage of accommodation, but prices in Zermatt can be a challenge and it's best to book well ahead. Many of the hotels are closed for part of the year (usually in the quieter months in late spring and late autumn). A comfortable and very welcoming hotel is the **Carina**, Untere Wiestistrasse 12, ☎ 027 966 40 66 (www.carinazermatt.ch), just a short walk from the station. Or try the friendly, family-run **Bella Vista**, Riedweg 15, ☎ 027 966 28 10 (www.bellavista-zermatt.ch). The **Hotel Parnass**, Vispastr. 4, ☎ 027 967 11 79 (www.parnass-zermatt.ch), is another good, central option.

Route 43: Swiss lakes and mountains

CITIES: ★ CULTURE: ★★ HISTORY: ★ SCENERY: ★★★
COUNTRIES COVERED: SWITZERLAND (CH)
JOURNEY TIME: 7 HRS 30 MINS | DISTANCE: 338 KM | MAP: WWW.EBRWEB.EU/18MAP43

In our opinion, this is one of the finest one-day train journeys in Switzerland, certainly on a par with the much-vaunted **Glacier Express** from St Moritz to Zermatt (the route of which is described in the preceding journey in this book). When **Thomas Cook** escorted his first tours to Switzerland, his itineraries focused on the territory traversed by this route. To English travellers in the Victorian period, Switzerland meant the Alps. This understanding of Switzerland was not peculiar to the English. The Alps are still as essential an element as ever of the Swiss psyche, even though more Swiss citizens now live in city apartment blocks than on farms in remote Alpine valleys. The myth of the *Dörfli* under the shadow of an alp is a very powerful image, and many Swiss who live in cities still assert that their hearts lie in a small village in the hills.

This route nicely explores the Switzerland of the imagination – a place full of **Alpine meadows**, cow bells and snow-capped peaks. With some of Europe's most efficient rail services running even into remote Alpine valleys, there is plenty of scope for really getting off the beaten track. We start in **Zurich**, heading south for a brief but tantalising encounter with Lake Lucerne, before striking south-west into one of the most serenely beautiful parts of the Alps. You'll see a lot of the **Bernese Oberland** on this route.

Our favourite section is the steep drop down to Montreux on the shores of Lake Geneva. West from Montreux we cruise through the **Lavaux Vineyards** to reach Lausanne, before embarking on the final leg along the lakeshore to Geneva.

THOUGHTS ON AN ITINERARY
We have twice in recent years made this journey from end to end without an overnight stop – once in each direction. It's a long ride, seven to eight hours, but it's **utterly captivating**. If you want to split the journey into two, then Interlaken is a good place to stop. With a two-night stop in Interlaken you might use the free day to travel to the **Jungfraujoch** (see the Sidetracks feature on p394). Towards the end of Route 43, you might think of spending a

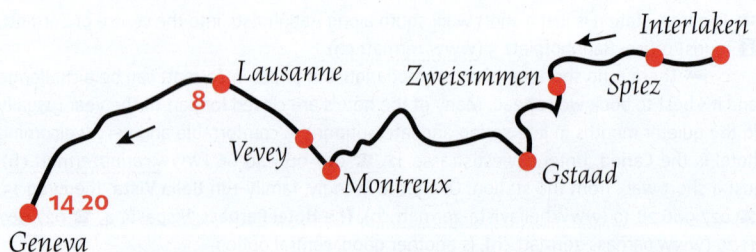

Route 43: Swiss lakes and mountains | 387

night in Lausanne, well worth exploring in its own right, but also a perfect jumping-off point for visiting the Lavaux Vineyard region or for **excursions by boat** on Lake Geneva.

Journeys on the Lucerne – Interlaken – Montreux axis, the central portion of Route 43, are now being marketed under the banal name *GoldenPass Line* (www.goldenpassline.ch). New trains on the stretch from Interlaken to Montreux have a very posh Prestige class, so some trains now offer a Glacier-Express-style packaged tourist experience. Stick to the regular trains if possible.

On the first part of the run out of **Zurich** (see p124) the train speeds under the balconies of multicoloured apartment blocks, before plunging into a long tunnel. There are stops in lakeside **Thalwil** and affluent **Zug** before, less than an hour after leaving Zurich, the train arrives at Lucerne for the first of several changes of train along the route.

Route details

Zurich to Lucerne
Frequency	Journey time	Notes
2 per hr	0h45–0h50	

Lucerne to Meiringen
Frequency	Journey time	Notes
Hourly	1h10	

Meiringen to Interlaken Ost
Frequency	Journey time	Notes
2 per hr	0h35	

Interlaken Ost to Spiez
Frequency	Journey time	Notes
2–3 per hr	0h25	

Spiez to Zweisimmen
Frequency	Journey time	Notes
1–2 per hr	0h45	

Zweisimmen to Montreux
Frequency	Journey time	Notes
Hourly	2h10	

Route details (cont.)

Montreux to Lausanne
Frequency	Journey time	Notes
4–5 per hr	0h25–0h35	

Lausanne to Geneva
Frequency	Journey time	Notes
4–6 per hr	0h35–0h50	

Lucerne straddles the River Reuss, itself crossed by quaintly roofed mediaeval footbridges, at the end of Lake Lucerne. Characteristic of Old Lucerne are its many elaborately painted houses, its cobbled squares, its fountains, its Renaissance town hall by the Kornmarkt, and the two bridges over the Reuss. The city's mascot, the **Löwendenkmal** (Lion Memorial), Löwenstr., is a massive but movingly portrayed dying lion carved in the cliff-side, commemorating the Swiss Guards massacred at the Tuileries in Paris during the French Revolution. Nearby is the **Gletschergarten** (Glacier Garden), Denkmalstr. 4, a bed of smooth rocks pitted with holes, created by glacial erosion. There's an ingenious mirror-maze here too.

Anyone with an interest in transport in all its guises and vintages should make for the **Verkehrshaus** (Swiss Transport Museum), Lidostr. 5 (www.verkehrshaus.ch), 2 km east of town, reached by a pleasant lakeside walk (or 🚌 6/8/24); it's one of Europe's leading museums on the theme, with exhibits covering locos, vintage cycles, space rockets and more, plus an IMAX movie theatre, a 360-degree cinema with a huge, almost vertigo-inducing screen.

The Zentralbahn

The **narrow-gauge railway** from Lucerne to Interlaken is called the Zentralbahn (literally Central Railway) or sometimes the **Brünig Railway**, taking that name from the line's summit. The old surface line through Lucerne's suburbs was rerouted underground in 2012. Soon we are above ground again, with the hills slowly closing in. After skirting the **Sarnersee**, the railway climbs steeply to Brünig Pass, where the summit station is called **Brünig-Hasliberg**.

This is an extraordinary spot, not so much for the scenery as for the huge bric-a-brac shop now housed in the station buildings. Austrian cook Josef Hechenberger ('Brünig Sepp') has run the place for 25 years, and when

All a question of width

There is an oddity about this journey which may appeal to rail buffs but may be judged a modest inconvenience by others. You will have to change trains along the way. There are **two narrow-gauge sections** of line: 74 kilometres from Lucerne to Interlaken Ost and a further stretch of 62 kilometres from Zweisimmen via Gstaad to Montreux. The railway company which plies that westernmost narrow-gauge section, the Montreux-Berner Oberland-Bahn (MOB), for years aspired to introduce direct trains from Montreux to Interlaken, obviating the need to change trains in Zweisimmen. In summer 2023, they introduced new rolling stock with wheels which slip ingeniously from standard-gauge to narrow-gauge track and back again – a piece of engineering magic which has proved imperfect in practice. In July 2024, a train derailed on the gauge-changer at Zweisimmen. Services were quickly restored and four trains each day now run through without any need for a change.

Boat trips on Swiss lakes

On a journey that celebrates Swiss lakes (as well as mountains), you might be inclined to spend some time afloat. In an earlier route in this book, we extolled the merits of **Lake Lucerne** (see p376). This current route also gives the opportunity for excursions on that same lake. Holders of Interrail and Eurail passes are entitled to a 50% discount on fares for journeys on Lake Lucerne and **Lake Geneva** (without any need to validate a pass day on flexi passes).

From Lausanne on the current route, there is a fine network of boat services. You may care to venture to **Château de Chillon**, the lakeshore castle at the eastern extremity of Lake Geneva, where Byron and Gogol both rather cheekily carved their names on pillars in the dungeon. Don't try and follow their example. Historic **belle époque paddle steamers** ply the route in summer (information at www.cgn.ch).

Or, if having followed Route 43 all the way from Zurich, you can forsake the train in **Lausanne** and travel by boat to Geneva. This longer hop is only possible from April till October. It takes 3 hrs 40 mins. But many boat services run year-round. For example, from the quays at Lausanne Ouchy, it's just 35 mins on a fast ferry over to **Évian-les-Bains** and 50 mins to Thonon. Both towns are on the French bank of the lake and these ferries are a year-round mainstay of the local transport infrastructure.

---

we stopped off at Brünig a few years ago, Hechenberger's stock included a ship's bell, an artificial leg, a life-size model of Jesus Christ with a penguin, and a fabulous collection of books ranging from Karl May to Karl Marx (plus a very handsome edition of *Sexual Splendours of the Erotic East*). This delicious emporium is open every day of the year.

From Brünig, it's downhill all the way to **Meiringen**, a town that claims to be the birthplace of meringue (the confection rather than the Caribbean musical genre). From Meiringen, opt for a seat on the left for lovely lake views on the run west, skirting the north shore of the **Brienzersee**, to Interlaken.

Interlaken (suggested stopover)

This **lively resort**, strategically placed between two lakes, boomed in the 19th century when it became popular with British visitors as a base for exploring the mountains, and fanciful hotels sprang up along the **Höheweg**, the town's principal avenue (which links the two stations). It's still virtually unrivalled in the country as a centre for scenic excursions.

You don't need transport for getting around town, but hiring a bike to explore the adjacent lakeshores can be fun. From the Höheweg a wonderful, uninterrupted view extends across the undeveloped meadow where the original 12th-century monastic site of the town once stood, to **Jungfrau** (4,158 m) and other peaks looming beyond – especially magnificent in the later afternoon Alpenglow (see also our Sidetrack feature on p394).

One of the period pieces in town is the distinctive 19th-century **Kursaal** (Casino), which in addition to gambling stages concerts and folklore evenings. Across the River Aare is the old part of town known as Unterseen, with the oldest buildings in the region. Cross the bridge and walk along the river to Obere Gasse, with its 17th-century **town hall and palace**, 14th-century church and the **Tourismuseum**. The latter charts the rise of Interlaken's tourist industry (www.tourismuseum.ch; open May–Oct, Wed–Sun 14.00–17.00; Dec–Apr Wed & Sun 14.00–17.00).

Arrival, information, accommodation

✈ Ostbahnhof at the western end of Höheweg, a 10-min walk from the centre. Westbahnhof is central. The two stations are 15 mins apart on foot, 4 mins by rail. It is the Ostbahnhof that connects with the railway to Jungfraujoch. From Berne, Westbahnhof is the first stop and the journey, by hourly trains, averages 50 mins. 🛈 Tourist office: Marktgasse 1 (www.interlaken.ch).

🛏 There's no shortage of hotels, many catering largely for tour operators, but private rooms can be better value. A reasonably priced and comfortable hotel is **Arnold's Bed & Breakfast**, Parkstr. 3, ☎ 033 823 64 21 (www.arnolds.ch). Or try the cozy **Adventure Guesthouse**, Helvetiastr. 29, ☎ 077 456 23 38 (www.adventure-guesthouse.ch), in Unterseen. More upmarket, in a great location between the two stations on the far side of the River Aare is the family-run **Aparthotel Goldey**, Obere Goldey 85, ☎ 079 385 77 86 (www.goldey.ch).

To Spiez and beyond

Our train runs west from Interlaken to **Spiez** with fine views over the Thunersee en route (sit on the right). Crossing the main Brig to Berne railway at Spiez, the railway then climbs the **Simmen Valley**.

At **Zweisimmen** travellers change onto a narrow-gauge train. Hills roll into more hills and the train traverses several ridges, passing the resort town of Gstaad, before a spectacular descent down to Montreux on the shores of Lake Geneva. Stylish **Gstaad** is a pleasant spot to pause for a couple of hours. For an overnight stay here, the small, family-owned Hotel Restaurant Alphorn, Gsteigstrasse 51, ☎ 033 748 45 45 (www.alphorn-gstaad.ch), is a good option.

Montreux is the best-preserved of the Lake Geneva resorts and blessed with a mild climate, with palm trees, magnolias and cypresses along its long waterfront promenade – a lovely place for strolling. Smart hotels make the most of the views, while the rest of the town rises in tiers up the hillside. The effect is slightly spoiled by a garish casino.

Our route west from Montreux skirts Switzerland's largest lake for much of the 85-km journey to Geneva. The best of the scenery is between Vevey and Lausanne where the railway skirts the **Lavaux Vineyard Terraces**, affording good views of a cultural landscape that dates back to mediaeval times (read more in our box 'Train des Vignes'). The Lavaux Vineyard is included on UNESCO's World Heritage List. There are some lovely set-piece villages which are delightful places to stop. Our favourite on the main lakeshore railway is **Saint-Saphorin**, the first stop west of Vevey. The place is served only by hourly local trains (service S5).

Lausanne (suggested stopover)

A city of two moods, half Alpine and half Riviera, Lausanne is perched on the **hills above Lake Geneva**. Some of the best views of this university city are from the cathedral high above the Old Town. The steepness of the place is part of its appeal, and if you don't fancy the trudge up from the lakeshore suburb of Ouchy, with its grand hotels and large park, up to the Old Town, there's a **useful metro** linking the top, middle and lakeshore districts of Lausanne. The partly pedestrianised **Old Town** is small enough to be explored on foot.

The upper metro terminal (Flon) is located just south of the main area of interest and dominated by the 15th-century steeple of the Église St-François (St Francis' Church). The **Cathédrale de Notre-Dame**, a 10-min walk up into the town, was consecrated in 1275. Italian, Flemish and French craftsmen all had a hand in its construction, and it is accepted as a perfect example of Gothic architecture. The night watch is still called from the steeple every hour from 22.00 to 02.00, a ritual which became even more varied in late 2021 with the first-ever female appointed to dutifully call out the hours.

Escaliers du marché, a wooden-roofed mediaeval staircase, links the cathedral square to Pl. de la Palud, an ancient square surrounded by old houses. West of the cathedral, the Palais de Rumine, Pl. de la Riponne, was built by a Russian family at the turn of the last century. It now houses a number of museums, including the cantonal museum of fine art. Take a 10-min walk north-west (or 🚌 3/21) to the **Collection de l'Art Brut**, av. des Bergières 11 (www.artbrut.ch), housed in the Château de Beaulieu (closed Mon except July–Aug). This compelling post-war gallery was founded by

---

TRAIN DES VIGNES

The journey from **Vevey to Lausanne** along the lakeshore is all too brief. Even the stopping trains take only 20 minutes. For much better views of the Lavaux area, take the *Train des Vignes* (service R7) which runs slightly higher up the hillside and cuts through the middle of the vineyards. The *Train des Vignes* runs hourly from Vevey to **Puidoux**, where there's an easy connection onto the R5, R6 or R9 which drop back down through Grandvaux to Lausanne.

For something really special consider an overnight stay at the **Auberge de la Gare** which is right by the railway station at **Grandvaux** (just one stop along the line from Puidoux). It's a place to try the delicate fillets of perch which are a Lake Geneva speciality and local Lavaux region wines. Check out the chasselas (white) and pinot noir (red). With a great view over the railway, it is also a sure hit with train spotters (☎ 021 799 26 86; www.aubergegrandvaux.ch).

a local collector, who sought the works of anyone who was not a trained or formal painter, from amateur dabblers to the criminally insane.

The **quai de Belgique** is a shady, flower-lined, waterside promenade, looking towards the Savoy Alps. The 13th-century keep of Château d'Ouchy is now a hotel. Baron Pierre de Coubertin, founder of the modern Olympics in 1915, chose Lausanne as the headquarters of the International Olympic Committee. The **Musée Olympique**, quai d'Ouchy 1, is a large modern complex, cleverly designed to retain the natural beauty of its surrounding park (www.olympics.com/musee). Boats can be hired near the 'cruise' pier.

Arrival, information, accommodation

⇒ Between the centre and Ouchy, connected by metro. Left luggage facilities and bike rental. ℹ Tourist office: in the main hall of the railway station (www.lausanne-tourisme.ch). ⛴ Close to the railway station and within walking distance of the centre, the Best Western Plus **Hotel Mirabeau**, av. de la Gare 31, ☎ 021 341 42 43 (www.mirabeau.ch) is a good option. Or try the **Hotel Élite**, av. Sainte-Luce 1, ☎ 021 320 23 61 (www.elite-lausanne.ch), just north of the station. Located in a quiet neighbourhood in the Old Town, just a few minutes walk from the Flon metro station is the boutique **Hotel des Voyageurs**, r. Grand-St-Jean 19, ☎ 021 319 91 11 (www.voyageurs.ch).

Connections from Lausanne

In Lausanne, you can connect onto **Route 8** in this book, following it back through France to the Low Countries. There are fast trains north from Lausanne to Berne and Zurich. Or follow the lakeshore railway west to Geneva. **Compagnie Générale de Navigation sur le lac Léman** (CGN), av. de Rhodanie 17, ☎ 0848 81 18 48 (www.cgn.ch), operate ferries from Lausanne Ouchy to Geneva, Montreux, Thonon and Évian-les-Bains – the latter two across the lake in France, both with connections onto the French rail network.

Our onward journey from Lausanne follows the north **shore of Lake Geneva** (Lac Léman) all the way to Geneva itself. Sit on the left for the best views of the lake. This is a fine last leg of our Swiss lakes and mountains adventure. But now the summits away to the south, on the far side of the lake, are French rather than Swiss. On a clear day, this is your chance to see **Mont Blanc**, at 4,800 metres the highest peak in western Europe.

Geneva (Genève, Genf)

Geneva is a cosmopolitan, comfortably prosperous city, with promenades and parks beautifying the shores of Lake Geneva. The River Rhône splits the city into two distinct sections, with the international area on the **Rive Droite** (right bank, to the north) and the compact Old Town on the **Rive Gauche** (left bank, to the south).

On Rive Droite (🚌 5/8/15/F) is Pl. des Nations, near which most of the international organisations are grouped. The **Musée International de la Croix-Rouge et du Croissant-Rouge**, av. de la Paix 17 (www.redcrossmuseum.ch; closed Mon), is a stern building with high-tech exhibits tracing the history of the Red Cross and its Islamic offshoot, the Red Crescent. Profoundly moving, it covers natural disasters and man's inhumanity to man. Close by, the **Palais des Nations**, av. de la Paix 14, is home to the European headquarters of the United Nations, which replaced the League of Nations in 1945; there are guided tours. Between here and the lake is the lovely **Jardin Botanique**, a perfect place for a quiet stroll (once you're away from the main road) and featuring a rock garden, a deer and llama park and an aviary. On Rive Gauche, south of the centre, the **Jardin Anglais**, on the waterfront, is famous for its Horloge Fleurie (floral clock), while the city's trademark, the 140-m high fountain (**Jet d'Eau**), spouts from a nearby pier.

At the heart of the Old Town is the lively **Place du Bourg-de-Four**, Geneva's oldest square. Take rue de l'Hôtel de Ville to the 16th-century Hôtel de Ville (town hall), where the first Geneva Convention was signed in 1864. Adjacent is the former arsenal and the 12th-century **Maison Tavel**, Geneva's oldest house and now an evocative museum, with several period rooms and exhibits covering the 14th–19th centuries. Calvin preached in the **Cathédrale de St-Pierre** and his chair has been saved for posterity. The north tower, reached by a 157-step spiral staircase, offers a great view of the Old Town. Beneath the cathedral is the *Site Archéologique*, where catwalks allow you to see the result of extensive excavations, including among others a 4th-century baptistery and a 5th-century mosaic floor.

Arrival, information, accommodation

Gare de Cornavin is the main station, a 10-min walk north of the centre (5/8/9). The airport has its own station (Genève Aéroport), with frequent trains into central Geneva taking 6 mins; services continue to all major cities in Switzerland. Tourist office: quai du Mont-Blanc 2 (www.geneve.com). When staying in a hotel, campsite or youth hostel in Geneva, you get free use of local public transport (transport info at www.unireso.com).

Most hotels are expensive, but there are plenty of hostels and private rooms. During summer, the **CAR** (Coordination Accueil Renseignement à Genève), located in a blue trailer in the pedestrian area opposite the station, offers accommodation booking and other advice to young people. A simple but comfortable option in the Old Town close to the r. de Rive is the **Bel' Espérance**, r. Mina Audemars 1, ☎ 022 818 37 37 (www.hotel-bel-esperance.ch). A bit more upmarket is the welcoming boutique hotel **La Cour des Augustins**, r. Jean-Violette 15, ☎ 022 322 21 00 (www.lacourdesaugustins.com). Well regarded and conveniently located close to the railway station is the **Kipling**, r. de la Navigation 27, ☎ 022 544 40 40 (www.hotelkiplinggeneva.com). Capitalising on the proximity to France, Geneva claims to be the culinary centre of Switzerland. Look for reasonably priced restaurants on the r. de Lausanne (turn left out of Gare de Cornavin) and around place du Cirque (blvd Georges-Favon). A great place for tapas and mezzes is the very relaxed **Cottage Café** by the Brunswick Monument (www.cottagecafe.ch).

Connections from Geneva

Geneva is the starting point for **Route 20** in this book, which leads across France to Spain. Or follow **Route 14** in reverse to Paris. There are regular TGVs to Paris and Eurocity services to Milan and Venice. French regional TER trains shuttle west to Lyon. Connections with France were much improved with the opening in 2019 of the Léman Express regional rail network which has the Gare de Cornavin in central Geneva as its hub. There are regular Léman Express trains to Évian-les-Bains, Annecy and Saint-Gervais-les-Bains.

Sidetracks: To the top of Europe

Interlaken, midway along **Route 43**, is the jumping-off point for myriad mountain excursions. One of our favourites is the short ride on the funicular up to Harder Kulm (1305m). It starts on the north side of the **Beaurivage Bridge** near Interlaken Ost station. From Harder, there's a tremendous panorama over the town and, away to the south, a great sweep of the Bernese Alps, dominated by a number of peaks over 4,000 metres. From that viewpoint it's easy to appreciate why early railway engineers saw the latent possibilities of the Lütschine Valley which runs up into the hills to the south of Interlaken.

A railway was indeed built up the **Lütschine Valley**, with the trains operated by the **Berner-Oberland-Bahn (BOB)**. There are easy connections onto BOB services from the narrow-gauge Zentralbahn trains from Lucerne and the various mainline services which reach Interlaken from the west. BOB trains leave Interlaken Ost every 30 minutes. For crowds of overseas visitors riding south from Interlaken, the blue-and-yellow BOB train is the overture to the excursion to Europe's highest railway station at Jungfraujoch, loftily perched at 3,454 metres. The summit of the Jungfrau is actually over 700 metres higher.

The **Jungfraujoch** excursion is easily done as a day trip and it's mightily expensive. In autumn 2024 the regular round-trip fare from Interlaken is 259.80 Swiss francs (about €270). Nevertheless, almost a million visitors made the round trip in 2023. This rail excursion remains a fine example of how modern tourism is shaped by branding and marketing. "Ride to the top of Europe" – thus reads the blurb for the Jungfraujoch trip, sidestepping the fact that Europe's highest summit, **Mount Elbrus** at 5,642 metres, is a whole lot higher.

Our view is that the BOB train up the Lütschine Valley is certainly the prelude to a fine range of excursions but we think you could do better than just dashing to Jungfraujoch and back – but if your heart is set on the latter then check out special deals for early morning departures. There are also sometimes multi-day passes covering a wider area which include the **Jungfraujoch railway**. When in Interlaken in early 2024, we spotted a three-day pass for 190 Swiss francs, only valid until late April 2024, covering all local railways plus the new fast cableway from **Grindelwald** to Eigergletscher. The latter, branded the *Eiger Express*, carried its first passengers in December 2020. This pass offers a Jungfraujoch add-on for just 63 Swiss francs – a remarkable low-season bargain.

For a less touristy experience that starts in the Lütschine Valley, we recommend an early departure from Interlaken for a leisurely ride on slow trains, travelling out with the BOB to **Lauterbrunnen**, from there making a detour to car-free **Mürren** and back, before continuing an anticlockwise rail circuit to Wengen and **Kleine Scheidegg**, the highest point of the route at 2,060 metres. Here, the Hôtel Bellevue des Alpes lives up to its name; it's a great spot for lunch on the terrace (or an overnight stay, details on www.scheidegg-hotels.ch). For the return to Interlaken, continue via Grindelwald and Lütschental to Interlaken. This round trip costs about 120 Swiss francs (including the side journey to Mürren and back). A new concession for 2024 is that Interrail and Eurail pass holders can now travel for free from Interlaken as far as Grindelwald and Lauterbrunnen, from where a pass gives a 25% discount on the onward journey to Jungfraujoch.

ITALY AND THE ADRIATIC
An introduction

In our revamping of routes over recent editions of *Europe by Rail*, we have amalgamated pure Italian journeys with routes that also link that country with Slovenia, Croatia and Greece, thereby providing a sharp focus on the **wider Adriatic region**. But not, it has to be said, to the detriment of Italy. We include a route from Venice to Athens which runs down Italy's Adriatic coast from Rimini to Bari before hopping on a ship for onward travel to Greece – so avoiding the need for travelling to Greece via the Balkans where cross-border rail links are abysmal.

We also have a route to **Trieste** from Vienna, which Habsburg purists might plausibly suggest belongs more properly with central Europe. But we include it here as Trieste is certainly an Adriatic gateway.

As to Italy itself, don't underestimate its size. The direct train from Palermo to Milan takes 22 hrs 29 mins, which must surely rate as the **longest domestic journey** on a single train in any EU country. That's not to suggest that all Italian trains are slow. Far from it; the fastest expresses regularly dash the 938 km from Turin to Naples in under six hours. If money is no object, you could book an Executive Class ticket on one of the smart NTV Italo trains. Sink deep into one of the train's posh leather armchairs and let yourself be pampered with complimentary coffee and snacks while losing yourself in Italo's entertainment system. It'll surely be a fun ride, but Italy won't stand centre stage in your memories of the trip. We've never travelled in Italo's Executive Class, but we have **meandered through Italy** on the slowest of slow trains, stopping off here and there along the way.

The fast train services in Italy are very fast, and seats always need to be booked in advance. The slow trains are wonderfully cheap and rarely need reservations. Just buy a ticket, hop on and ride. Slow trains are a chance to see the real Italy. When we visited Apulia, we were very impressed with the **Ferrovie del Sud Est** (FSE) services which run down to the heel of Italy from Bari. If you are tempted to explore those we can thoroughly recommend a slow trundle on FSE trains from Bari to Gagliano Leuca, changing along the way at Martina Franca and Navoli. There are also many deliciously slow journeys around Sibari and Crotone in Calabria.

The **eastern side of the Adriatic** isn't easy for rail travellers. The last train left Dubrovnik in 1976. The rail networks of Montenegro and Albania are minimal. But there are ferries aplenty and this section of *Europe by Rail* includes two longish ferry legs. This is not a covert plot to lure readers away from trains but more a matter of necessity in areas where trains are wanting. Let's face it; anyone who insists on sticking only to trains would never get to **Greece** these days. ■

Route 44: Habsburg connections

CITIES: ★★★ CULTURE: ★★ HISTORY: ★★ SCENERY: ★★★
COUNTRIES COVERED: AUSTRIA (AT), SLOVENIA (SI), ITALY (IT)
JOURNEY TIME: 9 HRS | DISTANCE: 576 KM | MAP: WWW.EBRWEB.EU/18MAP44

This is a tremendous journey over one of **Europe's first mountain rail routes** and links two very fine cities: Vienna and Trieste. The railway between the two was nurtured by imperial ambition, with the Austrian authorities keen to see a rail link between the capital and the country's principal commercial port at Trieste. But the notion of building a main-line railway over the rugged Alpine terrain south-west of Vienna was daunting. In 1844 **Carlo Ghega** stepped up to the challenge. Ghega was born in Venice of Albanian parents; as a young engineer he worked on several railway projects in Moravia.

The **Semmering Railway** opened in 1854. In 1998, it was inscribed on UNESCO's World Heritage List. The citation commends the route as "one of the greatest feats of civil engineering during the pioneering phase of railway building. Set against a spectacular mountain landscape, the railway line remains in use today thanks to the quality of its tunnels, viaducts, and other works."

Some **Alpine excursions** in this book (eg. **Route 40, 42 & 43**) follow routes which are wholly or partly narrow-gauge. The Semmering is different: it was designed from the outset as a main-line route carrying heavy passenger trains and lots of goods traffic. It is the best route in this book for capturing that sense of cruising gently through the Alps on a comfortable long-distance train.

Today, the Semmering Railway is well used by regular **Railjet trains** from Vienna to **Graz** and Klagenfurt, respectively the provincial capitals of Styria and Carinthia. It carries night trains from Vienna to over a dozen cities in Italy. The 2024 schedules allow you to sample the Semmering from the comfort of Austrian, Slovenian, Czech or Hungarian restaurant cars. This route, first included in *Europe by Rail* in 2022, has a dash of *Mitteleuropa* style.

ITINERARY HINTS

It was the introduction in June 2021 of a **new direct once-daily Eurocity** train from Vienna to Trieste which prompted the inclusion of this route in *Europe by Rail*. It's a wonderful trip to make in a single day, a real piece of scenic cinema which unfolds over a nine-hour journey, culminating in **superb views of the Adriatic** on the final approach to Trieste. Just note that the Slovenian restaurant car on the train is available only from departure from Vienna until about 13.15. Note it takes cash only, no cards. The restaurant car is detached from the train in Ljubljana. If you are minded to stop off along the way, the two key en-route cities that warrant a stop are Graz and Ljubljana; if you have time for just one, Ljubljana most certainly gets our vote.

Don't just think of this as a route only for getting to **Trieste**. We also recommend this new route for all daytime journeys from Vienna to anywhere in northern Italy. It's altogether

Route 44: Habsburg connections | 397

Route details

Vienna Hbf to Graz Hbf		
Frequency	Journey time	Notes
Hourly	2h35	
Graz Hbf to Ljubljana		
Frequency	Journey time	Notes
2 per day	3h25	M
Ljubljana to Trieste Centrale		
Frequency	Journey time	Notes
3 per day	2h45	X

Notes

The direct Eurocity train from Vienna to Trieste leaves Wien Hbf each morning at 07.58. Departure from Trieste Centrale for Vienna is at 12.52. This timetable information is correct as of October 2024.

There are good connections in Trieste between the Eurocity train to / from Vienna and a Trenitalia Frecciarossa service to / from Venice Mestre, Padua, Verona and Milan. It is possible that a direct Frecciarossa between Ljubljana and Milan will be introduced in 2025.

M – Additional options, taking up to an hour longer, with changes of train in Spielfeld-Straß and Maribor.
X – A change of train at Villa Opicina may sometimes be necessary when using the local trains from Ljubljana to Trieste. The once-daily Eurocity runs right through from Ljubljana to Trieste.

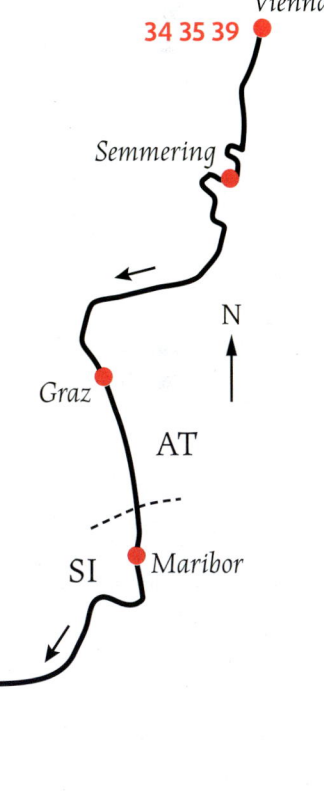

more interesting than the Pontebbana Railway which is followed by the direct Railjet trains from Vienna to Venice (although the latter do of course include the Semmering in the first part of their journey from Vienna). So if you are bound for Venice or beyond, do consider taking this route via Trieste, a city so unfailingly interesting that it certainly warrants a stop.

Over the Semmering

Our journey to Trieste starts at Vienna's striking new main station (Wien Hauptbahnhof). For more on **Vienna** itself see our comments on the city on p365. This is, from the outset, a journey with great promise. Escaping the suburbs, there are fine views of the Wienerwald hills to the right, the lower slopes close to the railway draped with vineyards. After a stop at **Wiener Neustadt**, the railway begins to climb the first ripples of the Alps. The next hour is superb, with the line skirting the Schwarza and Auerbach Valleys to gain height. The landscape is in constant flux, here and there dense forest interspersed with fleeting views of dramatic mountains and Alpine meadows.

The **Semmering Tunnel** marks the summit of the line. The villages close to the railway display a fine mix of architectural styles, with some fabulous turn-of-the-century villas built for wealthy Viennese who were delighted that the new railway brought the Alps within striking distance of the capital. These communities assumed immense importance in the literary and cultural imagination of *fin de siècle* Vienna, as artists and writers discovered the mountains – in much the same way as in Poland the Tatra resort of Zakopane (see p347) was crucial in reshaping Polish identity. Semmering was a rural annex to the coffee houses and salons of the capital. Freud was a regular in Semmering. So too was Arthur Schnitzler. Semmering was not an *escape* from Vienna. It *was* Vienna in the mountains (just as Trieste was Vienna by the sea). From Semmering, the railway drops down towards the **Mürz Valley**, following the river towards Bruck an der Mur with the elongated profile of the Fischbach Alps away to the left.

Bruck an der Mur connections
Our route towards Trieste turns south off the main line at Bruck. There are hourly trains which continue west on that main line to Klagenfurt and Villach, some of these services running on to Lienz in Austria's lovely Osttirol region and others routing into Italy via the Pontebbana Railway to Venice. With a population of only about 15,000, Bruck an der Mur gets our nomination for **Europe's best-connected small town**. It has direct trains to such far-flung points as Berlin, Milan, Rome, Zürich, Warsaw and Przemyśl. The direct train to Przemyśl currently (autumn 2024) even includes a stylish Swiss first-class panorama carriage.

South through Styria

From Bruck an der Mur, our route tracks south through **Styria**, the first part of the journey following the River Mur downstream through the hills to Graz. This is a part of Austria which strongly plays the regional card, with even otherwise very reasonable people taking every opportunity to don local Styrian costume. It's a region that oozes self-confidence and, despite the fad for dressing up, comes with some quite progressive politics. The city's first communist mayor, Elke Kahr, took office in November 2021.

Graz is Austria's second city and a place that is easily underestimated from the train which enters and leaves the city on the west side of the River Mur. The city centre, with its bustling market square, fine **Stadtpark** and the **Schlossberg**, is a 15-minute walk from the station. With its largely pedestrianised central area (car-free but mind the trams!), Graz makes a good one-night stop. You might enjoy staying at the art-loving Schlossberghotel, Kaiser-Franz-Josef-Kai 30, ☎ 031 680 700 (www.schlossberghotel.at) next to the river and close to the Old Town.

Connections from Graz
Graz lies at the eastern end of Austria's boldest venture into high-speed rail. When the **Koralm Railway** opens in December 2025, trains will dash from Graz to Klagenfurt in under an hour. Until then, this conspicuous gap in Austria's rail network is filled by buses run by rail operator ÖBB. The bus journey takes two hours and Interrail passes are accepted.

There is a **fine local line** which runs east from Graz via the Raab Valley to reach Hungarian territory at Szentgotthárd (which really sounds as though it should be in Switzerland). Services were upgraded on this route in late 2021 with the introduction of twice-daily Intercity trains to **Budapest**.

For those looking to distant horizons, Graz is the starting point for the daily Eurocity *Transalpin* which runs via Innsbruck to **Zürich**. It's a wonderful 9 hrs 35 mins journey on a train which has a Swiss panorama coach and a good Austrian restaurant car. There is also a night sleeper to Zürich.

Leaving Graz, the train follows the **Mur Valley** south for another 47 km to **Spielfeld-Straß**, at that point leaving the valley and almost immediately crossing the Slovenian border. The change in landscape at the border is quite dramatic, although in fairness this range of hills (often called the Slovene Hills) does extend across the border into Austria, where it is called the Windische Bühel. The railway cuts through these low hills to reach the Drava Valley where the first stop is in **Maribor**.

Slovenia's second city is often overlooked. As part of the former Duchy of Styria, Maribor shares a common history with Austrian Styria to the north, so it's no surprise that Maribor has a real Austrian feel. If you share our affection for rural railways, make time for the delightful **Drava Valley Railway**. Trains run west from Maribor four times daily (less often at weekends) to Dravograd, then crossing back into Austria and terminating at Bleiburg, where there is an onward connection to Klangenfurt.

The main line south from Maribor, followed by trains to Ljubljana, initially crosses flatter terrain then again takes to the hills to reach **Celje**. The next stretch, following the Savinja downstream from Celje, offers very fine valley scenery, passing the spa town of Laško (as famous for its beer as for regular spa offerings like massages and facials). Before long, we reach Ljubljana.

Ljubljana (suggested stopover)

The capital of Slovenia is a lively university town dominated by a hilltop fortress. The **River Ljubljanica** divides the city into two parts, joined in the city centre by an attractive and unique triple bridge, the Tromostovje. This links the city's old heart, Stari Trg, on the right bank, built below the hilltop castle, to Novi Trg on the left bank.

The **Old Town**, on the right bank, is an inviting maze of cobbled streets with historic buildings. Recent years have witnessed a renaissance with the opening of numerous shops, restaurants and bars, many with river views and generally reasonably priced. It is a gentle stroll up to the castle, which gives a good view of the city below. Beyond, on Vodnikov Trg, lies the **central food market** (closed Sun); good for picnic shopping.

On the river's left bank, the 17th-century Franciscan church dominates Prešernov Trg. The left bank of the city serves a generous portion of museums, including the **Museum of Contemporary Art Metelkova** and the **Museum of Modern Art** (both at www.mg-lj.si; closed Mon).

Arrival, information, accommodation

⇌ Trg Osvobodilne Fronte 6, a short walk south to the Old Town. = Ljubljana Jože Pučnik Airport, 24 km north-west of Ljubljana, 45 mins by bus (hourly Mon–Fri 05.20–20.10; every 2 hrs Sat & Sun 09.00–19.00; www.lju-airport.si). 🛈 Tourist office: Adamič-Lundrovo nabrežje 2 (www.visitljubljana.com).

🛏 Opened in 2021, the **Hotel Heritage**, Čevljarska ulica 2, ☎ 01 421 14 00 (www.hotelheritage.si) combines boutique style with a great location in a listed building in the city's Old Town. The **Hostel Celica**, Metelkova ul. 8, ☎ 01 230 9700 (www.hostelcelica.com), is housed in a former prison and is an excellent choice located in the heart of the popular artist-run Metelkova quarter. More upmarket and perfectly located close to the Old Town is the friendly and stylish boutique hotel **Cubo**, Slovenska cesta 15, ☎ 01 425 60 00 (www.cubogroup.si). ✕ The riverside zone between Stari Trg and Novi Trg is the centre for friendly bars and reasonably priced eating places.

Connections from Ljubljana

A main line runs north-west up the Sava Valley to Bled and beyond. Regular local trains run as far as Jesenice, with a limited number of trains (normally 5 per day) continuing to **Villach** in Austria. These include night trains to Zürich and Munich. There is also a useful direct daytime train to Munich, Stuttgart and Frankfurt.

To the Adriatic

The final section of this route – from **Ljubljana to Trieste** – really is magnificent. In a journey of little more than two-and-a-half hours, there's

Crossing the karst

Few of the passengers on the train even noticed **Gornje Ležeče**. The train had twisted and turned through valleys where the hillsides tilted sharper and sharper, screeches of wheels on ancient rails, and the wind blowing madly through open carriage windows. And then, after a long climb, just on the edge of the karst, the slow train stopped. The wind dropped, and for a moment, there was just the rasping sound of a lone cicada in the distance. A goat crossed the railway and paused beside the tracks to glance at the train before running off to safety behind a mountain ash laden with red berries. For a while, we were alone in the Slovenian karst, Vremščica's gentle slopes to the north and, in the opposite direction, the land tumbling away to the Reka Valley far below. A hundred years ago, Gornje Ležeče was at the hub of a great system of aqueducts that provided water to this arid land of potholed limestone. Here, the steam engines of the **Austrian Southern Railway**, labouring through the mountains and valleys from Trieste to Vienna, would stop for water. Near the railway tracks, a handsome building with blue doors housed the old water reservoir. Today it is half covered in ivy – a silent tribute to a wonderful piece of Habsburg hydrological engineering that made it possible for steam trains to traverse the arid karst.

Our slow train waits at Gornje Ležeče in the late summer sunshine. A minute stretches into five, and then, as the cicada ticks away the seconds and the dregs of morning coffee are drained, the door of the white station building opens and a clean-shaven man in a smart green uniform and red cap emerges. He walks with slow precision across to our train and gives a wave. Suddenly we are rattling along once more, heading west towards **Trieste**.

a real sense of drama to the changing landscape, culminating in a quite remarkable descent into Trieste. Leaving Ljubljana, the train crosses a beautiful area of seasonally **flooded marshland** which looks as wonderful on a misty spring morning as it does in deep midwinter when all is frozen. Slowly the railway gains height, swapping the serenity of the valley for the more challenging environment of the arid limestone hills. This is the **Slovenian karst** – the latter a geomorphological term which refers to the distinctive landscape assemblage found in these porous limestone regions.

All trains stop at **Postojna**, and that's the place to stop off to see the remarkable cave complex, which is open daily and is a 25 min walk from the station. Check details on www.postojnska-jama.eu. Apart from being a fun diversion, a tour of the caves is a nice tutorial on how *karst* landscapes develop.

Coastal connections

From **Pivka**, a remote railway junction 13 km south of Postojna, there are twice-daily trains running down to the coast at Rijeka, whence there are deliciously slow trains running inland to **Zagreb**. Rijeka is of course the jumping-off point for excursions to many **Croatian islands**, and a seasonal fast catamaran service down to Zadar. Just beyond Pivka, there's another junction at Divača, with year-round trains to the Slovenian port of Koper (the occasional trains being supplemented by buses) and a summer-season train to **Pula** in Croatia. **Koper** and Pula are both good gateways for wider explorations of the Istrian region.

The last stop in Slovenia is at **Sežana**, a pleasant border town and a last chance to taste burek, for once over the frontier you are definitely in pizza country. There are memorials to the **Yugoslav Partisans** (who liberated Sežana). The botanical park at the top end of town is a nice spot to while away an hour while waiting for the onward train. Sežana lies at the southern end of a rural rail route to Bled and Jesenice; we rate it as perhaps the finest in Slovenia.

From Sežana, it is just 10 mins to **Villa Opicina**, the first stop in Italy. The station is a shadow of its former self, but has still not quite lost the sense of intrigue and mystery which surrounded it in the Cold War years. If you delve into spy novels, Villa Opicina plays a bit-part role in many plots – often featuring under its former name Poggioreale Campagna. The station name was changed to Villa Opicina in the late 1960s. When **Ian Fleming** wrote about James Bond's arrival from across the border in *From Russia with Love*, the station revealed "the first smell of the soft life with the happy jabbering Italian officials and the carefree upturned faces of the station crowd." How times have changed. When we last were at Villa Opicina, the platform was deserted and we were the only people to board the evening train across the border.

There's an old **Habsburg-era tramway** from Villa Opicina down to Trieste, but it's been closed following an accident in August 2016. More than eight years on, the Triestini are beginning to despair that their antiquated but much-loved tram will ever be reinstated. But the train is fun, as it makes a great loop to descend down to the coast, entering Trieste from the northwest and passing **Miramare Castle** along the way (for more on that final run into Trieste see p426).

Trieste

Italy's atmospheric easternmost city looks more Austrian than Italian, a reminder of its former role as the entrepôt of the Austro-Hungarian Empire (up to 1918). Rebuilt in the 19th century in a **grand gridiron plan**, it relishes its role as a crossroads between East and West. Trieste is stately rather than intimate, with six-storey palazzi, **art nouveau** and classical façades. It's set on a beautifully curving bay, with the rugged limestone heights of the **arid Carso** an impressive backdrop to the city.

Trieste is a place which makes you think about issues of identity and heritage. **Habsburg history** is just one part of the Trieste mix. Today, the Slavic and Latin worlds mingle in Trieste. The city has a substantial Slovene minority. Throw in a dash of Italian flair and you begin to see why Trieste is so appealing. The 'must read' book for any visit to the city is the late Jan Morris' *Trieste and the Meaning of Nowhere* (published in 2001 by Faber & Faber).

Boat connections from Trieste

Trieste is the jumping-off point for some wonderful local boat trips. For a short excursion take the ferry over to **Muggia** (30 mins), a characteristic community on the far side of the bay, close to the Slovene border. The seasonal ferry services to the beautiful Slovenian port of **Piran** and direct sailings to Poreč and Rovinj – both towns in Croatian Istria – make wonderful excursions from Trieste. Timings for 2025 have not yet been announced. As befits a great port, there are also some long-distance shipping links from Trieste. Adria Ferries (www.adriaferries.com) has a weekly sailing, usually on Tuesdays, to **Durrës** in Albania.

The port of Trieste has long been important in the **coffee trade**, so it's no surprise that the Triestini cherish their city's café culture. Perhaps the most evocative café, one much favoured by the literary set, is the Caffè San Marco, Via Cesare Battisti 18, with its high-ceilinged art nouveau interior. One of Trieste's oldest cafés, the **Caffè degli Specchi** (1839), is on the majestic central square, Pza dell'Unità d'Italia, presided over by the vast **Palazzo del Comune del Governo**, aglow with its mosaic ornamentation.

A pleasant area for strolling is the Capitoline Hill, the heart of Roman and mediaeval Trieste. On top, beside the remains of the Roman forum, stands the 11th-century Cathedral of San Giusto, founded in the 5th century on the site of a Roman temple. It contains early mediaeval mosaics and frescos.

A short bus ride west from Trieste (🚌 6 towards Grignano) leads to **Miramare Castle**, a white marble pile in a stunning coastal location. Built 1856–60 for Maximilian of Habsburg as a love nest for him and Charlotte of Belgium, it reveals astonishingly ornate marquetry interiors. There's free entry to the surrounding park, which slopes down from the main road (get off the bus after going through two tunnels; retrace through one tunnel to reach the park gates). It is laced with trails and has many rare Mediterranean broadleaf trees, as well as a pond and a grotto.

Arrival, information, accommodation

🚆 Stazione Centrale, Pza della Libertà 8. Adjacent to the bus station. 🛈 Tourist office: Pza Unità d'Italia 4/b (www.turismofvg.it).

🛏 A very comfortable and friendly B&B not far from the station is **Atelier Lidia Polla**, Via del Coroneo 1, ☎ 0334 715 0231 (www.atelierlidiapolla.com). More upmarket, but also very close to Pza dell'Unità Italia is the design-centric **Urban**, Androna Chiusa 4, ☎ 040 302 065 (www.urbanhotel.it). Or try the similarly central and stylish hotel **Vis à Vis**, Pza dello Squero Vecchio 1, ☎ 040 760 0011 (www.hotelvisavis.net).

Onward by train

From Trieste Centrale, there are four direct daily trains to Bologna and **Rome** (one of them running overnight with sleeping cars). There are twice daily fast trains to **Verona** and Milan, with one of those services continuing to Turin. Rail passes are accepted on all these services. There's also a direct NTV Italo service to Naples (passes not accepted). In addition to these long-distance trains, there are plenty of local services including good links to Udine and **Venice**.

Sidetracks: World Heritage

Securing a coveted place on UNESCO's World Heritage List is just one of many ways in which countries stage their identity. The decision about what sites to propose for inclusion is **deeply political**, but also speaks volumes about how a country perceives itself and its achievements on a global stage.

Railways have long been a component of successful **World Heritage applications**. In 1986, Britain made its first successful applications and Ironbridge Gorge in Shropshire was inscribed on UNESCO's List. The site is a fine example of creative ingenuity in the **Industrial Revolution**, and railways are part of that story. But the intention of that listing was to do far more than showcase a primitive railway network – and much the same would be true of the listing of the industrial landscapes of Blaenavon in Wales, which were added to the World Heritage List in 2000. Here too, railways are important, but not centrally so. What is perhaps surprising is that Britain has never proposed the various sites around the **Liverpool and Manchester Railway**. Opened in 1830, this was the world's first railway linking two cities. Is this not the Chartres of railway history, something which would be as deserving of recognition as Europe's great Gothic cathedrals or mediaeval townscapes?

Austria and India made the first successful nominations in which **railways stood centre stage**. In 1998, the *Semmering Railway* (see **Route 44**) was the first railway to secure UNESCO recognition, followed by the narrow-gauge *Darjeeling Himalayan Railway*, added to the list in 1999. That latter citation has since been extended to include two other mountain railways in India.

Another railway citation focuses on the **Rhaetian Railway** network in eastern Switzerland. The specific lines are the *Albula Railway* (the opening section of **Route 42** in this book) and the *Bernina Railway* (which forms part of **Route 40**). So, of the first six railways to get a mention on UNESCO's list, all but the Semmering are narrow-gauge routes. The latest railway addition to UNESCO's list is the Trans-Iranian Railway which was inscribed in 2021.

There have been some interesting **rail-related inscriptions**, among them the exuberant Gothic revival style Chhatrapati Shivaji Terminus in Mumbai and the **Forth Rail Bridge** in Scotland. The latter is not the only case of a World Heritage Site which is particularly well seen from a train. The final stretch of **Route 37**, as it climbs south from Kraków towards the Tatra Mountains, cuts through the middle of a remarkable cultural landscape of huge spiritual significance. This is the park at **Kalwaria Zebrzydowska**, where the landscape has been shaped into a symbolic representation of the events and scenes of Christ's passion.

In Budapest, the long-standing UNESCO listing covering the banks of the Danube and the Buda Castle complex was extended to include the first line of Budapest's underground railway. But wouldn't it be good to see **Moscow's fabulous metro stations** being added to the World Heritage List? The *art deco* columns at Mayakovskaya and the ornamentation at Kiyevskaya are just two examples from the heyday of Soviet design that might easily be grouped into a single nomination.

But Russia's priorities today lie elsewhere and the Moscow metro could probably not compete with an ancient convent or monastery.

Route 45: From the Riviera to Florence

CITIES: ★★ CULTURE: ★★ HISTORY: ★★ SCENERY: ★★★
COUNTRIES COVERED: FRANCE (FR), MONACO (MC), ITALY (IT)
JOURNEY TIME: 7 HRS 50 MINS | DISTANCE: 482 KM | MAP: WWW.EBRWEB.EU/18MAP45

Travel writers rarely attain celebrity status nowadays. But in the early 19th century, as continental Europe once again became accessible to English travellers in the new political equilibrium which prevailed after the Napoleonic Wars, a number of British writers became household names for their tenacity in exploring far and wide and for their diligence in recording their experiences for the public. The **Riviera coast** attracted many budding guidebook authors, and one of the first and most successful was **Mariana Starke**. Her perceptive accounts of Italy ran to many editions, all published by the illustrious John Murray. Of the journey from **Nice to Pisa** along the coast, Starke remarked that the rough terrain was in many places impassable for carriages and the route was suitable only for mules.

The railway created the Riviera and by 1874 it was possible to travel by train all the way from Nice to Pisa. Mariana Starke never lived to see the day. When she died in 1838, Italy did not have a single railway. Our journey from Nice to Pisa and beyond needs no mules and there are no arduous feats of endurance. Just grab a seat on the **seaward side of the train** and sit back as we rattle east along a coast where the place names alone conjure up images of style and elegance: Monte Carlo, Sanremo, Portofino and more.

Along this entire route, the hills rise steeply into **wild country**, but the coastal littoral itself is seductively mellow. Vineyards, olive groves and palms flourish in the mild climes that attracted English visitors to Alpes-Maritimes and Liguria in the 19th century. Genoa is gritty but engrossing, Pisa a fine introduction to **Tuscany**, and Florence is just irresistible.

ITINERARY NOTES

There is some **wonderful scenery** on this short journey, though to see the best of it, you'll really need to get off the train and linger. Genoa is an obvious choice for an **overnight stop**, but you may want to be more creative and choose one or two smaller communities to stay for a day or two. Smaller towns which are among our personal favourites are Menton, Sanremo, Albenga, Santa Margherita Ligure and Vernazza, though the last of these is so formidably busy in summer that we would not even think of stopping there other than in the depths of winter. Slowish regional trains run at least every couple of hours along every section of this route, so it's perfectly possible to **travel spontaneously** and just buy tickets along the way. If you are in a rush, you can travel from Nice to Florence in about nine hours, using local trains for that entire journey.

Cruising the Riviera

This journey from Nice is a natural extension of **Route 15** in this book which runs from Marseille east through Provence to Nice. If you were taken with the scenery on that journey, then you'll find the coast east from Nice in many ways even more impressive. Hardly has the train left **Nice** (more on which on p169) than it reaches **Villefranche-sur-Mer** with its precariously tall ochre houses and one of the deepest harbours on the coast. Once leased to the Russian Navy, it's now a favoured stop for cruise ships. Away to the right you'll see **Saint-Jean-Cap-Ferrat**, a peninsula with gorgeous beaches plus some of the world's most expensive and closely guarded properties. **Beaulieu-sur-Mer** means 'beautiful place' – the name was bestowed by Napoleon. It's a tranquil spot full of affluent retired people, and palms flourish profusely in its mild climate.

Now we reach the tiny **Principality of Monaco** which has been a sovereign state ruled since 1297 by the Grimaldis, a family of Genoese descent. Later the family grew rich on gambling and banking, and now high-rise buildings crowd round the harbour, some built on reclaimed land which extends into the sea. Whatever the geographical and aesthetic limitations of the place, its curiosity value is undeniable.

Old Monaco is the touristy part, but still very much worth a wander with its narrow streets, the much-restored **Grimaldi Palace**, and the 19th-century Cathédrale de Monaco, containing the tombs of the royals, including Princess Grace. In av. St-Martin is the **Musée océanographique**, in the basement of which is one of the world's great aquariums, developed by Jacques Cousteau (www.oceano.org). Monte Carlo is the swanky part, with its palatial hotels, luxury shops and the unmissable, world-famous **Casino Café de Paris**, pl. du Casino, which is worth a look for the interior gilt alone. Oddly, you'll see none of this from the train. Land is so expensive in Monaco that the railway was long ago buried underground. The sole railway station in the principality is called Monaco-Monte Carlo.

Back on French territory (albeit only briefly), **Menton** is a retirement town full of Italianate charm, endowed with long stony beaches and full of lemon, orange and olive trees. Wander around the **hilly Old Town**, built by the Grimaldi family in the 15th century. The former summer residence of the

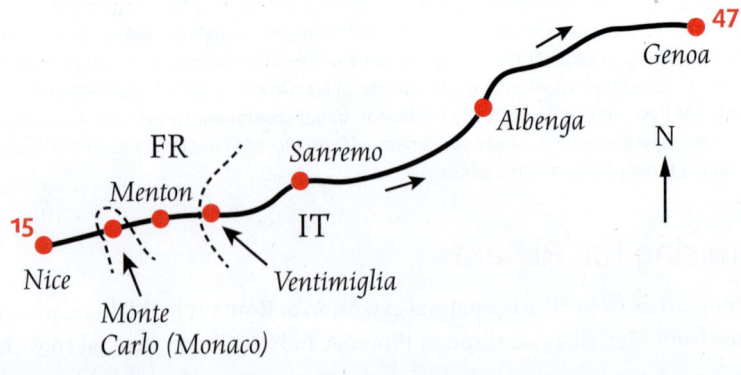

Grimaldis, the **Palais Carnolès** at 3 av. de la Madone, is an excellent museum of fine art (currently under renovation). For a very different take on art, visit the **Jean Cocteau museum** (www.museecocteaumenton.fr; closed Tues) by the Covered Market. In summer, the short curve of beach between the port and the marina is lined with bars, some of them pulling the rich and famous, others more the preserve of those who *wish* they were rich and famous.

Route details

Nice-Ville to Menton		
Frequency	Journey time	Notes
2–3 per hr	0h30–0h40	A
Menton to Ventimiglia		
Frequency	Journey time	Notes
1–2 per hr	0h15	

Notes

The direct Thello Eurocity trains from Nice to Genoa no longer run. All journeys from Nice to Genoa now require a change of train at Ventimiglia (referred to as Vintimille in French timetables).

A – All trains between Nice and Menton serve Monaco-Monte Carlo.
B – Many journeys between Santa Margherita Ligure and La Spezia require a change of train at Sestri Levante.

Route details (cont.)

Ventimiglia to Sanremo		
Frequency	Journey time	Notes
1–2 per hr	0h15–0h20	
Sanremo to Genoa Piazza Principe		
Frequency	Journey time	Notes
Every 1–2 hrs	1h45–2h	
Genoa Piazza Principe to Santa Margherita Ligure		
Frequency	Journey time	Notes
Hourly	0h30–0h45	
Santa Margherita Ligure to La Spezia Centrale		
Frequency	Journey time	Notes
Hourly	0h55–1h15	B
La Spezia Centrale to Pisa Centrale		
Frequency	Journey time	Notes
1–2 per hr	0h40–1h10	
Pisa Centrale to Lucca		
Frequency	Journey time	Notes
Hourly	0h30	
Lucca to Florence SMN		
Frequency	Journey time	Notes
Hourly	1h20–1h45	

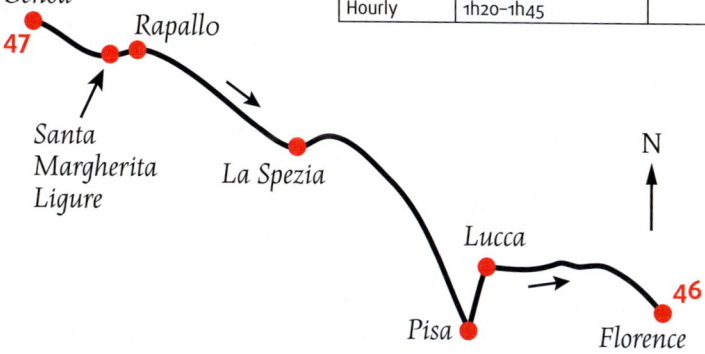

From Menton it is not far to the rather scruffy frontier town of **Ventimiglia**, the first station in Italy, always packed on Friday mornings when the French invade the town for its busy market. There is a crumbling steep Old Town, a thriving cut-flower and olive-oil industry, but little to detain visitors beyond the superb market, the place to stock up on bags, clothes, Parmesan cheese, oil and picnic lunches.

INLAND FROM VENTIMIGLIA

Twice-daily trains run inland from Ventimiglia along a railway through fierce mountainous terrain to Tende (in France) and Cuneo (back in Italy). This **border-hopping railway** is a very fine excursion. At Cuneo there are good onward connections to Turin. If you do not want to go that far, consider travelling inland just as far as **Breil-sur-Roya**, from where trains run every hour or two back down to the coast at Nice. If you take this route, the small town of **Sospel** in the Bévéra Valley is definitely worth a stop.

Sanremo (sometimes spelt San Remo) is the grande dame of the Ligurian Riviera — it's set in the long gentle arc of a bay. As in Monaco, the railway has been banished underground here and arriving at Sanremo station is nowadays a rather surreal experience. The old seafront route of the railway is now a pedestrian and cycle route. It's a nice thought that you can walk on the very ground over which tsars and emperors once travelled en route to Riviera holidays. Sanremo has an intriguing old quarter called **La Pigna**, full of shadowy streets, steep steps and a growing number of artisans and cafés. The **Villa Nobel**, C. Cavallotti 116, was the house of the Swedish inventor Alfred Nobel, who established the international prizes named after him; it is open to the public. In February each year the town is filled with singers and musicians for a massively popular and peculiarly Italian musical event: the **Festival della canzone italiana di Sanremo**.

Beyond Sanremo the railway escapes subterranean confinement and tracks east along the coast through Imperia to Alássio and Albenga. This stretch of the Ligurian coast, from the French border to Genoa is called the **Riviera di Ponente**. Beyond Genoa, it is called the Riviera di Levante. Both sides have their highs and lows, but along the Riviera di Ponente the most immediately appealing community is the old Roman town of **Albenga**. Just before you reach it on the train, there's a stunning view to the right of beautiful Gallinara Island, a one-time monastic retreat which is today a nature reserve.

Genoa (Genova) – (suggested stopover)

Sandwiched between the mountains and the sea, Genoa is a concertina of a city, with slate-topped palaces and squat churches bearing down on the old port. 'La Superba' is Italy's foremost seaport and was once, like Venice, a proud maritime republic ruled by a Doge, or elected ruler. As one of the most densely packed historic centres in Europe, Genoa is unfathomable. **Renzo Piano**, the renowned architect, sees his hometown as a 'secret, inward-looking Kasbah city'. Following the tragic collapse of the Morandi bridge in 2018, a new viaduct designed by Renzo Piano opened in 2020.

After the **restoration of the waterfront**, Genoa now has a port worthy of a maritime republic. Clustered around the Porto Antico are a traditional Genoese galleon, the **Museum of the Sea** (www.galatamuseodelmare.it; closed Mon Nov–Feb) and the superb Aquarium, designed to resemble a ship setting sail. Further west is the Lanterna (1544), Italy's oldest lighthouse. **Porto Antico**, the redesigned waterfront, functions as a new city piazza, with bars tucked into mediaeval arcades along the landward side. Much of the centre is pedestrianised, set among a maze of mediaeval alleys.

The most patrician street is **Via Garibaldi**, lined with Renaissance palaces, including Palazzo Bianco (No. 11) and Palazzo Rosso (No. 18), both galleries bursting with Flemish and Italian masterpieces. The **Cattedrale di San Lorenzo**, which survived bombing by the British, is one of the most engaging churches. Pza Banchi is a lively pocket of old Genoa, with cheap cafés nearby and places to try typical pasta and pesto dishes. A funicular from Pza del Portello whisks you to Sant'Anna, high on the hill. If you fancy a swim, there are a few *bagni*, private beaches with facilities such as showers, on Corso Italia (Albaro area), like Bagni Nuovo Lido at No. 13.

Arrival, information, accommodation

✈ There are two main stations: Principe and Stazione Brignole further east. Trains to the north use both stations; use the metro to transfer between them and to get into the city centre. 🅘 Tourist office: V. Garibaldi 12r (www.visitgenoa.it).

🛏 Cheap accommodation is easy to find, but can be tacky. Try the outskirts of the Old Town, near Brignole. Close to the Pza Banchi in the Old Town is **Le Nuvole Residenza d'Epoca**, Pza delle Vigne 6, ☎ 010 251 00 18 (www.hotellenuvole.it). Conveniently located close to Stazione Principe and with that Riviera look is **Hotel Continental**, V. Arsenale di Terra 1, ☎ 010 26 16 41 (www.hotelcontinentalgenova.it). A friendly B&B right in the Old Town is the **Genova Porto Antico**, V. San Luca 1/15A, ☎ 010 301 39 05 (www.bbgenovaportoantico.it). ✘ The cheapest places for lunch are in the dock area, but most close in the evening. For Saturday night fever, head for the student-filled Via di San Bernardo and Stradone di Sant'Agostino, or stroll down the pedestrianised Via di San Lorenzo.

Connections from Genoa

From Genoa, follow **Route 47** in this book via Milan to Verona, Venice and Trieste. Genoa lies well away from any of Italy's high-speed lines. There's a token appearance of a Trenitalia **Frecciarossa** train with an early morning departure to Venice. Not to be outdone, rival operator NTV Italo also makes a once-daily appearance in Genoa with a direct train to Naples. Milan and Turin are both within striking distance with regular regional or Intercity trains from Genoa. There are direct Eurocity trains to Lugano and Zürich, and you can climb aboard a **Nightjet** and awaken next morning in Vienna or Munich.

The Riviera di Levante

The stretch of coast from Genoa down to La Spezia is dedicated to mass tourism, but that's not to say that it's not very attractive. Stop off, if you

> ## Cinque Terre: the five lands
>
> Five villages just up the coast from La Spezia are often lauded as the most delectable on the entire coast of **Liguria**. The Cinque Terre coast is indisputably beautiful. Just imagine a summer evening in a rocky cove on this coast, preparing sauteed anchovies with wild fennel and garlic over a simple open fire of pine cones and twigs. Beautiful, yes? The problem is that thousands of others might well have the same idea.
>
> Each of the five villages has **its own railway station**. Running from north to south they are Monterosso, Vernazza, Corniglia, Manarola and Riomaggiore. In high-season local trains stop two or three times each hour at all five stations.

have time, at **Santa Margherita Ligure**, a laid-back resort which pulls the yacht crowd. From there it's but a short hop on a boat to impossibly beautiful **Portofino**. Back on the railway, a string of *belle époque* hotels overlook the palm-shaded promenade that defines Rapallo's long seafront. Anchoring the far end of this classic Riviera scene is a picture-perfect stone castle almost surrounded by water.

In time, we come to the **Cinque Terre** coast where, prior to the coming of the railway, a string of villages clinging to the cliffs relied entirely on boats for their connection with the outside world. Early travellers remarked on "the primitive simplicity of the inhabitants" – the words are from John Murray's 1866 guide. One hundred and fifty years later, that primitive simplicity is long gone. So too are the traditional occupations of wine making and fishing. The Cinque Terre villages are dedicated entirely to **tourism** and a visit to the region is a rite of passage for well-heeled Americans.

In recent years, cruise tourism has added greatly to the pressures on Cinque Terre. Large **cruise ships** anchor at La Spezia, from where smaller boats ferry passengers up the coast to Cinque Terre. A long sequence of tunnels means that you'll see little of the area from the train, but take time to stop and explore. Vernazza is a good base; it's the prettiest of the villages and from there you can take a boat along the coast. Choose carefully and you'll find it's not all impossibly expensive. Albergo Barbara in Vernazza, Pza Marconi 30, ☎ 0187 81 23 98 (www.albergobarbara.it) has several grades of room, all at reasonable prices, with the more expensive rooms having fine views over the harbour.

Beyond Cinque Terre, the railway passes through **La Spezia**, but there's no special reason to stop until Pisa. Shortly after La Spezia, the railway enters Tuscany at Carrara, source of the celebrated white **Carrara marble**, which is quarried in this area. Then a string of uninspiring resorts (the Riviera della Versilia) lead us down to Pisa.

Pisa

The Leaning Tower of Pisa rates among the world's most familiar landmarks, part of a magnificent triumvirate of buildings around the **Campo** dei Miracoli (Field of Miracles), by the Cathedral and Baptistry. The 11th-century, four-tiered **Duomo**, one of Italy's finest cathedrals, was the first Tuscan building to use marble in horizontal stripes, a design device popularised by the Moors. The **Leaning Tower** (Torre Pendente) began life in 1173, as a campanile for the Duomo. When it was 10 m high it began to tilt and the architect fled. Construction continued, however, with successive architects trying unsuccessfully to restore the balance.

ARRIVAL, INFORMATION, ACCOMMODATION
⇌ Centrale, south of the River Arno and a 20-min walk from the Leaning Tower, or take LAM Rossa. **?** Tourist office: Piazza Vittorio Emanuele II 16 (www.aboutpisa.info). ⌭ Just a short walk from the station and well placed for the city centre is the highly regarded **Alessandro della Spina**, V. Alessandro della Spina 5/7/9, ☎ 050 50 27 77 (www.hoteldellaspina.it). Equally well located is the welcoming B&B **Five Roses**, Corso Italia 156, ☎ 050 50 14 92 (www.fiveroses.it). Or try the comfortable and friendly B&B **Cuore di Pisa**, Pza San Frediano 6, ☎ 0345 60 88 677 (www.bedbreakfastcuoredipisa.com).

Moving inland

A railway runs east from **Pisa**, following the valley of the River Arno upstream to Florence. It's boring. You would do better by taking the alternative route via **Lucca**, which adds a little time to your journey, but gives a nicer introduction to Tuscany. The railway skirts Monte Pisano to reach Lucca, which is one of the finest small towns in the region. Even if you just stop for an hour or two, you'll be entranced by Lucca. It's just a five-minute walk from the railway station through the city's impressive bastions to the cathedral and **Piazza San Michele**. Despite its considerable beauty, Lucca never feels overrun, and the town has a leisurely, provincial feel.

From Lucca, the railway runs east, **Tuscan villas** and gardens slowly giving way to industrial estates as the train approaches **Florence**, where you'll arrive at Santa Maria Novella station (often shown as 'Firenze SMN' in booking systems), which is one of those buildings you'll either love or hate. It is acclaimed by some as a fine example of Italian Modernism; others take a less positive view. For more on Florence, see p413.

ITALIAN HIGH-SPEED: FLORENCE CONNECTIONS
If you have followed our route from Nice to Florence, it's likely the Santa Maria Novella (SMN) station in Florence is your first serious encounter with **Italian high-speed trains**. This is a place to watch the ultra-modern Italo and Frecciarossa trains come and go. If you are tempted to hop on one, just remember that Italian high-speed services all require advance booking. Some of these trains have **three or four classes**, the most luxurious of which is for those who evidently cannot leave home without having every possible creature comfort.

There's a range of high-speed trains serving Florence SMN. You can speed north to Bologna, Bolzano, Verona, Venice, Milan and Turin. Or make tracks for Rome, Naples and Italy's deep south. The fastest trains take less than 100 minutes to reach Milan or Rome. Interrail and Eurail passes can be used on Trenitalia's high-speed trains (only with advance reservation and a supplement of €13). Those passes may not be used on NTV Italo services.

Route 46: Tuscany and Umbria

Cities: ★★★ Culture: ★★★ History: ★★ Scenery: ★★
Countries covered: Italy (IT)
Journey time: 6 hrs 45 mins | Distance: 562 km | Map: www.ebrweb.eu/18map46

Some journeys in this volume come with advice about the wisdom of procuring visas or making other special arrangements before setting out. This current journey from Bologna through Tuscany to Rome comes with its own health warning – and it's nothing to do with COVID-19. When the French author **Stendhal** visited Florence in 1817 he endured a bout of illness after looking at too much art. The malady, nowadays known as Stendhal syndrome, finds expression in dizzy spells and fainting.

Be warned! One can overdose on culture. It's not compulsory to see every painting in the Uffizi Gallery in **Florence**, nor is it necessary to explore every back alley in **Siena**. A little goes a long way in Tuscany. Bear in mind that the fact there is no conspicuous queue *outside* a church or art gallery does *not* mean that there is nothing worth seeing *inside*. Nowhere is the flocking instinct of tourists more dramatically displayed than in **Tuscany**. We have never understood why thousands of visitors huddle in San Gimignano, when a score of other hilltop towns in Tuscany are every bit as beautiful as San Gimignano, but less assailed by crowds.

So let's set off on a journey **through green hills**, striped with olive groves and vineyards, stopping off at historic towns and cities overflowing with **Renaissance art** and architecture.

Itinerary suggestions

Florence and Siena are the obvious **overnight stops**, but you may also want to make space for Orvieto, a city which is a little off the beaten track.

You could, if you wish, do this entire route relying only on local and regional train services – where there's no need to pre-book, fares are cheap and holders of rail passes are not burdened with supplements. If you need to cover ground quickly, then why not use a fast service for the first part of the journey? Choose between fast Trenitalia or NTV Italo trains. Either will speed you from **Verona to Florence** in about 95 minutes, with a risk of course of missing some of the detail of the landscape.

Over the last dozen years, the railway between **Verona** (more on which on p356) and Bologna has been much improved, with long sections of single track being doubled and a new bridge constructed over the **River Po**. These Po Valley landscapes have been tamed by extensive land reclamation, and there is none of the sense of wilderness which early settlers would have encountered. The **drainage of the swamplands** took place from the 1880s and was the prelude to railway construction in this region.

But the latter proceeded in a lazy way; indeed the final link in the line from Verona to Bologna, namely the first bridge of the River Po between **Ostiglia** and Revere, was not completed until 1911. With dry land and access to railways, the region developed into a major agricultural area with thousands of acres devoted to wheat and sugar beet. Today, this has become a favoured region for urbanites seeking to escape city life, and increasing numbers of single-family villas (normally accompanied by a token olive grove) creep across the plains.

There is no particular reason to stop until **Bologna** which is the capital of Emilia-Romagna. The city's long-standing role as a major transport hub has been enhanced by its location on Italy's *alta velocità* spinal rail route linking the cities of the north with Rome and Naples. The city mastered the art of living in mediaeval times, when a pink-bricked settlement clustered around **Europe's oldest university**, founded in 1088. In terms of tourism, the only reason that Bologna has languished is because Florence is a looming presence over the hills. The Bologna streetscape has real dignity in its **arcades**, red- and ochre-coloured buildings, stucco facades, greatly varied porticos, church spires, palaces and **mediaeval towers**, the latter built as status symbols by the city's wealthy nobles. Connect in Bologna into **Route 49** to Athens.

Bologna Stazione Centrale is a distinctive neoclassical building. It's not by chance that the main station clock no longer works and forever reads 10.25. That was the moment on the morning of 2 August 1980 when a bomb exploded killing 85 people. A memorial to the victims stands by the renovated station entrance.

Into Tuscany

Three different rail routes between Bologna and Florence attest to the challenge of building a railway through the rugged **Apennines**.

The **Porrettana Railway** with its complex spiral tunnels was opened in 1864, cutting the travel time between the cities to five hours. Seventy years later, the *Direttissima* was built and the travel time tumbled to under two hours. In 2009, yet a third line was opened and the fastest trains now run non-stop from Bologna to Florence in just 35 minutes. All three lines are still in use.

If you opt for the new high-speed route, your train will depart from the underground platforms at Bologna Centrale. That sets the tone for what's to come. It's a 92-kilometre journey, of which more than 70 kilometres are in tunnels. If you believe in staying above ground, you may prefer to opt for the *Direttissima*, which is still served by a handful of Intercity and local trains. If a train is shown as stopping at Prato, then it follows the *Direttissima*.

Florence (suggested stopover)

Fast trains from the north arrive at **Santa Maria Novella station** in Florence. See what you make of the station's bold rationalist lines. Feted by some as a

414 | ITALY AND THE ADRIATIC

Route details

Verona Porta Nuova to Bologna Centrale

Frequency	Journey time	Notes
Every 1–2 hrs	0h55–1h35	

Bologna Centrale to Florence SMN

Frequency	Journey time	Notes
3 per hr	0h35–1h40	F

Florence SMN to Siena

Frequency	Journey time	Notes
Hourly	1h30	E

Siena to Chiusi–Chianciano Terme

Frequency	Journey time	Notes
11 per day	1h20–1h35	

Chiusi–Chianciano Terme to Orvieto

Frequency	Journey time	Notes
Every 1–2 hrs	0h25–0h30	

Orvieto to Rome Termini

Frequency	Journey time	Notes
Every 1–2 hrs	1h10–1h50	

Notes

E – There are additional journeys between Florence and Siena with a change of trains at Empoli.

F – A travel time of less than 45 mins between Bologna and Florence indicates that the train is routed via the new high-speed line, which is largely in tunnels. A longer travel time suggests that the train uses the *Direttissima* route. We think the latter is the better choice if you want to see something of the Tuscan scenery on the approach to Florence.

The **numbers in red** adjacent to some cities on our route maps refer to other routes in this book which also include that particular city.

marvel, but derided by others, it's a building which always evokes a strong reaction. Too many travellers arriving in Florence for the first time just dash though the station, keen to see their first Michelangelo or Giotto. The station is itself one of the city's most striking sights.

One of the greatest of Italy's old city-states, Florence has one of the richest legacies of art and architecture in Europe. Stendhal found in Florence a city of reason, intellect and order – the **epitome of Renaissance virtue**. Generations of travellers have flocked to Florence. It is so popular that, from Easter till autumn, its narrow streets are tightly crammed and major sights get extremely crowded during this period. Be prepared to wait in line to enter the **Galleria Uffizi** (www.uffizi.it) – Italy's premier art gallery – or to see Michelangelo's *David* in the **Galleria dell'Accademia** (www.accademia.org). Nevertheless, few would omit Florence from a tour of Tuscany, and it's really rewarding providing you don't overdo the sightseeing and take an afternoon siesta.

There are plenty of other galleries of world status if you cannot cope with the Uffizi crowds. Try the **Museo dell'Opera del Duomo**, the Palazzo Pitti museums or the Bargello. Enjoy the city by walking around: take in the **Ponte Vecchio**, the Duomo, the banks of the Arno or the huge **Piazza Santo Spirito**. The latter is on the south side of the river in an area known at Oltrarno. This is our favourite area of Florence; it's a little tamer than the north bank, where the main sights cluster. Wander the streets of **Oltrarno** in the evening and there is a reassuring sense of normality. It is an antidote to the over-hyped Florence-on-show style of the north bank.

ARRIVAL, INFORMATION, ACCOMMODATION

≥ Santa Maria Novella (SMN) is Florence's main rail hub. A new station for high-speed trains is under construction at Belfiore. It is a short walk from SMU to the city centre.

Florence's buses have been run by *Azienda Trasporti dell'Area Fiorentine* (ATAF) since 1945. That changed on 1 November 2021 when Autolinee Toscane (www.at-bus.it) took over. Tickets need to be pre-purchased (at machines or online) and are valid for 90 mins. Validate them in the machine immediately upon boarding. Florence also has two tram lines. Tourist office: Via Camillo Cavour 1r and at the station (www.feelflorence.it).

Florence is one of Europe's most popular tourist destinations, and although this means that there is plenty of accommodation on offer, things can get pretty full during the summer months. Near the station is the family-run **Hotel Nuova Italia**, Via Faenza 26, ☎ 055 287 508 (www.hotel-nuovaitalia.com). Equally handy for SMN station and good value for money is the **Hotel Fiorita**, Via Fiume 20, ☎ 055 265 43 76 (www.hotelfiorita.com). Very upmarket, the **Gallery Hotel Art**, Vicolo dell'Oro 5, ☎ 055 272 63 (www.lungarnocollection.com), is a boutique design hotel just off the north end of the Ponte Vecchio.

FLORENTINE CONNECTIONS

From Florence you can also follow **Route 45** in reverse, visiting Italy's Cinque Terre coast and then continuing through Liguria to the French Riviera.

Yet if all you want to do is head south in a hurry, a **high-speed train** will get you to Rome in 90 minutes and Naples is under three hours. Florence has direct night trains to Munich, Vienna and southern Italy.

Routes to Rome

The slowish journey from **Florence to Rome** described in this route is one of many alternative options to a fast dash south on the high-speed line. Another slow saunter south from Florence through central Italy has featured in earlier editions of *Europe by Rail* and we make just brief mention of it here. From Florence, there's a pleasant route up the Arno Valley, with its chestnut groves and olive orchards, to Arezzo. There the railway crosses into Umbria, skirting Lake Trasimeno to reach **Perugia**, the capital of Umbria.

From there the railway continues south-east, passing **Assisi** and Spello (both worth a stop), to join the main line from Ancona to Rome at Foligno. From Foligno, there are plenty of trains down to Rome. You may want to break your journey at arty Spoleto or, if you are a diehard romantic, then Terni might appeal, it being the one-time home of Saint Valentine. Romance apart, the **Marmore Waterfalls** which are entirely artificial and have been created more than 2000 years ago are worth a visit. They are 7 km east of Terni and can be reached by 🚌 E621.

The train to Siena initially runs west down the Arno Valley to **Empoli**, then turns south and climbs slowly into the hills. As you head towards Siena, the hillsides close in and you have a sense of travelling back in time. There are glimpses of **hilltop villages** and before long you arrive in Siena.

Siena (suggested stopover)

Spread over low hills and filled with robust terracotta-coloured buildings, Siena has changed little since mediaeval times. Indeed, this most beautiful of Tuscan cities is still contained within its **ancient walls** – look out from just behind the Campo, the main square, and there's a vista down a green, rural valley.

The city was Florence's tireless enemy for much of the Middle Ages, competing with it for supremacy politically, economically and artistically. Now it's a **delightful place to visit**, for its artistic treasures as well as just for the pleasures of discovering its myriad sloping alleys.

The fan-shaped **Piazza del Campo** dates from 1347 and is regarded as the focus of the city's life. The arcaded and turreted **Palazzo Pubblico**, on the south side, still performs its traditional role as the town hall, and its bell tower, the 102-m **Torre del Mangia**, soars above the town, with dizzying views. Part of the Palazzo Pubblico houses the Museo Civico, the Sala della Pace and Sala del Mappamondo which contain treasures of Lorenzetti and Martini among others. To the west stands the **Duomo**, the cathedral, with its striped marble facade studded with Renaissance sculptures. **Terzo di Città** (south-west of the Campo) has some of the city's finest private palaces, such as the Palazzo Chigi-Saracini, Via di Città 89.

Arrival, information, accommodation

🚆 2 km north-east (in a valley below the town). There are regular city buses into the centre (tickets from the machine by the entrance). You could also take a sequence of elevators that lead from the shopping centre opposite Siena station up to Porta Camolia, just opposite the city walls.

ℹ Tourist office: at the railway station (www.tourism-siena.com). 🛏 Private rooms are best value, but you often have to stay at least a week and they can be full of students in term time. A good, central B&B is the **Antica Residenza Cicogna**, V. delle Terme 76, ☎ 0577 285 613 (www.anticaresidenzacicogna.it). Another nice & comfortable B&B with large rooms, located not far from the Campo is the **Palazzo Bulgarini**, V. Pantaneto 93, ☎ 0391 396 85 71 (www.bbpalazzobulgarini.com). Even closer to the Campo is the stylish B&B **Il Corso**, V. Banchi di Sopra 6, ☎ 07 9180 34 58 (www.ilcorsosiena.it), in a lively neighbourhood.

In a route that has a lot of only middling scenery, the stretch running southeast from Siena is quite exceptional. This area, known as *crete senesi*, is classic peaceful **Tuscan countryside**. The 70-kilometre stretch from Siena via Asciano to **Montepulciano** is simply magnificent – in our view perhaps the finest one-hour train journey in the entire region. Many of the stations are far distant from the towns they serve; passengers alighting at Montepulciano, for example, might be surprised to find that the station is ten kilometres away from the town it serves. Buses run up to the exquisite hilltop town.

Through Umbria to Rome

Rejoining a main railway at **Chiusi**, close to the border with Umbria, it's not far to **Orvieto**. Set in a valley of vineyards, this striking cliffside town is perched above a raised tufa-stone plateau. Dominating the town is the vividly striped **Duomo**, Pza Duomo, built in honour of a 13th-century miracle. With its triple-gabled exterior of gilded mosaics, bronze doors and bas-relief by Lorenzo Maitani, as well as its outstanding interior frescos by Luca Signorelli depicting the Last Judgement, it is one of the great churches of Umbria.

Not far beyond Orvieto, the main railway towards **Rome** reaches the valley of the **River Tiber** (Tevere in Italian), which it then follows downstream all the way to the capital, in many places running parallel to the new high-speed line. The approach into Rome is through a predictable medley of motorways and industrial estates. Most trains stop first at Tiburtina station and then continue on to Roma Termini.

Rome (Roma)

The Romans have an inbuilt resistance to schedules and short lunch breaks. Life is too Latin for a Protestant work ethic. Indeed, they have no qualms about playing the tourist in their own city, from eating ice creams on **Piazza Navona** to tossing a coin in the Trevi Fountain, visiting the Vatican museums on a Vespa, lolling around the Villa Borghese Gardens, or peeking into the

Pantheon while on a café crawl. In Italy's most bewildering but beguiling city, it has somehow never made more sense to 'do as the Romans do'.

The Eternal City, dominated by its seven hills, is cut by the fast-flowing River Tiber. Don't expect Rome's legendary 'seven hills' to stand out as landmarks: they are too gentle, and merge into one another. Instead, treat the **Colosseum** and the **Forum** as the city centre, set on the east bank of the Tiber, with the Pantheon just north, and the chic Spanish Steps beyond. On the west bank of the Tiber lies bohemian Trastevere, a great restaurant and nightlife centre, with the mausoleum-fortress of **Castel Sant'Angelo** further north, and the Vatican City to the west. If this sounds exhausting (and it is), **Villa Borghese** is Rome's green heart, but with baroque fountains and galleries attached – you'll find there's no escape from several millennia of art and architecture in a city that spawned a civilisation.

Arrival, information, accommodation

≋ **Termini**, Pza dei Cinquecento, is Rome's largest station, handling all the main national and international lines; well served by buses and at the hub of the metro system. **Tiburtina**, Pza della Stazione Tiburtina, serves some long-distance north–south trains. ✈ **Leonardo da Vinci** (Fiumicino) is 36 km south-west of Rome (www.adr.it). There's a fast train service, every 15 mins (every 30 mins late evenings, Sun and holidays), to Tiburtina. Trenitalia also runs the *Leonardo Express* every 15 mins, taking 30 mins to Termini; **Ciampino** is just 16 km south-east of Rome with frequent shuttle buses to Termini station. Individual combined bus/metro tickets, called BIT (*biglietto integrato a tempo*, €1.50), are valid for 100 mins. 1–3 day tickets are also available. Tickets can be bought at newsstands and tobacconists or at railway and underground stations and bus termini. Validate the ticket on the bus, tram or trolleybus or at metro entrances. 🛈 Tourist information points throughout the city, e.g. at Termini station (www.turismoroma.it).

🛏 Hotels range from the opulent – mainly located close to the Spanish Steps and the Via Veneto – to the basic, largely clustered around the Via Nazionale and Termini station. Central, reasonably-priced hotels get booked quickly so reserve ahead. The very welcoming **Condotti Inn**, Via del Cancello 12, ☎ 06 683 920 50 (www.condottiinn.com) is in a great, quiet location north of Piazza Navona. Comfortable and tucked away in a quiet side street is the well located **Modigliani**, V. della Purificazione 42, ☎ 06 428 152 26 (www.hotelmodigliani.com). For those looking to splash out, the **Isa**, V. Cicerone 39, ☎ 06 321 26 10 (www.hotelisa.net), is a boutique hotel close to the Spanish Steps.

Rome connections

To continue further south, **Route 48** will escort you all the way to Sicily. Rome has good connections with south-east Italy, with several direct trains each day to Bari (on **Route 49**), most of which continue on through Apulia to Lecce. There are also direct trains to Taranto via Potenza. Of the lesser routes out of Rome, the one we especially like is the railway via Sulmona to Pescara on Italy's Adriatic coast.

Rome has a useful range of **night trains**, with southbound departures every evening for Palermo and Siracusa (both in Sicily). Heading north, there are direct night trains to Turin, Milan, Venice, Trieste, Bolzano, Vienna and Munich.

Bear in mind that a long hop on a **ferry** can be used to create itineraries which combine very different regions of Europe. The port of **Civitavecchia**, just 45 minutes from Rome by fast train, has departures almost every evening for Barcelona. There are also direct ferries from Civitavecchia to Sicily, Sardinia and Tunisia.

Route 47: North Italian cities

CITIES: ★★★ CULTURE: ★★★ HISTORY: ★★ SCENERY: ★
COUNTRIES COVERED: ITALY (IT)
JOURNEY TIME: 7 HRS 30 MINS | DISTANCE: 615 KM | MAP: www.ebrweb.eu/18map47

This route takes in several glorious north Italian cities from **Genoa** in the west to Trieste in the east – a veritable feast of art and architecture, along the way swapping the Mediterranean for the Adriatic. With such illustrious art and culture hot spots as **Milan**, Verona, Vicenza and **Venice** along the way, this route is, at one level, quintessential Italy. If you really are a city lover, then Route 47 is for you.

But there's much here too for those who discern beauty in the gentle alluvial landscapes of northern Italy: the rice fields between the Ticino and Po rivers, the lakes and meadows of the Mincio Valley at **Mantua**, the Lessini Hills dancing on the horizon as you approach Verona from the south-west and the quiet drama of the Veneto. The final leg takes us along the very shore of the **Adriatic** with a theatrical approach into **Trieste**.

As our start and end points we have two ports with very different histories, both shaped by maritime trade routes and both relying on railways to seal their status as great hubs of global commerce. Read more on these two contrasting cities in the box on p422. Meanwhile, let's hop on the train and travel from Genoa to Trieste.

ITINERARY SUGGESTIONS
Although this route has more constituent legs than many journeys in this book, each leg is quite short. With so **many fine cities**, it would easily be possible to spin this route out to a week or more. The train journeys are undemanding, each onward hop to the next city taking no more than an hour or two. As a bare minimum, think of stopping off in Milan, Mantua, Verona and Venice. The beauty of this route is that it can be followed using only regional trains. This means that even if you want to **travel totally spontaneously** and not book any train tickets in advance, you'll still not pay the earth for the entire journey from Genoa to Trieste. If you want to pre-book tickets, Trenitalia (www.trenitalia.com) sells tickets for all component legs of the journey for a total of about €50.

Through Piedmont to Lombardy

The hills which rise up immediately behind the **Ligurian coast** were a formidable barrier to railway magnates wanting to link **Genoa** (see p408) with the great inland cities of northern Italy. In 1853, the line running north from Genoa was eventually opened, cutting through the most rugged portion of the mountains in the **Giovi Tunnel** which, although less than four kilometres in length, was then the longest tunnel in the world.

There was widespread apprehension as to whether drivers and passengers might die of suffocation. Two catastrophic incidents in the early days of this railway demonstrated that such fears were well founded. A driver was overcome by smoke and fell from his cab; his train sped out of the steeply sloping tunnel and ploughed into a waiting passenger train at Busalla. Some years later, ten passengers died of fumes in the tunnel.

With such a painful history, the journey inland from Genoa nowadays seems all too easy. Even longer stretches now are in tunnels, but soon you emerge into Piedmont sunshine and track north towards Milan. The train crosses the **River Po**, skirting one of the most important areas of rice production outside Asia. Then we bridge the River Ticino to reach Pavia, a lovely city of quiet piazzas, and one which might reasonably claim to be the risotto capital of the world. Just north of Pavia, to the left of the railway, you'll see one of the most notable buildings of Renaissance Italy: the Carthusian charterhouse, served by a railway station (local trains only) called **Certosa di Pavia**. It is open to visitors (free entry; closed Mon).

Approaching Milan, the railway cuts through areas where industrial premises have nudged aside ancient orchards and olive groves. There are pylons, piles of pallets and container parks. This is the detritus of modernity which even sophisticated landscaping can never totally conceal. The train speeds past unsung **Lombardy** communities which have long succumbed to the enveloping reach of the city.

Milan (Milano) – (suggested stopover)

Italy's second largest city is the country's **economic powerhouse** as well as its commercial, banking, fashion and design centre. Milan is less aesthetically appealing than Florence or Rome. But Italy's most cosmopolitan city boasts Romanesque churches, grand galleries, a superb museum of Northern Italian art (the Brera) and one of the boldest cathedrals in Christendom.

Milan's signature building is the **Duomo**. This extravagant Gothic cathedral, overflowing with belfries, statues and pinnacles, has stairs leading to rooftop views. Leading off the square is the **Galleria Vittorio Emanuele II**, an iconic 19th-century iron and glass shopping arcade lined with chic

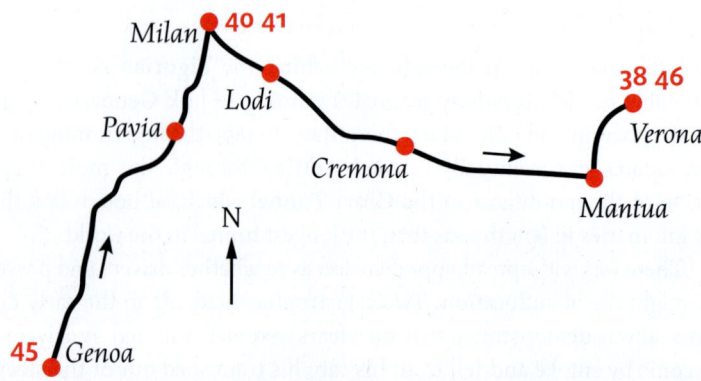

cafés and boutiques. Beyond lies Pza Scala, home of **La Scala**, the world's most celebrated opera house (www.teatroallascala.org).

Milan's finest art gallery is the **Pinacoteca di Brera**, Via Brera 28 (www.pinacotecabrera.org; closed Mon), featuring Italian artists of the 14th–19th centuries, including pieces by Mantegna, Raphael and Caravaggio. The Brera district is worth a wander for its relaxed and slightly alternative feel.

Milan's **most celebrated work of art** is Leonardo da Vinci's *Last Supper* (1495–1498), occupying a wall of a Dominican monastery refectory next to Santa Maria delle Grazie. Tickets must be booked ahead (www.vivaticket.it). Before leaving Milan, escape the urban chaos by visiting Milan's most beloved church – not the cathedral but the largely Romanesque Sant'Ambrogio, a

Notes

The fastest trains from Milan to Verona and Venice take the main line running east from Milan to Verona, so they do not serve Cremona and Mantua. East of Verona, they follow the line described in Route 47, normally stopping at Vicenza and Padua on the way to Venice.

V – Most direct trains from Verona Porta Nuova to Venice Santa Lucia stop at both Vicenza and Padua along the way.
X – Some trains on this leg are premium services (eg. Frecciarossa or Eurocity trains) where a seat reservation is compulsory. There are however also local or regional trains, usually a little slower, where no prior reservation is needed (or even possible).

Route details

Genoa Piazza Principe to Milan C		
Frequency	Journey time	Notes
Every 1–2 hrs	1h30–1h50	X
Milan C to Cremona		
Frequency	Journey time	Notes
Every 2 hrs	1h10	
Cremona to Mantua		
Frequency	Journey time	Notes
1–2 per hr	0h40–1h30	
Mantua to Verona Porta Nuova (PN)		
Frequency	Journey time	Notes
Every 1–2 hrs	0h45–0h50	
Verona PN to Venice Santa Lucia (SL)		
Frequency	Journey time	Notes
2–3 per hr	1h10–1h30	V, X
Venice SL to Trieste Centrale		
Frequency	Journey time	Notes
Hourly	2h5	

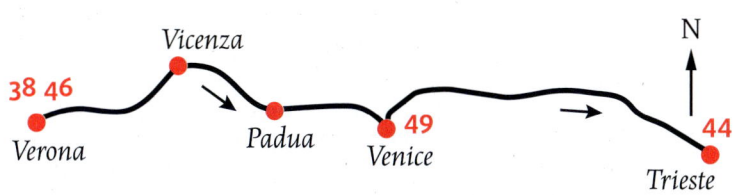

basilica founded in the late 4th century by St Ambrose, Milan's patron saint and former bishop. So smooth in speech was St Ambrose that a honey liqueur was named after him.

Arrival, information, accommodation

🚆 Most long-distance trains arrive at Stazione Centrale, Piazza Duca d'Aosta, although a limited number of services use Porta Garibaldi. Both stations are north of the city centre.

🛈 The tourist offices are at V. dei Mercati 8 and Pza Duomo 14 (www.yesmilano.it).

🛏 A comfortable and well regarded hotel close to Porta Garibaldi station is the **Berna**, V. Napo Torriani 18, ☎ 02 677 311 (www.hotelberna.com). A good central option is the hotel **Gran Duca di York**, V. Moneta 1, ☎ 02 874 863 (www.ducadiyork.com) in a quiet side street. Or try the highly regarded **Milan Suite Hotel**, V. Varesina 124, ☎ 02 334 316 18 (www.milansuitehotel.com), located about 4 km north-west of the city centre close to Villapizzone Railway Station. A bus outside the hotel runs into town.

Milan connections

All services mentioned here depart from **Milan Centrale** station unless otherwise mentioned. Eurocity services tunnel north through the Alps, via both the **Simplon** and new **Gotthard Base Tunnel** routes to major Swiss cities.

There are **night trains** to Calabria, Sicily and Apulia. International night trains are limited to those to Vienna and Munich, which both leave from Milan Rogoredo. A direct daytime train to Frankfurt-am-Main in Germany was reinstated in September 2024. The fast cross-border trains into France were suspended in 2023 following a **landslide** on the Fréjus route. They will be reinstated in mid-2025 with both Frecciarossa and TGV trains running to Chambéry and Paris. High-speed trains from two Italian operators, Trenitalia and Italo, dash south from Milan Centrale to **Florence** and **Rome**.

There are also direct daytime trains to many cities around the Italian Adriatic, including Ancona, Bari and Brindisi. Milan is a hub for regional train services to cities across Lombardy, into neighbouring Piedmont and into the Ticino canton of Switzerland. You can

A tale of two port cities

Route 47 may well make you think about the makings of modern Italy. We start in **Genoa**, where **Giuseppe Garibaldi** embarked in 1860 on the *Spedizione dei Mille* – the military adventure that led to the acquisition of Sicily and Naples, which paved the way for Italian unification in 1861. Genoa, as part of the House of Savoy, had already bought into Garibaldi's grand plan for unification, even if some movers and shakers in Genoa perhaps hankered after the pre-Napoleonic order when the proudly independent Genoese Republic exerted great maritime influence extending to the Black Sea, Iberia and the eastern Mediterranean. We see a far-flung mark of Genoese authority in the lighthouse in Constanța, mentioned on p322.

Trieste, the endpoint of Route 47, is so very different from Genoa, and strangely non-Italian. It is a great port, an imperial creation of the **Habsburgs**, a place with an history more Austrian than Italian. Had events taken a different turn after the Second World War, Trieste could so easily have ended up as part of Yugoslavia. In 1954 it was definitively assigned to Italy, though its hinterland was part of Yugoslavia, leaving Trieste on a finger of land that is only tenuously connected to the rest of Italy. For decades Trieste was what the late **Jan Morris** described as "an allegory of limbo" – and for Jan it always remained that. But with the opening of Europe's borders and Trieste's reconnection to places around, we see a new Trieste, an city that nicely bridges the Latin and Slavic worlds, and a place that embodies the European spirit.

follow **Route 40** (in reverse) up the Adda Valley to join the Bernina Railway in Tirano. There are trains at least hourly from Milan to Turin and Bergamo.

From Milan, the railway runs south-east across flat terrain to **Lodi**, then broadly follows the River Adda downstream to Cremona, where the railway station is as handsome as the small city it serves. To musicians, **Cremona** means one thing: violins. Antonio Stradivari lived his entire life in Cremona. Still today, Cremonese violin making is held in worldwide esteem. It's a delightful small town, well worth a few hours even if you have no interest in violins. Local life centres on the **Piazza del Comune**, less than ten minutes on foot south of the railway station. From Cremona it is just a short hop east to Mantua, following a pleasant rural railway which is now being upgraded in parts from single to double track.

Mantua (Mantova) – (suggested stopover)

Mantua is one of the finest small inland cities on the North Italian Plain. It is a world removed from the self-conscious style of Milan and thankfully less crowded than Verona. Arriving in town on the train from Cremona, you get a hint of what makes Mantua so special: its **lakeshore setting**. The railway station by Lago Superiore is a short walk west of the city centre. The city is on a wedge of land surrounded on three sides by water.

A quartet of pleasant squares are the spaces where Mantovani of all ages convivially gather. Visitors usually head first for the **Palazzo Ducale**, which occupies a big chunk of land in the north-east corner of the Old Town. This one-time home of the Gonzaga family (closed Mon) is packed with Italian Renaissance art – though, let's face it, one can have too many Renaissance crucifixions, so you'll find respite in some especially beautiful Flemish tapestries. The other 'must-see' attraction is the **Palazzo del Te** (www.palazzote.it), also a Gonzaga palace, but dedicated entirely to relaxation and the good life. Don't miss the magnificent Mannerist frescoes.

The real appeal of Mantua lies beyond the formal sights. It is a delightful place to just spend a couple of days doing nothing more demanding than enjoying good food, walks and boat trips. **Shakespeare** made a fine job of inscribing Mantua on the English imagination. There is a famous Mantua scene in *Romeo and Juliet*, though we learn little about Mantua itself. And there is a nice scene in *The Taming of the Shrew* where Tranio suggests to a Mantua pedant that leaving the town brings only death. It is a point to ponder as you stand on the station platform waiting for the train from Mantua to Verona.

ARRIVAL, INFORMATION, ACCOMMODATION

≈ The train station is just a short walk west of the centre. **ℹ** Tourist office: Pza Andrea Mantegna 6 (www.turismo.mantova.it). ⋈ A friendly, central and family-run B&B in a historic building is the **Palazzo Arrivabene**, V. Fratelli Bandiera 20, ☎ 0376 328 685 (www.palazzoarrivabene.net). The **Agorà**, V. Leon d'Oro 13, ☎ 0376 368 254 (www.agoraresidenza.it), is another comfortable option in the Old Town. The **Residenza Bibiena**, Pza Arche 5, ☎ 0376 355 699 (www.residenzabibiena.it), is a good B&B in a quiet area.

From Mantua the train stays to the east of the River Mincio as it travels north through vineyards to Verona (see p356), where you can connect onto two other journeys in this book: **Route 38**, which runs north through the Tyrol to Bavaria, and **Route 46** which tracks south through Tuscany to Rome.

Approaching Vicenza

From Verona our route runs due east to Vicenza, with fine views of the hills to the left, their lower slopes draped with vineyards. One of the wine-producing villages you can see from the train is **Soave**, well-known for its reliable dry whites and its attractive castle. As we approach Vicenza, the Berici Hills rear up to the right of the railway. This little mountain outlier is surprisingly rugged. If you've time to explore, you find landscapes of rare beauty tucked away in these hills.

Prosperous **Vicenza** was largely rebuilt in the 16th century to designs by Andrea di Pietro della Gondola, better known as **Palladio**, who moved here from Padua at the age of 16 to become an apprentice stonemason. He gave his name to the Palladian style of architecture, which applied elegant Romanesque concepts to classical forms. Corso Palladio, the long, straight, main street, is lined with palaces. The **Teatro Olimpico** at the eastern end was Palladio's finest work. Based on the design of ancient Roman theatres and opened in 1585, it is the oldest indoor theatre in Europe and still in use from May to early July, and from September to early October. Palladio's most famous villa, **La Rotonda**, is on a hillside about 1.5 km south-east of the centre. It has a round interior under a dome set in a cube of classical porticoes, a design often copied.

From Vicenza, the railway runs south-east across the plain to **Padua** (Padova in Italian) where the dignified Old Town in Padua has attractive arcaded streets and traffic-free squares. Prato della Valle, Italy's largest square, hosts a Saturday market. In the University, founded in 1222, you can see the wooden desk used by **Galileo**, who taught physics there, and visit the old anatomical theatre. Padua is the natural point to slip away south on **Route 49**, which will lead you to Bologna and down Italy's Adriatic coast.

From Padua the railway runs straight as an arrow across the plain to **Mestre**, the dismal industrial town which sits on the mainland just across the lagoon from Venice. But don't despair. The train continues, to terminate in Venice itself at Santa Lucia station by the Canal Grande.

If you are skipping Venice, you can change in Mestre for the onward train to Trieste. But surely no-one passes the chance to visit Venice.

Venice (Venezia)

Venice can play cultural one-upmanship better than most cities. Even the cafés of **St Mark's Square** (Piazza San Marco) are awash with famous ghosts, and tourism is almost as ancient as the city itself. Built on 118 tiny islands, this former **maritime republic** once held sway over an empire stretching from northern Italy to Cyprus. Around 1,000 residents leave each year, driven out by exorbitant rents. Ironically, for a city built on water, Venice numbers around 450 souvenir shops but fewer than ten plumbers. Most day trippers fail to stray far from Piazza San Marco with its famous basilica, which is a huge mistake. Beyond the crowds at the major sights, especially around St Mark's and the **Rialto Bridge**, Venice exudes a village-like calm. Even a 15-minutes walk from the main drag can deposit you alone in a Gothic square, with just pigeons for company.

Surprisingly for a city built on water, the best way to explore is on foot. Prepare yourself for serious walking as there are 400 bridges and around 180 canals to discover. Expect to get lost, especially at night, which is part and parcel of the charm of this mysterious lagoon world. However, you're never far from the **Grand Canal**, which snakes through the centre, and Venice is perfectly safe. The best way to feel the spirit of the city is simply to wander its narrow streets (*calli*), popping into churches as you pass and pausing to sit at a waterside café whenever the whim takes you.

A visit to the tiny islands of **Murano** and **Burano** (from Fondamente Nove by *vaporetti* 12 to Burano and 4.1/4.2 to Murano) reveals that the traditional skills of glass- and lace-making still thrive today. Pay a visit to Venice's finest collection of modern art in the **Peggy Guggenheim Collection** on the Grand Canal at Dorsoduro no. 704 (closed Tues & Wed).

Arrival, information, accommodation

Mestre station is on the mainland; to get to Venice itself, take a train to **Santa Lucia** station. A local service operates between the two stations (vaporetto stop, at the northwest end of the Grand Canal). **Marco Polo International Airport** is 13 km north-east of Venice (www.veneziaairport.it). The regular motorboat service of Alilaguna operates from the airport (year-round, www.alilaguna.it) via the Lido to the Pza San Marco in the heart of Venice, and costs €15 for a one-way trip.

Venice's sturdy **waterbuses** (*vaporetti*) are operated by ACTV (actv.avmspa.it) and run at 12- to 20-min intervals in daytime with a break from about 23.30–04.30. Line 1 runs the length of the Grand Canal, connecting Santa Lucia station to Pza San Marco. Piers bear the line numbers – but make sure you go in the right direction. The city's 400 gondolas, which can take up to six passengers each, provide a costly, conceivably romantic, means of getting around. Rates are fixed. You can also try the short gondola ride on the *traghetto* (gondola ferry), which crosses the Grand Canal at eight points (signposted traghetto) for €2 (residents pay less). Tourist office: Pza San Marco 71/f and at Santa Lucia station (www.veneziaunica.it).

The **Agli Alboretti**, Dorsoduro, 884 Rio Terrà Foscarini, ☎ 041 523 0058 (www.aglialboretti.com), is a popular hotel with a good restaurant and pleasant rooms. A recommended B&B within walking distance of the station is **Campiello Zen**, Santa Croce

> ## VENICE: WHERE THE 'REAL' PEOPLE LIVE
>
> The **Strada Nova** is a broad, hectic street running along the Grand Canal, leading from the Rialto Bridge to the Ca' d'Oro museum and packed with shops and cafés as well as tourists. Equally bustling is the Lista di Spagna near the railway station, full of touristy cafés and shops. To see a bit more of the 'real' Venice you have to venture away from these streets.
>
> The district of **Cannaregio**, once Venice's main manufacturing area, is spacious and pleasant with broad canal sides and a fairly simple layout. Shops, bars and hotels tend to be cheaper and the area is more popular with locals than the city centre. The backstreets here in Cannaregio, where over a third of the city's population live, are where you will find the 'real' people in Venice.
>
> The Fondamenta della Sensa and the parallel Fondamenta della Misericordia both offer **peaceful walks**. From the quayside of Fondamente Nove you can get fine views of the lagoon, the cemetery island of San Michele and, beyond it, Murano.

1285 Rio Terà, ☎ 041 710 365 (www.campiellozen.com). Splurgers should head for the **Novecento Boutique Hotel**, San Marco 2683/84, ☎ 041 241 3765 (www.novecento.biz), a small, family-run place in a central but quiet location.

VENICE CONNECTIONS

If you are not sticking with us on Route 47 right through to Trieste, Venice is the optimal point to cut away. There are twice daily Railjets via the **Pontebbana Railway** to Vienna, along the way giving good connections in Villach for Salzburg. There are direct night sleeper trains to Vienna, Munich and Rome.

Daytime **high-speed trains** run south from Venice to Rome and Naples, and nowadays Venice even has direct daytime trains to Italy's deep south: a daily Frecciarossa to Reggio di Calabria and twice-daily Frecciabianca trains to **Lecce**. You can also connect in Venice into **Route 49**, which will escort you south via Italy's east coast all the way to Bari for an onward leg by ship to Greece.

East to Trieste

The final leg of our journey means retracing our tracks back across the rail causeway to Mestre, then turning east. This unsung eastern part of the Veneto is a little off the beaten track. We cross a litany of rivers that drain down through these **marshy flatlands** into the Adriatic: the Piave, the Livenza, the Tagliamento and more. But of the Adriatic there are no real views until well after we cross the **River Izonzo** where the railways climbs onto the flank of the limestone hills to give fine views down to Duino and Sistiana on the coast.

The railway line then drops back down almost to the seashore and the final run into **Trieste** (for more on the city see p402) is pretty magical, with tantalising views of Miramare Castle and across to the Slovenian coast beyond. This is truly one of Europe's great arrivals, as befits a city that has morphed from Habsburg celebrity, through being a staging post for difficult journeys to the Balkans, into being a symbol of a new Europe. If you are inclined to venture beyond Trieste, then **Route 44** awaits, ready to escort you into Slovenia and beyond.

Route 48: South to Sicily

Cities: ★★ Culture: ★★ History: ★★ Scenery: ★★★
Countries covered: Italy (IT)
Journey time: 11 hrs | Distance: 858 km | Map: www.ebrweb.eu/18map48

Is it not extraordinary how some travel trends persist over centuries? In the heyday of the Grand Tour, privileged travellers from northern Europe travelled south in their thousands to **Naples**, but very few ever went far beyond. That's still largely true today.

In the 18th and 19th centuries the city of Naples, although raucous and scruffy, tugged irresistibly on the north European imagination – and it still does today. The French poet and librettist **Auguste Creuzé de Lesser** had words for the city. "Europe ends at Naples – and it ends there quite badly," he wrote 200 years ago. Naples has tidied itself up, but not completely. The noise and bustle of the city is complemented by the dramatic landscapes of the **Sorrento peninsula** and the islands of Ischia and Capri, with the entire ensemble presided over by temperamental Vesuvius which still spits at intervals.

Our journey takes in these Neapolitan staples to be sure, but the real appeal of Route 48 lies *beyond* Naples. This is a journey which ventures past the point where most rail travellers visiting Italy turn round and head back home. It gives a taste of the fiery harsh lands of **Basilicata** and it takes in a great sweep of the **Calabrian coast**. In a word, this is the finest coastal rail journey in this book – though that's not to diminish the appeal of **Route 15 and 45**, which between them lead from Provence through Liguria to Tuscany, sticking to the Mediterranean coast for much of the way.

Route 48 includes a short **hop on a ferry** from Villa San Giovanni, at the toe of the Italian mainland, to the Sicilian port of Messina. Five trains each day are shunted onto ferries for the crossing over the Strait of Messina. The **endgame is Sicily**, the largest island in the Mediterranean (just beating Sardinia to that record). Successive invasions by Greeks, Romans, Arabs, Normans, French and Spanish have shaped the Sicilian character; the land is a strange mixture of fertile plains, volcanic lava fields and rocky desert, while Mount Etna, the great volcano, is omnipresent, smoking in the background.

Itinerary suggestions

You can board an Intercity train in Rome in the morning and alight in Siracusa just 11 hours later. It would most certainly be a very enjoyable journey and it needn't be expensive. **Trenitalia** (www.trenitalia.com) often have tickets for the direct daytime trains from Rome to Siracusa for about €30. But to really catch the flavours of southern Italy, it's best to take this trip slowly with one or more stops en route. **Local trains** run the entire length of the journey.

If you are really **pushed for time** and want to focus on the coastal scenery well south of Naples, you can fast-track the first third of this route by taking a high-speed train which

428 | Italy and the Adriatic

Route details

Rome Termini to Naples Centrale (via Formia)

Frequency	Journey time	Notes
Hourly	1h45–3h	

Naples Centrale to Villa San Giovanni

Frequency	Journey time	Notes
Every 2 hrs	4h20–6h	X

Villa San Giovanni to Messina Marittima*

Frequency	Journey time	Notes
Every 40 mins	0h30	S

Messina Centrale* to Taormina Giardini

Frequency	Journey time	Notes
Every 1–2 hrs	0h40–1h10	

Taormina Giardini to Siracusa

Frequency	Journey time	Notes
Every 2 hrs	2h–2h30	

Notes

The dashed line on the map indicates an alternative route mentioned in our journey description.

S – Only very occasional trains are transported across the Strait of Messina to Sicily. But passenger and car ferries are frequent. The one-way fare as a foot passenger on the ferry from Villa San Giovanni to Messina Marittima is €2.50.

X – Some services require a change of train at Salerno.

* – If you arrive in Sicily as a foot passenger on the boat from the mainland, you'll need to walk (5 mins) from Messina Marittima to Centrale station for the onward train journey.

runs from Rome to Salerno in just two hours. There's a choice of Frecciarossa and Italo trains for that initial fast hop.

Naples is an obvious choice for an **overnight stop**. If you want to break your journey on the Calabrian coast, then we suggest either Diamante or Tropea. Once in Sicily, the 'must-see' community on our journey down the east coast of the island is Taormina.

South to Naples

Our route follows the main line from Rome via Formia to Naples. This railway was conceived as a pioneering experiment in high-speed travel. So tortuous and slow was the old inland route through Cassino (still used) that a new line closer to the coast was completed in 1927. Nowadays, the high-speed trains use an even newer line which opened in 2005, but we think the Formia route is the best prelude to this Sicilian adventure.

Escaping from **Rome** (see p417), you have a good view of the volcanic **Alban Hills** away to the left, then the railway skirts the wooded Lepini Hills (also to the left), before tunnelling under the great limestone massif of the Aurunci Mountains to reach the sea at **Formia**. There's no particular reason to stop, unless you want to visit Ponza, a very beautiful island served by hydrofoils from Formia. The railway briefly skirts the coast then heads in a straight line to Naples. The manner in which this railway from the 1920s defies the lie of the land is a very early example of an approach to railway engineering which returned to fashion in the new-build high-speed railways of the 1980s and thereafter.

Naples (Napoli) – (suggested stopover)

There's nowhere quite like Naples – the city is a **glorious assault on your senses**. It may have a notorious reputation as a city of crime, but its ebullience, history, cuisine and range of treasures make it a compelling stop on a southern Italian journey. The old central axis, known as **Spaccanapoli**, is a superb immersion into the Neapolitan maelstrom, so break yourself in with a pizza and a peaceful gallery visit first.

Then venture out and explore dark, crumbling, **mediaeval alleys**, with washing lines strung above and cooking smells everywhere. Watch housewives haul up bucketfuls of shopping by ropes hanging from high tenement windows. Out on the streets, you can wander for hours in the city's various districts, such as the **Sanità**, and be entertained by the performative style of daily life.

All this comes with an important caveat. Petty crime is rife, notably pickpocketing and bag-snatching, so take care, especially after dark. Avoid hanging around near the Stazione Centrale. But it's by no means all edgy. Wander down to sedate **Santa Lucia**, the waterfront district to the south of the city centre, where there is a good choice of seafood restaurants.

Day trips from Naples

Naples is somewhat upstaged by its surroundings, notably the **Neapolitan Riviera** – including the beautiful but often crowded resorts of Sorrento, Positano and Amalfi, and the island of Capri, just a short boat ride away – as well as the astonishing Roman remains of **Herculaneum** and **Pompeii**.

Exploring the area is easily done by train, bus and ferry. The **Circumvesuviana** is a private venture operating local trains (half-hourly service on most routes) linking Naples, Sorrento, Pompeii and Ercolano (for Herculaneum). The **Sorrento Peninsula** is unbeatable if you like beaches, ancient sites, boat trips and stunning coastal scenery. Take the boat or train from Naples to Sorrento. Scenically, **Amalfi** on the south side of the peninsula has the edge over Sorrento. There are some great walks in and around Amalfi. Take the frequent bus from Amalfi up to Ravello and return by one of several very attractive paths. This delicious hilltop village has stupendous views. Lying just off the Sorrento Peninsula, the island of **Capri** has a wonderful setting, with bougainvillea, cacti and jasmine growing everywhere around the Greek-looking dome-roofed white houses.

Arrival, information, accommodation

All trains from Rome (whichever of the three lines you use) arrive at **Stazione Centrale**, which is the hub for most long-distance trains. Most Circumvesuviana services, including those to Pompeii and Sorrento, start at **Napoli Porta Nolana** station (often locally referred to as Circumvesuviana) and then stop 2 mins later at Piazza **Garibaldi**, which is very close to the main-line station at Centrale. The two stations are linked by a moving walkway.

Tourist office: Via San Carlo 9 (www.visit-napoli.com).

The city centre is best explored on foot, but if you tire there is an excellent metro network. Four **funicular railways** (Funicolare di Montesanto, Centrale, Mergellina and Chiaia) link the Old City with the cooler Vomero Hill – take the funicular from Montesanto metro station to admire the views. Buy train tickets at kiosks and validate them in the machines near each platform. Buy bus tickets from news kiosks, tobacconists and bars.

If you like to experience the flavour of a lively neighbourhood full of local colour, try the friendly Hotel **Il Convento**, V. Speranzella,137/a, ☎ 081 403 977 (www.hotelilconvento.it), located in Naples' Spanish Quarter. The **Hotel Piazza Bellini**, Via SM di Constantinopoli 101, ☎ 081 451 732 (www.hotelpiazzabellini.com), is in a good, central location. Some of the higher rooms have balconies. For a dash of antique flair, try the family-run and very comfortable **Atmosfere del Centro Storico**, Corso Umberto I, 23, ☎ 0339 300 00 56 (http://bbatmosfere.blogspot.com), near the university.

The Tyrrhenian coast

Most trains running south-east from Naples duck round the back of **Vesuvius**, passing to the north of the volcano. A small number of trains (mainly local services to Salerno) take the old coastal railway, which is slower but much recommended. Opened in 1839, this was the very first railway in Italy. The slopes of Vesuvius rise up to the left and there are fine views to the right across the **Gulf of Naples** to Sorrento and Capri. The way to discern if a train takes the coastal line is to see if it stops at Torre Annunziata. If a train doesn't stop there, then it almost certainly follows the less interesting inland route.

Whichever way you skirt Vesuvius, the two routes from Naples converge in **Salerno**, a port city which is altogether more ordered than Naples. Salerno marks the start of the best section of this route. The Intercity trains take about four hours for the run south down the coast to **Villa San Giovanni**. Choose a seat on the right side of the train for great sea views. If you really want to make the most of the journey, consider using one of the slower trains on this route. The semi-fast *regionale veloce (RV)* services add a couple of hours to the overall journey time and require a change of trains at Paola.

True **slow travel aficionados** might opt for the local trains which run the whole way down the coast. With four dozen intermediate stations between Salerno and Villa San Giovanni, it'll take a day or two and you'll need to change trains several times along the way.

The railway heads inland, turning south at Battipaglia, where in the distance – on the lower slopes of the **Monti Picentini** – you'll glimpse **Eboli**, the village which inspired Carlo Levi's *Christ Stopped at Eboli*. When Levi arrived in handcuffs in remote Basilicata in 1935, the locals were quick to remind him that theirs was a region beyond the edge of civilisation, abandoned by God and the authorities. For the writer-in-exile, this was another world, one "hedged in by custom and sorrow, cut off from history and the State, eternally patient." Italy's southern provinces of **Basilicata** and **Calabria** have benefited in recent years from massive investment, not least in transport infrastructure and that sense of isolation from civilisation, captured so well by Carlo Levi, is no longer very evident. But it is still a place apart, a region where the values and norms of the north seem very foreign.

To the right of the railway is the small walled town of **Paestum**, once one of the most important cities of **Magna Graecia**, the territory of the ancient Greeks which included Sicily and the southernmost shores of mainland Italy. Beyond Paestum, the railway cuts through **Cilento National Park**, a wilderness area of rare beauty which figures centrally in Greek mythology. The appeal of this stretch of the railway is the manner in which it plays cat and mouse with the coast, swapping views of azure seas for glimpses of wild defiles and mountain streams.

The province of Basilicata touches the **Tyrrhenian coast** only briefly (though it has beaches aplenty away to the east on its Ionian coast), but it presents in **Maratea** a good spot to break the journey. A huge statue of Cristo Redentore (Christ the Redeemer) dominates the town; it is easily visible from the train. One glance at the marina – which has its own small railway station just south of Maratea itself – will convince you that this short stretch of Basilicata coast has been discovered by the chic set.

South of Maratea, the railway sticks firmly to the coast until Gizzeria, a stretch of about 130 kilometres. Only occasional tunnels interrupt the sea views. Of the various small communities along the coast, **Diamante** is the best choice for an overnight stop. Citrons and peperoncini are culinary staples in Diamante and you'll find **seafood aplenty** in this engaging small town. A safe hotel choice is the Stella Maris, V. Cavour 12, ☎ 0985 87 70 52 (www.stellamarisdiamante.it), on the seafront, where it is definitely worth paying the small supplement to secure a room with sea view.

Much further down the coast, another fine spot to stop off for a day or two is **Tropea**. With a fine setting on a rugged stretch of coast, this is a resort justifiably popular with Italians. It is worth checking accommodation availability before arriving. We've never stayed in Tropea ourselves, but hear good reports of the Residenza Il Barone, Largo Barone, ☎ 0963 60 71 81 (www.residenzailbarone.it). Note that only slower trains serve Tropea; the faster services cut south from Pizzo, avoiding the coastal loop around Capo Vaticano which serves Tropea and a number of other beach communities. The two lines converge again at Rosarno.

Beyond **Rosarno**, there are many more tunnels but still sufficient open stretches, as the train skirts the Costa Viola, to afford fine views across to Sicily. At **Villa San Giovanni**, there is the rare pleasure of watching your train being shunted onto a ferry for the short voyage to Sicily.

Sicily

Messina, Sicily's nearest port to the mainland, was the victim of an earthquake in 1908 that shook for two months and claimed 84,000 lives, and of a massive attack by US bombers in 1943. But even those events could not take away its glorious setting beneath the mountains. Much has been rebuilt in a stable, squat style. Trains from the mainland arrive on the ferry at Stazione Marittima, and continue to Stazione Centrale.

CONNECTIONS FROM MESSINA AND MILAZZO
From Messina Centrale, a railway runs along the north coast of Sicily to the island's capital at **Palermo**, along the way stopping at Milazzo, the departure point for the ferries and hydrofoils to Lipari and its neighbouring islands.

If you have travelled all the way to Sicily by train and fancy returning to **Naples by boat**, we especially recommend the twice-weekly ship (operated by *Siremar*) from Milazzo to Naples (www.carontetourist.it). The 18-hour journey starts with an afternoon cruise through the Aeolian Islands, stopping off at four or five small ports along the way. The last island stop is at Stromboli, from where the vessel continues overnight to Naples. Sicily is also well placed for onward travel to **Sardinia** (see our **Sidetracks** feature on p206).

Sit on the left side of the train for the onward journey to Siracusa. Once we escape Messina's dismal suburbs, there are fine views over the **Ionian Sea**. The first place of note is **Taormina**, a pretty town on a hillside overlooking Sicily's east coast with some striking Greek and Roman ruins. Mount Etna makes a beautiful backdrop to the south. Taormina is a picture-postcard spot. It is the ideal place to slip into the slow Sicilian way of life.

Taormina's only drawback is that the railway station (called Taormina Giardini) is on the coast way below the town itself. But you'll be rewarded for your effort in climbing up to the town by **breathtaking views**. And, if you don't fancy the climb, there's a useful shuttle bus that connects the station with the centre of Taormina. If you are minded to stay overnight, we can recommend the Villa Fiorita, V. L Pirandello 39, ☎ 0942 24 984 (www.villafioritahotel.com), which is very comfortable and has ample, well-furnished public spaces.

Beyond Taormina, you may want to shift to the right side of the train for views of **Mount Etna**. The last two hours of the journey, from Taormina down to Siracusa are dominated by the volcano. The principal city is **Catania** where you can connect onto a local railway which circles around the back of Mount Etna. It's a brilliant circuit, affording views of Etna from all angles.

South of Catania, the railway slips by the **Gulf of Augusta**, its coast much despoiled by some hideous chemical plants. It makes arrival in Siracusa seem all the better.

Siracusa

The city marking the end of our long journey from Rome is superb, one which in its history captures the entire Mediterranean experience. For **Cicero**, Siracusa was "the greatest Greek city and the most beautiful of them all." The sights are all gathered on **Ortygia Island**, just a short walk southeast of the main railway station and linked by two bridges to the mainland. There is a lively **daily fish market** on V Emanuele de Benedictis as you cross from the mainland onto Ortygia. Vegetables, fruit and dairy products are traded too, but fish stands centre stage.

Don't miss the impressive **cathedral**; it is essentially a baroque design, but it incorporates ancient columns which were once part of a Greek temple on the same site. That building encapsulates what is so very special about Siracusa. It is a city which has reinvented itself a dozen times over the centuries. Had the devotees of the **Grand Tour** ever ventured beyond Naples and come this far south, they would have discovered something well worth writing home about.

ARRIVAL, INFORMATION, ACCOMMODATION

⇌ On the mainland, north-west of the Old Town. 🛈 Tourist office: V. Roma 31 (www.siracusaturismo.net).
⇌ A friendly B&B on the Island of Ortygia, overlooking the channel between the island and the mainland is **L'Approdo delle Sirene**, Riva Giuseppe Garibaldi 15, ☎ 0931 248 57 (www.apprododellesirene.com). Also a good option right in the heart of the Old Town is the **Archimede Vacanze** B&B, Pza Archimede 2, ☎ 0339 140 98 09. Or try the stylish **Palazzo del Sale B&B**, V. Santa Teresa 25, ☎ 0931 659 58 (www.palazzodelsale.com), on the western side of Ortygia, well placed for the evening *passeggiata* along the Foro Vittorio Emanuele II.

Route 49: By rail and ship to Greece

Cities: ★★ Culture: ★★ History: ★ Scenery: ★
Countries covered: Italy (IT), Greece (GR)
Journey time: 28 hrs 20 | Distance: 1,444 km | Map: www.ebrweb.eu/18map49

This journey links two places which were both premier-league city-states. There were times when **Venice and Athens** wielded great influence through maritime power. Purists may suggest that the only sensible way to travel from Venice to Greece is by ship. And that is indeed possible. Several times each week, a comfortable cruise ferry leaves Venice for the voyage to the Greek port of Patras (Πάτρα), typically taking 32 hours for the long journey down the Adriatic.

For this **completely new route** for *Europe by Rail*, we offer an alternative to the direct ship from Venice to Greece, travelling down Italy's Adriatic coast and then taking the ferry from Bari to Patras, from where it is just a short hop on to Athens.

Itinerary hints

There are twice-daily direct trains from **Venice to Bari**, both Frecciarossa services, the first of which arrives in Bari in good time to connect with an evening sailing to Greece (when there is one). In truth, of course, it's better not to dash. Some of the most appealing stops on this journey involve detours off the main route. We highlight such opportunities in the route description. One we especially like is **San Marino**, easily reached by bus from Rimini, and only worth a visit if you have time to stay overnight (read more on that on p438). Another potential highpoint is an overnight stop at **Ascoli Piceno**, a small town set back from the coast and easily reached by train on a branch line. Later in the route, we especially like Trani. It makes a great overnight stay before hopping on the ferry from Bari to Greece. If you prefer the buzz of a bigger city then Bari itself is a good option.

You may consider a side trip by boat from Termoli to the Tremiti Islands – wee specks of land in the Adriatic which can be impossibly overcrowded in midsummer but are a delight off season. Or make time for the pine trees and limestone coves of the **Gargano Peninsula**. The choice is yours.

Leaving Venice

Venezia Santa Lucia railway station is made for grand departures. Some deplore its rationalist pose, others welcome its assertive modernism. Take a moment to compare it with the adjacent Carmelite church (Santa Maria di Nazareth) which is full of baroque affectation. Somehow that view, with the church and adjacent railway station, captures the conundrum which makes Italy so engaging (more on Venice on p425). Our train slips over the causeway to reach the mainland and then runs dead-straight across flat Veneto landscape to reach **Padua** (see p424). This stretch of railway also forms part of **Route 47** in this book.

After a stop in Padua, our train swings south, dashing on straight track towards the River Po. On the right there's a low ripple of hills. These

Route 49: By rail and ship to Greece | 435

Notes

A – Change trains in Ancona or San Benedetto del Tronto.
B – Change trains in San Benedetto del Tronto

Route details

Venice Santa Lucia to Bologna
Frequency	Journey time	Notes
2 per hr	1h35–2h15	

Bologna to Rimini
Frequency	Journey time	Notes
2–3 per hr	1h–1h40	

Rimini to Ascoli Piceno
Frequency	Journey time	Notes
Every 1–2 hrs	3h–3h30	A

Ascoli Piceno to Trani
Frequency	Journey time	Notes
5 per day	4h–5h20	B

Trani to Bari
Frequency	Journey time	Notes
1–3 per hr	0h30–0h45	

Bari to Patras
Frequency	Journey time	Notes
1 per day	17h–19h	By boat

Patras to Kiato
Frequency	Journey time	Notes
Every 2 hrs	1h30	By bus

Kiato to Athens Lárisa
Frequency	Journey time	Notes
Hourly	1h20	

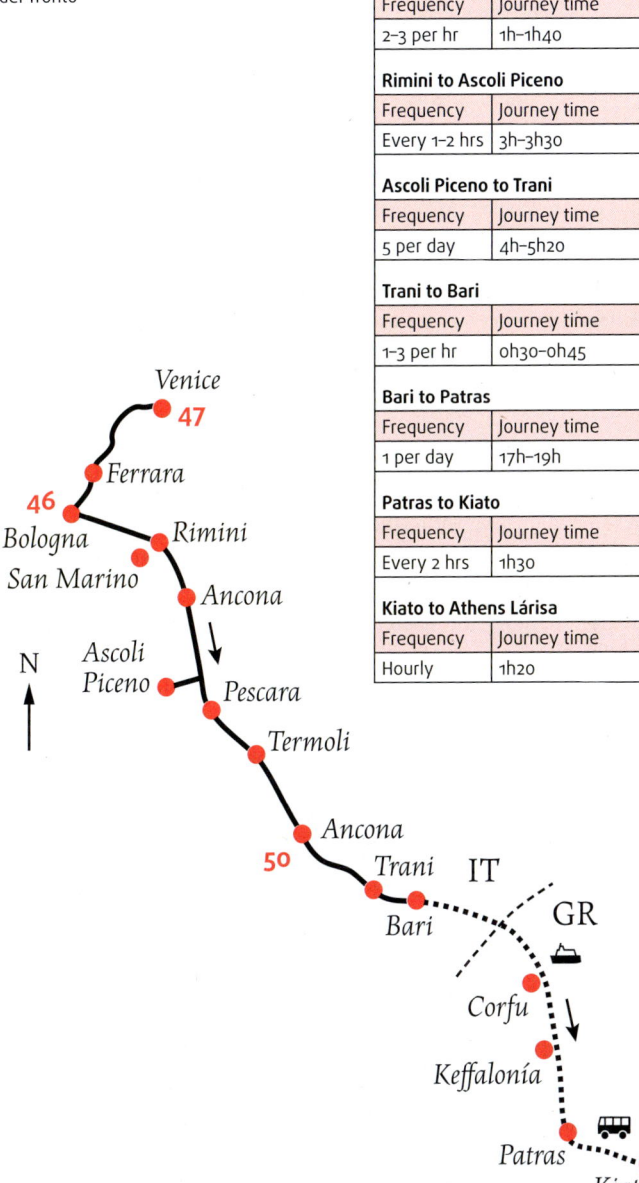

The 'Greek Problem'

We shall attribute our first grey hairs to the challenge of keeping Greece in successive editions of *Europe by Rail*. There were times when Greece enjoyed good rail connections with Turkey and Bulgaria via eastern Thrace. There were also direct trains to Thessaloniki from Sofia via the beautiful **Struma Valley rail route**, crossing from Bulgaria into Greece at Kulata. And for many years there was a reliable train service from Belgrade to Thessaloniki via the country we these days know as North Macedonia. All these routes have featured in various editions of this book.

Yet over the last dozen years, the ambition of the Greek national rail operator **TrainOSE** (ΤραινΟΣΕ) has flagged at borders. Be it Greek financial woes (in 2011), worries over refugees (in 2015) or latterly the COVID-19 pandemic, TrainOSE seems to take every opportunity to axe cross-border rail links. We hoped things might improve when TrainOSE was acquired by Italian national operator Trenitalia in 2017. It hasn't. For some years, TrainOSE's sole international effort has been a once-daily bus connection from Strymon in Greece to Kulata in Bulgaria. Even that cross-border bus disappeared from the timetables in 2024.

Faced with Greece's isolation from the rest of Europe's rail network, we decided to bite the proverbial bullet and introduce a **completely new route** to Greece, now relying on a ferry link from Italy rather than a cross-border rail service. Let's hope it proves a more enduring solution to what we affectionately refer to as 'our Greek problem'. But if the trains return, we'll most certainly react with a new route.

are the **Colli Euganei** (Euganean Hills) where Shelley hid away and wrote memorable stanzas about a green isle in "a deep, wide sea of misery." This is of course a fairly damning indictment of the flatlands of northern Italy, even if the green Euganean Hills survive the poetic encounter without blemish.

Around the northern and eastern edges of the Euganean Hills are a number of small spa towns noted for their mineral-rich thermal waters. They have always been popular and have over the years pulled their fair share of literary celebs. Stendhal and Heine both had recuperative stays at **Battaglia Terme** through which the train speeds about a dozen minutes after leaving Padua. Before long, we cross the River Po and reach the university city of **Ferrara**.

The expansion in the late 15th century of the original mediaeval city of Ferrara under the patronage of Duke Ercole I d'Este gives the city a special place in the history of European town planning. The development of entire new areas north of the historic heart of the city was a fine early example of Renaissance ideas of the *città ideale* (an ideal or model city). To us, Ferrara always seems like one of the most liveable cities in northern Italy. It's never quite been on the mainstream tourist trail. If you are minded to stop, the eminently walkable city centre with its **Piazza del Municipio** (and the cathedral just beyond) is just one km south-east of the railway station.

From Ferrara, it's another half hour down to **Bologna**, where you can connect onto **Route 46** in this book.

Ferrara and Bologna connections

There's a fine rural rail route that runs south-east from Ferrara, skirting the Comacchio wetlands to reach **Ravenna** with its celebrated UNESCO-listed Byzantine mosaics. From Ravenna there are hourly local trains down the coast to **Rimini** where you can rejoin our main route down the coast to Ancona and beyond.

Bologna is one of Italy's **largest rail hubs**. High-speed trains generally depart from the lower level platforms (numbered 16 to 19), with other trains serving the street-level platforms. NTV Italo and Trenitalia compete on the dash south to Florence and Rome, and also on the high-speed line to Milan and Turin. There's a new direct daytime train to Zürich (via the Gotthard route), complementing the regular trains to Innsbruck and Munich, the latter all upgraded from late 2024 to Railjets.

The Adriatic Coast

Running south-east from Bologna, the land to the south rises up to the **Apennines**, but the railway sticks firmly to the plain, passing through Imola (of motor-racing fame) and Faenza (whence comes the distinctive tin-glazed pottery called *faïence*) to reach the coast at **Rimini**, where there is no real reason to pause unless you want to visit **San Marino** (see box on p438).

Never underestimate the distances when exploring Italy's **Adriatic coast**. It is 539 km from Rimini down to Bari by train. You may choose to do this by local train. With 67 stops along the way, this would be a slow travel epic, but it is just about doable in a day with four changes of train along the way. Or you may prefer to cruise down the coast enjoying Executive Class comfort (champagne-coloured leather seats and free meals) or humbler accommodation in a Trenitalia Frecciarossa train, the fastest of which make only four intermediate stops along the way and reach Bari in little more than four-and-a-half hours. Slow or fast, the view so it happens is exactly the same with the sea to your left and undulating hills to the right of the train.

There are four occasions in which the railway veers inland from the coast, and these add interest to the journey. But the effect of these four diversions, which cumulatively means that the railway misses the finest stretches of the coast, is to communicate the impression that Italy's Adriatic littoral is a long ribbon of tourist resorts. It's better than that.

The first inland digression is between Cattolica and Pesaro, where the **San Bartolo hills** dominate the coast for a stretch of about 15 km. The second is immediately after Ancona where the railway runs inland of Monte Conero, a great limestone massif which tumbles precipitously into the Adriatic. The third stretch of coast you miss from the train, bar for fleeting glimpses, is the particularly fine part between Ortona and Vasto, where there are several tunnels. The last and by far the longest of the four deviations is when the railway cuts inland with the rugged **Gargano Promontory** away to the left. If you are on the hunt for good coastal scenery, these stretches where the railway forsakes the coast are where to look. Our top choice is definitely the last. Change at San Severo or **Foggia** for the local train – operated by

Ferrovie del Gargano – to Peschici, sublimely located on the north side of Gargano. From Peschici it is a short hop by bus or seasonal boat on to Vieste.

Overnight stops on the Adriatic coast

If truth be told, we wouldn't especially rate the main cities along the rail route to Bari as optimal stopovers. **Ancona** is a good jumping-off point for visiting the beautiful Monte Conero coast, and it is of course a major transport hub. You can connect in Ancona with the final journey in this book (**Route 50**), crossing the Adriatic to Split then heading on by train through Croatia to Hungary. Ancona also has direct ferries to Greece and in late 2021 a weekly link to Çeşme in Turkey was restored.

But if you are prepared to leave the main railway, we heartily recommend a one or two night stop in **Ascoli Piceno**, a handsome small town in the Tronto Valley, and easily reached by local trains which shuttle up the valley from San Benedetto del Tronto on the main line. Ascoli Piceno is far from being a sleepy backwater. It is surprising hip and boasts a number of excellent restaurants. If you are keen to stay overnight, try the centrally located and welcoming Albergo Sant'Emidio, Via Minucia 10 (www.albergosantemidio.it).

Further down the coast, Termoli isn't quite as brash as some of the other resorts, and a night here might be considered, but better still head out to the **Tremiti Islands** for a

San Marino

The Rimini to San Marino shuttle bus is run by Bonelli (www.bonellibus.it); it departs eight times a day from outside Rimini station (less often on winter weekends) for the 50-min ride up into San Marino, the little republic that clusters around Mount Titano in the hills above Rimini. The one-way fare is €5.

Terrain has been the greatest ally of the *Serenissima Repubblica di San Marino*, deterring invaders and safeguarding the territory's independence. That said, it is a surprisingly easy ride up from Rimini. The 'bus' is actually a very smart coach, which takes travellers in air-conditioned comfort through Rimini's unlovely urban sprawl and out into the Ausa Valley. The main road, a multi-lane affair that curves gently up towards the hills, is ideal for drivers aspiring to enter a Grand Prix.

The centre of San Marino is a riotous combination of exquisite buildings, glorious scenery and a feast of tawdry commerce. No other town we know boasts quite the same density of shops selling replica guns, real knives and fake mediaeval weaponry. Multilingual signs assault the senses. "Cheap booze and free drinks," shouts a placard in a street that climbs up steeply behind the city gate. There are shop windows overflowing with handbags and jewellery. There are watches, furs and perfumes.

The great majority of visitors who go to San Marino make only short visits, and the commercial rhythm of the capital beats to the pulse of a daily influx of day trippers. Few of these visitors ever stay on into the evening. Those who do are in for a treat. From the ramparts of Mount Titano, there are tremendous views east over the Adriatic, with the islands of Croatia visible on a clear evening. West, looking towards the setting sun, are wave upon wave of hills receding into the distance. Small towns balance on many of the hilltops. The view is a reminder of a lost Europe and San Marino is a relic from another age. It is the only surviving secular city-state on the Italian peninsula. No other republic on earth can claim such a long history and the principles of civic autonomy and self-governance fostered in San Marino have inspired the wider world. It is most definitely worth a visit, but we think only if you can make an overnight stay. We stayed at the Hotel Joli, Viale Federico D'Urbino 36B (www.hoteljoli.sm), an excellent three star hotel just outside the old city walls in the capital (and just steps from the bus stop for the coach back to Rimini).

day or two of insular retreat – this is ideally a shoulder-season option as the islands can be formidably crowded in mid-summer.

Just short of Bari – and actually on the main coastal railway – is the very appealing town of **Trani**. It combines style, even a touch of grandeur in its **magnificent seaside cathedral**, with still more than a hint of the traditional fishing community it once was. A good B&B is Le Marinelle, Vico Forno Vecchio 7 (www.lemarinelletrani.it). There are trains at least hourly (at certain times even as many as four per hour) to Bari, just 40 mins away.

Bari and the ferry

Okay, so did you take a week to explore the coast from Rimini down to Bari? Or dash down south in an afternoon? No worries, whatever you did, we're here and ready for what many regard as the finest part of this journey. First a word on **ferry options**, then we'll take a look around Bari. There are multiple ferry operators running from **Bari to Greece**. Some, like Superfast Ferries who operate in cooperation with ANEK Lines, offer discounts to holders of Interrail and Eurail passes. Our advice is to be guided by schedule, and to think carefully whether you just want to get to Greece or whether you want to make an occasion of the crossing by taking some food treats on board and / or perhaps booking a luxury cabin.

"Be guided by schedule." What does that mean? There's a choice of early afternoon and evening departures, respectively giving a crack of dawn or an early afternoon arrival in the **Greek port of Patras**. We tend to favour the evening option, as it means that the finest part of the journey is then in daylight the following day. Mind you, you have to be an early riser to enjoy the dawn views of **Corfu**. You can turn this stretch of the journey into a mini-cruise by stopping off in Corfu for a day or two.

Even if you don't break your journey, we do tend to favour crossings which make intermediate stops, as then you get more inshore cruising close to the shore. In summer Ventouris Ferries have often offered a direct Monday evening sailing from Bari to Sami on **Kefallonía**, which calls at Corfu and Igoumenitsa along the way. After a night on Kefallonía you can then continue to Patras next morning.

On those sailings from Bari giving an early afternoon arrival in Patras, you can anticipate an interesting morning of maritime sightseeing that, depending on the route taken, includes the Albanian coast (perhaps while some still sleep), the eastern shores of Corfu and many of the **Ionian islands**, including Paxi, Lefkádha and Itháki.

With ferry tickets sorted, take time to explore **Bari** where the oldest part of the city (called **Bari Vecchia**) is on a promontory that projects north with the ferry port, close to the old city walls, on the west side of that peninsula. Bari Vecchia has a labyrinthine quality, a maze of atmospheric alleys, but the centrepiece is the striking castle-like, part-Romanesque basilica dedicated to St Nicholas. The ferry terminal is a 20-min walk north from the station (or take 🚌 50). A good overnight option in the old town is the friendly B&B La Muraglia, Strada Annunziata 2 (www.lamuragliabari.it).

BARI CONNECTIONS
There are year-round sailings from **Bari to Durrës** in Albania and from April to November also sailings to Dubrovnik in Croatia. Plus of course multiple routes to Greece. The seasonal service from Bari to **Bar** in Montenegro has been very much an on-off affair. As this 18th edition of *Europe by Rail* goes to press, it has not been confirmed if this service will operate in 2025. We have found the **Morfimare agency** in Bari, on Corso Tullio just by the port, very helpful in making ferry bookings (www.morfimare.it).

Bari is good for trains too, with fast daytime trains to Rome (now with a choice of Trenitalia and NTV Italo services on the route). If you are heading back north, Bari has direct night trains to Milan and Turin. Closer to hand, Bari is the gateway to **Apulia**, served by an excellent network of minor railways operated by Ferrovie del Sud Est (no Sunday services) as well as Trenitalia services to **Lecce** and **Taranto**, the latter a staging post on routes to Calabria. Finally, Ferrovie Appulo Lucane tracks west into the hills to reach Matera.

The last hour on the **ferry into Patras** is very special. On the left the sumpy flatlands of the Akheloös delta, tucked away in which are the ruins of ancient Oeniadae, a silted-up port that was once the premier entrepôt for western Greece. No longer – these days it is Patras over on the Peloponnese side of the Gulf of Patras which takes the seaborne trade. As you approach Patras you'll see the four pylons of the spectacular **Rion-Antirion road bridge**, beyond which lies the narrow Gulf of Corinth.

Some ferry companies offer a direct **express bus** from the Patras ferry terminal to central Athens. It may not be the cheapest option, but it's quick and convenient. Alternatively, it's a short bus ride into town from where regular express coaches leave from the KTEL bus station, taking 2 hrs 30 mins for the **ride to Athens**. Or follow our example and take the OSE Greek Railways bus from Patras railway station to **Kiato** to connect with the hourly train to Athens' main railway station which is called Lárisa.

Don't underestimate this journey from Patras to Athens. It's wonderful – whether you take the bus the whole way or opt for the train-and-bus combo which we commend above. Sit on the left side of the bus or train for superb views across the **Gulf of Corinth** towards Mt Giona and Mt Parnassos. The journey bridges the Corinth Canal and then skirts the north shore of the Saronic Gulf to reach Athens.

Athens (Αθήνα)

For many, Athens' greatest appeal is rooted in the sights of the ancient city where Western democracy, science and philosophy were born. The **Acropolis** with its surrounding monuments is by far the best known of these. Don't miss the **National Archeological Museum** (www.namuseum.gr; closed Mon) which traces the history of ancient Greece in its excellent collections. At the centre of the city, a 4-km pedestrian walkway connects ancient sights and museums including the **Acropolis Museum** (www.theacropolismuseum.gr; closed Mon) near the start of the landscaped walk and the Theatre of Dionysus. The walk was created for the 2004 Olympics.

Yet Athens is not all history as the Greek capital is a bustling and exhilarating place with an abundance of trendy bars and restaurants. The **Pláka district**, the oldest part of Athens at the foot of the Acropolis, is very touristy, but it's also very attractive with its many cafés, shops and alleyways. It's nowadays largely pedestrianised. **Syntagma Square** is the city's central square and the place where the Greek Parliament is located.

For panoramic views over the city, take the **Lycabettus Funicular** (www.lycabettushill.com) up to Mount Lycabettus, the city's highest elevation. The closest metro stop is Evangelismos, about 600 metres away. It's a three-minute ride through a tunnel to the top. If you feel energetic, you can decend using a footpath. On top there is a restaurant and observation deck as well as church of Agios Georgios.

Arrival, information, accommodation

⇌ The main train station is called **Lárisa**. The closest metro station is Strathmós Larísis which connects the train station with central Athens and also the port of **Piraeus** which is about 8 km south-west of Athens.

✈ Eleftherios Venizelos Airport (www.aia.gr), 27 km east of Athens, is also served by the metro. **OASA** (www.oasa.gr) runs the public transport in Athens which consists of three metro lines, trams, trolleybuses and buses. Reloadable tickets can be purchased from vending machines and ticket counters and cover all urban transport. They are available for different periods, for example 90-min (€1.20), 24-hour (€4.10; including the X80 bus), 5-days (€8.29) and a 3-day tourist ticket (€20) that includes a journey to and from the airport. 🛈 Tourist information: Tsocha 7 (www.thisisathens.org); an information point is also near Syntagma Square at Amalias 26.

🛏 An excellent choice close to Syntagma Square is **Inn Athens**, Georgiou Sourri 3 & Filellinon, ☎ 0210 325 85 55 (www.innathens.com). Enjoy the stylish and comfortable **The Artist Athens** hotel, Kalamida Str. 7, ☎ 0210 323 80 12 (www.theartistathens.com) in the city's Psiri district. Well located in the Monastiraki district, **The Moon and Stars** boutique hotel, Plateia Agion Asomaton, ☎ 0211 412 03 29 (www.moonandstarsathens.com) has five individually furbished rooms in a beautiful, carefully renovated art deco building.

Beyond Athens

Although Greece is a disaster when it comes to international rail links (see box on p436), don't write off the domestic train services. The fastest trains to **Thessaloniki**, over 500 km away to the north, take five hours. Beyond Thessaloniki, all services east into Thrace are currently operated by buses rather than trains. But trains are running along the very scenic route west from Thessaloniki to Florina, a journey of over three hours.

Few other countries can touch Greece when it comes to the fine range of **domestic shipping services**. Whether you are heading for Crete or the Cyclades or venturing as far as the Dodecanese, the port of Piraeus is your point of embarkation (easily reached by metro from central Athens). We often dream of wandering along the **Piraeus** quaysides, randomly choosing an immediate departure for an island which we've never visited. Lipsi, Tinos or Symi perhaps? Or, better still, let's plan ahead and book the twice-weekly ferry from Piraeus to **Kastellorizo**. It stops at Lipsi, Tinos, Symi and lots of other places on the 23-hour voyage to Greece's easternmost island. Hope you'll join us.

Route 50: From the Danube to the Adriatic

CITIES: ★ CULTURE: ★ HISTORY: ★ SCENERY: ★★
COUNTRIES COVERED: HUNGARY (HU), CROATIA (HR), ITALY (IT)
JOURNEY TIME: 22 HRS 40 MINS | DISTANCE: 1,051 KM | MAP: WWW.EBRWEB.EU/18MAP50

Have you noticed that many of the routes in this book tend to lead the reader from west to east? We travelled east to Warsaw in **Route 31** and **36**, east to Košice in **Route 35** and east to Romania's Black Sea coast in **Route 34**. Let's make amends. This last route in *Europe by Rail* moves west, reflecting the manner in which Hungarians have often looked towards the Adriatic. Until the First World War, Hungary effectively controlled the seaport of Fiume (nowadays Rijeka in Croatia), with Budapest financiers promoting Fiume as a rival to the great Austrian port of Trieste (see p402 and p426).

But **Hungarian affection for the Adriatic** was not just a matter of commerce. The tradition of leaving the Budapest heat and decanting to the coast for the summer was as established a seasonal migration as the Parisian flight to the Riviera. Those who could afford it followed the Hungarian nobility to the resort they called Abbázia, still as lovely a place as ever, and now known more widely by its Croatian name Opatija. Other Hungarians would make for resorts down the Dalmatian coast: Crikvenica, Zadar, Šibenik or Split.

This journey for *Europe by Rail* retraces a pilgrimage of yesteryear – but one which remains enduringly popular with residents of Budapest today. It is a mark of Hungarians' continuing affection for the Adriatic that there are special summer-only direct trains from Budapest to Adriatic resorts. Of course, not everyone can afford to travel so far, but closer to home is **Lake Balaton**, often affectionately referred to as the Hungarian Sea. Landlocked countries have to use their watery assets as best they can.

So, on our journey from **Budapest to Split**, we shall cruise the south shore of Lake Balaton and stop off in the largest city on the way to the Adriatic: Zagreb. We'll then take the slow train down to the coast at Split and conclude the journey by travelling by ship across the Adriatic to **Ancona** in Italy, giving a seamless connection with the previous journey in this book.

BY DAY OR BY NIGHT: THOUGHTS ON ITINERARY

For an authentic meet-the-locals experience, you could book a seat on a summer season holiday train from **Budapest to Split**. One such train is called the *Adria* which in summer 2024 ran thrice weekly from mid-June to the end of September. The Friday departure from Budapest is your chance to catch the *Adria* at its surreal best. It is packed to the gills with families looking forward to a week of sun, sea and sand.

As the train tracks out through Budapest suburbs, hearty picnics are being shared and before long parents are telling their kids bedtime stories. But no one sleeps and neither will you. After a 15-hour journey, you'll arrive in Split dog-tired in the morning.

So, yes, you could take the *Adria*. But you probably won't, because there are sensible daytime alternatives. In summer, there is a good crack-of-dawn train from Budapest to Zagreb which takes the **lakeshore route** past Balaton. The year-round afternoon train from

ROUTE 50: FROM THE DANUBE TO THE ADRIATIC | 443

Route details

Budapest Déli to Zagreb glavni		
Frequency	Journey time	Notes
1–2 per day	5h30–6h20	

Zagreb glavni to Split		
Frequency	Journey time	Notes
1–3 per day	6h10–8h	

Split to Ancona		
Frequency	Journey time	Notes
2–8 per week	11h	

SUMMER SPECIALS TO SPLIT

Split has long been the end point for some of Europe's most ambitious night trains, all of them seasonal services bringing **holiday crowds** from far-flung cities. Fifty years ago, British holidaymakers looking for summer sun in Yugoslavia could travel by ferry to Oostende in Belgium and there join a train which would take them all the way to Split. That connection is long gone, but recent years have seen plenty of **exotic summer trains** in Split, with arrivals even from Minsk and Moscow. Split's enduring appeal attracted some new trains during the pandemic as travellers switched from planes to trains. **RegioJet** stepped in with a hastily organized direct link from Prague which in 2022 ran from early June to late September. A link from Vienna and Bratislava has been revived (a joint Austrian-Slovak operation). This service also transports cars. In 2025, it will run twice or thrice weekly from early May.

Budapest to Zagreb used to take a less interesting route which missed the lake, but for 2024 it's happily back running by Lake Balaton. Stop off in Zagreb, continuing at will by day train to Split and then on by boat to Ancona. That's usually an overnight crossing on the ferry to Italy, but in the summer there are also a limited number of daytime sailings.

If you don't fancy continuing to Italy, you can of course leave this route at **Split**, from where in the summer there's a good onward connection by **boat to Dubrovnik** – a wonderful city further down the coast which since 1976 has not been reachable by train. There's also a year-round bus service down the coast road from Split to Dubrovnik which at Neum cuts through a slither of Bosnian territory.

Heading for Lake Balaton

The seasonal early train from **Budapest to Zagreb** is called the *Gradec*. The year-round afternoon departure is called the *Agram*, recalling the name which German-speaking elites in Vienna often used for Zagreb. It's not a name which ever found favour with the locals, so there's a touch of imperial posturing in using it today as a train name. When we last used the *Agram*, there was a mix of older Hungarian and Croatian carriages, some with separate compartments, others open-plan. If you are inclined to travel first class, bear in mind that the seating there is entirely in compartments – if you don't like compartments, it's definitely not worth paying the extra. For good views of **Lake Balaton**, sit on the right side of the train. Trains to Zagreb leaves from the Déli station in Budapest: it has none of the antique grace of the city's two other main termini. For more on Budapest see p311.

35 minutes after leaving Budapest, you'll be cruising along a lakeshore. This is **Lake Valencei**. The name actually means Venice in Hungarian. A fine lake though it may be, there's no similarity with Venice. But Valencei is the warm-up act for Lake Balaton, a lake about which we always have mixed feelings. It's not always a pretty sight. Our route tracks along the southern shore of the lake which was the focus for intense organised tourism in the **socialist period** of the last century. Workers needing a well-earned vacation, along with their families, would flock to cheap accommodation around the lake. The lucky ones had vouchers which guaranteed an all-expenses-paid holiday – no frills, of course. Comradely solidarity has since been eclipsed by capitalist avarice and the area has paid a heavy price for overdevelopment.

> ### Balaton diversions
>
> Don't write off **Lake Balaton** entirely. If you have time, take the minor railway around the north side of the lake, changing trains at Tapolca and rejoining our main route at Balatonszentgyörgy, a railway junction at the south-west corner of the lake. Of the many resorts on that north bank, the one we most like is the former spa town of **Balatonfüred**. It's also worth stopping at Badacsony, a lakeshore railway station in a fine setting by the eponymous basalt butte. The latter draws visitors from far and wide to admire its distinctive **columnar jointing**, which doesn't quite have the romance of the similar formations on the Scottish island of Staffa or at the Giant's Causeway in Ireland.

See the box on the previous page for a more positive take on Hungary's premier region for domestic tourism. Once past Balaton, it's not far to the **Croatian border**, where there's still occasionally a quick check of passports. Croatia joined the Schengen region in 2023 and that should in theory have marked the end of routine checks. Over the border, the train cuts through the hills separating the Drava from the Sava Valley to reach Zagreb.

Zagreb (suggested stopover)

The north of Zagreb is the posh side of the railway tracks. The distinguished Croatian writer **Miroslav Krleža** wrote a damning essay on social (and spatial) divides in Zagreb in 1937. To the north of the station, he found "hot water, roulette, lifts, *on parle français*, Europe, good!" Over on the south side of the railway there were "open cesspits, malaria... Balkan, a sorry province." To Krleža, those quarters of Zagreb beyond the railway were "the back of beyond, Asia." That from a left-leaning writer who was keen to shock the Zagreb bourgeoisie – all by definition residing north of the railway – out of their complacency.

Nowadays, the cesspits south of the tracks are long gone and the district between the railway and the river, while not pretty, is an edgy part of town where activists protest against real estate speculators. Even Zagreb has its rebel zone. If you incline towards more sedate cityscapes, stick to the north side of the station where the **Esplanade Hotel** still has uniformed bellboys and the Paviljon restaurant attracts an affluent elite who like elaborate cakes. Both the Esplanade and the Paviljon are visible from the front of the station. Any visit to Zagreb these days is necessarily coloured by the aftermath of the **terrible earthquake** of March 2020. Two years on, some of the city's landmark buildings are now being restored. The most-affected part of the city is the so-called Kaptol area, particularly in and around the cathedral – precisely that part of Zagreb upon which many visitors to the city focus. The **Kaptol** district as well as the wider *Gornji grad* (Upper Town) still have a certain Austro-Hungarian flavour, and the city paid a heavy price in seeing many Habsburg-era buildings damaged by the earthquake.

If your real interest is in sacred architecture and you are itching to see the inside of Zagreb's wonderful **range of churches**, then a visit just now may end in disappointment. The combination of earthquake and pandemic led to many churches, museums and other public buildings being closed for tourist visits. However, if your intent is more on getting a feel for this welcoming city, then don't be deterred from stopping off for a day or two. Zagreb is vibrant, fun and never too expensive. With a few hours in Zagreb, one could easily wander through the **Upper Town** and still have time to explore the boulevards and gardens of the more formal *Donji Grad* (Lower Town), the present layout of which dates back to very extensive reconstruction after an earlier earthquake in 1880 – modest consolation, perhaps, that earthquakes can pave the way to major urban regeneration projects which benefit subsequent generations of residents and visitors.

Arrival, information, accommodation
≊ In the centre of town. ℹ Tourist offices: Trg Bana J Jelačića 11 (www.infozagreb.hr).
⊨ Try the **Jägerhorn**, Ilica 14, ☎ 01 483 3877 (www.hotel-jagerhorn.hr), Zagreb's oldest hotel, in the heart of the Old Town. Close to the main square and within walking distance of museums, eateries and cafés is **Hotel Dubrovnik**, Ljudevita Gaja 1, ☎ 01 486 35 12 (www.hotel-dubrovnik.hr). The boutique B&B **Pod Zidom Rooms**, Pod Zidom 5, ☎ 099 387 48 36 (www.podzidom.hr) offers comfortable, modern rooms in a quiet location not far from the cathedral. ✘ The central and certainly most obvious destination for coffee by day and beer by night is popular Tkalčićeva street, leading from Trg Bana J Jelačića up to Gornji grad.

Zagreb connections
There are very useful **overnight trains** from Zagreb to Munich and Zurich. There are daytime services to Ljubljana, Vienna and Villach (with a good onward connection in Villach to Munich). The rail service to Belgrade was suspended during the pandemic, but a thrice-weekly train to **Serbia** may possibly be reinstated in 2025. There is also vague talk of a restored rail link to Banja Luka and Sarajevo in Bosnia in due course.

Over the hills to Split

In the depths of winter, the long leg from **Zagreb to Split** can be a stunning ride. In mid-summer, the train is often very crowded. The train journey to Split has become a rite of passage for large numbers of young travellers from western Europe. Anyway, this is a route where you should definitely reserve a seat in advance, even if only on the eve of your departure from Zagreb.

The railway parallels the motorway as far as **Karlovac** and then takes to the hills. The journey up the Mrežnica Valley is very pretty, but the best is yet to come. South of Oštarije, the train runs the entire length of the **Lika Railway** (*Lička pruga* in Croatian) through formidably desolate terrain which can be very snowy in winter. The summit of the line at Rudopolje is at 870 metres above sea level. As the railway drops down towards the **Krka Valley**, the train crosses territory which in the 1990s was part of the Republic of Serbian Krajina (RSK). It was formally assimilated back into Croatia in 1998. It is still a region where the scars of the terrible war years are all too evident. All trains stop at **Knin**, the former RSK capital. It is an unloved town, but it does have a useful bus connection to Zadar. From Knin, it is less than two hours down to the coast. From the right side of the train you'll get good views of Split on the approach.

Split (suggested stopover)
Split's old core is built around the remains of **Diocletian's Palace** which was constructed 2,000 years ago for the Roman emperor's retirement. The

South from Split

Well may you wonder why the Croatian coast beyond Split is so poorly connected by rail. If you want to head down to **Dubrovnik** from Split, you need to rely on connections by both bus or boat. The latter wins hands-down but it's a summer-only option. There is also a railway to the Croatian port of **Ploče** from Bosnia.

In recent years, the trains have run from Sarajevo down through Mostar and then stubbornly stopped at Čapljina, the last community in Bosnia & Herzegovina before the Croatian border. But from early June to early September 2024, a thrice-weekly Bosnian Talgo train again ran on beyond Čapljina to Ploče. A welcome development, though there's little prospect of seeing trains return to Dubrovnik, where the last train departed in 1976.

The railway to Dubrovnik was part of an extensive **narrow-gauge network** which once extended through southern Yugoslavia. Travel was never fast. In 1965, the fastest train from Dubrovnik to Sarajevo took over ten hours. In 1966 the narrow-gauge line from Sarajevo to Mostar and Ploče was converted to standard gauge, leaving only peripheral fragments of the old narrow-gauge network (like the Dubrovnik branch).

These narrow-gauge railways of the region were a legacy of Austro-Hungarian influence. The demise of that network was born of good intentions. In Tito's **Yugoslavia**, there was a strong commitment to renewing aged rail infrastructure and building new lines – of which the most celebrated was the line from Belgrade to Bar. The new line to Bar opened in May 1976 in the same week as the last train ran to Dubrovnik. Had the Bosnian narrow-gauge network survived, it would surely today be a cherished asset in promoting tourism – much like the Rhaetian Railway network in eastern Switzerland.

---

waterfront Riva buzzes all day with a string of pavement cafés. The traffic-free Old Town consists of narrow paved alleys, opening out onto ancient piazzas. From here the tourist office's self-guided walk leads through town; a series of information boards highlight Split's Roman roots, the **Cathedral of St Duje**, and the various buildings dating back to the times of Venetian and Austro-Hungarian rule. Climb the cathedral bell tower for fine views.

Continue through the area of **Varoš**, where steep winding steps take you to the wooded Marjan peninsula. One of Split's best museums is the **Meštrović Museum** (www.mestrovic.hr) in Šetalište Ivana Meštrovića 46. Ivan Meštrović was a Split-born sculptor whose work can be seen all over the country and overseas, with one of the most striking examples being the hulking statue of Grgur of Nin on the northern edge of Diocletian's Palace.

The UNESCO World Heritage-listed city of **Trogir** lies just 30 km west of Split. 🚌 37 leaves from Split's main bus station every 30 mins, taking half an hour for the ride. Wander around Trogir's narrow cobbled streets, stopping off at the cathedral and the Kamerlengo Fortress. The waterfront fills at night with pavement cafés and seafood restaurants in summer and there are regular boat excursions to the nearby islands.

Arrival, information, accommodation
🚆 Trains, buses and ferries all arrive in the same area, overlooking Gradska Luka, the town's harbour. The historic centre is just 100 m away to the north-west.

🛈 Tourist office: Peristil bb (www.visitsplit.com). ⛴ A friendly B&B, close to the harbour on the edge of the Old Town, is **Kastel 1700**, Mihovilova Sirina 5, ☎ 021 343 912 (www.kastelsplit.com). It varies from quite affordable to pricey depending on season. Family-run and highly regarded, the small **Hotel Villa Diana**, Kuzmanića 3, ☎ 021 482 460 (www.villadiana.hr) is very well placed for both the Old Town and the promenade. Or try the welcoming and comfortable boutique hotel **Splendida** Palace, Rokova 26, ☎ 021 838 485 (www.splendidapalace.com) equally well located.

By ship to Italy

Two companies compete on the shipping route from **Split to Ancona**. Jadrolinija (www.jadrolinjia.hr) sails year round, though winter sailings are only twice-weekly. Italian ferry company SNAV (www.snav.it) sails only from mid-April to the end of September. Both rely on older vessels which have seen service in Scandinavian waters. The fact that the SNAV ferry is decorated with images of Bugs Bunny and Dodo the Duck plays no part in our prejudice that Jadrolinija might be the better bet, if only for their year-round loyalty to the route. We used the Jadrolinija vessel in mid-winter; it is called *Marco Polo*. It was just us, a few truck drivers and a huge group of Italian **Catholic pilgrims**, returning home after a visit to the Marian shrine at Međugorje, who were very determined to make an occasion of their last night away from home. The one thing that might make you opt for the SNAV boat is that on Saturdays in June, July and August they offer a day-time crossing. All other sailings are overnight.

As ferry crossings go, this route from Ancona to Split has a lot going for it. With a crossing time of 11 hours (but less for that summer Saturday daytime sailing), there's time for a decent night's sleep. The departure from Split is excellent, as the vessel slips past the islands of Šolta to port and **Drvenik Veli** to starboard. Then it's open sailing to the Italian coast, where on the approach to Ancona there are very fine views of the rugged **Conero coast** off to port. Then the ship rounds a headland dominated by Ancona's squat cathedral, dedicated to Saint Cyriacus. Suddenly we are there by the quayside. There are connections onward by train, following **Route 49** either up or down the coast. There are also direct trains to Rome. If the voyage from Split hasn't dampened your enthusiasm for **ferry travel**, you can connect in Ancona onto ships bound for Greece and Turkey. If you want to stay over night in Ancona, an upmarket option close to the Old Town is the elegant Seeport Hotel, Rupi di Via XXIX Settembre 12, ☎ 071 971 51 00 (www.seeporthotel.com) with views across the harbour. They also have a good restaurant.

Congratulations on making landfall in Italy. Ancona marks the very end of the final route in *Europe by Rail*. If you have followed all 50 routes in this book you are now an expert. The next 50 journeys are for you alone to decide. The world is your oyster.

SIDETRACKS: THROUGH ALBANIA

Comb the various online travel forums that focus on Adriatic travel and there is one question that recurs with unfailing regularity: "How do I get from southern Croatia to Greece without going through Albania?" And of course the travel pundits who lurk around those virtual communities give all the right advice. Jadrolinija offer direct ferries (April to October) from **Dubrovnik to Bari**, from where there is an onward ship to Greece, part of **Route 49** in this book, serving Corfu, Igoumenitsa (in the Thesprotia area of north-west Greece) and Patras (in the northern Peloponnese, about 200 km west of Athens). But few on those online forums query why one would ever want to avoid Albania. True, a couple of days making an Adriatic dog-leg to **reach Greece by ship** from Dubrovnik would surely be very relaxing. But to skip Albania (and for that matter Montenegro too) is to miss two of Europe's most intriguing countries.

If you might have followed **Route 50** to Split, you'll very likely make your way by boat or bus down the coast to lovely Dubrovnik. How do you head further down the coast? And can you really **cut through Albania** to reach Greece? The answer to that last question is yes. And here's how to do it.

You can make the entire journey south from Dubrovnik through Montenegro into Albania on local buses. But we suggest relying instead on longer-distance bus services; it means you spend less time sitting on buses, but it does still require a couple of overnight stops with plenty of time for sightseeing. Those overnight stops are probably best made in Kotor and Tiranë.

Times given here are correct in September 2024. There are direct buses (3 to 8 times daily) from **Dubrovnik to Kotor**. The journey takes about two hours. Tickets (usually about €30) can be booked on www.buscroatia.com. The beautiful Bay of Kotor is a real highlight of Montenegro, and the UNESCO-listed town of Kotor on the shores of a great fjord surrounded by high mountains is stunning. If you have time, spend two nights in Kotor and use the intervening day to make a side trip to the mountain town of **Cetinje** (Цетиње), which flourished in the late 19th century as the capital and principal centre of Montenegrin culture. It is not for nothing that many Montenegrins still refer to Cetinje as the honorary capital of their country.

From Kotor, there is a direct bus at 08.00 every morning to Tiranë. The 270-km journey costs €27 and takes six hours. The bus is operated by *Jadran Ekspres* and runs via Podgorica to enter Albania by the north-east corner of **Lake Shkodër**. Book on www.flixbus.com. From Tiranë there are direct coaches to Athens, but that's the boring option. Far better to take the Tisa Travel bus service (€15.50) which runs several times daily from **Tiranë to Sarandë**. Book this on travel.gjirafa.com. The bus takes 4 hrs 15 mins to reach Sarandë from where there is now a year-round direct ferry to Corfu. The crossing takes anything from 30 to 75 mins, depending on whether it is a hydrofoil or a car ferry, with fares running from €12 to €25. You'll find details on www.finikas-lines.com.

Once in **Corfu**, you can plot your onward journey to the Greek mainland, whether with just a short ferry hop over to Igoumenitsa or a longer sea passage down to Patras. Whatever you decide, you'll have the satisfaction of having made a journey through a part of Europe which is well off the beaten track.

Gazetteer
Countries from A to Z

Albania Andorra Austria Belarus Belgium Bosnia and Herzegovina Bulgaria Croatia Cyprus Czech Republic Denmark Estonia Faroe Islands Finland France Germany Great Britain Greece Hungary Iceland Ireland Italy Kosovo Latvia Liechtenstein Lithuania Luxembourg Malta Moldova Monaco Montenegro Netherlands North Macedonia Norway Poland Portugal Romania Russia San Marino Serbia Slovakia Slovenia Spain Sweden Switzerland Turkey Ukraine Vatican City

There is some information that is best presented on a **country-by-country basis**. In our gazetteer we give a cameo account of most European territories with key data such as language, time zone and currency. We also indicate which electrical plug types are used in the respective country. The letters A-N each represent a plug type. See www.iec.ch/world-plugs for details – a truly wonderful website. For countries that feature in our **50 rail routes**, we give additional travel information. Remember that, as with everything in this book, the *European Rail Timetable* (ERT) and the accompanying *Rail Map Europe* or Mike Ball's *European Railway Atlas* all make **good companions** to this gazetteer. And these days you'll most certainly want to download a public transport app or two for each country you visit. You'll find a list of key apps and websites on p524.

We are very aware that many readers of this book travel on tight budgets so, where appropriate in this gazetteer, we make brief mention of the availability of independent hostels – which are increasingly a canny choice for travellers looking for something different from a traditional hotel. Other types of budget accommodation are also mentioned.

Albania

The small republic in the **eastern Adriatic** features on few tourist itineraries, but there is no reason why it should not, for Albania offers remarkable old Ottoman towns, stunning beaches and some of Europe's finest mountain scenery. And it boasts some deliciously antiquated trains. Timetables change unpredictably. No passenger trains cross the country's borders, so the Albanian rail network is effectively isolated from the rest of Europe. Read more in our **Sidetracks** on p449.

Essentials: Local name: Shqipëria – Population: 2.9m – Capital: Tiranë – Currency: Lek (ALL) – Languages: Albanian (Italian and English often understood in main towns) – Accommodation costs: generally low – Plug types: C, F – Time zone: winter GMT+1, summer GMT+2 – International dialling code: +355 – Public holidays: 1, 2 Jan; 14, 21 Mar; Easter Mon (Catholic and Orthodox); 1 May; Eid-al-Fitr; Eid-al-Adha; 19 Oct; 28, 29 Nov; 8, 25 Dec.

Andorra

The mountain principality in the **Pyrenees** is one of just a handful of rail-free countries in mainland Europe. Tacky shops and concrete aplenty in the capital but fine hiking and skiing in the hills around. The nearest you'll get to Andorra by train is Andorre-L'Hospitalet, just three kilometres from the border. There is no regular bus connection from that station. So your best bet from France is the express bus from Toulouse (thrice daily, taking 4 hrs). There are also **direct buses** to Andorra from Barcelona city centre and airport.

Essentials: Local name: Andorra – Population: 77k – Capital: Andorra la Vella – Currency: Euro (EUR) – Languages: Catalan (Spanish, Portuguese and French also widely spoken) – Accommodation costs: generally high – Plug types: C, F – Time zone: winter GMT+1, summer GMT+2 – International dialling code: +376 – Public holidays: 1, 6 Jan; 8 Feb; 14 Mar; Good Friday; Easter Mon; 1 May; Ascension Day; Whit Mon; 15 Aug; 8 Sep; 1 Nov; 8, 25, 26 Dec.

Austria

Austria feels very much at the **centre of Europe**. Staples in the promotional literature designed to woo visitors are lush green Alpine meadows, steep-roofed chalets with heavy wooden balconies full of geraniums, and onion-domed churches. But Austria has much more, with extremely beautiful lake regions and fine historic cities such as Salzburg and Vienna.

Essentials: Local name: Österreich – Population: 8.9m – Capital: Vienna/Wien – Currency: Euro (EUR) – Languages: German (English is widely spoken in tourist areas, Slovene minority in Carinthia) – Accommodation costs: generally high – Plug types: C, F – Time zone: winter GMT+1, summer GMT+2 – International dialling code: +43 – Public holidays: 1, 6 Jan; Easter Mon; 1 May; Ascension Day; Whit Mon; Corpus Christi; 15 Aug; 26 Oct; 1 Nov; 8, 25, 26 Dec.

Travel in Austria

Austria is most conspicuously included in this book in **Route 39** and **44**. In addition, **Route 38** crosses the country from north to south. Rail travel in Austria is very efficient. Trains are generally clean and modern, and the great majority of internal services run precisely to time. A big plus point for touring Austria by rail is that there are no compulsory reservations or supplements on day trains, including **Railjet high-speed trains**. International services (particularly night trains) arriving in Austria from Croatia, Slovenia, Romania and Hungary are prone to delays, and you should be cautious about relying on too tight connecting times when arriving on these trains.

There is an impressive programme of **infrastructure renewal**. The Koralm railway, a 130 km new route linking Styria and Carinthia is due to open in 2026. The country's principal operator is **Österreichische Bundesbahnen (ÖBB)**. ÖBB's impressive range of **night trains**, branded *Nightjet*, have done so much to revitalise Europe's night-train network – with Vienna very much the hub of that developing network. ÖBB has also been proactive in developing new daytime connections like the Eurocity service to Trieste which prompted Route 44 in this book.

Private operator **Westbahn (WB)** runs trains between Vienna and Bregenz (www.westbahn.at). **RegioJet** (novy.regiojet.cz) offers fast trains from Vienna to Prague, its bright yellow trains competing with Austrian and Czech Railjet services. Intercity Express (ICE) trains offer connections to and from Germany. The national rail website at www.oebb.at has a good journey planner and downloadable timetables.

Rail passes

Both Eurail and Interrail passes are valid (not just on ÖBB trains, but also on Westbahn and RegioJet services). Many areas within Austria have regional passes, some of which include private railways and local buses. For travel throughout the whole country, the **Einfach-Raus-Ticket** gives a day's second-class travel on regional trains for groups of 2–5 people from €36 (not before 09.00 Mon–Fri).

Other public transport options

Austria's long-distance bus network is run by Österreichische Bundesbahnen (ÖBB) under the **Postbus** brand. Bus stations are usually based by rail stations/post offices. International services are offered by Eurolines, RegioJet, Leo Express, Flixbus and others. City transport: tickets are cheaper from Tabak/Trafik booths. Taxis are metered.

Further information

Main website for tourist information: www.austria.info. In cities, look for green 'i' sign which indicates a tourist office (called a *Fremdenverkehrsbüro*).

Accommodation

Standards of cleanliness and comfort are usually high even in simpler places. *Gasthaus/Gasthof* indicates an inn and *Frühstückspension* a bed and breakfast place. **Independent hostels** are a good bet for both private rooms and beds in dorms, although they are mainly limited to the major cities and principal tourist destinations. More widespread, but more institutional, are *Jugendherbergen* (youth hostels), of which there are more than 100 around the country (www.oejhv.at).

Food and drink

Food tends towards the **hearty**, with wholesome soups and meat-dominated main courses (famously *Wiener Schnitzel* – a thin slice of fried veal or pork), while *Gulasch* (of Hungarian origin) and dumplings are also prevalent. Cakes may be sinfully cream-laden, high in calories, but are rarely sickly; *Apfelstrudel* is the best option for those watching their waistlines. Beer and wine are equally popular. The Austrians also take their **coffee** seriously.

Belarus

The Republic of Belarus gets into the news for all the wrong reasons. For some the country is a reminder of what the Soviet Union was like in its heyday. Events in early 2022 showed how Belarus is still very much subject to dictates from Moscow. **Disputed elections** in summer 2020 led to prolonged civil unrest. It's probably not high on your travel wish list so we have retired routes through Belarus for this 18th of *Europe by Rail*.

Essentials: Local name: Belarus/Беларусь – Population: 9.4m – Capital: Minsk/Мінск – Currency: Belarusian new rouble (BYN) – Languages: Russian and Belarusian (young people in urban areas might speak some English)

Travel in Belarus

There are **high-quality daytime services** on principal axes, and slow overnight trains linking provincial centres at opposite corners of the country. Reservation is compulsory on almost all long-distance trains. The website of **Belarusian Railways** (www.rw.by) is in Belarusian, Russian and English with good timetable information. Note that as of October 2024, all **international trains** (bar for those to and from Russia) remain suspended. Trains between Minsk and Russia's Baltic exclave in Kaliningrad travel through Lithuania without any scheduled stops.

Belgium

If people have told you Belgium is dull, ignore them! Belgium is homely, intimate and **immensely interesting**. It is a place to really explore, from the surreal urban landscapes of the coast, through historic cities like Bruges and Brussels, to the hill country of the Ardennes in the east and south-east of the country. You will find edgy modern culture cheek by jowl with magnificent mediaeval squares. Throw in some of Europe's finest **art nouveau architecture** and design, a population that is enviably multilingual, and you have a beguiling mix.

Essentials: Local name: Belgique/België – Population: 11.5m – Capital: Brussels/Bruxelles/Brussel – Currency: Euro (EUR) – Languages: Dutch (north), French (south), German (east); many speak both French and Dutch plus often English and/or German – Accommodation costs: generally high – Plug types: C, E – Time zone: winter GMT+1, summer GMT+2 – International dialling code: +32 – Public holidays: 1 Jan; Easter Mon; 1 May; Ascension Day; Whit Mon; 21 July; 15 Aug; 1, 11 Nov; 25 Dec.

Travel in Belgium

Belgium is on **Route 6** and **7** in his book. The country has a busy and efficient rail network, extending to the remotest corners of Belgium. All routes are served by frequent trains. In Brussels the **main hub** is the Midi/Zuid station. No reservations are required for domestic services, but seat reservations are compulsory on all Eurostar services. The national rail operator is **SNCB** (in French) or **NMBS** (in Dutch) and has its website at www.belgianrail.be. There are two sets of timetables, one for Mondays to Fridays and another for weekends. Beware that only Dutch or French spellings may be shown on departure boards; for example, the French city of Lille may be rendered at Dutch-speaking stations as Rijsel. Train categories: fast international trains connecting Belgium with its neighbours are Eurostars, Intercity Express trains (ICE) and TGVs. Night trains from Belgium are operated by **European Sleeper** and **Nightjet**. Otherwise you'll encounter regional Intercity (IC) trains and local stopping services.

Rail passes

Both Interrail and Eurail are valid. There are a number of discounted passes for people under the age of 26. **Weekend tickets** give 50% discount, and there is an off-peak fare cap for senior citizens.

Other public transport options

National bus companies are **De Lijn** (Flanders), **TEC** (Wallonia, i.e. the French-speaking area), and **STIB** (Brussels); there are only a few long-distance buses. Buses, trams and metros: board at any door with ticket or buy ticket from driver. Fares depend on length of journey, but are cheaper if bought before boarding. Tram and bus stops: red and white signs (all stops are request only – raise your hand).

Further information
Websites: www.walloniebelgiquetourisme.be (Wallonia and Brussels), www.visitflanders.com (Flanders). *Office du Tourisme* (French), *Toerisme* (Dutch) and *Verkehrsamt* (German).

Accommodation
Hotels tend to be **pricey**, and during the summer months it is advisable to book ahead when visiting the main cities and tourist destinations. In business hubs like Brussels and Antwerp, hotels might offer greatly discounted prices on weekends. If you arrive without a reservation, the tourist office can help find a bed.

As with many things in Belgium there are two official youth hostel organisations, the Vlaamse Jeugdherbergen (www.jeugdherbergen.be) and the **Les Auberges de Jeunesse** (www.lesaubergesdejeunesse.be). Independent hostels are often more relaxed and friendly.

Food and drink
Most restaurants have good-value fixed-price menus (*plat du jour, tourist menu, dagschotel*). Establishments in the main squares can charge two or three times as much as similar places in nearby streets. Try waffles (*wafels/gaufres*) and sweet or savoury pancakes (*crêpes*), mussels (*moules*) and freshly baked pastries. The **most common snacks** are *frieten/frites* (French fries with mayonnaise or other sauce). Belgium produces literally hundreds of types of **beer** (both dark and light); wheat beer (*blanche*) comes with a slice of lemon in it in the summer.

Bosnia and Herzegovina

'The heart-shaped land' claim the tourist brochures produced by the Sarajevo government, trying to give a suitably warm and cuddly feel to a country that has had a very difficult time since the demise of socialist Yugoslavia. The country has two 'entities' which operate in many respects as independent states. One is referred to as the **Federation** and the other as **Republika Srpska**. The tiny **Brčko district** remains apart from either entity. But cut through the troubled politics and you'll discover a country with a rich Ottoman history, superb landscape and, in Sarajevo, one of Europe's most interesting capital cities.

Essentials: Local name: Bosna i Hercegovina/Босна и Херцеговина – Population: 3.8m – Capital: Sarajevo – Currency: Convertible mark (BAM) – Languages: Bosnian, Croatian, Serbian (young people will speak some English; try German in northern Bosnia & western Herzegovina) – Accommodation costs: generally low – Plug types: C, F – Time zone: winter GMT+1, summer GMT+2 – International dialling code: +387

Travel in Bosnia and Herzegovina

Sarajevo has no significant international train services. The Talgo trains from the capital to Mostar were extended to Ploče on the Croatian coast at weekends in summer 2024. The only station with year-round international departures in the country is Štrpci on the **Belgrade to Bar railway**. Given this lack of international connectivity, we have not included any journeys for Bosnia and Herzegovina in this 18th edition of *Europe by Rail*. But if the woeful state of cross-border rail in the western Balkans improves, then we shall most certainly reintroduce routes in the next edition of this book.

Rail passes
Eurail and Interrail global passes are valid, but there are no Interrail or Eurail one-country passes for Bosnia and Herzegovina. Domestic rail fares are very cheap.

Other public transport options
Both public and private bus companies (and *marshrutkas*) connect every city and most villages within the country. One long-standing company with a good bus network hubbed on Sarajevo is **Centrotrans-Eurolines** (www.centrotrans.com).

Bulgaria

Bulgaria joined the EU in 2007, and then was admitted to the Schengen area in spring 2024. The **Black Sea nation** which has come a long way since political plurality was introduced in November 1989. The Bulgarian coast has long been popular with summer visitors, but now travellers are discovering the beauty of the Bulgarian mountains. There are remarkable **monasteries and old cities**, the latter often revealing a rich vein of Ottoman influence.

Essentials: Local name: Balgarija/България – Population: 6.9m – Capital: Sofia/София – Currency: Lev (BGN); credit cards increasingly accepted – Languages: Bulgarian (English, German, Russian and French in tourist areas); nodding the head indicates 'no', shaking it means 'yes' – Accommodation costs: generally low – Plug types: C, F – Time zone: winter GMT+2, summer GMT+3 – International dialling code: +359 – Public holidays: 1 Jan; 3 Mar; Orthodox Easter Sunday and Monday; 1, 6, 24 May; 6, 22 Sept; 25, 26 Dec.

Travel in Bulgaria

Bulgaria might not have the fastest, most modern or most frequent services in Europe, but the network covers the major cities and there are good services linking Sofia with the Black Sea resorts. International rail links are abysmal. As of October 2024, there are no regular passenger services on the cross border railways into Greece and Serbia. Your choice is limited to one train each day to Turkey and two to Romania – one from Ruse and the other from Vidin which uses the **New Europe Bridge** over the Danube. It is scandalous that this new bridge isn't used by more trains.

Rail passes
Interrail is valid, as is Eurail and the Balkan Flexipass. Domestic rail fares are cheap.

OTHER PUBLIC TRANSPORT OPTIONS
There is a **good bus network**, with buses often slightly more expensive than trains. Yet both modes of transport are very cheap compared with western Europe. Sofia: buses and trams use the same ticket but note that there are different tickets for the subway. Punch your ticket at machines after boarding and get a new ticket if you change.

FURTHER INFORMATION
The website of the Bulgarian tourist association is at www.bulgariatravel.org.

CROATIA

First of the countries to break from the Yugoslav fold by controversially declaring independence in 1991, Croatia joined the European Union in July 2013. This deeply Catholic country is blessed with a vast stretch of **Adriatic coast**. Over a thousand islands are dotted along Croatia's sinewy littoral. The area north and west of the capital, Zagreb, is mountainous, while to the east are the vast Slavonian plains, the area worst hit by the 1990s war.

Essentials: Local name: Hrvatska – Population: 3.9m – Capital: Zagreb – Currency: Kuna (HRK) – Languages: Croatian (English, German and Italian spoken in tourist areas) – Accommodation costs: medium – Plug types: C, F – Time zone: winter GMT+1, summer GMT+2 – International dialling code: +385 – Public holidays: 1, 6 Jan; Good Friday; Easter Mon; 1 May; Corpus Christi; 22, 25 June; 5, 15 Aug; 8 Oct; 1 Nov; 25–26 Dec. Many local saints' holidays.

TRAVEL IN CROATIA

Croatia is on **Route 50** in this edition of *Europe by Rail*. Hubbed on Zagreb, the Croatian rail network covers the main towns but services can be infrequent, particularly on the superbly scenic Zagreb to Split route (see Route 50). The modern air-conditioned diesel trains on this route (tilting trains, classified ICN) require compulsory reservation, as do a handful of Intercity (IC) trains elsewhere. For **Dubrovnik** you will need to take a bus or ferry from Split. The national railway company is **Hrvatske Željeznice (HŽ)** with its website at www.hzpp.hr. In recent years, the Croatian rail network has been substantially trimmed due to public spending cuts. This has particularly affected international services. As of October 2024, passenger train services with both Serbia and Bosnia are suspended. But there are daytime connections to Slovenia and Austria, and in summer 2024 a new direct service from **Rijeka** to Italy was introduced. Train categories: apart from ICN and IC trains, there is a limited number of Eurocity (EC) services linking Croatia with Austria.

RAIL PASSES
Interrail and Eurail passes are valid; domestic rail fares are cheap.

OTHER PUBLIC TRANSPORT OPTIONS
Jadrolinija (www.jadrolinija.hr) runs many **domestic ferry lines** with hubs in Rijeka, Split and Dubrovnik. You can use the complex network of ferry services along the Dalmatian

coast to create some great sightseeing mini-cruises. The seasonal Split to Dubrovnik ferry service is one of the best. Another of our favourites is the Zadar to Rijeka route, which gives 11 hours afloat and requires an overnight stop at the island port of Mali Lošinj (a community which was Italian until 1947). **Long-distance buses** are often faster than trains.

Further information
The website of the Croatian National Tourist Board is at www.croatia.hr.

Accommodation
Hotel prices, especially along the coast in high season, can be expensive, although if you travel at other times of the year some incredible bargains can be had. For those on a real budget, there are an increasing number of **hostels in Croatia**, both official (www.hicroatia.com) and independent – although the latter are concentrated in Zagreb, Dubrovnik and Split, with a handful on the islands. Private rooms (*sobe*) are also a good option, both for price and the chance to get to know your hosts.

Food and drink
Along the **Dalmatian coast**, fish and other seafood predominate. Inland, meat in all its guises and dairy produce rule. Look out for roadside restaurants serving *janjetina* (lamb) roasted whole on a spit. Another traditional method of preparing meat is in a *peka*, a large iron pot with a dome-shaped lid, buried to cook under glowing embers. You can get excellent fresh produce in **local markets**. Top-of-the-range **wines** are pricey but can be excellent. Try Croatia's distinctive orange wine. Mix red wine with still water and enjoy *bevanda* – a less headache-inducing method of savouring **rich red wine** under the Adriatic sun. White wine can have similar treatment with sparkling water to make refreshing *gemišt*. Coffee (*kava*) is often served as espresso or cappuccino in bars, though some families prepare it Turkish-style at home.

Cyprus

It's over 70 years since the last passenger trains ran in Cyprus. A 122-km **narrow-gauge line** ran across the centre of the island from west to east. Interestingly, it broadly paralleled the Green Line (and the UN administered buffer zone) which now divides the Turkish Republic of North Cyprus (TRNC) from the Greek-dominated southern half of the island. Had the trains not been axed for economic reasons in 1951, the railway would almost certainly have become the victim of politics in the 1970s. The heyday of the Cyprus Government Railway (CGR) is recalled in the **Cyprus Railways Museum**, housed in the beautifully restored former railway station near Evrychou in the Troodos mountains. Nowadays, the best way to get around Cyprus is by bus.

Essentials (Cyprus): Local name: Κυπριακή Δημοκρατία – Population: 1.1m – Capital: Nicosia – Currency: Euro (EUR) – Languages: Greek (English widely spoken) – Accommodation costs: medium – Plug type: G – Time zone: winter GMT+2, summer GMT+3 – International dialling code: +357 – Public holidays: 1,6 Jan; Orthodox Ash Monday; 25 Mar; 1 Apr; Orthodox Good Friday and Easter Monday; 1 May; Orthodox Whit Monday; 15 Aug; 1, 28 Oct; 25-26 Dec.

Essentials (TRNC): Local name: Kuzey Kıbrıs Türk Cumhuriyeti – Population: 0.32m – Capital: North Nicosia – Currency: Turkish lira (TRY) – Languages: Turkish – Accommodation costs: generally low – Plug type: G – Time zone: winter GMT+2, summer GMT+3 – International dialling code: +90392 – Public holidays: 1 Jan; 23 Apr; 1, 19 May; 20 July; 1, 30 Aug; 29 Oct; 15 Nov; Mawlid; Eid al-Fitr, Eid al-Adha.

Czech Republic

One half of former Czechoslovakia which, having defiantly despatched a lacklustre communist government with the **Velvet Revolution** in autumn 1989, then proceeded to a Velvet Divorce less than four years later. With that split from Slovakia, the Czech Republic was born. The move to a market economy hasn't always been easy.

An urban elite in Prague has undoubtedly made good, but in more rural areas the supposed benefits of capitalism are not so evident. You'll run across stunning areas of **mountains and forests**, towns with delightful squares, sleepy villages and imposing castles.

Essentials: Local name: Česká republika – Population: 10.7m – Capital: Prague/Praha – Currency: Czech koruna (CZK) – Languages: Czech (English is widely spoken among young people, especially in the cities. German and Russian are also encountered, particularly among older folk) – Accommodation costs: medium – Plug types: C, E – Time zone: winter GMT+1, summer GMT+2 – International dialling code: +420 – Public holidays: 1 Jan; Good Friday; Easter Mon; 1, 8 May; 5, 6 July; 28 Sept; 28 Oct; 17 Nov; 24–26 Dec.

Travel in the Czech Republic

Route 32 and **33** both traverse the Czech Republic, connecting with each other in Prague. The well-run and generally punctual rail network covers every corner of the country, with express trains hourly or every two hours on most routes. **High-speed trains** classified SuperCity (SC) are the only trains to require compulsory reservation. Smart **Railjet** (RJ) trains are used on the Prague – Brno – Vienna axis. If you have time on your hands, however, there is no better way to explore than on the many slow and rural routes, often operated by **vintage railcars**, which criss-cross the countryside.

The national rail company is **České Dráhy (ČD)** with its website at www.cd.cz. The winds of competition are bringing change. ČD now competes with private operators **RegioJet** (www.regiojet.cz) and **Leo Express** (www.le.cz) on the route from Prague to Ostrava. Train categories: apart from high-speed SC and RJ trains, the Czech Republic operates fast trains ('R' for rychlík), semi-fast trains ('Sp' for spešný) and slow, local trains ('Os' for osobný).

Rail passes
Interrail and Eurail passes are both valid. A wide range of great-value regional day passes is available, including several which include border areas of Germany or Poland. A *celodenní jízdenka* **one-day countrywide** ticket costs (2024 price) just 699 Czech crowns (about €29).

Other public transport options
The Czech Republic has a good long-distance **bus network**, run by **RegioJet** (www.regiojet.cz) and other private companies. You can buy tickets from the driver.

Further information
The website of the Czech tourism association is at www.visitczechrepublic.com.

Accommodation
There is a **wide choice of accommodation types** in the Czech Republic, from standard hotels to private rooms and pensions, and an ever-increasing number of hostels (www.czechhostels.com). Quality in the more budget hotels can often leave a lot to be desired, so for the cost-conscious a private room might be a better choice. The well-developed network of independent hostels concentrates on favourite backpacker destinations such as Prague, Olomouc, Brno and Český Krumlov.

Food and drink
Czech cuisine is **hearty**, and features lashings of meat with cream-based sauces, but vegetarian options include fried cheese (*smažený sýr*), risotto and salads. **Pork with cabbage and dumplings** (*vepřová pečeně s knedlíkem a sezelím*) is on virtually every menu, as is *guláš*, a bland beef stew. The cost of eating and drinking is reasonable. *Kavárny* and *cukrány* serve coffee and very sweet pastries. Pubs (*pivnice*) and wine bars (*vinárny*) are good places to eat. Czech beers are excellent, as is Moravian wine.

Denmark
Situated between the Baltic and the North Sea, watery Denmark incorporates **some 400 islands**, 75 of which are inhabited, as well as the peninsula of Jutland. It is low-lying and undramatic terrain, where you sense you're never far from the sea. The **long maritime tradition** inflects the townscapes too, a reminder that even towns that now seem well inland (like Roskilde) once lived from the sea. While an impressive programme of bridge-building has linked many of Denmark's islands, you will still need to take to ferries to reach remote islands – the most distinctive of which is Bornholm.

Essentials: Local name: Danmark – Population: 5.9m – Capital: Copenhagen/ København – Currency: Danish kroner (DKK) – Languages: Danish (English is almost universally spoken) – Accommodation costs: generally high – Plug Types: C, E, F, K – Time zone: winter GMT+1, summer GMT+2 – International dialling code: +45 – Public holidays: 1 Jan; Maundy Thursday–Easter Monday; Common Prayer Day (4th Fri after Easter); Ascension Day; Whit Mon; 5 June; 24–26 Dec.

Travel in Denmark

Denmark features on **Route 25** and **26** in this book. **Route 27** starts in Denmark but then immediately crosses the Øresund into Sweden and continues to Norway. Denmark's efficient rail network relies on modern and frequent Intercity (IC) services that fan out from Copenhagen's main station, usually abbreviated to København H, which also has frequent trains **across the Øresund** to Malmö in Sweden. There is a rail-sea link to the Danish island of **Bornholm** via Ystad. There is currently quite some investment in national transport infrastructure Wk is underway on a new tunnel from Rødby to the German island of Fehmarn. You don't need to reserve on Intercity trains but it is recommended at busy times. Most IC trains have refreshment trolleys.

Danske Statsbaner (DSB), www.dsb.dk, is the principal operator, although ever more regional services are run by private operators such as **Arriva** (www.arriva.dk). There is a national multi-modal **journey planner** at www.rejseplanen.dk which includes an English and a German version. Train categories: Denmark's IC services are complemented by fast Intercity Lyn (ICL) trains – which stop less frequently than ICs – and frequent, but slower RE services.

Rail passes
Interrail and Eurail are valid.

Other public transport options
Long-distance travel is easiest by train but there are also excellent regional and city bus services, many dovetailing with trains. **Ferries** or bridges link all the big islands.

Further information
The website of the Danish National Tourist Board is at www.visitdenmark.com.

Accommodation

Hotels in Denmark are of a high standard, and can be expensive. In rural areas the **old inns**, known as *kros*, are charming places to stay and often have good restaurants serving traditional food. There are around 100 official (HI) hostels (*vandrerhjem*), and the general standard is excellent, which might explain why the growth of independent hostels in the country has not been as dramatic as elsewhere. Check out www.danhostel.dk for more details. If you enjoy **camping**, you will find a wide choice of campsites, many of which also offer self-catering cabins which can work out great value for those travelling in a small group.

Food and drink

Danish cuisine is simple, based on **excellent local produce**; standards are uniformly high, but with prices to match. Look for *dagens ret* (today's special), which is noticeably cheaper than eating à la carte. **Fish** features a lot – most commonly herring served in a sauce. *Smørrebrød* are elaborately topped open sandwiches of meat, fish or cheese with accompaniments, served on *rugbrød* (rye bread) or *franskbrød* (wheat bread). You can also try filling up on the ubiquitous *frikadeller* (pork meatballs). There are many **local lagers** in addition to the internationally known Carlsberg and Tuborg. The local firewater is akvavit. All alcohol is expensive.

Estonia

Smallest of the three **Baltic States**, Estonia joined the European Union in 2004. The country looks more to Finland than its Baltic neighbours to the south. Estonia offers a fetching mixture of forests with old manorial estates. You will also find some strikingly beautiful coast, desolate islands and appealing lake country. Relations with **adjacent Russia** are very tense following Russia's invasion of Ukraine in February 2022, and all cross-border rail services into Russia are suspended. Limited bus services are still operating.

Essentials: Local name: Eesti – Population: 1.3m – Capital: Tallinn – Currency: Euro (EUR) – Languages: Estonian, Russian (English is widely spoken, though less so in rural areas) – Accommodation costs: medium – Plug types: C, F – Time zone: winter GMT+2, summer GMT+3 – International dialling code: +372 – Public holidays: 1 Jan; 24 Feb; Good Fri; 1 May; 23 June (Victory Day), 24 June; 20 Aug; 24–26 Dec.

Travel in Estonia

Estonia has a reasonable network of regional railways radiating from Tallinn. Trains run east to Narva and south-east via Tartu to Koidula. The excursion from Tallinn to Koidula and back makes a fine excursion from the capital. Another route south via Tartu runs to **Valga**, on the Latvian border, whence there is a slow onward connection to Riga. That once-daily opportunity to escape into Latvia is Estonia's sole international rail offering.

Rail passes
Eurail and Interrail are valid. There are no local rail passes, but fares are cheap.

Other public transport options
Bus services are often fast, clean and more efficient than rail services (see web.peatus.ee for routes and timetables). Book international services in advance from bus stations or online at www.luxexpress.eu. Pay the driver at rural stops or small towns.

Further information
The official tourism website is at www.visitestonia.com.

Accommodation

There should be no problem with accommodation in Estonia, which has a variety of hostels and **inexpensive hotels**. Prices in Tallinn are often twice as high as elsewhere. Home stays offer accommodation in farmhouses, summer cottages, homes and small boarding houses. For hostels, the **Estonian Youth Hostel Association** can make reservations at 40 hostels throughout the country (www.hostels.ee), whilst Tallinn in particular has seen a massive growth in independent, backpacker-orientated establishments.

FOOD AND DRINK

Particularly outside Tallinn, many **restaurants close early** in the evenings, so you may think of lunch as a main meal opportunity. For value, look to the dish of the day (*päevapraad*). Cheap cuts of meat, particularly pork, with potatoes and bread are staples. Not a place for the sweet-toothed or for vegetarians. Estonian **beers** (both dark and light) have a growing reputation.

FAROE ISLANDS

This curious little island polity in the **North Atlantic** has loose links to Denmark, but enjoys a high measure of independence with its own parliament. There are stunning wild mountain and coastal landscapes across 17 inhabited islands which are linked by efficient ferries, bridges and undersea road tunnels. Railways do not really feature, the sole exception being a winch-operated incline railway at the harbour in Gjógr on the island of Eysturoy. The Faroes are easily reached by ship from Hirtshals in Denmark (see **Route 26**). Also see our Sidetracks feature on p254.

Essentials: Local name: Føroyar – Population: 53k – Capital: Tórshavn – Currency: Faroese króna – Language: Faroese, Danish (English widely understood) – Accommodation costs: generally high – Plug Types: C, E, F, K – Time zone: winter GMT, summer GMT+1 – International dialling code: +298 – Public holidays: 1 Jan; Maundy Thur; Good Friday; Easter Mon; 22, 25 April; Prayer Day (4th Fri after Easter); 5 May; Whit Mon; 29 July; 24–26, 31 Dec.

FINLAND

Often classified as part of Scandinavia, Finland is a world apart from the two Scandinavian neighbours with which it shares common borders, Norway and Sweden. The cultural landscape reflects Finland's historic links with Russia, even to the extent that the Orthodox Church is an official state church. The **Grand Duchy of Finland** was part of the Russian Empire until 1917. The west of the country has a good dose of Swedish influence. Pure air, glistening lakes, an **abundance of wildlife** and deep winter snow all help sustain Finland's appeal to travellers.

Essentials: Local name: Suomi – Population: 5.5m – Capital: Helsinki – Currency: Euro (EUR) – Languages: Finnish (Sámi in the north, Swedish on the west coast); Swedish, the country's second official language, often appears on signs after the Finnish (English widely spoken, esp. in Helsinki) – Accommodation costs: generally high – Plug Types: C, F – Time zone: winter GMT+2, summer GMT+3 – International dialling code: +358 – Public holidays: 1, 6 Jan; Good Friday; Easter Mon; 1 May; Ascension Day; Whit Sun; Midsummer's Day (Sat falling 20–26 June); 1 Nov; 6, 25–26 Dec.

Travel in Finland

Finland has a very efficient rail network, with **national operator VR** (www.vr.fi) running comfortable Pendolino, Intercity and night sleeper trains radiating out from Helsinki to regional centres across the country. Two lines in Finland extend beyond the **Arctic Circle**. These are the railways to Kolari and Kemijärvi, both served directly by overnight trains from the capital, in each case a journey of more than 13 hours. Don't underestimate the size of Finland. What is other countries would normally be referred to as first and second class are brands Ekstra and Eco respectively in Finland.

On longer-distance trains, including many overnight services, you will find **excellent restaurant cars**. For a small premium over the regular fare, you can reserve a seat in the restaurant area. There's not a lot of high-speed running, although the Pendolinos do dash along at over 200 kph on the line out of Helsinki towards Lahti. There are no cross-border rail services.

Rail passes
Both Interrail and Eurail are valid.

Other public transport options
There's a good long-distance bus network run in the main by **Matkahuolto** (www.matkahuolto.fi) and **Expressbus** (www.expressbus.fi). Timetables for trains, buses and boats dovetail conveniently. Matkahuolto has timetables online. Buses: stops are usually identified by the symbol of a black bus on a yellow background (for local services) and a white bus on a blue background for longer distances. It is cheaper to buy tickets from stations or agents than on board. Bus stations usually have good facilities.

Further information
Main website of Finnish tourism association is at www.visitfinland.com.

Accommodation

Hotels tend to be stylish, **immaculate and pricey**. Budget travellers might want to check out *matkustajakoti* (relatively cheap guesthouses) or the nearly 50 hostels (*retkeilymajat*) that are well spread across the country (www.hostellit.fi). Note that not all hostels are open year-round. **Campsites** are widespread too (about 350; around 200 belong to the Finnish Campingsite Association www.camping.fi). Rough camping is generally allowed providing you keep 150 m from residents and remove any trace of your stay.

Food and drink

Fixed-price menus in a *ravintola* (upmarket restaurant) are the best value, or you may want to try a *grilli* (fast-food stand), *kahvila* (self-service cafeteria) or a *baari* (snack bar). For self-caterers, try Alepa, Siwa, K-market or Valintatalo supermarkets. Some specials are *muikunmäti* (a **freshwater fish roe** served with onions and cream and accompanied by toast or pancakes) and for dessert *kiisseli* (literally 'berry fool'). Finns are very dedicated coffee drinkers. Lower-alcohol beers are sold in supermarkets, but for stronger beers and all wines and spirits, turn to **Alko**, the aptly named state-owned distributor of stronger drinks.

FRANCE

France boasts such **varied culture and heritage**, so rich a mix of scenery and architecture, that you could comfortably return every year of a long life and still discover something new. Impressive mediaeval cities in the north, although humdrum landscapes. Move to the centre for wilderness, east for the **Alps**, and south for sun, sea and sand. Throw in fine food and wine to create the perfect ensemble. But be warned! Try it once and you may become an addict who can never be weaned off the country that is by far the most popular destination for tourists on the planet. We have greatly improved our coverage of France in this 18th edition of *Europe by Rail*.

Essentials: Local name: France – Population: 67.4m – Capital: Paris – Currency: Euro (EUR) – Language: French (many people speak some English, particularly in Paris) – Accommodation costs: generally high – Plug Types: C, E – Time zone: winter GMT+1, summer GMT+2 – International dialling code: +33 – Public holidays: 1 Jan; Easter Mon; 1, 8 May; Ascension Day; Whit Mon; 14 July; 15 Aug; 1, 11 Nov; 25 Dec. If on Thur, many places also close Mon or Fri.

TRAVEL IN FRANCE

France is on **Route 13 to 19** in this book. In addition, **Route 6, 7** and **45** all start in France but then quickly cross into neighbouring countries. France's well-developed **high-speed network** means we now take for granted that journeys such as Paris to Marseille (750 km) take little more than three hours. Many parts of France have similarly impressive journey times from Paris by high-speed TGV, although in contrast cross-country routes can often be slow and infrequent. France is not a country for hopping on and off trains at will, since reservation is compulsory on almost all **TGV** and most **Intercité** services; some TGV trains have only a limited allocation of seats for pass holders. Fares are higher during peak travel periods. Tickets (not passes) must be validated in the orange composteurs at the entrance to platforms. Domestic **night trains** have couchettes (and often reclining seats), sleeping cars being confined to the Nightjet services from Paris to Berlin and Vienna.

The national operator is *Société Nationale des Chemins de fer Français* or **SNCF** for short with its website www.sncf-connect.com. Train categories: apart from high-speed TGV services, France has Intercité trains which are long-distance services running at slower speeds (they do not use the high-speed lines which are the backbone of the TGV network). In 2024, SNCF further extended its offering of TGVs running under the **low-cost Ouigo** brand. These can be very cheap, but Interrail and Eurail passes are not accepted at all. The country also has a good network of slower **regional**

services (TER) and creative travellers (or pass holders who have an ideological objection to paying for seat reservations on high-speed services) can devise itineraries which cross the entire country on TER trains. In our view, those services – though never fast – often offer the very best rail travel in France.

Rail passes
Interrail and Eurail passes are valid, but beware the supplements on French TGV services. Note that the price of a **pass-holder's supplement** depends on many routes on how full a train is. So it is worth booking well in advance.

Other public transport options
The **métro systems in Paris** and several other major cities are clean, efficient and relatively cheap. For urban and peri-urban transport, carnets (multiple-ticket packs) are cheaper than individual tickets. Bus and train timetables are available from bus and train stations and tourist offices; usually free. Always ask if your rail pass is valid on local transport. Bus services may be infrequent after 20.30 and on Sun. Rural areas are often poorly served.

Further information
The official website for French tourism is at www.france.fr.

Accommodation

For hotels, **half-board** (i.e. breakfast and evening meal included) can be excellent value in smaller towns and villages. As elsewhere in Europe, budget hotels are often clustered near stations. In summer, it is advisable to book ahead in larger towns and resort areas. **Gîtes de France** produces directories of B&Bs, *gîtes d'étape*, farm accommodation and holiday house rentals for each département (www.gites-de-france.com).

There are hundreds of **hostels** in France, including those which are members of Hostelling International (HI; www.fuaj.org) and those more independently minded. The useful website www.hostelz.com offers listings of both types. **Camping** is a national obsession, and there are hundreds of campsites all across France. Camping municipal is usually basic but cheap.

Food and drink

France's **gastronomic reputation** often lives up to its promise, providing you're prepared to look beyond mere tourist fodder such as *steak frites* (steak and fries). In restaurants, eating à la carte can be expensive, but the menu (set menu, of which there may be several) or the plat du jour (dish of the day) is often superb value, especially at lunchtime.

Coffees and beers can be surprisingly expensive: **wine** is generally cheaper – order a *pichet* of house red (*rouge*), white (*blanc*) or *rosé*. If you ask for *café*, you'll get a small black coffee; coffee with milk is *café crème*. Tea is usually served black. Beer is mostly yellow, cold, French and fizzy, though gourmet and **foreign beers are popular**. *Une pression* or *un demi* is draught beer, better value than bottled. Baguettes with a variety of fillings from cafés and stalls are cheap – as are *crêpes* and *galettes* (sweet and savoury pancakes). **Morning markets** are excellent for stocking up on picnic items.

GERMANY

Germany, bang in the middle of Europe, is hard to miss. Nor should anyone wish to: from the heathlands of the north to the Alpine peaks of the south there is **scenery galore**. There are idyllic offshore islands and sandy beaches on both the North Sea and the Baltic coasts, great tracts of lakes and forests, especially in the north-east, and **three of Europe's great rivers**: the Rhine, the Danube and the Elbe. Plus a galaxy of historic cities including Cologne, Hamburg, Munich, Berlin and Dresden.

Essentials: Local name: Deutschland – Population: 83m – Capital: Berlin – Currency: Euro (EUR) – Language: German (English and French widely spoken in the west, less so in the east) – Accommodation costs: medium – Plug types: C, F – Time zone: winter GMT+1, summer GMT+2 – International dialling code: +49 – Public holidays: 1, 6* Jan; Good Friday; Easter Mon; 1 May, Ascension Day; Whit Mon; Corpus Christi*, 15 Aug*; 3, 31 Oct*; 1 Nov*; 25, 26 Dec; (*religious feasts celebrated as public holiday only in certain German states.)

TRAVEL IN GERMANY

Germany features principally on **Route 9 to 12** in this volume. In addition, **Route 7, 31, 32, 33, 36, 37** and **38** all touch German territory as part of longer international journeys. The country's comprehensive and generally efficient rail network is served by many different types of train, from sleek **high-speed Intercity Express** (ICE) trains and the less modern Intercity (IC) and Eurocity (EC) services to **sleepy rural branch lines** winding along picturesque river valleys. There are no compulsory reservations on daytime trains and no supplements for pass holders. ICE services generally have on-board refreshments (either a restaurant car or a board bistro), IC and EC trains often have a board bistro. There are good facilities at main-line stations, such as showers and lockers. Principal operator is **Deutsche Bahn (DB)**, www.bahn.de, but there are also many private operators of regional trains, which in terms of fares and timetables are fully integrated into the national rail system. The long-distance operator **Flixtrain** stands apart; it has its own ticketing system. DB runs some overnight ICE and IC trains, but has pulled out of the market for proper night trains (ie. with sleepers and couchettes). The latter are run mainly by ÖBB under their **Nightjet** brand with routes from Düsseldorf, Cologne and Hamburg to Innsbruck, Vienna and Zurich. There are also **overnight services** from Berlin to south-west Germany and Switzerland, from Berlin to Paris, Vienna, Stockholm and Budapest, as well as from Munich to Italy, Croatia and Hungary.

RAIL PASSES

The full range of Interrail and Eurail passes are valid on all trains other than those operated by Flixtrain. A **German Rail Pass** is available for those living outside Europe; residents of Europe can buy the Interrail One-Country Pass. A range of regional **Ländertickets** is available (from €22 for one person, from €33 for groups of up to 5 people), giving the freedom to roam any day of the week on all but the fastest trains through one or more of the federal states of Germany or often even over Germany's borders.

OTHER PUBLIC TRANSPORT OPTIONS
Most large cities have U-Bahn (U) underground railway and S-Bahn (S) urban rail services. **City travel passes** cover both and other public transport, including ferries in some cities. International passes usually cover S-Bahn. A day card (*Tagesnetzkarte*) or multi-ride ticket (*Mehrfahrtenkarte*) usually pays its way if you take more than three rides.

FURTHER INFORMATION
The website of the German National Tourist Office is at www.germany.travel. Tourist offices (marked by white 'i' on a blue background) are usually near stations and have English-speaking staff. Most offer room-finding services.

ACCOMMODATION

You'll find a range of accommodation options at **all price levels** in Germany, but prices for rooms of comparable standards vary enormously across the country. Areas that were, until 1990, part of the GDR still offer the best value, and Berlin is noticeably cheaper than, say, Munich. *Pensionen* (pensions) and *Privatzimmer* (private rooms) are particularly good value. In many cities, a new generation of design-orientated budget hotels are providing rooms of high quality at reasonable prices. Hostel accommodation is widely available in Germany, and the country has a network of **independent hostels** (www.german-hostels.de). There are also around 600 official (HI) Jugendherbergen (youth hostels) which often cater to school groups and can have an institutional feel. The **Deutscher Camping-Club** (DCC) (www.camping-club.de), compiles each year a list of 1,600 camping sites.

FOOD AND DRINK

Germans tend to have biological clocks that run in advance of the rest of Europe. Families at home eat early, with supper often done and dusted by soon after six. In restaurants, hotels and hostels expect breakfast from 06.30 to 10.00. Lunch is around 12.00–14.00 (from 11.30 in rural areas) and dinner 18.00–20.30 (but much later in cities). Breakfast is often substantial (and usually included in the price of a room), consisting of a variety of bread, cheese, cold meats and often eggs. For lunch, the best value is the **daily menu** (*Tageskarte*); in rural parts of southern Germany, there's often a **snack menu** (*Vesperkarte*) from mid-afternoon onwards.

Traditional German cuisine is widespread, both in towns and rural areas, and traditional recipes, which vary greatly by region, are produced with pride. Expect **hearty** fare, with large portions, and often **good value**. Look for home-made soups, high-quality meat, piquant marinated pot roasts (known as *Sauerbraten*) and creamy sauces. For really cheap but generally appetising eats, there are *Imbisse* (stalls) serving *Kartoffelsalat* (potato salad) and *Wurst* (sausage) in its numerous variations, plus fish in the north. Rural Germany can be quite challenging for vegetarians.

Great Britain

Great Britain consists of three countries: **England, Wales and Scotland**. **Route 1 to 5** and **13** all have an English dimension. **Route 2** and **3** showcase some of Scotland's finest railways, while **Route 4** and **5** traverse rural Wales. A stunning variety of landscapes and a lavish dose of history help make any visit to Britain very rewarding. But it can also provoke reflection. Britain stands curiously apart from the mainstream of European life. English nationalism, even isolationism, challenges the liberal consensus which has fostered European integration over the last half-century. After **having left the European Union** (in 2020) and then suffering terribly in the pandemic, Britain is forging a new future under a new government in 2024. It is a risky and uncertain time. Yet travel is a great way of fostering understanding – and it's for that very reason that we hope that rail travellers from the continent will soon be venturing to Britain again.

As of autumn 2024, residents of some European countries outside the European Union (and EEA) require **visas** to enter any part of the United Kingdom, and those visas are among the most expensive in the world. **Post-Brexit Britain** maintains strict border controls, and there's a national preoccupation with security. For many Europeans, a visit to Britain is like entering another world, but it's definitely interesting. Make time to explore beyond the big cities, and if you can visit **rural communities** in Yorkshire, south-west England, Wales or Scotland then you're in for a treat.

Essentials: Local name: United Kingdom – Population: 60.8m – Capital: London – Currency: Pound sterling (GBP) – Languages: English, Welsh, Gaelic – Accommodation costs: generally high – Plug type: G – Time zone: winter GMT, summer GMT+1 – International dialling code: +44 – Public holidays: 1 Jan; Good Friday; first and last Mon in May; 25–26 Dec. Further regional holidays.

Travel in Britain

Britain has an **extensive rail network**, and services are by no means as bad as most British residents would have you believe. Railways extend even to the distant extremities of the British mainland and those willing to book in advance can secure some of the cheapest tickets in Europe for long-distance journeys. The downside is crowded trains. That said, the first-class service on some main-line trains is often very good. Check www.nationalrail.co.uk for prices and to buy tickets.

The system of rail franchising effectively collapsed during the pandemic and there are now plans to take the railways back into public ownership. For now, train services are sill run by more than **two dozen different operators**, but there's a fully integrated national ticketing scheme. Unless you board a train at a station with no facilities for ticket purchase, you are required to have a ticket before boarding the train. The penalties for infringement are unusually severe. Compared with some other countries, trains in Britain can be noisy spaces. Security announcements on trains on some routes have become a veritable litany of terror.

Rail passes

Britain has been a long-standing member of the Interrail programme, and since 2019 Eurail passes are now also accepted. While you may wish to reserve a seat on busy routes, there's no obligation to do so, and the good news is that, bar for overnight sleeper services, there are absolutely **no rail pass supplements** in Britain. For travellers visiting only Great Britain, the **Britrail Pass** can be an excellent choice.

Other public transport options

For **long-distance coach travel** in England, check www.nationalexpress.com. For main Scottish bus routes see www.citylink.co.uk. Principal Welsh bus services are covered by www.trawscymru.info (with free travel available at weekends on many Welsh routes). Britain has one of Europe's best networks of local bus services. Find times at www.traveline.info.

As befits a maritime nation, there's a good network of ferry services in and around Britain's coastal waters. In Cornwall, for example, there are more than a dozen ferry routes which form part of the regular public transport network. Services in the Clyde and Hebrides area are provided by **CalMac** (www.calmac.co.uk) while ferry services to Orkney and Shetland are provided by **NorthLink** (www.northlinkferries.co.uk).

Further information

The official tourism website of Great Britain is available at www.visitbritain.com.

Accommodation

The British seem to particularly favour the major chains of budget hotels which are cheap but soulless. We find that small owner-managed hotels are a much better choice, but they are often not cheap. There is an excellent range of accommodation in **pubs and inns**. Major online reservations channels like www.booking.com cover the full range of options. There's a buoyant independent hostels movement (see www.independenthostels.co.uk). **B&Bs** are an especially good option in smaller communities.

Food and drink

Standards and choice have greatly improved in recent years. The best of British cuisine now draws on a medley of Mediterranean and more exotic influences, and it's now one of the easiest regions to find top-quality **vegan and vegetarian choices**. The absence of good street markets means that many visitors are thrown back to shopping in supermarkets where too many products are chilled and pre-packed in plastic. But good, fresh produce is available and the best restaurants and inns have led the way in giving a much-needed creative edge to British dining. Expect a **brilliant range of**

beers, a good choice of wines (often imported from outside Europe), endless good cups of tea and some of Europe's most insipid coffee.

Greece

Still inexpensive, friendly and beautiful, and with a wonderful array of archaeological sites, Greece offers a seductive mix of **culture and relaxation**, with plenty of opportunity to linger in tavernas or laze on a beach as well as visiting ancient ruins. There is an edgy buzz about the capital, but it is easy to **escape to the islands**, some of which are full of cosmopolitan glitz, while others are refreshingly unspoilt and provincial.

Essentials: Local name: Elláda/Ελλάδα – Population: 10.6m – Capital: Athens/Αθήνα – Currency: Euro (EUR) – Language: Greek (English widely spoken in Athens and tourist areas; some German, French or Italian too, but less so in remote mainland areas) – Accommodation costs: medium – Plug types: C, F – Time zone: winter GMT+2, summer GMT+3 – International dialling code: +30 – Public holidays: 1, 6 Jan; Shrove Mon; 25 Mar; Orthodox Good Friday; Orthodox Easter Mon; 1 May; Whit Mon; 15 Aug; 28 Oct; 25, 26 Dec.

Travel in Greece

The state of rail travel in Greece reached an all-time low in the 2010s. Read our lament in the box on p436. The acquisition in 2017 of the national operator, **TrainOSE** (www.trainose.gr), by Trenitalia paved the way for renewal. Since then services on the main axis from **Thessaloniki to Athens** are much improved. The downside is that as a cost-saving measure there are no longer sleeping cars on the overnight service between these cities. An **entirely new railway** is being built along the south side of the Gulf of Corinth, replacing the old narrow-gauge railway which once linked Athens with Patras. With the opening in summer 2020 of the latest stretch, it now extends from Athens to Aigio. Yet the absence of any **international rail services** is a problem. The lines to North Macedonia, Bulgaria and Turkey are there, but there are no passenger trains. That's why, on the only journey to Greece in this book (**Route 49**), you arrive in the Hellenic Republic on a boat.

Rail passes
Interrail, Eurail and the Balkan Flexipass are all valid. The high supplements for pass holders were happily scrapped in 2019.

Other public transport options
KTEL buses (www.ktelbus.com) provide fast, punctual, fairly comfortable long-distance services; well-organised stations in most towns (tickets available from bus terminals). The Greek islands are connected by **ferries and hydrofoils**. City transport: bus or (in Athens) trolleybus, metro and electric rail; services are crowded.

Further information
Website of the Greek National Tourism Organisation: www.visitgreece.gr.

Accommodation

Greece is over-supplied with accommodation. You should have **no problem finding a bed** in Athens, Pátra or Thessaloniki even in high summer (though the very cheapest Athens dorms and pensions are often very crowded in July and Aug). Rooms are hardest to find over the Greek Easter period (note this date is different from Easter in western Europe, as it's based on the Orthodox calendar), so try to book ahead. The **youth hostel network** is sparse, but you will find hostels in Athens, Corfu and some of the more popular islands. **Campsites** at major sights (including Delphi, Mistra and Olympia) can be good value with excellent facilities.

Food and drink

Greeks rarely eat breakfast. Traditional Greek meals are unstructured, with lots of dishes brought at once or in no particular order. Lunch is any time between 12.00 and 15.00, after which most restaurants close until around 19.30. Greeks dine late, and you will find plenty of restaurants open until well after midnight. The best Greek **food is fresh**, seasonal and simply prepared. Fresh fish dishes are usually the most expensive. Pork, chicken and squid are relatively cheap, and traditional salad – olives, tomatoes, cucumber, onions, peppers and feta cheese drowned in oil, served with bread – is a meal in itself (though Greeks eat it as a side dish). Aniseed-flavoured ouzo is a favourite aperitif. Greek brandy, Metaxa, is on the sweet side. **Draught lager** is not widely available and is neither as good nor as cheap as bottled beer: Amstel, Heineken and Mythos, brewed in Greece and sold in half-litre bottles.

Hungary

Melding central European panache with a dash of Balkan style, Hungary is assertively different from any of its neighbouring countries. The **Great Plain**, *Alföld*, extends across more than half this landlocked country, with the most appreciable hills rising in the far north. Hungary's most scenic moments occur along **Lake Balaton** and the Danube Bend just north of Budapest, with a trio of fine towns – Szentendre, Visegrád and Esztergom (the latter dominated by a huge basilica – see p311).

Essentials: Local name: Magyarország – Population: 9.7m – Capital: Budapest – Currency: Forint (HUF) – Language: Hungarian (English and German widely understood) – Accommodation costs: medium – Plug types: C, F – Time zone: winter GMT+1, summer GMT+2 – International dialling code: +36 – Public holidays: 1 Jan; 15 Mar; Easter Mon; 1 May; Whit Mon; 20 Aug; 23 Oct; 1 Nov; 25, 26 Dec.

Travel in Hungary

Hungary is on **Route 33, 34, 35** and **50** in this book. In recent years the country has developed its Intercity (IC) network to link all the main towns and cities and **Railjet** (RJ) services from ÖBB are also used on international journeys from Budapest to Vienna, Munich and Zurich. Yet there are plenty of slower trains from which to savour Hungary's largely rural nature, in particular along the north and south shores of Lake Balaton. **International services** to Serbia are currently suspended bar for four trains each day from Szeged to Subotica. The Budapest to Belgrade route, currently closed for reconstruction, will reopen in 2026.

Intercity trains require reservation and a supplement, whilst most of the international Eurocity trains have a supplement but no compulsory reservation. Domestic journeys on international EC/IC/RJ/EN trains require a supplement and sometimes a seat reservation. **International sleepers** should be booked well in advance, particularly in summer. EU pensioners over 65 can enjoy **free second-class travel** on all trains (but not on cross-border services), including those run by GySEV (any supplements applicable to premium services do still need to be paid). **Hungarian State Railways (MÁV)** owns the network and MÁV-Start runs the trains (www.mavcsoport.hu).

Rail passes
Interrail and Eurail passes are valid, as is the Balkan Flexipass.

Other public transport options
Long-distance buses operated by **Volánbusz** (www.volanbusz.hu). There are many local boat services along the Danube.

Further information
The website of the National Tourist Board is available online at https://visithungary.com. *Tourinform* branches exist throughout Hungary.

Accommodation

There is a wide range of accommodation. For the medium to lower price bracket, **private rooms** are very good value, as are small pensions. Steer clear of the old Communist-era tourist hotels and youth hostels as they are very basic with limited facilities.

However, in Budapest especially, a new generation of **independent hostels** are offering dorm rooms at a much higher standard. Campsites are, on the whole, very good and can be found near the main resorts. Many have cabins to rent.

Food and drink

Cuisine has been much influenced by Austria, Germany and Turkey. Most restaurants offer a cheap fixed-price menu. Lunch is the main meal of the day, and a bowl of *gulyás* (goulash) laced with potatoes and **spiced with paprika** is a 'must'. Try smoked sausages, soups (sour cherry soup is superb) and paprika noodles or pike-perch. Hungary has some decent wines, such as *Tokaji* and *Egri Bikavér* (Bull's Blood), while *pálinka* is a fiery schnapps.

Iceland

This remote **North Atlantic island** did a great favour to railway operators over much of Europe in spring 2010 by exporting so much volcanic ash that flights across Europe were paralysed. Of course, you'll not get to Iceland by train but there is an excellent **ferry link** from Hirtshals in Denmark (on **Route 26**). A land of wild fjords and volcanoes awaits. And it is not quite devoid of trains. On the dockside in Reykjavík you'll see a preserved steam locomotive that once ran on the local harbour railway. Read more about travelling to Iceland by boat in our Sidetracks feature on p254.

Essentials: Local name: Ísland – Population: 0.37m – Capital: Reykjavík – Currency: Icelandic króna (ISK) – Language: Icelandic (Danish and English are widely spoken) – Accommodation costs: generally high – Plug types: C, F – Time zone: winter and summer GMT – International dialling code: +354 – Public holidays: 1 Jan; Maundy Thursday; Easter Monday; 21 Apr; 1 May; Ascension Day; Whit Monday; 17 June; 25–26 Dec.

Ireland

More than merely Britain's sidekick, the Republic of Ireland is assertively independent and the Dublin government punches far above its weight on the European stage. Six counties in the north of Ireland continue to be part of the UK and have a very moody assembly in Belfast (reinstated in 2024), yet many aspects of economic, cultural and sporting life in Northern Ireland and the Republic are seamlessly integrated. There are **fine landscapes** across Ireland from the Antrim glens in the north to the rugged Atlantic coast.

Essentials: Local name: Poblacht na hÉireann (or Éire for short) – Population: 5m – Capital: Dublin – Currency: Euro (EUR) – Languages: Gaeilge (Irish), English – Accommodation costs: medium – Plug type: G – Time zone: winter GMT, summer GMT+1 – International dialling code: +353 – Public holidays: 1 Jan; 17 Mar; Easter Mon; 1st Mon in May; 1st Mon in June; 1st Mon in Aug; last Mon in Oct; 25–26 Dec.

Travel in Ireland

Route 4 and **5** in *Europe by Rail* explore Ireland, with one of them having originated in Rotterdam and the other in London. Ireland has a modern rail network hubbed on Dublin with one route extending across the border to Belfast (for an onward connection by rail to Derry).

Rail passes

Eurail and Interrail are both valid, not just throughout the Republic but in **neighbouring Northern Ireland** too. Before investing in a first-class pass, note that first-class seating is only routine on fast trains from Dublin to Belfast or Cork. For the purposes of One-Country Passes, Northern Ireland is combined with the Republic in a single unit. That means that the One-Country Pass Great Britain (and all Britrail Passes) are not valid in any part of Ireland.

Other public transport options

Cross-country rail travel in Ireland is limited, with most rail routes leading to or from Dublin or Belfast. The very comfortable Bus Éireann **long-distance coaches** nicely fill the gaps in the rail network (www.buseireann.ie). Good ferry links with Roscoff and Cherbourg (the latter on **Route 16**) allow a visit to Ireland conveniently to be combined with France.

FURTHER INFORMATION

The website of the national tourist board is online at www.discoverireland.ie.

ACCOMMODATION

Hotels are generally of a very high standard with a price tag to match. There are many **independent hotels**, the best of them full of character, which knock spots off the faceless chain hotels. There's a good selection at www.originalirishhotels.com. **An Óige** (www.anoige.ie) manages a network of about two dozen youth hostels and there's also a lively independent hostels scene (see www.independenthostelsireland.com).

FOOD AND DRINK

The **Irish breakfast** is legendary and packed with enough calories to set you up for the day. Irish beef and lamb are renowned staples, complemented by excellent fish and seafood in coastal areas and all major cities. There are plenty of good quality cheeses, many from independent producers. As to drinks, don't miss the creamy stout (of which **Guinness** is just one example) and Irish whiskey. Despite the first class ingredients to hand, Ireland still serves up some culinary disasters. Anyone for lasagne with garlic fries?

ITALY

Italy has been on the tourist trail since the days of the 18th-century 'Grand Tour', offering a mix of **art, history and landscape** arguably unrivalled in any other European country. It is not for nothing that the pundits say 'see Rome and die'. But Italian passion and flair comes with a nice dose of chaos too, and for unhurried travellers prepared to slip gently into the Italian way of life, the country is deeply seductive.

Essentials: Local name: Italia – Population: 60.3m – Capital: Rome/Roma – Currency: Euro (EUR) – Language: Italian, German in Alto Adige (many speak English in cities and tourist areas) – Accommodation costs: medium – Plug types: C, F, L – Time zone: winter GMT+1, summer GMT+2 – International dialling code: +39 – Public holidays: 1, 6 Jan; Easter Monday; 25 Apr; 1 May; 2 June; 15 Aug; 1 Nov; 8, 25, 26 Dec. Regional saints' days: 25 Apr in Venice; 24 June in Florence, Genoa and Turin; 29 June in Rome; 11 July in Palermo; 19 Sept in Naples; 4 Oct in Bologna; 6 Dec in Bari; 7 Dec in Milan.

TRAVEL IN ITALY

Italy features principally on **Route 45 to 49** in this book. In addition, **Route 38, 40, 41, 44** and **50**, while more focused on territory beyond Italy's borders, start or end in Italy. Although headlined by its showpiece 1,000-km-long Torino to Salerno **high-speed line** via Milan, Rome and Naples, with sleek

Frecciarossa and Frecciargento trains linking the principal cities in double-quick time, there is also no shortage of railways of the slow and scenic variety in Italy. The fastest trains (at premium fares) are classified *Alta Velocità (AV)* services, and all **Frecciarossa** trains need advance reservation, as do the Eurocity trains to Austria via Bolzano and the Brenner Pass. Frecciabianca trains are fast premium services which run on traditional rail lines. There are refreshments on most **long-distance trains**. Italy has a good night train network with first and second class in both sleeping and couchette compartments. Train travel in Italy is generally good value. For the best fares, book long-distance journeys well in advance.

The national rail company is **Trenitalia** (www.trenitalia.com), a division of *Ferrovie dello Stato (FS)*. Private operator **NTV Italo** (www.italotreno.it) competes with Trenitalia on the high-speed routes from Turin, Milan and Venice to Rome and Naples. **Trenord** operates local services mainly in the Lombardia region (www.trenord.it). Direct EC trains to northern Italy arrive from Geneva, Zurich, Basel, Frankfurt, Munich and Vienna.

Rail passes
Interrail and Eurail are both valid. There are no locally sold national passes, but some city passes include trains and cover a wide area extending well beyond the municipal border.

Other public transport options
Various regional bus companies operate. Buses are often crowded, but regular and serve many areas inaccessible by rail. Services are however drastically reduced at weekends.

Further information
The website of the Italian Tourist Baord is at www.italia.it.

Accommodation

Venice, Florence and Amalfi Coast are particularly pricey. Most establishments style themselves hotel or albergo, but some more basic hotels are still called locande. **B&Bs** are booming, with lists available from tourist offices. HI youth hostels are plentiful, with around 80 members; prices include sheets and breakfast (www.hihostels.com). Independent hostels, of varying standards, can be found in all the main tourist destinations. Farm stays and B&B in cottages and estates is well-established. **Agriturismo** (www.agriturismo.it) is a good first port of call.

Food and drink

In Italy, meals are an **important social occasion**, but food is far more varied than the pasta and pizza stereotypes. A full meal may consist of *antipasti* (cold cuts, grilled vegetables, bruschetta), followed by pasta, a main course, then fruit, cheese or a *semi-freddo* (cold desserts, like tiramisu) or superb ice cream (*gelato*). Much of the **pleasure of eating** in Italy is derived from the sheer freshness and quality of the ingredients. *Trattoria* are simple establishments and are cheaper than *ristoranti* while *osterie* vary from simple and unpretentious to pricey gentrified-rustic restaurants. For drinking, try an *enoteca* (wine bar), which may do light meals. Coffee comes in tiny shots of espresso. There are many **fine Italian wines**. Bars are good places to get a snack, like a roll or toasted sandwich. In restaurants, be aware of cover charges (*coperto*) and service (*servizio*), both of which will be added to your bill.

Kosovo

Europe's **newest nation state**, Kosovo controversially seceded from Serbia in 2008, leaving the international community divided on whether the upstart country deserved recognition. As of autumn 2024, just over half of UN members recognise Kosovo as a legitimate sovereign state. Even the EU is divided on the issue, but 22 of the Union's 27 members have recognised Kosovo. Limited train services within Kosovo are operated by **Trainkos** (www.trainkos.com). An excellent website on the affairs of the Kosovan railways is run by RJ Krammer (www.kosrail.de; only in German). Kosovo offers a **very retro railway experience**. Enjoy it while it lasts. Sadly, as of autumn 2024 there are no cross-border train services.

Essentials: Local name: Kosovë/Kosovo (Косово) – Population: 1.9m – Capital: Prishtinë/Priština – Currency: Euro (EUR) – Languages: Albanian, Serbian, Romani, Gorani – Accommodation costs: generally low – Plug types: C, F – Time zone: winter GMT+1, summer GMT+2 – International dialling code: +383 – Public holidays: 1 Jan; Orthodox Christmas; 17 Feb; Catholic Easter Mon; 9 Apr; 1, 9 May; Orthodox Easter Mon; Eid al-Fitr; Eid al-Adha; 25 Dec.

Latvia

Latvia secured independence from the Soviet Union in 1991 and joined the EU in 2004. Silvery beaches, the **finest forests** you've ever seen and some showpiece cities combine to make affordable Latvia one of Europe's most promising destinations. You'll find an interesting ethnic mix, with about one third of the population speaking Russian and preserving many aspects of Russian culture and customs. The paucity of cross-border rail services means that we are not currently covering Latvia in *Europe by Rail*, but that may change if rail links improve.

Essentials: Local name: Latvija – Population: 2m – Capital: Riga/Rīga – Currency: Euro (EUR) – Languages: Latvian (spoken by two thirds of the population), Russian (English spoken by younger people) – Accommodation costs: medium – Plug types: C, F – Time zone: winter GMT+2, summer GMT+3 – International dialling code: +371 – Public holidays: 1 Jan; Good Fri; Easter Monday; 1, 4 May; 23–24 June; 18 Nov; 25, 26, 31 Dec.

Travel in Latvia

The country uses the Russian broader gauge rather than the western European standard gauge. Domestic train services are sparse. Services to

Russia and Belarus are suspended. However, a once-daily train from Riga to Vilnius in Lithuania was reintroduced in late December 2023. Your one opportunity to escape north from Latvia by train is a once-daily connection from **Riga to Tallinn** with a four-hour wait when you change trains at the border station of Valga. Latvia's national rail operator is **Pasažieru vilciens (PV)** and has a website at www.pv.lv.

Rail passes
Latvia is a newcomer to both Interrail and Eurail; both passes have been accepted since January 2020. There are no local passes, but rail fares are unbelievably cheap.

Other public transport options
Buses provide a more extensive service than trains for domestic Latvian and international journeys. Bus tickets can be purchased at bus stations or directly from the driver. **Lux Express** (www.luxexpress.eu) buses connect Riga with Vilnius, Tallinn, Warsaw and Pärnu.

Further information
Website: www.latvia.travel.

Liechtenstein

The bite-sized alpine Principality of Liechtenstein is set between the River Rhine and the mountains to the east. Enigmatic Liechtenstein shares borders with Austria and Switzerland and is traversed by **Route 39** which takes in the only railway line to cross Liechtenstein territory. All rail passes valid in Austria are deemed to also include Liechtenstein.

Essentials: Local name: Fürstentum Liechtenstein – Population: 39k – Capital: Vaduz – Currency: Swiss franc (CHF) – Language: German (English is widely spoken) – Accommodation costs: generally high – Plug types: C, J – Time zone: winter GMT+1, summer GMT+2 – International dialling code: +423 – Public holidays: 1, 6 Jan; Easter Monday; 1 May; Ascension Day; Whit Monday; Corpus Christi; 15 Aug; 8 Sept; 1 Nov; 8, 25–26 Dec.

Lithuania

Largest of the three **Baltic States** (though only fractionally larger than Latvia), Lithuania is able to refer back to a more glorious history than its Baltic neighbours, having been part of the influential Polish-Lithuanian Commonwealth from 1569 to 1795. Nowadays a place for sculptural stork nests, Europe's finest sand spit and a glorious capital city in Vilnius, Lithuania is cheap, friendly and desperate to welcome visitors. The fact that there are only once-daily direct trains to **Latvia and Poland** respectively means that it is still a challenge to reach Lithuania by rail.

Essentials: Local name: Lietuva – Population: 2.8m – Capital: Vilnius – Currency: Euro (EUR) – Languages: Lithuanian, Russian (English is widely spoken, as is German on the coast) – Accommodation costs: medium – Plug types: C, F – Time zone: winter GMT+2, summer GMT+3 – International dialling code: +370 – Public holidays: 1 Jan; 16 Feb; 11 Mar; Easter Monday; 1 May; 24 June; 6 July; 15 Aug; 1 Nov; 25, 26 Dec.

Travel in Lithuania

Lithuania does not feature on any of our 50 routes. The country has a **sparse domestic rail network** with services from Vilnius to Kaunas, Klaipėda and Turmantas and a new link to Vilnius airport. The national operator is **Lietuvos Geležinkeliai (GZ)** with a website at www.litrail.lt. Most railway lines are of the Russian broad gauge. The line to Poland has been rebuilt, as part of the Rail Baltica project (see p297). It is served by one train each day. Passenger trains between Russian cities and Kaliningrad transit Lithuania without stopping.

Rail passes
Both Eurail and Interrail are valid. There are no local passes, but rail fares are very cheap.

Other public transport options
Cheap for Westerners. Long-distance buses operated by **Lux Express** (www.luxexpress.eu) provide links from Vilnius to Riga, Warsaw, Tallinn, Suwałki and St Petersburg.

Further information
The Lithuanian State Department of Tourism has a website at www.lithuania.travel.

Luxembourg

The Grand Duchy of Luxembourg covers some pretty terrain for hiking, with river valleys, forests and hills, giving way to a more industrial landscape along the southern border (with neighbouring France). The **forested sandstone hills** of the north-east, abutting onto Germany, are an oasis of calm rurality in an otherwise rather crowded part of Europe. The country's eponymous capital has a dramatic and picturesque setting, straddling two gorges.

Essentials: Local name: Luxembourg/Lëtzebuerg – Population: 0.63m – Capital: Luxem¬bourg/Luxemburg – Currency: Euro (EUR) – Languages: Lëtzebuergesch, French and German (most people speak some English) – Accommodation costs: generally high – Plug types: C, F – Time zone: winter GMT+1, summer GMT+2 – International dialling code: +352 – Public holidays: 1 Jan; Easter Monday; 1 May; Ascension Day; Whit Monday; 23 June; 15 Aug; 1 Nov; 25, 26 Dec.

Travel in Luxembourg

The small, modern and efficient rail network links Luxembourg city with most areas, the longest line being the picturesque route northwards to the Belgian border at Gouvy and on to Liège (part of **Route 8** in this book). The national rail company is *Société Nationale des Chemins de fer Luxembourgeois* (**CFL**), www.cfl.lu. On 29 February 2020, Luxembourg became the first country in the world to make public transport free when using buses or trains (applies only to second-class travel).

Rail passes
Both Eurail and Interrail are valid.

OTHER PUBLIC TRANSPORT OPTIONS
Good bus network linking Luxembourg city with towns and villages across the Grand Duchy and into neighbouring countries. Timetables are online at www.mobiliteit.lu.

FURTHER INFORMATION
Luxembourg City Tourist Office, 30 place Guillaume II (www.luxembourg-city.com). The National Tourist Office has a website at www.visitluxembourg.com.

ACCOMMODATION

The National Tourist Office has free brochures featuring hotels (of all grades, plus restaurants), holiday apartments, farm holidays and camping in the Grand Duchy, plus a bed and breakfast booklet that covers all three Benelux countries. There are nine **youth hostels**. See www.youthhostels.lu for details.

FOOD AND DRINK

Cuisine has been pithily described as 'French quality, German quantity', but **eating out is pricey**. Keep costs down by making lunch your main meal and looking out for special deals: *plat du jour* (single course) or *menu* (two to three courses). Local specialities include: Ardennes ham, *träipen* (black pudding), *gromperekichelcher* (fried potato patties) and in September *quetschentaart* (a flan featuring dark plums).

MALTA

Island archipelago (with three inhabited islands) in the Mediterranean. Explore the densely populated main island (Malta itself) and you'll find old railway stations in Mdina and Birkirkara. But the railway line that linked them was closed in 1931 and Malta is now a country without trains, although recent government announcements hint of a possible light rail network. Malta has good ferry **links from Sicily**, so you can extend **Route 48** with a sea voyage to Malta from the port of Pozzallo, south-west of Siracusa.

Essentials: Local name: Repubblika ta' Malta – Population: 0.5m – Capital: Valletta – Currency: Euro (EUR) – Languages: Maltese, English (Italian widely understood) – Accommodation costs: medium – Plug type: G – Time zone: winter GMT+1, summer GMT+2 – International dialling code: +356 – Public holidays: 1 Jan; 10 Feb; 19 Mar; Good Friday; 31 Mar; 1 May; 7, 29 June; 15 Aug; 8, 21 Sept; 8, 13, 25 Dec.

MOLDOVA

The **landlocked country** of Moldova just touches the Danube and shares common borders with Ukraine and Romania. Moldova slipped quietly to independence as the Soviet Union was preoccupied with the August 1991 coup attempt in Moscow, and has been riven by strife ever since with the easternmost part of the country, called Transnistria, insisting that it is a separate state. Despite those difficulties, Moldova is an engagingly different place to visit with some beautiful wetlands, amazing old monasteries and **charmingly antiquated railways**. A paradise for those who appreciate slow travel! Limited cross-border services to Romania with an overnight sleeper to Bucharest.

Essentials: Local name: Republica Moldova – Population: 2.6m – Capital: Chișinău – Currency: Moldovan leu (MDL) – Language: Moldovan, Romanian, Russian – Accommodation costs: generally low – Plug types: C, F – Time zone: winter GMT+2, summer GMT+3 – International dialling code: +373 – Public holidays: 1 Jan; Orthodox Christmas; 8 Mar; 1 May; Orthodox Easter Monday; 9 May; 27, 31 Aug; 25 Dec.

MONACO

This tiny sovereign city state, a **constitutional monarchy** presided over by the Grimaldi family, is tucked away on a prime strip of real estate in the middle of the French Riviera. The main railway line from Nice to the Italian border at Ventimiglia (on **Route 45** in this book) cuts through Monaco or, more properly, under Monaco for most of this stretch is buried away in a tunnel. So not a lot of potential for sightseeing by train, but you can stop off at the sole station, called **Monaco-Monte Carlo**. All rail passes valid for France are deemed to include Monaco.

Essentials: Local name: Principauté de Monaco – Population: 38k – Capital: Monaco Ville – Currency: Euro (EUR) – Languages: French, Monégasque, Italian (English commonly understood) – Accommodation costs: generally high – Plug types: C, D, E, F – Time zone: winter GMT+1, summer GMT+2 – International dialling code: +377 – Public holidays: 1, 27 Jan; Easter Monday; 1 May; Ascension Day; Whit Monday; Corpus Christi; 15 Aug; 1, 19 Nov; 8, 25 Dec.

MONTENEGRO

The small **Adriatic republic** of Montenegro was part of socialist Yugoslavia. Upon the demise of the latter, it remained in a loose union with Serbia. Montenegro eventually split from Serbia in 2006 (without any of the problems associated with the secession of Kosovo, for Montenegro was never politically integrated into Serbia). A new government in the capital **Podgorica**, elected in 2023, walks a political tightrope as it pursues policies to edge closer to the European Union. The country has fabulous coastal scenery, backed by the wild mountain landscapes of the Dinaric Alps. In the Bay of Kotor, Montenegro boasts the most spectacular fjord-like landscape of the entire Mediterranean region.

There has been some unflattering ribbon development in some of the coastal resorts, but even on the coast it's still possible to find unspoilt areas. One example is the **Luštica Peninsula** just by the entrance to the Bay of Kotor. In the far south of the country, Montenegro shares southern Europe's largest lake with neighbouring Albania. It's called *Skadarsko jezero* in Montenegrin (Lake Skadar). A dash of **Venetian influence**, especially on the coast, along with the legacy of Habsburg and Ottoman adventurers, all combine to make Montenegro immensely appealing. We did have a route through Montenegro in the 17th edition of *Europe by Rail*, running from Belgrade to Bar. We've paused it in this 18th edition merely because Serbia now has no regular long-distance trains to Hungary or Croatia, so making impossible to create longer itineraries across Europe which include either Serbia or Montenegro.

Essentials: Local name: Crna Gora/Црна Гора – Population: 0.62m – Capital: Podgorica – Currency: Euro (EUR) – Languages: Montenegrin, Serbian (English and Italian widely understood in coastal resorts) – Accommodation costs: generally low – Plug types: C, F – Time zone: winter GMT+1, summer GMT+2 – International dialling code: +382 – Public holidays: 1, 2 Jan; Orthodox Christmas; Orthodox Good Friday; 1 May; Orthodox Easter Monday; 21 May; 13, 14 July.

Travel in Montenegro

Montenegro is one of Europe's last frontiers and features in this edition of *Europe by Rail* with a journey from Belgrade to the port of Bar. The country is only served by direct trains from Belgrade. The only other passenger railway within the country is from Podgorica to Montenegro's second city of Nikšić. The now abandoned railway across the border into Albania has never carried passenger traffic. There are direct buses from Bar and Kotor to Dubrovnik. Passenger trains are operated by **Željeznički prevoz Crne Gore** (www.zcg-prevoz.me) and the only international rail link that exists is with Serbia. Fares are extremely cheap, with the maximum one-way fare for any domestic journey being only €7.60 (with a €1 supplement if purchased on the train).

Rail passes
Interrail and Eurail Global Passes are both valid, as is the Balkan Flexipass. With such a sparse rail network, it's no surprise that there is no Interrail and Eurail One-Country Pass for Montenegro.

Other public transport options
There is a good network of **long-distance buses**, hubbed on the capital city of Podgorica. Air-conditioning is not always available, but the system is otherwise very reliable. You can see which carriers operate a route and buy tickets online at www.busticket4.me. Since Montenegro is not part of the European Union, chances are that border formalities will take a bit longer when crossing into neighbouring countries by bus. During the summer season, privately owned minibuses help tourists get around.

Further information
The website of the national tourist organisation is online at www.visit-montenegro.com.

Netherlands

Canals and 17th- and 18th-century gabled buildings are abiding memories of a visit to the Netherlands, whose numerous historic towns and cities have a strikingly uniform appearance. In between, the **bulb fields and windmills**

NETHERLANDS | 483

lend the Dutch farmland a distinctive character. Amsterdam, laid-back and bustling at the same time, justifiably draws most visitors.

Essentials: Local name: Nederland – Population: 17.7m – Administrative Capital: Amsterdam, Legislative Capital: The Hague/Den Haag – Currency: Euro (EUR) – Language: Dutch (English and German widely spoken) – Accommodation costs: generally high – Plug types: C, F – Time zone: winter GMT+1, summer GMT+2 – International dialling code: +31 – Public holidays: 1 Jan; Easter Monday; 27 Apr; Ascension Day; Whit Monday; 25, 26 Dec.

TRAVEL IN THE NETHERLANDS

The Netherlands are on **Route 6, 8** and **25** in this book. Frequent electric trains, many of which are double-deckers, whizz around the country's dense rail network, linking well-kept stations, some completely modernised, others retaining traditional features such as Delft Blue tiles. Domestic services fall into three categories: Intercity Direct, Intercity and local trains known as Sprinter or Stoptrein. Intercity Direct services are run on the **high-speed line** from Amsterdam to Schiphol, Rotterdam and Breda. A small supplement is compulsory if your route includes the stretch between Schiphol Airport and Rotterdam. Seat reservations are not necessary except on high-speed international services such as Eurostar. Direct Eurostar trains from Amsterdam and Rotterdam to London will be reinstated in early 2025 (obviating the need to change in Brussels). **International sleeper services** are run by Nightjet and European Sleeper. Most domestic services are run by the national rail company **Nederlandse Spoorwegen (NS)**, www.ns.nl. Tickets are mostly sold from machines, or online with e-tickets being printed at home. A contactless smartcard, OV-chipkaart, has been introduced for all public transport.

RAIL PASSES
Both Interrail and Eurail are valid. The barcode on your pass cover will open the gates at Dutch stations. The **NS Dagkaart** allows unlimited travel for one day on all NS trains.

OTHER PUBLIC TRANSPORT OPTIONS
Personalised and anonymous OV-chipkaarts are available for use on the entire public transport system.

FURTHER INFORMATION
A useful website is at www.holland.com. Tourist offices (*VVV – Vereniging voor Vreemdelingenverkeer*) bear signs showing a triangle with three Vs.

ACCOMMODATION

Hotel standards are high and lower prices reflect limited facilities rather than poor quality. Booking is advisable. As a backpacker-magnet, Amsterdam has a wide range of independent hostels to choose from, although elsewhere in the country a better bet are the official **Stayokay youth hostels** (www.stayokay.com). Tourist offices (VVV) have listings of bed and breakfast accommodation in their area, where it exists.

Food and drink

Dutch cuisine is mainly **simple and substantial**: fish or meat, potatoes and vegetables. Many Indonesian restaurants offer spicy food and in cities a good variety of international cuisine is available. Most cheaper eating joints stay open all day. Some restaurants in smaller places take last orders by 21.30 or 22.00. Look for boards saying *dagschotel* (a very economical 'special'). 'Brown cafés' (traditional pubs) also serve good-value food. Specialities include apple pie (heavy on cinnamon and sultanas), herring marinated in brine, smoked eels, *poffertjes* (tiny puff-pancakes with icing sugar) and *pannenkoeken* (pancakes: try bacon with syrup). **Street stalls** for snacks abound, options invariably including *frites/patates* (a cross between French fries and British chips) with mayonnaise or other sauces. **Excellent coffee** everywhere, often topped with whipped cream – *slagroom*. Dutch beer is topped by two fingers of froth. Most local liqueurs are excellent. The main spirit is **Jenever**, a strong, slightly oily gin made from juniper berries.

NORTH MACEDONIA

The Republic of North Macedonia is one of several countries that appeared on the political map of Europe following the break-up of Yugoslavia. The country had an ongoing spat with neighbouring Greece over the use of the name Macedonia which was amicably resolved in 2019 when the country adopted the name North Macedonia. Too often overlooked by travellers, North Macedonia is a wonderful kaleidoscope of **Balkan life and culture**. It just needs and deserves some international train services. As of October 2024, there are simply none at all. Slow and infrequent domestic services link Skopje with Bitola (Битола), Kočani (Кочани), Kičevo (Кичево), Tetovo (Тетово) and Prilep (Прилеп). In late 2017, a funding package was agreed for a new line from Skopje to the Bulgarian border. The North Macedonian national rail operator **Makedonski Železnici**, has a website at www.mzt.mk. Interrail, Eurail and the Balkan Flexipass are all valid.

Essentials: Local name: Republika Severna Makedonija/Република Северна Македонија – Population: 1.8m – Capital: Skopje/Скопје – Currency: Macedonian denar (MKD) – Languages: Macedonian, Albanian – Accommodation costs: generally low – Plug types: C, F – Time zone: winter GMT+1, summer GMT+2 – International dialling code: +389 – Public holidays: 1 Jan; Orthodox Christmas; Orthodox Easter Monday; 1, 24 May; Ramazan Bajram; 2 Aug; 8 Sept; 11, 23 Oct; 8 Dec.

NORWAY

Stretching far **beyond the Arctic Circle** and as far east as a shared frontier with Russia, Norway is one of Europe's great natural wonderlands. The country's majestic fjords – massive watery corridors created scouring glaciers – make up one of the finest coastlines in the world, backed by wild mountainous terrain. The downside is the cost. Prices are higher than in most of the rest of Europe, and even by camping or hostelling and living frugally, you'll inevitably notice the difference. Be sure to stock up on the essentials before you go.

Essentials: Local name: Norge – Population: 5.2m – Capital: Oslo – Currency: Norwegian krone (NOK) – Language: Norwegian, i.e. Bokmål and Nynorsk (English widely spoken) – Accommodation costs: generally high – Plug types: C, F – Time zone: winter GMT+1, summer GMT+2 – International dialling code: +47 – Public holidays: 1 Jan; Maundy Thursday; Good Friday; Easter Monday; 1, 17 May; Ascension Day; Whit Monday; 25, 26 Dec.

TRAVEL IN NORWAY

Norway is blessed with some of the most scenic railway lines in Europe. A selection of those feature on **Route 26, 27, 28** and **29** in this book. The liberalisation of Norway's railways, using a franchising system, was abruptly halted in October 2021 as a new left-leaning government announced a major reorganisation of and **investment in passenger rail**.

The national operator is **Vy** (www.vy.no). Seat reservations are recommended on long-distance trains. In addition to standard class, many long- and medium-distance trains have NSB Komfort areas (equivalent to first class) for a fixed supplement, which includes complimentary tea and coffee. Reserved seats are not marked other than on your confirmation. There's a good **night train network** and sleeping cars have two-berth compartments, all available with a standard-class ticket plus a supplement. Long-distance trains convey a bistro car serving hot and cold meals, drinks and snacks.

RAIL PASSES
Norway is covered by the Interrail and Eurail schemes. The **Flåm railway** is treated like a private line – Interrail and Eurail pass holders are however granted a 30% discount on the fare.

OTHER PUBLIC TRANSPORT OPTIONS
Train, boat and bus schedules are interlinked to provide good connections. Often worth using buses or boats to connect two dead-end lines (e.g. Bergen and Stavanger), rather than retracing your route. Rail passes sometimes offer good discounts, even free travel, on linking services. **NOR-WAY Bussekspress** (www.nor-way.no) and **Vy buss** (www.vybuss.com) are two big express bus operators. Long-distance buses: comfortable, with reclining seats, ample leg room. Tickets: buy on board or reserve.

FURTHER INFORMATION
Website: www.visitnorway.com. Tourist offices (*Turistinformasjon*) and tourist boards (*Reiselivslag*) can be found in virtually all towns; free maps, brochures etc available.

ACCOMMODATION

Because Norway is so expensive, the **youth hostel network** is a real asset if you don't want to break the bank. There are some 75 hostels (*vandrerhjem*), many of which are unfortunately only open between mid-June and mid-

August. The standard of hostel accommodation is very high, with singles, doubles and dormitories, and there's a good geographical spread. Booking ahead is highly recommended, especially in summer (www.hihostels.no). Private houses can be quite good value, and in some cases almost the same price as hostels. More upscale are guesthouses and pensions.

Hotels are generally very pricey, but many cut rates at weekends and in summer. **Advance booking** is important, especially in Oslo, Bergen and Stavanger. Many of the more than 1,200 official **campsites** have cabins (*hytter*), sleeping two–four people and are equipped with a kitchen and maybe a bathroom. Rough camping is permitted as long as you don't intrude on residents (you must be 150 m from them) and leave no trace of your stay. Never light fires in summer.

FOOD AND DRINK

Eating out is **very pricey** and you will save a lot by self-catering. Stock up at supermarkets and at *konditori* (bakeries), which often serve sandwiches and pastries cheaply. Restaurants sometimes have *dagens rett* (daily specials), relatively inexpensive full meals. Self-service cafeterias are also generally reasonable. Bigger towns have the usual array of fast food joints, plus hot dog and baked-potato stalls on the street; you may find *smørbrød*, the ubiquitous and diverse open sandwich, more appetising.

Lunch is normally 12.00–15.00, and sometimes features all-you-can-eat *koldtbord* at a fixed price, for a lot less than the equivalent evening meal. Dinner is 18.00–22.00 in towns, but may end earlier in rural areas. **Fresh fish** is abundant, with numerous dishes based on salmon and trout. Meat is generally costlier, and includes *elg* (elk) and *reinsdyr* (reindeer), as well as hearty stews, sausages and *kjøttkaker* (meatballs). Anything above an alcohol content of 4.75% is sold at the state-run **Vinmonopolet** stores. Bottles of wines and spirits are quite reasonable when purchased there, while purchasing a glass of wine at a restaurant or bar is universally expensive.

POLAND

In the space of just a few years, Poland has established itself as one of Europe's **prime travel destinations**. Superb old city squares, many quite Italianate in character, and some dazzling Baltic beaches are just the start. There are stunning lake landscapes (especially in Masuria), memorably beautiful mountains (in the south of the country), tremendous nightlife and enough shrines to keep a shine on your rosary.

Essentials: Local name: Polska – Population: 38.2m – Capital: Warsaw/Warszawa – Currency: Złoty (PLN) – Language: Polish (English spoken by younger Poles, German by older ones) – Accommodation costs: medium – Plug types: C, E – Time zone: winter GMT+1, summer GMT+2 – International dialling code: +48 – Public holidays: 1, 6 Jan; Easter Monday; 1, 3 May; Corpus Christi; 15 Aug; 1, 11 Nov; 25-26 Dec.

Travel in Poland

Poland features on **Route 31, 36** and **37** in *Europe by Rail*. The country has a decent rail network linking all major cities, though services in some rural areas can be infrequent. Timetables change with disconcerting frequency and the various rail operators lurch from one financial crisis to the next. There are two separate subsidiaries of the national railway: **PKP Intercity** (www.intercity.pl) operates Express Intercity (EIC), Express Intercity Premium (EIP), Intercity (IC) and TLK trains, in addition to international Eurocity (EC) and EuroNight (EN) services, whilst **Przewozy Regionalne** (www.polregio.pl) operates the slower and more local REGIO (R), InterREGIO (IR) and REGIO Ekspres (RE) trains, some of which nevertheless cover quite long distances. TLK trains are cheaper daytime and overnight services. Reservation is compulsory on EIC, EC and some TLK trains. Not all long-distance trains have refreshments. **Night trains** have first and second-class sleepers, second-class couchettes and seated accommodation.

Rail passes
Both Interrail and Eurail are valid. PKP Intercity has a **weekend ticket** valid 19.00 Friday to 06.00 Monday.

Other public transport options
PKS Express buses are cheap and practical. Tickets normally include seat reservations (book at bus station). In rural areas, bus drivers often halt between official stops if you wave them down. For longer-distance journeys, both within Poland and internationally, **PolskiBus** offers improbably cheap fares to those prepared to book a week or two in advance (www.flixbus.pl/polskibus).

Further information
The Polish Tourist Board has a website at www.poland.travel. Tourist offices can usually help with accommodation.

Accommodation

Expect **huge variations in prices**. A Kraków hotel in high season might charge several times more than a comparable place in a grim industrial city. There is a growing range of **pensions** (*pensjonaty*), which can be great value, but note that breakfast is often charged as an extra. Rooms in private houses (*kwatera prywatna*), often touted to young travellers at main railway stations, are a bit hit and miss. Check you won't be staying out in some distant estate before committing. Youth hostels are often lacklustre and spartan, but there are a growing number of **independent hostels**, especially in Kraków, Wrocław, Warsaw and Zakopane.

Food and drink

Kiosks and cafés serve the ubiquitous pizzas, chips and unappealing burgers. A common Polish fast food is *zapiekanka* (cheese and mushrooms on toast).

The **wholesome local food** is often excellent value. Look particularly for pierogi (tiny dumplings often filled with vegetables or meat), fried or grilled pork, and a great range of soups. Barszcz is one of the classics. Beer and vodka are very cheap, the latter coming in a thousand varieties. Try vodka flavoured with honey, juniper or lemon.

PORTUGAL

Portugal once prospered as a **great maritime power** and ruled a far-flung empire across Africa, the Far East and South America. Much of northern Portugal looks positively lush, with landscapes of rolling hills with orange, lemon and olive groves. Head inland to **explore hill country**, dotted with ancient fortified towns, and south to the Algarve for sun, sea and sand.

Essentials: Local name: República Portuguesa – Population: 10.3m – Capital: Lisbon/Lisboa – Currency: Euro (EUR) – Languages: Portuguese, Mirandese (English is a good bet, French or Spanish may be understood) – Accommodation costs: medium – Plug types: C, F – Time zone: winter GMT, summer GMT+1 – International dialling code: +351 – Public holidays: 1 Jan; Good Friday; 25 Apr; 1 May; 10 June; Corpus Christi; 15 Aug; 5 Oct; 1 Nov; 1, 8, 25 Dec. Many local saints' holidays.

TRAVEL IN PORTUGAL

Travel to Portugal by train, following **Route 24** in this book. Extensive modernisation in recent years has given Portugal a first-rate rail network, at least on the main lines, with tilting AP (**Alfa Pendular**) trains providing the fastest services on the core Porto-Lisbon-Faro route, alongside Intercity trains. AP and IC (Intercidades) trains all require compulsory reservation and a supplement is payable. Regional and semi-fast Inter Regional (IR) trains also run on many routes, including the picturesque **Douro Valley line** to Régua and Pocinho. National operator is **Comboios de Portugal (CP)**, www.cp.pt. The overnight trains to Spain and France were withdrawn in 2020.

RAIL PASSES

Apart from Interrail and Eurail, there is also a rail pass for non-residents valid on the entire Portuguese rail network (and also urban trains) for either three (€73) or seven (€129) days in a month (prices are for 2nd class). It is called the **Portugal Rail Pass**.

OTHER PUBLIC TRANSPORT OPTIONS

There is a good domestic express bus network run by **Rede expressos** (www.rede-expressos.pt). Buy long-distance bus tickets before boarding. Extend your arm to stop a bus.

FURTHER INFORMATION

Website of the Portuguese Tourist Board: www.visitportugal.com.

ACCOMMODATION

A good bet in most places is to find rooms (*quartos* or *dormidas*) in a private house, or in a **pension** (*pensão* – more of a business than a house, and graded from 1 to 3 stars). Other inexpensive places are boarding houses (*hospedarias/ casas de hóspedes*) and 1-star hotels. *Pousadas* are state-run places in four categories, with some of them being converted national historic monuments (*Pousadas Históricas*, Historic Pousadas) while others are, for example, in remote locations (*Pousadas Natureza*). More information at www.pousadas.pt. To find out about youth hostels see www.pousadasjuventude.pt. For campsites contact the **Federação de Campismo e Montanhismo de Portugal** (www.fcmportugal.com).

Food and drink

The Portuguese pattern of eating is to have a fairly frugal breakfast and two big main meals: lunch (12.00–15.00) and dinner (19.30–22.30). Eating is not expensive but, if your budget is strained, go for the meal of the day, *prato do día* or *menú*. Eating is taken seriously, the cuisine flavoured with herbs rather than spices and rather heavy on olive oil. There is lots of **delicious seafood**, such as grilled sardines and several varieties of *caldeirada* (fish stew). Other local dishes are *bacalhau* (dried salted cod in various guises) and *leitão* (roasted suckling pig). The most popular pudding is a sweet egg custard. Portugal is, of course, the home of port, but there are also several excellent (and often inexpensive) **wines**, such as the *vinho verde* 'green' wines and the rich reds of the Dão and Bairrada regions. Do not be surprised if you are charged for pre-dinner bread, olives or other nibbles that are brought to your table unordered. If you don't want them, say so.

Romania

A member of the EU since 2007, and still hoping to be admitted to the Schengen area, Romania is a world apart from its neighbours. Its linguistic and cultural heritage is more Romance than Slavic, and many rural areas of the country are caught in a time warp. This is Europe as it used to be. Travel comes with a few inevitable frustrations, but stay cool and take time to interact with the warmly hospitable locals. The country covers a remarkable range of landscapes from the **rugged Carpathians** to the wetlands of the Danube delta.

Essentials: Local name: România – Population: 19.2m – Capital: Bucharest/București – Currency: Romanian Leu (RON) – Language: Romanian (English understood by younger people, plus some German, and Hungarian throughout Transylvania) – Accommodation costs: generally low – Plug types: C, F – Time zone: winter GMT+2, summer GMT+3 – International dialling code: +40 – Public holidays: 1, 2, 24 Jan; Orthodox Easter Monday; 1 May; Orthodox Pentecost Monday; 15 Aug; 30 Nov; 1, 25, 26 Dec.

Travel in Romania

The natural landscapes and historic cities of Romania are easily explored by rail, with 11,000 km of track to chose from. In this book we feature Romania in **Route 34**. With only a small number of Intercity trains, services can be quite slow, particularly on branch lines. Reservations are required for **long-distance trains**, either at the station or CFR agents. Fares for locally-purchased tickets depend on the type of train; there's a speed supplement for all but local trains. There are *trende persoane* (very slow services), *accelerat* (rather slow), *rapid* and IC services (that's the fastest and most expensive category). Food is only available on IC and some rapid trains, but drinks are occasionally available.

Night trains offer sleepers and couchettes. The national railway is *Societatea Natională de Transport Feroviar de Călători* (**CFR**), www.cfrcalatori.ro, but some services are run by private operators, including some longer distance trains. Among them are **Regio Călători** (www.regiocalatori.ro) and **Astra Trans Carpatic** (www.astratranscarpatic.ro). Tickets are not interchangeable between companies.

Rail passes
Interrail and Eurail are valid. The Balkan Flexipass is accepted but only on Regio Călători services.

Other public transport options
There are a number of long-distance bus companies which provide inexpensive links between the country's main cities (see www.autogari.ro).

Further information
The Romanian National Tourism Authority has a website at www.romaniatourism.com.

Accommodation

At the bottom end, hotels can be basic and inexpensive, while some match the highest international standards and prices. **Private rooms** may be booked at tourist offices in some towns, and in a few tourist areas touts will meet trains at the station to offer their rooms – which may be centrally located in attractive old houses, or far out in grim suburban tower blocks, so make sure you know what you're agreeing to. Book in advance for hotels on the **Black Sea coast** in summer and in mountain ski resorts at winter weekends. There are a few decent hostels: see www.hostelz.com for an overview.

Food and drink

A small piece of meat (*cotlet*) and chips is staple fare in many restaurants. You could do a lot better by samping sarmale which are tasty stuffed cabbage leaves, often without meat. Try the **local soup** (*ciorbă*), stews and rissoles. And if all else fails, there are plenty of takeaway stalls and pizzerias.

Cafés serve **excellent cakes** (*prăjitură*), soft drinks, beer and coffee; *turceasca* is Turkish-style ground coffee, while ness is instant coffee. Wines are superb and very cheap. Try the plum brandy known as *țuică* (pronounced 'tswica'), or its double-distilled version *pálinca*.

Russian Federation

That part of the Russian Federation which lies within Europe (viz. west of the Ural Mountains) is very much larger than the entire European Union. Russia is Europe's *terra incognita*, and has hardly helped its own case through its **invasion of Ukraine**. Recent months have seen the wholesale transformation of the security landscape in eastern Europe, and we suspect that few readers of *Europe by Rail* will have any appetite for travel to Russia any time soon.

But let's not forget Russia. As our friends at the excellent *Russian Life* magazine nicely put it: "Love the people. Loathe the regime." Russia is so immensely varied. Even the European part of the country includes constituent republics that hardly figure in Europe's collective consciousness. When did you last hear of Komi, Mordovia or Chuvashia in the news?

Essentials: Local name: Rossiya/Россия – Population: 145m – Capital: Moscow/Москва – Currency: Russian rouble (RUB) – Language: Russian. Several other languages are co-official in various regions (English or German are widely spoken by young people in larger cities) – Accommodation costs: medium – Plug types: C, F – Time zone (for the area covered in this book): GMT+3 (summer and winter) – International dialling code: +7 – Public holidays: 1–6 Jan; Orthodox Christmas; 23 Feb; 8 Mar; 1, 9 May; 12 June; 4 Nov.

Travel in Russia

Almost all Russian railway lines are of the Russian broad gauge. The train was the making of the Russian Empire in tsarist times, and trains were a mainstay of Soviet life – hardly surprising given the essential roadlessness of much of the country in the first decades after the revolution. The **vast distances** covered have dictated that the traditional Russian train is one of sleeping cars of various grades (even including dormitory-style bunks in many cases), designed for daytime use as well as overnight.

New double-deck sleeper trains have revolutionised domestic overnight services, although some travellers still hanker after the old-style **communal carriages** (see our Sidetracks feature on p287). A revolution has taken place, however, on the 650-km long Moscow to St Petersburg line with the introduction of **Sapsan high-speed trains** on daytime services, the fastest taking just four hours. Trains in Russia are operated by **RZD** (www.rzd.ru). All except suburban trains require advance reservation. Some long-distance services run only on alternate days. Note that as of October 2024, train services between the Russian Federation and the European Union remain suspended.

Rail passes
Eurail and Interrail are not valid.

Further information
Website: www.visitrussia.com. Tourist offices exist in major cities.

San Marino

Serenissima Repubblica di San Marino. What a gracious name for a country! The Most Serene Republic of San Marino. Serene is not quite the word that springs to mind on a hot summer day when this little micro state is packed with tourists. This affluent territory, **enclaved within eastern Italy**, is not a member of the EU. Stunning scenery and its quirky political status pull the crowds, and it is well worth a visit. The railway from the Italian city of Rimini to San Marino has long gone, so you'll have to take a bus nowadays (and we suggest just that as part of **Route 49**). Although the territory is now trainless, you see **relics of the old railway** at several places in San Marino and some former railway tunnels have now been converted for pedestrian use.

Essentials: Local name: San Marino – Population: 34k – Capital: City of San Marino – Currency: Euro (EUR) – Language: Italian – Accommodation costs: medium – Plug types: C, F, L – Time zone: winter GMT+1, summer GMT+2 – International dialling code: +378 – Public holidays: 1, 6 Jan; 5 Feb; 25 Mar; Easter Monday; 1 Apr; 1 May; Corpus Christi; 28 July; 15 Aug; 3 Sept; 1 Oct; 1, 2 Nov; 8, 25, 26, 31 Dec.

Serbia

Landlocked Serbia is a country that has reinvented itself. In 1999, NATO was pounding Serbia with aerial bombardment, and the Belgrade government was widely denigrated, at least in the West, for its renegade ways.

How times change! Now Serbia is hip, and angling to become a member of the European Union. It may be short on beaches, but it offers other ingredients that make for great travel. The country has good affordable food, a famously vibrant nightlife, **mountain scenery aplenty** (with some decent skiing), some remarkable Orthodox churches and monasteries and bags of **cultural history**.

Essentials: Local name: Republika Srbija/Република Србија – Population: 6.8m – Capital: Belgrade/Београд – Currency: Serbian dinar (RSD) – Languages: Serbian (in the Vojvodina region also Hungarian, Slovak, Croatian, Rusyn and Romanian); note that Serbian is generally written in the Cyrillic alphabet (many younger Serbs know at least some English) – Accommodation costs: generally low – Plug types: C, F – Time zone: winter GMT+1, summer GMT+2 – International dialling code: +381 – Public holidays: 1, 2 Jan; Orthodox Christmas; 15, 16 Feb; 1, 2 May; Orthodox Good Friday and Easter Monday; 11 Nov.

Travel in Serbia

Ten years ago, we were so proud that Serbia featured on four new routes in *Europe by Rail*. Since then Serbia has axed all its main-line **international train services**. All of them! So we have paused our Serbian coverage for this 18th edition of the book. But in fairness, there is a lot of investment in Serbian rail infrastructure at the moment, and things are looking good for the reopening of the main line from Belgrade to Budapest in 2026. So watch this space. Meanwhile, there is a limited domestic network still operating.

The national rail operator is **Železnice Srbije (ZS)**, www.zeleznicesrbije.com. The country's timetable and booking site at www.srbvoz.rs. Neither site has much English content.

RAIL PASSES
Interrail and Eurail are valid as is the Balkan Flexipass.

OTHER PUBLIC TRANSPORT OPTIONS
Good network of buses connecting towns throughout the country with main hubs in Belgrade and Novi Sad. Buy tickets in advance at the bus station. Buses are usually comfortable though they might get very crowded on popular routes.

FURTHER INFORMATION
The official Tourist Board website is available at www.serbia.travel. The excellent **Bradt Guide to Serbia** by Laurence Mitchell – currently in its 6th edition – is also a helpful travel companion.

SLOVAKIA

Slovakia has progressed enormously since joining the EU in 2004, adopting the euro in advance of most of its neighbours. Easy to get around, tourist-friendly and still good value, Slovakia is beginning to cut a dash on the central European travel circuit. For real highlights, look to the **High Tatras** for fabulous mountain scenery and **Carpatho-Ruthenia** for picture-perfect wooden churches and the remarkable Rusyn culture.

Essentials: Local name: Slovensko – Population: 5.4m – Capital: Bratislava – Currency: Euro (EUR) – Languages: Slovak (German, Hungarian in the south; some English and French is spoken) – Accommodation costs: medium – Plug types: C, E – Time zone: winter GMT+1, summer GMT+2 – International dialling code: +421 – Public holidays: 1, 6 Jan; Good Fri; Easter Mon; 1, 8 May; 5 July; 29 Aug; 1, 15 Sept; 1, 17 Nov; 24–26 Dec.

TRAVEL IN SLOVAKIA

The country is included in **Route 33** and **35** in this book. Slovakia's main trunk route from Bratislava to Košice through Žilina and the foothills of the impressive Tatra Mountains at Poprad-Tatry is well provided for, with fast trains every two hours. A good network covers the rest of the country. An excellent **narrow-gauge network** covers the Tatra Mountain resorts. EU citizens aged 62 and above can register for free rail travel in Slovakia. Trains can be crowded, so reservation is recommended on express and night trains (at station counters marked R). Local services (*osobný*) are very slow. There are also faster Intercity (IC), *expresný* (Ex) and *rýchlik* (R) trains. Domestic **night trains** run from Bratislava to each of Humenné, Prešov and Košice. Night trains offer sleeping cars, couchettes and seated accommodation. **Železničná spoločnosť Slovensko (ŽSSK)** is the national operator (www.zssk.sk), using the network of ŽSR. Private operators include **Regiojet** (www.regiojet.sk) and **Leo Express** (www.le.cz).

Rail passes
Eurail and Interrail passes are valid, plus the European East pass for non-European residents.

Other public transport options
Comprehensive long-distance bus network, often more direct than rail in upland areas. You can buy tickets from driver, though priority might be given to those with bookings. For international bus connections see www.eurobus.sk and www.slovaklines.sk.

Further information
The website of the Slovakian Tourist Board is available at www.slovakia.travel.

Accommodation
There is a wide choice of hotels, private rooms and pensions, and, at a much more basic level, **hostels and inns** with a few spartan rooms, plus *chaty* (simple chalets) and *chalupy* (traditional cottages) in the countryside. Bratislava has an increasing number of stylish independent hostels.

Food and drink
Slovak food has a lot in common with Hungarian food; a typical dish is *bryndzové halušky*, gnocchi with grated bryndza, a ewes' milk cheese that's only produced in Slovakia and Romania. You'll find *rezeň* (*schnitzel*, usually pork), fried chicken and goulash-style stews everywhere, the latter often accompanied by **steamed dumplings** (tasty, even though the habit of serving them in slices looks distinctly unappetising). Good local beers, and decent local wines, many of which are rarely seen outside Slovakia.

Slovenia

Slovenia, a pocket-sized land of **beautiful Alpine mountains and lakes**, undulating farmland and vineyards, blends Mediterranean style with central European efficiency. Not quite the first breakaway from the Yugoslav fold, for Croatia declared independence one day earlier, Slovenia was the first part of former Yugoslavia to join the EU and in 2007 the country also became party to the Schengen Agreement. The country has made fast progress economically. The real surprise for many visitors is to discover a European country so dedicated to the outdoors and adventure.

Essentials: Local name: Republika Slovenija – Population: 2.1m – Capital: Ljubljana – Currency: Euro (EUR) – Language: Slovene (English, German and Italian often spoken in tourist areas) – Accommodation costs: medium – Plug types: C, F – Time zone: winter GMT+1, summer GMT+2 – International dialling code: +386 – Public holidays: 1 Jan; 8 Feb; Easter Mon; 27 Apr; 1–2 May; 25 June; 15 Aug; 31 Oct; 1 Nov; 25–26 Dec.

Travel in Slovenia
Slovenia features in **Route 44** in this book. The country's small and efficient rail network hubbed on Ljubljana mixes the traditional and charming aspects

of this mountainous country with more modern features, such as the tilting ICS trains on the Maribor to Ljubljana route. The national operator is **Slovenske železnice (SŽ)**, https://potniski.sz.si. ICS trains have compulsory reservation. Other train types include domestic and international long-distance services (IC and EC), international MV trains, EuroNight services (EN) and regional and other local trains (RG, LV). **Catering services** are available on most IC and EC trains and all ICSs.

Rail passes
Interrail and Eurail passes are valid.

Other public transport options
A number of companies offer **express bus** connections from as far as Sweden and Denmark to Slovenia. Long-distance bus services are frequent and inexpensive; usually buy ticket on boarding.

Further information
The website of the Slovenian Tourist Board is at www.slovenia.info.

Accommodation
Refurbished hotels and high standards make for prices comparable to those of other EU countries. Private rooms are an option for the budget conscious, as are hostels. The official **youth hostel organisation** can be found at www.youth-hostel.si, although the hostel network is concentrated on the alpine north, plus a few options – including independent hostels – in Ljubljana. There are numerous small but well-equipped **campsites**.

Food and drink
A restaurant where you are served by a waitress is a *restvracija*, while a *gostilna* is an inn, which typically serves national dishes in a rustic setting. Both sometimes have a set menu (*dnevna kosila*) at lunch, which is usually the least expensive option. Slovenian cuisine reflects historic ties with Vienna. **Meat and dairy products** predominate: *Wiener schnitzel* (veal in breadcrumbs) is a **speciality**, as is *pohana piška* (breaded fried chicken), and French fries are served with almost everything. **Coffee shops** offer a wide range of pastries, cakes and ice creams. A *zavitek* is a light pastry filled with cream cheese, either sweet or savoury.

Spain

Inexpensive to travel in and blessed with a warm climate, Spain is **astonishingly varied**, ranging from the fashion-conscious sophistication and pulsing atmospheres of Madrid and Barcelona to rural scenes that look as if they might belong to another continent, or even another century. It's not consistently beautiful – views from the train might take in ugly high-rise developments or monotonous cereal plains, while on much of the coast there are concrete resorts that sprang up in the 1950s and 1960s to provide cheap holidays. But the **classic Spanish elements** are there too: parched landscapes dotted with cypresses and cacti, backed by rugged sierras; lines of poplars receding to hazy horizons, and red-roofed fortified towns clustered around castles. Some scenes are peculiarly regional: the luxuriant greenness of Galicia; the snowy pinnacles of the **Picos de Europa**; the canyon-like badlands of Aragon on the southern fringes of the Pyrenees.

Essentials: Local name: España – Population: 47.5m – Capital: Madrid – Currency: Euro (EUR) – Languages: Castilian Spanish (most widely spoken), Catalan (east), Galego (north-west), Euskera (Basque country) (English widely spoken) – Accommodation costs: medium – Plug types: C, F – Time zone: winter GMT+1, summer GMT+2 – International dialling code: +34 – Public holidays: 1, 6 Jan; Good Friday; 1 May; 15 Aug; 12 Oct; 1 Nov; 6, 8, 25 Dec. Many other regional and local saints' holidays.

Travel in Spain

You'll find Spain featured principally on **Route 21 to 24** – and we have three journeys through France leading to Spain (viz. **Route 17 to 20**). Massive **investment in high-speed rail** has put Spain in the major league of European high-speed players, most notably with the Madrid to Barcelona line and the long-established line to Seville, which opened 30 years ago in 1992. In Spain 'high-speed' doesn't necessarily mean 'boring'. **Route 22**, a giant leap from Barcelona to Málaga, is unusual in being one of only two routes in *Europe by Rail* which rely entirely on high-speed trains (the other one being **Route 7**). There are high-speed trains linking Barcelona with Paris and a dozen other French cities. All major Spanish cities have good connections to Madrid and there are many useful cross-country and regional links. The Spanish high-speed rail network uses the western standard gauge, while traditional lines run on the **Iberian broad gauge**. There are different train categories, AVE being the principal high-speed trains, along with Avant, Alvia and Altaria trains (the latter two can switch between both gauge types). Media Distancia (MD) trains provide regional services. Nowadays restricted to secondary routes are the slower long-distance Talgo services. *Regionales* are local stopping services and Cercanías suburban trains. There are no domestic night sleeper services in Spain. **Reservation is essential** on the majority of trains, including some regional services, whilst pass holders must purchase seat reservations (often pricey) on all high-speed and certain other long-distance trains.

At main stations you'll need to check in and be on the platform a few minutes before the advertised departure time. The national railway company is **Renfe** (www.renfe.com). Of several **narrow-gauge railways** the largest network is that branded as **FEVE**, in the northern coastal provinces.

Rail passes
Interrail and Eurail passes are valid. Note that many trains require seat reservations.

OTHER PUBLIC TRANSPORT OPTIONS
Numerous regional bus companies (*empresas*) provide fairly comprehensive and cheap service. Check routes and book **express buses** on www.movelia.es/en.

FURTHER INFORMATION
The website of the Spanish Tourist Board is at www.spain.info. *Oficinas de Turismo* (tourist offices) can provide maps and information on accommodation and sightseeing, and generally have English-speaking staff. Regional offices stock information on the whole region, municipal offices cover only that city; larger towns have both types of office.

Accommodation

There's generally no problem finding somewhere to stay outside major festivals and other peak periods; however, some large cities (notably Madrid and Barcelona) can be problematic. Thanks to a useful hierarchy imposed by regional tourist authorities, **accommodation is graded** according to facilities, from *albergues juveniles* (youth hostels) via basic boarding houses, known variously as *fondas* (look for plaques marked F), *pensiones* (P), *posadas, ventas* and *casas de huéspedes*; then come *hostales* (HS) and *hostales residencias* (HR) up to *hoteles* (H), ranging from 1 to 5 stars. *Casas rurales* are farmhouses and *refugios* are mountain huts. The hostel scene in Spain is developing fast. There are dozens of **HI youth hostels** around the country (www.reaj.com), as well as an increasing number of independent hostels. Barcelona, Madrid, Sevilla, San Sebastián and Granada all have a particularly good choice of hostel options.

Food and drink

The locals take a light breakfast: coffee or hot chocolate with rolls or a *pan con tomate* (toasted bread rubbed with a ripe tomato, and sometimes garlic, and then drizzled with olive oil) or perhaps *churros* (deep-fried fritters dipped in hot chocolate). The main meal is lunch. Dinner is a little lighter, and is eaten around 22.00 in towns. *Platos combinados* and *menú del día* are both good value. If you want an **inexpensive light meal**, ask for *raciones*, a larger portion of *tapas* (little more than nibbles, intended as aperitifs). The best-known Spanish dish is *paella*. Another famous summer dish is *gazpacho* (chilled tomato soup), which originated in Andalucía and is found mainly in the south. Choose your **drinking place** according to what you want to consume. For beer, you need a bar or *cervecería*, for wine a *taberna* or *bodega*. For cider (in the north), you need a *sidrería*. There are some excellent wines (notably, though by no means exclusively, from the Rioja and Ribera del Duero regions) and Jerez is, of course, the home of sherry.

Sweden

Scandinavia's largest country includes **huge tracts of forest** and thousands of lakes, with mildly rolling, fertile terrain to the south, and excitingly rugged uplands spilling over the Norwegian border and beyond the Arctic Circle into Lapland. The sheer amount of space is positively exhilarating, and it's the northern stretches that are easily the least populated.

Essentials: Local name: Sverige – Population: 10.4m – Capital: Stockholm – Currency: Swedish krona (SEK) – Languages: Swedish (English widely spoken); Sami and Finnish-speaking minorities – Accommodation costs: generally high – Plug types: C, F – Time zone: winter GMT+1, summer GMT+2 – International dialling code: +46 – Public holidays: 1, 6 Jan; Good Friday; Easter Monday; 1 May; Ascension Day; Whit Monday; 6 June; Midsummer's Eve Day; 25, 26 Dec.

Travel in Sweden

You will find Sweden included in **Route 25, 26, 27, 29** and **30** in this book. The fastest services are operated by **high-speed Snabbtåg** trains, whilst the new **Botniabanan** has begun to revolutionise services from Stockholm to the north. Services are efficient and frequent, though understandably sparse in the far north. Seat reservations are compulsory on night trains and Snabbtåg, the latter also requiring a supplement. Most long-distance trains have refreshments, some also have play areas for children. The national rail company is **SJ AB** (www.sj.se). Several other operators are involved on certain routes, as for example **Inlandsbanan AB** (www.inlandsbanan.se), which run the route from Mora to Gällivare or **Vy Tåg AB** (www.vy.se) which since 2020 have run the night train from Sweden to Narvik which appears as **Route 29** in this edition of *Europe by Rail*.

Rail passes
Interrail and Eurail passes are valid.

Other public transport options
Transport system is highly efficient; ferries are covered (in whole or part) by rail passes and city transport cards. Sweden's biggest operator of long-distance buses is **Swebus Express**, now part of **Flixbus** (www.flixbus.se). Advance booking is required on some routes and always advisable in summer; bus terminals usually adjoin train stations.

Further information
Sweden's tourism website is at www.visitsweden.com. Tourist offices are called Turistbyrå.

Accommodation

You can sleep in fair comfort at a reasonable price in Sweden. Tourist offices have listings of most places to stay and charge a small booking fee. Hotel standards are high and the cost usually includes breakfast. There are more than 300 **HI hostels** (*vandrarhem*), about half of which open only in summer. Family rooms are available (www.swedishtouristassociation.com). There are also more than 190 independent hostels operated by **Sveriges Vandrarhem i Förening (SVIF)** (www.svif.se). Room-only accommodation in private houses is a good budget alternative (contact local tourist offices). Sveriges

Campingvärdars Riksförbund (SCR), **Swedish Camping Site Owners' Association** (www.camping.se) lists more than 600 campsites.

Food and drink

Hearty buffet breakfasts are a good start to the day. Cafés and fast-food outlets are budget options for later on. *Pytt i panna* is a hefty fry-up; other **traditional dishes** are pea soup served with pancakes, and *Jansson's temptation* (potatoes, onions and anchovies). **Systembolaget** is the state-owned outlet for alcohol – shoppers must be over 20, but you can buy alcoholic beverages in some restaurants, pubs and bars at 18.

Switzerland

Even by European standards, Switzerland packs a lot into a small space, and, despite its **admirable transport system**, it can take a surprisingly long time to explore the country thoroughly, though it's predominantly scenery rather than cities that attracts the appreciable crowds. There are marked regional differences, and four separate official languages.

Essentials: Local name: Schweiz/Suisse/Svizzera – Population: 8.5m – Capital: Berne/Bern – Currency: Swiss Franc (CHF) – Languages: German, French, Italian, Romansch (English is widespread) – Accommodation costs: generally high – Plug types: C, J – Time zone: winter GMT+1, summer GMT+2 – International dialling code: +41 – Public holidays: 1 Jan; Ascension Day; 1 Aug; 25 Dec. Various additional regional public holidays.

Travel in Switzerland

Switzerland features principally on **Route 39 to 43** in this volume. **Route 8 and 9** lead south through the Rhine Valley to Switzerland and **Route 14** runs from Paris to Geneva. The country's reputation for being spotlessly clean, efficient, and above all punctual, certainly holds true on the **extensive Swiss rail system**, which covers every town and valley. Of course, if there's a mountain, there will often be a railway involved, with incredible views thrown in. But beware the **long tunnels**; there is not a lot of landscape to be seen in the new 57-km long Gotthard Base Tunnel. The main operator is **Swiss Federal Railways (SBB/CFF/FFS)**, www.sbb.ch. There are many small private or regionally run railways, particularly in mountainous areas. There is no compulsory reservation on domestic services, except for journeys on the popular *Glacier Express*, the *Bernina Express* and the new Gotthard Panorama tourist trains.

Rail passes

Interrail and Eurail passes are valid, but do note that there are restrictions on their use on many mountain railways. The **Swiss Travel Pass** gives non-residents consecutive days on Swiss Railways, boats and buses, plus discounts on mountain railways; valid for 3, 4, 6, 8 or 15 days. The **Swiss Travel Pass Flex** is similar but valid for 3, 4, 6, 8 or 15 days within one month.

Other public transport options
Swiss buses are famously punctual. Yellow **postbuses** (www.postauto.ch) stop at rail stations.

Further information
The official tourism website is at www.myswitzerland.com. Tourist offices in almost every town or village. The standard of information is excellent.

Accommodation
Swiss hotels have high standards but are expensive. In rural areas and Alpine resorts, it is often possible to get rooms in **private houses** (look for 'Zimmer frei' signs posted in windows and gardens), but these are few and far between in cities. Budget travellers (unless they are camping) rely heavily on **youth hostels** – so book these as far ahead as possible. The standard of hostel accommodation in Switzerland is excellent, and there are two organisations worth checking out. The Swiss Hostels Association (www.swisshostels.com) is an organisation of privately-run independent hostels, that have agreed to a set criteria of standards, whilst the official youth hostel organisation **Schweizer Jugendherbergen** has locations across the country (www.youthhostel.ch). Mountain backpackers can stay at huts of the **Swiss Alpine Club (SAC)/ Schweizer Alpenclub** (www.sac-cas.ch); these are primarily climbing huts based at the start of climbing routes, but walkers are welcome. There are also (in more accessible locations) mountain inns known as *Berghotels* or *Auberges de Montagne*, with simple dormitory accommodation as well as private rooms ranging from basic to relatively luxurious.

Food and drink
Pork and veal are common menu items, but in the lake areas you'll also find fresh fish. **Swiss cheese** is often an ingredient in local dishes; the classic Swiss fondue, for instance, is bread dipped into a pot containing melted cheese, garlic, wine and kirsch. *Raclette*, a speciality of the canton of Valais, is simply melted cheese, served with boiled potatoes, gherkins and onions. The ubiquitous meal accompaniment in German-speaking areas is Rösti, fried potatoes and onions, while French Switzerland goes in for stronger tastes, such as smoked sausages. *Bündnerfleisch* is a tasty raw smoked beef, sliced very thin. Don't miss the UNESCO-listed **Lavaux Vineyards** along the north shore of Lake Geneva (mentioned in **Route 8** and **43**) which produce some of the finest Swiss wines.

Turkey

Europe meets Asia in Turkey. But before you write off Turkey as not being really European at all, bear it mind that it has in Istanbul the largest city anywhere in Europe. Even on the west side of the **Bosphorus**, you will find mosques, Islamic monuments and oriental-style bazaars and it is important to remember that Islam has been an important aspect of the cultural fabric of Europe for many centuries. Turkey has outstanding relics of Greek and Roman settlement, superb mountain and coastal scenery and a population that is ever welcoming to visitors.

Essentials: Local name: Türkiye – Population: 73.6m – Capital: Ankara – Currency: Turkish Lira (TL) – Language: Turkish (English and German often understood) – Accommodation costs: generally low – Plug types: C, F – Time zone: GMT+3 – International dialling code: +90 – Public holidays: 1 Jan; 23 Apr; 1, 19 May; Ramadan; 30 Aug; Bayram; 29 Oct.

Travel in Turkey

Turkey does not feature in this edition of *Europe by Rail*. Many journeys by train are still tortuously slow, but new **high-speed lines** are transforming Turkish rail travel. When the new Ankara to Konya route opened in 2011, it cut the journey time from over ten hours to less than two. A new rail tunnel for suburban services under the Bosphorus opened in 2013, linking the Asian and European parts of the country. The final sections of the Ankara to Istanbul high-speed line opened in 2019. Services are operated by **Turkish State Railways (TCDD)**. Fares and timetables are at www.tcdd.gov.tr.

Rail passes
In addition to Interrail and Eurail passes, the Balkan Flexipass is valid.

Other public transport options
Excellent long-distance bus system (generally quicker than rail), run by competing companies, for example **Kamil Koç** (www.flixbus.com.tr). Shorter rides are available via dolmuş (shared taxis) that pick up passengers like a taxi, but only along a specified route and much cheaper. **IDO** runs the ferries (www.ido.com.tr). Ankara and Istanbul have a modern metro line, Istanbul also has a light-rail and tram route.

Further information
The official website of the Turkish Ministry of Tourism is at www.goturkeytourism.com.

Accommodation

Turkey's accommodation spectrum is as varied and colourful as the country itself. You can hang your hat in converted Ottoman palaces (known as 'Special Licence Hotels') that aren't as expensive as you might think and almost define the word 'atmospheric'. Or try an international hotel that will deliver neither nice surprises nor hideous shocks, or go for a hostel. The **Turkish hostel scene** is particularly well developed and organised. *Pansiyons* (small guesthouses) are a good and affordable overnight option.

Food and drink

Turkish cuisine has many fans, and generally the fare is more varied than in Greece. Try **vegetable stews**, *shish* (lamb) kebabs, pizza and spicy meat dishes, or for a real blowout the all-encompassing meze, with a bit of everything. **Tea** is the national drink, but there are good-value wines and beers, and raki is the highly distinctive aniseed-flavoured brandy.

UKRAINE

Assertively independent since 1991, Ukraine is the largest country entirely within Europe. The **rich, fertile steppes** so often associated with Ukraine give way to the **Carpathian hills** in the west and wetlands on the Black Sea coast. Ukraine has a lot to offer and is remarkably good value. But Russia's invasion of Ukraine has sidelined tourism – at least for now. Better times will surely come. We have just one journey into Ukraine and that's **Route 36** which starts in Berlin and ends in Lviv. Ukrainians now look to the west as never before and, once the political and military situation permits, those who venture to Ukraine will surely receive a warm welcome. Meanwhile, caution is advised. Once travel becomes possible again, stick to areas which are reliably conflict free and just be a little wary about venturing too far off the beaten track.

Essentials: Local name: Ukraina/Україна – Population: 41.3m – Capital: Kyiv/Київ – Currency: Hryvnia (UAH) – Languages: Ukrainian, Russian; Hungarian-speaking minority (English spoken especially by younger people in major cities) – Accommodation costs: generally low – Plug types: C, F – Time zone: winter GMT+2, summer GMT+3 (Luhansk, Donetsk & Crimea are on GMT+3 all year) – International dialling code: +380 – Public holidays: 1 Jan; 8 Mar; Good Friday; Easter Monday; 1, 2, 9 May; Pentecost Monday; 28 June; 24 Aug; 14 Oct; 25 Dec; some Orthodox feast days are still recognised.

TRAVEL IN UKRAINE

Rail connections between unoccupied areas of Ukraine and both the Russian Federation and Belarus are currently suspended. Limited services between Russian occupied areas of Ukraine and the Russian Federation have been reinstated. There are no rail services across the front line between occupied and free Ukraine. Recent years have seen improvements in train services between western Ukraine and the EU. There are **new services across the border** into Slovakia, Hungary and Poland as well as longer-distance overnight trains. Vienna has a direct overnight train to Lviv and Kyiv. **Long-distance trains** in Ukraine have sleeping accommodation designed for both night and daytime use. There is a growing number of Intercity (IC) trains with seated accommodation. Advance reservation is essential. The national operator is **Ukrainski Zaliznytsi** (UZ; www.uz.gov.ua). Tickets can be booked at https://booking.uz.gov.ua/en. There is also a ticket booking site run by Kyiv-based travel agent **SoloEast Travel** (www.trainticketsukraine.com).

RAIL PASSES

Neither Interrail nor Eurail are valid. Fares are very cheap.

OTHER PUBLIC TRANSPORT OPTIONS
Extensive and cheap bus network with buses of varying comfort level. Marshrutkas (minibuses) are also used. Buy tickets at bus stations in advance or directly from the driver.

ACCOMMODATION

Inexpensive, but frankly uninspiring, hotels aplenty in the main cities, many of them concrete blocks that have had little maintenance since the day, long ago, when they first opened their doors to the public. A short-lived spate of entrepreneurialism has fostered many new **small privately owned hotels**, particularly in Kyiv and western Ukraine, many of which are excellent value and offer every possible convenience. There is a nascent independent hostel movement, most conspicuously in Kyiv, Lviv and the Ukrainian Carpathian region.

FOOD AND DRINK

Fertile Ukraine produces a wealth of vegetables that find their way into soups and stews – of which the most celebrated is *borscht* (beetroot soup). Crescent-shaped dumplings called *vareniki* are a Ukrainian staple, usually served stuffed with cabbage, potato or cheese. Pork and chicken dishes aplenty, though many Ukrainians may eat meat only rarely. Drinkwise, vodka rules. But there are **good local beers** and some splendid hefty red **wines** from the Black Sea region. Try the sweet **kagor**, produced in southern Ukraine or imported from neighbouring Moldova.

VATICAN CITY (HOLY SEE)

Tiny theocratic state that survives as a political island within the Italian capital, and the sole remaining territory of the once much more extensive Stato Pontificio or Papal States. Churches, fabulous art collections and remarkable gardens characterise the planet's smallest country. And there is something for rail travellers too. The Vatican has a few hundred metres of **railway line** and its own train station – in days past generally used only by the Pope. But Pope Francis has brought a breath of fresh air to Vatican transport, when he permitted a regular Saturday morning train from Città del Vaticano to Castel Gandolfo, only bookable as part of a tour. Even if you don't take that train, Vatican City's sole railway station deserves a visit. It's a graceful white marble affair, which these days houses the Vatican coin and stamp collections (open to the public).

Essentials: Local name: Stato della Città del Vaticano/Status Civitatis Vaticanae – Population: 453 – Capital: Vatican City – Currency: Euro (EUR) – Language: Latin, Italian (English and French spoken) – Plug types: C, F, L —Time zone: winter GMT+1, summer GMT+2 – International dialling code: +3906 – Public holidays: 1, 6 Jan; 11 Feb; 19 Mar; Easter Monday; 1 May; 29 June; 15 Aug; 1 Nov; 8, 25, 26 Dec.

Reference Section

The reference section that follows is packed with factual detail to assist in **journey planning**. You'll surely also want to refer back to this section while travelling. Top of the list are our city links tables, which start overleaf. Use them to check how long it will take to travel by direct train between key cities across Europe.

A word on place names

To kick off this final section of the book, we throw in a thought on a topic which confounds many novice travellers. **Place names** are infinitely mutable. Even within a country you will find multiple renderings of the same place name. Luik, Lüttich and Liège are all the same place — the town in eastern Belgium that English speakers most commonly refer to as Liège.

The city you knew as Cologne when you were planning your journey turns out to be Köln when you reach it. The Viennese, it transpires, don't call their city Vienna, but favour Wien. And the Danish capital is København. Where a city has a very well established **English version** of its place name, then we have used that rather than the native version in this book: so Prague rather than Praha, Munich rather than München, Seville rather than Sevilla.

Before you throw up your hands in despair, rest assured that you'll quickly get used to these **various renderings**. With just a little practice, you'll master the knack of mapping one version onto the other, and by the time you get back home you'll be referring to Venezia and Firenze rather than Venice and Florence. In areas which use the **Cyrillic alphabet**, you'll pick up some interesting variations. Russia's second city (Санкт-Петербург to the locals) is commonly called St Petersburg by English speakers. A more accurate transliteration of the Cyrillic would be Sankt Peterburg.

While you are travelling, you'll almost certainly run across some **odd exonyms**, ie. names used by speakers of other languages to refer to a particular city. Italians often speak of a city called Monaco di Baviera (or sometimes just Monaco) which is in fact Munich. If you catch a train from Hungary to Bratislava, the chances are that it'll be signed as going to Pozsony — that's the Hungarian name for the Slovak capital.

City links

On the following pages, we give the fastest travel times by **direct train** between various European cities. There are many more journeys which can be done with a single seamless change of train. Examples are Zagreb to Vienna with an easy change in Graz. Or Warsaw to Vilnius with a cross-platform change in Mockava. Whilst we only show a direct night train from Munich to Ljubljana, that journey can also be done by day with a change of train in Villach – and it's faster than by night. It's a guaranteed connection that works well. But we don't list that daytime option as it's not direct.

Our listings show where there are direct trains between 66 cities and rail hubs in those parts of Europe covered by this edition of *Europe by Rail*. For each city pair, we give the fastest travel time by a direct train service. The data are derived from timetables for autumn 2024.

The **numbers in brackets** after the emboldened name of a departure city show on which routes in this book that city features. A handful of our 66 departure cities don't feature on any route. For each departure city, we give a selection of places served by direct **overnight train (N), daytime train (D) or ferry (F)**. These letters follow the destination name. We only include an overnight train if it has proper sleeping accommodation on board. That usually means sleeping cars, but there are a handful of services which have only couchettes. We do not include overnight trains which only offer seats because, let's face it, that's not a comfortable way of spending the night. For other notes used in the city links tables, see the boxed inset on p506.

The **fastest travel time** by direct train (in hours and minutes) is rounded up to the closest ten minutes. Faster travel times may be available by indirect services with one or more changes of train along the way. Just bear in mind that on many routes with multiple direct trains each day, not all journeys will be equally fast. So if we say four hours is the fastest, that won't necessarily apply to every train, and you may well find yourself on a direct train that takes five hours or even longer. Indeed, that fastest travel time may apply to only one or two trains each day.

Overnight trains are generally slower than daytime trains – a sensible timetabling strategy which nicely allows travellers to sleep longer. So for city pairs with a choice of daytime and overnight direct links, you can be pretty sure that travel times quoted relate to daytime services. Finally, just be aware that timetables do change from time to time.

Key abbreviations

D – A direct daytime train links these two cities.
F – A direct daytime or overnight shipping connection links these two cities.
N – A direct overnight train with sleepers and/or couchettes links these two cities.

Amsterdam (6, 8, 25)
Basel N (10h)
Berlin N* D (6h)
Brussels D (2h)
Cologne D (2h40)
Frankfurt D (4h)
Innsbruck N (14h20)
Lille D (2h40)
London D**X** (4h10)
Marseille D* (7h10)
Munich N D (7h10)
Paris D (3h20)
Prague N* (12h30)
Vienna N (14h20)
Zurich N (11h40)

Athens (49)
Thessaloniki D (5h)

Bar
Belgrade N D* (10h30)

Barcelona (18, 20, 21, 22)
Cádiz D (13h40)
Lyon D (5h)
Madrid D (2h30)
Marseille D (4h50)
Paris D (6h50)

Bari (49)
Milan N D (7h)
Rome D (4h)
Venice D (7h40)

Basel (8, 41)
Amsterdam N (10h)
Berlin N D (7h30)
Cologne N D (3h50)
Frankfurt D (2h50)
Hamburg N D (6h30)
Milan D (4h20)
Munich D (5h)
Paris D (3h10)
Prague N (12h10)
Zurich D (1h)

Belgrade
Bar N D* (11h)

Bergen (27)
Oslo N D (6h40)

Berlin (10, 12, 33, 36)
Amsterdam N* D (6h)
Basel N D (7h30)
Bratislava N D (8h50)
Brussels N (10h40)
Budapest N D (11h20)
Cologne D (4h)
Copenhagen N* (9h50)
Frankfurt D (4h)
Hamburg D (2h30)
Innsbruck D (12h40)
Kraków D (7h20)
Munich D (3h50)
Paris N* (14h10)
Prague D (4h10)
Przemyśl D (10h)
Stockholm N (15h20)
Vienna N D (7h50)
Warsaw D (5h10)
Zurich N D (8h40)

Bordeaux (17)
Lille D (4h50)
Marseille D (6h20)
Paris D (2h10)

Bratislava (33, 35)
Berlin N D (8h50)
Budapest N D (2h30)
Hamburg D**Y** (11h20)
Innsbruck D (5h20)
Košice N D (5h50)
Kraków N D (5h30)
Prague D (4h20)
Przemyśl D (8h50)
Salzburg D (3h50)
Split N* (16h50)
Vienna D (1h10)
Warsaw N D (8h40)
Zurich D (8h50)

Brussels (7)
Amsterdam D (2h)
Berlin N (11h)
Cologne D (1h50)
Frankfurt D (3h10)
Lille D (0h40)
London D (2h)
Lyon D (3h40)
Marseille D (5h30)
Munich N* (11h)
Paris D (1h30)
Prague N* (15h40)
Salzburg N* (12h20)
Vienna N* (15h40)

Bucharest (34)
Budapest N D (15h20)
Constanța D (2h10)
Sofia D* (9h40)
Vienna N (18h40)

Notes

The following notes are shown in **red** or **black** in our city links listings:

D – A direct daytime train links these two cities.
F – A direct daytime or overnight shipping connection links these two cities.
N – A direct overnight train with sleepers and/or couchettes links these two cities.
X – Amsterdam to London resumes in early 2025. Meanwhile change at Brussels Midi.
Y – Currently suspended. Due to be reinstated in the first half of 2025.
* – Direct trains between these two cities operate **only seasonally** or run on **less than six days or six nights each week**. The asterisk is placed next to the D (for day train) or N (for night train) to indicate which is the seasonal or irregular service.

Budapest (32–35, 50)
Berlin N D (11h20)
Bratislava D (2h30)
Bucharest N D (15h)
Hamburg D**Y** (13h50)
Innsbruck N D (7h10)
Košice D (3h40)
Kraków N D (8h20)
Ljubljana D (7h50)
Lviv N (13h30)
Munich N D (7h)
Prague N D (6h50)
Przemyśl D (11h40)
Salzburg D (5h20)
Split N* (15h10)
Vienna D (2h40)
Warsaw N D (11h30)
Zagreb D (6h30)
Zurich N D (10h40)

Cádiz (21)
Barcelona D (12h50)
Madrid D (4h30)

Cherbourg (16)
Dublin F* (19h20)
Paris D (3h10)

Cologne (7, 9, 10)
Amsterdam D (2h50)
Basel D (4h)
Berlin D (4h)
Brussels D (2h)
Frankfurt D (1h10)
Hamburg D (3h40)
Innsbruck N (11h30)
Munich N D (4h30)
Paris D (3h20)
Salzburg N* (9h30)
Vienna N* D (9h)
Zurich N D (6h10)

Constanța (34)
Bucharest D (2h10)

Copenhagen (25, 27)
Berlin N (9h20)
Göteborg D (3h50)
Hamburg D (4h40)
Oslo F (19h)
Stockholm D (5h20)

Cork
Dublin D (2h20)

Dublin (4, 5)
Cherbourg F* (18h)
Cork D (2h30)

Edinburgh (2, 3)
Fort William D (5h10)
London N D (4h)
Penzance D (10h30)
York D (2h30)

Florence (45, 46)
Milan D (2h)
Munich N (10h50)
Rome D (1h40)
Trieste D (5h)
Venice D (2h20)
Vienna N (11h)

Fort William (3)
Edinburgh D (5h20)
London N (12h10)

Frankfurt
Amsterdam D (4h)
Basel D (2h50)
Berlin D (4h)
Brussels D (3h10)
Cologne D (1h10)
Hamburg D (3h40)
Innsbruck D (6h20)
Lyon D (6h)
Marseille D (7h50)
Munich D (3h20)
Paris D (3h50)
Vienna D (6h30)
Zurich D (4h)

Göteborg (27)
Copenhagen D (3h50)
Oslo D (3h30)
Stockholm D (3h)

Hamburg (25, 31, 33)
Basel N D (6h30)
Berlin D (2h30)
Bratislava D**Y** (11h20)
Budapest D**Y** (13h40)
Cologne D (3h40)
Copenhagen D (4h40)

Frankfurt D (3h30)
Innsbruck N D (10h)
Munich N D (5h40)
Prague D**Y** (6h40)
Stockholm N (11h20)
Vienna N D (8h50)
Zurich N D (7h40)

Helsinki (30)
Rovaniemi N D (8h10)
Stockholm F (17h50)
Tallinn F (2h10)

Innsbruck (38, 39)
Amsterdam N (13h20)
Berlin D (12h30)
Bratislava D (5h10)
Budapest N D (7h10)
Cologne N (10h10)
Frankfurt D (6h20)
Hamburg N D (10h)
Ljubljana N (7h10)
Munich D (1h50)
Salzburg D (1h50)
Venice D (5h10)
Vienna D (4h20)
Zagreb N (9h40)
Zurich D (3h40)

Košice (35)
Bratislava N D (5h)
Budapest D (3h50)
Prague N D (7h50)
Vienna D (5h50)

Kraków (36, 37)
Berlin D (7h)
Bratislava N D (6h)
Budapest N D (8h40)
Munich N (11h30)
Prague N D (5h50)
Przemyśl D (2h40)
Salzburg N (9h40)
Vienna N D (5h20)
Warsaw D (2h20)

Lille (6, 7, 13)
Amsterdam D (2h50)
Bordeaux D (4h50)
Brussels D (0h40)
London D (1h30)

Lyon D (3h)
Marseille D (4h50)
Paris D (1h20)

Lisbon (24)
Porto D (3h)

Ljubljana (44)
Budapest D (7h30)
Innsbruck N (6h40)
Munich N (7h40)
Trieste D (2h50)
Vienna D (6h)
Zagreb D (2h10)
Zurich N (11h20)

London (1, 2, 5, 13)
Amsterdam D (4h)
Brussels D (2h)
Edinburgh N D (4h20)
Fort William N (12h50)
Lille D (1h30)
Paris D (2h20)
Penzance N D (5h10)
York D (2h)

Lviv (36)
Budapest N (13h20)
Przemyśl D (2h)
Vienna N (16h20)

Lyon (14, 19)
Barcelona D (5h)
Brussels D (3h50)
Frankfurt D (6h)
Lille D (3h)
Marseille D (1h40)
Milan DY (4h50)
Nice D (4h30)
Paris D (2h)

Madrid (22, 23)
Barcelona D (2h30)
Cádiz D (4h30)
Marseille D (8h)

Marseille (13, 15)
Amsterdam D* (7h20)
Barcelona D (4h40)
Bordeaux D (6h10)
Brussels D (5h30)
Frankfurt D (7h50)
Lille D (4h50)

Lyon D (1h50)
Madrid D (7h50)
Nice D (2h30)
Paris N D (3h10)

Milan (40, 41, 47)
Bari N D (6h50)
Basel D (4h20)
Florence D (2h)
Lyon DY (4h20)
Munich N (12h)
Paris DY (6h40)
Rome N D (3h)
Trieste D (4h10)
Venice D (2h30)
Vienna N (11h40)
Zurich D (3h20)

Munich (12, 38)
Amsterdam N D (7h10)
Basel D (5h)
Berlin D (3h50)
Brussels N* (11h)
Budapest N D (6h50)
Cologne N D (4h40)
Florence N (10h50)
Frankfurt D (3h20)
Hamburg N D (5h40)
Innsbruck D (1h50)
Kraków N (11h40)
Ljubljana N (8h20)
Milan N (11h40)
Paris N D (5h50)
Prague D (5h40)
Rome N (15h)
Salzburg D (1h30)
Venice N D (7h)
Vienna N D (4h10)
Warsaw N (14h20)
Zagreb N (10h50)
Zurich D (3h40)

Narvik (29)
Stockholm N (19h)

Nice (15, 45)
Lyon D (4h30)
Marseille D (2h30)
Paris N D (5h40)

Oslo (26, 27, 28)
Bergen N D (6h40)

Copenhagen F (19h)
Göteborg D (3h30)
Stockholm D (5h20)

Paris (13, 14, 16, 17, 18)
Amsterdam D (3h20)
Barcelona D (6h50)
Basel D (3h10)
Berlin N* (13h20)
Bordeaux D (2h10)
Brussels D (1h30)
Cherbourg D (3h10)
Cologne D (3h20)
Frankfurt D (3h50)
Lille D (1h20)
London D (2h20)
Lyon D (2h)
Marseille N D (3h10)
Milan DY (6h50)
Munich N D (5h40)
Nice N D (5h40)
Salzburg N* (12h20)
Vienna N* (15h10)
Zurich D (4h10)

Penzance (1)
Edinburgh D (10h30)
London N D (5h)
York D (7h50)

Porto (24)
Lisbon D (3h)

Prague (32, 33)
Amsterdam N* (12h20)
Basel N (13h)
Berlin D (4h20)
Bratislava D (4h20)
Brussels N* (15h30)
Budapest N D (6h50)
Hamburg DY (6h50)
Košice N D (8h)
Kraków N D (6h)
Munich D (5h50)
Przemyśl N D (9h30)
Vienna D (4h)
Warsaw N D (8h10)
Zurich N (14h)

Przemyśl (36)
Berlin D (9h50)
Bratislava D (8h50)

City links | 509

Budapest D (11h40)
Kraków D (2h40)
Lviv D (1h50)
Prague N D (9h30)
Vienna D (8h30)

Riga
Vilnius D (4h30)

Rome (46, 48)
Bari N D (4h)
Florence D (1h40)
Milan N D (3h)
Munich N (16h)
Trieste N D (5h30)
Venice N D (3h30)
Vienna N (12h50)

Rovaniemi
Helsinki N D (8h)

Salzburg (12, 39)
Bratislava D (3h50)
Brussels N* (11h40)
Budapest D (5h20)
Cologne N* D (7h50)
Innsbruck D (1h50)
Kraków N (9h50)
Munich D (1h40)
Paris N* (12h50)
Vienna D (2h30)
Warsaw N (12h40)
Zurich D (5h30)

Sofia
Bucharest D* (10h20)

Split (50)
Bratislava N* (16h20)
Budapest N* (15h40)
Vienna N* (15h30)
Zagreb N* D (6h50)

Stockholm (25, 26, 29, 30)
Berlin N (15h50)
Copenhagen D (5h20)
Göteborg D (3h)
Hamburg N (12h30)
Helsinki F (16h40)
Narvik N (18h40)
Oslo D (5h20)

Tallinn
Helsinki F (2h10)

Thessaloniki
Athens D (5h)

Trieste (44, 47)
Florence D (5h)
Ljubljana D (2h50)
Milan D (4h)
Rome N D (5h20)
Venice D (2h10)
Vienna D (9h10)

Venice (47, 49)
Bari D (7h30)
Florence D (2h20)
Innsbruck D (5h10)
Milan D (2h30)
Munich N D (7h)
Rome N D (3h30)
Trieste D (2h10)
Vienna N D (7h50)
Zurich D (7h10)

Vienna (34, 35, 39, 44)
Amsterdam N (13h50)
Berlin N D (7h40)
Bratislava D (1h10)
Brussels N* (14h50)
Bucharest N (18h30)
Budapest D (2h40)
Cologne N* D (9h)
Florence N (11h40)
Frankfurt D (6h30)
Hamburg N D (8h50)
Innsbruck D (4h20)
Košice D (5h50)
Kraków N D (5h10)
Ljubljana D (6h)
Lviv N (16h30)
Milan N (12h30)
Munich N D (4h10)
Paris N* (14h)
Prague D (4h10)
Przemyśl D (8h30)
Rome N (14h)
Salzburg D (2h30)
Split N* (14h10)
Trieste D (9h20)
Venice N D (7h50)
Warsaw N D (7h40)
Zurich N D (8h)

Vilnius
Riga D (4h20)

Warsaw (31, 36)
Berlin D (5h10)
Bratislava N D (8h30)
Budapest N D (11h20)
Kraków D (2h20)
Munich N (14h10)
Prague N D (8h10)
Salzburg N (12h30)
Vienna N D (7h30)

York (2, 3)
Edinburgh D (2h30)
London D (1h50)
Penzance D (8h)

Zagreb (50)
Budapest D (5h50)
Innsbruck N (9h20)
Ljubljana D (2h10)
Munich N (10h20)
Split N* D (6h40)
Zurich N (13h50)

Zurich (9, 39, 40, 43)
Amsterdam N (11h40)
Basel D (1h)
Berlin N D (8h40)
Bratislava D (8h50)
Budapest N D (10h40)
Cologne D (6h10)
Frankfurt D (4h)
Hamburg N D (7h40)
Innsbruck D (3h40)
Ljubljana N (12h30)
Milan D (3h20)
Munich D (3h30)
Paris D (4h10)
Prague N (13h30)
Salzburg D (5h30)
Venice D (7h10)
Vienna N D (8h)
Zagreb N (14h)

> Our listings are based on timetables valid in autumn 2024. Schedules for 2025 and beyond may vary slightly.

Tickets and rail passes

For almost any traveller exploring Europe by rail, train tickets will be one of the two principal categories of expenditure, the other of course being accommodation. How much you spend on tickets will be determined by your itinerary, whether you opt for second or first class and – in many countries – whether you can **book well in advance**. Across large parts of Europe, this last factor will dramatically influence how much you pay.

As you have reached this section of the book, the chances are that you have already decided where you want to travel, or have at least started to narrow down options. Perhaps you are already thinking about tickets for an upcoming journey. This may all prove extremely easy. If so, you are one of the lucky ones. For many, the whole process of reviewing ticket options and then booking turns out to be a hassle. In this section of *Europe by Rail*, we share a few thoughts on **how best to get tickets** for the sort of journeys described in this book.

RAIL PASSES VERSUS POINT-TO-POINT TICKETS

Let's get a **few basics** out of the way first of all. If you are planning on a fair amount of rail travel outside your home country within a month or two, then it is well worth considering buying a rail pass. Interrail and Eurail are the two main options here. Interrail is only for residents of Europe. Eurail is for travellers resident outside Europe.

If you are making more limited journeys, know exactly where and when you want to travel, and don't need flexibility, then regular train tickets may be an ideal solution. These are often referred to as **point-to-point tickets**. If in doubt, we tend to go for passes – and sometimes we may do that even where we know that point-to-point tickets might have been marginally cheaper. Why? Well, sometimes a pass may bring a little more flexibility and, let's face it, sometimes it is too much hassle getting point-to-point tickets.

To put it bluntly, **European rail ticketing is a mess**. Buying tickets for complex journeys can be immensely frustrating. In many European countries, people often complain that tariffs and tickets for domestic rail travel are far too complicated. This is a refrain we have heard from rail travellers in Great Britain, Germany, France and more widely. It is small wonder then that, if rail tickets for travel at home seem complicated, tickets for **cross-border journeys** are often even more daunting.

MAKING CROSS-BORDER TICKETING EASIER

In July 2024 the **president of the European Commission**, Ursula von der Leyen, called for a major reform of international rail ticketing. "Cross-border train travel is still too difficult for many citizens," said von der Leyen, as she highlighted the difficulties that passengers face with fragmented tariffs.

Byway Travel

If you are one of those people who just **love travel** but hate the whole process of researching and booking trips, then help is at hand from a **fast growing tour operator** which will offer a tailor-made trip for readers of *Europe by Rail* wanting to book a journey shaped around one or more routes in this book. The company is called Byway Travel. If you have not explored Europe by train before, then Byway Travel may be a good partner in booking a first trip. Or if day-to-day life is just too frenetic and leaves no time for **trip planning or making bookings**, then talk to the team at Byway Travel. They will not handle merely the rail ticketing alone; their license as a tour operator means that there needs to be some accommodation element. On longer trips the hotel bookings need not cover the entire holiday.

Under the dynamic leadership of CEO **Cat Jones**, Byway offers flight-free journeys across Europe. Be it a round trip or a one-way journey, starting anywhere in Europe, Byway will **develop a detailed itinerary** for you to approve. Once you've agreed, they will take care of rail and ferry tickets, plus your hotel bookings, for the entire trip. We have worked closely with Byway for four years, advising the company on the best itineraries. Byway Travel offers off-the-shelf holidays which **can be booked online** (see www.byway.travel/europebyrail) but for most trips following routes in this book your best bet is to opt for Byway's concierge service.

Just in case you wonder, we don't receive or accept any affiliate fees or kickback when you book with companies mentioned in this book. So we recommend Byway Travel because we find what they are doing extremely interesting. Of course, using a tour operator usually means some mark-up over what you might pay if you make all the rail, ferry and hotel bookings yourself. But it certainly saves a lot of headaches and you have the assurance that **help is at hand** when your journey is disrupted, with free rerouting and hotels rebooked as necessary at no extra cost to you.

So the European Commission is, in von der Leyen's words, pressing for an integrated booking system so that "Europeans can buy one single ticket on one single platform and get passengers' rights for their whole trip." The rights referred to here are **guarantees about ticket acceptance** right through to the final destination when trains are delayed or cancelled – and compensation when things go badly wrong.

How long it will take for all this to come to pass is anyone's guess. It won't happen tomorrow. But national rail operators are being nudged into getting their act together. Too often their **ambition flags at frontiers**. Some are trying. Deutsche Bahn will already sell you a ticket from Amsterdam to Lugano or from Bratislava to Brussels.

Meanwhile, this imperative to service demand for **cross-border ticketing**, particularly for longer itineraries, is fuelling the growth of independent ticket retailers who link together tickets from different sources to allow you to make a complex trip across Europe. The Paris-based company **Rail Europe** does just this, allowing you to book tickets from Manchester to Marseille or from Madrid to Amsterdam. Download their app or play around on their website at www.raileurope.com.

Rail Europe is what's known as an aggregator. There are others. **Trainline** (www.thetrainline.com) is well known in Britain and the company is very good at many cross-border itineraries (including some where Rail Europe stumbles), but curiously Trainline won't manage a through booking from a station in Britain (other than London) to continental Europe. The Berlin-based aggregator **Omio** (www.omio.com) is another player in this area. As things currently stand, Rail Europe is the pick of the bunch. Some transactions may incur a fee, though as we go to press with this new edition all purchases made in sterling with Rail Europe are still fee-free. That may change of course, but we would argue that a modest fee may be a price worth paying to secure a ticket that is not easily available elsewhere.

For simple journeys, particularly where a through ticket is available from the relevant rail operator, we tend to **book directly with the operator** if they have a half-decent website. There is anecdotal evidence that buying directly from the operator may be slightly advantageous when things go wrong. With major disruptions, operators may refer passengers who have booked through agents back to those sales channels for refunds or exchanges.

Getting the best deals on tickets

For those with the patience to check out a variety of different websites and agents, there are some fabulous deals there for the taking, especially for **early bookers**. Checking in September 2024, we find tickets from Zurich to Malmö available for under €60. Or from Rotterdam to Salzburg for under €40. These are exceptional offers and sometimes one might have to pay much more for the same trips. On p524, we **list some of the principal websites and agencies** that we have found useful in researching and buying rail tickets and passes for travel around Europe.

The secret to getting the cheapest fares is to book ages in advance, to avoid travel at peak times and on peak days, and to show some flexibility about what kind of train you want to take. This doesn't mean to say that slower trains are always cheaper. But we have noticed that on a day when the very fastest ICEs from Berlin to Munich have second class tickets for €70, a seat on a slightly slower ICE on that same route may be only €35.

How far in advance can I book?

The key to securing the best fares is usually to book your tickets the moment they become available. One small caveat is that, in a few countries, premium fares aimed at the business market may become available slightly prior to discounted tariffs. The **forward booking horizon** for rail operators across continental Europe generally varies from two to six months.

Some operators (like Deutsche Bahn) open bookings on a **day by day basis** with the booking period advancing by one day in the early hours of each morning. Others (like Renfe in Spain) **release tickets in waves**, with

Booking tips

One thing that's clear from our review of rail tickets is that fares and ticketing are complicated matters, the high theology of which is understood by only a handful of people on the entire planet. The average travel agent will not be able to help you a lot, so if you need help, it is best to turn to specialists. A good source of online advice is **Mark Smith**, the much-quoted **Man in Seat Sixty-One**, whose comprehensive website at www.seat61.com gives rock-solid information on the best fares and where to book.

For booking **Interrail or Eurail passes**, we suggest that you first take a look at those schemes' official websites: www.interrail.eu and www.eurail.com. You can purchase passes on those sites, but our top tip for buying Interrail passes is **All Aboard** (www.AllAboard.eu). This Swedish company prices in euros and sells only mobile passes. All Aboard doesn't charge a refund fee if you change your travel plans and decide not to use your pass – provided of course the pass has not been activated for use.

Most **national rail websites** give reliable timetable information and allow online booking for domestic and in some instances also for international tickets (see our overview of booking sites and apps on p524 for further details). It's worth bearing in mind that the great majority of European train tickets are purchased through sales channels without the addition of any **booking fees**. Some websites may levy a booking fee. If it's an unusual ticket not available elsewhere, or if there's some real added value (such as first-class customer service), then paying a fee may be money well spent. We leave you to decide.

It is worth bearing in mind that **e-tickets** are now very much the norm. When you present your ticket for inspection on the train, you may need to show a passport (or other form of identification). **Mobile tickets** are also on the rise with many operators. These have a matrix barcode (usually a QR or Aztec code) and are presented to the conductor on board straight from your mobile device.

With such a fragmented market, the Holy Grail in European rail ticketing has been to create a platform that integrates fares data from a variety of vendors to create through itineraries. We said a few words about that on p510. **Rail Europe** is always worth a look. See www.raileurope.com for more complex itineraries which cannot be booked on individual operators' websites. And just a reminder that if you are overwhelmed by the whole business of planning and booking, there are agents who offer packages for travellers following many of the routes in this book, selling rail tickets and hotels as an all-in bundle. See the box on p511 in which we mention **Byway Travel** (www.byway.travel) where Cat Jones and her team will put together a travel plus accommodation package for many of the routes in this book (or indeed for other European journeys). Many Byway packages rely on Interrail passes. Two other companies worth checking out are **Tailor Made Rail** (www.tailormaderail.com) and **Original Travel** (www.originaltravel.co.uk). If you really like planning things yourself, and just need a bit of help on the ticketing side, you might like to turn to **Ffestiniog Travel** (www.ffestiniogtravel.com, ☎ +44 1766 512 400) or **International Rail** (www.internationalrail.com). Although both agents are in Britain, they are able to handle enquiries and bookings for clients based outside Britain.

each new wave covering a month or two. So you may search in vain for tickets for a journey just six weeks hence, but then bookings open all at once for the entire summer. Yet others, like **SNCF in France**, generally follow a fixed booking horizon (three months for SNCF) but may release tickets for mid-summer travel in a single wave. In Croatia and Denmark, tickets for domestic journeys go on sale just two months in advance. At the other extreme is *Caledonian Sleeper*, operator of Anglo-Scottish overnight trains, where you can book your ticket a full year in advance.

Whenever there are **major timetable changes**, generally on the second weekend in December each year across much of western and central Europe, ticket sales for the new timetable period will not open until the new schedules have been confirmed, and that may mean that, for a spell each autumn, the forward booking horizon is shorter than normal.

BIG REWARDS FOR EARLY BOOKERS

Across much of continental Europe, though less so in eastern Europe and the Balkans, there has been a **revolution in rail tariffs** over the last ten years. Fares were traditionally based on the length of your proposed journey. While these kilometre-based tariffs still often apply to passengers who purchase their tickets on the day of travel, many countries now offer a vast range of cheaper options.

Let's take two routes of similar length. The regular **distance-based fares** from both Paris to Leipzig and Amsterdam to Salzburg (each journeys of about 1,000 km) are similar: in each case about €165 to €185. The precise amount payable varies by the route you elect to follow. But canny travellers on a budget always book well ahead. Commit yourself in the few days after ticket sales open and you will almost certainly pay under €50 for either of our two sample journeys above. Even if you book just a week in advance, there is still a very good chance of **bagging a good deal** – probably under €100.

Most rail operators in western Europe have fallen in love with **market pricing**, where the fare on offer is carefully tuned to reflect anticipated demand, and where the customer prepared to book well in advance and – most importantly – **commit to a particular itinerary** and specific trains can travel for a fraction of the regular fare. The best deals are always on off-peak services.

Of course, our Paris to Leipzig and Amsterdam to Salzburg examples both come from an area of Europe where rail tariffs are pricier than elsewhere across the continent. Move east a little and €175 will buy you a **fully flexible** ticket for a journey of over 2,000 km from Prague to Turkey. No need to book in advance and you can even stop off as often as you wish along the way within the period your ticket is valid.

Our general rule of thumb is that, in those areas where market pricing gives **advantages to early bookers**, you can normally expect to pay about one quarter of the regular fare if you book within a week or two of tickets being released for sale. The names given to these early deals vary confusingly by country and rail operator.

Youth and senior discounts

While every country offers child discounts, there are few **across-the-board discounts** for young people, students or seniors. Where such discounts do exist, they are usually calculated as a percentage reduction on the regular full fare, and are rarely as cheap as the bargain-basement fares available to anyone who books well in advance.

Eurostar is a happy exception and offers discounts to young people and seniors even on many discounted standard-class fares. And **Hungary** is a wonderful example to all of Europe, offering free rail travel (on all but a small number of express services) to all EU citizens aged 65 or older. There are also railcards geared to specific market segments (eg. youth or senior travellers). Read more about those below.

Railcards

Many European rail operators offer **reductions on their regular tariffs**, and sometimes also on their discounted early-booking fares, to holders of selected railcards. Most of these cards are actively marketed only within the countries where they are valid. These railcards are usually valid for one year and **can be purchased by anyone**, so you do not need to be a local resident.

Examples are the Swiss *Halbtax* card, the Czech *In Karta*, the French *Carte Avantage*, the German *BahnCard* and the Dutch *Voordeelurenkaart*. Many countries have specific railcards aimed at the youth and senior-citizen markets. In **Britain**, for example, there are railcards aimed at 16–25 year olds, at those who are aged 26–30 and at the 60+ market. Other countries sell their national railcards to youths, couples and seniors at a reduced price. The Austrian *Vorteilscard*, for example, normally costs €99 for a year, but those under 26 years of age pay just €19 and seniors (those older than 64) pay €29. Note that the **RailPlus scheme**, which gave modest discounts on certain rail fares across multiple European countries was discontinued in 2023.

You have to be doing a lot of travelling over an extended period to make the purchase of such railcards worthwhile. They are however an attractive option for residents or for those who frequently visit one particular country. For example, many British residents who are regular Channel-hoppers have realised that a French railcard can be a very sensible investment. Most rail cards are annual cards, but there are one or two exceptions. The Swiss *Halbtax* card is essentially designed as an annual card, but for **visitors from outside Switzerland** there is one-month version (often marketed under the English name *Swiss Half Fare Card*). This gives a 50% discount on public transport across Switzerland for one month. It costs 120 Swiss francs.

First-class comfort

First-class carriages may offer **better legroom, extra space for luggage** and a higher level of service. That may include snacks and drinks served at your seat (often at a price), complimentary newspapers, power sockets and free wi-fi access. Quite what you actually get for the extra outlay **varies greatly by country and category of train**. The COVID-19 pandemic has made some travellers particularly value the extra space available in many first-class carriages. With the real drop in business travel since 2020, many first-class seats are these days taken by travellers keen to maintain social distancing.

On a very small number of trains, passengers in first or premium classes may receive a complimentary snack or meal. Examples of where you can enjoy such perks include TGV Lyria trains between France and Switzerland in their business premier class and Eurostar trains, where passengers in Eurostar plus are offered complimentary snacks and drinks while Eurostar premier **travellers enjoy substantial meals** complemented by fine wines.

Whether you think it worth splashing out for first class is really a matter of personal choice. Bear in mind that first class affords much **less opportunity for contact with locals**. The availability of first-class seating may be very limited on some routes. On certain long-distance daytime trains in central Europe and the Balkans, for example, just a small part of a single carriage is designated as first class – Munich to Zagreb and Budapest to Cluj-Napoca are examples.

The extra you pay for first class varies greatly. As a general rule, expect to pay about 50% more than for a second-class fare. In some countries you just pay a flat fare supplement on top of the regular price. Austria is an instance of this, where for holders of a first-class Interrail pass or a first-class ticket an upgrade to business class costs €15, whatever the length of journey.

The question of class is **more complex on night trains**, where the basic distinction is between seats, couchettes and sleeping compartments. The highest sleeping compartment category will usually only be available to holders of first-class tickets (plus the sleeper supplement). For more on night trains see pp22–24.

Second class or first class?

Most European local trains are one class only. Many regional trains and most express or long-distance services offer **two classes of service**, often called second and first. The names vary. On many Finnish trains for example, the two classes are called Eco and Extra respectively. In many countries, second class may be marketed as economy or standard.

If you are buying tickets at a railway station, and you don't specify to the contrary, the booking clerk will generally assume that you wish to travel second class. Most booking websites also take second (or standard) class as the default or norm.

A small number of trains offer **three levels of services**. On such trains, the middle of the three classes is usually roughly equivalent to first class, and the highest class is a premium product. **Eurostar's services** have Eurostar standard, Eurostar plus and Eurostar premier. **NTV Italo** pretentiously asserts (at www.italotreno.com) that they do not have classes, but three travel ambiences: smart, prima business and club executive.

Some Italian high-speed rail services have no less than **four different classes of travel**. On Trenitalia's Frecciarossa trains the four classes are marketed as standard, premium, business and executive. The last of these is clearly designed for travellers who only very reluctantly leave their private jet at home. In **Spain** things get even more complicated with operator *iryo* offering a choice of seats in Inicial, Singular, Singular Only You and Infinita Bistró. We'll leave you to fathom those out.

Unless you really value **creature comforts**, the regular second-class (or standard-class) carriages are more than adequate on most day trains (see the box on p516 to find out more about what to expect in first class). The question of **comfort levels on night trains** is more complicated, and the simple distinction between first and second class no longer applies. See our feature on night trains on pages 22–24.

First class bargains

The real surprise for many travellers is that there are times when first-class **tickets may be cheaper** than second class. Early bookers can sometimes take advantage of special offers, usually only available online, for heavily discounted first-class tickets. We have noted many instances of journeys in western Europe where the cheapest available ticket is in first class. Travelling from Paris to Berlin last May, we found that Deutsche Bahn was offering first-class tickets at a fare which undercut anything available in second.

You are most likely to encounter this oddity some time after bookings first open, when **budget-conscious travellers** have already snapped up all the cheap second-class seats, but bookings in first class are still very light. This is most likely at weekends and during summer holidays – so when budget leisure travel is in high demand but there are fewer business travellers on the move.

Is it really worth getting a rail pass?

The question that many travellers ponder endlessly before, during and even after exploring Europe by rail is whether **investing in a rail pass** makes good financial sense. Cast back 50 years and the first generation of Interrail pass holders explored Europe's principal cities by day and slept by night on trains making long nocturnal hops across Europe. Others partied by night and slept on trains by day. Either way, the Interrail pass was a fine investment. Young backpackers with stamina could criss-cross Europe for a month and hardly pay a cent for accommodation.

Times have changed. Many European railway administrations have **introduced supplementary charges** for pass holders wishing to use even the most basic category of accommodation on overnight services. Some countries also levy a supplement for pass holders using premium daytime express trains. These supplements must usually be purchased prior to boarding. The

Rail pass supplements

A rail pass does not necessarily entitle you to totally free travel. **Many trains require that you pay a supplement**. And be aware that on selected trains (eg. on TGV and Eurostar services), there may be only a limited contingent of seats available for pass holders. Travellers who hop aboard without pre-checking availability, and without having paid for the necessary supplement, may be in for a big surprise as they are charged the full fare for their journey.

A supplement of €10 or €20 is payable on **TGV services** within France. Whether you pay the lower or higher fee depends on how busy the train is in your preferred class of travel. For international journeys on TGVs, the supplements may be very much more, even up to about €50 for first-class journeys from **Paris to Barcelona**, Geneva or Zurich. From Paris or Lyon to Turin or Milan, when the direct TGVs are reinstated in 2025, the supplement for holders of an Interrail pass will probably be €31 second class or €45 first class.

For domestic journeys on **Trenitalia high-speed trains** in Italy a supplement of €13 is the norm. Not bad for a long-distance leap across Italy, but pricey if you are just making a short hop. The fastest trains in **Sweden** charge 65 SEK or 150 SEK for second and first class reservations respectively – and you have no choice but to get a reservation. For **AVE trains in Spain**, where reservation is also compulsory, the fees are €10 (Elige Estándar), €13 (Elige Confort) and €23.50 (Prémium). The Brenner route Railjet trains (on **Route 38**) have supplements of €13 and €10 in first and second class respectively.

All that sounds like bad news. But choose your trains and routes carefully and it is possible to roam around Europe for a month or more **without having to pay a single supplement**. Britain, Ireland, Denmark, Germany, Switzerland and Austria are all very Interrail-friendly with few daytime trains where pass holders must pay a supplement. And, across much of central Europe (including the Czech Republic, Slovakia and Hungary), supplements – where they exist at all – are no more than a couple of euros.

Interrail and Eurail passes are also accepted on **Eurostar trains**, though a supplement is payable: €30 for travel in standard class and, for holders of first-class passes, €38 for a seat in Eurostar plus (standard premier). These fares are valid on Eurostar trains from London to Brussels and Paris. Prices are €5 more on journeys from London to Rotterdam and Amsterdam. Eurostar supplements between Brussels and Cologne or Paris and Brussels are €27 in standard and €32 in Eurostar plus (standard premier). The best place to purchase passholder supplements, including for Eurostar, is Rail Europe (www.raileurope.com).

Most **night trains** require advance reservation and some sort of extra payment, even if you are willing to spend the entire night in a seat. Trade up to a couchette or sleeping berth and even pass holders will face a substantial supplement. In Italy, for example, pass holders might typically pay €58 for a berth in a shared sleeper or €122 for sole occupancy of that sleeper compartment. We have been struck by how variable these supplements are. On the *Alpine Pearls* night train from Zurich to Zagreb, pass holders may pay as little as €19 for a couchette or €39 for a sleeping berth. Read more about night trains on pp22–24 and see our list of pass supplements at www.ebrweb.eu/rps.

growing number of supplements may undermine the value of a pass, as the holder can no longer breeze through the station and avoid the queues at the ticket office. You can read more about supplements on the page opposite.

A pass may make very good sense if you really intend to **travel very intensively** and cover long distances in those countries where rail tariffs are generally high. Bear in mind that Europe-wide passes (often referred to as global passes) are priced at a level that reflects the high prices of **flexible walk-up tickets** in countries such as Norway, Denmark, the Netherlands, France, Germany, Switzerland and Great Britain.

If your travel horizons lead you further east to areas where even flexible tickets are cheap, then a rail pass may be a poor investment. Even in Italy, they are not such a good deal – in part because the regular fares are very modestly priced, and also due to the supplement demanded of pass holders using Trenitalia's express services in Italy. And passes are not valid at all on Italo trains in Italy; these are high-speed trains run by an independent operator which often offers **very attractive deals on point-to-point tickets**.

In those areas of Europe where market pricing offers potentially great deals for early bookers, travellers prepared to commit two or three months in advance will almost certainly pay less than pass holders. And yet every year, thousands of travellers do buy rail passes and never regret that decision.

The nub of the argument is that with a rail pass you purchase enormous flexibility. The **freedom to roam at will** does not come cheap, but can be incredibly liberating. Yet for those committed to keeping costs to a minimum, provided they are prepared to book well in advance and not change their itinerary, a rail pass may seem an expensive luxury.

Our comments on the relative merits of rail passes versus regular tickets relate mainly to **global passes** that cover a large part of Europe. If your geographical horizons are more limited, restricted to one country or even just one part of a country, you may well find a more restricted pass that meets your needs perfectly.

At this stage, you may want to note just the bare facts. **Interrail** is designed for **residents of Europe**, while **Eurail** is designed for those who live outside Europe. Both Interrail and Eurail Global Passes now have identical geographical validity. They both cover all European rail networks (plus Turkey) bar for six countries: Belarus, Russia, Ukraine, Albania, Moldova and Kosovo. There are some passes that are valid for a single country or just part of a country. You will find mention of these under the relevant country entry in the gazetteer section of this book (see pages 449–503).

Ultimately, the key decision – one which should be made before buying any tickets or passes – is about the **style and manner of travel** which best suits you. Do you value the security of having everything booked in advance or do you prefer to retain a measure of spontaneity? If the latter is important, then a rail pass may well be the best option.

An even deeper dive into passes

There were big changes in the Interrail and Eurail schemes in 2019, with the **two pass programmes** effectively converging. So there are now common conditions for both Eurail and Interrail, although promotional offers (eg. low-season discounts) are still geared to particular passes and target specific market segments.

Mobile pass variants of the passes are now available for both Interrail and Eurail and are used in conjunction with Eurail's wonderful **Rail Planner app**. Once purchased, they normally must be activated within an eleven-month period. But there may be restricted activation dates for passes sold in some promotions designed to encourage low-season travel. **Paper passes** are also still available, but to be honest we really recommend the mobile (or digital) passes. This is mature tech which works well on all modern smart phones and using a mobile pass brings many advantages — one of which is not needing to specify the first date of validity when purchasing your pass.

Interrail passes can only be purchased by residents of Europe (this includes citizens of Turkey, Cyprus and the Russian Federation). Eurail is the parallel scheme for those who don't meet the conditions to buy an Interrail pass. Learn more about the two schemes at www.interrail.eu and www.eurail.com. You'll find **up-to-date prices** for passes on those two websites, where you can also purchase passes. Prices quoted below are valid for autumn 2024, but do note that **seasonal promotions** may offer discounts of as much as 20%. Sometimes even more. A promo sale for Interrail in May 2022 offered 50% off certain passes, while Eurail passes were available with 25% off during a 2024 promo.

Global Passes

The classic Interrail product is the Global Pass and that's now also true of Eurail. The Eurail Select Pass range has been dropped. For both schemes, there are now **ten varieties of Global Pass**. Five are valid for a **fixed number of days** within a one-month period (4, 5 or 7 days), or a two month period (10

Seduced by freedom

The seductive appeal of a **Eurail or Interrail Global Pass** lies in the chance to roam freely across Europe. Of course this freedom can be illusory as in some countries railway operators nowadays demand hefty supplements of pass holders. But the very idea of being able to speed from Hamburg to Budapest on a mere whim is **quite tantalising**. We know of one young Irish traveller who had never once set foot outside his home country until he purchased a Interrail Global Pass. He set off from Cork by ferry for France and a month later was back, having visited 31 countries in 31 days. It was, he said, the worst month of his entire life. As far as we know, he has not once set foot on a train since.

or 15 days respectively). With those variants of the Global Pass you choose exactly which days you want to use the pass. You don't need to decide in advance. You can enter the date in the relevant space on your paper pass or activate a mobile-pass day in the Rail Planner app, then head off knowing that you can enjoy unlimited travel for the rest of that day.

Apart from the five types of passes valid for selected days within a defined period, there are five Global Passes valid for **continuous travel**. No one insists you actually use them every day, but these passes really do allow you to hop on and off trains at will for the entire period that the pass is valid. The periods on offer are 15 or 22 days, and then one, two or three months. We can only wonder if anyone really travels continuously for three months by train and still stays sane.

Global Pass area of validity

The Global Passes – both Interrail and Eurail – are valid across much of Europe. Note that the area of validity was enlarged in 2020, with both passes now accepted in Latvia and Estonia. Since 2019 Eurail has been accepted in Great Britain (where previously only Interrail was valid). The European countries with railways where the passes are **not valid** now number just six: Moldova, Albania, Kosovo, Belarus, Ukraine and the Russian Federation.

With a Global Pass you can roam from Finland to Portugal, from Scotland to Sicily or from Greece to Ireland. It covers in total **three dozen countries** – even including diminutive Monaco and lovely Liechtenstein. And Global Passes are also valid in Turkey, so you can use your pass all the way to Turkey's eastern border with Iran, though we do just wonder if the staff at Kapıköy – that's Turkey's easternmost railway station – have ever actually seen an Interrail or Eurail pass. The westernmost station in Europe where passes are accepted is Tralee in Ireland.

There's an **important caveat for Interrail**, namely that passes are not valid in the pass holder's country of residence, although a recent welcome concession is that Global Pass holders may make two journeys within their home country. **Supplements** are payable on many high-speed and premium-priced trains in a small number of countries, notably France, Spain, Sweden, Italy and Portugal and also on Eurostar and Lyria services (see the box on p518 for further information on these supplements and reservation fees).

As well as the national rail operators, passes are often valid on **private or locally run railways**, or in some cases the latter may offer a discount to pass holders. Occasionally there is no discount at all, for example on some Swiss mountain railways. Many ferry companies give **discounts**, and in fact the Global Pass gives free deck passage on the popular sailings between Italy and Greece operated by Superfast Ferries (you will, however, pay port taxes and there are high-season surcharges of €10 to €25 in summer). The pass may also give you discounts on tourist attractions, hostels, boat trips and even bike hire, so it's worth checking. There are good listings of these ancillary benefits on www.interrail.eu and www.eurail.com.

Global Pass prices

All passes come in **first and second-class variants**. Prices for Eurail and Interrail passes are the same. Expect to pay 30% more for first class; but there are sometimes special offers, usually in winter, where you can very occasionally snap up a first-class pass for the price of a second-class one. For Global Passes there's a 10% discount for **seniors** (aged over 59) and 25% off for **youths** (under 28). Children under 12 travelling with an adult pass holder receive an equivalent kid's pass for free. Additional discounts may be available in special promotions – and for Interrail such promo sales seem pretty frequent.

A first-class Global Pass for three months of continuous travel for an adult costs €1,214. A second-class pass valid for just four days in a month is €283 for an adult with the price for a five-day pass rising to €318. One long return journey across Europe can easily see you recouping the full cost of your pass, perhaps even leaving one or more free days on a four or five-day pass to enjoy an excursion by train from your destination.

A Global Pass valid for **15 days continuous travel** in first class is €605 for an adult (€545 for seniors, €454 for youths). A brilliant deal, but before dashing to purchase it, just consider whether the Global Pass valid for 15 days' travel in a two-month period may not be a far better deal. The price for the latter is about 15% more than the 15 day continuous pass.

One Country Passes (Eurail & Interrail)

Apart from the classic Global Pass products, both Interrail and Eurail offer passes **valid in just one country**. Some national rail administrations market their own passes. Let's look at the Interrail and Eurail offer first.

One Country Passes generally cover just one country, but there are exceptions. Belgium, the Netherlands and Luxembourg are combined together in the **BeNeLux Pass**. Perhaps presciently anticipating a political trend, the **Ireland Pass** covers both the Republic of Ireland and Northern Ireland. Eurail offer a **Scandinavia Pass** (covering Denmark, Norway, Sweden and Finland), but there's no equivalent for Interrail. There is no Eurail One Country Pass for Great Britain or Switzerland, but Interrail does offer One Country Passes for these territories. Visitors from outside Europe (who are not eligible to purchase Interrail) are nudged towards the one-country passes marketed by the **respective national rail administrations** (Britrail, Swiss Travel Pass and the German Rail Pass).

Eurail and Interrail One Country Passes are sold for a **fixed number of days** within one month (but of course nothing stops you from using your

> ## USING PASS DAYS WISELY
>
> With Interrail and Eurail passes that are only valid for a certain number of days within a longer period, direct **overnight trains or ferries** are reckoned by their departure date. So if you are using a Global Pass, for example, to roam through Austria for a day, you can then join an overnight train from Vienna to, say, Rome or Berlin and your pass will be valid for the entirety of that journey (subject to any sleeper supplements), even though you don't disembark until the following morning. If on the day of arrival, you are only making a short onward connecting journey, it may be wiser just to buy a regular ticket for that short onward hop. **Pass days are valuable** so if you have a pass just valid for a certain number of days in one or two months, consider carefully whether the extent of your proposed travel warrants use of a pass day.

travel days consecutively). In most countries, you can choose between 3, 4, 5, 6 or 8 travel days. The amount you'll pay depends on the size of the national rail network and the normal cost of rail travel in the country. Our view is that, for some of the cheaper countries, it may still be more economic to buy **point-to-point tickets** for the specific journeys you want to make. And for some of the top-tier countries, the price of a One Country Pass is similar to a Global Pass. For example, an Interrail One Country Pass for Britain for a youth (aged under 28), valid for four days, second-class travel in a month costs €207. That's not bad value for travel in a region where walk-up fares are pretty high. But the same traveller can pick up a Global Pass for just five euros more – so €212.

When you take into account that the **off-season discount promos** for Interrail are sometimes applicable only to Global Passes, it does mean that a Global Pass price can sometimes undercut the One Country Pass price for the equivalent number of travel days.

OTHER USEFUL PASSES

There are many other passes covering more than one country. These include the **Balkan Flexipass** (covers Bosnia & Herzegovina, Bulgaria, Greece, North Macedonia, Montenegro, Serbia and Turkey) and the European East Pass (Austria, Czech Republic, Hungary and Slovakia).

Useful one-country passes include the **Renfe Spain Pass**, a fine range of passes for Switzerland, the **German Rail Pass** (which includes many routes way beyond Germany's borders) and of course BritRail. This latter is a long-established scheme with many variants. The classic **BritRail Pass** covers England, Wales and Scotland, but there are passes covering just Scotland, just England and also more limited areas. They can be excellent value if you are planning a lot of travel within the designated pass area, all the more so if you value spontaneity and don't want to commit to a specific itinerary by booking much cheaper train tickets (known in Britain as Advance tickets) weeks prior to travel. Find out more about BritRail at www.britrail.com.

Know your apps

Near the very front of this book (see p19) we stressed the importance of **downloading key apps** prior to departure. And then keeping an eye open for others which you may wish to download and use along the way. Quite what you'll need will be driven first and foremost by geography. So public transport apps, whether with timetable data or real time running info, are often geared to special countries or even particular cities or regions.

There are some basic apps which most users of this book will find immensely useful. **Eurail's Rail Planner app** is top of our list of must-haves. It was designed first and foremost for travellers using Eurail and Interrail passes. If you are not using a pass you can just ignore the 'my pass' function in the *Rail Planner* app and still use the journey planner and the 'my trip' functions. This app is **brilliant for itinerary planning** and for checking timetables, and this can all be done without any need to be online. The *Rail Planner* app draws on a timetable database called MERITS. The *Rail Planner* is updated about twice monthly so keep your app up-to-date to be sure you are relying on the latest **MERITS data**. We like the map and listings functionality in 'my trip' on the *Rail Planner* app but it's not easy to export. If having a souvenir of your trip is important try *travelboast* which allows you to record itineraries and photos together in a single app.

For navigating your way across cities, it's hard to beat *Citymapper* for those areas it covers. It's perfect for urban maps, **public transport information** and walking routes. For wider online **mapping of railways** across Europe, we like the pdf versions of Mike Ball's *European Railway Atlas* (see also p222) and the *Railmap* app. Drawing on Open Railway Map data, the *Railmap* app has multiple data layers, so you can customize it to your interests (or, as we do, just flick between layers). For **timetable data**, we have already mentioned Eurail's *Rail Planner* app, but it's also good to have *DB Navigator* on your phone. Unlike the *Rail Planner* app, you need to be online to access timetable data through *DB Navigator*. It has timetables for most of Europe and also offers real-time running information for Germany and some services well beyond Germany's borders. Google will be your best friend in identifying other online sources of **live running data**. For Britain we use *Real Time Trains*, in France the *Ma Gare SNCF* app, in Spain the excellent *adif* app, in the Netherlands *9292*, in Austria *Scotty* and for Switzerland the *SBB Mobil* app works a treat. The list goes on. We can merely give a few pointers here.

There are some apps which will allow to **access your tickets**. We like the easy-to-use *Rail Europe* app which covers a range of tickets from multiple providers. The *Eurostar* app is good for entering **Advance Passenger Information** required for some Eurostar journeys. And the *Trenitalia* app has a useful check-in function which you will need with some Trenitalia tickets.

Planning overnight stays

The question of how much money you might need to explore Europe by train is a tough one. So much depends on **length of journey**, your expectations, the **level of comfort** to which you aspire or the degree of discomfort you are prepared to tolerate.

Train tickets booked three months in advance might cost only a quarter (or even less) of what you might pay if you buy tickets on the day of travel. We have made long journeys through Europe on just a pittance, taking advantage of special fare deals, opting for budget accommodation and surviving on a long litany of picnics. On other occasions, we have splashed out and enjoyed the comfort of crisp, clean sheets in air-conditioned sleeping cars and eaten in style in railway restaurant cars. We give more **advice on train fares and ticketing matters** in this book on pp510–23.

Here our focus is on **accommodation prices**. Hotel and hostel pricing policies vary considerably across Europe. In many countries dynamic pricing is the norm, which means that there is virtually no set price, and the rates paid for the same room may vary wildly according to season, day of the week, or even the weather. Britain follows this approach, and it means that travellers may encounter extraordinarily good low-season deals, while prices rocket at times of peak demand.

In many parts of Europe, the maximum price for which a room may be sold is clearly stipulated, and often subject to approval by the authorities. In some countries that may be the price that most travellers effectively pay. Elsewhere there is **regular discounting**, even to the extent that no one ever really pays the full list price.

Negotiating your way through the tariff jungle is not easy. Where deep discounts on room rates are available, they may be reserved for clients who book weeks (or even months) in advance and prepay the full cost of their stay. A growing range of online booking engines sometimes offer cheaper prices than those quoted by the hotel itself. But don't be too seduced by the power of the **online booking sites**. Many of our favourite hotels are small family-run places, which still simply cannot be booked through any of the major online agencies.

We realise that visitors to Europe sometimes place a certain premium on well-known hotel chains. But there are many areas of Europe where the international chains have no presence in the market. And in so far as Hilton or Marriott are there at all, perhaps in a capital city, their hotels are tailored to the international business market rather than to travellers eager to catch the pulse of local life. However, in **major commercial centres** – such as Brussels, Hamburg or Zurich – top-end business hotels may discount so heavily on Friday, Saturday and Sunday nights that travellers with only modest budgets can afford a weekend of rare luxury.

Throughout Europe, the most common way of pricing accommodation is by room. Although hostels sell beds in dorms on a per-bed basis, in most European countries hotels sell, in the main, **rooms for two people**. Where single rooms exist, they will generally cost much more than half the rate for a twin or double. Solo travel can be an expensive business.

Hotel accommodation in cities often costs more than in rural areas, though Europe's blossoming hostel sector, which offers discount accommodation in most cities, is less well represented in the rural regions of many countries. The new generation of **independent hostels** are not like the youth hostels of yesteryear. They attract clients of all ages and many offer private rooms, sometimes with en suite facilities.

Capital cities are often more expensive than elsewhere in the country, but this rule is not infallible. Hotels in Rome can often be better value than those in Florence or Venice. Berlin is often significantly cheaper than Munich or Cologne. We say a few words in the **gazetteer** (pp450–503) about accommodation issues in different countries.

Hotel rates do not always rise and fall in line with other costs. In Belarus and Russia rail travel is very cheap. Food, even in restaurants, can also be very affordable. But hotel prices are higher than you might expect. Folk flock to Andorra for cheap ciggies and alcohol, but that does not mean that hotels are any cheaper than in neighbouring Spain or France.

Not all who wander are lost

There are many journeys in this book, which can easily be taken without the need to book in advance. They follow routes where train tickets are economical. During low season, when few travellers are out and about, such journeys are well suited to travelling spontaneously. The **sense of freedom** that comes from travelling without knowing where you will rest that evening was a hallmark of travel in the early days of European railways. But it's not for everyone. The modern inclination is to plan every aspect of the journey to such a degree that every risk is minimised and every element of uncertainty banished.

But **some of our very best journeys** have been unstudied, unrehearsed and unplanned. We have set off with a map, the latest issue of the *European Rail Timetable*, a rail pass and a change of clothes. Not much more. And we have wandered. The point is not to plan, but to **savour the serendipity of chance**. To wander for its own sake. "Not all those who wander are lost," wrote Tolkien in *The Lord of the Rings*.

Our feeling is that many travellers have lost the capacity to wander. Travelling without knowing your precise destination or even your route is infinitely more exciting than following a well-mapped trail to a pre-booked hotel.

So, in the spirit of an earlier generation of travellers, we sometimes meander on the slowest of slow trains. We **pause at country stations** and eventually we stumble on a little pension, cheap but more than adequate, and there we stop overnight. The manner of the journey is more important than any specific destination. Without a guidebook and without expectation, we are led by a whim. It is a fine way of exploring Europe. Slow travel is fun. You might like to try it some time.

Cruise trains

The emphasis in this book is on independent travel. The rail journeys we recommend rely entirely on regular scheduled train services. We think that's a fine way to explore Europe by rail, but we understand that it is not for everyone. Some travellers prefer the feel of a specialist cruise train, so here we highlight just a couple of first-class ventures.

The most celebrated European cruise train is the **Venice Simplon-Orient-Express** (VSOE). Since 2019, it's been owned by LVMH (a Louis Vuitton Moët Hennessy marque), adding a bit of retro style to that company's daunting portfolio of classy brands. Paris to Venice is now VSOE's signature route. This route runs weekly in summer 2024. The 25-hour journey from London includes a night aboard an **elegant heritage train** with beautiful Lalique glass panels and art deco marquetry. Such style does not come cheap. One-way from Paris to Venice for a couple sharing a double compartment costs about €5,000 (including meals) and over €15,000 for one of the posh grand suites (which were introduced in 2020). VSOE offers connections between London and Paris with Eurostar.

VSOE's occasional showpiece trips from **Paris to Istanbul** are being offered twice in 2024. You can check schedules and fares on www.vsoe.com. With VSOE commanding those sorts of prices, it is no surprise that many entrepreneurs have tried to emulate the VSOE model.

Golden Eagle Luxury Trains is a British company founded in 1989 by Tim Littler, who in the 1990s organised pioneering steam-hauled trains across the former Soviet Union. Golden Eagle has been a very reliable operation which consistently offers the most adventurous cruise train itineraries in the European market (and beyond). The company's European trains include the *Golden Eagle*, the *Golden Eagle Danube Express*, the *Prestige Continental Express* and the *Glacier Pullman Express*.

The Golden Eagle itineraries are mouth-watering. If you want to ride the **Trans-Siberian Railway**, this is the way to do it in style. But take a look at some of their other offerings too: how about the October 2024 **Venice to Istanbul** rail cruise via Bosnia, North Macedonia and Bulgaria? Golden Eagle here includes a border crossing from Volinja in Croatia to Dobrljin in Bosnia — a rail route which since December 2016 has simply not been used by any scheduled passenger trains. The prices naturally reflect the upmarket product. A couple will pay from €33,690 for that 12-day Venice to Istanbul holiday.

Golden Eagle have suspended their cruise train operations in the Russian Federation, but there are still plenty of exotic journeys on offer including rail cruises to Armenia, Turkmenistan and central Asia. See p224 for a note on the **El Transcantábrico** cruise trains exploring minor rail routes in northern Spain.

When a train is not a train

There may be times when your train turns out not to be a train at all. Sometimes this might be because of a **festival of track maintenance**, meaning that for a day or two buses replace trains on a particular stretch of line. At other times **buses permanently replace trains** on a 'rail' journey. For example, some daytime services operated by Austrian Railways (ÖBB) from Venice to Villach or from Graz to Klagenfurt are not trains at all, but comfortable double-decker coaches. Similarly, the direct services between Luxembourg and Saarbrücken advertised by Deutsche Bahn are in fact buses. Here at least there is a choice, and devotees of rail travel will much prefer to use trains to travel from **Luxembourg to Germany**. The railway traverses pleasant agricultural country in south-east Luxembourg to reach Trier in Germany, from where it is a gorgeous journey up the winding Saar Valley to Saarbrücken.

Rail ferries

Train travellers may even find themselves unexpectedly afloat. On **Route 48** trains are loaded onto ships between the Italian mainland and Sicily. This is Europe's last remaining rail ferry still used for passenger trains. In 2019, three other rail ferry routes in Europea disappeared. The opening of the new **Kerch Strait Bridge** in late December 2019 meant that Russian passenger trains travelling to and from Crimea no longer had to be shipped on ferries. Another rail ferry route which disappeared in late 2019 was the **Fehmarn Strait route** between Germany and Denmark; trains from Hamburg to Copenhagen were rerouted via Jutland and Odense to avoid the ferry. The Malmö to Berlin night train also changed its route when the Trelleborg to Sassnitz ferry was axed, travelling through Denmark instead.

Missing links

On journeys around Europe you will occasionally need to use a bus to bridge a gap in Europe's rail network. One **missing link in the continent's rail infrastructure** is plugged by the bus across the Tatra Mountains between Slovakia and Poland. We now include it in **Route 37**.

Other gaps are between Split and Dubrovnik, on the stretch along the Norwegian coast between the railheads at Bodø and Narvik, on the border between Sweden and Finland on **Route 30** and between Poland and the Baltic States. The latter may (or may not) be ameliorated by the *Rail Baltica* project (read more on p297). In the Balkans there are so few cross-border rail services that travellers find themselves having to switch from train to bus with grim regularity. It is immensely frustrating that capital cities like Belgrade, Sarajevo and Skopje have few or no international train services. And you'll never get to Greece without resorting to a bus or a boat.

A–Z of travel in Europe

Bicycles

Before you start planning a comprehensive tour of Europe by train and bike, just be aware that many railway operators do not take an especially benign view of bicycles. Across much of Europe you can take a bike on many local and regional trains, although restrictions may apply in many urban areas during peak travel times. Usually this requires the purchase of a bicycle ticket – but sometimes taking your bike is free of charge. When boarding a train, look out for carriages marked with a bicycle icon.

Move to long-distance trains and the situation becomes much more varied. For example, most German ICE trains simply have no allocated bike space, so the only way you can transport your bicycle on those trains is if it is folded and carried in a proper bike bag. There is **limited space** for pre-booked bicycles on many German IC trains. Spain is a problem area with bikes barred from all daytime long-distance services, even if they are folded and packed in a **bike bag**. In Finland and the Czech Republic, bicycles can be transported on Pendolino services, but only if pre-booked.

There is a limited amount of space for **pre-booked bicycles** on Eurostar. Some TGVs have bike space, others do not. On Thalys, a bicycle must be folded and packed. Okay, so you get the idea. This is a formidably complicated subject – and you might see why many travellers decide to rent a bike at their destination. In summary, many local trains are bike-friendly, but if you are planning stretches on fast trains, you will need to research carefully what trains are able to take your bike and at what price. The respective rail operator's website is a good source of imformation.

Borders

Most travellers will need a **valid passport** to travel through Europe. A dispensation allows citizens of any of the 30 members of the **European Economic Area** (EEA), plus Switzerland too, to travel throughout the participating countries with just a National Identity Card.

In practice, passport checks are very low-key in much of Europe nowadays and the only occasions your documents are likely to be checked are at certain border pinch points, eg. entering Germany from Salzburg, crossing into Denmark from Flensburg or on the rail journey from Copenhagen to Malmö. Such exceptions apart, it's only around the edges of the **Schengen area** and beyond that passports are scrutinised. That area consists of more than two dozen countries which are party to the Schengen Agreement, allowing freedom of movement across their mutual borders.

The UK and Ireland are conspicuously not members of Schengen and the UK in particular maintains strict **border controls**, even to the extent that you must pass through UK immigration in Brussels, Paris or Lille before joining Eurostar trains bound for London.

So it is really only as you enter the UK, Russia, Belarus, Ukraine, Turkey and certain Balkan countries that you will encounter any significant **border bureaucracy**. See also **Visas** and **Customs checks** in this section.

Cellphones – see Telephones

Children

Kids and trains just go together. Many children will tolerate a much longer journey on a train than in a car. But don't test their patience too much. Too packed an itinerary just won't wash with most youngsters. On some trains, such as Thalys and selected German ICE services, you'll even find **dedicated family space**. Some trains in Scandinavia and Switzerland have a children's play area. Almost without exception, European rail operators offer **discounted fares** for children. In some countries accompanied children even travel for free.

Climate – see Seasons

Credit cards

If you come from a country with a strong credit card culture (such as the UK or USA), you may be surprised how little you can use your credit cards in some parts of Europe. Train ticket machines in some countries may not accept credit card payment and you may find that, especially once you get off the main tourist trails, hotels and restaurants will want payment in cash.

Of course in **major cities** payment with plastic is absolutely accepted, but just be aware that this may not apply to more **rural areas**. Where cards are accepted, VISA and MasterCard are your best bets. Some cards, such as AmEx and Diners Club, are quite unknown in many rural regions of Europe.

Cycles – see Bicycles

Currency

With the uncertainties affecting some of the peripheral countries in the **eurozone**, currency remains a hot topic. At least for now, the euro remains by far the most useful currency for travellers exploring Europe by train. You can draw cash from ATMs across Europe.

Proffering UK pounds or US dollars in continental Europe on the assumption that these are valued currencies in foreign countries often simply invites derision. There's really no substitute for local currencies. In central and eastern Europe, as also in the Balkan region, you will find many more countries that use currencies other than the euro. Our country gazetteer (pp450–503) gives currency details for every territory in Europe.

Customs checks

With the development of the single European market, customs checks are becoming a thing of the past. Just be aware that there are still strict limits on **importing cigarettes and alcohol** from non-EU areas into the European Union. No-one will quibble over 200 cigarettes and a bottle of spirits, but that's about the limit. It goes without saying that narcotics, weapons and pornographic publications can all get you into serious trouble. See also **Borders** in this section.

Disabilities

Travellers with disabilities need to take special care in planning their journeys. The exemplary service provided by **Eurostar** (even with concessionary fares) is not emulated across the continent. On premium long-distance services (TGV, AVE, ICE, etc) there is designated space for wheelchairs and boarding assistance is available if pre-booked. Move to regional and local trains and accessibility is much more patchy. It pays to check carefully before booking.

Electricity

The invisible stuff that comes out of plugs isn't quite the same the world over. Most of the planet, including Europe, uses a 220 to 240 volt system (230 volts is the EU standard). If you are travelling with dual voltage appliances such as a hair dryer, check that they are correctly set. More troublesome are **plugs which vary enormously**. A universal plug adaptor is a wise investment. See www.iec.ch/world-plugs for more on the wonderful world of plugs.

Health and travel insurance

COVID-19 has made us all much more health aware. Plan carefully and check quarantine requirements carefully, including any restrictions that might apply upon returning home. Don't be tempted to evade or ignore local health regulations.

If you live in the European Economic Area make sure you get a **European Health Insurance Card (EHIC)** before leaving home. That will cover some (but by no means all) emergency medical expenses within the EHIC area. UK residents may want to check out the GHIC card. Take out **travel insurance** to cover additional medical expenses (including repatriation if necessary) as well as theft or loss of your belongings. Remember to take out insurance at an early stage, as most policies only provide cancellation cover for transport bookings and hotel reservations made after you have taken out the insurance.

Language

Use our **gazetteer** (pp450–503) to check which languages are spoken in each country. English will get you a long way across most of Europe, but it is presumptuous to assume that everyone you meet speaks English. Make sure you master at least a few words of the local lingo. And as you head east, it is important you are able to decipher the **Cyrillic alphabet**, if only to be able to transliterate place names.

Mobile phones – see Telephones

Passports – see Borders

Plugs – see Electricity

Rail passes – see pages 525–28

Seasons

As an area significantly larger than the continental United States, it'll be no surprise that Europe encompasses a great range of **climate zones**. Mainland Europe alone takes in 65° of longitude and 35° of latitude. Of course you really can follow the routes in this book at any time of year, but there can be a special pleasure in travelling to places at times when there are fewer folk on the move. Trains in many parts of Europe are significantly quieter in winter than in summer (provided of course you can avoid the Christmas and New Year rush and you are not bound for the main skiing areas). Our view is that **spring and autumn** are the best seasons for exploring Europe by rail. So April, May, September and October. But bear in mind that the timing of seasons varies greatly across the continent. The southern areas of Spain and Italy may have idyllic spring weather in late March, while at the same time northern Scandinavia and the Alps may still have deep snow.

Smoking bans

A smoking ban on all **public transport** and in some **public places** has prevailed in some European countries for over 25 years, augmented over the last ten years with more bans extended to cover cafés, bars and restaurants. Most of Europe now has such bans, with smoking rarely allowed on trains.

Telephones

If your mobile phone (**cellphone**) is enabled for roaming (ask your provider before leaving home if you're unsure), you'll be able to use it anywhere in Europe where your phone picks up an adequate signal and can log onto a network. It is no longer always the case that you incur a charge to receive calls when abroad. Thanks to a European Union initiative, the costs of receiving and making calls and sending texts have plummeted in recent years. End-user roaming charges were abolished in 2017. This benefits only those with EU SIM cards and applies only to communications within the EU.

If you plan on making a lot of calls from one country, you might consider the merits of buying a local SIM card. **Payphones** are still available in cities and at major rail stations. Increasingly they rely on **prepaid cards** (commonly available from newsstands and in some countries from post offices) rather than cash. Avoid making long calls from phones in hotel rooms. They are invariably expensive.

TIME ZONES

Europe's great longitudinal spread from west to east means that it extends over **seven time zones** (from the Azores to European Russia). Bear in mind that several routes in the book cross time zone boundaries. You can check the time zone for each country in the **gazetteer** section of this book (see pages 446–511).

All but four countries mentioned in this book seasonally adjust their clocks, moving them forward an hour on the last Sunday in March and putting them back on the last Sunday in October. The four exceptions are Iceland, Belarus, Turkey and the Russian Federation.

TRAIN TICKETS – SEE PAGES 21–28

VISAS

EU passport holders can follow all fifty routes in this book without having to worry about visas. Much the same applies to citizens of EEA member states outside the EU, and passport holders from Switzerland, the United Kingdom, Japan, Australia, Canada and the United States. Yet even within these general precepts there are some intriguing exceptions. Australians, for example, need a visa to enter Ukraine (which features in **Route 36** in this book). Note that citizens of some European countries (outside the EEA or EU) require a visa to enter the United Kingdom. The process of securing a UK visa is laborious and expensive.

We live in a divided world and citizens of most African countries, as well as those from Asia (except for Japan and one or two others), will need to secure one or more visas for almost every route described in this book. The same applies to holders of passports from the **Commonwealth of Independent States** (including the Russian Federation) and some Latin American countries. If in doubt, check out what visas might be necessary before purchasing tickets. The consular departments of the embassies of countries you propose to visit will always advise.

Reference section

Index

In this index, we list the **principal places** mentioned in our 50 routes and elsewhere in this book. So this is first and foremost a geographical index. But we also include a small number of entries on **people** (for example Thomas Cook or Jan Morris) or **themes** (like night trains or visas) that crop up in the book.

With very few exceptions, we do not list country names in this index. So you'll not find Spain or Slovenia listed here. Any exceptions relate mainly to microstates (for example Liechtenstein or Vatican City) or small island nations (such as Iceland or Malta). You can check out broader country information in our **gazetteer** on pages 450 to 503. And to verify which countries feature in each of our fifty routes see our **route list** on pages 16 and 17.

A

Å 275
Aachen 104, 107
Aalborg 247, 249–50
Aarhus 247, 249
Aberdeen 65–66, 262
Abisko 273
accommodation 525–26
Achnasheen 67
A Coruña 226
Adler 287
Adlestrop 90
Aeolian Islands 32, 432
África Española 214
Agay 167
Ahlbeck 294
Ais Gill Summit 73
Aix-les-Bains 162, 200–201
Åland Islands 277, 286
Albacete-Los Llanos 210
Albenga 408
Albula Railway 370, 383, 404
Alcázar de San Juan 210–211
Aldermaston 55
Alençon 191
Alentejo 234
Alexisbad 136
Algeciras 214
Alicante 210
All Aboard 513
Alleyras 154
Almería 209–10
Alp Grüm 368, 371
Älvsbyn 270
Amalfi 430

Ambérieu-en-Bugey 162
Amersfoort 237
Amsterdam 69, 101–102, 110, 237
Ancona 438, 448
Ancy 159
Åndalsnes 265
Andermatt 378, 383–85
Andersen, Hans Christian 244, 372
Andorra 187
Angelsey 83
Angers 176, 178, 189, 191–192
Annecy 158, 162
Antequera 219, 220
Antibes 169
Antwerp 99–100, 235
Appleby 73
Apulia 395, 440
Apuseni Mountains 317
Arad 317
Aran Islands 95
Aranjuez 210, 217
Arcachon 180
Arctic Circle 263, 267, 269, 272–73, 280
Ardnamurchan 57
Argentan 191
Arlberg Railway 358–59, 361
Arles 154
Armadale 67–68, 77
Ascoli Piceno 434, 438
Ascona 379
Assisi 416
Athenry 95

Athens 434, 440–41
Athlone 95
Attadale 67
Augsburg 145
Augusta 433
Aviemore 65–66
Avignon 200–203
Ax-les-Thermes 186
Ayamonte 197, 234

B

Babylon 300
Badacsony 444
Badajoz 197, 234
Bad Bentheim 237, 239
Bad Doberan 292
Baden-Baden 122
Bad Schandau 308
Baedeker, Karl 9, 119, 371, 373, 381
Balatonfüred 444
Bâle see Basel
Balkan Flexipass 523
Ball Atlas see European Railway Atlas
Ballinasloe 95
Banavie 76
Bandol 165
Bangor 83
Banyuls 205
Bar 447
Barcelona 182, 187–88, 197–98, 205, 207–208, 215
Bardejov 331
Bari 41, 395, 439–40, 449
Barnstaple 56

INDEX | **535**

Barra 68
Basel 115–16, 373, 375–76
Battaglia Terme 436
Bauhaus architecture 137, 141–142
Bautzen 344
Bayerischer Wald 299
Bayeux 171, 173–74
Beattock Summit 73
Beaulieu-sur-Mer 406
Beaune 159–60
Beethoven, Ludwig van 119
Behaim, Martin 299
Belfast 84
Belgrade 447
Bellagio 372
Bellinzona 378
Belloc, Hilaire 50
Beni Enzar 214
Bergen 254–55, 261–62
Bergerac 180
Bergün 383
Berlin 96, 126, 128, 131–32, 138, 140, 307, 332
Berne 116, 377
Bernina Express (train) 350, 368, 381
Bernina Railway 27, 43, 368, 371–72, 380, 384, 404
Bernkastel 125
Berwick-upon-Tweed 64
Besançon 163
Betjeman, John 54, 150
Beverwijk 69, 71
Béziers 147, 153, 203
Białystok 297, 336–37
Biarritz 180
Bicester 89
bicycles 529
Bilbao 224
Bingen 119–20
Binz 293
Birmingham 81
Birnam Wood 65
Bischofshofen 363
Black Forest 96, 117, 121–122, 138
Blaenavon 404
Blair Atholl 65

Bleiburg 399
Boden 271–72, 279
Bodmin 58
Bodø 268, 274, 276, 528
Bohoniki 336
Bologna 40, 413, 437
Bolzano 351, 355, 357
Bonn 119
Boppard 119, 120
Bordeaux 176, 179–80
Boris Gleb 276
Bornholm 32, 257, 293, 460
Borromean Islands 373, 375, 378–80
Bourges 191, 193
Bourg-Madame 187
Braga 231
Brandenburg 130
Brașov 318, 319
Bratislava 311, 324–26
Braudel, Fernand 206
Breil-sur-Roya 170, 408
Bremen 239–40
Bremerhaven 239–40
Brenner Railway 28, 38, 355
Breskens 100
Briançon 155, 195
Brig 380, 384–85
BritRail 50, 523
Brno 310, 323
Broadford 67, 77
Brocken 133–36
Bruck an der Mur 398
Bruges 97–99
Brugge *see* Bruges
Brunel, Isambard Kingdom 52–55, 94
Brünig-Hasliberg 388–89
Brussels 37, 104–106
Brzeg 346
Bucharest 320
Buchs 360
Budapest 305, 311–12, 316, 323, 404, 442, 444
budget 18–19, 517
Bullay 125
Burano 425
Burgos 221, 223–25
Burnham Beeches 54

Bury St Edmunds 78, 80
Bușteni 319
Byron, GG 119, 389
Byway Travel 15, 511, 513

C

Cáceres 212
Cádiz 197, 213–14
Caen 173, 191
Cahors 185
Cairngorms 59, 66
Calais 150
Calatayud 215
Calatrava, Santiago 33, 106, 209, 232, 235
Caledonian Canal 76
Caledonian Sleeper (train) 60, 76, 514
Cambridge 78, 80
Canary Islands 214
Cannes 164, 168–69
Cannobio 379
Cape Finisterre 226
Capri 427, 430
Carbis Bay 58
Carlisle 63–64, 72–73
Carmarthen 82, 92
Carrara 410
carriage design 175, 287
Cassel 150
Cassis 164–65
Castel Gandolfo 503
Castle Cary 53, 55–56
Catalan Talgo (train) 198, 200
Catania 30, 433
Celje 399
Celta (train) 227, 229
Centovalli Railway 375, 378
Cerbère 205
Cerdanya 186–87
Certosa di Pavia 420
České Budějovice 304
Český Krumlov 304, 460
Cetinje 449
Ceuta 214
Chabowka 347
Chaika Express (train) 297
Chambéry 201
Chamborigaud 154

Chamonix 161
Channel Tunnel 25, 150
Chartres 176, 178, 404
Château de Chillon 389
Chauffailles 194
Cheb 299, 303
Chenonceaux 193
Cherbourg 84, 171, 174, 189
Chernivtsi 298
Chester 78, 81–82
Chiemgau 146
children, travel with 530
Chirk Aqueduct 81
Chișinău 320
Chiusi 417
Chomutov 304
Chop 312, 331
Chur 370, 384
Church Stretton 91
Cilento 431
Cinq-Mars-la-Pile 192
Cinque Terre 410
Ciudad Real 218
Civitavecchia 30, 188, 418
Clermont-Ferrand 153
Clervyus 113
Clifden 95
Cluj-Napoca 316–17
Cluny 27, 156
Cluses 161
Cochem 125
Coimbra 227, 232
Col-des-Roches 163
Colico 372
Collins, Wilkie 54
Collioure 200, 205
Colmar 115
Cologne 104, 107–108, 117, 126, 128
Como 372
Compagnie Internationle des Wagons-Lits 109, 156
Condrieu 195
Constable, John 80
Constanța 43, 320–22, 422
Conwy 82, 83
Cook, Thomas 96, 117, 119, 122–23, 280, 360, 381, 386

Copenhagen 42, 237, 245–46, 255
Copșa Mică 314, 317
Córdoba 211, 215, 219
Corfu 439, 449
Corinth Canal 440
Corniglia 410
Cornwall 52, 55, 57–58
corridor trains 285, 349
Corrour 76
Corsica 206
Cotentin Peninsula 174
Côte-Rôtie 195
COVID pandemic 367
Cowlairs Incline 75
Craven Arms 91
credit cards 19, 530
Cremona 423
Crete 206
Crianlarich 75
cross-city transfers 21, 196
Crotone 395
cruise trains 527
Culloden 66
Culoz 200
Cuneo 170, 349, 408
Curragh 85
currency 530
customs 531
Cuxhaven 240
Cyprus 206
Częstochowa 231, 346

D

Dalí, Salvador 203–205
Dalwhinnie 65
Darlington 64
Dawlish 57
De Haan 103
De Panne 103
Debrecen 330
Delémont 116, 163
Delft 96, 100
Den Haag 97, 100–101
Dent 73
Derry 50, 95
Despeñaperros 207, 211
Dessau 137, 141
Deventer 237
Devínska Nová Ves 325
Diaghilev, Sergei 313

Diamante 431
Dieppe 173
Digne-les-Bains 170
Digoin 194
Dijon 158–59
Dingle Peninsula 86–87
Dingwall 66
disabilities, travellers with 531
discounts (rail fares) 523
Disentis/Mustér 384
Domažlice 300–301
Dombås 265
Domodossola 375, 378
Doncaster 60, 62
Donostia see San Sebastián
Dostoyevsky, Fyodor 287
Douro Valley 231
Dover 29, 31
Drei Annen Hohne 133, 136
Dresden 308, 341
Drumochter Summit 65
Dublin 41, 50, 78, 83–85, 87–88, 93–94
Dubrovnik 444, 447, 449, 528
Dumbarton 75
Dún Laoghaire 87, 94
Dunkeld 65
Durham 60, 64
Durrës 31, 403, 440
Düsseldorf 126

E

Earl, George 59
Eboli 431
Edinburgh 59, 63–64, 69, 73–74
Eibsee 353
Eidsvoll 263, 265
Eiffel, Gustave 152
Eindhoven 112
Einstein, Albert 103
Eisfelder Talmühle 136
El Chorro Gorge 220
El Escorial 217
El Transcantábrico (train) 224
Elba 32
Ely 80

INDEX | 537

Emmental 377
Enghien 105
Enniscorthy 94
Enns 365
Enveitg 186
Épinal 115
Erfurt 142–43
Espinho 232
Esztergom 311
Euganean Hills 436
Eurail see Interrail
European Health Insurance Card (EHIC) 531
European Rail Timetable 10, 15, 18, 110, 451, 526
European Railway Atlas 10, 15, 222, 451, 524
Eurostar (train) 26, 51, 104, 106, 148, 150, 515–16, 518, 524
Evesham 90
Évian-les-Bains 389
Évora 234
Exeter 56

F

Faenza 437
Falmouth 58
Faro 234
Faroe Islands 254
Faslane 75
Fauske 268, 274
Fehmarn 290
Feldkirch 360–61
Ferrara 436–37
Ferrol 224
Fetești 320
FEVE Railway 224, 496
Ffestiniog Railway 82
Figueres 200, 205
first class travel 516–17
Fishguard 82, 92
Fisterra 226
Flåm 261
Flensburg 243
Florence 411–13, 415–16
Flüelen 377
Flying Scotsman (train) 63, 313
Foix 186
Fontainebleau 152, 158

Formia 429
Fort William 76
Forth Bridge 59, 65
Forth Rail Bridge 64, 404
Františkovy Lázně 303–304
Fredericia 243, 247
Fredrikstad 259
Fréjus 167
Frétin Triangle 105
Freudenstadt 122
Furka Base Tunnel 385
Furth im Wald 300–301
Füssen 145

G

Gagliano Leuca 395
Galashiels 73
Gällivare 272
Galway 88, 95
Gammelstad 277, 279
Gap 155
Gargano 437
Garibaldi, Giuseppe 423
Garmisch-Partenkirchen 351, 353
Garve 67
Gaudí, Antoni 188
Gdańsk 288, 296
Gdynia 296
Geilo 261
Geneva 158, 162, 198, 200, 392–93
Genoa 408–409, 419–20, 422
Gernrode 136
Ghega, Carlo 396
Ghent 99
Gien 152
Gièvres 193
Giovi Tunnel 419
Girona 205
Giverny 171–72
Glacier Express (train) 350, 381–84, 386
Glasgow 21, 69, 74–75
Glastonbury 56, 240
Glenfinnan Viaduct 33, 76–77
Glovelier 163
Gniezno 335
Gobowen 81

Goethe, Johann Wolfgang von 142
Golden Pass Railway 387
Goodwick 92
Görlitz 341, 343–44
Gornergrat Railway 385
Gornje Ležeče 401
Goslar 96, 135
Göteborg 257–59
Gothenburg *see* Göteborg
Gotland 246
Gotthard Railway 28, 350, 373, 375–76, 378, 384
Gottmadingen 123
Gouvy 113
Grandvaux 36, 116, 391
Grasse 169
Graun 357
Gray, Thomas 54
Graz 399
Great Malvern 90
Greifswald 294
Grindelwald 394
Grong 267
Groningen 235
Gstaad 390
Guimarães 231
Gunnislake 58
Gutenberg, Johannes 120
Győr 349

H

Halden 259
Halmstad 29
Hamar 265
Hamburg 237, 240–41, 288–89, 305, 307
Hämeenlinna 283
Hameln 129
Hannover 128–29
Hanseatic League 130, 237, 240, 288–90, 292, 294, 335
Haparanda 279–80
Hardy, Thomas 150
Harlech 50
Harlingen 96
Haro 195
Harrow-on-the-Hill 54
Harstad 275

Harwich 78–80
Harz Mountains 96, 126, 129, 133–37
Hauenstein Railway 28, 376
Heart of Wales Railway 91
Hebrides 32, 67–68, 76–77
Heidelberg 120–21
Heiligendamm 137, 292
Heine, Heinrich 27
Helgoland 240
Helmstedt 129–30
Helsingborg 245, 257
Helsingør 245, 257
Helsinki 47, 277, 283–85
Hendaye 180
Herculaneum 430
Hereford 88, 90–91
Heringsdorf 294
Hermitage 195
'herring girls' 77
Heuston, Seán 85
Hexham 72
Hidasnémeti 330
Hiddensee 293
Highland Chieftain (train) 59
high-speed railway 25
Hildesheim 135
Hirtshals 29, 250, 254, 262
Hjørring 250
Hoek van Holland 78–79
Hogwarts Express (train) 59
Holy Island 64
Holyhead 83, 88, 90
Horšovský Týn 301
Hrodna 337
Huelva 214
Hunawihr 115
Hungaria (train) 305, 307
Hurtigruten 236, 254, 262, 267–68, 275–76
Hyères 166

I

Ibiza 206
Iceland 254
Igoumenitsa 439, 449
IJmuiden 64, 69
Îles de Lérins 168

Imola 437
Imst 362
Inglis, HD 207
Inlandsbanan (train) 236
Innsbruck 351, 354, 359, 362
insurance 19, 531
Interlaken 389–90, 394
Interrail 9, 11–13, 21, 30, 50, 96, 133, 171, 240, 378, 383, 389, 394, 510, 513, 517–23
Inverness 59, 66
Ionesco, Eugène 316
Ionian Islands 439
Iron Curtain 128, 292, 299, 305, 309
Ironbridge 404
Irún 177, 181, 218
Ischia 427
Isles of Scilly 53, 56
itinerary planning 8–10, 18–20, 524

J

Jakobstad 277, 282
Jerez de la Frontera 213
Jesenice 350, 402
Joensuu 281, 283
Johanngeorgenstadt 304
Joyce, James 360
Juan-les-Pins 164, 169
Jungfraujoch 386, 394
Jupiter 315, 321
Jura 116, 147, 163

K

Kajaani 281
Kaliningrad 296
Kalix 279
Kalmar 246, 257
Kalsoy 254
Kalwaria Zebrzydowska 347, 404
Kandersteg 384
Kapıköy 32, 521
Karlovac 446
Karlovy Vary 303–304
Karlskrona 246, 257
Karlsruhe 121–22
Karlstad 252, 259

Kastellorizo 441
Katowice 346
Kaunas 297
Kefalloniá 439
Kemi 280
Kiel Canal 237, 242
Kiato 440
Kildare 85
Kilkenny 94
Killarney 84–86, 93
Kindertransport 78, 132
Kingussie 65
Kirkenes 236, 262, 265, 276
Kiruna 272
Kitzbühel 362
Kladno 304
Kleine Scheidegg 394
Knighton 91
Knin 446
Knock 231
Knokke 99, 103
Knoydart 77
Koblenz 119, 125
Kokkola 282
Kolari 280
Kolding 243
Kolín 310
Kongsberg 251
Kongsvoll 265–66
Königswinter 119
Konstanz 124
Koper 312, 401
Koralm Railway 399
Kortrijk 97
Košice 39, 328–331
Kotor 449
Kraków 36, 332, 337–38, 346
Krasnaya Strela (train) 313
Kreuzlingen 123
Kristiansand 250–251
Kristiansund 267
Krleža, Miroslav
Kruszyniany 336
Kufstein 349, 351
Kühlungsborn 137, 288, 292
Kulata 436
Kulturzug (train) 345
Kuopio 281

INDEX | **539**

Kutná Hora 310
Kyiv 340
Kyle of Lochalsh 59, 66–67, 77

L

La Baule-Escoublac 179
La Chaux-de-Fonds 163
La Rochelle 179
La Roche-sur-Foron 162
La Spezia 409, 410
Ladybank 65
Lake Balaton 442, 444–45
Lake Constance 32, 123, 353
Lake District 63
Lake Geneva 36, 110, 116, 162, 200, 386–87, 389–92
Lake Lucerne 373, 376–77, 386, 388–89
Lake Maggiore 373, 375, 378–80
Lake Trasimeno 416
Lake Valencei 444
Lake Van 32
Lake Vänern 236, 252, 259
Land's End 57
Landeck 357, 361
Landquart 370
Langeac 154
Langeais 191–92
Latour-de-Carol 182–84, 186–87, 204
Lausanne 116, 389, 391–92
Lauterbrunnen 394
Lavaux vineyards 36, 116, 386, 390–91, 500
Lawrence, DH 206
Laxå 252
Le Bris, Pierre 12
Le Capitole (train) 184
Le Mans 178, 191
Le Mistral (train) 156, 158
Lenné, Peter Joseph 131
Le Train Jaune (train) 204
Le Trayas 167
Lehliu-Gară 320
Leicester 81
Leiden 101
Leipzig 140–41

Lenin, Vladimir Illyich 123, 270–71, 277, 279–80, 282, 284, 347, 349
León 221
Les Arcs 166–67
Levi, Carlo 431
Levoča 329
Liechtenstein 360–61
Liège 33, 106–107, 109, 112–13
ligne de Cerdagne 204
ligne des Causses 147, 153
ligne des Cévennes 148, 153
ligne du Bourbonnais 148, 152, 194
Lika Railway 446
Lille 97, 104–105, 150
Lillehammer 265
Limerick 50, 85, 94
Limoges 184
Lincoln 60
Linköping 246
Linz 364, 365
Lisbon 44, 197, 227, 232–34
Lisieux 173
Liverpool 235
Ljubljana 396, 400–401
Llandovery 82, 88, 91–92
Llandrindod Wells 91
Llandudno Junction 82–83
Llanelli 92
Llanfair PG 83
Llívia 187
Locarno 373, 375, 377–79
Loch Ness 76
Lofoten Islands 236, 263, 274–75
London 21, 48, 51–52, 63, 148, 150
Longfellow, Henry Wadsworth 144
Looe 53, 58
Lorca, García 209
Loreley 120
Lötschberg Railway 384
Lübeck 46, 289–90
Lucca 411
Lucerne 38, 373, 376–77, 387–88
Ludlow 91

luggage 19
Luleå 279
Lund 246, 257
Lüneburg Heath 129
Luther, Martin 140
Lutherstadt Wittenberg 140
Luxembourg 113
Lviv 35, 298, 331–32, 338–40
Lyon 156, 160, 191, 194

M

Maassluis 78
Maastricht 112
MacGillycuddy's Reeks 85
Machynlleth 50
Madrid 197, 215–18, 221, 225
Magdeburg 130, 137
Maidenhead 54
Mainz 120
Málaga 214, 219–20
Malbork 288, 295–96
Mali Lošinj 458
Mallaig 67–69, 76–77
Malles 355, 357, 361
Mallin, Michael 87
Mallorca 206
Mallow 85
Malmö 246, 255, 257
Malta 29, 206
Man in Seat Sixty-One 18, 513
Man, Isle of 84
Manarola 410
Manet, Édouard 151, 171
Mangalia 322
Mantua 423–24
Maratea 431
Marchegg 324–25
Mariánské Lázně 301–304
Maribor 399
Mariehamn 286
Marienborn 130
Mariestad 259
Marmore Waterfalls 416
Marseille 154–55, 164
Martigny 161
Martina Franca 395
Marx, Karl 125

Matera 440
Medina del Campo 221
Međugorje 231
Medway Viaduct 150
Medzilaborce 331
Meggen 377
Meiringen 389
Melilla 214, 220
Melk 365
Mellrichstadt 143
Menorca 210
Menton 406–407
Merano 355, 357
Merida 212, 227, 234
Messina 206
Messina 32
Messina 427–28, 432
Metz 114
Middelburg 96, 100
Milan 45, 372, 379, 420–22
Millau 153
Millet, Jean François 158
Minden 128
Miskolc 330
Mittenwald 351, 353
Mo i Rana 267
Mockava 297, 337, 505
Monaco 406
Monet, Claude 151, 171
Montargis 152
Mont-Blanc Express (train) 161, 350
Monte Carlo 406
Monte Conero 437–38
Montélimar 201
Montepulciano 417
Monterosso 410
Montpellier 203
Montreux 47, 390
Morecambe Bay 63
Morokulien 252
Morris, Jan 82, 402, 422
Morvan 26
Moscow 235, 404
Moselle Valley 113, 115, 119–20, 125, 195
Mosjøen 267
Mouans-Sartoux 169
Moulins-sur-Allier 194
Mount Athos 286
Mousehole 57

Muggia 403
Mukachevo 312, 331, 339
Müller Lights 175
Munich 146, 351
Münster 127
Murmansk 276, 287
Mürren 394
Mussy Viaduct 48, 194
Muszyna 328
Myrdal 261

N

Nagelmackers, Georges 109
Nancy 114
Nantes 40, 178–79, 192
Naples 427, 429–30
Narvik 268, 272, 274, 276, 528
Nauders 357, 361
Neisse Viaduct 343–44
Neum 444
Neussargues 147
Nevers 152–53, 193–94
Newbury 55
Newcastle 64, 69, 72
Newhaven 173
Newlyn 57
Newquay 58
Nice 164, 169–70, 405–406
Night Ferry (train) 24
night trains 22–24, 109, 367, 516–18
Nîmes 154, 203
Norrköping 246
North Shields 64, 69, 71
Nowy Targ 347
Nuremberg 144–45, 299
Nurmes 281
Nyborg 244

O

O'Hanrahan, Michael 93
Oban 68, 75–76
Oberalp Pass 383
Oberwesel 120
Odense 243–44
Odesa 340
Okehampton 56
Olten 116, 376
Oostende see Ostend

Opatija 442
Opole 345–46
Orange 201
Orient Express (train) 27, 109, 114, 313, 358
Orkney Islands 65
Orléans 184
Orvieto 417
Oslo 251–252, 255, 259–61, 263
Osnabrück 127, 239
Ospizio Bernina 368
Ostend 99, 103
Östersund 266
Ostiglia 412
Oulu 277, 280–82
Ourense 225
Oviedo 224
Oxford 88–90

P

Padua 424, 434
Paestum 431
Pajares Base Tunnel 28
Palermo 206
Paray-le-Monial 193–94
Paris 21, 42, 150–52, 156, 158, 171, 176, 182, 184, 196
Patras 439–40, 449
Pavia 420
Peenemünde 294
Pembroke Dock 93
Penn, William 54
Penzance 57, 58
Perpignan 203–204
Perth 65
Perthus Tunnel 147, 182, 203–204
Perugia 416
Peterborough 60, 80
Pieštʹany 323, 327
Pinhão 231
Piraeus 441
Piran 403
Pisa 410–11
Pitlochry 65
place names 504
Ploče 447
Ploiești 320
Plymouth 57

INDEX | 541

Plzeň 301–302
Polcirkeln 273
Pompeii 430
Pontevedra 229
Pontresina 372
Ponza 429
Poprad 35, 328, 348
Porkkala 349
Porrettana Railway 413
Porta Westfalica 127
Portbou 203, 205
Porthmadog 82
Porto 197, 227, 230–32, 235
Portree 67
Postojna 401
Potsdam 130–131
Poznań 332–33, 335
Prague 299, 304, 309–10
Prato 413
Predeal 319
Przemyśl 338, 340, 349
Puigcerdà 187

Q

Quedlinburg 96, 133, 136–37
Quest-Ritson, Charles 131, 365
Quimper 179

R

Radebeul 137
Raftsundet 275
Rail Baltica 285, 297, 337, 528
railcards 515
Rail Europe 12, 104, 511–13, 518, 524
Rail Planner app 10, 14–15, 521, 524
rail-sail tickets 32, 50
Rannoch Moor 75–76
Rapallo 410
Rathmore 85
Ravenna 437
Reading 55
Redondela 230
Reichenau-Tamins 383–84
Rendsburg 237, 242
Retford 62
Reutte 353

Rhine Gorge 117, 120, 125, 138
Ribblehead 73
Ribe 243
Rigi 376–77
Rijeka 401, 442
Riksgränsen 273
Rimini 437–38
Riomaggiore 410
Riquewihr 115
Roermond 112
Rohan, Henri de 97
Rome 417–18
Røros 265
Roscoff 30
Roskilde 244
Rosslare 84, 92–93, 174
Rostock 29, 292
Rotterdam 78, 100
Rouen 171–73
Rovaniemi 280
Rovinj 403
Rügen 34, 123, 137, 242, 293–94
Ruse 320, 456
Ruskin, John 50, 381
Rusyns 331
Rütli 377
Ružomberok 328

S

Saarinen, Elien 283
Sablé-sur-Sarthe 178
Sagliains 369
Saimaa Canal 284
Saint-Gervais-les-Bains 161
Saint-Jean-Cap-Ferrat 406
Saint-Jean-de-Luz 180
Saint-Raphaël 167
Saint-Saphorin 391
Salerno 431
Salisbury 53, 56
Saltaire 73
Salzburg 138, 146, 359, 363–64
Samos 206
San Candido 355
San Marino 434, 437–38
San Sebastián 181, 221, 223–24

Sancerre 152
San Gimignano 412
Sankt Goarshausen 120
Sanremo 408
Santa Maria (Müstair) 357, 370
Santander 224
Santiago de Compostela 37, 221, 225–27
Sarandë 449
Sardinia 206
Sargans 360, 370
Sarlat 180
Saturn 315, 321
Saumur 178, 189, 191–92
Schaffhausen 117, 123
Scheeßel 240
Schengen 125
Scheveningen 101
Schivelbusch, Wolfgang 175
Schöna 309
Schwarzach-St Veit 362
Scuol-Tarasp 357
Sedrun 384
Segovia 225
Semmering Railway 28, 396, 398, 404
Sens 158–59
Settle & Carlisle Railway 63, 69, 72–73, 91
Seville 197, 211–12, 234
Seyðisfjörður 254
Seyssuel 194
Sežana 350, 402
Shelley, Mary 125
Shepherd, Nan 66
's Hertogenbosch 110
Shetland Islands 65, 252, 254, 262
Shrewsbury 50, 81
Sibari 395
Sibiu 318–19
Siena 44, 416–17
Sierra de Aralar 223
Sierra Morena 207, 211, 218
Sierra Nevada 219
Sighișoara 314, 316–18
Simplon Railway 380, 384
Sinaia 319
Singen 123

Siracusa 433
Skørping 249
Skye, Isle of 67, 77
Sligo 84
Slochd Summit 66
Slough 54
slow travel 10, 13, 25, 40
Soave 424
Sochi 287
Sóller 206
solo travel 18
Solway Firth 63
Sopot 296
Sorrento 427, 430
Sospel 170, 408
Southall 54
Spalding 60
Spielfeld-Straß 399
Spiez 390
Split 443, 446–49, 528
Spoleto 416
Sprogø 244
St Anton am Arlberg 361
St Davids 92
St Erth 58
St Ives 58
St Mawes 53, 58
St Moritz 368, 370–71, 381–384
St Petersburg 284, 287, 313
Stamford 78, 81
Starý Smokovec 327, 348
Stavanger 251, 254, 262
Steinkjer 267
Stephenson, George 317
Stevenson, RL 76, 166

Stockholm 237, 246, 252–53, 269, 286
Stoke Poges 54
Stoke Summit 60
Stoker, Bram 314, 318
Stonehenge 53
Storlien 266
Stralsund 292
Strasbourg 34, 114–15
Štrba 328
Štrbské Pleso 327
Stresa 379
Stromboli 32, 432
Štúrovo 311
Sugar Loaf 91
Suhl 143
Sundsvall 266, 269–70
Svolvær 268, 274–75
Świnoujście 294
Sylt 242
Szczecin 294–95
Szentgotthárd 399

T

Taizé 156
Tampere 277, 282–83
Tangier 214
Tanlay 159
Taormina 206, 432–33
Tarascon 154, 203
Tarifa 214
Tarragona 215
Tatra Mountains 323, 327–28, 332, 347–48, 404, 528
Tavira 234

Teignmouth 57
Telford, Thomas 65, 76
Teplá 303
Terni 416
Teruel 197, 210
Teutoburger Wald 239
The Hague *see* Den Haag
The Jacobite (train) 33, 76–77
Theroux, Paul 103
Thessaloniki 436, 441
Thionville 114
Thomas, Edward 50, 90
Thüringer Wald 143
Thurso 66
Tiranë 449
Tirano 372
Tokaj 195, 330
Toledo 217–18
Torneträsk 273
Tornio 280
Torre Annunziata 430
Torre del Oro (train) 208–209, 211
Tórshavn 254
Toruń 335
Toulon 164, 166
Toulouse 184–86
Tours 191–192
Traben-Trarbach 125
track gauge 87, 163, 183, 198, 224, 277, 297, 368, 388, 447
Train Bleu (train) 156, 313
train tickets 12, 510–23
Tralee 50, 86

Using this index effectively

In this index, we list the **principal places** mentioned in our 50 routes and elsewhere in this book. So this is first and foremost a geographical index. But we also include a small number of entries on **people** (for example Thomas Cook or Jan Morris) or **themes** (like night trains or visas) that crop up in the book.

With very few exceptions, we do not list country names in this index. So you'll not find Spain or Slovenia listed here. Any exceptions relate mainly to microstates (for example Liechtenstein or Vatican City) or small island nations (such as Iceland or Malta). You can check out broader country information in our **gazetteer** on pages 450 to 503. And to verify which countries feature in each of our fifty routes see our **route list** on pages 16 and 17.

Trani 439
Transalpin (train) 359, 399
Trans-Europe Express
  (train) 13, 116, 156, 376
travel apps 19, 21, 524
Travemünde 29, 31, 285
Trelleborg 29
Tremiti Islands 434, 438
Trenčín 327
Treno Gottardo (train) 27, 373–77
Trento 355
Triberg 122–123
Trier 125
Trieste 45, 298, 395–96, 402–403, 419, 422, 426
Trnava 327
Trollfjord 275
Tromsø 276
Trondheim 263, 266–67
Tropea 432
Troyes 159
Trubschachen 377
Tui 230
Turin 235
Turku 277, 285–86
Turner, JMW 54, 120
Tynemouth 72

U

Uimaharju 281
Uppsala 269
Usedom 293–94
Ústí nad Labem 304
Utrecht 110
Uzhhorod 331
Užok Pass 331

V

Valença 230
Valençay 193
Valence 194–95, 200–201
València 209–210
Valladolid 221, 225
Vallorcine 161
Varberg 257
Vardø 276
Varenna 372
Vejle 247
Venice 424–26
Venice 434

Venice Simplon-Orient-Express (train) 527
Ventimiglia 408
Venus 314–15, 321–22
Vernazza 410
Vernon 172
Verona 351, 356, 412, 424
Verviers 107
Vevey 391
Viana do Castelo 227, 230
Vicenza 424
Vichy 153
Vienna 46, 314, 316, 323–25, 358–59, 365–67, 396, 398
Vienne 194
Vierzon 184
Vigo 197, 227–29
Vila Real de Santo António 197, 234
Vilches 211
Villa Opicina 402
Villa San Giovanni 427, 431–32
Villach 505
Villefranche-de-Conflent 186
Villefranche-sur-Mer 406
Villefranche-Vernet-les-Bains 204
Vilnius 297, 337
visa requirements 19, 533
Visp 385
Vitoria-Gasteiz 223
Vlissingen 100
Vosges 27, 114–15
Voss 261
Vyborg 284

W

Wagner, Richard 313, 372
Warsaw 39, 288, 296, 335–36
Waterford 50, 85, 94
Watt, James 317
weather and climate 19
Weimar 141–42
Weißwurstgrenze 117, 138
Welkenraedt 107
Welwyn Viaduct 60
Wengen 394

Wernigerode 133, 135
Wexford 84, 88, 93–94
Whitby 63, 72
Whitehaven 72
Wick 66
Wicklow Hills 85, 94
Windsor Castle 54
wine tourism 195
Wismar 292
Wissembourg 147
Wittenberge 307
Wittstock 307
Wolfsburg 127, 129
Wolsztyn 333
Woolf, Virginia 165
Worcester 90
Worms 120
Wrocław 344–45
Würzburg 143–44

X

Xàtiva 210

Y

Yellow Train *see* Le Train Jaune
York 59–60, 62–64
Ystad 257

Z

Zadar 401, 442, 446, 458
Zagreb 445–46
Zakopane 327, 346–48, 398
Zamora 225
Zaragoza 215
Zbąszynek 333
Zeebrugge 29, 237
Zell am See 362
Zermatt 381–82, 385
Zernez 368, 370
Zgorzelec 343
Žilina 327
Zittau 137, 308, 349
Zola, Émile 151
Zug 287
Zugspitze 351
Zurich 124, 358, 370, 387
Zvolen 326–27
Zweig, Stefan 372
Zweisimmen 47, 388, 390

Postscript

We are always reviewing possible new routes for *Europe by Rail*. Cast back a dozen years and we introduced **Belgrade** as a Balkan hub. From Belgrade we had routes to Croatia, Hungary, Romania, Bulgaria and North Macedonia. The withdrawal of direct rail services from Belgrade to those five countries prompted a rethink. However, we have noted that Serbia is investing in its rail infrastructure, so we are quietly hopeful that things will improve in the **western Balkans**. We are also keen to improve our **Baltic region coverage**. The recent reinstatement of once-daily trains across Lithuania's borders with Poland and Latvia is encouraging.

Feedback from readers reveals real interest in more purposeful and conscious approaches to journeys. We sense that many people are valuing journeys for their own sake – as something to be enjoyed and cherished. Those who have written and spoken with enthusiasm about this book, and the travels it inspired, reiterate three messages. The first is that the **most memorable travel days** are those where speed is forsaken in favour of the slow train. The second is to have the courage to stop off here and there. The third is to avoid the tyranny that comes from excessive planning.

We post occasional updates on the dedicated website which accompanies this book. You'll find that at www.europebyrail.eu. There you can also check out the **specially prepared online maps** which accompany our 50 routes. The weblinks are shown at the very start of each route in this book (eg. www.ebrweb.eu/18map5 for R**oute 5**).

Feedback request

We hope you've valued using this book as much as we've enjoyed creating it. If you identify errors, or if you'd like to give some feedback, **we'd love to hear from you**. Which routes did you follow? What did you find good about the book? What worked less well? Just send your comments to the authors, Nicky Gardner and Susanne Kries, at editors@europebyrail.eu.

Also from hidden europe publications

Europe by Rail is a product of *hidden europe publications*, a Berlin-based publisher with a strong track record in promoting slow travel. The authors of this book, Susanne Kries and Nicky Gardner, have long campaigned for a particular style of travel – one which is mindful of the impact of tourism on communities. Their work found expression in the pages of *hidden europe*, a print periodical which over two decades and 70 issues celebrated fine journeys while exploring European culture, communities and landscapes

The final issue of *hidden europe* magazine was published in summer 2023. But you can still enjoy *hidden europe*, as a carefully curated collection of travel stories at www.hiddeneurope.eu. It's an online corpus of good writing evoking the spirit of landscape and a strong sense of place. No glitz, no gloss. And completely free.